D0410308

AMERICAN LABOR

FROM CONSPIRACY
TO
COLLECTIVE BARGAINING

LABOR PROBLEMS

Edgar S. Furniss
With the collaboration of Lawrence R. Guild

ARNO & THE NEW YORK TIMES
NEW YORK 1969

Reprint edition 1969 by Arno Press, Inc.

Library of Congress Catalog Card No. 71–89733

Reprinted from a copy in
The New York State Library

Manufactured in the United States of America

LABOR PROBLEMS

LABOR PROBLEMS

A BOOK OF MATERIALS FOR THEIR STUDY

BY

EDGAR S. FURNISS, PH.D.

PROFESSOR OF POLITICAL SCIENCE, YALE UNIVERSITY

WITH THE COLLABORATION OF

LAWRENCE R. GUILD, M.A.

GRADUATE FELLOW, YALE UNIVERSITY

HOUGHTON MIFFLIN COMPANY

BOSTON NEW YORK CHICAGO SAN FRANCISCO

The Riverside Press Cambridge

The Riverside Press
CAMBRIDGE · MASSACHUSETTS
PRINTED IN THE U.S.A.

PREFACE

THIS book is the result of many years of experiment in teaching the subject of Labor Problems in Yale College. Any attempt to cover this subject in a single comprehensive course of study presents a textbook problem of unusual difficulty. The field is a broad one, including many groups of problems which are more or less distinct from each other and more or less technical in character. During recent years, materials dealing with these special phases of the subject have multiplied rapidly, but chiefly in the form of technical monographs of limited scope which cannot be used as texts. The manuals which attempt to cover the entire field are too often superficial in many parts and leave important phases of the subject untouched. This book has been prepared in the belief that other teachers, like the authors, have found the existing materials unsatisfactory for classroom use.

The basis of this book is a collection of readings from the monographs which deal with special branches of the subject. It is the conviction of the authors that this material should be presented to the students since it represents the best work of technical experts. But in its present form it is not available for this purpose. Accordingly, the authors have attempted, through careful selection and editing, to bring its most useful parts together in compact form within the space of a single volume.

The book should be viewed, however, not as a collection of isolated excerpts from other writers, but as a textbook developing a continuous and connected course of study. All teachers are familiar with the faults of the ordinary collection of readings. It is too often scrappy and disjointed, confusing the student and leaving no coherent impression upon his mind. In this book, an effort has been made to avoid these errors. In the first place, the selections are all of considerable length, each a complete study in itself, and none duplicates of others. In many cases, a single selection will suffice for an ordinary class assignment. Where this is not true, the readings have been grouped together so that a given subject may be covered by a continuous series of selections.

In the second place, a large part of the book has been written by the editors for the purpose of filling gaps in the available materials and of welding the entire collection into a consistent whole. Finally, the collection has been assembled in logical order designed to carry the student through a progressive course of study until the entire field has been covered. In this way it is hoped that the book may possess the merit of containing the best thought of the authorities in the various technical phases of the subject without sacrificing the continuity and coherence essential to a successful textbook.

No claim is made that the authors have contributed anything new on the subject of Labor Problems. Their task has been only that of making available what is already known. Before publication the materials comprised in this book were used for two years in mimeographed form in the classroom at Yale. The present content and arrangement are the result of these experiments. All things considered, the authors are convinced that, both in subject-matter and in arrangement, the volume serves adequately the needs of the student in general courses of study in Labor Problems. It is published in the hope that other teachers will find it equally useful.

EDGAR S. FURNISS
LAWRENCE R. GUILD

CONTENTS

Part Two

THE ORGANIZED LABOR MOVEMENT

Part Three

AGENCIES OF INDUSTRIAL PEACE

Part Four

MODERN INDUSTRIAL RELATIONS POLICIES

EDITOR'S INTRODUCTION

PROFESSOR FURNISS'S book really needs no introduction. It carries its own credentials. Teachers of economics will be quick to appreciate the judgment and skill with which it has been put together.

Books of selected readings have come to be important adjuncts of the teaching of the social sciences. They have one outstanding advantage: they convey a just impression of the diversity of opinions, the opposition of interests, the range of concrete problems, which characterize this field of study and inquiry. Furthermore, with classes as large as they have come to be in many American colleges, it is difficult, often impossible, to give every individual student convenient access to all of the separate books which he ought to consult. The book of readings is a practicable and convenient partial substitute.

Economic problems, however, have their unity as well as their diversity. There is no mastery of them except as they can be seen in their relations and brought together into a consistent and manageable body of knowledge. A defect of some books of readings has been that they have emphasized diversity at the expense of unity. A collection of short excerpts, each torn from its own context, provides neither an alluring nor a profitable introduction to economic studies. A scrapbook is not a book.

The present volume is not a scrapbook. True, Professor Furniss has brought together a generous measure of excerpts, judiciously selected and skillfully arranged. But these, one might say, are no more than the building materials which have gone into a structure of which he is the architect. The sections that his own pen has furnished are not merely supplementary material, designed to fill up gaps. They bind the other materials together, so that the whole book has continuity and unity.

The unity thus achieved, the reader will find, is in no way artificial. The book begins by describing and defining a problem. Its successive chapters are concerned with the unfolding of the various aspects of that problem. Nowhere do the advantages of this method of approach appear more clearly than in the study of the particular problem, or related group of problems, with which Professor Furniss deals. Some economic problems, one may surmise, could be brought to a solution if all the pertinent facts were available and if correct reasoning could be assured. Not so with the labor problem. It calls, of course, for adequate information and for clear thinking. But it calls also for understanding.

Unfortunately, outside of the ranks of the special students of the labor problem and of men who are in close personal touch with the labor movement, any adequate comprehension or sympathetic understanding of the realities of that problem is rare. Professor Furniss's book is so planned as to give insight as well as knowledge.

Allyn A. Young

LABOR PROBLEMS

∴

PART ONE

PROBLEMS OF THE MODERN INDUSTRIAL WAGE-EARNER

LABOR PROBLEMS

CHAPTER I

THE BACKGROUND OF THE LABOR PROBLEM

The Labor Problem. When we speak of The Labor Problem, we have in mind a case of serious maladjustment which has developed in our industrial order. The desires, the policies, the mores of a large mass of the members of society are in conflict with certain basic institutions of society's economic structure. In the form of movements with conscious purposes, or of the irrational reactions of individuals, pressure is brought to bear upon these institutions. Conservative forces in society rally to their defense. Out of this develops a conflict which affects a wide range of economic activities and personal relationships. The future evolution of our economic institutions will be greatly affected by the outcome of this conflict. And in the meantime, the friction, bitterness and waste energy resulting from this disharmony reduces the efficiency of the industrial system and affects the economic welfare of all members of society. The chief purpose of the collection of materials contained in this book is to set forth the causes, present tendencies, and probable future results of this great problem of maladjustment.

Labor problems. Back of this major social problem, however, lies a complex of forces commonly called "labor problems." These are life problems of the individual worker — hazards, menaces, unpalatable conditions of life brought to bear upon him as a consequence of his position as a wage-earner. Unemployment, low wages, hazardous conditions of employment, exhausting hours, the labor of women and children may be cited as examples. Each of these problems arises from causes peculiar to itself, exerts its own peculiar effect upon the wage-earner, and, therefore, constitutes a special field of study. A preliminary study of these specific problems is indispensable to an understanding of the broader social aspects of the industrial conflict; for it is in reaction against their influences upon his life that the worker adopts practices which place him in opposition to a social order founded on the institutions of private property and individual enterprise.

The propertyless wage-earner is born to a life beset by many evil forces whose causes he does not understand and whose consequences he is, in general — especially if unaided by organized social support — powerless to escape. Even if he is so fortunate as to escape the most devastating of these menaces, the monotony and dreariness of his work may condemn him to a life from which he can draw no contentment. To the drabness of his labor is added an oppressive feeling of insecurity. Dependent for his existence upon his success in obtaining and retaining a job, he has neither the power of self-employment nor a guarantee of employment for others. In the case of many occupations, mutilation, sickness, sudden death are a commonplace experience of his group — by-products of machine industry. Labor spent under such conditions can return no psychical or spiritual rewards in partial compensation for the costs involved. The reward of the wage-earner consists solely in his wages; and these, in too many cases, are merely sufficient to maintain his family above the poverty line of existence.

Modern competitive society creates these problems for the propertyless worker, but makes little organized effort to lighten their effects upon him. Their solution is left to his own ingenuity. It is natural, therefore, that these facts of experience should constitute the determining forces shaping the worker's outlook on life, and his attitude toward his social environment.

It is the attempt of the great mass of industrial workers to guard against the hazards of life and to open up avenues of escape from the dreariness and misery of their lot that creates the conflict within society known as 'The Labor Problem.' The problem assumes many different aspects according to the standpoint from which it is viewed. To the employer it is evident in the disposition of his labor force to shirk and soldier on the job, to render inefficient service, to waste time, materials, equipment. The lawyer sees it in the tendency among common men to flout the law and the courts when they touch upon the relations of employee to employer; and to challenge the right of certain of our most honored judicial institutions — e.g., the Supreme Court — to exist. The general public cannot disregard it in these days of nation-wide strikes in essential industries. To the student of society these phenomena are manifestations of a single condition — a serious maladjustment within our order. Our institutions of contract, free competition, property rights are working badly because the mass of mankind upon whom their functioning depends either refuses outright to accept them, or else works them in such a spirit of resentment and antagonism that their functioning is crippled.

When we search for the roots of the modern labor problem we are led back to the Industrial Revolution out of which sprang our industrial order. The typical economic institution of to-day is the factory. The life of the typical wage-earner is confined within the walls of the factory and subjected to its discipline. Therefore, we may well begin our study of the labor problem with the following summary of the effects of the modern factory system in the words of an able student of the subject.[1]

The Social Revolution. The rise of the factory was coincident with a political and social revolution. In attempting to estimate the effects of mechanical industry upon the well-being of workers, it is accordingly necessary to distinguish between these two influences. It is manifestly impossible to say what might have happened to workers had water-power and the energy of steam never been harnessed to machines, but it is entirely clear that even prior to the invention of the basic machines which served to create the beginnings of the factory age the position of wage-workers in society had begun to be altered. Political and social tendencies were conspicuous, even though they had not already borne their full fruit when the first factories were built. These liberating political and social movements followed the logic of their own nature in spite of the sometimes conflicting influences generated by the new industrial system. The position of workers to-day is consequently the resultant of these diverse forces.

Artisans, mechanics, and laborers were largely unfree when the foundations of the first factories were being dug. No wage-earner, unless he was also a property-owner, could vote. South of Mason and Dixon's line artisans were slaves or indentured servants. In Pennsylvania much work was done by the so-called redemptioners, the German immigrants who paid for their passage overseas by giving four years' labor or more to employers who advanced the funds required for emigration. Industrially the United States was half slave and half free at the end of the eighteenth century, and the first President of the new nation was himself the master of an establishment where under the ancient handicraft system cloth was fabricated by bondswomen. Artisans of various crafts were offered for sale, the black men as slaves and

[1] From *Industry and Human Welfare*, by W. L. Chenery. Copyright by The Macmillan Company. Reprinted by permission.

the white as indentured servants. The unfree worker who quit his appointed tasks could be disciplined, and the man who ran away might be arrested and returned. The free workers of the Northern States were not represented politically and, if one may judge by the expressions of members of Congress and of delegates to constitutional conventions where suffrage was being considered, they were not highly regarded. The social and political status of workers has been revolutionized. Universal manhood and womanhood suffrage obtain and while in practice casual laborers and negroes are often deprived of the vote, race and a wandering life, rather than caste or property distinctions, maintain the barriers.

In the North the first manufacturers were often artisans who with money loaned by merchants or farmers were able to begin business in a small way. Reporting for Connecticut in 1832, H. L. Ellsworth, for example, informed Louis McLane, Secretary of the Treasury, that "many of the manufactories are small and carried on by the owner and his family, with little additional help." The figures submitted by Mr. Ellsworth substantiated this statement. Establishments employing three, four, five and six operatives were characteristic. In the North, merchants in the larger towns were the chief possessors of wealth. The rise of factories created a new and property-holding class, who in time were to dispute the supremacy of the merchants. The artisans who became the proprietors and managers of factories were obviously enormously bettered by the mechanical revolution but it is not with the well-being of those who rose to affluence that society is now chiefly concerned.

The fortunes of the men and women who did not emerge, and who in the mass have no prospect of emerging, are immediately significant. Not only, however, do the artisans and laborers of to-day enjoy political and social rights which were denied their forefathers, but also for them education has become general. A hundred years ago workers yearned vainly for the dignifying influence of a system of public schools. To-day attendance at school is compulsory, and certainly in the larger cities the opportunity for education is all but universal. The laborer of to-day thus not only exercises political privileges which were denied his predecessors four generations ago, but also through education he has been assisted in utilizing more intelligently the political opportunity accorded him. In saying this one does not forget the confusions and imperfections of the political and educational systems which have been created. Each falls far short of the desires of generous men and women, but each marks a vast advance over what existed at the beginnings of the factory age, and each has had a potent influence in determining the status of workers. In truth, it may be added that, with all their defects, the public schools and the democratic political system occasion much of the hope of the present. In them lies the inspiration and the avenue to release from unredressed evils. These gains, however, are mainly attributable to the political tendencies which exploded in the American and French revolutions. Had there never been a factory system, it is possible that manhood, if not womanhood, suffrage would have been established, and even popular education might have come. Such a leader as Thomas Jefferson was an advocate of these things. But how did industry itself affect the position of those workers who continued to be laborers and artisans?

The factory system. In general it is fair to say that the factory system has depressed the economic status of artisans and elevated the position of laborers. The experiences of the shoemakers or of the iron molders illustrate this. The extension of markets and the gradual adoption of machinery both tended to degrade the quality of the work done by journeymen cobblers. Prices were reduced in a competitive market and artisans found themselves in an impossible rivalry with factory-made goods and with the products of semi-skilled workers who were able and willing to live at a lower standard. Machinery hastened the process of substituting laborers for artisans. This has been accomplished unequally and at various times in different industries. As late as 1851 all labor on shoemaking was handwork. The McKay sole-sewing machine, introduced in 1862, however, did in one hour what the journeyman had required eighty hours to accomplish. At a stroke the skill of the shoemaker for manufacturing purposes was rendered obsolete. The spectacular development of the labor organization known as the Knights of St. Crispin, following the Civil War, was the protest of these craftsmen against the loss of a market for their skill, the substitution of laborers for craftsmen, and the consequent reduction of wages. The artisan able to perform all the operations of his craft has tended to disappear in many trades. Shoe factories ultimately divided the cobbler's work into many operations. Yet the manufacturing system itself created a demand for a new kind of skill. Specialized operations, such, for instance, as cutting, require an expertness in a limited field scarcely attained by the general workers of the handicraft days. The iron molders are an example of belated transfer from a handicraft to a machine basis of operation. The long and bitter struggle between the Iron Molders' Union and the National Founders' Association arose over the question of the installation of machinery and the resultant wage changes.

With a few exceptions, such as printers, artisans whose trades have been revolutionized by the invention of machines have been unable to maintain their relative position in the industrial community. It is indeed a curious and significant fact that the craftsmen of to-day are very largely men whose trades have not been seriously affected by the introduction of machinery, and that these handicraft workers compose the backbone of organized labor. The building trades workers have nearly the same skill as that attained by their forefathers, and the building trades workers are the most powerfully unionized. Other groups which have obtained great power are chiefly those who under machine conditions have still been able to acquire skill. The railroad brotherhoods are among the most potent labor organizations in the country. The strength of the railroad unions is to be found in the fact that locomotive engineers and trainmen are possessed of a peculiar skill which is not quickly imparted and which is not widely distributed. The miners are another instance of men securing skill and solidarity under new conditions. The clothing makers have completed a cycle. Tailors originally ranked in the aristocracy of artisanship. The introduction of machine methods and the extension of the competitive market made conditions worse for the workers, who largely lost their skill as journeymen to become specialists in particular operations. Trade union organization has in their case very recently restored much of the dignity and of the economic advantage which belonged to journeyman tailors. The textile industries, which first felt the influence of the factory system, show from the standpoint of craftsmanship as well as from that of reward a striking degradation of labor. The workers in the cotton and woolen and silk mills have never been able to effect a powerful organization for their own protection. New groups of workers have successively invaded this field. The skilled workers who first as craftsmen and afterwards as machine tenders were displaced by immigrants and others willing to work for lower wages suffered seriously by this change. Yet both for the daughters of American farmers who were attracted to the early mills and for the peasants of Europe who were subsequently drawn into the textile factories, the shift in the basis of the industry from a hand to power-machine process meant an advance. Again and again this contrast is found. Journeyman artisans were injured by machinery, while laborers were lifted to a higher level of living when they were drawn into new work. The reluctance of skilled workers to submit to changes which implied the sacrifice of the cunning of their hands as well as losses in income has been one of the tragic phases of the industrial revolution. It has been a struggle in the main to preserve status, and it has been a losing struggle. Old values were ruthlessly destroyed and those who suffered saw for themselves too often no compensation.

Men and women became machine tenders. Impersonal motors determined the speed of human effort. The leisurely quality of handwork was lost. Specialization at endlessly repetitive tasks performed at a high speed injected a new factor into the toil of men and women. Repetition of a single process eliminated the joy of the worker who has a sense of creation in his work. For most machine tenders the craftsman's pleasure of performance does not exist. Some trade union leaders and some manufacturers, however, now regard the matter without misgivings. They assert that repetitious work can never be rendered truly interesting. Happiness, accordingly, must be found outside of work. Consequently, they contend that hours should be shortened so that leisure may exist, and wages should be raised so that leisure may be enjoyed. That idea is in itself a child of the machine age. So far as men can now see there is in truth no prospect of a change from repetitious labor. The most productive factories are those in which standardization is furthest advanced. Such was the experience of the World War, during which much progress was made toward placing industry more completely on a foundation of machinery. With mechanical processes the United States can now produce more than it can consume, as was shown during 1918, but with a return to manual production it would be impossible to provide for the necessities of the population. It is improbable that the kind of pleasure in work of which William Morris was the prophet can ever be restored in factories where men and women spend their days and nights in the continual repetition of a single set of operations. The normal human mind is wearied by monotony. Hence it is true that relief and recreation, as well as rest, must be had beyond the working hours.

From this standpoint it can hardly be argued that the factory system has brought joy or dignity to workers. The hours of labor were longer before machinery imitated the deftness of human hands, and many tasks had almost infinitely to be repeated from the days when galley slaves propelled the vessels of their conquerors. But the impersonal beat of machinery has made demands, never before approximated, upon the men and women who serve it. In the textile industry, for example, the rate of production is determined by the speed of machines. It is impossible for the workers tending the separate operations to influence the rate. Human beings are subordinated not immediately to the will of other men — although, of course, some human will decides the rate at which the engines move but to the motion of machinery. That this has deleterious effects on the body as well as upon the spirit of man seems probable from the researches of Philip Sargent Florence and others for the United States Public Health Service. The rhythm of such machines as lathes in certain operations appears, furthermore, to drive workers onward regardless of the accumulating poisons of fatigue, and regardless even of their ability in some such cases to alter the speed of the machine.

Corporate enterprise. Not less influential than power machinery itself in affecting the status of workers has been the corporate form of organization which industry, trade and transportation have taken. In 1830, when the factory system was well established, industry seems principally to have been in the hands of individual owners whose establishments were small.

Certain Lynn shoe manufacturers reported in 1832 that their real estate and buildings varied in value from $200 to $2000. Factories with only two or three employees were common. An establishment with a hundred workers was large. In such circumstances the relationship between the manufacturer and his employees was similar to that which subsisted between the old master workman and his journeymen. The enactment of legislation designed to facilitate the growth of corporations tended to destroy this relationship. The corporation, and later the trust, created a new industrial environment, which influenced powerfully the position of workers. In the report to Secretary McLane in 1832, the accounts of ninety Pennsylvania iron manufactories are listed. Altogether they represented an investment of $3,200,000. The United States Steel Corporation alone was valued at $2,430,546,962.56 on December 31, 1920. S. Smith & Company's rolling mill and nail factory at Pittsburgh employed twenty-five men and six boys in 1832. The United States Steel Corporation had 267,345 on its rolls in 1920. The rolling mill of 1832 was managed by the owner. There were more than a hundred thousand stockholders of the United States Steel Corporation during 1921. Most owners can have little share in management.

In 1914 nearly a third of all wage-earners engaged in manufactures worked in establishments employing five hundred or more persons. Only about thirteen per cent of the wage-earners were employed in factories using twenty workers or fewer, according to the 1914 census of manufactures. The number of these small factories is large, composing as it did in 1914 upwards of seventy per cent of the entire number of industrial establishments in the country, but the proportion of workers employed is very small. On the other hand, enormous organizations are common. Corporations employing as many as ten thousand workers excite little comment, while the more conspicuous concerns utilize the energies of thirty, forty, fifty, and even a hundred thousand men and women.

Great power over the lives and fortunes of the men and women employed is possessed by the directors of such enterprises. Many large corporations have created cities, in which their factories are situated and their workers are housed. Often the corporation owns the entire community. In many of the "satellite" towns, workers employed by the dominant industry occupy houses owned by their employers, buy food and clothes and other necessities of life at stores owned by the employers, send their children to schools maintained by the employers, worship in churches established by their employers, and finally are buried in cemeteries located upon their employer's land. Many of the communities in which employers have provided the essential utilities of living, it must be admitted, are on the whole far more comfortable and decent than the localities which have been neglected. But while one is scrupulous in refraining from suggesting censure of those who have come into this great industrial power, it is impossible to refuse to observe the fact. The relationship between such companies as the United States Steel Corporation, the General Electric Company, the United States Rubber Company, the Ford Motor Company, the International Harvester Company, American Woolen Company, to cite only a few, and their employees, is a new social phenomenon. In theory the humblest citizen worker enjoys all the political and social rights of the richest and most potent industrial magnate. But the economic status of the employee of a large corporation is not, save in the industries where trade unionism has reached maturity, one of independence.

Position of the modern wage-earner. When we take a comprehensive view of this development, and attempt to estimate its effects upon the average propertyless man, it is easy to draw too dark a picture. In many respects the worker has shared in the gain resulting from the progress of industrial society. In terms of material comfort, his position has undoubtedly been improved. His standard of life contains numerous elements which on an earlier stage were the special prerogatives of the rich. Scientific progress has brought within his reach a degree of security against disease which was unknown even in the highest strata of society a century ago. Collective provision for education, sanitation, amusement have opened up sources of enjoyment at little or no cost to himself. These happier features of the Industrial Revolution are omitted from this account of its effects on labor, not because they do not exist or are unimportant, but because our immediate purpose is to account for the discontent and restlessness of the industrial workers; and this requires that we focus attention upon the darker aspects. From this point of view we may summarize the principal effects of the Industrial Revolution under the following heads: (*a*) employment; (*b*) craftsmanship; (*c*) control.

Employment. In terms of employment the rise of machine industry has had one overwhelming effect upon the propertyless man: it has deprived him of all power to employ himself. Even in its earlier stages, the tools with which men worked had grown so costly that the worker could no longer own them. To-day, few indeed are the remaining trades in which the workman, as a customary thing, equips himself with capital instruments. In many of the older countries, this process was accompanied by another which worked in the same direction: namely, the separation of the laborer from the land. In other countries where this change was not so noticeable, and in the United States where an abundance of free land delayed its effect until our own time, the workingman of to-day is, after all, in little better case. He is born landless and is rarely able to scrape together the money required to buy a portion of the earth's surface, however minute. Moreover, the growth of the factory system — an aspect of the Industrial Revolution which has been described in the preceding pages — has brought it about that small holdings of land scattered over the countryside, because of their remoteness from the scene of his day's work, have lost their effectiveness to supply a supplementary source of employment and income to the industrial worker.

The joint effect of these changes was to destroy the laborer's capital equipment and make him, as we find him to-day, almost entirely propertyless. Before they occurred, the tools of the average workman were in his home. In a sense, he was an enterpriser, setting himself to work upon a product which was either his own property or, at least, brought him into direct contact with the market. His little plot of ground supplied him with a resource which he could hold in reserve for exploitation in slack periods of trade, or could use as a supplementary source of income, thus fortifying him against disaster in case of a total loss of market for his primary product. In contrast with this, we find him to-day solely dependent upon some agency outside himself to supply him with a means of livelihood.

Hence, in a very real sense the propertyless worker has an insecure tenure on life. In our exchange economy the possession of a money income is the *sine qua non* of existence; and for the worker the possession of a job is the sole source of money income. Not only has the wage-earner no power to create the job for himself; he has no assurance or guarantee that any one else will supply him with one. No machinery exists in modern society to compel an unwilling employer, public or private, to hire the man out of work. The industrial wage-earner is successful in finding a job only if it profits some one else to provide it for him. This statement may be made with no intention to impugn the motives or the practices of employers as a class. The employer of to-day is not only behaving in accordance with the moral standards of his time when he refuses to provide work for the laborer unless it is profitable to himself to do so; but, what is more to the point, he would benefit no one — least of all the workingman — if he behaved in any other manner in a competitive society. To hire men at a loss is one sure road to bankruptcy, and the bankrupt employer ceases entirely to function as a supplier of jobs.

It must be clear, however, that these questions of motive do not alter the state of affairs from the standpoint of the workingman. In the matter of employment, the Industrial Revolution has presented the laborer with a problem of life whose solution is vital to his existence. Since the laborer is, after all, a man and not a beast of burden; and, moreover, a free man and not a slave, it is inevitable that he should experiment with policies calculated to protect himself from the evil effects of uncertainty of employment.

Craftsmanship. The progress of machine industry not only swept away the material capital of the workingman but, in the case of certain higher grades of workers, destroyed as well the value of his skill or craftsmanship. There are points of similarity between the skill of the workman and his material equipment; both, in a sense, may be called capital. They originate from human choices and efforts which are very much alike in essence. The accumulation of capital and the learning of a skilled trade result, alike, from a disposition to bear present costs and endure present sacrifices in the hope of reaping rewards in the future. The effect of each is to place its possessor in a position of competitive advantage as compared with his fellow men less well equipped. Now the steady advance of invention which has occurred throughout the Industrial Revolution has been marked by a refined division of labor, a substitution of simple and routine processes for a single complex performance, a nullification of an older skill of hand or brain. Crafts have been devoured by the machine. Skilled craftsmen have lost their immaterial capital and have been precipitated into the ranks of the unskilled.

During the earlier stages of the Revolution, when crafts were being destroyed wholesale and the earlier aristocracy of labor thrown en masse into the common fund of ordinary labor, the magnitude of this economic disaster found a permanent place in the annals of the times. The substitution of the labor of women and children for that of men; the degradation of the ancient and privileged crafts of the weaver, the bootmaker, the nailer; the increasing misery of workers who were formerly in a position of comparative comfort; the revolting details of the exploitation of desperate men and women and helpless children engaged in cut-throat competition for employment, are incidents of the Industrial Revolution which all may read who take the trouble to turn the pages of the Parliamentary Reports. In our own day, this process has grown less perceptible for many reasons. The rate of technical progress has become more gradual and continuous — less revolutionizing. Fewer of the ancient crafts remain to be affected by it. Yet contemporary industrial history is not lacking in illustrations of the destruction of craftsmanship by the machine. The disappearance of the ancient trade of typesetting before the advance of the linotype machine was an event of our own time. So, too, was the destruction of the skilled craft of the wood carver, the glass blower and others. Everywhere the iron man in industry encroaches on the domain of the craftsman. The beneficial results of this progress when measured in terms of general economic welfare may be incontestible; but for particular individuals, its immediate effects is usually loss of wages, increased intensity of competition for employment; sudden or gradual degradation.

Control. A third effect of the Industrial Revolution has been the loss of *control* by the workers over the ordinary circumstances of their lives. The trend of industrial organization described by Mr. Chenery has resulted in the supplanting of the small industrial unit by the factory system. This has involved a compounding of labor, similar to that of capital instruments, into large and compact units, and the concentration of these units upon narrow geographical areas which possess some peculiar cost-saving advantage — such as water power, or proximity to cheap and efficient transportation. Here we find organized and disciplined labor armies responding to the command of the owner of capital or his agent, controlled in many of the details of their lives — e.g. their hours of rising, or beginning and ending work, their mealtimes, the amount of their leisure, even their place of residence — by the will of a profit-making employer. The term "wage slavery," when it is not merely a demagogic utterance used for its emotional effect, is employed by the spokesman for labor to define this condition of unfreedom with respect to the habits and daily conduct of their lives, common to factory workers. It is true, of course, that workingmen have never been free; their range of choices has always been determined more or less narrowly by the exigencies of their lives, by their lack of reserves, by the economic and social environment within which their struggle to win subsistence has been confined. But it can scarcely be denied that the shifting of the scene of his labor from his own home, or from the small shop in the neighborhood, to the giant factory in which his identity is lost in the mass of the labor army, has decreased the laborer's power to exert control over the conditions of his life; and has correspondingly increased the influence of the owner, manager, or "captain of industry" over the lives and destinies of his fellow men.

Two consequences of this condition should be noted. In the first place, the modern factory provides an environment congenial to the development of group motives and group conduct among the workers, which run counter to the prevailing individualism of our day. Class-consciousness among free laborers is a distinctly modern phenomenon. There have been, it is true, sporadic outbursts of mass action among the laboring populations of earlier times; but their brief duration and the ease with which they broke down prove the absence of a cohering force strong enough to counteract the influences of self-interest which tend to disrupt all unions of men for a common end. To-day it is possible to effect a stable union among wage-earners largely because of the great similarity of their life conditions, and because of the regimentation of the factory which familiarizes the workers with the fact of their common needs and inclines them toward coöperative group action. The standards of right and wrong, of legal rights and obligations, which develop within an organized group are not in harmony with those which dominate in our individualistic, competitive order. Their presence among the industrial workers constitutes one of the elements in the Labor Problem.

In the second place, partly as a result of the increasing size of the labor force in the modern factory, partly for other reasons, the bond between the employer and the individual employee has been attenuated to such a degree that it is no longer effective in controlling the laborer's actions. We may suppose that, had other influences been in operation to join employer and worker in a close union of mutual interest, the worker's loss of interest in his job and his product might have been counteracted by his feeling of loyalty to his enterprise as a corporate venture. But the trend has been in the opposite direction. Until very recent years, when a deliberate attempt has been made to counteract the effects of this factor in certain enterprises, the organization of the factory has been such as to stifle within the worker any feeling that he might have of direct economic interest in the destinies of his employer. The older and more intimate relationships of master and servant were wiped out in the progress of the Revolution and in their place arose the impersonal and bloodless relationship of paymaster and wage-earner — the "cash nexus" of Carlyle. With complete control over the enterprise lodged in the hands of the owner of the material equipment or his representative, possessed of no opportunity to share in its councils or influence its policies, the workers have not unnaturally declined to believe that the enterprise was *theirs* in any sense, or that they shared responsibility for its welfare. Many of the policies of organized labor give evidence of a total lack of knowledge of modern business principles and of total inability to understand the problems of an employer in a competitive market. This is not unnatural when one remembers that the workers have always been excluded from contact with the problems and responsibilities of management.

CHAPTER II

THE PROBLEM OF UNEMPLOYMENT

1. Social Significance of Unemployment

Menace of unemployment. Unemployment must be ranked first in importance among the problems which confront the industrial worker to-day, whether we measure the seriousness of these problems by the numbers they affect, by their economic and psychological consequences, or by the losses they inflict upon society as a whole. With comparatively few exceptions, all wage-earners are subject to the influence of this great menace. Perhaps the majority of them have experienced its power to cut them off from the support of life for a longer or shorter period. And those who have been so fortunate as to escape its most disastrous economic effects have passed their lives in continuous apprehension of their insecurity.

The most far-reaching and serious effects of unemployment are traceable, not to the actual misery and suffering which it entails, but rather to the *fear* of its occurrence — a haunting, insistent dread which so colors the outlook on life and moulds the behavior of the great mass of wage-earners that its cost to society in terms of reduced productivity, discontent and open rebellion are incalculable. The relation of the problem to the Industrial Revolution has already been pointed out. In modern industrial society, where the right to life for the propertyless depends upon the possession of a money income and where money income is obtainable only at the pleasure of a profit-seeking employer, the great mass of mankind must, perforce, conceive it to be the chief business to win and hold a job. The job, not the product, has become the focal point of economic activity for the working people. Industrial enterprises of all sorts are viewed as job-making institutions. With no collective provision to aid them, either in the way of supplying work to the jobless or of guaranteeing the continuance of employment for those who are in possession of a job, the workers have not unnaturally devised policies of their own for the solution of this greatest of life's problems. These policies, though they differ much in detail, are alike in essence: they aim at "making work," either through the device of multiplying jobs within the industrial establishment or, by opposing various labor-saving expedients of the employer, of prolonging the life of the jobs already in existence. These policies are not the creation of organized labor; they originate spontaneously among all industrial wage-earners whose tenure of employment is uncertain. Condemn them as we may, we must view them as natural — though undesirable and, it is to be hoped remediable — by-products of the life conditions of the wage-earner in industrial society.

Nature of unemployment. Unemployment should be defined as "involuntary idleness on the part of a workman who is able to work." The unemployed, from the point of view of the student of social problems, do not include all those who are out of work at a given time; but a smaller group. Some workers are idle from choice, as, for example, those who are on strike, or those congenitally opposed to labor of any sort. Others, though involuntarily idle, are the victims of industrial accident or disease and should be considered as a separate group constituting a special social problem. The loss of the job which constituted unemployment as it is here defined always takes place through the exercise by the employer of his right to discharge or lay-off a member of his labor force. Every such action by the employer adds to the sum of unemployment for a longer or shorter period — if we except those discharges which result from such willful misconduct of the worker as would indicate an intention on his part to sacrifice his job, if need be, in order to satisfy his malice or indulge his laziness. True unemployment, then, has these characteristics: first, it is a condition not created by the worker nor controllable by him; secondly, it appears from the worker's viewpoint to result at the desire of the employer.

It is the purpose of this chapter to analyze the causes of unemployment, to present some indication of its effects, and to consider various expedients whereby it may be reduced in amount or entirely removed. Two major causes of unemployment will be considered: (1) causes inherent in the seasonality of industry; (2) those which spring from the business cycle. This is not presented as a complete catalogue of the causes of this problem but rather as a sample of the forces at work within our order. It omits from discussion two groups of the unemployed whom it is the practice of students of the problem to place in a class distinct from those we have enumerated. The first of these groups is the *unemployable* — that section of the propertyless for whom no place can be found in productive enterprise because of their physical, mental or moral defect. These we have chosen to exclude by definition from the category of the unemployed. The second group omitted from our analysis comprises those who are thrown out of work as a consequence of *technical changes in industry* — that is, the victims of the progress of invention, improvement of management, "labor-saving" devices of sundry sorts. The causes which create unemployment of this sort are sporadic, fluctuating, uncertain; the resulting unemployment is of a temporary nature and, to a large degree, a matter of chance. Though this aspect of unemployment is disregarded in the discussion which follows through lack of space, account must be taken of it in any attempt to understand the magnitude of this great social problem.

2. Seasonal Unemployment, General Considerations

Extent of seasonal unemployment. Seasonality — the ebb and flow of industrial activity — is a well-marked feature of modern economic enterprise. In the case of some trades these fluctuations are so well known as to be a commonplace; building operations, coal mining, the clothing trades, the manufacture of Christmas and other holiday specialties, must for reasons known to all vary in intensity with the season of the year. What is not so well known, however, is that a similar, though not synchronous, variation appears in almost all industries, from the basic operations of agriculture to those of manufacturing and transportation, and throughout the various specialized branches of the latter group of industries. So generally is this true that the foremost student of the problem has summarized the matter in the following brief statement of fact: "Detailed inquiry shows that it is almost the exception rather than the rule for any trade to maintain fairly equable activity throughout the year. Most trades have their regular alternation of busy months and slack months." [1]

It is very difficult to measure statistically the amount of unemployment normally traceable to this cause. Since the problem is governed by forces peculiar to each industry in which it appears, simple averages of the numbers unemployed at a given time because of seasonal fluctuation are meaningless or misleading. The following statistics are presented, therefore, rather as indices to the magnitude of the problem than as an exact measurement.

One source of information regarding the volume of seasonal unemployment is to be found in the record of their unemployed members kept by the trade unions. These figures, so far as they relate to four major groups of British unions — building trades, furnishing trades, engineers (machinists), and printers — have been analyzed for the decade ending 1906 by Mr. Beveridge with the following results: [2]

[1] From *Unemployment: A Problem of Industry*, by W. H. Beveridge, p. 29. Longmans, Green & Co., publishers.

[2] *Op. cit.*; adapted from Table VI, p. 30.

Building Trades: 80 per cent more unemployment during the slackest month (December) than during the busiest (August).

Furnishings: 3⅓ times as much unemployment during the slackest month (January) as during the busiest (April).

Machinists: 50 per cent more unemployment during the slackest month (December) than during the busiest (May).

Printers: Twice as much unemployment during the slackest month (August) as during the busiest (November).

For the United States trade-union statistics covering the State of New York for the years 1904–15 show an average unemployment in March seventy-five per cent higher than in September. And similar statistics for Massachusetts reveal an average unemployment in March eighty per cent higher than in September during the years 1908–19. For the country as a whole reliable studies indicate a total unemployment during the worst month one and one half millions in excess of that for the best month.

Causes and consequences. The following quotation from the same leading authority will serve as a summary of the salient causes and consequences of seasonal unemployment:[1]

The causes of seasonal fluctuations are sometimes classified as climatic or social. It is better perhaps to say that each type of cause is to be found in nearly every case. Climatic conditions necessarily give rise to social habits; indeed nearly all social habits involving regular annual fluctuation in the demand for labor may be traced ultimately to differences in temperature and weather. On the other hand, social habits once established generally go beyond climatic necessities. It is, for instance, not so much impossible as unusual to build in winter. Sometimes fluctuation combines purely climatic with purely customary influences. At the London docks, for instance, tea comes in at one season of the year, timber at another, fruit at another according to climate. The net result is to make the general level of employment higher in the months about Christmas and again in July than it is in the early spring or in August or September. But with this goes a

[1] *Op. cit.*, pp. 33 f.

fluctuation dependent upon the customary dates of the wool sales for which large masses of additional labor are required . . . sometimes, again — as is conspicuously the case with fluctuations of dock employment — the climate to be considered is not that of the United Kingdom but that of some other country whence goods come.

Seasonal fluctuations imply a falling off, in slack months, of the demand for labor. It is a cause of lack of employment entirely independent of the wishes and character of the individual workman, or, in general, of the individual employer. It does not, however, necessarily or commonly involve acute distress.

In the first place, seasonal fluctuation may not lead to the actual discharge of the workmen at all. In coal mining it is represented almost entirely by a reduction in the average number of days worked. In many other industries part, though not the whole, of the effect of seasonal fluctuation is carried off in this way — by shortening the working hours. . . . Part of the loss, by a reduction of working hours, is spread over all the men still employed.

In the second place, the difference in the period of fluctuation for different trades makes it possible for men thrown out of their usual occupation in a slack season to find a subsidiary occupation in some other industry which is then busy. Laborers engaged in the building trade or at the brickfield in the summer can and often do find winter occupation at the docks or in gas works. . . . There are plenty of men . . . who have been to the same farm for temporary work summer after summer. There are in the same way plenty of men who get taken on year after year by the Post Office or by some of the big shops to meet the Christmas pressure. This use of subsidiary trades in slack seasons has, no doubt, its limits. Practically it is confined to low-skilled or unskilled work. A man cannot be a cabinet-maker in April, a bricklayer in August and a compositor in November. . . .

In the third place, seasonal fluctuation, being so common and regular a phenomenon, is to a large extent provided for in the expenditure of wages. This is one of the functions of the unemployed benefit paid by many unions. One or two unions, it is curious to note, only pay this benefit during the slack season. Outside these unions the matter has of course to be dealt with and is very commonly dealt with by individual effort. . . . Even where the individual has made no provision for slack times beforehand he can often get through them by running into debt and clearing himself during the following busy season. This is a form of retrospective saving made possible and common by the institution of the pawnshop and the readiness of small shopkeepers and landlords to grant credit to men ordinarily out of work.

In practice, therefore, it is found that acute recurrent distress at times of seasonal depression is confined to the unskilled occupations, and even in them to men who at all times are largely irregularly employed. The natural remedy is for the fact of seasonal fluctuation to be recognized as a normal incident of the industry and to be allowed for in the standard both of expenditure and of wages. . . . That, of course, is the root of the trouble. The men who winter after winter are in acute distress are the men who summer after summer can only live from hand to mouth, men whose earnings even in the busy months are cut down by irregularity of employment. They have no reserves and no credit. They almost certainly do not spend to the best advantage even such money as they earn, for their whole life is an education in the futility of foresight. They find themselves at the first pinch in the streets.

Ultimately, therefore, seasonal fluctuation becomes a question not of unemployment but of wages. From an economic point of view no industry is self-supporting unless it pays wages sufficient to keep men, not only while they are at work, but also while they must stand idle and in reserve. Where in any occupation seasonal fluctuation year after year brings round acute distress, that occupation must be judged as one in which wages are too low or ill-spent, because they do not average out to a sufficiency for the slack months as well as for the busy ones. It is from this point of view that the problem must be regarded.

3. The Labor Reserve [1]

Cause of the reserve. The fact of the existence of chronic over-supplies of casual labor in various occupations, with resulting

[1] From *Unemployment*, by F. C. Mills, being no. 183 of the Columbia University Studies.

under-employment and destitution, has long been recognized. Booth and his co-workers, in their survey of the working people of London in the late 80's and early 90's describe it. Sidney Webb, writing at about the same time, testified to "the fearful daily struggle for bread at the dock gates." But the discovery of the reason for this "chronic and ubiquitous over-supply of casual labor," which the Webbs term "perhaps the most momentous of this generation in the realm of economic science," was only recently made. It is Beveridge who has made the most original and most intensive studies in this field. Of the contemporary writers, none have materially added to Mr. Beveridge's analysis of the problem.

There are these observed facts to be explained: The distress from want of employment is chronic. An "irreducible minimum" of unemployment exists in all trades at all times. Trade-union statistics prove that this unemployment is due to loss of time by many, not to the chronic idleness of a few. The typical applicant to distress committees, moreover, is not unemployable, but industrial, a casual laborer. That this unemployment is due to an excessively rapid increase of population is disproved by known facts — unemployment in rapidly growing industries, increasing productivity of labor, and the rising remuneration of labor, which proves it to be of increasing importance in production.

The explanation of the existence of this irreducible minimum of unemployment is found in the labor reserve which tends to accumulate in modern industries. This reserve of labor is made up of "the men who within any given period are liable to be called on sometimes but are not required continuously." Its size depends upon the number of separate employers, the irregularities of their separate businesses and of the industry as a whole, the relative mobility of labor, the average length of engagements, and the extent to which chance prevails in the hiring of workers. Conditions in any one of these respects may be such as to result in the development of a "stagnant pool" of labor in an industry; the size of the reserve may be increased by the cumulative action of any or all of the other factors. Beveridge's analysis of their separate and mutual effects upon the labor market may be briefly summarized:

The number of workers who gather in any given center of the

labor market will tend to equal the maximum number who may be able to obtain employment in that center. If each employer in a certain industry maintains his own center of employment, so that no man working for him works for any other employer in that industry, a separate reserve will be built up for each of them. If the volume of the business of each varies from day to day, week to week, or month to month, the number of workers employed and "at the gate" will tend to equal the maximum number employed during the busiest period. If the term of engagement is brief, and if the element of chance centers in the selection of workers, the matter is further complicated and the reserve is further swelled. With no discrimination whatsoever, every man will in the long run get as much employment as every other man. The number of competitors for positions in each given center of employment will, therefore, tend to increase until the average remuneration received by each reaches the subsistence level of the class of men employed. If the average pay be below this, certain men will have to withdraw; if it be above the subsistence level, newcomers, having equal chances for employment, will attach themselves to the industry.

Assume now that instead of each employer drawing his labor supply from his own reserve there is perfect mobility of labor within the given industry; the reserve will tend to equal the maximum number employed in the industry as a whole at the busiest season. The separate fluctuations of individual employers will here partially neutralize each other, and so cut down the necessary reserve. The author illustrates this point by assuming ten centers of casual employment, each employing a minimum of 50 men and a maximum of 100 men. A total force of 1000 men will thus be maintained. In the industry as a whole, however, the minimum number employed is 700, the maximum 800. With perfect fluidity of labor a reserve of 100 men will suffice, and the extra 200 men who have been living in an under-employed condition forced out. Thus, the greater the degree of mobility of labor, the smaller will be the necessary reserve maintained in an industry. An excessive element of chance, complete absence of selection in employment, would, of course, vitiate the favorable results of mobility in the cutting down of the reserve.

On the basis of this reasoning Beveridge distinguishes three elements in the total reserve of labor for any occupation; those men representing fluctuations in the total volume of work in the industry as a whole; those representing the element of friction in the labor market; and those "attracted and retained by the perpetual chance of work."

This tendency toward the accumulation of reserves exists in varying degrees of strength in practically all industries; though seen in its most vicious forms in the casual occupations. The reserve as such is a "normal industrial phenomenon," necessary in all the industries liable to fluctuations in volume. This needed power in a given industry may be maintained, without producing distress, either through a high wage level, unemployment insurance, or elasticity of hours. Usually, however, faulty methods of securing the reserve power are resorted to; the men of the reserve suffer a continuous "leakage of employment" and there results the demoralizing evil of under-employment — the reduction of earnings to, or even below the level of bare subsistence. Though all the members of a labor reserve are subject to irregularity of employment, it is only that element which is called on "often enough to be prevented from drifting away elsewhere, but not often enough to obtain a decent living" which constitute the "unemployed." It is in the casual occupation, to which entrance is free and in which every one has a chance of securing work, that the incessant competition of low subsistence standards works out in demoralizing under-employment.

Effects. The deteriorating effect of unemployment will be touched upon in considering the personal factor. The same vicious reaction upon personal character, the perpetuation and intensification of the conditions conducing to reduce individuals to casual work, is characteristic of under-employment. Wages are inefficiently spent; wives and children are forced into industry; the securing of public relief prompts a descent into the unemployable class. Finally, there is the fact that in a world where chance rules supreme, where "the good are not more successful in securing work than the evil," personal merit and honesty are almost drawbacks. "No class in the community," says the minority of the Poor Law Commission, "could withstand the demoralizing influence of such a view of life and such a system."

The rates in occupations giving irregular employment must be higher than those affording regular employment for two reasons — to compensate for greater uncertainty of employment, and to build up reserves which can be used in busy times. Thus the wage rate in fluctuating occupations will be such as to attach to such occupations "a number of work-people roughly intermediate between the number for whom employment at that rate can be found in good times and in bad times, respectively." Wage rates above normal are thus the prime cause of the creation of reserves of labor, according to Pigou's reasoning.

The minority of the Poor Law Commission accept Beveridge's analysis of labor reserves unqualifiedly. Both majority and minority reports condemn in strong words the system which creates these "stagnant pools" of labor, and subjects industrial workers to the enervating influence of chronic under-employment. Three sets of special investigators were sent out by the Royal Commission to work on unemployment and allied problems. "All these inquirers . . . starting on different lines of investigation and pursuing their researches independently all over the kingdom . . . came, without concert, to the same conclusion, namely, that of all the causes or conditions predisposing to pauperism, the most potent, the most certain, and the most extensive in its operation was this method of employment in odd jobs." "All these (other) conditions (low wages, insanitary conditions, excessive hours of labor, outdoor relief, drunkenness) injurious though they are in other respects, were not found, if combined with reasonable regularity of employment, to lead in any marked degree to the creation of pauperism."

4. Fluctuations in the Coal Industry [1]

Under-employment of miners. Perhaps no industry suffers more acutely from the malignant disease of unemployment than the mining of coal. Under-employment is chronic. Involuntary idleness became more and more aggravated during 1921. At the end of the year, according to what I believe to be a conservative estimate, only 10 per cent of the total number of miners engaged in the bituminous coal industry were working full time; 50 per cent worked part time, and over 40 per cent had no employment. Thousands of coal miners have not been able to get a single day's work during the whole year.

[1] From the *American Labor Legislation Review*, March, 1922, pp. 37-40.

Bituminous coal mining is notorious as an example of wasteful and costly under-employment. Out of a possible 308 days' work in a year, the miners have been given on the average only 215 days. In 1893, a year of severe depression, they worked only 171 days. During the past year, worst of all, they had work for only 170 days.

With only 215 days' work a year even in normal times, the coal miner's yearly earnings are never sufficient to enable him to save up against hard times, while in periods of industrial stagnation, like the present, he and his family suffer miserably in destitution.

An exhaustive investigation by the United States Immigration Commission in 1908–09, covering practically all of the mining sections of the country, disclosed that the average annual earnings of all the male heads of households was only $451. The average family income was only $577 a year. Only about two fifths of the families investigated derived their entire income from the earnings of husbands at the mines. The remaining three fifths found it necessary to supplement the earnings of the husband by taking boarders or lodgers or by putting the children to work.

Again, the United Mine Workers of America in the presentation of its wage case to the Bituminous Coal Commission appointed by the President to adjudicate the mine workers' strike of 1919, showed that even in that year, when wages and prices were at their peak, the wage rates prevailing at that time enabled the pick miners in all bituminous mines to make average annual earnings of approximately $1130. This figure is derived from the reports of the United States Bureau of Labor Statistics, and was published in the December, 1919, *Monthly Labor Review.* It was also shown during the hearings of this commission, according to the exhibits submitted by the coal operators themselves, that the average earnings of pick miners in northern Illinois were, during the year 1918–19, under $1000 a year.

It must be remembered that the earnings of the coal miners are considerably decreased by such customary deductions as contributions to the various fraternal organizations, death and accident funds, doctor's care and medical supplies, union dues, rents and payment for blacksmith.

Mr. Herbert Hoover, in his inaugural address before the American Institute of Mining and Metallurgical Engineers, February 17, 1920, said:

> Many of the questions of this industrial relationship involve large engineering problems, as an instance of which I know of no better example than the issue you plan for discussion to-morrow in connection with the soft-coal industry. Broadly, here is an industry functioning badly from an engineering and consequently from an economic and human standpoint. Owing to the intermittency of production, seasonal and local, this industry has been equipped to a peak load of 25 or 30 per cent over the average load. It has been provided with a 25 to 30 per cent larger labor complement than it would require if continuous operation could be brought about.... There lies in this intermittency not only a long train of human misery through intermittent employment, but the economic loss to the community of over 100,000 workers who could be applied to other production, and the cost of coal could be reduced to the consumer. This intermittency lies at the root of the last strike in the attempt of the employees to secure an equal division among themselves of this partial employment at a wage that could meet their view of a living return on full employment.

This statement of Mr. Hoover gets at the gist of the whole problem. The mine workers contend that the industry owes to them a living wage. This, they believe, they do not secure. The report of Robinson and Peale, the gentlemen who rendered the majority report of the 1919 Coal Commission, said that the principal causes of this irregularity of employment in the coal industry are the unusual character of the market, and the inadequate railroad car supply. However, there is another factor which cannot be overlooked — one of the two main causes of idleness — and that is the overdevelopment of the industry. The Bituminous Coal Commission appointed by President Wilson in 1919, in dealing with this subject, said:

> At the present time America requires less than five hundred million tons of bituminous coal a year, while the capac-

ity of the mines in operation is over seven hundred million tons. Under the stimulus of war demand many new mines were opened and many old ones expanded in order to secure sufficient coal to meet the exceptional and urgent national requirements. As a result, the coal industry, which you speculatively overdeveloped before the war, is still more overdeveloped now and employs more capital and more labor than is necessary to supply the present needs of the country. Full-time employment in the coal mine cannot, therefore, be expected until the industry is put on such a basis that only those mines remain in operation whose output is required to supply the needs of the country.

Remedial measures. Considerable difficulty has been experienced in the marketing of bituminous coal, due to the seasonal demand for it. The United States Bituminous Coal Commission, in suggesting a remedy for the evils resulting from overexpansion, and from seasonal irregularity, makes certain suggestions regarding the stabilizing of the marketing of coal. These suggestions are, briefly: that the railroads move their own coal in the otherwise dull months; that the public utilities and the large industries, such as steel, increase their storage capacity in order to purchase early in the season; that the Interstate Commerce Commission make necessary provision to permit the railroads to provide sufficient cars; that the banks consider eligible for rediscount a paper drawn against coal in storage.

These suggestions meet with the complete approval of the United Mine Workers of America, as we believe that if they were followed out in practice, it would result in the elimination of a great many of the evils growing out of the present irregularity of employment in the coal mining industry.

But despite the fact that the United States Bituminous Coal Commission recommended the adoption of this plan, yet so far as I know not one of these proposals has been carried out in sufficient earnestness to appreciably reduce the evils complained of. The only practical course to be followed in putting into effect this plan would be for the Government to adopt a drastic regulatory measure, and of course this could only be made practicable by making it financially profitable to all the parties affected to carry out their recommendations. A measure, such as this one, if carried out, would of course have for its purpose the safeguarding of the interests of not only the mine worker, but also those of the consumer and the employer.

For years, the question of guaranteeing greater continuity of work in the coal mines has been discussed, but so far nothing effective has been done. In my judgment the plan suggested by President John L. Lewis of the United Mine Workers of America to the President's Unemployment Conference at Washington is the best that has been presented to date as a remedy for the evils of unemployment in the coal industry. This plan calls upon the Federal Government to extend credit to the unemployed miner as an emergency measure to help tide him over his period of unemployment; it calls for Federal legislation requiring individuals and corporations engaged in interstate commerce to build up a reserve labor fund to be used to pay the wages of employees who would otherwise be summarily dropped for lack of work — a measure designed to prevent unemployment in the future; and urging an impartial investigation of labor costs and profits by the proper governmental authorities.

The need for stabilizing the coal industry is immediate and urgent. Practicable measures to this end should be undertaken at once. Every year the industry is destroying hundreds of millions of tons of the finest coal which would be saved to society by more thorough working of the mines. Along with that goes human waste — lost time, slack work, and unemployment. This leaves the worker with reduced efficiency because of worry, insecurity, and fear. The burden of unemployment in the mine is heavy on all users of coal, but it falls with crushing weight upon the miners and their families.

What the miner wants is not less work, but more work — a regularization of the industry that will insure steady employment. We earnestly hope that the American Association for Labor Legislation, which has done such magnificent work in this field, will succeed in bringing about the adoption of legislative measures that will result in the permanent prevention of unemployment and remove forever from the coal industry, as well as other industries, the menace of involuntary idleness.

5. The Business Cycle [1]

With whatever phase of the business cycle analysis begins, it must take for granted the conditions brought about by the preceding phase, postponing explanation of these assumptions until it has worked around the cycle and come again to its starting-point.

The upward swing. A revival of activity, then, starts with a legacy from depression: a level of prices low in comparison with the prices of prosperity, drastic reductions in the costs of doing business, narrow margins of profit, liberal bank reserves, a constructive policy in capitalizing business enterprises and in granting credits, moderate stocks of goods, and cautious buying.

Such conditions are accompanied by an expansion in the physical volume of trade. Though slow at first, this expansion is cumulative. In time an increase in the amount of business which grows more rapid as it proceeds will turn dullness into activity. Left to itself this transformation is effected by slow degrees; but it is often hastened by some propitious event, such as exceptionally profitable harvests, or heavy purchases of supplies by the Government.

A partial revival of industry soon spreads to all parts of the business field. For the active enterprises must buy materials and current supplies from other enterprises, the latter from still others, etc. Meanwhile all enterprises which become busier employ more labor, use more borrowed money, and make higher profits. There results an increase in family incomes and an expansion of consumers' demands, which likewise spreads out in ever-widening circles. Shopkeepers pass on larger orders to wholesale merchants, manufacturers, importers, and producers of raw materials. All these enterprises increase the sums they pay to employees, lenders, and proprietors. In time the expansion of orders reaches back to the enterprises from which the initial impetus was received, and then the whole complicated series of reactions begins afresh at a higher pitch of intensity. All this while the revival of activity is instilling a feeling of optimism among business men.

The cumulative expansion of the physical volume of trade stops

[1] Adapted from *Business Cycles*, by Wesley C. Mitchell, pp. 571–79. Copyright by the author. The University of California Press, publishers.

the fall in prices and starts a rise. For, when enterprises have in sight as much business as they can handle with existing facilities, they stand out for higher prices on additional orders. This policy prevails because additional orders can be executed only by breaking in new hands, starting new machinery, or buying new equipment. The expectation of its coming hastens the advance. Buyers are anxious to secure large supplies while the quotations continue low, and the first signs of an upward trend bring out a rush of orders.

The rise of prices spreads rapidly; for every advance puts pressure on some one to recoup himself by advancing the prices of what he has to sell. The resulting changes in price are far from even: retail prices lag behind wholesale, and the price of finished products behind the price of their raw materials. Among the last-mentioned the prices of mineral products reflect changed business conditions more regularly than do the prices of forest and farm products. Wages rise more promptly, but in less degree than wholesale prices; interest rates on long loans always move sluggishly in the earlier stages of revival, while the prices of stocks both precede and exceed commodity prices on the rise.

In a great majority of enterprises larger profits result from these divergent fluctuations coupled with the greater physical volume of sales. For while the prices of raw materials and of bank loans often rise faster than selling prices, the prices of labor lag far behind, and the prices making up supplementary costs are mainly stereotyped by old agreements.

The increase of profits, under the spell of optimism, leads to a marked expansion of investments. The heavy orders for machinery, the large contracts for new construction, etc., which result, swell still further the physical volume of business, and render yet stronger the forces which are driving prices upward.

Indeed, the salient characteristic of this phase of the business cycle is the cumulative working of the various processes which are converting a revival of trade into intense prosperity. Not only does every increase in the volume of trade cause other increases, every convert to optimism make new converts, and every advance in price furnish an incentive for new advances; but the growth of trade also helps to spread optimism and to raise prices, while optimism and rising prices support each other. Finally the changes going forward swell profits and encourage investments, while high profits and heavy investments react by augmenting trade, justifying optimism, and raising prices.

Causes of instability. While the processes just sketched work cumulatively for a time to enhance prosperity, they also cause a slow accumulation of stresses within the balanced system of business — stresses which ultimately undermine the conditions upon which prosperity rests.

Among these is the gradual increase in the cost of doing business. The decline in supplementary costs per unit ceases when enterprises have secured all the business they can handle with their standard equipment, and a slow increase in these costs begins when the expiration of old contracts makes necessary renewals at higher rates. Meanwhile prime costs rise at a relatively rapid rate. The price of labor rises both because of an advance in nominal wages and because of higher rates for overtime. More serious is a decline in the efficiency of labor, because of the employment of undesirables, and because crews cannot be driven at top speed when jobs are more numerous than men. The prices of raw material rise faster on the average than the selling prices of products. Finally numerous small wastes creep up when managers are hurried by the press of orders.

A second stress is the accumulating tension of investment and money markets. The supply of funds available at the old rates fails to keep pace with the swelling demand. It becomes difficult to negotiate new issues of securities except on onerous terms, and men of affairs complain of the "scarcity of capital." Nor does the supply of bank loans, limited by reserves, grow fast enough to keep up with the demand. Active trade keeps such an amount of money in circulation that the cash left in the banks increases rather slowly. On the other hand, the demand for loans grows, not only with the physical volume of trade, but also with the rise of prices, and with the desire of men of affairs to use their own funds for controlling as many businesses as possible.

Tension in the bond and money markets is unfavorable to the continuance of prosperity, not only because high rates of interest reduce the prospective margins of profit, but also because they check the expansion of the volume of trade out of which prosperity develops. Many projected ventures are relinquished because borrowers conclude that interest would absorb too much of their profits.

The group producing industrial equipment suffers especially. In the earlier stages of prosperity this group enjoys exceptional activity. But when the market for bonds becomes stringent and the cost of construction high, business enterprises defer the execution of plans for extending old or erecting new plants. As a result contracts for this kind of work become less numerous as the climax of prosperity approaches. Then the steel mills, foundries, machine factories, lumber mills, construction companies, etc., find their orders for future delivery falling off.

The larger the structure of prosperity, the more severe become these internal stresses. The only effective means of preventing disaster while continuing to build is to raise selling prices time after time high enough to offset the encroachment of costs upon profits, and to keep investors willing to contract for fresh industrial equipment.

But it is impossible to keep selling prices rising for an indefinite time. In default of other checks, the inadequacy of cash reserves would ultimately compel the banks to refuse a further expansion of loans on any terms. But before this stage has been reached, the rise of prices is stopped by the consequences of its own inevitable inequalities. These become more glaring the higher the general level is forced; after a time they threaten serious reductions of profits to certain business enterprises, and the troubles of these victims dissolve that confidence in the security of credits with which the whole towering structure of prosperity has been cemented.

In certain lines in which selling prices are stereotyped by law, by contracts, for long terms, by custom, or by business policy, selling prices cannot be raised to prevent a reduction of profits. In other lines prices are always subject to the incalculable chances of the harvests. In some lines the recent construction of new equipment has increased the capacity for production faster than the demand for the wares has expanded under the repressing influence of high prices. The unwillingness of investors to let fresh contracts threatens loss not only to the contracting firms but to the enterprises from which they buy materials. Finally the success of some enterprises in raising prices fast enough to defend their profits aggravates the difficulties of the men who are in trouble.

As prosperity approaches its height, then, a sharp contrast develops between the business prospects of different enterprises. Many are making more money than at any previous stage in the business cycle. But an important minority faces the prospect of declining profits. The more intense prosperity becomes, the larger grows this threatened group. In time these conditions bred by prosperity will force radical readjustment.

The downward swing. Such a decline of profits threatens consequences worse than the failure to realize expected dividends. For it arouses doubt about the future of outstanding credits. Business credit is based primarily upon the capitalized value of present and prospective profits, and the volume of credits outstanding at the zenith of prosperity is adjusted to the great expectations which prevail when affairs are optimistic. The rise of interest rates has already narrowed the margins of security behind credits by reducing the capitalized value of given profits. When profits begin to waver, creditors begin to fear lest the shrinkage in the market rating of business enterprises which owe them money will leave no adequate security for repayment. Hence they refuse renewals of old loans to enterprises which cannot stave off a decline in profits, and press for settlement of outstanding accounts.

Thus prosperity ultimately brings on conditions which start a liquidation of the huge credits which it has piled up. And in the course of this liquidation prosperity merges into crisis. Once begun the process of liquidation extends rapidly, partly because most enterprises called upon to settle put similar pressure on their own debtors, and partly because news presently leaks out and other creditors take alarm.

While this financial readjustment is under way, the problem of making profits is subordinated to the more vital problem of maintaining solvency. Business managers nurse their financial resources rather than push their sales. In consequence the volume of new orders falls off rapidly. The prospect of profits is dimmed. Expansion gives place to contraction. Discount rates rise higher than usual, securities and commodities fall in price, and working forces are reduced. But there is no epidemic of bankruptcy, no run upon banks, and no spasmodic interruption of ordinary business processes.

Crises, however, may degenerate into panics. When the process of liquidation reaches a weak link in the chain of interlocking credits and the bankruptcy of some conspicuous enterprise spreads unreasoning alarm, the banks are suddenly forced to meet a double strain — a sharp increase in the demand for loans and in the demand for repayment of deposits. If the banks meet both demands, the alarm quickly subsides. But if many solvent business men are refused accommodation at any price, and depositors are refused payment in full, the alarm turns into a panic. A restriction of payments by banks gives rise to a premium upon currency, to hoarding of cash, and to the use of various unlawful substitutes for money. Interest rates may go to three or four times their usual figures, causing forced suspensions and bankruptcies. There follow appeals to the Government for extraordinary aid, frantic efforts to import gold, the issue of clearing-house loan certificates and an increase in bank-note circulation as rapidly as the existing system permits. Collections fall into arrears, workmen are discharged, stocks fall to extremely low levels, commodity prices are disorganized by sacrifice sales, and the volume of business is violently contracted.

The depression. There follows a period during which depression spreads over the whole field of business and grows more severe. Consumers' demand declines in consequence of wholesale discharge of wage-earners. With it falls the business demand for raw materials, current supplies, and equipment. Still more severe is the shrinkage in the investors' demand for construction work of all kinds. The contraction in the physical volume of business which results from these shrinkages in demand is cumulative, since every reduction of employment causes a reduction in consumers' demand, thereby starting again the whole series of reactions at a high pitch of intensity.

With this contraction goes a fall in prices. For when current orders are insufficient to employ the existing equipment, competition for business becomes keener. This decline spreads through the regular commercial channels which connect one enterprise with another, and is cumulative, since every reduction in price facilitates reductions in other prices, and the latter reductions react to cause fresh reductions at the starting-point.

The fall in prices is characterized by certain regularly recurring differences in degree. Wholesale prices fall faster than retail, and the prices of raw materials faster than those of manufactured products. The prices of raw mineral products follow a more regular course than those of forest or farm products. Wages and interest on long-time loans decline in less degree than commodity prices. The only important group of prices to rise is high-grade bonds.

The contraction in the volume of trade and the fall in prices reduce the margin of present and prospective profits, spread discouragement, and check enterprise. But they also set in motion certain processes of readjustment by which the depression is overcome.

The prime costs of doing business are reduced by the fall in the prices of raw material and of bank loans, by the marked increases in the efficiency of labor which comes when employment is scarce, and by closer economy by managers. Supplementary costs are reduced by reduction of rentals and refunding of loans, by writing down depreciated properties, and by admitting that a recapitalization has been effected on the basis of lower profits.

While costs are being reduced, the demand for goods begins slowly to expand. Accumulated stocks left over from prosperity are exhausted, and current consumption requires current production. Clothing, furniture and machinery are discarded and replaced. New tastes appear among consumers and new methods among producers, giving rise to demand for novel products. Most important of all, the investment demand for industrial equipment revives. Capitalists become less timid as the crisis recedes into the past, the low rates of interest on long-time bonds encourages borrowing, and contracts can be let on most favorable conditions.

Once these forces have set the physical volume of trade to expanding, the increase proves cumulative. Business prospects become gradually brighter. Everything awaits a revival of activity which will begin when some fortunate circumstance gives a fillip to demand, or, in the absence of such an event, when the slow growth of the volume of business has filled order books and paved the way for a new rise in prices. Such is the stage of the business cycle with which the analysis begins, and, having accounted for its own beginning, the analysis ends.

6. Effect of the Business Cycle on Labor

Labor's interest in the cycle. The business cycle is one of the influences of the modern business world profoundly affecting the economic well-being of the propertyless wage-earner. On the whole, this influence is decidedly an evil one; indeed, it is impossible to estimate the extent of the injury done to the working population by reason of the constant uncertainty and distrust of the future generated by the business cycle, and to the entire productive structure of society through reaction of the workers to these conditions. From the preceding description of the cycle it is to be noted that the phenomena connected with it pass through three rather well-marked phases. There is, in the first place, the upward swing of the cycle known as the *prosperity* period, which culminates in the short and rather hectic experience of "boom times." Secondly, the sudden and acute breakdown of the industrial and credit structure at the climax of the cycle to which is given the name "*crisis*." Finally, the ensuing period of *depression* during which the economic organization of society is working toward a new point of equilibrium. These different phases do not all have the same effect upon labor.

The upward swing. It may even be said with substantial truth that the effect of the first period of the business cycle upon the welfare of labor is, on the whole, good. At this time, two conflicting tendencies are at work, the one to worsen the economic condition of the workingman, the other to better it; but the balance of these forces is usually on the positive side. The most prominent feature of the prosperity phase of the cycle is the inflation of prices, and this, if unbalanced by conflicting tendencies would work steadily toward a lowering of the real wages of the workingman and an undermining of his standard of life. Money wages are a species of price subject, like other prices, to the forces which tend to raise the price level. But the rise of money wages for the whole mass of workers is never rapid enough to keep pace with the prices of consumable goods which constitute the living costs of this group.

Decline of real wages. There are two major reasons for this. In the first place, money wages are controlled, to a greater or less degree, by contract. The term of employment, for all but the lowest grades of labor, is fixed or implied in the contract to cover a period extending from one week to a year, according to the custom of the business world with respect to the particular occupational group in question. During this period the question of a revision of the wage bargain does not arise automatically but must be pressed forward as an emergency issue by the employee in opposition to the general usage of the business world. This handicap is felt especially by the higher ranks of workers — the so-called "salariat" — whose money wage is usually assumed to be fixed for one year from the date of the wage contract. An alert and aggressive labor group not embraced in this custom of the yearly contract may succeed in shortening the gaps between the dates of the revision of the wage bargain. But even in their case, it is almost impossible to prevent some lag between the rise of their money income and the cost of living; for market prices rise continuously and without cessation, and money wages, adjusted periodically to equate the income of the worker to current living costs, are quickly left behind in the race.

The decline in real wages which results from this lack of correspondence between the rise of money wages and other prices, does not apply, therefore, in equal degree to all groups of workers, but varies with the practice of the business world in respect of the length of term embraced in the wage contract. There is, moreover, another factor tending to prevent this correspondence. Wage-earners may be viewed as sellers of a commodity whose price is, within broad limits, controlled by the forces of demand and supply. In the absence of restrictive time contracts, the influence which they might exert upon the price of their commodity — money wages — could only be exerted through an exercise of that power which any selling group possesses: namely, control over the supply of the commodity. For the wage-earner, under conditions of competition among buyers, this power consists fundamentally in his willingness and ability to withdraw his labor from one employer and offer it to another, whenever it is to his advantage to do so. It is by playing off one buyer against another in this fashion that enterprisers take advantage of rising prices to their own profit. But the position of the laborer as a seller is, in some respects, unique. He, alone of all sellers, must deliver himself with his commodity; and, if the transfer from one employer to another covers a geographical area of any size, the change involves a removal of his home and family to a new location. The costs involved in this change — money expenses of travel, the disrupting of neighborhood ties and of sentimental attachments to the old environment — operate to reduce the *mobility* of the workingman and, hence, to impair his effectiveness as a bargainer. It is probable that these forces are more strongly felt by the general class of salaried employees than by the recipients of day wages — by that class, in other words, whose money income is most subject to the repressive influence of the time contract. But immobility is, to a greater or less degree, the condition of all propertyless wage-earners. It is a factor which operates independently of the influence of the time contract to prevent a continuous readjustment of money income to mounting costs of living.

Evidence of the failure of general money wages to keep pace with a rising price level during a period of inflation is available in the record of the prosperity phase of the business cycle which culminated in the crisis of 1920. Statistics of money wages compiled by the Bureau of Labor Statistics of the Department of Labor show that, in the initial stages of the price inflation, the money income of the working population fell behind the mounting cost of living; and that this discrepancy continued in varying degree throughout the entire period. Taking 1913 as the base year in which, for purposes of comparison, both money wages and average prices may be assumed to be 100, a comparison of these two factors during the succeeding seven-year period is given in the following table:

INDEX — WAGES AND PRICES (UNION SCALES)

YEAR	WAGES PER HOUR	FULL TIME HOURS PER WEEK	RATE WAGES PER WEEK (FULL TIME)	PRICES	REAL WAGES
1907	90	103	92	94	98
1908	91	102	93	90	103+
1909	92	102	93	97	96
1910	94	101	95	101	94
1911	96	101	96	93	103
1912	98	101	98	99	99
1913	100	100	100	100	100
1914	102	100	102	98	104
1915	103	99	102	101	101
1916	107	99	106	127	84—
1917	114	98	112	177	63
1918	133	97	130	194	68
1919	155	95	148	206	72
1920	199	94	189	226	84—
1921	205	94	193	147	131

"Real wages" obtained by dividing weekly wage index by price index, thus obtaining purchasing power of weekly wage.

It was not until *after* the crisis of 1920 that money wages overtook the rising cost of living. Throughout the period of price inflation, the effect of rising prices was to reduce the real wages.

Compensating factors. Despite the testimony of these statistics, however, the net effect of the prosperity period of the business cycle upon the wage-earner is, as stated above, probably good. Statistics of money wages, like those contained in the foregoing table, take no account of the factor of unemployment which must be drawn into our calculations before we can estimate the *earnings* [1] of the wage-earner as distinct from his money wages. During the first phase of the business cycle unemployment sinks to a minimum, approaching the zero point for the only time in the normal course of the business world. It is a period of intense business activity with production proceeding at an accelerating rate in almost all lines of industry. With rare exceptions, every able-bodied wage-earner can find a job and hold it continuously at his pleasure. He can do more than this; in many industries he can work overtime at rates of pay frequently double the normal rates. Other perquisites come to him: bonuses for consistent service, shares in the profits, Christmas presents — bribes offered by an employer keen to reduce his labor turnover. Members of his family not usually employed, the wife and children, may be drawn into industry to replenish the exhausted supply of labor. From all these sources, the family earnings are increased to a point which, even allowing for the lowered purchasing power of money wages, make possible an elevation of the standard of living. It is to be noted that a part of these earnings is drawn from sources that, from the standpoint of social welfare, would be detrimental if continuously utilized. Nevertheless, there is a net gain for all concerned — to the other members of society no less than to the workingman himself — in the reduction of unemployment which characterizes this period.

It is impossible to prove statistically the extent, or even the reality, of this gain to labor through a diminution of unemployment during the prosperity phase of the cycle; for no adequate records are kept of the actual earnings of the industrial worker's family. General observation during the period of price inflation immediately preceding the crisis of 1920, however, gave consistent support to the opinion that the great bulk of wage-earners were enabled at this time to raise their standard of living. This opinion received further confirmation from the fact that most of those unemployed after the crisis found it possible to finance their own periods of idleness from accumulated savings without recourse to charity. Speaking in more general terms, the consistent reaction of workingmen in favor of "cheap money" is evidence that they, at least, consider the period of rising prices favorable to their interests.

[1] *Earnings* are the money wages actually received by the workman over a period of time. They are derived, obviously, by multiplying the money wages by the fraction which represents the average unemployment experience of the group. It requires no argument to prove that the economic welfare of any section of the population depends upon real earnings rather than upon real wages.

It is well, however, to accept this conclusion regarding the beneficial effects of the first phase of the business cycle with strong reservations, and to employ it as a basis for further inferences only with great caution. Obviously it does not apply to all labor. Those grades not normally subject to much unemployment — in general, the salaried group — gain through this factor very little offset to the decline in the purchasing power of their money income. Moreover, with regard to the other labor groups, it cannot be assumed with confidence that the gain from increased employment will necessarily outweigh the loss through the rising cost of living. This is especially doubtful during times of gradually rising prices when the inflation is not sufficiently pronounced to exert an appreciable effect upon business activity. And at best any favorable conclusion regarding the effect upon labor of the prosperity phase of the cycle, must be formed by divorcing this period from those which follow and considering it separately. As soon as it is placed in its proper relationship to the whole sequence of phenomena which constitute the business cycle, it becomes apparent that any possible gains are more than counterbalanced by the losses which follow.

The depression. From the standpoint of labor, the second and third phases of the business cycle differ only in the severity of their evil effects. Both are times of abnormal unemployment. During the crisis unemployment reaches its high-water mark; all enterprises are confronted with the urgent necessity of reducing current costs and resort to general dismissal or lay-off of their work forces as the most direct means of accomplishing this end. Since this condition is almost universal, the discharged workman can find no job to replace the one he has lost. The calamity comes without warning. An army of unemployed flocks to the cities, filling the park benches, thronging the streets in a weary round of job-hunting, crowding the dockets of the police courts with charges of begging and petty offenses against property. A graphic picture of this condition of unemployment is given in the following section which treats of the circumstances attending the crises of 1915 and 1920.

This condition of abnormal unemployment continues through the depression which follows in the wake of the crisis, but with diminishing severity. After the collapse of the industrial and credit structure business enterprise is slow to revive. At length, however, the accumulated stocks of commodities are worked off the market. The first halting recovery of production drains the labor market of a part of its excess supply and, with the gradual increase of business activity, unemployment subsides. The depression may cover a span of several years during which unemployment continues at an abnormally high figure. Though the total gradually falls, in the case of many families the experience of unemployment will be practically continuous and the suffering, consequently, progressive. These are times of labor unrest and radicalism. Desperation born of protracted misery and the apparently hopeless future may lead to open violence bordering on civil war.

The recovery at the end of the depression is never all-inclusive. The economic organization of society reaches a point of equilibrium through the process of finding a new balance between the various branches of production. On the new plane, some types of enterprise are permanently constricted within limits narrower than those which obtained before the crisis; others are expanded. A part of the labor committed to the former group of industries must be transferred to new occupational groups, bearing, usually without compensation, the costs involved in the process. Above all, the entire laboring population faces life with an increased burden of anxiety and fear.

7. Effects of the Crisis of 1920 [1]

Extent of unemployment. Unemployment in 1920–21 has been far greater in extent than in 1914–15. Six years ago the total number of workers forced into involuntary idleness was estimated at 2,000,000, with at least as many more on only part-time employment. In the industrial depression there were, by June 1, 1921, according to the highest official estimates 4,000,000 employees idle and at least as many more on part time.

About October, 1920, unemployment began to set in on an unmistakably large scale. On December 9 the United States Department of Labor announced that what is left of the Federal Employment Service would undertake to gather statistics of unemployment for the entire country, in coöperation with other federal and state agencies, the figures to be published at regular intervals. In accordance with this new plan the first number of the *Industrial Employment Survey Bulletin* was published by the United States Employment Service in January, 1921; the second number appeared in March, and later the *Bulletin* appeared monthly.

On January 25, 1921, according to the official government

[1] From the *American Labor Legislation Review*, September, 1921.

figures based on data from 182 principal industrial cities in 35 states and the District of Columbia, there were 3,500,000 fewer workers employed in the mechanical industries covered than in January, 1920 — a reduction of 36.9 per cent. The official figures fall short of disclosing the actual extent of unemployment in that they do not take into account the great railroad and mining groups and the smaller firms throughout the country employing less than 501 workers. In eight basic industrial groups the degree of unemployment in January, 1921, as compared with January, 1920, according to the official estimate, was as follows: Metal and products, machinery, electrical goods, foundry products, 30.5 per cent fewer employed; building trades, 52.4 per cent fewer employed; packing and food products, 19 per cent fewer employed; textiles and products, clothing, hosiery and underwear, 35.5 per cent fewer employed; leather, its products, boots and shoes, 34.9 per cent fewer employed; automobiles and accessories, 69.2 per cent fewer employed; lumber, house furniture, boxes and wood products, 32.3 per cent fewer employed; clay, glass, cement and stone products, 19.3 per cent fewer employed, which meant that in these great industries alone there were on the average as high as 35.5 per cent fewer persons at work than a year previous.

The American Federation of Labor on February 28 announced that a canvass under way by organized labor covering 917 cities indicated that approximately 4,000,000 were out of work.

On May Day the Associated Press reported that estimates from government, labor, and industrial officials showed more than 2,000,000 men unemployed in 19 States — a large proportion of those unable to obtain work being in the industrial sections of the Eastern and Central States — while reports from the remaining 29 States indicated that the total for the country was between 3,000,000 and 5,000,000 idle workers. On June 1 the "survey" published by the Guaranty Trust Company, relying upon "the most reliable estimates," placed the number of unemployed at between 3,000,000 and 4,000,000. These estimates were substantiated by a careful study of figures supplied by the Department of Labor which showed that the number of unemployed in August of this year totaled approximately three and a half million.

Here was an unemployment crisis of appalling magnitude. Following past experience with these ever-recurring depressions

— particularly the crisis of six years ago — the way has been opened this time alarmingly wide for the quick appearance of acute distress and destitution on a scale never before known. Yet as winter dragged out its course and gave way to spring, the reports from all sections, with but few exceptions, failed to record drastic resort to emergency relief measures or suffering among the families of unemployed at all commensurate with the extent of involuntary idleness. How was this to be explained?

Why so little distress. Unemployment in the winter of 1920–21, although twice as great in extent — according to highest official estimates — as during the previous depression of 1914–15, was accompanied by far less acute distress.

The outstanding reason given for this was the unprecedented degree to which unemployed workers tided themselves and their families over the first few months of idleness. By using up their savings and selling their Liberty Bonds, and to a less extent disposing of automobiles, victrolas, pianos, and other valuables acquired during the war and post-war boom — even in many instances sacrificing paid-for or partly-paid-for homes — the unemployed on the whole carried themselves over last winter's emergency for periods ranging from three to nine months.

Charitable and relief organizations, therefore, were to that extent freed from a burden that must otherwise have quickly overwhelmed their resources — although reporting that, as it was, they had to expand their activities greatly; in some cases toward spring their expenditures for material aid and temporary loans amounting to three or four times as much as in previous years without fully meeting the need for relief, while in many places it was found necessary to assist with charitable aid through city appropriations.

Preventive measures. Employers succeeded in preventing a large amount of complete unemployment by going on a part-time basis. Business associations reporting from 41 cities were almost unanimous in stating that the short day and the short week were used as a rule by manufacturers in their effort to avert as much joblessness as possible. Shifting and rotating employees, though to a less extent, were also used. There was some "making to stock," especially in basic industries, despite the uncertainty of price trends in raw materials and of the buyers' strike, and there were also a few attempts to utilize labor in making plant repairs or improvements. The reports warrant the estimate that if emergency plans for making available work go as far as possible had not been thus generally adopted by manufacturers there would have been twice as many without employment.

Public works were found to be effective for relief, serving as a sponge to absorb jobless workers. Out of 81 cities sending information, 24 had by June 1 provided bond issues and appropriations totaling nearly $10,000,000 expressly for the purpose of starting or pushing forward useful public works as an aid to the unemployed — a significant showing in view of the many cities reporting a disposition to delay even their regularly-planned public works pending cheaper transportation and construction costs. No city, however, had provided work enough to take care of all who applied — at least half in most cases being turned away. Direct hiring was the rule on city emergency work, as was also working the same hours and applying the same standards of efficiency as is required for regular city employment.

Cities generally had failed to make any efforts to reserve necessary improvements for bad seasons or bad years. Neither have they made any progress, the reports show, toward maintaining sinking funds to be used in starting emergency work when needed.

Public employment bureaus were helpful in relieving unemployment, most reports commending their services. Employers' associations in 19 out of 28 cities reporting expressed themselves as favorable to the public employment service, only 5 registering opposition. Some employers' bodies criticized the private fee-charging agencies for, as one expressed it, "collecting exorbitant fees on mythical jobs." The action of Congress a year ago in radically curtailing the appropriation for the United States Employment Service was criticized in many reports which declared that necessary offices had to be closed and that placement activities had thus been seriously crippled. In all cities reporting, where federal, state and city bureaus were in existence, they were found to be in close coöperation not only with each other but also with other agencies — private and public — dealing with the unemployed.

Community organization had by June 1 to a marked extent

taken the form of emergency committees representing both public and private agencies. In no less than 18 cities special unemployment committees appointed by mayors, or similar public-private bodies, were created. Activities of these groups ranged from specific campaigns for stimulating emergency public works and finding temporary jobs in private employment to the more general work of coördinating the efforts of all existing relief agencies. In 14 cities where organized work of emergency relief was confined to committees of private bodies or citizens, it was found that in most cases the committees were formed to bring about closer coöperation between existing relief agencies.

Nearly all cities that had any experience with the demoralizing results of "pauperization" sent in warnings to "avoid bread lines, soup kitchens, money gifts or other indiscriminate giving of charitable relief." Nine cities especially condemned the giving of undue publicity to relief plans or funds.

Several states in 1921, through legislation, expanded their systems of state employment bureaus, with generous additional appropriations. One or two authorized bond issues by cities for the relief of the unemployed. Some made provision for road construction. Unemployment insurance bills were introduced with strong, representative backing in two States, and in Wisconsin the bill was advanced to a favorable committee report in the Senate. Two States on opposite sides of the continent furnished a striking contrast; New York reorganized its labor department, on the ground of "economy," in such a way that a serious blow was struck at the state employment bureaus, and on the same plea of "retrenchment" refused to advance a resolution to create a legislative committee to coördinate all plans for public works, under way or contemplated throughout the State as a matter of first aid to the jobless; California, on the other hand, enacted a comprehensive law providing for permanent, advance planning of public works by state departments so that useful jobs may be made available at once whenever an unemployment emergency sets in.

Federal action, aside from Secretary Hoover's appeal to the states to help by letting contracts for road building in the autumn wherever practicable, instead of waiting until next spring, was less in evidence. Our Government suffered in this respect in comparison with Canada, where the Government, already provided with a well-organized national-state employment service, announced that it will push forward public works scheduled for next summer so that they will be available during the coming winter to combat unemployment. Canadian government officials, too, called a conference at Vancouver, August 10, of 50 representative employers and government and municipal officials to work out a definite program whereby industry would assist in providing jobs for the unemployed.

Looking immediately ahead, reports from many sections in the United States warned that cities must prepare for severe unemployment during the coming winter. Relief agencies not only pointed out that the unemployed have exhausted their own savings and valuables and cannot continue to help themselves as they did last winter, but they also found that unemployment has been increasing faster than community activities have been planned to combat it. While an encouraging number of cities, the reports show, have taken measures to relieve the unemployed, still the great majority face the coming winter with no program at all or merely the feeble beginnings of constructive relief. The opinion is widely held that unless the industrial cities promptly "dig in" unemployment in many sections will become unmanageable with the advent of cold weather.

Definite conclusions as to the proper measures for combating unemployment were forthcoming out of the experiences of 66 cities. Of these, 23 laid stress upon expansion of public works as the most successful measure within their experience; 16 emphasized temporary jobs and the giving of material relief, where necessary, only when earned; 15 regarded proper community organizations, including "mayors" committees as a prime necessity; 14 were especially aided by the efforts of employers to provide part time employment by means of the short day, short week and the "making to stock"; and 8 secured notably good results through public employment bureaus.

CHAPTER III

REMEDIES FOR UNEMPLOYMENT

1. The Labor Exchange

Function of the labor exchange. A large part of the total unemployment existing at any time may be attributed to the failure of the labor market to work out a precise adjustment of the supply of labor to the demand for it. In a static industrial society where processes were stereotyped and unchanging, the location of industries fixed, and the various lines of productive activity permanently held in a state of equilibrium, this problem of maladjustment would either not arise at all or would work out its own correctives in short order. But our world is not of that kind. On the contrary, there is continual change and transition from one technical process, or from one geographical location to another; the ownership of our enterprises is constantly in a state of flux with resulting changes in method and direction; the proportions which the quantities of different kinds of goods and services bear to one another are never in stable equilibrium. Hence it follows that the amounts of labor demanded at a given rate of wages in a given locality, or by a given employer, or in a particular productive group are constantly rising or falling; and the supply of labor must fluctuate in harmony with these changes in demand if unemployment is not to occur in certain industrial centers. This necessity is especially urgent during that period of readjustment which follows a crisis; but it is never entirely absent even when industry is proceeding on even keel.

Now labor is not a highly mobile commodity. When changes in the amounts or kinds of labor demanded in different communities at stable rates of wages occur with any degree of suddenness, the workmen are slow to adjust themselves to the new conditions of the labor market. In part, this lethargy of the labor supply is due to inertia, to the bonds of sentiment which attach the wage-earner to his neighborhood, or to other forces which influence the behavior of the workman in common with all other human beings. But in some measure it is caused by mere ignorance of the conditions of the labor market outside the workman's own locality. The unemployed of one city simply do not know that jobs are available elsewhere and, if left to their own devices, have no inexpensive and effective means of finding out. The labor exchange fits into the situation at this point. It is a clearing-house for information regarding the demand and supply of labor. As a part of a nation-wide organization, it registers and classifies both the unemployed and the available jobs in each locality with a view toward bringing together, with a minimum of delay and friction, the unfilled jobs and the idle workmen of the entire district. Whatever effect it may have upon the problem of unemployment must be exerted through the device of increasing the mobility of labor.

In the absence of public provision for labor exchanges, this function will be undertaken by private enterprisers as a profit-making activity. A string of registration offices will be set up in the industrial centers of a state or region to which idle workmen may apply for jobs. These offices pool the information they gather, thus working out an adjustment of demand and supply in the labor market over a wide area. Since they are organized for profit, they charge the workman who uses their facilities fees in excess of the cost of service.

Evils of the private exchange. Experience with the private labor exchange has proved that this institution tends to abuse its power. The social interest demands that all such devices serve the primary purpose of reducing and preventing unemployment, rather than palliate the evil after it has developed. But the private owner of a system of labor exchanges has no interest in reducing unemployment; on the contrary, his profit varies directly with its amount. He is tempted to increase the disease from the treatment of which he draws his revenue. In many cases it has been found that this temptation has led the private exchange into practices of the most unscrupulous kind. For example, instances have been discovered of collusion between the owners of an exchange in one city and the foremen or employment managers in another, the intention being to maintain a constant demand for labor from the city in question. The foreman's part in this partnership of iniquity was to force the newly employed workmen to vacate their jobs in the shortest possible space of time; the manager of the exchange, for his part, was to keep a stream of applicants on the way to the distant city, charging fees for this service which he divided with the foreman.

The history of the private exchange is filled with similar examples of sharp practice. The manager of such an institution is essentially a broker and should be bound, by moral and ethical considerations if not legally, to demand a fee from but one of the two parties whom he serves. But many of the exchanges have charged fees from both, not for providing service but merely for registering the applicant for employment, on the one hand, and the employer, on the other. This has enabled them to levy a double tribute upon those suffering from the evil of unemployment merely because of their suffering, and not for the relief of it. Other examples could be given. Private employment agencies have been known to send the unemployed workman on a futile journey to a distant point where no employment existed, equipping him with cards of introduction to fictitious employers. Many times the fees charged have been exorbitant, and this has been especially true in times of acute distress among the unemployed. The private exchanges have, also, worked in collusion with loan sharks who advanced the money required for rail fares on chattel mortgages which placed the workman under a permanent bondage of debt. In short, experience with this institution has proved again what society has learned from bitter experience in other lines of enterprise: that it is unsafe to entrust the solution of a social maladjustment to a private enterpriser who draws his profit from its continuance.

Organized labor has a grievance against the private labor exchange which has not yet been discussed. The system easily lends itself to the purpose of strike breaking, and has often been used to serve this purpose. An employer whose men are on strike can send to another city a requisition for an entirely new set of workmen, perhaps concealing the reason for his demand for labor. The manager of the exchange quite naturally welcomes this kind of business since it creates a large harvest of fees. If he knows that the demand is virtually a demand for strike breakers, he may either make up a force of strong-arm men who are informed as to the true nature of their position and welcome the opportunity to exercise their turbulent dispositions; or, suppressing the information about the strike, he may send workmen — even union men — who take their employment in good faith and are surprised when they discover that they have unwittingly adopted the rôle of "scabs." Quite apart from the bearing of this activity on the success of the strike, the unions have found that it creates internal dissension among their members. Idle members of a local union may, without intention, contribute to the defeat of their fellow members in another place. When the system is used to recruit professional strike breakers, on the other hand, it is functioning to promote the bitterness and violence which follow inevitably in the path of that species of modern free-booter.

Regulation of the private exchange. Because of these abuses, most of our States[1] — thirty-eight in all — have statutes regulat-

[1] Summarized from an article on "Legislation on Private Employment Agencies" in the *Monthly Labor Review*, October, 1922.

ing the private employment agency. Some of these statutes are thirty years old, but most of them were enacted during the last decade. There are certain features common to these laws. The agencies are licensed and open to inspection by government authorities; they are required to keep records of their transactions; and to make reports at intervals setting forth the details of their activities.

The regulatory features common to these statutes relate to the fees charged by the employment agencies and to their obligations to the payer of these fees. It is a common requirement that receipts be given for all fees collected and that the fee be returned to the applicant if he has failed to obtain the position to which he was referred. Similarly the unemployed workman is usually allowed to recover any registration fee he may have paid if he is not furnished with work through the agency within a specified time. Where applicants are sent out of town and then fail to get work, the laws of some States provide that the agency pay their traveling expenses in addition to returning the fees. In many cases, in addition to providing for refunds, the laws place restrictions on the amount of the fees which may be charged.

Most of the laws contain a list of "acts forbidden" which is illuminating since it shows the lengths to which the unregulated agency may go in abusing its power. The most frequent of these prohibitions are: misrepresentations of the conditions of employment; falsifying records; trying to convey the impression in advertisements that no fees are charged; sending women to immoral resorts; allowing questionable characters to frequent the agency; splitting fees with employers or foremen; sending applicants to positions without having bona fide order from employer; inducing workmen to leave positions in order to seek employment through the agency; endeavoring to secure the discharge of employees. The usual penalty for these offenses is fine and imprisonment.

The public exchange. In addition to the regulation of private employment exchanges, the States have taken steps to discharge this function through publicly owned agencies. Before the World War there were in existence upwards of eighty public exchanges, maintained by twenty-three States and a number of municipalities. Because of insufficient financial provision, or because the work was handled by mail through a single employment office in one place, the system in some of these States — West Virginia, Maryland, Nebraska might be mentioned as examples — was virtually impotent to discharge its functions. But many other States, including the large industrial commonwealths of New York, Massachusetts, Illinois, Wisconsin, and

Ohio, have set up machinery which is functioning with a large degree of success. A good illustration of these more effective systems of public labor exchanges is afforded by the machinery set up in New York by the statute of 1914.[1]

"By this statute a bureau of employment is established in the state department of labor, under the immediate charge of a director who must be under civil service and who must have 'recognized executive and managerial ability, technical and scientific knowledge upon the subject of unemployment and administration of public employment offices and recognized ability to direct investigations of unemployment.' The industrial commission may establish such local offices as it deems necessary, each to be in charge of a superintendent under the general supervision of the director. These local offices are to register applications from those seeking employment or employers seeking workmen, and make periodic reports to the director. Any office may be subdivided into departments for men, women, and juveniles, or other class of workmen. The service is to be free and penalties are prescribed for the acceptance of fees by officials. A coördination of the activities of the local bureaus is to be facilitated by a labor market bulletin and the interchange and publication of lists of vacancies. Partial recognition is given to the European policy of joint control by directing the commissioner of labor to appoint for each office a representative committee composed of employers and employees, with a chairman agreed upon by the majority. On the request of a majority of either side the voting on any question must be so conducted that there shall be an equality of voting power between employers and employees, notwithstanding the absence of any member."

Similar comprehensive statutes have been passed in the industrial States of Illinois, Ohio, Wisconsin, Massachusetts and Pennsylvania. As stated below, the efforts of these organizations are, however, hampered by the absence of any system covering the national area in a unified manner. The Federal Government, it is true, has made some attempts to meet this problem. In connection with the effort to place immigrants on the farms, an employment service was set up in the Bureau of Immigration in 1907. As a part of the war policy, and in order to reduce the great turnover of labor which resulted from uncontrolled competition among employers working on government contracts, this service was widened in 1918 to cover the entire country and to embrace all types of labor. At that time the service was separated from the Bureau of Immigration and taken over by the

[1] See Commons and Andrews: *Principles of Labor Legislation*, p. 298. Harper and Brothers, publishers.

Department of Labor. During 1918 a rapid expansion occurred in the number of offices — the total rising to 832 concentrated in the principal industrial centers — and in the geographical area covered.

Improvement of the public exchange. The testimony of experts who have studied the operations of the Federal Employment agencies during this period leave no doubt as to its effectiveness. Between January, 1918, and March, 1919, 5,323,509 unemployed workmen were registered, while applications were received from employers totaling 10,164,000. Of the registered workmen almost 5,000,000 were referred to positions, of whom 3,776,750 were successful in obtaining employment. Yet in the spirit of economy which followed the conclusion of the War, the appropriations for this service were so drastically reduced that it was forced to discontinue its local operations entirely and has at the present day virtually ceased to exist. The reasons for the necessity of a federal service to supplement and coöperate with the state bureaus are thus stated by the leading authorities on the subject:[1]

Notwithstanding the good work of a few, however, the state and municipal bureaus are still far from furnishing an adequate medium for the exchange of information on opportunities for employment. Only about half the States are represented. Due to lack of civil-service requirements many of the managers are political place-holders of worse than mediocre ability. Some of the offices exist, as has been seen, only on paper; others are poorly located, in out-of-the-way places; and inadequately heated, lighted, and ventilated. Many have therefore driven away the better class of workers, and deal only with casuals. Appropriations are usually too small for efficiency. A uniform method of record-keeping has yet to be adopted. Statistics are non-comparable, and frequently unreliable, if not wholly valueless. There is practically no interchange of information between various offices in a State, or between States. In short, workmen are still undergoing want, hardship, and discouragement even though often within easy reach of the work which would support them, if they but knew where to find it.

Nor does the evil end there. Every one who has studied the problem realizes that method and system in putting men and opportunities for work in touch with each other will not of them-

[1] Commons and Andrews: *Principles of Labor Legislation*, p. 302 f. Harper and Brothers, publishers.

selves prevent over-supply of labor or of jobs. They will do so no more than the cotton exchanges guard against an over- or under-supply of cotton. They will serve merely as levelers in the scales of labor supply and labor demand. Besides the unemployment which is due to the failure of men and jobs to find each other, there is much due to other causes which even the best system of employment exchanges would not directly eliminate.

But close students agree that these other causes of unemployment cannot be successfully attacked without a basis in comprehensive, conscientiously collected information such as cannot be furnished by our present machinery for dealing with the problem. Under present methods there exists no automatic, cumulative means for collecting facts. This results, of course, in exaggerated statements in both directions. Our paucity of information on this complex and vital question has continued, even though labor problems in one form or another have taken the lead as subjects for legislation. Any scientific lawmaking on the programs of social insurance — especially unemployment insurance — and of vocational guidance must be grounded on facts of relative employment and unemployment of the workers, by trades, by sexes, and by ages. Without a nation-wide system of labor exchanges, no basis can exist for anticipating in an accurate manner the ebbs and flows of the demand for labor. Without concentration of the information now collected and now held separately in thousands of separate organizations throughout the land, the possibility of looking into the future, or of profiting by the past, is out of the question.

2. A Labor Exchange at Work [1]

New York Exchange. It is fortunate that a great industrial state like New York has, at this time, the beginnings of an adequate public employment office system — an organized bureau which cannot only be of great direct aid in the present emergency, but, what is of far more importance, an organization which can bring together up-to-the-minute data on the labor situation and thus be in a position to suggest ways, both to employers and employees, in which some of the present difficulties can be overcome, and point to remedies which will relieve the situation.

[1] From an article by C. B. Barnes, "Employment and the Labor Market," in the *American Economic Review*, vol. 8, Supplement. 1918.

The organization of a State Bureau of Employment in New York was commenced in 1915, and at the present time the Bureau has offices in Buffalo, Rochester, Syracuse, Albany, and New York City, with small branches in Auburn, Oswego, Williamsburgh, and Long Island City. The Bureau has an administrative office in New York City, to which are sent daily reports from each office throughout the State. These reports from the large industrial centers of the State enable the main office to get a good general view of the labor situation.

As evidencing the activity of the offices in direct placement work, I quote you a few figures from the monthly statistics. During the past twelve months these offices have registered (both men and women) a few over 90,000 people, and received requests from employers for nearly 114,000 workers. The offices referred out to jobs over 111,000 persons. Up to this time, of the 111,000 persons referred, it has been definitely learned that 73,370 have actually secured jobs. Dividing these placements according to trades and occupations, we find that a few over one half of them are in the manufacturing and mercantile pursuits, about one third are casuals, domestics and hotel workers, and nearly 12 per cent agricultural. It will be noted that only 90,000 people were registered, while over 111,000 were sent out. The difference here is accounted for by the fact that the offices had many thousands of names on the registration lists prior to the twelve months' period for which we are giving the figures. The offices have been visited in this past year by many thousands more than the 90,000 spoken of. The pressure of work on our limited force at the present time does not allow the registering of each worker who comes to us, unless there is a job ready waiting to which he can be sent.

During the past two weeks, our offices in both the men's and women's departments have been visited by hundreds of workers. There is no office that does not report more than 100 applicants for work a day, and some of the offices report from 300 to 400 seekers for jobs. In spite of this fact, we hear on every hand about the shortage of labor. There is said to be a shortage of workers in the shipyards, a shortage of workers in the munitions factories, a shortage of workers in the knitting mills, and in many other places where war supplies are being made. Some of these reports are true, and others are mere exaggeration. In some cases employers give out the word that they will need 300 or 3000 workers, meaning thereby that they expect, in the course of the next six weeks or six months, to take on this number of workers, but the man who writes up the story knows that it does not sound "good" to spread the demand out over such a long time, and so we read in the headlines that such and such a place is needing hundreds of thousands of workers. For instance, on a certain day about the first of November, an article appeared in hundreds of newspapers, telling that 400,000 workers were needed in shipyards. About three days after this there appeared in the *New York Times* a triple-headed article to the effect that the Port Newark Terminal Shipyard needed 12,000 men and requested all men able to do work in this line to give up their jobs and go to the shipyards. On reading this article I first ascertained that our New York office had on that day between 400 and 500 men who were capable of doing work of this kind. I called up the United States Emergency Fleet Corporation, and got their employment manager. On stating that we were ready to send them men, I was informed by Mr. Brady that they did not need any men. When I quoted the newspaper article he said it was exaggerated. I then offered to send him a few skilled men in certain specific lines, which brought out the fact that he was troubled by personal requests of workers at the gates, and that he actually had over 4000 registrations on his books, and was turning away men every day. This is but a single example, but we can duplicate this in every office throughout the State, so that this one case can be multiplied many times.

Difficulties. It is true we have, in the past few months, been unable to fill many orders, but mainly because these orders have called for certain technically trained workers in a line in which there is such a demand that all of the highly skilled in that particular line have been taken on.

Where we have investigated scarcity of labor, we have found three predominant factors; either the call was for trained workers in technical lines; or the demand was for husky laborers to do work calling for strong physique and endurance; or investigation showed that the employer was offering too low a wage, often coupled with long hours and bad working conditions.

The cure for the last factor of low wages and bad conditions is too self-evident to call for any comment.

As to the second factor, the call for laborers, especially laborers of strong physique, is a very fluctuating one, with the demand in most cases exceeding the supply. There would seem to be good reason to believe that there is an actual shortage in this line. Immigration of Huns, Poles, and Slavs has practically ceased. Many Greek and Italian reservists returned to their countries soon after the outbreak of the war. We have depended largely upon these races for our laborers and very few native-born Americans go into this field. In spite of all this, however, we have time and again in our different offices been able to fill orders for laborers where the wages offered were high. Apparently some of these applicants had left semi-skilled jobs because the wages offered for laborers were sufficiently above those paid for semi-skilled work to make the common labor attractive.

As regards the first factor, the call for skilled and semi-skilled workers in technical lines, there is a steady and persistent demand for the very highly trained men. This, however, does not indicate a real shortage of labor. There is no real shortage of labor in this country as yet. There is, however, an apparent shortage which can be remedied by adapting ourselves to our changed conditions. Let us look into the facts as regards the labor loss resulting from the war, in New York State. The state census of 1915 showed a total population of 9,687,000. Calculating from the percentage of workers shown by the United States Census of 1910, there are at the present time in the State of New York about 3,300,000 persons engaged in gainful occupations. On the other hand, from the figures given out as well as from liberal estimates made, the Army, Navy and the Red Cross have taken about 140,000 men out of this total of over 3,000,000 workers. Another heavy military draft will have to be made before the labor power of the State is materially affected.

The truth of the matter is that until a very short time ago there has been a great loss of man power in this State because of unemployment. Every one is aware of the fact that until three years ago an advertisement offering any position with fairly attractive wages would bring to factory or plant gates a large crowd of eager applicants. It is also well known that from all the work places in every industrial community there were turned away each morning hundreds of men willing to work. This meant a great loss of man power to the country, for these hundreds and thousands of workers lost anywhere from three days to three months finding a proper job, and the total loss of days' work calculated in man power was appalling. Society passed over this loss without notice save when it was emphasized by bread lines and soup kitchens. Now we realize what we were wasting and are commencing to take up the slack, though even yet hundreds are turned away from various plants every morning.

"But," says the employer, "these men are not trained or are unfit and I must have trained men right away." Granted that a small percentage of the men are unfit and that only a few of them are technically trained, then the only answer is that employers at their own or at government expense must train these men. The United States is just now teaching thousands of men how to shoot a gun and handle a bayonet. Is it not just as desirable, in this emergency, to teach men how to handle a tool and a machine? Many thousands of the soldiers are at this time just as unfamiliar with the rifle and the bayonet as are thousands of workers with the tool and the machine. More men than are now trained will be needed to do the technical work coming into existence through the needs of the war. There are enough human beings to do this work and now is the time to prepare for the training. The necessity for this training is not just now so apparent, because the real labor shortage is not yet here. This, as we have already said, is not only shown by the number of workers coming to our employment offices, but in the last few weeks we are constantly hearing from our offices throughout the State of this plant here and that plant there laying off men. Sometimes it is only 20 or 30 men. Other times it is from 300 to 500. We have the actual data of the name of the firm and the number laid off in hundreds of cases. Various causes are assigned. Lack of materials — generally steel or coal — is the main reason given. Some plants tell that the Government has requested them to reduce their output because it is non-essential. Then, too, it is a transition period. Certain plants have closed down so that they may change their machinery to make a product they have not heretofore produced.

It is at this point that the usefulness of the public employment offices becomes so apparent. When men are laid off at one place, there should be a common center to which they can turn to learn all about the openings either in their own vicinity or in the country at large, to the end that there shall be as little loss of time between jobs as possible. The importance of public employment offices is now recognized on every hand. The American Federation of Labor at Buffalo demanded the establishment of a national bureau of employment, not only for the present needs, but for future aid in the demobilizing of our army. The creation of such a bureau is called for by the American Association for Labor Legislation, by the United States Labor Department, and by the United States Shipping Board.

In the meantime the newspapers continue to proclaim a great shortage of labor and to recite stories of abnormal earnings, especially in munition factories. This adds to the general restlessness caused by the fact that we are at war and results in much shifting of workers, with great increase of "turnover" and the loss of man power. In many cases where labor shortage is spoken of, what is really meant is the "turnover." A worker reading of labor shortage and of large earnings gets restless, quits his job, and goes hunting the wage El Dorado. In truth such places are not many. Where a contractor has a government job on a cost-plus-profit basis there is the temptation to make the labor item high, for his percentage comes from this item as well as the item of materials. But inquiry as to wages made in a large munitions plant with a straight government contract brought the answer that the average wage of the 3000 employees was "about $3.00 per day."

To sum up: There are in this country enough human beings potentially capable of doing all the work required, and that too without materially (as yet) increasing our number of women workers. But large bodies of workmen will have to be trained and retrained to meet new technical needs, and employers must face the problem of doing this training. It should be faced now, for until it is done the method will be for one employer to steal workers from the other, a method more than wasteful. This is already being done to such an extent that whole communities are hiring so-called employment experts, whose only experience is shown in stealing trained workers from other communities.

While we are doing this stealing in our effort to avoid spending the time and money to train men, we are jeopardizing the lives of our boys in the French trenches. When employers have been approached on the subject of training men they have refused on the ground that as soon as they get them trained the men will be stolen from them.

The only remedy is coöperation. Might I suggest that a conference of employers and representatives of labor be called in each industrial center, or for the country as a whole? This conference should consider the subject of training workers, the number necessary in each industry, the number to be trained by the different plants, and the aid which could be given by those industries not then needing trained workers. Not only could workers be trained in the factory, but every plant turning out machines could train workers as the machine was building, so that with every machine sent out there would also go a trained operative. In order to lessen the necessity for all-around mechanics who require long training, the subdivision of work into operations ought to be carefully considered. Government contracts should not be allotted beyond the ability of the section to furnish the necessary labor, thus saving the shifting of workers. A firm with a contract which must be finished in six months sends out an appeal asking that hundreds of workers be sent from another community. Work is more mobile than labor.

Correct principles of labor exchanges.[1] The principle of a labor exchange has been excellently illustrated by the manager of an employers' labor bureau in Indianapolis:

> These bureaus are (he said) what our Soldiers' and Sailors' Monument was to the travel-stained carpenter who recently applied for a job to a contractor engaged in building some houses in a suburb of Indianapolis. In answer to the contractor's query, "How far have you come?" the man replied, "I've walked from Soldiers' Monument," explaining that he had spent his last penny in reaching its summit, where he could obtain a view of the surrounding country in the hope of locating new work in the course of construction. Like the

[1] From an article by W. M. Leiserson, "The Movement for Public Labor Exchanges" in the *Journal of Political Economy*, vol. 23, 1915. University of Chicago Press, publishers.

monument, these bureaus are "pinnacles of observation," constituting the shortest cut between supply and demand.

But it is easy to say that the monuments shall be built; it is quite another thing and a much more difficult task to erect them so that they will actually stand up and serve the whole community as "Pinnacles of Observation."

Recent experience has shown that the essential administrative machinery required to make a state or a national system of labor exchanges successful must include:

1. A civil service provision that will make tenure of office secure for every member of the staff, including the director, that will eliminate the incompetent political worker and attract capable people to make a career of employment in the service.

2. A joint committee of representative employers and workers to advise in determining all policies of management, and to assist in the selection of the staff under civil service, so that they may have confidence that the members of the staff will conduct the work impartially as between capital and labor. The members of the committee should be designated by the interests which they are chosen to represent.

3. An accurate and reliable system of records designed to show quickly and completely the character of the work of the offices and to furnish authoritative statistics on the problem of unemployment.

4. Uniform methods and records for the whole system of exchanges and coöperation and interchange of information among the offices, so that comparisons could be made easily and labor transferred quickly from place to place through the offices.

These essential administrative requirements cannot, of course, be absolutely insured, but no bill ought to be sponsored — least of all by organizations of social reformers — that does not contain these provisions. They have been developed in the States which are successfully conducting public employment offices, sometimes in spite of the laws, by strong personalities, and failure has resulted invariably where they have not been made a part of the management. It is disconcerting, to say the least, to see students and organizations continuing to advocate before legislatures bills which do nothing more than establish the general principle of labor exchanges, when this is now recognized in more than half the States, and when the greatest need is to work out methods of effective administration. Under exceptional circumstances such laws might become effective, as when administered by powerful and enthusiastic personalities; but ordinarily they result only in dismal failures, discreditable to the whole movement. It were much better to have no new legislation at all than to enact laws now that do not contain the proper administrative safeguards.

Opposition to public exchanges. While it is generally conceded that public employment offices need to be standardized and united into a national system, there is considerable opposition to the movement that rarely comes out in the open. The opposition comes from some of the strongly organized employers' associations and from highly organized skilled trades. It is an opposition that is based on misconceptions and is not likely to prevail. The employers' associations have organized central employment bureaus of their own in many cities and they find these most effective weapons in fighting organizations among their employees. They therefore do not want them supplanted. Strongly organized trade unions, on the other hand, themselves serve as employment offices for their members, and they fear that public offices might tend to weaken their organizations.

But, on the one side, far-seeing employers are recognizing that the movement for public labor exchanges is inevitable as an efficiency measure which will organize the labor market on a modern, business-like basis, as other markets have been organized; and they take the position that since we are sure to have public labor exchanges they had better coöperate and see that the offices are efficiently conducted. On the other side the workers in the unorganized and weakly organized trades see in this movement an attempt of the government to help them by organizing the search for work. Even among the skilled trades, union men are beginning to see that the alternative to a national system of labor exchanges is not an ideal condition in which the unions find work for all their members and thus protect themselves against the competition of unorganized and immigrant workers. The real condition is that private labor agencies and the increasing number of employers' labor bureaus are entirely uncontrolled in placing these people, and it works out most disadvantageously both to union and to non-union workers. They are, therefore, demanding that the Government shall conduct the labor exchanges and give them an equal share with employers in the management, and thus insure impartiality. More and more of the state federations of labor are taking this view and they are urging their views on the legislatures.

It may be noted in passing that the same kind of opposition was encountered by the European labor exchanges in their early stages, but experience removed it and resulted in the formation of joint committees of employers and workers to assist in the management of public offices. In the highly organized trades the practice has developed of including a provision for an employment exchange in the trade agreements between employers and employees. These are conducted by representatives of both sides and very often they maintain their offices in connection with the public labor exchanges. This is a development which may reasonably be expected in this country as soon as a national bureau of employment succeeds in establishing the work of the public employment offices on an efficient basis.

In concluding, a significant tendency may be noted showing that labor exchanges are gaining in public favor and esteem. Until very recently they were called in this country "free employment offices," and were considered by the public largely as more or less charitable institutions. Now there is a strong tendency to substitute the word "public" for the word "free." The New York laws call its exchanges public employment offices, and the New York City office is known as the Public Employment Bureau. Most of the bills now pending before the state legislatures have also dropped the use of the word "free." It was just so with our school systems. They were at first known as "free schools" and were then considered largely as charitable institutions. When they became generally used they became "public schools." The movement for public labor exchanges has now acquired such a momentum that the word "free" is rapidly being eliminated and public employment offices are patronized by all classes of workers.

3. Public Works

It has long been urged by students of the problem of unemployment that the various departments of government might well use their power as employers of labor to mitigate in some measure the extent of this evil. In its crudest form, this proposal is but a phase of the "make-work" fallacy so inherent in the reasoning of wage-earners, and, as such, is worthy of very little consideration. But the policy, if carefully worked out and safeguarded against mistaken philanthropy, would, without doubt, afford some relief from the effects of industrial fluctuation.

Essentials to success. A program of public works as a partial solution of unemployment must not attempt too much. Its aim should be, not the relief of distress, but the steadying of the labor market by making the demand in one direction — that of public bodies — expand or contract as the demand in other directions contracts or expands. Every governmental body is to some extent an employer of wage-earners and the larger units of government constitute perhaps the greatest single source of demand for labor. With the increase of governmental activity and the assumption of new functions by States and municipalities, this demand for the services of ordinary wage-labor of various grades must increase. With a little planning these activities of government could be made to coincide with the normal slack periods of employment in private enterprise; the construction, repair and painting of public buildings, the paving of streets, digging of sewers, planning of parks — to mention some of the more routine activities of government — could be carried on when seasonal unemployment was at a high point. The larger undertakings of the State, such as irrigation, reclamation, reforestation, shipbuilding, railroad construction and the like, could be carried through during the period of depression which follows in the wake of a crisis.

Certain prerequisites, both of purpose and method, must be present to make such a policy effective. As regards purpose, it is essential that the entire program be carried through on the lines mapped out by strict business principles. No motives of charity or philanthropy must be allowed to conflict with efficient management and economical financing of the enterprise. No unnecessary work should be undertaken as a means of relieving distress. It must be borne in mind that the Government can acquire purchasing power only through the process of diminishing by taxation or borrowing that of its citizens; and that to transfer this purchasing power from private hands to public only to have it wasted in footless undertakings must, in the long run, impair the economic position of the working population.

With regard to method, the experience of European governments has established certain useful principles in the way of working rules. In the first place, the policy is effective only as a part of a more thorough and comprehensive program for the solution of the problem of unemployment. It must be founded upon a system of statistical research carried on over a sufficiently long period of time to afford reliable information regarding the trend of seasonal and cyclical unemployment percentages. Only with this information at hand can any government plan to distribute its future demand for labor in such a manner as to offset the effects of industrial fluctuations. Given this essential foundation, the next step is to budget public work over a period of considerable length — say ten years — providing for the financing of the program by means of reserves for that purpose from the ordinary revenues of government. Moreover, the plan should work in coöperation with a system of public labor exchanges through which the demand of the Government for labor can be made available in those localities where unemployment is most acute. Under these conditions, a program of the amount of public work contemplated for several years in advance may be pushed ahead in lean years and in the months when private employment is at a low ebb. It is essential to the success of the plan that the work be done in the ordinary way, the workers being employed at the standard wage and under the usual working conditions and hired on the basis of efficiency, not merely because they happen to be unemployed.

British Labor Party. The place which the policy holds in the program of the British Labor Party is shown in the following selection from a draft report on reconstruction drawn up by a committee of the party in 1918: "It is the duty of the Government to adopt a policy of deliberately and systematically preventing the occurrence of unemployment, instead of (as heretofore) letting unemployment occur, and then seeking, vainly and expensively, to relieve the unemployed. It is now known that the Government can, if it chooses, arrange the Public Works and orders of National Departments and Local Authorities in such a way as to maintain the aggregate demand for labor in the whole kingdom (including that of capitalist employers) approximately at a uniform level from year to year; and it is therefore a primary obligation of the Government to prevent any considerable or widespread fluctuation in the total numbers employed in times of good or bad trade. . . . Moreover in order to relieve any pressure of an overstocked labor market, the opportunity should be taken, if unemployment should threaten to become widespread, (*a*) immediately to raise this school-leaving age to sixteen; (*b*) greatly to increase the number of scholarships and bursaries for Secondary and Higher Education; and (*c*) substantially to shorten the hours of labor of all young persons, even to a greater extent than the eight hours per week contemplated in the new Education Bill, in order to enable them to attend technical and other classes in the daytime. Finally, wherever practicable, the hours of adult labor should be reduced to not more than forty-eight hours per week, without reduction of the Standard Rate of Wages. There can be no economic or other justification for keeping any man or woman to work for long hours, or at overtime, whilst others are unemployed."

4. An Employer's Solution [1]

The notion that the employer has any element at all of responsibility for unemployment which requires consideration upon his part, though accepted by some of them, has not yet lost its novelty. The principal obstacle to its more general acceptance is the fact that the moral responsibility for unemployment cannot invariably and entirely be laid at the door of the employer. Nevertheless the employer can both reduce, by skillful management, the amount of unemployment among his employees, and can mitigate the hardship of such unemployment as cannot be avoided by making reservations for contingencies beyond his control.

The Dennison Manufacturing Company is undertaking to work out measures for meeting this twofold responsibility. Briefly outlined the principles applied for PREVENTION and the plan adopted for RELIEF are as follows:

Measures for the prevention of unemployment. The fluctuation of employment due to seasonal conditions of demand is always a bugbear to any manufacturing business that is endeavoring to operate harmoniously. Through it the working force is disorganized; some capable employees drift away or lose their keenness; and newcomers at the next period of increased production have to be familiarized with their duties and with local conditions. It is true that the seasonal decline affords an opportunity of ridding the organization of those whose services are least

[1] From the *American Labor Legislation Review*, Reprint XI, pp. 9–14.

profitable to retain, and here and there an employer might be found who would consider the uncertainty of tenure as working out to his own advantage; but since the significance of labor turnover has become apparent, and the spirit of coöperation is found to work, not only justly but profitably, there has been a widespread desire to stabilize employment, and to reduce the seasonal variation to a minimum.

At the plant of the Dennison Manufacturing Company a marked reduction of seasonal employment has been effected by the application of certain clearly conceived principles. These principles were not put at once into sudden and complete operation, but were given a practical try-out, and were extended first in one direction and then in another, as conditions made possible. In the nature of things, any very considerable reduction must be a matter of gradual development. It is, indeed, going on here to-day, with the goal far ahead of present attainment; but results so tangible have been secured that the means through which they have been achieved are no longer untested. The five principles applied include:

a. Reduction of seasonal orders by getting customers to order at least a minimum amount, well in advance of the season.

This has been accomplished partly by merely asking for the business, partly by persuasive salesmanship and partly by promising a greater security as to delivery. For example, originally paper box production was exceedingly seasonal. Orders would not come in in any large number until late in the summer, and then there would be a painful rush of work until Christmas. As a result of modified sales policies, however, we now secure a considerable number of our holiday orders in January, and even get a fairly large proportion of orders for Christmas delivery in November and December of the preceding year. Similar results have been accomplished in the crêpe line.

b. The increase of the proportion of non-seasonal orders with a long delivery time.

These orders are either "hold orders," not to be delivered until a certain date, or orders to be delivered when ready. This increase is brought about by the same methods of selling that proved effective in securing the transfer of the seasonal orders to the next seasonal period as outlined in (*a*) above.

c. The planning of all stock items more than a year in advance.

The general method is as follows: Over a year in advance a detailed statement of just what stock items are wanted is placed with our Warehousing Department. The Warehousing Department works out a minimum monthly schedule, based on the distribution of the last year's sales. Except that production must be kept up to this minimum, the producing department can distribute the work as seems best.

d. The planning of inter-departmental needs well in advance.

Thus the orders of our Gummed Label Department for boxes are placed at the beginning of the year.

By the means suggested in the foregoing principles, we have converted all possible seasonal and time-limited orders into articles on which we have long delivery time, and can thus be produced according to a schedule based on production rather than delivery needs. It would, however, probably be impossible to realize benefits as fully as at the present time, if we were in a trade characterized by sharp style variations; but even under such conditions it is probable that some benefits could be received.

e. The building-up of "out-of-season" items and the varying of our lines so as to balance one demand against another.

For example, we are developing new paper box items of a sort that are not used for holiday purposes, so that we can make and sell them for delivery at times when the holiday work is light. Items, too, that are securely staple in nature, can safely be made at any time for stock. It is our policy to increase up to the point of a healthful adjustment the number of such items.

Measures of this type are attempts to build the normal business of a concern up toward the peak level of the busy season. They aim not at removing the peaks, but at filling up the hollows. They constitute a healthy, leveling-up process, which achieves a positive increase of the total output, at the same time that it decreases the fluctuations.

Besides these methods of decreasing the pressure of seasonal demands, and evening out the inequalities, we can meet seasonal employment by conforming ourselves somewhat to it. We can balance the decrease in work of one department against the surplus of another. We can transfer operatives not needed in one line to another where there is work on hand. In doing so, we make it a rule to transfer our operatives to the same off-season work each time, so that they will develop proficiency in these off-season trades. We can go a step further: we can plan to adjust the work of one department so as to use to advantage the unemployed operatives of another department.

An illustration of this is found in the sample work of our crêpe-paper department. This requires little special training, and can be handled well by the paper-box makers in their dull season. As a matter of deliberate policy, this work is always saved up for December and January, when the slack season of the box makers is at hand.

This method often works incidentally to our advantage in other ways besides those which have led to its adoption. It tends, for example, toward producing a more versatile operating force, from whose numbers emergency transfers may at other times more easily be made. As a still further measure, we have even arranged to transfer operatives to outside industries. This course of action we resort to only in extreme cases. It has the disadvantage of relaxing the bond of connection between the employee and our company; but it has been found to preserve a certain relation of considerable advantage over complete discharge, or incurring the risk that employees whom we might wish later to take on again might be led to obtain other continuous employment during the period while we were unable to furnish them work.

Measures for the relief of unemployment. Not primarily because the employer is in a position to mitigate the hardship of unemployment by making reservations for that contingency, but rather because the employer is so largely able to reduce the amount of unemployment by proper management is it desirable that he should assume the responsibility for its relief. For in the long run the assumption of such responsibility by the employer will tend to urge him forward in the prevention of unemployment through wise management.

With this conception Dennison Manufacturing Company has begun the task of working out a policy for the relief of unemployment by the company. The impossibility of determining now the proper fixed charge or ratio of charge to be made against unemployment and the advisability of budgeting charges capable of so elastic an application have led to the creation of an Unemployment Fund, set aside by the directors out of the profits, and accumulated over a period of approximately five years.

It is necessary to bear in mind at the start the status of this fund, both because the status represents the adjustment to a new industrial concept and because the reaction to the program which this fund involves will be determined in no small degree by the conception of it which prevails.

In the first place, it is not charity; it has a business basis and must rest upon considerations of mutual advantage, with mutual self-respect. This business basis it must find in securing and retaining better employees, in better work on the part of the employees, due to their release from the risk of periodic total loss of income through unemployment, and in a steadier working force due to the abrogation of the risk that the employees will find permanent work elsewhere during times when he is unemployed.

In the second place, our establishment of an Unemployment Fund is not a guarantee either of permanence of employment or of maintenance of the regular rate. In the lack of knowledge on the subject, we provide a fund, setting emphasis on its wise use, and stating plainly that we do not guarantee its renewal.

After the directors had established a fund, the matter of working out provisions for its administration was placed in the hands of a special joint committee, of which two of the members are chosen by representatives of the employees themselves from the General Works Committee of employees, and two from the Management.

This committee in drafting the rules governing the use of the fund gave to the term "unemployment" a broad interpretation, not regarding total or even partial idleness as necessary in order to establish unemployment within the intent of the fund, but regarding any loss involved by the inability of a willing worker to continue employment at his normal and qualified duties, while being retained on the books of the company, as creating a field of unemployment loss. Thus those transfers because of lack of work, previously referred to as a policy of the management for the prevention of unemployment, are under this conception of "unemployment" part of the problem of relief of unemployment.

Accordingly the program the unemployment committee has mapped out provides at the start that in the event of employment shortage in any part of the plant, the actual laying-off of any employees shall be avoided whenever possible by temporarily transferring those for whom there is no work to other parts of the plant where there is work. If this results in a materially lowered wage rate, it is recognized as constituting a basis for a claim upon the Unemployment Fund. Therefore, if any "unemployment" exists, there may be both a class in which there is complete lack of work, and a class in which the unemployment claim is really a claim for loss by reason of diminished returns. Employees, regardless of length of service, are paid for all unemployment of one-half day at a time or over. No lay-off or transfer of less than half a day at one time is considered unemployment.

As has previously been stated the fund is not a guarantee of the regular wage rate. It is felt that at least in the first experiments the burden of unemployment should be jointly shared by the employer and the employee and the fund used as far as it is capable of doing so in relieving the worst distress of unemployment. Furthermore, there is a certain healthy effect upon the employee in thus knowing that in unemployment relief, as in fire insurance, there is an appreciable factor of co-insurance, for this will remove any possibility of the fund tending to motivate against a feeling of responsibility on the part of the employee as to his own financial security.

Accordingly, whenever there is actual unemployment, the fund is set in operation for the relief of distress in the following manner:

Employees who are temporarily laid off receive 90 per cent of their regular wages if they have dependents and 60 per cent if they have no dependents. Both classes of employees, when they secure temporary work outside, are entitled to 10 per cent of their outside earnings plus 90 per cent of their earnings with the Dennison Company, the unemployment fund being used to make up the difference between this amount and what they receive outside. Employees who are transferred inside to other work are paid their full wages if they are time workers and 90 per cent of their six weeks' average if piece workers. Whatever they are worth on their new job is charged to operating expenses and the rest is made up out of the unemployment fund. At any time after six days' payments have been made the Unemployment Fund Committee may stop payments to any who in its opinion are not making proper efforts to secure outside work.

Thus in all cases where the employee's earning power is temporarily reduced because of lack of employment, whether the employee is rendered idle or secures temporary employment in some other work inside or outside the factory, he is protected against any severe hardship.

Moreover, of necessity, the company retains the right, if it deems best, to discharge employees; but discharge because of shortage of work — besides being regarded as the last resort, to be had recourse to only when the shortage cannot safely be considered temporary — is not permitted to create an unemployment problem for which there has been no warning. An employee cannot be summarily projected because of lack of employment outside all safeguards which the Dennison system has created without receiving two weeks' notice or its pay equivalent, thus assuring the employee two weeks to place himself to better advantage.

Thus, by its efforts to prevent seasonal unemployment — that phase of unemployment which is largely controllable by the employer — and by budgeting unemployment relief and working with its employees in testing out relief methods, this company is endeavoring to develop a scientific method of solving the greatest evil of present working conditions. However, although a clearly defined working principle has been mapped out in the entire field of compensation, all practices are but tentative hypotheses which are put into practice merely to feel out, step by step, the true principles that control this new field.

In this endeavor this company has kept two fundamental principles constantly in mind. The first is that the highest goal is always the prevention, not the relief of unemployment. The second is that what will do most to prevent relief from having a tendency to pauperize the employees and check their efforts to safeguard their future, and what will do most to make the giving of relief a stimulus to the employer to prevent unemployment is the distribution of the expense of unemployment so that those who share in the responsibility for unemployment — the employer, the employee, and the consumer of the products of the industry in question — will each share in the burdens of unemployment as far as possible in such a manner that the amount of the burden they share will be reduced in proportion to the extent to which they successfully assume their responsibility for the prevention of unemployment. Just as fire insurance is one of the strongest incentives to fire prevention, the relief of unemployment will then become one of the principal incentives to the prevention of unemployment.

5. Experiments in the Clothing Industry [1]

A seasonal industry. One is tempted to dismiss the subject of continuity of production in the clothing industry in the classical manner of the author of the famous report on snakes in Ireland. There is no such thing in our industry.

And if that is true of the men's clothing industry, it applies with tenfold force to the women's garment industry, embracing the manufacture of women's cloaks, suits, dresses and waists, in which the frequent changes of style turn the normal seasonal fluctuations of industry into a frenzy of feverish activity — a mad effort to meet the immediate demand for a momentarily popular model — succeeded by industrial paralysis due to lack of demand and total destruction of market value of models no longer popular and for which the manufacturer cannot get a price that would reimburse him for the cost of materials and labor.

Under the circumstances, it would seem utter folly to speak of continuity of employment in the clothing industry. Yet it is not impossible. It has been achieved in at least three clothing plants in this country with which I am personally familiar, and there is a growing feeling among efficiency engineers that it can be accomplished throughout the industrial field. A definite movement has now been launched by the Taylor Society in this direction, from which much good is expected.

The three plants referred to are those of Joseph and Feiss

[1] From an article by N. I. Stone, "Continuity of Production in the Clothing Industry," in the *American Labor Legislation Review*, Reprint XI, pp. 15–23.

Company of Cleveland, and Hickey-Freeman Company of Rochester (both in the men's clothing industry), and of the Printz-Biederman Company of Cleveland, in the women's. In these three plants continuous production has been carried on for the last few years for a period of from forty-five to fifty-one weeks a year. Varying methods have been used to achieve this result.

The Joseph and Feiss Company has attained this end by standardizing its products, adjusting it to the needs of a large class of consumers who value durability and service above style. By concentrating its advertising on this product, by giving proper inducements to its retail distributors in return for their accepting deliveries over an extended period instead of at the opening of the season, as is the custom, they have been able to carry on their manufacture on an even keel throughout the year.

The firm with which I am connected, although manufacturing clothing at the other end of the scale, catering to the most fastidious trade and strongly influenced by considerations of style and individual tastes among its customers, has managed to insure continuity of production by filling in the dull periods between seasons with work done partly for stock on conservative models not affected much by variations of styles and partly by securing orders for mid-season sales at prices which leave no profit, but which are considered desirable from a business standpoint inasmuch as they help to cover overhead expense — a total loss were the plant closed — and help to maintain our organization intact and provide remunerative employment for our help.

The Printz-Biederman Company which manufactures quality clothes for women is one of the few concerns in any industry which has deliberately adopted the principle of close coördination of its selling policy with its production policy under scientific management. Although manufacturing an article in which style is the determining factor, it follows the rule of "selling what it makes" as against the ordinary opportunistic policy of drift known in the trade as "making what you sell."

Months in advance of the selling season it selects and orders its cloths, determining the number and kind of garments it wants to make the following season in order to keep its plant at capacity production. Then it instructs its designers to make the necessary models. As soon as these are approved by the firm, quantity manufacture is commenced, before any customers have placed orders or have even seen the models. Through years of consistent maintenance of its policy the company has inspired its retailers with confidence in its judgment, reliability of its promises and value of its merchandise. Its salesmen in different territories are given their respective quota which they are expected to dispose of and which they usually do. In this they are helped not a little by the fact that the goods of the company are sold under a trade mark which is widely known among the consuming public through national advertising. While occasionally the firm may lose out on a model and be obliged to sell it at a loss, in the long run it has been eminently successful in maintaining production for fifty-one weeks in the year, one week being devoted to plant repair during which the workers enjoy a vacation with pay.

Peculiar difficulties. What has been accomplished by these three concerns could be done by others, not necessarily by imitating their methods in detail, but by applying similar principles in their sales policies. The complete attainment of this goal, however, is impossible unless we can secure the coöperation of the consumer, the retailer, and the manufacturer. The chief difficulty lies in the peculiar conditions prevailing in the two clothing industries. One is the prevalence of the sub-contracting system; the other is the custom of frequent changes in style unduly and artificially stimulated under the stress of competition.

The sub-contracting evil is common to both the women's and men's clothing industries. In the men's clothing industry it is especially rampant in New York City, which makes about 60 per cent of all the ready-made clothing in the country. It has been entirely done away with by several of the large houses in Chicago, Rochester and Baltimore, and is no longer an important factor in these markets. In New York City, however, the contract shop is the predominating type of manufacturing establishment, and as long as it continues to dominate the industry it will hang like a millstone about the neck of the industry in the rest of the country, a menace to the progressive manufacturer who carries on his work in a large modern plant.

The companies which own these plants have a compelling economic reason for maintaining steady production: they have large overhead expenses for plant maintenance, they have a large executive personnel, sales managers, production managers, labor managers, each with their staffs, factory superintendents with foremen and assistants, all of whom are carried on the payroll in dull seasons as well as in busy periods. While the labor force is not paid when laid off, there is always the loss in efficiency in starting up the plant after a shut-down, when a part of the force may have drifted to other plants or other industries and new workers have to be trained to their jobs and "broken into" the plant organization. The progressive, responsible firm is, therefore, interested from a business as well as a humanitarian motive in maintaining continuity of production. Not so with the house which contracts out its output.

The typical New York clothing house maintains at most a cutting and shipping department and an office. Many dispense even with a cutting department. All the manufacturing is done by contractors running small shops at their own risk. The manufacturers are thus relieved of the necessity of investing in factory buildings and machinery, of the expense of plant maintenance, of overhead expense in maintaining executive staffs. Not coming in direct contact with their help, they are not concerned about maintaining their plant organization. The contractor is at their beck and call, ready to take up work at a moment's notice. Ambitious workers are encouraged to start up new shops and competition is thus maintained among contractors to a point where the ordinary profit of the average small contractor is not much in excess and often not quite as large as the salary of a foreman in a large Rochester or Chicago factory. With this type of industrial organization there is no incentive for the manufacturer to try to maintain steady work. On the contrary, the periodic shut-downs keep the contractor on the anxious seat and hungry for business. So long as he can squeeze the profit out of the reserve army of workers as anxious for work as himself, he is willing to accept work on any terms.

Service of trade unions. The building-up of a strong trade union has been the sole check upon this primitive method of doing business, thereby preventing unfair competition with other markets. But beyond raising wages, the union has not been able to check the contracting evil. On the contrary, the absence of large modern plants, with competent managerial staffs and other equipment which makes for efficient handling of men and production, redounded to the injury of both the employers and the union. The small contractor was in no position to maintain discipline in his shop, and to exact efficient workmanship. With piece work eliminated, and the unusual demand for labor which prevailed in the clothing industry in the last two or three years, there was no restraining factor to impress upon the workers their responsibility to industry and society beyond Mr. Hillman's earnest pronouncements on the subject. In the end both the employers and workers have come to grief, as they were bound to do.

Without attempting to anticipate the results of the present strike in New York, it is safe to say that so long as the contracting system remains in force as the prevailing type of industrial organization in the largest center of the clothing industry, it will be idle to expect continuity of production in that industry. Every consideration and motive which prompts owners of large plants in other centers to reduce the periods of idleness, favors the maintenance of the cat and mouse policy of periodic shut-downs to keep otherwise unmanageable contractors and workers in check. And the retailers' practice of demanding deliveries at two peak seasons of the year furnishes a favorable economic background for such a policy.

Effects of fashion. The evil of frequent changes in style — the other factor that strongly militates against continuity of employment — is less serious in the men's clothing industry than in the women's. Yet, even in the former it is sufficiently strong to make the manufacture of stock a hazardous undertaking, except in the case of a few conservative models and only by firms that are sure of their trade.

In the women's clothing industry the matter of style dominates the entire situation. We all know, of course, that Dame Fashion is fickle; but to be fair to our women, it is very doubtful whether this incessant grinding out of new styles by an army of highly paid designers is at all necessary to gratify woman's æsthetic taste and desire for variety and change in dress. More than nine tenths of women belong to the middle and working classes whose husbands or themselves enjoy but moderate incomes and who would be satisfied, like their men folks, with such variety in dress as is developed from season to season. The remaining less than one tenth of women do not buy ready-made clothing in any event. But competition prompts the quick imitation and reproduction of a model which happens to strike a popular fancy. This policy is encouraged by the retailers in their effort to beat down the price of the successful manufacturer who originated the model. He in turn finds it necessary to keep ahead of the procession by developing new models. Thus the process of multiplication of models goes merrily on, not from season to season, but from week to week. In the long run, the consuming public pays the cost of this mad race for styles. In this wild scramble the individual manufacturer or retailer gets ahead or thinks he is getting ahead of his competitor, yet in the end the aggregate sales of clothing are no greater than they would be if the Printz-Biederman policy were followed by everybody in the trade. The very multiplicity of models and the frequency with which they succeed one another in the show windows create such a bewildering variety that no one can tell which is the more up-to-date style and milady is rather pleased at wearing "something that is different."

But the effect on the industry is demoralizing. Because of the uncertainty of the style situation, the retailer will not order any model in quantity until he has had a chance to see how the public will take to the different models. The manufacturer, therefore, is unable to manufacture stock and so manufacturing is done on a small scale and can be carried on much more economically in a small contract shop than in a large modern plant with its heavy overhead expenses.

On the other hand, if there were greater steadiness in styles in women's clothing, the retailers would order their goods in larger quantities as they do in men's clothing and manufacturing on a large scale would be more economical than at present and could be conducted over longer periods of time.

In the light of these facts, the conclusion seems warranted that while continuity of production in the clothing industry is not beyond the range of possibility, the industry as a whole is far from being in a position to realize this desirable end in the near future. The chief obstacle is the lack of an economic incentive which would overcome the financial advantages of intermittent production inherent in the contract shop system. If a condition could be created which would make it unprofitable or at least more costly to work intermittently than working continuously, it would go far toward undermining the contract system and would make continuity of production in the clothing industry a practical possibility.

Public action necessary. Since it is not within the power of the other clothing centers to reform New York conditions, only the Government, state or national, can provide the necessary incentive. Such an incentive could be furnished by a system of unemployment insurance. By grading the insurance premium in proportion to the continuity of production, carried on by each concern, it would be made to the interest of each house to maintain production as steadily as possible. Once this incentive were provided, the ingenuity of every manufacturer would be exercised to the utmost in this direction, and what has proven possible in the case of the three concerns mentioned, would be even more easy of attainment in the industry as a whole, once the united efforts of the entire industry were turned in this direction.

The effect of workmen's compensation laws in stimulating the "safety first" movement and making safety pay, is an earnest system based on the principle of a premium graded on the basis of what might be expected from an unemployment insurance of continuity of employment. Such a system of insurance would at the same time put an end to the injustice of throwing the burden of maladjustment of supply and demand upon the poorest class of the community, which is least able financially to bear it.

It would also lay at rest one of the principal obstacles to increased efficiency on the part of workers and that is the fear on the part of the average worker that by working more efficiently he works himself out of a job. As a labor manager who is called upon to deal constantly with this problem, I venture to express the opinion that the gain in efficiency on this score alone would far outweigh the cost of the unemployment insurance premium which the employer would have to pay.

In adopting unemployment insurance, we would not be entering upon an untrodden path. We would merely be following in the footsteps of Great Britain and other advanced industrial nations. The only departure would be the suggested grading of the premium according to the steadiness of employment furnished by each employer, whereas in England the payment is based solely on the number of persons employed.

It would be difficult to expect, however, that our national or state governments would act in the matter until the American people and their representatives in the legislatures are aroused to the seriousness of the situation; until they are made conscious not only of the grave injustice inflicted upon our most numerous and at the same time most helpless class of people financially, but also of the costliness to society as a whole of letting things drift as they are. It therefore may be pertinent to present an estimate of the losses caused by unemployment which I had the privilege to submit to the Efficiency Society in 1915 when unemployment was seriously disturbing the country.

Loss through fluctuation. According to the figures of the federal census for 1900 there were nearly six and one half million people unemployed during the year of 1899 for periods varying from one to twelve months each. Allowing an average wage of only $10 a week and assuming that the average period of unemployment was four months, the American Association for Labor Legislation estimated the total annual loss of wages of these people at over one billion dollars. This billion dollars had to be covered by the nation in the form of charitable and public relief as well as out of the savings of the unemployed, and, in so far as not so covered, the deficit resulted in the deterioration or total destruction of the physique of the working people, representing a loss in the productive power of the nation. A part of the wage-deficit was covered by crime with the additional loss to society represented by such otherwise unnecessary expenditures as those for prisons, police, prosecuting attorneys and judges. Finally, there was the loss of wealth which the idle workers would have produced in return for the billion dollars of wages they would have earned, if employed, which may be estimated at three billion dollars on the basis of census statistics of manufactures.

How great is the loss of wealth caused by the impairment of the worker's efficiency on account of deterioration of his physique, the loss of regular habits of work, and, most of all, through the "laying down" on the job caused by the fear that by working efficiently he will be merely working himself out of a job, it is impossible to estimate even approximately. From personal investigation in industry, confirmed by the experience of industrial engineers generally, I can state that a loss of production of from 10 per cent to 50 per cent is due to the "laying down" process alone.

Apart from individual efficiency, there is plant efficiency: all engineers, as well as practical manufacturers, are familiar with the loss of momentum caused by the gradual shutting down of a plant and the difficulty of bringing it up to normal in starting up after a shut-down. If all these factors could be accounted for, the additional loss of wealth would run into billions and greatly swell, if not double, the three billion dollar estimate. The havoc wrought by unemployment may, therefore, be said to rival in magnitude that caused by war. But there is this difference: wars are necessarily of more or less duration and are followed by long periods of peace and recuperation, while unemployment adds its cumulative destructive effect year by year.

Once this condition is realized, no effort will be thought too great, no measure too ambitious which will hold out the promise of an effective cure of this greatest of our economic ills, carrying in its train grave social and political evils.

6. Unemployment Insurance [1]

It seems to be agreed that the regularization of private industry is a necessary and important step in the prevention of unemployment. Some progressive manufacturers have already found it possible to regularize production. But how are we to persuade industry as a whole to regularize? Last winter's crisis brought forth the suggestion that "If unemployment insurance was in force there would be much less unemployment than there is now, because greater efforts would be made to regularize industry and keep the labor forces employed."

At present the only unemployment insurance in force in this country is that of the trade unions which give out-of-work benefits to tide their members over periods of unemployment. For instance, Blacksmiths' Helpers' Local No. 1, which gives $5 a week, runs an employment exchange in connection with the local, while Brewers' Union No. 1 requires members receiving benefits to report at least once a week during the daytime so as to prevent

[1] From the *American Labor Legislation Review*, November, 1915, pp. 589–92.

fraud. The latter give $4 weekly for 12 weeks, or $48 annually, for two years, and after that a member must have paid dues for a full year before he will be again entitled to benefits. Other unions give smaller benefits, some contenting themselves with exempting unemployed members from dues. But however small the benefits given, they sufficed to account in some measure for the fact that comparatively few of the unemployed seeking charity last winter were union men. From St. Paul, Minn., the secretary of the United Charities writes that "trade unions with benefit features have been the saving grace in the situation here." The secretary of the Boston Associated Charities recommended their extension as a "fundamental remedy." Much help is also given unemployed members by locals without benefit systems. The building trades unions of New York report that they had no regularly established system of unemployment benefits but that "assistance is rendered in all cases of distress either by loans or donations. No worthy applicant is turned away. The building trades unions are estimated to have spent over $250,000 of union funds in these ways — some lending their mortuary benefit surplus to the general fund for this purpose."

Recognizing the possibility of administering benefit funds through unions, many members believe that the system should be extended through government aid. Fred French, business agent of the Milwaukee Patternmakers' Association, suggested that we "should take into consideration" the Ghent system under which many European cities and state subdivisions supplement trade union out-of-work benefits by generous government subsidies. However, he admitted that "a large number of members of our union favor the English plan." Compulsory unemployment insurance went into effect in England in seven selected trades in July, 1912. It is supported by joint contributions from employers, employees and the State. Workmen involuntarily unemployed receive cash benefits from the second to the sixteenth week of unemployment in each year. They must register with the labor exchange and must accept work of equal value if found for them by the exchange. Less than 2 per cent of all the cases are still out of work at the end of the sixteenth week. The incentive to regularization is provided through an annual rebate to employers for each employee given forty-five weeks of work during the year. It is the English method of administering unemployment insurance which is favored by most publicists, because of its success, because it includes non-union men and because it gives the employer an incentive to regularize his business.

Unemployment insurance is favored as the most practical method of dealing with the wage losses due to lack of work. Early in 1915 the Chicago Industrial Commission astonished the business community by an estimate that it would cost $500,000 to tide their unemployed over the winter through charity. Thereupon constructive measures were demanded as more economical. The commission replied: "The emergency relief work with charitable funds is at best a sorry makeshift. Generally it is wasteful. We are satisfied the business community does not approve this plan. Hence — we call for systems of unemployment insurance by State or Nation." On February 20, 1915, Professor Roswell C. McCrea, dean of the Wharton School of Economics, University of Pennsylvania, pointed out the expediency of unemployment insurance saying: "Poverty is an aspect of modern industry, and must be treated in this light."

Expediency was not the only reason given for advocating unemployment insurance. Robert G. Valentine, of Boston, in addressing the Central Philanthropic Council of Massachusetts, argued its abstract justice, saying: "Unemployment is a problem of industry — it is an inherent aspect of business management. Employers must realize that they owe a duty to the pool of labor from which they draw men as they need them. They must devise a means (unemployment insurance) so that men thrown back into this pool because of unemployment through no fault of their own shall not suffer." Similar conclusions were reached by Rabbi Stephen S. Wise in New York and by the Mayor's Committee on Unemployment of Spokane which reported on February 20, 1915: "Reserves of labor are necessary under present industrial conditions for the full expansion of industry in busy times, and can be fully taken care of during periods of depression only through a system of state and national unemployment insurance."

Prospects in the United States. Preparation is being made in many quarters for the introduction of legislation. On March 24, 1915, a meeting was held in Ford Hall, Boston, to discuss unemployment insurance. All present favored drafting a bill which should provide for some contribution by the State. Accordingly the Massachusetts Committee on Unemployment is working on a bill to be introduced into the legislature at an early date. The Massachusetts Federation of Labor at its annual convention adopted resolutions favoring the plan, and the Republican Party platform in that State, adopted in October, 1915, contains the declaration:

> We favor . . . the development of such industrial organizations as will tend to minimize unemployment and to distribute its effects when unavoidable over the entire industrial field. We call to the attention of the legislature the subject of social insurance and the consideration and investigation of some system which will protect the home life against the hazards of . . . irregular employment.

Further resolutions in favor of unemployment insurance were adopted by the International Typographical Union, 70,000 strong, and by the New England Typographical Union at their conventions in the summer of 1915.

In sympathy with the enlightened demand for unemployment insurance, the Social Insurance Committee of the American Association for Labor Legislation last winter began work upon the draft of a bill for compulsory insurance, which will probably be introduced in 1916 in several state legislatures. In December, 1914, the California Commission of Immigration and Housing recommended the "appointment of a special committee or designation of an existing committee to conduct an extended investigation into the wisdom of devising some scheme for out-of-work insurance that will not have the effect of drawing into California the unemployed of the nation." Following this recommendation, $20,000 was appropriated by the California legislature for a commission to investigate social insurance. A bill for a similar investigation was introduced in the Ohio legislature, but failed to pass. In New York the Socialist Party executive committee appointed a committee to draft an unemployment insurance bill and the state federation of labor and the Committee on Constitutional Convention of the American Association for Labor Legislation made an effort to have a clause permitting unemployment insurance embodied in the proposed new constitution.

However, unemployment insurance is as yet hardly beyond the agitation stage. The fact that very little was heard against it is in itself evidence that the plan is just emerging as a practical policy. But it is probable, as Ida Tarbell says, that "The day is coming when it will be as universal as compensation is rapidly becoming." Like workmen's compensation, it is a movement for prevention rather than cure. The feeling is not only that it is socially more just and economical than charity; but that as industrial accident insurance laws have caused employers to find that they can prevent accidents, and sickness insurance laws are in several countries inducing them to protect their workers against processes injurious to health, so unemployment insurance in America as well as elsewhere will lead them to turn their attention to regularizing employment.

A plea for unemployment insurance.[1] I know that in some quarters there is a strong feeling against unemployment insurance. I believe that feeling is based upon unsound beliefs and arguments. It is frequently asserted in America that unemployment insurance has been a failure in England.

But that is far from being the case. Rather, our scheme of insurance, inadequate as it is, has, in my opinion, saved us from something like a revolution, and at the least from very serious civil riots. It must be borne in mind that there is nothing intrinsically demoralizing in unemployment insurance. Its reactions largely depend on the nature of the scheme. In England, insurance benefits do not drop down from the skies for every lazy workman. The method is one of mutual insurance, to which the workman, every week when he is in work, pays 14 cents, and the employer pays 16 cents. When the man is out of work, he gets about $3.60 a week. It is no more demoralizing to receive it than it is to receive a pension paid for in part by ones self and in part by one's employers.

What *is* demoralizing, what *is* dangerous, is a state of things in which this terrible menace of unemployment is constantly hanging, like a black cloud, over the worker's life — in which he is

[1] From an article by B. S. Rowntree, "Unemployment and its Alleviation," in the *Annals* of the American Academy of Political and Social Science, vol. 100, March, 1922.

completely at the mercy of fluctuations in trade over which he has no shadow of control. They may, indeed, be owing to some seasonal calamity at the other side of the world, which is beyond human control altogether. No matter how capable, how honest, or how industrious the individual may be, he cannot escape from this black cloud. We may say: "He can live on his savings when unemployment comes." But the evil may come perhaps in early middle life, when the expenses of his household are at the maximum, and he has been unable to save. If, on the other hand, it comes later, a period of unemployment will soon eat up the small provision he has made against old age. This is not fair.

It is sometimes said that many workingmen "will not give a full day's work." Now, I put this question to you. If you were a bricklayer with a wife and family, and it was winter time, and you knew that when the job on which you were engaged was finished you had little hope of another — would you work at top speed? Or would you dawdle and slack, and make excuses, and try to "nurse the job"? You would "nurse" it, if you were human, and so would I. What is more, I would recommend my "mates" to do the same!

Now we can dissipate the black cloud of anxiety from the workingman's horizon if we take a little trouble and use a little common sense. Let me remind you that taking the average over a number of normal years, there are ninety-five workers employed to five unemployed. What does this mean? Simply that an addition of 5 per cent to the wage bill would suffice to pay each unemployed worker his full wages during unemployment. Therefore, the financial difficulty is not insuperable. I am not for a moment suggesting that the above course should be pursued. Human nature is not yet so far evolved that it would be wise to pay a man the same wage when he is not working as when he is working. At the same time, he should be paid sufficient to secure him and his family against serious privation or hardship.

A practical scheme. To come to what I consider practical politics, I will very briefly outline a scheme for unemployment insurance drawn up by an unofficial committee of employers, economists and labor men which met many times in London and of which I was a member. We suggested that under this scheme every unemployed worker should receive, for a maximum period of twenty-six weeks in any one year, half of his average earnings when at work. A married man should receive in addition 10 per cent of such earnings for a dependent wife, and 5 per cent for each dependent child under 16, with a maximum of 75 per cent of his average earnings. Calculations showed that the cost of providing these benefits in Britain for 5 per cent of the workers (the figure taken as the proportion of unemployed persons over a number of years) would amount to about 282 million dollars per annum or 4 per cent of the wage bill.

The question — "Who will pay the premiums?" — was discussed a long while by the committee before, in true English fashion, we decided on a compromise, and proposed that the cost of the scheme should be borne jointly, as at present, by the state, the worker and the employer. Briefly, the plan was this:

1. Premiums equal to 2½ per cent of the wage bill (or 185 million dollars) would be paid by the employers.

2. Premiums of a little under 1 cent on every dollar of their earnings (equal to 75 million dollars) would be paid by the workers.

3. Twenty-two million dollars a year would be paid by the state, which would also bear the cost of administration. This 22 millions was the sum already being paid by the state for unemployment insurance when the scheme was worked out.

A successful experiment. We hoped that the Government would see fit to introduce this scheme, leaving industries free to contract out of it if they could guarantee equal or better benefits. This hope has not yet been realized, but my own firm came to the conclusion that, while waiting for the Government, we ourselves could do something, so we introduced a similar scheme in our own factory in York. We set aside 1 per cent on our wage bill (in addition, of course, to the contributions we make under the National Insurance Act) and we undertook to continue to set this aside till the sum amounted to 5 per cent of the wage bill, after which our contributions would be altered to the sum necessary to maintain the fund at 5 per cent of the wage bill, with a maximum liability in any one year of 1 per cent of the wages. The majority of our employees belong to a trade union which, for a payment of 4 cents a week, allows them $1.40 weekly when unemployed. Thus, when the scheme was inaugurated, an unemployed man already got $5 ($3.60 from the State and $1.40 from his union), and an unemployed woman got $4.32 ($2.88 from the State and $1.44 from the union). We calculated that a premium of 1 per cent on the wage bill would be sufficient to bring the benefits up to those mentioned in the scheme above described — i.e. half the average earnings, with an additional 10 per cent for a dependent wife and 5 per cent for each dependent child, up to a maximum of 75 per cent of the average earnings.

One important condition in our scheme is that though we guarantee to pay an agreed premium we do not guarantee the benefits which, if the scheme were abused, might have to be reduced or even temporarily suspended. It is obviously in the interest of the employed workers who feel that they themselves may one day be in need of benefit, to guard against any contingency that might unduly deplete the fund. Its administration is in the hands of the workers, who can therefore take whatever steps they consider necessary to check abuse.

I may add that the match industry in Great Britain has recently adopted a similar scheme.

Now, while I am deeply desirous of seeing a system of national insurance against unemployment, with really adequate benefits, established in every industrialized country, and while I hope that the League of Nations and all individual governments will devote thought and energy to this most important matter, I am anxious to recommend individual employers to introduce some measure of insurance in their own factories. Some may say that they cannot afford it. But purely from a business point of view, I believe that it pays to give the workers comparative security. How can we expect them, without it, to work faithfully and to "put their heart" into what they are doing?

CHAPTER IV

THE PROBLEM OF WAGES

1. The Economic Law of Wages

From the standpoint of its importance to the industrial worker, the problem of wages is second only to that of unemployment. Indeed, if we base our judgment of the relative importance of these problems upon the part they have played in determining the policies and programs of labor, wages would be ranked first. Wages have a tangible reality, their bearing upon the worker's welfare being direct and obvious; while unemployment, in the laborer's mind, takes the form of a great and terrifying menace, ever present yet imperfectly understood, whose action does not seem to be amenable to prediction. Again, wages are determined in the first instance by bargain and, hence, seem to be under the control of human volition; while unemployment seems to result from the operation of sinister forces which its victims are powerless to control. These attributes have given wages a place of peculiar prominence in the thinking of the laboring population and in the programs of the unions.

Wages are the remuneration given to the laborer by the employer for the work which has been done. The reason why wages are paid needs no explanation; they are a natural resultant of the industrial order in which we find ourselves. The problem is to explain why they stand at a certain level; that is, what determines the amount of wages? The problem is very complex; no single rule or formula will cover the entire situation. The ranks of labor are far from homogeneous; there are many different grades of worker, from the unskilled man who shovels cinders to the highly efficient and intelligent electrician who keeps the motors and dynamos going. Furthermore, because the problem involves such vital human relationships, it is apt to be obscured by theories of what ought to be, to the exclusion of clear thinking regarding the causes of what is. For this reason, if for no other, it is desirable to become acquainted with the underlying economic theory of the determination of wages, before proceeding to the practical problems of the wage contract.

The marginal productivity theory. The theory of money wages commonly held by economists is called the "marginal productivity theory." The purport of this theory, to state the matter in non-technical terms, is that the economic forces of a competitive and non-regulated industrial order such as ours tend to give each worker a money wage equal to the value of his contribution to the product of industry. When stated in the abstract, this theory seeks to measure the amount by which the social income would decrease through the withdrawal from industry of one hired worker, and to show that the *value* of this fragment of the social income fixes the rate of wages for all workers who fall into the same group as the one in question. The economic law, therefore, goes to prove that when men work for a private employer, they tend to get what they are worth to society as a whole, in their character as producers of income. This theory has been subjected to much ridicule as a bit of academic reasoning which does not square with the facts of life. The complexities, maladjustments, and aberrations of the business world make such criticism of theoretical reasoning easy and speciously convincing. Nevertheless, the marginal productivity theory of wages contains a kernel of truth of much importance in explaining the workings of our competitive world. It is well to understand just what the economic law implies and within what limits it holds true, before we attempt to solve practical problems arising out of the wage contract.

The independent worker. If all workmen to-day were independent laborers, directing their own labor and marketing their products, their money incomes would be determined roughly by the marginal productivity law. These incomes would be drawn directly from the sale of their goods and services on the market at prices which measured the utility of these goods to the consumers. The prices which governed the money incomes of the different occupational groups would themselves be determined by the numbers of workers in these groups in relation to the demand for their services. Hence the situation would result in returning to each worker a rough equivalent of his worth as a producer, the test being applied by the ultimate consumer of his product. Such is now the case with many of those who follow the so-called "liberal" professions — medicine, music, law, and the like.

The case of the wage-earner. The typical worker to-day, however, is not an independent laborer, but a wage-earner receiving his money income from an employer who voluntarily contracts to pay him stated amounts at definite intervals. This typical worker does not sell a product and derive his money income from the sale. Indeed, to separate the result of his labor from that of the other workers who cöoperate with him and market it by itself is manifestly impossible. It is valueless except as a part of the whole process which carries the product through its many stages until its final emergence in a form suitable for the satisfaction of human wants. In the case of the ordinary wage contract, therefore, we must take account of two complicating factors: first, the intricate division of labor which conceals the product of any given worker and makes its exact measurement very difficult if not impossible; secondly, the intermediation of the employer who stands between this worker and the ultimate consumer. Do these complications suffice to overthrow the marginal productivity law of wages? A little analysis will convince us that they do not overthrow this law, though they do require certain qualifications.

It is characteristic of our economic order that no propertyless man can find employment unless it is profitable to some one else to hire him. As the worker sees the situation, his money income depends merely upon the willingness and ability of the employer to pay it. But the employer looks upon wages as a species of cost, differing in no important regard from the cost of light, heat, raw materials, and the other elements consumed in his business. Despite the statement of moralists that "labor is not to be considered an article of commerce," the business man applies to his purchase of labor the same canons of business prudence which govern his expenditures on these other categories of materials. The employer will agree to bear the cost of wages only if he is confident of his ability to recover it from the sale of his product. Indeed, if he fails to do this, his business will presently become bankrupt and his demand for labor will disappear. Good management demands that each worker contribute as much to the corporate income as his wage subtracts from that income. In any chosen instance, the wage-earner's product may be intangible and nonmensurable in the physical sense; but he does, none the less, have the power to expand the gross money income of the enterprise. This is the "produce" of the workingman as viewed by his employer. It serves at the same time to create the employer's desire to add this worker to his payroll, and to set a limit to the amount of money wages which he is willing to pay for his services.

We see, then, that the money wages of the hired worker and those of the independent laborer are controlled by essentially similar forces. In the broadest sense, each workingman throughout the whole field of industry is a servant of the consumer of goods, coöperating with others to satisfy human wants. A true measure of his economic worth as a producer is that value which the ultimate buyers of goods and services place upon his contribution — however slight and intangible it may be — to the product of industry. Our system of private enterprise thrusts the employer between the worker and the consumers; but the appraisal of the consumers is still the determining factor. The employer derives his demand for labor from the consumers' demand for the products of his industry; and he derives his *demand price* for any given kind of labor from the market's evaluation of that portion of the industry's product attributable to this labor group. Reducing these relationships to their simplest terms, it appears that the rôle of the employer is to take over the worker's product and sell it on the market, transmitting to the worker his share of the proceeds of the sale. Continuing this simplified view of the matter, we may take any article of wealth bought in the market and regard that part of its purchase price, not absorbed in the necessary costs of interest, rent, and insurance against risk, as the consumers' reward for all the labor which has contributed to the production of the article in its final form. The ten dollars which one pays for a pair of shoes, for example, is a composite reward; in part, a remuneration for the capital and land used in production; in part, a payment for the labor of the farmer, the tanner, the factory workers, the railway men, the middlemen, and all other persons who, either by manual labor or managerial skill, have played a part in turning out the product.

Practical difficulties. Now it is freely admitted that we have simplified the situation far more than is true of the actual world of affairs. If we attempt to deduce any law of wages from the behavior of a single employer, it will be extremely difficult to arrive at any general statement which would hold true outside the enterprise in question. Employers are situated very dissimilarly as regards their ability to pay a given rate of wages and recover the outlay through the sale price of their product. For one thing, they differ as to their own efficiency as managers; for another, as to the efficiency of their mechanical equipment; again, as to the intensity of the competition to which they are subjected. As far as the individual employer is concerned, the rate of wages is one of the facts of industry, determined by forces which he does not understand, though he may attempt to influence them to his own profit. Nevertheless, he will admit that there is an upper limit to his wage offer, and that this limit is set by the necessity of compelling his employees to earn their own costs. Moreover, if he carries his thought far enough, he will agree that the determination of this upper limit does not rest solely with him, but must be referred in the final analysis to the market which fixes a price upon the goods which he offers for sale.

It is, however, when we direct our attention to the whole of industry rather than to the conditions of an isolated enterprise, that we see most clearly this relationship between the money wages of the worker and the market price of his product. The entire supply of a given kind of labor can find employment in the open market only if the purchasers of goods are willing to buy all the product of their efforts. To disentangle that portion of the product attributable to the wage-earners as distinct from the other productive factors, we must assume that the shares accruing to landlords, capitalists and managers are determined by competitive forces. Then it will appear that the terms upon which any labor group can find employment will be subjected, as a limiting condition, to the test of the money appraisal which consumers place upon their services as producers.

Diminishing productivity. One other element must be added before this analysis of the forces which govern the wage rate can be used in our study of the labor problem. Employing the terms used in abstract economics, we may say that labor, like all other factors of production, conforms to the *law of diminishing marginal productivity.* This means that when the supply of labor of any kind increases, other things — capital supply, land, supplies of other types of labor — remaining constant, the productivity of the *individual member* of that group of laborers declines, after the increase has passed a certain point. This statement holds true whether it be applied to the entire working force, or to any one group within the working force; and whether the attention be focussed on a single enterprise or upon the entire range of industry. If a modern factory increases its total complement of workers — executive, clerical, skilled, unskilled — without increasing its land and capital equipment, though the output of the factory will probably increase it will do so at a progressively slower rate after a certain point has been reached in the process of expansion. If, on the other hand, the increase in the working forces takes place within any one group of workers — let us say, the clerical staff — while all other factors remain constant, there will be evidence of the same principle of diminishing productivity per unit as applied to the increasing factor. The compelling cause of this phenomenon is this: as the number of workers increases, other things constant, each will receive less effective coöperation from the other productive factors. A given capital equipment, a given supply of land and managerial ability can be utilized with maximum effectiveness from the standpoint of the wage-earner, when the labor force has grown to a certain size. If the number of workers expands beyond this point, each will be less well equipped with capital and less well directed than before, and, consequently, each can produce less.

How it works in practice. When the economist states this principle of diminishing marginal productivity in the peculiar language of his craft, the "practical" business man is wont to reply that it conforms to no business principle with which he is familiar. But the difficulty here lies in the language and not in the principle itself; for, like the man who was surprised to discover that he had been talking prose all his life, the business man can be made to see that he has habitually adjusted his operations to the law of diminishing marginal productivity. To illustrate, let us assume that an employer hires a certain number of clerks at a wage of fifteen dollars a week. But why a "certain number"? Having once begun to hire clerks at this rate, why does he not continue indefinitely to do so? If the first ones hired were "worth their wages," why is not the twentieth or the fiftieth or the thousandth? Obviously, it is because the worth of any clerk to the business man depends in some manner upon how many he already has at work; as the number increases beyond a certain point, the economic worth of each clerk begins to decline. The business man would probably say, somewhat bluntly, that he stops hiring clerks when he has all that he needs; but he will readily admit, upon pursuing the matter further, that he does not mean this literally. For, if the wages paid to clerks as compared to those paid other types of labor should decline, he will find it profitable to employ more of them; or, to state the converse, if their wages rise far enough, he will begin to reduce the number on his payroll. This, at any rate, is the reaction of business men in general to fluctuations in wage rates. In other words, employers do not have a fixed demand for a certain definite number of workers of any sort, but a demand which varies with the cost of the workers. And it is universally true that the economic worth to the employer of the individual member of a labor group falls as the number of that group on his payroll increases, until a time comes when an additional worker would not produce enough to equal his wage cost. This is the law of diminishing marginal productivity as viewed from the standpoint of the individual employer.

The effect on labor. Now this factor of diminishing marginal productivity has an important influence upon the welfare of the wage-earner. If we can call before our minds the image of some group of workers — let us say, ordinary machine operatives — increasing in number faster than the other factors of production, it will be easy for us to see that the late comers who join the group will be worth less to their employers than those who came before them. Because of this diminishing economic worth, the employer, even if he paid over to them the entire value of their contribution to his enterprise, would be compelled to take on these later comers at lower rates of money wages than he has been in the habit of paying. We might not see so clearly, however, that the *older* members of the group were also worth less now than before, and that, again on the assumption that money wages were equal to the value of the worker's product, their wages must fall, too. But a little reflection will convince us that this would be the effect of business practice if not of justice. For, as the employer views the situation, in a homogeneous group one member of which can be substituted for another, the economic worth of one laborer depends upon what it costs to hire another man to take his place. And if the wage rate for men outside the plant who can do the same work is going down, those who now hold jobs must presently suffer a reduction of wages, else they will be dismissed and their places filled by the newcomers. If they are dismissed and, consequently, are themselves put under the necessity of applying for work as additional members of some other employer's labor force, their reduced economic worth will become apparent.

If we follow the illustration used in the preceding paragraph a little farther, it will be seen that the ultimate effect of this disproportionate increase in the number of workers is to lower somewhat the prices of the goods they produce and thus redound to the benefit of consumers. It still holds true that the workers' money wages are determined by the value placed on their contribution to the product in the market. But, if the increase in the number of workers has been appreciable, the supply of the product upon which they are engaged will have increased, with a consequent fall in the *price per unit* at which it is sold. At the same time, as we have seen, the productive effectiveness of the individuals in the group will have declined. These two factors, therefore, combine to reduce the money wages of any type of labor which is increasing out of proportion to the other factors of production.

The law stated. If, now, we gather together the results of this rather abstract discussion, we have these considerations governing the rate of money wages: first, the hiring of men being optional with the employer, he will offer employment only on such terms as are remunerative to himself; secondly, since the employer can recover what he expends in wages only through the sale of his product, any attempt that he makes to appraise the economic worth of the worker to his enterprise must be stated in terms of the worker's contribution to this product; thirdly, the economic worth of any member of a given general class of labor varies inversely with the supply of labor of that type (other things equal). The economic law of wages, then, is stated as follows: "Each worker will receive in money wages the equivalent of his contribution to the product of industry, the amount of this contribution being equal to the productivity of the 'marginal' man in his group." This law rests upon those assumptions regarding the free play of competition which underlie the reasoning of the economists regarding all market prices; it assumes, particularly, that the working population falls into certain well-defined homogeneous groups within which the individuals may be substituted for each other at will; that the members of these groups are in perfect competition with one another for employment; and that a similarly perfect competition dominates the dealings of the employers in the labor market.

The bargaining factor. If we examine this law of wages with these assumptions in mind, we shall see that it is, at best, not a statement of what the wage rate in any given case *will be*, but rather a statement of *the highest rate which employers will pay.* No employer will pay more than the amount determined by this law, since to do so would turn the wage bargain into a net loss for him. But they all will gladly pay less, and as much less as is possible through shrewd bargaining. The economist's law of money wages — called the "marginal productivity theory" — has, in general, been repudiated by labor leaders; but its fault lies not so much in its incorrectness as in the false impression of exactness which it gives and in the faith it reposes in the power of competition to compel employers to pay the highest demand price when hiring workers.

Now, there are many reasons why we cannot conclude that wage rates will automatically rise to the level determined by this law. In the first place, complex division of labor resulting, as it does, in the splitting-up of processes into minute fractions of the whole, makes it quite impossible to fix any precise value upon that fragment of the composite product which is attributable to the labor of a single workman. How would we undertake, for example, to state in dollars and cents how much a given stenographer adds to the corporate income of an enterprise; how much a night watchman; how much a stock clerk; or a machinist, an accountant, an elevator boy, or any other single worker? With the best of intentions, and with the application of the most exact methods of modern cost accounting, neither workman nor employer, nor both working in coöperation with each other, can settle a value for these services which will be recognized by all as fair. Since this cannot be done in any individual case, we must, in order to have confidence in the correct working of the economic law of wages, assume that these valuations result, in some way, from the operation of competitive forces in the general industrial world. If we can make this assumption, then it can be said that each employer by adopting this rate will pay to the worker his maximum value to industry as a whole, even if this does not conform to his exact economic worth in the employer's own enterprise.

Such an assumption rests upon a belief that competition works as freely on one side of the wage contract as on the other. But this is untrue; and here we find a second reason why the economic law of wages is inapplicable in practice to specific cases. For wage-earners, as one will be convinced by even a superficial examination of the facts, are usually not in position to take full advantage of competition among employers. To do so they must be able to play off one employer against another; to move about at will from one locality to another; to discard one line of occupation and undertake a different one whenever it is to their immediate financial advantage to do so. All of this requires a degree of mobility in the ranks of labor which the average workman does not possess, and which he is prevented from acquiring because (to mention but one factor among many) of the mere cost of transportation for himself, his family, and his household effects.

The sphere of bargaining. For these reasons alone we cannot conclude that the actual wage rate for any particular workman or class of workmen will conform exactly to the prescriptions of economic theory. In fact, we must accept this law of marginal productivity for what, in truth, it is: a statement of the upper limit of the wage rate under given conditions as to the efficiency of industry. The rate of wages in any specific enterprise for any class of workers cannot rise above the point determined by this law, but may fall below it; where it actually rests will be settled by bargaining between employer and workman. It would aid us to delimit the scope of this bargain if we could ascertain with precision the *lower* limit of the wage rate — the point below which all workers will refuse employment. It is safe to say that there is such a lower limit at any given time, but it is fixed by forces too complex to be gathered up in a simple formula: forces of emotion as well as of reason, of sentiment, of pride, of tradition and loyalty, as well as of economic interest. Within the boundaries of the two limits thus marked out — the upper limit equal to the value of the workman's product, and the lower limit represented by that vague line below which free men will cease to labor — lies the sphere of bargaining. And within this sphere the actual rate of wages is determined by the relative bargaining power of the two parties to the wage contract.

2. National Prosperity and the Wage Rate [1]

The subject of the relationship between national productivity and real wages has a direct bearing on wage determinations, because it involves the application of a modern academic theory of wages and the validity of several arguments or "principles" recently invoked in wage adjustments.

The academic theory in question is the explanation of the distributive process known as the "theory of marginal" or "specific productivity." My hearers are undoubtedly familiar with this varied and intricate theory, and so I shall not attempt to summarize it except by saying roughly that it contends that there is a close relationship between what each group engaged in production contributes to the national grab-bag and what it receives back.

The other arguments referred to are of a more popular nature, and are usually found in propaganda representing special interests or in the proceedings before wage arbitration boards.

There is the argument that the standard of living of the wage-earners increases with the efficiency of the modern productive process, and that if the workers want higher real wages they should buckle down and work harder instead of asking for higher money wages or striking or restricting production in other ways. This argument usually embraces the contention that real wages cannot be increased by any other method than by an increase in national productivity.

There is the argument that wages should be adjusted up or down in direct ratio to a cost-of-living index. This is usually advanced by wage-earners in times of rising prices to prevent a decrease in real wages, and by employers in times of falling prices to prevent an increase in real wages.

There is the argument, akin to the first-mentioned, that the real wages of one group of workers can be increased only at the expense of another group of workers, and that if such a readjustment occurs it creates an abnormal relationship in the fabric of wages and prices, and so prevents the arrival of general prosperity.

There is the argument that, the national income being what

[1] From an article by Geo. Soule, "The Productivity Factor in Wage Determinations," in *The American Economic Review*, vol. 13, supplement.

it is, there can be no marked or general increase in real wages, because such an increase would necessitate an increase in the national income. This argument, together with the preceding one, has recently had a wide vogue, and was sanctioned by the United States Railroad Labor Board in its last wage decision, in which it attacked the principle of the living wage.

The subject also has a bearing on the reasonable expectations of wage-earners under the present economic order, and hence on the desirability of maintaining this order unchanged from the point of view of the wage-earner. Marxian Socialists, for instance, contend that under the present order real wages have a tendency to fall, and cannot be increased. In this contention they are at one with those who argue that money wages should not rise more rapidly than the cost of living, and with those who argue that real wages cannot be increased without disaster to the economic fabric. Such arguments, it will be noted, are incompatible with the theory that real wages do increase with a growth in productivity. We shall, I believe, find light on these various contradictory assumptions only by a quantitative investigation of the facts.

The national income. Several studies of the course of the physical production in the United States, not including a complete list of products, but nevertheless on a wide basis of fundamental data, have been independently made, notably by Professor Walter W. Stewart, late of Amherst and now of the Federal Reserve System, and Professor Edmund E. Day of Harvard. These studies agree substantially with each other. Dr. Day's index indicates that between 1899 and 1920 production of all classes of commodities increased from 64.6 to 117.0, the base, or 100, being an average of production for the years 1909 to 1913. This is an increase of about 80 per cent for the 22 years. During the same years manufacturing production alone increased at a slightly higher rate, or from 58.4 to 115.0. The population during these years increased from about 75 millions to about 105 millions, or about 40 per cent. Thus it is clear that total production increased about twice as rapidly as the population between 1899 and 1920, and that manufacturing production increased at a rate even slightly higher. If we divide the index of production by an index of population, we find that production per capita of the population increased from

84 to 107, or about 28 per cent, and that manufacturing production per capita of the population increased from 76 to 105, or about 39 per cent.

It is thus clear that, over a considerable recent period concerning which fairly complete and accurate data are obtainable, the national product increased so much more rapidly than the population that each man, woman, and child in the country might have received from 30 to 40 per cent more goods per year at the end of the period than each one received at the beginning. If we smooth out the fluctuations of production incidental to the business cycle, we find that the average per-capita increment to national production was slightly under 2 per cent a year. This means that the real wages of all wage-earners might have been increased at the rate of a little less than 2 per cent every year, or between 30 and 40 per cent for the period in question, while the real incomes of all other persons were being increased in like proportion. This includes, of course, incomes classified under the heads of land and capital.

To put the matter in another way, every person in 1899 received a certain share of the national product. We need not question here whether that sharing was just or proper; we know only that it existed and hence was possible. Now if every one had continued to receive the same share year after year, each person's real income would have increased as the national product per capita increased. If wage-earners, for instance, had continued to receive the same per-capita share of the national product year after year, average real wages would have increased in direct ratio to the increase in per-capita production, and this without any relative loss to the shares of other classes of the population or to land and capital. What, as a matter of fact, happened?

Trend of real wages. Before the period above mentioned we have only data of the most general nature — production figures of pig iron, for instance, wage rates in some occupations, an index of retail food prices. In general it seems reasonable to suppose from what we know that both production and real wages increased between 1870 and 1896. We have not enough data to make possible a detailed comparison between the two factors in this earlier period.

All studies of the subject, however, indicate that real wages began to fall about 1896 and continued to fall up to 1914 and perhaps for two or three years more. The most comprehensive and satisfactory data from which to calculate the trend of wages come from the United States Census of Manufactures. The Census of Manufactures covers all wage-earners in factories and it gives the material for calculating annual earnings instead of wage rates, thus including the effects of part-time and seasonal unemployment. It has been, to be sure, compiled only every five years and thus misses much of the fluctuation of the business cycle, but over a period of twenty years we ought to be able to discover a trend within reasonable limits even from five-yearly data. An index of real wages, made by comparing the census figures with the index of retail food prices, shows the following result, if we take 1889 as the base:

Index of Real Wages (in Food)

Year	Index
1889	100
1899	99
1904	99
1914	89
1919	98

Thus, while per-capita production was increasing more than 30 per cent, real wages first fell 10 per cent and then recovered to a position slightly below the levels of 1889 and 1899. It is thus evident that wage-earners not only did not receive the same share per capita of the increased product year after year, but actually were receiving at the end of the period slightly less goods than at the beginning. If real wages had increased in direct ratio to the increase in per-capita production, the index number of real wages in 1919 would have been nearer 140 than 98.

The index of retail food prices was used in arriving at these figures because it is the only good index of retail prices we have over the whole period. It may not be closely indicative of the trend of the cost of living as a whole, but since food occupies nearly 40 per cent of the wage-earner's family budget, we are justified in assuming, I think, that the error is slight before 1914. It certainly is not large enough to invalidate the broad conclusion that the trend of real wages was quite different from the trend of productivity.

More detailed figures on the course of money wages and on the cost of living are available between 1914 and the present. It is well to examine these, not only to secure an index of real wages for 1920, 1921, and 1922, but to check up any error that may be involved in using the retail food index since 1914 when, on account of the disturbance of price relationships incident to the war inflation and deflation, food prices fluctuated more widely than other retail prices.

The best sources for money wages year by year since 1914 are the figures of average weekly earnings published by the States of New York and Wisconsin. Both cover a wide range of industries and a large sample of the factory workers of the respective States. That the movement of New York wages in particular may be considered closely indicative of factory wages throughout the country is indicated by the census figures, which show an increase of average yearly factory wages between 1914 and 1919 of 99.04 per cent for New York, and of 99.8 per cent for the Nation.

INDEX OF REAL WAGES (COST OF LIVING) FOR NEW YORK AND WISCONSIN

Year	Index
1914	100.0
1915	101.7
1916	102.2
1917	93.5
1918	96.6
1919	101.2
1920	110.1
1921	114.7
1922 (10 mos.)	117.3

This would indicate an increase in real wages of about 17 per cent between 1914 and the present year. If we join this new series with our former series derived from the census, however, and reduce it to the base of 1889, we find that real wages at present have increased only a little over 4 per cent above 1889, or about 5 per cent above 1899. The index number on the 1889 base is 104.4.

Thus, even taking into consideration the recent rise in real wages, due chiefly to the more rapid drop of prices than of wage rates since 1920, we have only a 5 per cent increase in the per-capita purchasing power of factory wages to compare with a 30 or

40 per cent increase in per-capita production in the last twenty-five years. Making the utmost possible allowance for error in the real wage figures, it is hardly conceivable that this gap would be bridged.

What groups have gained? What became of the augmented production of physical goods between 1899 and the present which wage-earners failed to receive? The first thought is, naturally, that they may have gone to other elements engaged in manufacturing. Both the Marxian and classical economists, having in mind the great increase in productive capital, might expect to see the share of profits and interest enlarged. The census figures, however, seem to prove that this is not the case, at least to any great degree. If we calculate the percentages of "Value Added by Manufacture" which were paid in wages, in salaries, and in the margin which went for profits, interest, depreciation, and miscellaneous expenses, we find that wages very nearly if not quite held their own, that salaries increased somewhat, and that the property interest decreased slightly. Dr. King's emendation of my table on this point is as follows:

Year	Wages (per cent)	Salaries (per cent)	Profits, Interest, Depreciation, Rent, and Miscellaneous (per cent)
1889	44	8	48
1899	42	8	50
1904	41	9	50
1909	40	11	49
1914	41	13	46
1919	42	12	46

The distributors. My first suggestion was that the extra products were absorbed by those engaged in the distributing process, and by the "overhead" trades or those not engaged in the production of physical goods. This inference is made reasonable by the fact that retail prices before the war seem to have risen more than wholesale prices. Between 1899 and 1914, for instance, retail prices of food increased 50 per cent, while wholesale prices of food increased only 37 per cent. Unfortunately we have no other good series of retail prices to compare with wholesale prices before

1914. The same inference is indicated by the rapidly increasing percentage of the population engaged in trade and finance, the numbers in such occupations having grown from 6.4 per cent of the gainfully employed in 1890 to 10.2 per cent in 1920. The evidence, however, is inadequate on this point, and although it seems probable that the merchants, bankers, advertising men, and the like have in part been responsible for absorbing the addition to the national income lost by those engaged in manufacture, they could hardly have absorbed all of it.

The agriculturalists. Dr. King is responsible for the data which appear to show that the bulk of the increase in production went to those dependent on agriculture for their livelihood. On the basis of his estimates of the national money income, he finds that the share of the total income of the United States going to those engaged in agriculture increased from about 13 per cent in 1889 to about 20 per cent in 1918. During the same period, the share of the total income going to those engaged in manufacture fell a little and then increased slightly, or from about 26 per cent in 1889 to about 29 per cent in 1918. The percentage of mining income showed only a slight increase, while transportation fell slightly.

Meanwhile the number of persons engaged in agriculture had not increased nearly so rapidly as the numbers engaged in the other occupations. And so the larger share of income which agriculture received was divided among a smaller percentage of the gainfully employed population. From these figures it is difficult to avoid the conclusion that the per-capita real income of those engaged in agriculture rose so rapidly between 1899 and 1919 as to absorb most of the increment to national production which, as we have seen, was not shared by factory workers. Dr. King's tables on these points are here repeated for the convenience of the reader on page 107.

It would be improper to infer from these figures that the increase in the average per-capita agricultural income was wholly reflected in the prosperity of actual working farmers. If we bear in mind the enormous increases in the value of good farming land, and the large number of tenant farmers and farm mortgages, we must conclude that a great part of this new income did not bring full benefit to actual tillers of the soil.

PERCENTAGE OF THE TOTAL INCOME OF THE UNITED STATES

	1889	1899	1909	1918
Attributed to value product of:				
Agriculture	12.8	14.1	16.2	20.4
Mining	2.5	3.1	3.1	3.3
Manufacturing	25.6	23.1	23.5	29.4
Transportation	10.4	9.2	9.6	8.7
Total	51.3	49.5	52.4	61.8

PERCENTAGES OF TOTAL NUMBER OF PERSONS HAVING GAINFUL OCCUPATIONS

	1890	1900	1910	1920
Attributed to:				
Agriculture	39	36	33	26
Mining	1.7	1.9	2.4	2.6
Manufacturing	18	18	22	27
Transportation	4.7	5	6.2	7.4
Total	63	61	64	63

The drastic fall in agricultural income in 1920 and 1921 coincides with the recent increase in real wages of factory workers. But it should be remembered that real wages have apparently not yet risen sufficiently to indicate that factory workers are receiving as large a per-capita share of the national product as in 1899. As far as their improvement of status is concerned, the agricultural real income per capita might still be more than 40 per cent greater than in 1899. If the farmers are therefore suffering from extreme deflation, they should look elsewhere than to high wages for the cause. If the share of the national income now received by factory wage-earners is unwonted or "abnormal" according to the standards of twenty-five years ago, it is so only by virtue of being too small.

Summary. A summary of the preceding sections shows that while the national per-capita product was increasing steadily (of course with minor fluctuations due to the business cycle) manufacturing wage-earners experienced the following four periods:

(*a*) A period (between 1870 and 1896) about which little is known in detail except that real wages increased.

(*b*) A period (between 1896 and 1914) in which real wages decreased. The new surplus of production, plus what the wage-earners lost, was absorbed in part by manufacturing salary-earners, in part by the distributing and overhead trades, but chiefly by agriculture.

(*c*) A period (between 1914 and 1919) in which real wages showed a net increase, but not increase enough to absorb any of the increase in per-capita production since 1899. During this period the real per-capita incomes of those engaged in agriculture increased as well.

(*d*) A period (between 1919 and the present) in which real wages showed a more rapid rise than before. Measured from 1899, however, the present wage level does not show as great an increase as the increase in per-capita production during the same period. This recent rapid rise in real wages was accompanied by a rapid decline in agricultural income, and in the per-capita income of farmers. Probably, however, the present share per capita of agriculture in the national income is still larger than in 1899.

During the course of each of the above periods there were fluctuations in wages.

Bearing on wage theory. It is difficult to say without more data whether these conclusions tend to bear out the theory of marginal productivity. They do show, however, that under actual conditions this principle, if it is true, does not operate in any automatic way so as to bring about results which can be recognized as just or desirable. Were there any changes in the relative contributions of factory labor to the productive process which made it just that real wages should increase from 1870 to 1896, should decrease from 1896 to 1914, and should increase again from 1914 to 1922, though not in proportion to the increase in per-capita production? It does not seem reasonable to suppose so.

As to the argument that real wages do increase and can increase only by increasing productivity, and hence that wage-earners would do well to concentrate on improved efficiency, the facts do not seem to establish any great reality for such an incentive. The connection between productivity and wages is not close enough to act as a stimulus. The most that can be said is that increased productivity enlarges the possibility of higher wages. Whether this possibility is to be realized evidently depends either on the blind play of economic forces, or on a higher degree of social control than has been exercised in the past.

The argument that money wages should be adjusted up or down in direct ratio to a cost-of-living index does not seem to be confirmed. Wages have not moved in any such way in the past. It is, to be sure, necessary that money wages should increase at least as rapidly as the cost of living, if real wages are not to fall. But it is neither desirable nor necessary that money wages should fall with the cost of living. If wage-earners are to benefit by increased productivity, money wages must increase more than the cost of living in the long run.

It is obviously not true that the real wages of one group of workers can be increased only at the expense of another group of workers. Such shifts in the distribution of the national income do, indeed, appear to occur. But it would be possible to preserve any given status of distribution by increasing the real incomes of all persons in direct ratio to the increase in per-capita production. The increase in productivity alone has been rapid enough to furnish substantial increases in income to every one, without robbing Peter to pay Paul. This is not to say that it might not be desirable to award a larger share of the national income to the wage-earners than in the past. No one has yet proved that the rate of capital accumulation, for instance, ought to be as rapid as it is, or that society benefits from large increases in agricultural rents. But we do not need to go into such questions to see that increases in purchasing power of wage-earners might reasonably keep even pace at least with increases in per-capita production.

Even if shifts in the distribution of the national income do occur, that fact by itself offers no assurance that a new basis of sharing may not arrive without upsetting any so-called "normal" balance of wages and prices. Where are we to look for such a "normal" year? In 1919? But that differed from 1914. In 1914? But that differed from 1899. Such a balance, as a matter of fact, has apparently not been preserved without change through any considerable part of the period we have had under consideration.

The argument that, the national income being what it is, there can be no general increase in real wages is erroneous, for the reasons stated above. If we mean by the national income merely an estimated total of dollars, such an estimate is arrived at by adding up the money incomes of individuals or groups, and the argument amounts to a meaningless mathematical identity. If we mean by the national income an annual total production of goods and services, that can and does increase, and might under proper control increase faster than it has in the past. Furthermore, readjustments in the distribution of this income have occurred and can occur in the future.

Finally, the evidence is not conclusive with regard to the desirability of the present economic order from the point of view of the wage-earner. It does not bear out the Marxian theory that real wages must fall, neither does it bear out the opposing argument that real wages must rise with technical progress. It would appear, nevertheless, that if the wage-earner is to receive a minimum of justice his share of the national income should not be diminished over any considerable period. If this end is to be achieved, average real wages must be increased at least in direct ratio to a smoothed index of national per-capita production.

Is such a goal beyond the power of conscious social control? The answer will depend in part on an analysis of the causes which lie behind the observed phenomena. It may be that there is a significance in the falling price level which accompanied the rise in real wages from 1770 to 1896 and from 1920 to 1922, in the rising price level which accompanied the drop in real wages between 1896 and 1914. It may be that there is a significance in the large volume of immigration between the nineties and 1914, and in the falling off of immigration between 1914 and the present. Perhaps the rapid increase in trade-union organization since 1914 is a factor. Possibly the processes of distribution can be organized more efficiently, or the national overhead can be decreased. The working farmers may find some way of reducing agricultural rents or interest. At any rate those engaged in making wage determinations, so far as they hope to accomplish anything besides registering the aimless play of the market, may find the beginning of a guide for the use of reason in the course of national productivity.

3. The Standard of Living and the Wage Rate

Labor's wage theory. If it can be said with truth that the industrial workers hold any particular theory of wages, that theory consists in a rather vague conviction that wages either are, or ought to be, determined by the worker's standard of living. For the most part, the stress is laid upon what is fair and just rather than upon what is economically possible. The wage-earner is viewed, not as a means of production, but as a human being whose welfare constitutes the end and purpose of all industry. In accordance with this point of view, wages are not looked upon as a *rental* paid for a productive instrument, whose amount is to be measured out by impersonal economic forces, but rather as the source of life and the sole means toward happiness of a human soul. Any theory to be in harmony with this conception of the worker's relation to industry must be stated in terms of living standards and costs.

Nevertheless, this standard-of-living theory of wages is sometimes advanced as an attempt to explain things as they are, rather than as an assertion of what, on moral grounds, ought to be true; and as such it vies with the economist's theory of marginal productivity. It is not to be expected, of course, that any theory or explanation which arises from the thinking of the mass of men in industry should have been worked out with scientific exactness. Underlying the wage theory, we usually find unexpressed the belief that the employer's remuneration to his employee is determined autocratically, or, at any rate, arbitrarily; and that it tends to gravitate toward some cost-of-subsistence minimum, where its decline is arrested either by the forces of sentiment — public sentiment or the employer's compassion — or by the sheer impossibility of providing a supply of workers for a wage smaller than is required to keep them alive. For over a century the wage-earners have rebelled against the efforts of social workers to reduce their cost of living by means of frugal expenditure, cheaper diet, thrifty budgeting of costs and income, and similar devices, believing that any gains resulting from these expedients would be appropriated by the employer through a reduction of the wage rate. In the reverse direction, many workers have favored extravagant living for their group, especially when it took the form of including in the normal standard of life expensive items of consumption. It has been held that such expenses, as soon as they become habitual, will play their part in determining the wage rate. The fallacy of the crudest of these corollaries of the standard-of-living theory of wages is so obvious that they merit no discussion. Nevertheless, there is an element of truth in the theory itself which should be clearly understood by the student of labor problems, especially in these days when it is popular to attempt to fix wages with reference to the cost of living.

As we have seen, the thing of fundamental importance with regard to the determination of the wage rate is the fact that wages are paid out of the product of industry. Now, when we take things as we find them at a given time under the prevailing conditions of industrial efficiency, it is clear that the *real* wages of all *workers* cannot be raised permanently above the amount of their product. Things must be produced before they can be consumed. As long as factors making for industrial efficiency remain unchanged, bargaining over the *division* of the product will not increase the amount to be distributed. Looking at the matter from another angle, it is also easy to see that, in an industrial order where employment is optional with the employer, and the supplying of land, capital and managerial ability to productive enterprise is voluntary on the part of the possessors of these factors, the employer will not pay to a given workman more than that workman adds to the income of the enterprise. Indeed, the employer *cannot* pay more than this in a *competitive* industry except at the possible cost of driving himself into bankruptcy. Consequently, if the standard of living is to have any influence upon the wage rate it must work out its effects in harmony with the factor of marginal productivity and not in opposition to it.

Standard of living may affect bargaining power. Nevertheless, there are two ways in which a high standard of living may be effective in raising the wage rate or preventing its decline. In the first place, it must be repeated that the marginal productivity wage is merely the ideal maximum above which the rate will not rise in an industrial order operated for profit. The actual wage is fixed by bargaining at this point, or below it, though never above it. If the result of this bargain is to give the wage-earner a rate lower than that determined by the marginal productivity of his group, he is being *exploited* in the sense that his wage is less than the industry is able to pay him, less than his economic worth to society; while, ipso facto, some other factor of production is drawing a revenue in excess of its economic worth. In such a situation, a firmly entrenched standard of living may operate to increase the bargaining power of the workers. To have this effect, the worker must be so firmly attached to his standard by ties of tradition and sentiment that he will refuse to work at a wage which involves a worsening of this traditional mode of life. When this is true the standard of living sets the lower limit to the wage bargain and fixes a point below which the wage rate is not allowed to fall, at least over short-run periods. A gradually rising standard of living will elevate this lower boundary to the sphere of bargaining, thus reducing the range of the wage contract and causing the actual rate to approach more closely, and adhere more permanently, to the point determined by the factor of productivity. Since there can be little doubt that the propertyless worker, especially when unorganized, is a timid and necessitous bargainer, there is reason to believe that his hand has sometimes been strengthened against an unscrupulous employer through the emotional influence of his standard of life.

Evidence in support of this conclusion is to be found during those periods when there is a tendency of the real wage for an occupational group to fall. Wage-earners in many cases have been known to reject the offer of employment at less than a "white man's wage"; in other words, to prefer idleness and slow starvation to a deliberate degradation of their standard. Obviously, such a reaction is a short-run phenomenon; if the decline of the wage rate is determined by fundamental and enduring economic forces, the workers must submit eventually to a worsening of their standard and fall back upon some lower minimum. On the other hand, when the trend of economic change is in the other direction — toward an improvement of the real wages of labor — a rising standard of living may aid the workers in gaining more quickly the advantage which is theirs by virtue of these underlying forces. We need not conclude that the standard of living, operating through its influence upon the bargaining power of the wage-earner, can nullify the controlling influence of the productivity factor. Nevertheless, there are times when it may affect the wage rate in a way beneficial to the workingman.

A rising standard may increase productivity. In the second place, the standard of living must be viewed as one of the elements determining the marginal productivity of the workers, in which character it plays a part in the complex of economic forces which fix the upper limit to the wage bargain. It is common knowledge that a close correlation exists between the productivity of the worker and those phases of his standard of living which consist of physical maintenance — food, shelter, clothing. But we are now beginning to learn that less tangible elements in his mode of life play a similar part; that wholesome home life, freedom from worry, leisure for intellectual and spiritual development, a hopeful prospect of social advancement for his children, all contribute to the worker's productivity. The argument in support of the "economy of high wages" rests upon such considerations as these, tending to prove that when once the wage of the low-paid worker has been raised he automatically becomes "worth" the increased reward. We need not push very far our analysis of this phase of the standard-of-living theory in order to appreciate its truth, and, also, to grasp its limitations. Obviously, there are bounds set to the power of good living to improve the worth of the worker, considering him solely in the rôle of a productive machine. But within these bounds there is room for the standard-of-living factor to operate to raise wages.

The long-run influence. There is another reason for believing that the standard of living is a factor of fundamental importance in determining the marginal productivity of any wage-earning group. By stressing the word "marginal" in the economist's formula for the law of wages, we remind ourselves that the rate of wages received by any individual member of a group is equated, through the influence of the principle of substitution, to the productivity of the so-called "last man" of the group; that is to say, that man, or group of men, whose labor can be used least effectively when the entire group is employed in industry. Because labor conforms to the law of diminishing marginal productivity, this determinant of the wage rate varies inversely with the supply of labor of the kind in question; rising when that supply shrinks (other things constant), and falling when it expands. This maximum wage of the members of a given occupational group is governed, therefore, not solely by the physical fitness and productive energy of these workers but also by the bare fact of their number in relation to the supplies of other productive factors in society.

Now, from the broadest point of view, the standard of living, operating over long-run periods, sets limits to the numbers of workers in the different occupational groups as well as to the total number who seek employment in industry. Viewed from this broad social standpoint the standard of living is defined as "that quantum of physical and psychical enjoyments which the individual demands in preference to marriage or the procreation of children after marriage." It operates as a limitation on the birth rate, stimulating the "preventive" checks to population which form a part of the Malthusian doctrine: postponement of marriage and the deliberate control of births. By advancing its standard of living, a given labor group not subject to infiltration from other classes of workers may make itself, progressively, a "short factor" in industry, raising its marginal productivity over a long-run period of time, and, consequently, advancing its economic worth. Indeed, it is conceivable that the entire body of wage-earners may accomplish somewhat the same result by applying the same method; though in this case, the *real* wages of the different classes would be, in part, held down by the off-setting effects of the policy of the other groups. The beneficial effect of limitation on numbers for the entire laboring population would come at the expense of the other major factors of production, land and capital, and thus affect fundamentally the distribution of wealth within society, though in a way impossible of exact prediction.

We will not attempt an analysis of the bearing of this relation of the standard of living to the marginal-productivity wage upon the welfare of the entire laboring population. For certain wage-earning groups, however, this implication of the standard-of-living theory has a very practical meaning. The higher grades of wage-earners began long ago to give evidence of the influence of their standard upon their rate of increase, with the result that it has become a commonplace among social students to attribute to this influence some of the credit for that rise of families in the social scale which has characterized society since the Industrial Revolution. Unfortunately for our hopes of social progress, it has been found that the influence of the standard of life upon the birth-rate varies directly as the existing economic condition of the different grades of workers. The most necessitous groups, whose poverty is due essentially to their excessive numbers and, consequently, their low marginal productivity, are least affected as to their increase through the birth-rate by the standard of living; at the other end of the scale, those groups which are already prosperous are most inclined to elevate their standard of living in preference to increasing their birth-rates. In effect, this aspect of the standard-of-living theory may be summed up by stating that it operates more in the way of *maintaining* existing high wages — and, over long-run periods, slowly advancing them — than by raising a low wage rate now current.

Summary. In summing up this discussion, we find that the standard-of-living theory of wages, to the extent that it is not fallacious, is not a disproof of, or a qualification upon, the marginal-productivity theory; that, nevertheless, the standard of living may act as a force raising wages; first, through a strengthening of the bargaining power of the workers and, thus, to raise the lower limit of the range of the wage contract; secondly, by reason of its effectiveness to increase the marginal productivity of the workers, through (*a*) an improvement of their physical and psychological fitness; (*b*) a limitation of their numbers. This analysis should be kept in mind when reading the discussion, immediately following, which treats of the recent experience in America with attempts to equate the wage rate to hypothetical ideal standards of living.

4. The American Standard of Living [1]

Recent applications of the standard of living. The standard of living as a factor in setting wages came to be of considerable importance during the war when prices were rising. Previously, interest in this aspect of wages had come about through the study of poverty, through the normal growth of budget studies, and through the development of state minimum wage laws for women. During the war period, the first use of the standard of living as a basis of wage settlements was, I believe, by the President of the American Economic Association, Professor Seager, who was then the Secretary of the Shipbuilding Labor Adjustment Board.

During the war, the standard of living and earnings became in a very vivid manner the interest of every one, and a matter of public knowledge. Wage adjustments were frequent, and turned on the standard-of-living issue, so that never before had the standard of living been given so much consideration as a wage factor.

Since the depression of 1920 these standards have dropped out of discussion, and similarly their use in setting wages. Wage-earners, and particularly their chief spokesmen, the skilled workmen, said little about the cost of living, because since they argued for increased wages when prices were rising it might be expected that they would take a reduction in wages when prices were falling. Employers, who in general have never shown enthusiastic interest in cost-of-living statistics, particularly in budget details, have tried very little to base their wages on the standard of living. With the pressure of rising prices removed, the public has not been so much interested.

Practical difficulties. I think it can be said that during the war public policy did try to regulate wages on the basis of living costs. This experience showed that at that time the consideration of the standard of living as a basis of wage settlements was practical, but this experience also showed that the application of the stand-

[1] From an article by W. F. Ogburn, "The Standard of Living Factor in Wages," in *The American Economic Review*, vol. 13, supplement.

ard-of-living factor to wage settlements involved a fairly complicated technique, which was not always clearly understood. It seems desirable at this time to pass in review a few of these points about which there is a confusion, as judged from our recent experience, in the interests of facilitating the use of cost-of-living figures in future wage adjustments.

What is meant by cost of living? In the recent wage adjustments in the coal industry and in the railroad industry, it was quite evident that there was much confusion in the mind of the public over the standard-of-living budgets. This confusion arose from the fact that there are several different levels of living and not just one standard of living. Two of these levels of living have been particularly well studied. They are the minimum-subsistence level and the minimum-comfort level. The minimum-subsistence standard of living is supposed to provide just a bare subsistence. It can be determined in terms of death-rates, sickness rates, and calorie needs. It is that wage that is thought of when we speak of requiring industry to pay a living wage and say that otherwise it is parasitic and ought not to be permitted to exist.

So drastic a policy has never been urged for the minimum-comfort wage, however desirable it may be socially to raise the standard of living. Condemning an industry for not paying a living wage depends upon what living wage, whether the minimum-subsistence wage or some higher level, is meant. Very frequently the minimum-comfort wage has been erroneously called the minimum-subsistence wage.

Another use of standard-of-living figures that has made it seem impractical is the tendency to apply standards worked out in one locality to another and different locality. It is frequently said that it costs a certain sum for a family of five to live in the United States to-day. There is, of course, not just one single cost for the United States. There are many, varying from locality to locality.

Just how great a variation there is between different regions cannot be told without special investigation. But from the data collected by the United States Bureau of Labor Statistics from all regions of the United States, the difference in cost of living according to sections of the Nation appears to be slight; perhaps it is a little lower on the Pacific Coast.

The variability is somewhat greater, however, by size of the particular locality. The cost of living in the very large city is not greatly different from the cost of living of the large city. But there seems to be a good deal of difference between the cost of living in the large city and in the small town or village. We have very little statistical data concerning cost-of-living standards on the farm. But whatever these differences may be, it should be remembered that there are these variations. The best way of finding out is by special cost-of-living surveys, but of course those are expensive and take time. It is quite possible, I think, for some such agency as the United States Bureau of Labor Statistics to establish differentials according to locality which would very probably be stable over time. In lieu of such differentials, a very useful and practical device has been to take some standard quantity budget and price it in different localities, making such variations here and there in the budget as are found necessary according to custom, climate, and other factors.

When an industry extends over many different localities, variations in levels of living are obstacles to uniformity in wages, if the standard of living is taken as a basic factor. There is, however, such a thing as regional wages.

A third source of confusion in the technique of using standards of living in setting wages has been the failure to differentiate between the two concepts, actual budgets and standard budgets. Actual expenditures are sometimes called the plane of living, while standards of expenditure, showing what ought to be spent to get a bare subsistence or a minimum of comfort, are called standard budgets. It is, of course, easy to see that what a family spends may be less than a minimum of subsistence, although the Railroad Labor Board seems to have been confused on this point. At the minimum-comfort levels, the failure to differentiate between actual and standard budgets has been greater than at the minimum-of-subsistence level.

It has frequently been asserted that the standard budgets are too high, that families can and do live on a smaller amount. This assertion is in part due to the fact that a minimum-comfort "standard" is compared with a minimum-of-subsistence "plane" of living. I am inclined to think that there is more danger of a minimum-of-subsistence standard being set too low rather than too high.

The reason is this. Framers of standard budgets at the minimum-of-subsistence level tend to estimate standards for each separate segment of a budget, as for instance, for food, for clothing, for rent, for fuel and light, and for certain miscellaneous expenditures. They then add up these standards. If this is done, the separate standards add up to some sum, say $1300. But does it follow that $1300 will actually be spent by the wage-earner's family in the same proportions that the framers allow? There is a tendency for standard budgets so made to minimize the miscellaneous expenditures. There is much evidence to show that workers' families will go without the necessary food, clothing, and warmth in order to get recreation or purchase services or goods that have to do with social standing.

For instance, in Chicago, in the latter part of 1918, families of husband, wife, and three children aged 2, 5, and 11 years, did not buy food yielding as much as 3500 calories per man per day until the total expenditure was $1800 a year. Standard budgets recommend 3500 calories per average adult male wage-earner; yet a standard minimum-of-subsistence budget for Chicago in the latter part of 1918 would surely have been set at less than $1800 by several hundred dollars. (With $1600 families of this size bought an amount of food yielding 3300 calories, and with $1400 they bought food yielding 3100 calories.) Of course, in setting wages according to standards of living, we must not assume the families to possess superhuman will power or extraordinary rationality. We must take human nature as we find it. We should not forget that desires for recreation and social approval are just as integral a part of our legitimate desires as is the desire for bread. For these reasons, it is thought, any error that may be found in minimum-of-subsistence standards is likely to make the standard too low rather than too high.

Why the family of five? A fourth practical difficulty in using the standard of living as a basic factor in wage settlements is the adjustment to the varying composition in sex, age, and family of the working-class population of a particular plant. Standard budgets are customarily drawn for a family of five. Employers have at times argued that their wage-earners' families are smaller, averaging, say, two children per family. The theory back of the selection of three children as a standard average is, however, more or less irrelevant, except, of course, in broad limits, of the actual number of children in a family, in very much the same way that the standard minimum-of-subsistence wage is more or less irrelevant to the actual wage received. Public sentiment has, however, supported the family-of-five standard, since in order that the race may maintain itself two children must grow to maturity, marry, and in turn bear children. Three children are simply a recognition of the undoubted chance of death, of non-marriage, and of infertility. Actually the average number of children at any one time in workingmen's families is not far removed from five, as has been shown by Miss Stecker. It may be true that the children of a wage-earner are not all of or under school age, but the excellent researches of Rowntree indicate that the inclusion of children of a young age does not unduly swell the budget because of other obligations and dependents not allowed for in these standard budgets. But of course it is very easy to scale down or up a standard budget according to variations in the size of the family if a situation is found to warrant it. In industries where very young men only are employed, or where unmarried men are the rule, or in industries where large proportions of women are employed along with men, it may be necessary to make some special adjustment.

In concluding these comments on certain practical difficulties which recent experience has uncovered, in the application of budget data to wages, I should like to point out the great desirability of having more studies and researches made on the standard of living so that the material will be readily available. The United States Bureau of Labor Statistics has continued its excellent wartime practice of supplying at short intervals the index numbers of the cost of living as measured in items of the family budget. It would be very desirable if this Bureau would also continue its standard-of-living work, making further researches and bringing up to date estimates of standards.

The American standard. I have now reviewed the outstanding difficulties found by several years' experience in the use of cost-of-living data in setting wages. These difficulties have not been found to be serious, certainly not serious enough to account for the diminished use of the standard of living as a factor in setting wages. The real reason why there has been a diminishing use of standard-of-living data seems to have been the business depression and falling prices. But falling prices and a business depression, however, do not justify a lack of interest in the standard of living. Of course, if the cost of living falls faster in a business depression than wages, as I think is customarily thought, then there is a rise in the standard of living and no undue concern exists for those interested in human betterment. But there is evidence that, contrary to common assumption, wages have fallen farther than the cost of living, and hence there has been a lowering of the standard of living.

Let us look into the evidence. The cost of living reached its peak in June, 1920, approximately. By September, 1922, it had fallen on the average, for the 32 cities for which we have data, 23 per cent, according to the index number of the United States Bureau of Labor Statistics, and 24 per cent according to the estimates of the National Industrial Conference Board. The cost of living has therefore fallen about 25 per cent, less, it is noted, than wholesale prices or retail prices of food.

It is difficult to get good measures of the decline in wages. According to the published figures of earnings in New York factories, the present earnings of $25.71[1] per week in September, 1922, are a decline of only 11 per cent from the peak. Their greatest decline has been 15 per cent.

In Wisconsin factories, the decline in average weekly earnings was greater than in New York, their maximum decline being 29 per cent, and in September, 1922, they were 24 per cent lower than their peak. Weekly earnings in factories in Wisconsin have fallen more than the cost of living there. The data for New York and for Wisconsin are for all types of labor.

As to union labor in the skilled trades, their wage rates have not fallen as much as the cost of living. The rates of wages for the principal organized trades in the large industrial centers had by May, 1922, as reported by the United States Bureau of Statistics, fallen only 6 per cent, while the cost of living by that time had fallen over 20 per cent. It is somewhat questionable how representative the wage rates are of earnings. We think earnings even in the unionized trades must have fallen more. Still the union

[1] This figure is high because of increased earnings in railway repair shops as a result of the strike and because of the high seasonal wages in the clothing trades.

wage rates for the unionized trades had fallen less than the cost of living by May, 1922.

However, the standard of living is of more social concern in connection with the lower-paid, unskilled labor. Mr. Burgess,[1] of the Federal Reserve Bank of New York, has worked out an index of average weekly earnings of common labor in Federal Reserve District No. 2. His figures show that the weekly earnings of common labor had fallen 29 per cent by January, 1922.

The United States Department of Commerce publishes the hourly rate of common labor employed by the United States Steel Corporation, and from these figures we find common labor hourly wage rates have fallen 29 per cent.

A declining standard. It therefore appears that the real wages of common labor, as measured by their rate of earning in terms of what can be bought, have fallen since June, 1920; for the rate of earnings has fallen 29 per cent, while the cost of living fell only 23 per cent. It should be noted in passing that it has in the past been customary to compute changes in real wages by comparing the change in money wages with wholesale prices, or with monthly retail food prices. By this method we find wholesale prices have declined 38 per cent and retail food prices have declined 36 per cent, while the rate of earnings of common labor has declined only 29 per cent; therefore according to this method real wages have risen, some 15 per cent on the basis of wholesale prices and 11 per cent on the basis of retail food prices. But in reality, that is, when money wages are contrasted with cost of living, real wages have declined 9 per cent.

There are therefore large numbers of wage-earners whose standard of living has fallen. Their standard of living has fallen more than the figures of rate of earnings indicate, since the yearly earnings from wages is less now than when wages were higher, because of the unemployment and irregularity of employment, and lack of bonus and overtime.

Although the standard of living is not being considered very much in the midst of the liquidation of labor during a period of falling prices, there is evidently need that it should be considered

[1] W. Randolph Burgess, "Index Numbers for the Wages of Common Labor," *Journal of the American Statistical Association*, March, 1922, p. 101.

because of the decline in the standard of living that has taken place, particularly among the families of unskilled labor.

We do not, of course, realize in social values nor appreciate the human significance of a fall in the standard of living of the most poorly paid laborers. I would like to call your attention, however, to what has happened to the families of certain poorly paid laborers when their standard of living fell. In the winter of 1917–18, Dr. Harris,[1] of the Department of Health of New York City, made a survey of 2000 families whose standard of living had been reduced, and his data show what happens when real wages fall and how the family meets the problem.

Of Dr. Harris's 2000 families, 9 per cent [2] sought charity for the first time. In 9 per cent of the families, women sought work for the first time; 18 per cent of the families went into debt as a direct result of the lowered real wages; 6 per cent took in boarders, never having taken in boarders before; 2000 cases of illness were recorded, an average of one per family; 13 per cent of these cases of illness were definitely retarded because of the low standard of living; 37 per cent of the families eliminated meat from their diet, and in 17 per cent more the amount of meat was reduced. In 40 per cent of the families eggs were eliminated from the diet; in 30 per cent, butter; 6 per cent gave up sugar; and, what is perhaps worst of all, 300 families gave up bottled milk, because of the fall in real wages. It seems very probable that when the standard of living of poorly paid laborers is lowered, sacrifices and adjustments follow somewhat the lines recorded by Dr. Harris in his data of 1917–18.

Even greater need is shown for considering the standard of living if we approach the problem from the point of view of what is a subsistence wage. I do not know what is a subsistence wage at the present time. Practically no valuable standard-of-living studies have been made since 1918 or 1919. I should guess that the minimum-of-subsistence standard would be for New York City to-day in the neighborhood of $1300, and very nearly the

[1] L. I. Harris, "Some Medical Aspects of the High Cost of Living," *The American Journal of Public Health*, July, 1919.

[2] While I give Dr. Harris's data in percentages, the numerical terms are not of interest to us here as measures of degree, because we do not know relatively how much the standard of living had fallen for his 2000 families in comparison with the fall in the standard of living of common labor during the past two years.

same for Chicago. Miss Lucy Gillett, of the New York Association for Improving the Condition of the Poor, has secured prices of a minimum food budget as of December 1, 1922, in New York City, and finds that such food cost $10.39 a week, or at the rate of $540 a year. Such an allotment of food gives adequate nourishment for a family with three children under working age, provided they follow detailed instructions and buy as the Association for Improving the Condition of the Poor says to buy. If a family does not follow instructions, Miss Gillett thinks such an adequate allowance of food would cost $600 or more. If food be considered 43 per cent of the total budget, then the minimum-subsistence budget in New York in December, 1922, must be nearly $1400 a year. In many other regions and localities of the country this level would be somewhat lower.

We know common labor is hired to-day in the northeastern part of the United States at about 37 cents an hour. But of course this does not tell us what the annual earnings are. The annual earnings might conceivably be as high as $1100 a year. At one time in the summer of 1921 the rate of wages of common labor in the United States Steel Corporation plants went as low as 30 cents an hour, which would mean at maximum employment about $900 a year. Chairman Hooper, of the Railroad Labor Board, has estimated the average earnings of the maintenance-of-way men to be 32.7 cents per hour which, it has been variously estimated, would mean only $800 a year or thereabout. Mr. Burgess's studies of earnings of common labor showed for January, 1922, average weekly earnings of $18.06. At 50 weeks' employment per year, common labor in the second Federal Reserve District would earn only $900 a year.

In regard to women's wages, the most comprehensive data come from the studies of general industries in certain States by the Women's Bureau of the United States Department of Labor.

These reports show that one half of the women working in Kansas in 1919–20 received less than $11.80 a week; in Georgia one half received less than $12.20 a week in the winter of 1920–21; in Rhode Island the median wage was $16.85 in the fall of 1920; and in Kentucky in the fall of 1921, the median wage was $11.05. In Missouri, the median earnings were (May–June, 1922) $12.65 a week; in South Carolina (fall, 1921) $9.55; in Alabama (fall,

1921) $8.80; and in Arkansas (spring, 1922) the median weekly earnings were $11.60. The fact that half of the women engaged in industry in these States received less than these median wages means that many must be receiving less than a minimum wage, although we do not know definitely what the living wages are in these States. In general, the minimum-wage boards in States with minimum-wage laws for women have in force to-day minimum wages at figures varying from $12.00 to $16.50 a week.

Can workers live on less than "living wages"? It appears from these comparisons that large numbers of wage-earners are not getting a living wage. The question naturally arises as to how they live if they do not get a living wage. Judging from the recent pronunciamento of the Railroad Labor Board on the living wage, there is current the opinion that any wage which workers work for is a living wage, since in order to work they must be alive.

The answer is that workers trying to live on less than a living wage do not live on it. It should be remembered that the wage is for the family as well as the wage-earner. In the first place, the family income is sometimes a little larger than the earnings of the chief wage-earner, perhaps 10 per cent greater on the average. This may have undesirable social consequences for the family and the children, but it does add something to the amount to be spent. But even 10 per cent added to the average earnings of common labor probably in many cases does not bring it up to a bare subsistence standard of living. Furthermore, not all unskilled laborers are married, nor do all have three children.

Although the chief wage-earner of a family may live, it does not follow that this is true of the family. There is some evidence to lead us to think that poverty falls the least hard on the husband and harder on the wife. The only records of expenditure for which we have individual accounts is clothing, and when the standard of living falls, standards of clothing of the wife are sacrificed before the standards of clothing of the husband.

Besides, living and death are not determined by the heartbeat. Customarily we say if the heart beats one lives; if not, one is dead. But there is such a thing as deterioration and sickness that make death more probable. I have already referred to the high sickness rate found by Dr. Harris in his survey. Inferior feeding also leads to deterioration. The idea of the living wage in that of maintenance, and, in the case of children, of growth. Boas has shown that children of poor parents on the average are smaller than children of well-to-do parents and their rate of growth is definitely retarded. The fact, therefore, that a wage-earner lives and works is not proof of the fact that his family is living. Nor is it proof of the fact that he is not deteriorating more rapidly than the normal process of decay.

The fact that families do not live on less than a living wage is very well shown by the infantile death-rate studies of the Children's Bureau of the United States Department of Labor. Woodbury has published the infant mortality rate, for eight cities, according to the earnings of the father. The highest rate is 157, for families where the father earns $450 or less a year. The figures of income are pre-war figures; $750 now will buy what $450 bought then. The death-rate decreases more or less continuously as the earnings of the father increase. The rates for the graded income classes fall as follows:

$450 or less	156.7
450 to 549	118.0
550 to 649	108.8
650 to 849	96
850 to 1049	71.5
1050 to 1249	66.6
1250 to 1449	64.0
1450 to 1849	86.3
1850 to	37.2

We see, therefore, that at the very low income groups the death-rate for infants under one year is extremely high. We know the correlation of the general death-rate with the infant mortality rate is about 0.8 and we think that the health and disease rate is closely correlated with the death-rate. Dr. Woodbury's data suggest the possible adoption of a new nomenclature. We might call certain low earnings a dying wage, instead of a living wage.

We have shown that during the phenomenal rise of prices of 1916–20 the standard of living came to be considered a most important factor in setting wages; but that with the fall in prices since the summer of 1920 the standard of living has been largely neglected in such considerations. The effect has been a fall in the standard of living of those least able to bear such a fall, with a result that a large number of unskilled laborers are trying to live on less than a living wage and that the standard of living has probably been lowered for some skilled workers.

The living wage a possibility. For a country with a per-capita annual income of around $500 per year, such a policy is all the more unjustifiable. While there may be forces connected with the business cycle that tend to make the standard of living an important factor in wages during prosperity, and that tend to minimize the standard of living as a factor during a depression, it seems unnecessary and deplorable that the standard of living should be so neglected during a business depression.

There is no question that our industries could pay a living wage. The recent report of Secretary Hoover's Committee on Waste in Industry showed a percentage of waste in six of our major industries varying from 29 per cent to 64 per cent. Even if the added payment in wages in consideration of the standard of living should not come out of profit, there is certainly abundant opportunity for such a raise in wages to be met through the elimination of waste, which amounts on the average to about 40 per cent. Of this waste, more than 50 per cent is due to the fault of management and less than 25 per cent to labor. The most efficient plant in an industry is usually two or three times as efficient as the average plant.

The issue of the standard of living and wages is largely an issue of social policy. It seems wholly desirable that all wages below a bare subsistence level should be raised at least to the subsistence level and that in time the standard of living for all wage-earners be progressively raised.

It would, of course, be possible to enact state minimum-wage legislation which should apply to adult males, just as there are now in some States minimum-wage laws for women. There is, however, no practical movement toward this end in the United States at present.

On the other hand, it is possible for public sentiment regarding the importance of standard of living as a factor in wages, by becoming strong, to affect arbitrators in decisions, to affect the bargaining strength of wage-earners. It is conceivable that appreciation of the standard-of-living factor may become so strong as to become part of the mores, just as anti-slavery or monogamy is a part of the mores. It would, of course, take some time for the standard-of-living idea to become strongly implanted in the mores. But certainly to the extent that public sentiment supports the idea, to that extent will it come to affect the wages set in negotiations and arbitrations.

While it is probably true that with the upward trend of the business cycle the public attitude toward a consideration of standards of living is favorable, and that with the downward trend of the business cycle public opinion on the matter is indifferent, still it would be most unfortunate to have as much lost on the downward curve of the cycle as is gained on the upward curve. If public opinion be aroused in favor of considerations of standards of living in periods of depression, then not so much would be lost as was gained when the cycle was moving upward, so that the long-time trend of sentiment in favor of considering standards of living would be upward.

5. The Theory of the Minimum Wage [1]

Minimum wages not maximum wages. We must first get clearly before us the distinction between the fixing and enforcing of a Minimum, and the fixing and enforcing of a wage. What is here in question (as in all factory legislation) is a Minimum, not a Maximum — still less any actual decision that the wage shall be such or such sum. It ought not to be necessary to point this out. But the ignorance and stupidity of people calling themselves educated is, in this matter, beyond belief. Nearly every day I am told, or I read, that this Minimum-Wage legislation is merely a revival of the mediæval fixing of wages by the Justices of the Peace, or the eighteenth-century fixing of wages by the Tailors' Acts or the Spitalfields Weavers' Acts, which had, it is asserted, such disastrous consequences. I wonder how long it will take before such people (economists, I am afraid, not wholly excluded) will realize that they are, in making such statements, simply making fools of themselves, revealing an ignorance of the subject so abysmal as to put themselves beyond the pale. The ancient legislation to which they refer, by definitely prescribing the actual rates to be paid, fixed maximum wages, not merely a mini-

[1] From "The Economic Theory of a Legal Minimum Wage," by Sidney Webb, in *Journal of Political Economy*, vol. 20, 1912. University of Chicago Press, publishers.

mum. There is no sort of resemblance or analogy between prescribing that the work-people shall under no circumstances get more than a specified rate, and merely enacting that they shall under no circumstances get less. The whole economic and social consequences and results of the two types of legislation, and their effects on employers and on industry, are as different as chalk is from cheese.

The principal question for the economist to consider is how the adoption and enforcement of a definite minimum of wages in particular trades is likely to affect, both immediately and in the long run, the productivity of those trades, and of the Nation's industry as a whole.

Minimum wage increases efficiency of labor. Now upon this point the verdict of economic theory, whatever it may be worth, is, I submit, emphatic and clear. To the modern economist there seems nothing in the device of a legal minimum of wages, especially where (as would in the great majority of trades be the case) it takes the form of a standard piecework list, that is in any way calculated to diminish productivity. On the contrary, all experience, as well as all theory, seems to show that, as compared with no regulation of wages, or with leaving the employer free to deal individually with each operative, it must tend actually to increase the productivity of the industry. Here we have, in fact, the lesson of actual experience from a whole century of industrial history. It is only necessary to watch the operation, in trade after trade, of analogous common rules, many of them enforced by law. These common rules, like the legal minimum wage, are always minima, not maxima. Every employer naturally prefers to be free to do whatever he chooses; to compete in any way he pleases, on the downward way as well as on the upward way. But the enforcement in any industry, whether by law or by public opinion, or by strong trade-unionism, or a standard rate, a normal day, and prescribed conditions of sanitation and safety, does not prevent the employer's choice of one man rather than another, or forbid him to pick, out of the crowd of applicants, the strongest, the most skillful, or the best-conducted workman. The universal enforcement of a legal minimum wage in no way abolishes competition for employment. It does not even limit the intensity of such competition, or the freedom of the employer to take advantage of it. All that it does is to transfer the pressure from one element in the bargain to the other: from the wage to the work, from price to quality. In fact, this exclusion from influence on the contract of all degradation of price, whether it takes the form of lower rates of wages, longer hours of labor, or worse conditions of sanitation and safety, necessarily heightens the relative influence on the contract of all the elements that are left. If the conditions of employment are unregulated, it will frequently "pay" an employer (though it does not pay the community for him to do so) *not to select the best workman*, but to give the preference to an incompetent or infirm man, a "boozer" or a person of bad character, provided that he can hire him at a sufficiently low wage, make him work excessive and irregular hours, or subject him to insanitary or dangerous conditions. In short, the employer may (in the absence of definitely fixed minimum conditions) make more profit, though less product, out of inefficient workmen than out of good workmen. With a legal minimum wage, and with similarly fixed hours and sanitary conditions, this frequent lowering of productivity is prevented. If the employer cannot go below a common minimum rate, and is unable to grade the other conditions of employment down to the level of the lowest and most necessitous wage-earner in his establishment, he is economically impelled to do his utmost to raise the level of efficiency of his workers, so as to get the best possible return for the fixed conditions.

This is the basis of the oft-repeated accusation brought by the sentimental lady or charity worker against the trade-union standard rate, and now, in England, by foolish persons against the Workmen's Compensation Act, that it prevents an employer from preferentially selecting an old man, or a physical or moral invalid, when there is a vacancy to be filled. But it is clear that the aggregate efficiency of the Nation's industry is promoted by every situation being filled by the best available candidate. If the old man is engaged instead of the man in the prime of life, because he can be hired at a lower rate, the man of irregular habits rather than the steady worker, because the former is prepared to take smaller wages, there is a clear loss all round. From the point of view of the economist, concerned to secure the highest efficiency of the national industry, it must be counted to the credit of the legal minimum wage that it compels the employer, in his choice of men to fill vacancies, seeing that he cannot get a "cheap hand," for the price that he has to pay, to be always striving to exact greater strength and skill, a higher standard of sobriety and regular attendance, and a superior capacity for responsibility and initiative. This is exactly what has happened in Victoria under the Minimum Wage Law, as it has happened in Great Britain where a definitely fixed minimum has been substituted for the irregular competitive rates, which, in the absence of a common rule, the sharp or "cutting" employer can enforce on the weakest or most necessitous workers. Thus, a legal minimum wage positively increases the productivity of the Nation's industry, by insuring that the surplus of unemployed workmen shall be exclusively the least efficient workmen; or, to put it in another way, by insuring that all the situations shall be filled by the most efficient operatives who are available. This is plainly not the case under "free competition" where there is no fixed minimum.

But the enforcement of a legal minimum wage does more than act as a perpetual stimulus to the selection of the fittest men for employment. The fact that the employer's mind — no longer able to seek profit by "nibbling" at wages — is constantly intent on getting the best possible workmen, silently and imperceptibly reacts on the wage-earners. The young workman, knowing that he cannot secure a preference for employment by offering to put up with worse conditions than the standard, seeks to commend himself by a good character, technical skill, and general intelligence. Under a legal minimum wage there is secured what under perfectly free competition is not secured, not only a constant selection of the most efficient but also a positive stimulus to the whole class to become more and more efficient. It is unnecessary here to dwell on the enormous moral advantage of such a permanently acting, all-pervasive influence on character. But this, too, has an economic value, in increasing productivity.

So far we have considered merely the effect upon productivity of enforcing a minimum wage, quite irrespective of this involving a positive increase of wages. But to enforce a minimum is actually to raise the wages of, at any rate, some of the worst paid operatives. We have, therefore, to consider also the effect on the living human being of the more adequate wages that the enforcement of a legal minimum would involve in the lowest grades. If unrestricted individual competition among the wage-earners resulted in the universal prevalence of a high standard of physical and mental activity, it would be difficult to argue that a mere improvement of sanitation, a mere shortening of the hours of labor, or a mere increase in the amount of food and clothing obtained by the workers or their families, would of itself increase their industrial efficiency. But such ideal conditions are far from prevailing in any country. In the United Kingdom at least eight millions of the population — over one million of them, as Mr. Charles Booth tells us, in London alone — are at the present time existing under conditions represented by family earnings of less than five dollars a week. It is notorious that even in the United States there are millions of families unable to earn regularly throughout the whole year as much as ten dollars a week: a sum which does not afford, at present prices, in the slums of New York or Chicago, Pittsburgh or Cincinnati, enough for a physiologically healthy existence. The unskilled, and especially the casually hired laborer, who is inadequately fed, whose clothing is scanty and inappropriate to the season, who lives with his wife and children in a single room in a slum tenement, and whose spirit is broken by the ever-recurring irregularity of employment, cannot by any incentive be stimulated to much greater intensity of effort, for the simple reason that his method of life makes him incapable of either the physical or mental energy that would be involved. Even the average mechanic or factory operative, who earns in the United Kingdom from five to ten dollars a week, seldom obtains enough nourishing food, an adequate amount of sleep, or sufficiently comfortable surroundings to allow him to put forth the full physical and mental energy of which his frame is capable. The cool observer of the conditions of life of that half of the American people who have to live on family earnings that do not exceed five hundred dollars in a year, cannot refrain from placing them in the same case. No "intellectual" who has lived for any length of time in households of typical factory operatives or artisans in England or in the United States, can have failed to become painfully aware of their far lower standard of nutrition, clothing, and rest than his own, and also of their lower standard of vitality and physical and mental exertion. It has accordingly been pointed out by many economists, from J. R. M'Culloch to Alfred Marshall, that, at any rate so far as the weakest and most necessitous workers are concerned, improved conditions of employment bring with them a positive increase of production. "A rise in the standard of life for the whole population," we are expressly told, "will much increase the national dividend, and the share of it which accrues to each trade." We see, therefore, that a legal minimum wage, so far as the wage-earner is concerned, is calculated — at any rate if it takes the form of a standard piecework list — to promote the action of both forces of evolutionary progress; it tends constantly to the selection of the fittest, and at the same time provides both the mental stimulus and the material conditions necessary for functional adaptation to a higher level of skill and energy.

Minimum wage a stimulus to management. But we have got into the habit of thinking that the productivity of industry depends more upon the efficiency of the brains and machinery employed, than upon the quality of the manual laborers. Let us, therefore, consider the probable effects of a legal minimum wage upon the brain-workers, including under this term all who are concerned in the direction of industry. Here the actual experience of the Factory Acts and of strong trade-unionism is very instructive. When all the employers in a trade find themselves precluded, by the existence of a common rule, from worsening the conditions of employment — when, for instance, they are legally prohibited from crowding more operatives into their mills or keeping them at work for longer hours, or, when they find it impossible, owing to a strictly enforced piecework list, to nibble at wages — they are driven in their competitive struggle with each other, to seek advantage in other ways. We arrive, therefore, at the unexpected result that the enforcement of definite minimum conditions of employment as compared with a state of absolute freedom to the employer to do as he likes, positively stimulates the invention and adoption of new processes of manufacture. This is no new paradox, but has been repeatedly remarked by the opponents of trade-unionism. Thus Babbage, in 1832, described in detail how the invention and adoption of new methods of forging and welding gun-barrels was directly caused by the combined insistence on better conditions of employment by all the workmen engaged in the old process

In this difficulty [he says] the contractors resorted to a mode of welding the gun-barrel according to a plan for which a patent had been taken out by them some years before the event. It had not then succeeded so well as to come into general use, *in consequence of the cheapness of the usual mode of welding by hand labour*, combined with some other difficulties with which the patentee had to contend. But *the stimulus produced by the combination* of the workmen for this advance of wages induced him to make a few trials, and he was enabled to introduce such a facility in welding gun-barrels by roller, and such perfection in the work itself, that in all probability very few will in future be welded by hand labour. Similar examples [continues Babbage] must have presented themselves to those who are familiar with the details of our manufactories, but these are sufficient to illustrate one of the results of combinations. . . . It is quite evident that they have all this tendency; it is also certain that considerable stimulus must be applied to induce a man to contrive a new and expensive process; and *that in both these cases unless the fear of pecuniary loss had acted powerfully the improvement would not have been made*

The Lancashire cotton trade supplied the same generation with a classic instance of "trade-union folly" of this kind. Almost every contemporary observer declares that the adoption of the "self-acting" mule was a direct result of the repeated strikes of the cotton spinners, between 1829 and 1836, to enforce their standard piecework lists, and that many other improvements in this industry sprang from the same stimulus. The *Edinburgh Review* went so far as to say, in 1835, that "if from the discovery of the spinning frame up to the present, wages had remained at a level, and workers' coalitions and strikes had remained unknown, we can without exaggeration assert that the industry would not have made half the progress." And, coming down to our own day, I have myself had the experience of being conducted over a huge steel works in Scotland by the late Sir Charles Tennant, one of the ablest and most successful of our captains of industry, and being shown one improvement after another, which had been devised and adopted expressly because the workmen engaged at the old processes had, through their powerful trade unions, enforced a definite minimum standard wage. To the old economist, accustomed to the handicraftsman's blind hostility to machinery, this insistence on a uniform minimum standard rate seemed a proof of the shortsightedness of trade-union action. The modern student perceives that the trade unions, in fighting for better conditions of employment than would have been yielded by individual bargaining, and, in particular, for a compulsory minimum, were building "better than they knew." To the wage-earners as a class it is of the utmost importance that the other factors in production — capital and brain power — should always be working at their highest possible efficiency, in order that the common product, on which wages no less than profits depend, may be as large as possible. The enforcement of the common rule on all establishments concentrates the pressure of competition on the brains of the employers, and keeps them always on the stretch. "Mankind," says Emerson, "is as lazy as it dares to be," and so long as an employer can meet the pressure of the wholesale trader, or of foreign competition, by nibbling at wages or "cribbing time," he is not likely to undertake the "intolerable toil of thought" that would be required to discover a genuine improvement in the productive process, or even, as Babbage candidly admits, to introduce improvements that have already been invented. Hence the mere existence of a legal minimum wage, by debarring the hard-pressed employer from the most obvious form of relief — one which is of no advantage to the community — positively drives him to other means of lowering the costs of production, which almost inevitably take the form of increasing productivity.

Thus, the probable effect of a legal minimum wage on the organization of industry, like its effect on the manual laborer and the brain-working manager or entrepreneur, is all in the direction of increasing efficiency. Its effect on the personal character of the operative is in the right direction. It in no way abolishes competition, or lessens its intensity. What it does is perpetually to stimulate the selection, for the Nation's business, of the most efficient workmen, the best-equipped employers, and the most advantageous forms of industry. It in no way deteriorates any of the factors of production; on the contrary, its influence acts as a constant incentive to the further improvement of the manual laborers, the machinery, and the organizing ability used in industry. In short, whether with regard to labor or capital, invention or organizing ability, the mere existence of a legal minimum wage in any industry promotes alike the selection of the most efficient factors of production, their progressive functional adaptation to a higher level, and their combination in the most advanced type of industrial organization. And these results are permanent and cumulative. However slight may be the effect upon the character or physical efficiency of the wage-earner or the employer; however gradual may be the improvement in processes or in the organization of the industry, these results endure and go on intensifying themselves, so that the smallest step forward becomes, in time, an advance of the utmost importance. I do not see how any instructed economist can doubt, in the fact of economic theory on the one hand, and of the ascertained experience of Victoria and Great Britain on the other, that the enactment and enforcement of a legal minimum wage, like that of an ordinary factory law, positively increases the productivity of industry.

Parasitic trades. I pass to a more interesting point. What would be the result of a legal minimum wage on the employer's persistent desire to use boy labor, girl labor, married women's labor, the labor of old men, of the feeble-minded, of the decrepit and broken-down invalids and all the other alternatives to the engagement of competent male adult workers at a full standard rate? What would be the effect, in short, upon the present employment, at wages far below a decent level, of workers who at present cannot (or at any rate do not) obtain a full subsistence wage?

To put it shortly, all such labor is parasitic on other classes of the community, and is at present employed in this way only because it is parasitic.

When an employer, without imparting any adequate instruction in a skilled craft, gets his work done by boys and girls who live with their parents and work practically for pocket money, he is clearly receiving a subsidy or bounty, which gives his process an economic advantage over those worked by fully paid labor. But this is not all. Even if he pays the boys or girls a wage sufficient to cover the cost of their food, clothing, and lodging so long as they are in their teens, and dismisses them as soon as they become adults, he is in the same case. For the cost of boys and girls to the community includes not only their daily bread between thirteen and twenty-one, but also their nurture from birth to the age of beginning work, and their maintenance as adult citizens and parents. If a trade is carried on entirely by the labor of boys and girls, and is supplied with successive relays who are dismissed as soon as they become adults, the mere fact that the employers pay what seems a subsistence wage to the young people does not prevent the trade from being economically parasitic. The employer of adult women is in the same case, where, as is usual, he pays them a wage insufficient to keep them in full efficiency, irrespective of what they receive from their parents, husbands, or lovers. In all these instances the efficiency of the services rendered by the young persons or women is being kept up out of the earnings of some other class. These trades are therefore as clearly receiving a subsidy as if the workers in them were being given a "rate in aid of wages." The employer of partially subsidized woman or child labor gains actually a double advantage over the self-supporting trades; he gets, without cost to himself, the extra energy due to the extra food for which his wages do not pay, and he abstracts — possibly from the workers at a rival process, or in a competing industry — some of the income which might have increased the energy put into the other trade.

But there is a far more vicious form of parasitism than this partial maintenance by another class. The continued efficiency of a nation's industry obviously depends on the continuance of its citizens in health and strength. For an industry to be economically self-supporting, it must, therefore, maintain its full establishment of workers, unimpaired in numbers and vigor, with a sufficient number of children to fill all vacancies caused by death or superannuation. If the employers in a particular trade are able to take such advantage of the necessities of their workpeople as to hire them for wages actually insufficient to provide enough food, clothing, and shelter to maintain them permanently in average health; if they are able to work them for hours so long as to deprive them of adequate rest and recreation; or if they can subject them to conditions so dangerous or insanitary as positively to shorten their lives, that trade is clearly obtaining a supply of labor force which it does not pay for. If the workers thus used up were horses — as, for instance, on the horse-cars of an old street railroad, or like those that the English stage-coaches formerly "used up" in three years' galloping — the employers would have to provide, in addition to the daily modicum of food, shelter, and rest, the whole cost of breeding and training the successive relays necessary to keep up their establishments. In the case of free human beings, who are not purchased by the employer, this capital value of the new generation of workers is placed gratuitously at his disposal, on payment merely of subsistence from day to day. Such parasitic trades are not drawing any money subsidy from the incomes of other classes. But in thus deteriorating the physique, intelligence, and character of their operatives, they are drawing on the capital stock of the nation. And even if the using-up is not actually so rapid as to prevent the "sweated" workers from producing a new generation to replace them, the trade is none the less parasitic. In persistently deteriorating the stock it employs, it is subtly draining away the vital energy of the community. It is taking from these workers, week by week, more than its wages can restore to them. A whole community might conceivably thus become parasitic on itself, or, rather, upon its future. If we imagine all the employers in all the industries of the nation to be, in this sense, "sweating" their labor, the entire nation would, generation by generation, steadily degrade in character and industrial efficiency. And in human society, as in the animal world, the lower type developed by parasitism, characterized as it is by the possession of smaller faculties and fewer desires, does not necessarily tend to be eliminated by free competition. The degenerate forms may, on the contrary, flourish in their degradation, and depart farther and farther from the higher type. Evolution, in a word, if unchecked by man's selective power, may result in degeneration as well as in what we choose to call progress. It is to prevent this result that every civilized nation has been driven, by a whole century of experiment, to the adoption of stringent factory legislation as regards sanitation and hours of labor. But water-closets and leisure do not, of themselves, maintain the Nation's workers in health and efficiency, or prevent industrial parasitism. Just as it is against public policy to allow an employer to engage a woman to work excessive hours or under insanitary conditions, so it is equally against public policy to permit him to engage her for wages insufficient to provide the food and shelter without which she cannot continue in health. Once we begin to prescribe the minimum conditions under which an employer should be permitted to open a factory, there is no logical distinction to be drawn between the several causes of the wage contract. From the point of view of the employer, one way of increasing his expenses is the same as another, while to the economist and the statesman concerned with the permanent efficiency of industry and the maintenance of national health, adequate food is at least as important as reasonable hours or good drainage. To be completely effectual the same policy will, therefore, have to be applied to wages. Thus, to the economist, the enforcement of a legal minimum wage appears but as the latest of the long series of common rules, which experience has proved to be (*a*) necessary to prevent national degradation; and (*b*) positively advantageous to industrial efficiency.

Effect on sweated trades. Does this mean that the enforcement of a legal minimum wage in any sweated industry will involve the destruction of that industry? By no means.

When any particular way of carrying on an industry is favored by a bounty or subsidy, this way will almost certainly be chosen, to the exclusion of other methods of conducting the business. If the subsidy is withdrawn, it often happens that the industry falls back on another process, which, less immediately profitable to the capitalists than the bounty-fed method, proves positively more advantageous to the industry in the long run. This result, familiar to the free trader, is even more probable when the bounty or subsidy take the form, not of a protective tariff, an exemption from taxation, or a direct money grant, but of the privilege of exacting from the manual workers more labor-force than is replaced by the wages and other conditions of employment. The existence of negro slavery in the Southern States of America made, while it lasted, any other method of carrying on industry economically impossible; but it was not really an economic advantage to cotton-growing. The "white slavery" of the early factory system of Lancashire a century ago stood, so long as it was permitted, in the way of any manufacturer adopting more humane conditions of employment; but when these more humane conditions were forced upon the Lancashire mill-owners, they were discovered to be more profitable than those which unlimited freedom of competition had dictated. The low wages to which, in the unregulated trades, the stream of competitive pressure forces employers and operatives alike, are not in themselves any more economically advantageous to the industry than the long hours and the absence of sanitary precautions were to the early cotton mills of Lancashire. To put it plumply, if the employers paid more, the labor would be worth more. In so far as this proves to be the case, the legal minimum wage would have raised the standard of life without loss of trade, without cost to the employer, and without disadvantage to the community. Moreover, the mere fact that employers are at present paying lower wages than the proposed minimum is no proof that the labor is not "worth" more to them and to the customers; for the wages of the lowest grade of labor are fixed, not by the "worth," in any sense — not even the possible "value in exchange" — of the individual laborer, but (as we must nowadays sadly concede) largely by the urgent necessities of the "marginal" man, or, rather, the "marginal" woman. It may well be that, rather than go without the particular commodity produced, the community would willingly pay much more for it, and yet consume as much or nearly as much of it, as it now does. Nevertheless, so long as the wage-earner can be squeezed down to a subsistence wage, or, more correctly, a parasitic wage, the pressure of competition will compel the employer so to squeeze him, whether the consumer desires it or not.

The question then arises what effect the prohibition of parasitism would have on the individuals at present working in the sweated trades. We need not dwell on the individual personal hardships incidental to any shifting of industry or change of process. Any deliberate improvement in the distribution of the nation's industry ought, out of regard for these hardships, to be brought about gradually, and with equitable consideration of the persons injuriously affected. But there is no need to assume that anything like all those now receiving less than the legal minimum wage would be displaced by its enactment.

We see, in the first place, that the very leveling up of the standard conditions of sanitation, hours, and wages would, in some directions, positively increase the demand for labor. The contraction of the employment of boys, and girls, brought about by the needful raising of the age for full and half time respectively, would, in itself, increase the number of situations to be filled by adults. The enforcement of the normal day, by stopping the excessive hours of labor now worked by the most necessitous operatives, and the overtime resorted to whenever it suits the momentary convenience of each particular employer — quite irrespective of whether the community as a whole is in a hurry, or not — would automatically absorb the best of the unemployed workers in their own and allied occupations, and would create a new demand for learners. Finally, the abandonment of that irregularity of employment which so disastrously affects the New York outworkers and the London dock-laborers, and indeed most other occupations, would result in the enrollment of a new permanent staff. All these changes would bring into regular work, at or above the legal minimum, whole classes of operatives selected from among those now only partially or fitfully employed. Thus, all the most capable and best conducted would certainly obtain regular situations. But this concentration of employment would, it must be admitted, imply the total exclusion of others, who might, in the absence of regulation, have "picked up" some sort of partial livelihood. In so far as the persons thus rendered permanently unemployed consisted merely of children removed from industrial work to the schoolroom, few (and certainly no economist) would doubt that the change would be wholly advantageous to national productivity and economic efficiency. And there are many who would welcome a reorganization of industry, which, by concentrating employment exclusively among those in regular attendance, would tend automatically to exclude from wage labor, and to set free for domestic duties, an ever-increasing proportion of the women having young children to attend to. There would still remain to be considered the remnant, who, notwithstanding the increased demand for adult male labor and independent female labor, proved to be incapable of earning the legal minimum in any capacity whatsoever. We should, in fact, be brought face to face with the problem, not of the unemployed but of the unemployable: those whom no employer would employ at the legal minimum even if trade was booming and he could get nobody else.

How to handle the unemployable. The unemployable, to put it bluntly, do not and cannot under any circumstances earn their keep. What we have to do with them is to see that as few as possible of them are produced; that such of them as can be cured are (almost at whatever cost) treated so as promptly to remove their incapacity, and that the remnant are provided for at the public expense, as wisely, humanely, and inexpensively as possible.

I cannot here enter into the appropriate social regimen and curative treatment best calculated to minimize the production of the unemployable in each subdivision, and to expedite the recovery of such as are produced. Such a regimen and such a treatment have been elaborately expounded for the United Kingdom in the Minority Report of the Poor Law Commission, which is, in my judgment, essentially, applicable to the United States in much the same way as to the United Kingdom. Once such unfortunate products of social anarchy exist, these physical and moral weaklings and degenerates must somehow be maintained, at the expense of other persons. They may be provided for from their own property or savings, by charity, or from public funds, with or without being set to work in whatever ways are within their capacity. But, of all ways of dealing with these unfortunate parasites, the most ruinous to the community is to allow them unrestrainedly to compete as wage-earners for situations. For this at once prevents competition from resulting in the selection of the most fit, and thus defeats its very object. In the absence of any common rule, it will, as we have seen, often "pay" an employer to select a physical or moral invalid, who offers his services for a parasitic wage, rather than the most efficient workman, who stands out for the conditions necessary for the maintenance of his efficiency. In the same way a whole industry may, if permitted, batten on parasitic labor, diverting the nation's capital and brains from more productive processes, and undermining the position of its more capable artisans. And where the industrial parasitism takes the form of irregular employment, as, for instance, among the sweated outworkers or homeworkers in all great cities, and the casual dock-laborers, its effect is actually to extend the area of the disease. The consumers' demand — which governs the employers' requirements — would suffice to keep in regular work, at something like adequate weekly earnings, a certain proportion of these casual workers. But because it is distributed, as partial employment and partial maintenance, among the entire class, its insufficiency and irregularity demoralize all alike, and render whole sections of the population of the great cities of the twentieth century permanently incapable of regular conduct and continuous work. Thus, the disease perpetuates itself, and becomes by its very vastness incapable of being isolated and properly treated. A dim appreciation of the evil effects of any mixing of degenerates in daily life, joined, of course, with motives of humanity, has caused the sick and the infirm, the imbeciles and the lunatics, even the cripples and the epileptics, to be, in all civilized communities, increasingly removed from the competitive labor market, and scientifically dealt with according to their capacities and their needs. The "labor colonies" of Holland and Germany are, from this point of view, an extension of the same policy. To maintain our industrial invalids, even in idleness, from public funds, involves a definite and known burden on the community. To allow them to remain at large, in parasitic competition with those who are whole, is to contaminate the labor market; and means a disastrous lowering of the standard of life and standard of conduct, not for them alone, but for the entire wage-earning class.

The economist has therefore to point out to the statesman that the adoption of a legal minimum wage would in no way increase the amount of maintenance which has to be provided by the community, in one form or another, for persons incapable of producing their own keep. It would, on the contrary, tend steadily to reduce it, both by diminishing the number of weaklings or degenerates annually produced, and by definitely marking out such as exist, so that they may be isolated and properly treated.

6. An Attack on the Minimum Wage

The following article, written in 1913 when our States were beginning to pass laws establishing minimum rates of pay for women in industry and commerce, states the case of the laissez-faire economists against the attempt to raise wages by law. The major thesis of the writer is fundamentally sound: i.e., that in an order based on free enterprise attempts to advance wages without regard to the worker's productivity are both futile and injurious. However, in applying the logic of this position to any specific minimum-wage law, two considerations, both overlooked by this writer, must be borne in mind. In the first place, we have no assurance that the prevailing wage rate, especially as applied to unorganized women workers in certain trades, represents the full product of the worker. The actual rate is fixed by the bargaining process; the *productivity* wage is merely an ideal maximum toward which wages tend to rise under competition. The writer assumes that the shopgirl's $5 per week, for some reason, must automatically measure her full worth as a producer. But weak and timid bargainers may be victimized into accepting less than they are worth to the employer and to society. When this is true, it is obvious that the wage of the group in question may be raised by law — provided the increase is not pushed too far — without conflicting at all with the position of the writer.

Secondly, an initial rise of wages for any especially low-paid group may bring about reactions which so far improve the productivity of the group as to justify the higher wage on the very grounds laid down by the writer. Undernourishment, anxiety, resentment against the employer, to say nothing of the effects of vice indulged in as a means of supplementary income, are, for obvious reasons, destructive of the productive efficiency of any class of workers. Relief from these handicaps, it may be argued, will inevitably improve the service of the wage-earner in industry; and an advance of wages which works toward this end — even if at the outset the advance is wholly arbitrary — need not in the long run conflict with the productivity theory of wages. Experience with the minimum wage in this country and others has proved that this consideration is not merely of theoretical importance.

[1] The hysterical agitation for a minimum wage (to-day urged chiefly for women) has in it no conception of a relation between wages and producing power. It is unsound for several reasons which touch the very interests of the laborers themselves.

It introduces a new and unjustifiable basis of wages — that wages shall be paid on the basis of what it costs the recipient to live. If it is urged, for instance, that a woman cannot live on $5.00 a week but can live on $8.00 and hence her minimum wage should be $8.00, the whole case has not been considered. If we accept — what we should not accept — the principle that wages

[1] Adapted from an article by J. Laurence Laughlin, "A Monopoly of Labor," in the *Atlantic Monthly*, vol. CXII, pp. 551–53.

should be related to the cost of living, and if it is accepted that the woman should live on $8.00 a week, on what grounds should she ever receive more than $8.00 a week? On what grounds could any one get $18.00 a week? At present $18.00 is paid on the ground that it is earned, that is, on the basis of a relation between wages and producing power. No other basis can stand for a moment in the actual work of industry. Men go into business to gain profit; if, in their opinion, the employee is not worth $8.00 a week, she will not be retained, no matter what it costs to live. If she is worth to the business $18.00, that will be the wage. No law can force any one to remain in a business that does not pay.

The theory of a minimum wage based on the cost of living is flatly inconsistent with the facts of daily life and preparation for any occupation. At what age or point is a beginner, or apprentice, to receive the full legal wage? Is no boy, or apprentice, to be allowed to receive a partial reward till he is a full-fledged adult workman? How about the woman, who, in the economic rôle of domestic labor, knits stockings in odd hours in order to add a little to the family income — shall she receive nothing if not the full legal wage? Shall the boy, or even a young lawyer just entering an office, be forbidden to receive the small stipend of the preparatory period?

Suppose it were required by law to pay shopgirls $8.00 a week instead of $5.00 on the ground that the insufficient $5.00 leads to vice: then, since no ordinary business would pay $8.00 unless it were earned, those who did not earn $8.00 would inevitably be dropped from employment without even the help of $5.00 to save them. If $5.00 is no protection from vice, how much less is no wage at all? This proposal of a minimum wage is directly opposed in practice to the very self-interest of the girls themselves.

It is crass to try to remedy wages which are admittedly too low by fixing a legal minimum wage, which can never be enforced unless private business establishments are to be regarded as state institutions. In a state factory, wages may possibly be determined by law, but not in open competitive business conditions, where the supply of labor has as much influence on wages as the demand. If the supply of women wage-earners converges on only certain kinds of work, wages will be lowered by the very large supply of the workers. There is no exit by this door of legal enactment as to the amount of wages.

The true and immediate remedy is the creation of ready means by which the industrial capacity of the wage-earning women will be increased. The wrong situation — of which low wages, possible starvation, and the temptation to vice are only symptoms — is due primarily to the fact that women thrown on their own resources know no trade and crowd each other in the market for unskilled labor. The remedy lies in the creation of places of instruction where any woman (no matter how poor) shall be taught a trade and have skill given to her by which she can obtain a living wage.

The remedy lies in preventing a congestion of unskilled feminine labor by industrial education. There is no other rational or permanent or human way out of the present wretched situation, if we have the real interest of the workers at heart and are not interested chiefly in getting some cheap political notoriety.

This conclusion applies to men as well as to women. Is not a skilled carpenter worth more than a blunderer? In any business, does not every one agree that it is fair to give a very energetic, live, active, skillful salesman more than a stupid? If he is skilled he earns more, because he brings in more business. That being settled we do not fix his wages on what it costs him to live. He has a right to spend his income as he pleases. Hence if we were to adopt the theory of the minimum wage we should be adopting a new theory of wages, which would justify the refusal to pay higher wages based on efficiency.

The only real permanent aid to low wages is to increase the productivity and skill of the persons at the bottom. Instead of talking of such injurious palliatives as minimum wages, create institutions at once where those persons can be given a trade or training for a gainful occupation. The cry for a minimum wage is evidence of the industrial incapacity, the lack of producing power, in masses of our people. The concrete ways of increasing the productive power of each man and woman are not unknown. Moreover, the captain of industry can introduce carefully worked out plans for helping his operatives to rise in life; to better conditions by welfare work; to encourage savings and thrift; to introduce the stimulus of profit-sharing; and above all, establish civil-service methods devised to pick out and promote the promising youth so that the path from the bottom to the top is open to every employee. Under unrestricted competition, there will be seen the inevitable results of "natural monopoly" by which superiority comes to its own and wages are in some proportion to productive power.

7. The Minimum Wage in Operation [1]

England. The fixing of a minimum wage by law — making it a penal offense to hire labor at a lower rate than that fixed by the law — is now an accomplished fact, of which the world has had half a generation of experience. In this matter of the legal minimum wage the sixteen years' actual trial by Victoria is full of instruction. Victoria, which is a highly developed industrial state, of great and growing prosperity, had long had factory laws, much after the English fashion. In 1896, largely out of humanitarian feeling for five specially "sweated" trades, provision was made for the enforcement in those trades of a legal minimum wage. Naturally this was opposed by all the arguments with which we are familiar — that it was "against the laws of political economy," that it would cause the most hardly pressed businesses to shut down, that it would restrict employment, that it would drive away capital, that it would be cruel to the aged worker and the poor widow, that it could not be carried out in practice, and so on and so forth. Naturally, too, all sorts of criticisms have since been leveled at the administration and working of the law; and over and over again eager opponents, both in England and on the spot, have hastened to report that it had broken down. But what had been the result? In the five sweated trades to which the law was first applied sixteen years ago, wages have gone up from 12 to 35 per cent, the hours of labor have invariably been reduced, and the actual number of persons employed, far from falling, has in all cases, relatively to the total population, greatly increased. Thus the legal minimum wage does not necessarily spell ruin, either for the employers or for the operatives. But, of course, it is open to any theorist to urge that we do not know

[1] From "The Economic Theory of a Legal Minimum Wage," by Sidney Webb, in the *Journal of Political Economy*, vol. 20, 1912. University of Chicago Press, publishers.

how much better off these trades might have been without the Act. The only test here is what the people say who are directly concerned, who see with their own eyes the law actually at work, and who are forced daily to compare the trades to which it applies with those to which it does not apply. First, let us notice that the Act of 1896 (like the British Trade Boards Act of 1909) was only a temporary one. It has during the past sixteen years been incessantly discussed; it has been over and over again made the subject of special inquiry; it has been repeatedly considered by the Legislature; and, as a result, it has been five successive times renewed by consent of both Houses. Can it be that all this is a mistake? Still more convincing, however, are the continuous demands from the other trades, as they witnessed the actual results of the legal minimum wage where it was in force, to be brought under the same law.

Provision is made for this extension by resolutions which have to be passed by both Houses of the Legislature. The first trades to which the law was applied were those of bootmaking and baking (employing mainly men), clothing, shirts, and underclothing (employing mainly women), and the very troublesome furniture trade, in which the Chinese have gained a secure footing. It naturally took some time to get the law to work, to overcome the inevitable difficulties and to demonstrate any results. Accordingly for four years there was no extension. In 1900, however, we had the brickmakers coming in, and the butchers, the cigar makers and the confectioners, the coopers and the engravers, the fellmongers, the jewelers, and the jam trade, the makers of millet brooms and the pastrycooks, the plate glass manufacturers and the potters, the saddlers and the tanners, the tinsmiths and the wood-workers, the woolen manufacturers and, perhaps most significant of all, the strongly organized printers, including the compositors in the great newspaper offices. In the following year (1901), so far from there being any signs of repentance, there was an equal rush of extensions of the law to industries of all kinds — the aerated water makers and the manufacturers of artificial manure, brass-workers and the bedstead makers, the brewers and the brush-workers, the ironmoulders and the makers of leather goods, the malsters and the oven makers, the stonecutters and the workers in wicker. For three years there was then a pause, the legal minimum wage being only demanded by and extended to the dressmakers in 1903. In 1906 came another rush of trades, the agricultural implement makers, the cardboard box makers, the candle makers, the cycle trade, the farriers and the flour millers, the milliners and the paper bag makers, the manufacturers of starch, soap, and soda, and the makers of waterproof clothing. In the following year (1907), only the glass-workers and the picture frame makers came in. The year 1908 saw the application of the law to the bread carters, the hairdressers, the manufacturers of ice and the wire-workers. In 1909 it was extended to the carpenters, the carriage builders, the carters, the drapers, the electro-platers, the grocers, the ham and bacon curers, the dealers in coal, wood, hay and chaff, the makers of men's clothing, the organ builders, the painters, the manufacturers of polish, the plumbers, the quarrymen, the makers of rubber goods, and that mysterious craft the tuck-pointers. During 1910 there came in the boiler makers, the boot makers, the bricklayers, the coal miners, the electrical engineers, the factory and mining engine drivers, the gold miners, the hardware makers and the hotel employees, the marine-store dealers, the plasterers, the stationers, the teapackers, the tilers, the watchmakers, the slaughterers for export, the undertakers and even the lift attendants. What occupations were left to come in during 1911 and 1912 I do not yet know.

Now, in this remarkable popular demonstration of the success of the Act, tested by the not inconsiderable period of sixteen years, extending over years of relative trade depression as well as over years of boom, some features deserve mention. First, the extensions have frequently — indeed, it may be said usually — taken place at the request, or with the willing acquiescence, of the employers in a trade, as well as of the wage-earners. What the employers appreciate is, as they have themselves told me, the very fact, that the minimum wage is fixed by law and therefore really forced on all employers: the security that the Act accordingly gives them against being undercut by the dishonest or disloyal competitors, who simply will not (in Victoria as in the Port of London) adhere to the common rules agreed upon by collective bargaining. We must notice, too, that the application of the law has been demanded by skilled trades as well as by unskilled, by men as well as by women, by highly paid craftsmen and by sweated workers, by the strongly organized trades as well as by those having no unions at all. One is tempted, indeed, to believe that little remains now outside its scope except the agricultural occupations and domestic service! Nor can it be said to be confined to industries enjoying a protective tariff, for there are no import duties to shield the gold miners, or the quarrymen, or the slaughterers for export; and no fiscal protection helps the carters or the butchers, the drapers' assistants or the engine drivers, the newspaper printers or the potters, the grocers or the hairdressers, the hotel employees or the lift attendants. And it is difficult to believe that the enforcement of a legal minimum wage in all these hundred different industries, employing 110,000 persons (being, with their families, more than a quarter of the entire population of the state), has interfered with the profitableness of industry, when the number of factories has increased, in the sixteen years, by no less than 60 per cent, and the numbers of workers in them have more than doubled. Certainly, no statesman, no economist, no political party nor any responsible newspaper of Victoria, however much a critic of details, ever dreams now of undoing the Minimum Wage Law itself.

Since the publication of the foregoing article in 1912, an expansion of minimum-wage legislation has occurred which must be taken into account in any effort to grasp the extent to which this device is now employed. The following summary of developments in Great Britain and the United States since 1912 should be read in conjunction with that of Mr. Webb.

In that very year a disastrous strike paralyzed the British coal industry. The miners were frankly dissatisfied with their conditions; among their demands they insisted upon a flat rate weekly minimum wage. Previous to this time the minimum wage had been a device used primarily in the sweated industries; now the Government was forced, by the exigencies of the situation, to yield so far as to establish by legal enactment representative district boards to fix minimum wages and other working conditions. This act did not prove so useful in practice as had been hoped, but it certainly showed that workers in a well-organized industry were not averse to supplementing their own strength in this manner.

During the Great War it was of course necessary to make numerous adjustments in the various awards for the nine sweated trades dealt with under the original Act; these increases did not, as a rule, keep pace with the rising cost of living. In 1917 and 1918 the Act was extended, both to improve conditions at the time, and to aid in stabilizing wages during the transition from war to peace. The 1918 Act applied to various industries; it provided speedier action and also greater flexibility. In the first place, boards might be formed wherever wages were "unduly low," rather than in those cases only where wages were "exceptionally low," as formerly. The formation of these boards proceeded rapidly, after the termination of the war, and by the end of 1920 twenty-five additional industries were represented. These were: aerated waters; boot and shoe repairing; brush and broom; button-making; coffin furniture; corset; dressmaking and women's light clothing; flax and hemp; fur; general waste reclamation; grocery and provisions; hair, bass, and fiber; hat, cap, and millinery; jute; laundry; linen and cotton handkerchief and household goods, and linen piece goods; milk distribution; paper bag; perambulator and invalid carriage; pin, hook and eye, and snap fastener; rope, twine, and net; stamped and pressed metal ware; tobacco; toy; and wholesale mantle and costume. Notice had also been given that special orders were to be applied to still more trades; viz: boot and shoe polish; hairdressers; sack and bag; fish, poultry, and game distribution; fruit, flower, and vegetable distribution; made-up textiles; and ostrich and fancy feather and artificial flower trade.

The other Act, chronologically preceding that of 1918, was the Corn Production Act of 1917, which provided, among other things, for minimum rates among agricultural workers. Rates were fixed by law, subject to local variations by representative "agricultural wage boards." By the end of 1919 the boards had fixed minimum wages for men, women, and children, throughout practically all of England and Wales.

In the United States the status of minimum-wage legislation is less extensive; however, the year 1920 saw minimum-wage laws in operation in thirteen States, as well as the District of Columbia and Porto Rico. In three States, California, Ohio, and Nebraska, special provision is made in the state constitution for such legislation, although California alone had taken advantage of it.

Minimum-wage legislation in the United States has been limited almost entirely to women and minors. There are several reasons for this. One is the inflexibility of our written constitutions, which not infrequently impose obstacles to the passage of such a law, or at least to any extension of the principle. It is possible to care for the women and children under the police power of the

State, because of the evident inability of this class of workers to protect themselves. But men are not so regarded. Nor do they wish to be, as most of the labor organizations feel that they can obtain better wages by their own efforts than any legislation could get for them. In this they are not mistaken.

In brief, then, minimum-wage laws in the United States have never been regarded as anything more than a remedy for exceptional conditions; when enacted, they have sought to provide only a bare subsistence wage for those who were not receiving it. There is some indication of a broadening of this viewpoint, as evidenced by an unsuccessful bill introduced into the Wisconsin Legislature in 1919, which would have extended the minimum wage to men; this failed by a small margin. It remains to be seen whether the natural and legal difficulties which this country presents to such legislation will prevent the general extension of the minimum wage or merely retard it.

CHAPTER V

HOURS OF LABOR

1. Problem of Hours

Conflict of interest. The problem of the length of the working-day began to attract public attention early in the progress of the Industrial Revolution, and still remains one of the points of conflict in the field of industrial relations. With the passage of time, however, the emphasis has shifted from the solution of the problem in the interests of women and children by public action, to the attempts of organized male workers to solve the problem for themselves through their own bargaining power. A century of agitation for the shorter working-day, carried on by the public reformer and the trade union, has brought to light two aspects of the problem which are of importance to the social student.

In the first place, the long struggle to limit hours of work for women and children has made it clear that the length of the work-day is one of the phases of our economic activity in which individual self-interest and the welfare of society do not always coincide. During the earlier stages in the development of the modern industrial order, most men who gave thought to the matter believed that society as a whole would prosper most completely if its members were left free to pursue their own profit by any means which commended themselves to their intelligence. Division of labor had brought it to pass that the individual could serve himself by serving others; hence a maximum of zeal in pursuit of personal advantage must result in a maximum of social welfare. So ran the logic of laissez faire. But it was soon discovered that this reliance upon the profit motive was likely to betray the social interest at two points. On the one hand, in respect of a great many services of vital importance to society, the profit to the individual might be *too small* to induce any man to render the service. The lighthouses, hospitals, public schools, and many other institutions of similar importance in terms of social welfare are examples of types of service which would either not be performed at all by private initiative, or would be supplied in inadequate quantity. In such cases the spur of private profit must be supplemented by collective action if society as a whole is to prosper. On the other hand, and at the opposite extreme, there are fields of activity in which the spur of immediate private profit is *too strong* to serve the long-run interests of the group. The temptation of the individual to reap the maximum advantage in the present may induce him to employ means which impoverish future generations of the community. In America we have been made familiar with this menace through the movement to conserve our natural resources. Long, exhausting hours of labor, especially for women and children — though sometimes, also, in the case of men — are another example of this conflict between individual and social interest. In such cases the exercise of private initiative must be restricted by the establishment of collective standards.

Legal restriction of hours of labor for children has always implied the truth of this statement that individual and social interest do not coincide. These laws usually appear in conjunction with provisions for the compulsory education of children below certain ages and are intended to prevent the employer's interest in cheap labor and the selfishness of parents from nullifying the efforts of society to insure a minimum standard of intelligence in the rising generation. That this is an appropriate exercise of the sovereign power of the State has never seriously been questioned; the "constitutionality" of these laws — to employ the term most frequently used in the United States — is unchallenged, so far as concerns the legislation of the several States of the Union. Similar attempts to shorten the working-day for women, or to prohibit labor at certain specific hours when the hazards to the morals and health of the workers were most serious, have had to win their way against the assumption of the courts that *adults* are the best judges of their own interests. As long as these laws were based upon an acknowledged desire to benefit the women to whom they applied, they were in general declared unconstitutional. As soon, however, as their protagonists, recognizing the conflict between social and individual interest of which we have spoken, began to base their argument on considerations of public health, morals, and safety, and to call for an exercise of the police power of the State, reasonable limitation of the working-day for women won the approval of the courts. To-day these laws frankly disclaim the motive of conferring benefit upon any section of the population and rest their case solely on the grounds of the long-run welfare of society as a whole.

Hours laws for child workers. "To-day there is general agreement that legislation, at the very least, besides keeping children under fourteen out of the factory and in the schoolroom, should prevent night work by all boys and girls under sixteen and limit their working hours to eight. Beginning with Illinois in 1903, this standard has been reached by about half the States, including the majority of those of industrial importance. Of the remaining States, about half have nine-hour laws for children and the rest allow a work-day of ten hours or more. In some of the Southern cotton-mill States, however, it is legal for children to work at night and eleven hours a day, and such poor laws as exist are reported not to be well enforced. All but five States had laws limiting the daily or weekly hours for women at the beginning of 1922. The ten-hour day was still the most frequent, but the eight-hour day was in force in nine Western States, the District of Columbia and Porto Rico, and a nine-hour day in more than a dozen of the remaining States, including the important industrial areas of New York, Ohio and Missouri. A few States have daily limits of from ten and a quarter to twelve hours. Most States fixed weekly as well as daily limits, which varied from forty-eight to sixty hours."

Limitation of hours of male workers. In connection with this phase of the problem of hours of labor it is in point to note that the same considerations of social interest may justify forcible limitation of the working day for men in specific industries. Employers are wont to attack the program for the limitation of hours in their enterprises by asserting that "the men, themselves, prefer the longer day." But this argument is not impressive, even when the truth of the statement can be granted. The worker, no less than the employer, may pursue immediate gain to a point detrimental to social welfare. This fact has been recognized in connection with industries peculiarly affected with public interest and those in which the hazard to the worker is especially great.

"With railroad employees, excessive hours mean not only danger to their own health and safety, but also a greater risk of accidents which may endanger the lives and property of passengers. Almost every State in the Union, as well as the United States for interstate employees, has placed hour restrictions on two classes of railroad workers — firemen, engineers, conductors and others engaged in actual handling of trains, and those who direct train movements, such as telegraphers, and train dispatchers. For those handling trains, sixteen hours, to be followed by at least eight or ten hours' rest, is generally set as the limit of a day's work. Telegraphers may be restricted to eight hours under a three-shift system if employment is continuous, or at small stations to twelve or thirteen hours followed by a rest period of eight or ten hours. But the necessary permission to work overtime in 'emergencies' leaves a loophole through which these laws may be evaded. . . . About a dozen States have scattering laws affecting men's hours in other special lines of work. Laundries, electric plants, firing of stationary boilers, cement mills, sawmills, brickyards, and drug and grocery stores, have all appeared to some legislators to demand special protection against the dangers of overwork. . . . The eight-hour day in mines, where dangers to health and safety are many, has been secured by law in most of the important mining States."

Attitude of labor. Legal restriction of the work-day illustrates the need of collective action to set bounds to the exercise of individual initiative in cases where personal and social interests cross. This consideration, however, does not entirely cover the modern problem of the hours of labor; for the great mass of male workers in America have not sought the aid of the law in their efforts to shorten the work-day, nor have they limited their demands to occupations clearly affected with a public interest. On the contrary, at the present time it is the practice of organized labor to press the demand for a reduction of hours whenever and wherever it feels strong enough to do so. For a full half-century, the eight-hour day was the goal of the organized workers, and this in respect of all types of occupation regardless of the menace to health and safety or the general welfare. Having won this concession in many industries, the more aggressive unions are now attempting to move forward to the forty-four-hour week; while at least one group — the mine-workers — has set the six-hour day as its goal. The motive power behind this incessant struggle for a shorter day is clearly not to be explained on the same principles as those we have been discussing with reference to legal restriction of hours.

The demand of organized labor for a reduction of hours must be viewed, in part, as a means toward the solution of an apparently unrelated problem of the wage-earner — the problem of unemployment. The reasoning behind this policy is often defined as the "lump of labor theory." Leaders of the labor movement who are given at all to theorizing in broad general terms have sometimes reached the conclusion that there is in society at any given time only a certain fixed quantity of work to be done, and that this work must be parceled out among the whole body of men who are seeking employment. In this view of the matter, unemployment results from an exhaustion of the quantity of work to be done, or, in common parlance, by the wage-earner's "working himself out of a job." Such reasoning lends support to many of the "make-work" fallacies of the laboring population. With especial reference to the matter we are considering, it leads to the conviction that a shortening of the work-day for all those employed will provide jobs for men who otherwise would not be employed at all. Workingmen who are not at all given to theorizing reach a similar conclusion by a more direct and "common-sense" route.

To the man of average intelligence there seems to be no moral or economic justification for a state of affairs in industry which keeps one group at long hours of labor while others are forced to remain idle. It must be admitted that this device of limiting hours is not without its merits as a remedy for the problem of unemployment peculiar to some kinds of industry. Those occupations which suffer particularly from seasonal fluctuations may be stabilized to some degree by the refusal of the workers to supply the extra labor required during the rush season. In the clothing trades, the forty-four-hour week accompanied by a refusal to work overtime or on holidays, provided it is rigidly enforced, must have the effect of compelling the enterprisers to devise means of attaining greater continuity in the volume of production. Similarly, the demand for the six-hour day by the miners is intended primarily to stabilize employment in an industry which suffers severely from seasonal fluctuations.

But the shorter day in the program of organized labor is not merely a means toward an end; it is an end in itself. The attempt to reduce hours for the sake of increasing the amount of leisure time at the disposal of the wage-earner is, in reality, a phase of the relative prosperity of modern industrial workers. High wages cause the worker to raise his standard of life; and, especially, to add to the range of his wants those physical satisfactions which are available only to one released from the drudgery of routine duties. That this preference for leisure as compared with a higher money income is so widespread among the wage-earners of modern society as to create an almost universal drive for a shorter work-day, brings to light another aspect of our industrial order — the second of the considerations of fundamental importance with which we opened this discussion of hours.

The truth is that the productive life of the propertyless man in the industrial structure as it is now organized is, on the whole, a thing of almost intolerable monotony and dreariness. The incessant repetition of a meaningless process; the almost military discipline of the factory; the total absence of interest in either the product or the fortunes of the enterprise, combine to thwart and stifle any desire for self-expression, any urge toward impressing his personality upon his social environment, which the worker might have. The hours spent in the factory are a period of servitude in the interest of a taskmaster; the job is the property of another, as is the product; the giving of orders, the planning and direction of the venture are prerogatives in which the worker does not share. Too often that minute portion of the entire process on which he is engaged makes no appeal to his standards of workmanship and contributes nothing to his sense of the artistic. This is the background of the wage-earner's attitude toward his employer and his job. No one can hope to understand labor psychology who does not approach the problem with an appreciation of this fact, for it colors the wage-earner's thinking and shapes his policy in regard to all phases of industrial relations. His struggle to reduce his hours of service is but one symptom of this underlying condition; to the student of society, this is the chief significance of the demand for the shorter day on the part of organized workingmen.

2. Union Scale of Hours [1]

Index Numbers
Union Wage-Rates and Hours of Labor
1907–1921

	Rate per Hour	Hours per Week	Full-Time Wages per Week
1907	100	100	100
1908	101	100	101
1909	102	99	102
1910	105	99	104
1911	107	98	105
1912	109	98	107
1913	111	97	109
1914	114	97	111
1915	115	97	112
1916	119	96	116
1917	127	96	123
1918	148	95	142
1919	172	92	162
1920	222	91	206
1921	229	92	211

3. The Eight-Hour Day Defined [2]

Different meanings of the term. Discussion of the eight-hour day is characterized by much vagueness and confusion because of the different senses in which the term is used. The phrase has no clearly defined or universally accepted significance. It has at least three separate meanings:

1. A straight eight-hour day under which overtime is eliminated or even prohibited, except in extraordinary emergency.

[1] From United States Bureau of Labor Statistics, Bulletin 302, *Wages and Hours of Labor*. 1921.

[2] From Research Report No. 11 of the National Industrial Conference Board.

2. An eight-hour shift with three work periods daily of eight hours each for as many different sets of workers. This arrangement may extend over six or seven days of the week.
3. A basic eight-hour day in which eight hours is made the basis or measure for service or payment, but under which overtime is permitted.

These definitions reveal the distinctions which exist between the different meanings of the so-called eight-hour day. When the straight eight-hour day is meant, overtime is prohibited and the work-week contains forty-eight hours or, if a Saturday half holiday is observed, only forty-four hours. Under the eight-hour shift system, overtime is practically eliminated by the nature of the arrangement; if the industry operates continuously seven days in the week, the work-week totals fifty-six hours. In the case of the basic eight-hour day, the *nominal* work-week may consist of forty-eight or forty-four hours, dependent upon the observance or non-observance of the Saturday half holiday, but since overtime is permitted, no limit is imposed on the number of actual hours per week.

In discussing these distinctions it should be recognized at the outset that a "straight" eight-hour day with overtime prohibited differs from a "basic" eight-hour day with overtime permitted, not only in the number of work-hours but also in principle. This applies equally to consideration of the straight forty-eight hour week and the basic forty-eight hour week.

The eight-hour day in its rigid sense with prohibition of overtime is founded on the theory that such limitation of work-hours is demanded on grounds of health and social advantage. The contention is also often made that the straight eight-hour day is more productive than a longer work-day. With these underlying premises for limitation of hours of work, overtime is inconsistent. Clearly, if the health of the worker or his social rights demand that he shall work not more than eight hours per day, permission of overtime labor, except in extraordinary emergency, is illogical. If the straight eight-hour day is really more productive than a longer work-day, overtime is absurd.

The social grounds on which the eight-hour day is advocated do not permit of precise measurement. The factor of leisure is clearly not adapted to statistical evaluation. In regard to the health and well-being of workers, except for industries subject to peculiar health hazards or unusual physical or mental strain, only vague generalizations are available. The contention that a straight eight-hour day increases output lends itself better to the test of definite measurement, but clear distinction must be made between hourly output and total weekly output. In occupations where hours were previously unduly long, reduction has at times been followed by an increase in hourly output. But such an increase frequently does not mean an increase or even maintenance of total weekly output. Obviously, the economic result of the straight eight-hour day must be ascertained by measuring the total production achieved.

Effects of straight eight-hour day. The straight eight-hour day has been brought about chiefly by legislation. It was first applied to women and children; later it was extended to men in certain hazardous occupations. Still later it was made applicable to employees on public works or contracts for the State and last to certain private enterprises. At the present time an eight-hour day is established by law in many of the States to govern the hours of labor of men and women in public employment, or in private employment on contract work for national, state, or municipal governments. Fourteen States enforce the eight-hour day for miners, eight States enforce it for men employed in smelting operations. Eleven States apply it to men in certain other private employments most of which involve special hazards.

Federal legislation providing for an eight-hour day in certain government contract work existed prior to 1892, but the provisions were vaguely worded and their practical application was uncertain. By an Act of August 1, 1892, however, Congress definitely adopted the principle of a straight eight-hour day for laborers and mechanics employed by the Government or contractors or sub-contractors upon public works. The hours of work in such cases were definitely limited to eight in any calendar day, except in case of extraordinary emergency. A later act of June 19, 1912, commonly referred to as the Federal Eight-Hour Act, provided for the insertion in certain classes of government contracts of a more specific condition. No laborer or mechanic was to be required or permitted to work upon the subject-matter of such contracts more than eight hours in any calendar day. A penalty of $6.00 a day for each mechanic or laborer illegally employed in excess of such hours was imposed. The eight-hour day enforced by this Act was a straight eight-hour day.

The eight-hour shift system is in accord with the motive of the straight eight-hour day. Essentially, however, it is an arrangement for securing greater efficiency in production. It is quantitatively determined by the fact that since the calendar day consists of twenty-four hours, the only practicable choice in a continuous industry lies between two shifts of twelve hours each or three shifts of eight hours each. In many occupations requiring continuous activity or high nervous tension, the twelve-hour shift has proved excessive; hence the system of three shifts of eight hours each has been adopted as the only alternative.

This system does not involve any organized overtime. While its adoption may be based in part on the same grounds as are urged for the straight eight-hour day, it is a product of industrial organization and not of legislative enactment. Its effect upon output is radically different from that of the straight eight-hour day, while as a wage measure it differs from the basic eight-hour day. As against either of these arrangements, the eight-hour shift system obviously increases total production, while it lessens production cost by offsetting the burden of idle machinery and other overhead expense.

Basic eight-hour day a wage policy. The basic eight-hour day, on the other hand, is essentially a wage issue. Eight hours of work are taken as a convenient standard by which to measure service, any hours in excess of these in a calendar day being paid for as overtime, usually at higher rates, but sometimes on a prorata basis.

That the basic eight-hour day is primarily a matter of wages is clearly recognized in the Adamson Law, which provides that "eight hours shall, in contracts for labor and service, be deemed a day's work and the measure or standard of a day's work for the *purpose of reckoning the compensation for services* of all employees."

The phrase "for the purpose of reckoning compensation for services" obviously means that this legislation relates to wages, while the fact that overtime is permitted under it removes the Act from the category of legislation primarily designed to protect the health or social welfare of workers. Its effect was similar to its intent. The railroads, faced with the alternative of changing their methods or paying for overtime, found the latter policy the cheaper, especially in their freight service. That this legislation is recognized as a matter of wages, is shown by the report of the Eight-Hour Day Commission, appointed in pursuance of the Adamson Law to report upon the operation of that statute, which states: "the same payment is now made for a minimum day of eight hours as was formerly made for a minimum day of ten hours. . . . The increase in pay which the observance of the law brings to the employee is chiefly in the form of payment for more hours of overtime at an increased rate per hour."

The practical effect of this legislation was to make overtime operative at the end of an eight-hour period without generally shortening hours of work. The wage previously paid for ten hours of daily service is now paid for eight hours, which means, of course, an increase in the hourly rate. This increased hourly rate, however, applies alike to regular and to overtime work; overtime is not penalized by extra rates.

Even clearer evidence that the basic eight-hour day is essentially a wages matter is found in the operation of the Federal Eight-Hour Act, as modified to meet wartime exigencies. As already shown, the Federal Eight-Hour Act of 1912 provided for a straight eight-hour day under which overtime was prohibited. But the war altered the situation. Because of the enormous demands on production the Government deemed it imperative in many instances to increase hours of work. Such an emergency was clearly contemplated by the Act itself, which contained a provision that "The President, by Executive order, may waive the provisions and stipulations in this Act as to any specific contract or contracts during time of war or at a time when war is imminent, and until January 1, 1915, as to any contract or contracts entered into in connection with the construction of the Isthmian Canal."

As originally framed, this provision simply contemplated the abandonment of the eight-hour limitation. The Naval Appropriation Act of March 4, 1917, however, introduced a new condition defining the circumstances under which such suspension could be made. It provides: "That in case of national emergency the President is authorized to suspend provisions of law prohibiting more than eight hours labor in any one day of persons engaged upon work covered by contracts with the United States; provided further, That the wages of persons employed upon such contracts shall be computed on a basic day rate of eight hours work, with overtime rate to be paid for at not less than time and one half for all hours work in excess of eight hours."

The practical effect of the insertion of this provision for increased overtime rates was to change the character of the Federal Eight-Hour Act from an hours-of-service to a wage statute, and by legislation to introduce the basic eight-hour day with penal rates for overtime.

Thus in the Adamson Law and in the modified federal eight-hour statute, the terminology of the legislation shows that the basic eight-hour day is a wage question.

Even in advance of legislation on this subject, some employers had already voluntarily applied the basic-day principle with increased rates for overtime. Usually this plan was predicated on a work-day of nine or more hours, and overtime rates were from twenty-five to fifty per cent higher than regular rates.

Increased rates for overtime are obviously designed to discourage employers from resorting to it. To this extent, the provision is related to the problem of health and social relaxation. In practice, however, these penal rates have proved an incentive to overtime work by the employee and thus tend to defeat any desire to promote his health or increase his leisure. Therefore, these rates, though ostensibly a penalty on the employer, are in reality a premium to the employee. So far as such an incentive induces the worker to work a longer day than is justified on the grounds of health, it is clearly warranted only by unusual emergency. In such cases overtime is physically undesirable, and overtime rates mean extra compensation for diminished productivity. Furthermore, experience has shown that the overtime rate tends to increase the amount of absenteeism during regular hours, for with premium overtime rates workers can earn their usual wages in shorter time and are thus more inclined to "lay off."

As an illustration of these effects, a study of 20,000 shipyard workers in San Francisco during April, 1918, may be cited. For a group of over 3600 workmen employed at a wage of $5.80 per day, working under the basic eight-hour day during the month of April, 1918, overtime constituted 11.8 per cent of the total hours worked. Nevertheless, these workers lost so much regular time that, even when their overtime was taken into account, they were still 19.4 per cent behind the full time which continuous work for the regular eight-hour period each day would have yielded. Yet, by working at double rates an amount of overtime equal to about one half of the total regular time lost, these workmen earned 99 per cent of the wages they would have received for full-time regular work. Similarly, in the case of over 5700 other shipyard workers engaged at $3.57 a day, 25 per cent of total regular time was lost, even when credit was given for all overtime. In this instance, however, overtime earnings of these workers, though at double rates, made up only 49 per cent of the wages lost during regular hours. It is clear that these men were not using the provision of the basic eight-hour day to increase either their own total earnings or the total output of the establishment; it simply increased the cost of production and decreased the output.

The eight-hour day, whether straight or basic in character, implies as a corollary a certain length of work-week. The straight eight-hour day naturally leads to the forty-eight-hour week, with eight hours of work for six days, and with overtime beyond forty-eight hours prohibited save in emergency. The practice of working only half a day on Saturday at times leads to a compensating lengthening of hours of work during the first days of the week so as to offset the loss on Saturday. But where the Saturday half holiday is coupled with the straight eight-hour day for the first five days of the week, the work-week is automatically reduced to forty-four hours. Where the Saturday half holiday is observed there is sometimes a sentiment in favor of entire cessation of work on that day, thereby creating a nominal forty-hour week. Thus, the straight eight-hour day in combination with the Saturday half holiday has a tendency towards a five-day week.

The basic eight-hour day implies a nominal forty-eight-hour or forty-four-hour week according to whether or not a Saturday half holiday is observed. But overtime is permitted and paid for at overtime rates if the work on any day extends beyond eight hours. In some cases overtime rates are paid for Saturday afternoon work.

In contrast with the basic eight-hour day, granting overtime rates every day for any overtime work on that day even though no work or only partial work is done on subsequent days, the basic forty-eight-hour week allows overtime rates only after a total of forty-eight hours has been worked during the week at regular rates. Thus, overtime may have been worked on one or more days, but if an equal amount of time has been taken off on other days, no extra allowance for overtime will be made at the end of the week. To prevent any day's work being unduly extended, overtime rates are sometimes made to apply to each specific day when overtime beyond a certain limit is required. Several decisions of the National War Labor Board contain this provision.

Contrast between two concepts. The basic forty-eight-hour week differs sharply from the basic eight-hour day in principle. By requiring forty-eight hours of work before overtime rates are paid, it robs overtime largely of its premium advantage. For the same reason it lessens the incentive to the worker to take time off unnecessarily. In consequence, the basic forty-eight-hour week tends to become less a measure for adjusting wages than one for securing efficiency.

Clarity in discussion of the eight-hour day issue depends ultimately on recognition of the fundamental distinction between the straight and the basic eight-hour day. Recognition of this difference is equally essential to intelligent discussion of the work-week. Most aspects of the eight-hour shift system also admit of similar distinction.

In practice, the essential difference between the straight eight-hour day and the basic eight-hour day arises in connection with overtime. The straight eight-hour day under no circumstances encourages overtime and, as enforced by legislation, prohibits it. The basic eight-hour day allows overtime, under penal rates which are intended to discourage it. Their practical effect, however, is to encourage what they are designed to prevent.

In principle the straight eight-hour day is a matter of social policy based on regard for the health, welfare, and leisure of the workers. The basic eight-hour day is a measure of service and reward. The former regulates hours of service, the latter is a form of wage arrangement.

This essential difference is in a measure reflected in the methods by which limitation on work-hours has been brought about. Legislation has been the most general method for the introduction of the straight eight-hour day. Such legislation has usually been promoted by those who give weight to social considerations, while action by employers or by labor unions has generally favored the basic day. In any event, labor organizations have repeatedly opposed legislative limitation of hours of work on the ground that such legislation would weaken their economic strength. Thus the American Federation of Labor, at its conventions in 1914 and 1915, defeated resolutions favoring the enforcement of a straight eight-hour day by law. The Adamson law for railroad employees providing for a basic eight-hour day, was, on the other hand, forced by the demands of organized labor.

The basic eight-hour day with premium rates for overtime theoretically and practically violates the principle of the straight eight-hour day. The laborer who demands the eight-hour day on grounds of recreation, home life, and intellectual development, but who welcomes overtime, shows that to him the eight-hour day is in reality a question of earnings. To be consistent, advocates of the straight eight-hour day should oppose the basic eight-hour day. As matters stand at present, the social need for recreation and home life is made the basis for a provision which, instead of shortening hours, merely increases wages. The straight eight-hour day thus becomes a fiction; the basic eight-hour day becomes an artificial means for demanding increased compensation.

4. The Case for the Shorter Work-Day [1]

The case for the shorter work-day may be outlined under three separate aspects; the dangers of long hours, the benefits of short hours, and the economic aspects of reducing hours. In each of these phases it will appear that a work-day of reasonable length is desirable and advantageous.

The dangers of long hours. Science teaches that immunity from disease is due chiefly to the individual's adequate power of resistance. Health is preserved not by absence of exposure, but by the power of resisting the ever-present chances of disease.

The first study of so-called "occupational diseases" was begun two hundred years ago. It has long been recognized that workers

[1] Adapted from Felix Frankfurter and Josephine Goldmark: *The Case for the Shorter Work-Day.* National Consumers' League.

in certain occupations, clearly subject to special dangers, succumb to special forms of disease and premature death.

Obviously, workers in the dangerous trades who are overfatigued and exhausted, are more readily attacked by occupational diseases. Fatigue intensifies all the special dangers and lessens all the chances of escaping the peculiar hazards of the trade. It was formerly supposed therefore that only in occupations subject to such special risks was special protection needed for the workers.

More recent investigations show that not only in the dangerous trades, but in all industries, a permanent predisposition to disease and premature death exists in the common phenomenon of fatigue and exhaustion. This is a danger common to all workers, even under good working conditions, in practically all manufacturing industries, as distinguished from the specially hazardous occupations.

Fatigue. In ordinary factory work, where no special occupational disease threatens, fatigue in itself constitutes the most imminent danger to the health of the workers because, if unrepaired, it undermines vitality and thus lays the foundations for many diseases.

Overfatigue predisposes to the infectious as well as to general diseases. Scientific laboratory experiments prove that fatigue markedly diminishes the power of the blood to overcome bacteria and their toxic products. Thus, for instance, of two groups of animals, one resting and the other fatigued by muscular work and both inoculated by pathogenic bacteria, the fatigued animals succumb more quickly and in larger numbers. The resting animals may wholly resist the infection.

Hence overfatigue constitutes a danger to the public health, as well as to the individual, since working people who are overfatigued more readily take and spread infectious disease.

Overfatigue from excessive working hours not only renders overtaxed workers susceptible to general and infectious diseases, it predisposes them effectually to more subtle nervous disorders, especially neurasthenia in its various forms. These diseases are due to overstrain of the nervous system. Intense and long lasting fatigue are characteristics, and disorders of the heart, circulation, the special senses and the digestive apparatus are common symptoms.

Nervous exhaustion, considered until recently a disorder of brain-workers and the well-to-do solely, has been found by physicians and physiologists to be alarmingly prevalent among industrial workers, subject to the strain of overlong hours.

Adults are more susceptible to nervous disorders than young persons. Liability to these diseases is found highest between the ages of twenty and forty-five years. Hence adults, as well as young persons, must be guarded from excessive overstrain, which engenders nervous exhaustion.

A predisposition to nervous disorders may be transmitted, and may constitute a marked disability in the second generation. The protection of workers from the excessive fatigue which may lead to nervous disorders is needed for the preservation of the race.

The onset of nervous exhaustion is often unperceived. A special danger to health arises when, after excessive work, this form of overfatigue shows itself in unnatural stimulation, which conceals fatigue and creates a false exhilaration. Only after health is seriously threatened does the overstrain become apparent, overstimulation being succeeded by reaction and exhaustion.

The fatigue which follows excessive working hours may become chronic and result in general deterioration of health. While it may not result in immediate disease, it undermines the vitality of the worker and leads to general weakness, anæmia, or premature old age.

Continuous overexertion has proved even more disastrous to health than a certain amount of privation; and lack of work in industrial crises has entailed less injury to health than long continued overwork. The excessive length of working hours, therefore, constitutes in itself a menace to health.

Serious injury to the eyes results also from excessive working hours. The danger of eye-strain from overlong hours is intensified by the lack of proper and adequate lighting of workrooms. Shorter working hours not only relieve the strain upon the eyes, but diminish the necessary time for working with artificial light.

Various incidents of industrial life, such as extremes of heat and cold, dust, fumes, etc., are injurious to the organs of hearing. Loud and intense noise in manufacture is an important cause of impaired hearing, especially among machinists, boilermakers, and metalworkers. Recent experiments show a distinct lowering of the acuity of hearing among fatigued workers.

Whenever the nature of a worker's employment or the position required by the work makes particular demands upon any organ of the body, that organ or part of the body first tends to become overstrained. Excessive length of hours intensifies such overuse of particular organs or parts of the body in the different trades, and only the establishment of shorter hours can lessen the danger of such overstrain.

The length of working hours, irrespective of the nature of the occupation, is in itself a menace to health. Industries not intrinsically dangerous and conducted under good sanitary conditions may become harmful through sheer lengthening of the working hours. Even the lightest work becomes totally exhausting when carried on for an excessive length of time.

A decrease of the intensity of exertion in industry is not feasible. The needed protection, therefore, can be afforded only through shortening the hours of labor.

Increasing danger of fatigue. Modern industry is characterized by increased strain. Machinery is increasingly speeded up, the number of machines tended by individual workers grows larger, processes become more and more complex as more operations are performed simultaneously. All these changes involve correspondingly greater physical strain upon the worker. Though there is little work which requires great muscular strength or exertion in our factories, yet the alertness and exactness of attention and constant application required exhaust the nervous vitality very rapidly.

Besides the physical strain due to speed and complexity of machinery, health is injured by the extreme monotony of many branches of industry. Specialization has been carried so far that change and variety of work have been reduced to a minimum. Minute division of labor results in the constant repetition of similar motions and processes by the same worker, favoring the onset of fatigue and requiring for relief the establishment of a shorter work-day.

So far as labor consists in specialized routine, absorbing the main current of productive energy, it is the enemy of organic health. It is hostile in two ways: first, in denying to man opportunity for the exercise of his other productive faculties; secondly, in overtaxing and degrading by servile repetition the single faculty that is employed.

All the evils of speed and monotony in industrial establishments are intensified by the abuses of piece-work. When each worker aims to work faster for the sake of a slight increase in wages, a premium is put upon feverish activity, regardless of the physical cost to the worker. With the increased efficiency of the piece-worker, the price per piece of work turned out is commonly decreased, so that a greater and increasingly more intense effort is necessary to reach the individual's maximum reward for his labor. It needs no argument to convince even a sturdy advocate of that new idol, called efficiency, that such methods are bound, in the long run, to use up the worker.

Physiological basis for the shorter day. The fundamental need of limiting excessive working hours is based on the physiological nature of man. For medical science has demonstrated that while fatigue is a normal phenomenon — the natural result of bodily and mental exertion — excessive fatigue or exhaustion is abnormal — the result of overexertion of work pursued beyond the capacities of the organism.

Two processes are continually carried on in the living body: assimilation or building up; dissimilation or breaking down material into simpler chemical form, ultimately expelled as waste products. Upon these two processes together, known as metabolism, life itself depends, and to this fundamental basis of life we must turn for an explanation of what fatigue is.

During activity, the products of chemical change increase. An overtired person is literally a poisoned person, poisoned by his own waste products. These wastes are poisonous impurities arising from the chemical processes of cellular life. They circulate in the blood, poisoning brain and nervous system, muscles, glands and other organs until normally burned up by the oxygen brought by the blood, removed by the liver or kidneys, or eliminated through the lungs.

When these waste products accumulate in the blood, fatigue ensues. When they exceed their physiological or normal amount, exhaustion results and health is impaired. After excessive labor there is also a consumption of energy-yielding material, essential for activity. The processes of dissimilation are in excess of those of assimilation.

The need of limiting excessive working hours is further emphasized by recent medical research, which asserts that fatigue is due not only to actual poisoning, but to a specific poison or toxin of fatigue, analogous in chemical and physical nature to other bacterial toxins such as the diphtheria toxin. This theory asserts that when artificially injected into animals in large amounts the fatigue toxin causes death.

The dangers of excessive working hours are increased by the fact that the onset of fatigue is often unperceived by the worker. Not until the damage is done and health is impaired by the strain of overlong hours is the injury manifest. Measurements of muscular contraction by the ergograph show first a progressively increased power of contraction of the muscle and then a steady diminution, the rate and regularity of the diminution varying with individuals. After a certain degree of fatigue has set in, the muscle becomes incapable of performing further work unless a lighter weight or less tension is involved, or its contractility is restored either by artificially irrigating the muscle or by allowing an interval of adequate rest to intervene before renewed exertion. If fatigue has not proceeded too far, this suffices to remove the toxic fatigue products which have been produced in the muscle. After exhaustion has set in, a much longer period of rest is required to restore the muscle to use, or it may become wholly incapacitated. To prevent injurious accumulation of unperceived fatigue, therefore, overexertion through excessive working hours must be prevented.

The greatest strain is attendant upon work continued after fatigue has set in. When the hours of labor are so long that work must be continued after fatigue has set in, the dangers to health are correspondingly increased. Greater injury results from work done by fatigued muscles than from severer labor accomplished before the worker is tired. This is because strain, or the continued exertion of will power to keep up, is more exhausting than work in itself.

During rest, fatigue disappears. Rest is thus a physiological necessity. With the intensity of modern industry, the individual worker can keep up efficient labor only on condition that the fatigue engendered on one day is completely repaired before the next day. If fatigue is not balanced by adequate rest, a deficit remains which may be little noticed at first, but which inevitably accumulates, and after a shorter or longer period results in physical breakdown.

When the individual has worked to exhaustion through excessive hours of labor, normal rest does not suffice for repair. He has literally "used himself up."

During work, the products of chemical change increase. Some idea of the combustion or chemical process carried on within our muscles is shown by the fact that at every breath, air inspired loses about one fifth of its oxygen and increases in the gas carbon dioxide more than one hundred fold. A well-known scientific experiment has shown that during a day of work a man expires almost twice as much carbon dioxide as during a day of rest. The internal combustion is more rapid. But during rest, the processes of tissue repair are in the ascendant. The noxious products of activity are more quickly eliminated and tissue is rebuilt. This is the main reason why lack of rest is detrimental to the organism.

Fatigue and accident. Emphasis is laid upon the need of limiting excessive working hours by the increased danger from accidents arising from the varying effects of fatigue. The statistics of all countries which have recorded the hours in which industrial accidents occur, show that the number of accidents tends to rise after a certain number of hours of work. According to a recent investigation, the number of accidents is usually highest during the penultimate hour of work, when muscular contraction and attention are at their lowest. During the last hour of work the accident rate may fall, owing to the decreased rate of output and anticipation of rest. The following table of the hours of accident occurrence in Illinois in 1910 is a sample which could be many times paralleled.

Accident-Hours (Illinois, 1910)

Hours	Accidents	Hours	Accidents
7:00– 7:59 A.M.	79	1:00–1:59 P.M.	111
8:00– 8:59	150	2:00–2:59	156
9:00– 9:59	193	3:00–3:59	227
10:00–10:59	246	4:00–4:59	260
11:00–11:59	257	5:00–5:59	145
12:00–12:59 P.M.	49	All other hours	289

After fatigue has set in, the faculty of attention is in inverse ratio to the duration and intensity of work undertaken. Attention is always accompanied by a sensation of effort, and fatigue of attention is due to the continuance of the efforts and the difficulty of sustaining them. When the brain is fatigued, attention lags and reaction time is retarded. Hence, after overexertion fatigued workmen are subject to increased danger when reaction time is slowest and attention at its minimum.

Moral effects of fatigue. The dangers attendant upon excessive working hours are shown also by the moral degeneration which results from over-fatigue. Laxity of moral fiber follows physical debility. After excessive labor the overtaxed worker is left stupefied or responds most readily to coarse pleasures and excitements. Bodily exhaustion is evidently unfavorable to the exercise of self-control. The man who is too tired to exert himself at all on days of rest is also too tired to interest himself in questions affecting his physical welfare and that of his family and fellow-citizens.

When the working-day is so long that no time is left for a minimum of leisure and recreation, relief from the strain of work is often sought in alcoholic stimulants. Among industrial workers the desire for drink is often due to the physical incidents of factory work, such as exposure to extreme heat, or the inhalation of dust or fluff in the many trades involving such hazards. Intemperance often results also from the worker's craving for some stimulant or support for exhausted energies.

The experience of manufacturing countries has illustrated the evil effect of overwork upon the general welfare. Health is the foundation of the state. No nation can progress if its workers are crippled by continuous overexertion. The loss of human energy, due to excessive working-hours, is a national loss, and must inevitably result in lowering the nation's prosperity.

The loss of moral restraints and intellectual ambition on the part of workers exhausted by excessive labor is a social loss. Family life, essential for the welfare of the Nation, is destroyed. After overlong hours, the workers scarcely see their young children, and have neither time nor energy after working-hours to share the family interests. They are too much spent to make use of the advantages for development offered by enlightened communities, such as public libraries, lectures, recreation centers, etc. This must necessarily react disastrously upon the community as well as the individual. For the deterioration of any large portion of the population inevitably lowers the entire community, physically, mentally, and morally.

The benefits of short hours. The good effects of shorter working-hours on the uses of leisure is conspicuously shown in the growth of temperance where working-hours have been reduced. With better health and a higher moral tone due to the shorter working-day, temperance in the use of alcoholic stimulants results automatically. The proposition that without variation the elimination of intemperance, poverty, pauperism, ignorance, crime, and their accompanying evils move parallel with and proportionate to the increase of social opportunities stands without impeachment of its historical accuracy. It costs the Nation hard cash to attend to these evils.

History, which has illustrated the deterioration due to long hours, bears witness no less clearly to the regeneration due to the shorter working day. To the individual and society alike, shorter hours have been a benefit wherever introduced and have raised all the standards of living. Wherever sufficient time has elapsed since the establishment of the shorter working-day, the succeeding generation has shown extraordinary improvement in physique, intelligence, and morals. The prominent facts may be briefly summarized:

Greater relative vigor to the workman, in connection with the imperative obligation to reduce time from the exhausted portion of the day. Less loss of time in consequence of a sensible relief in the daily duration of labor. Greater healthfulness, especially during the summer season. A quicker return to labor, and a more rapid recovery of strength after sickness. The increased respectability of labor, which retains many in production. An approximate equalization of the day's work, which has largely contributed to diffuse employment over the year, and thus diminished distress during the winter season. Multiplied inventions, subdivisions in trades, and, generally, a more intellectual and progressive impetus to production. Openings for the industrial classes in evening exercises of a religious, reformatory, political, and miscellaneous character.

After continuous work, a certain amount of leisure and recreation is a physiological necessity. The worker's condition determines in large measure whether or not he takes advantage of opportunities for self-improvement or legitimate enjoyment. The worker who has not exhausted his energies by overexertion turns instinctively to the better uses of leisure.

Of these opportunities the most striking modern instances are the new forms of recreation and education open to wage-earners. Practically every large city in the United States and many small ones are making increasingly large expenditures for public recreation. The growth of this movement has been phenomenal. Side by side with the recreation movement for adults, new opportunities for popular education are developing. Besides regular night schools and public evening lectures within the school system, the extension classes of state and privately endowed universities are growing rapidly.

The best examples of the benefits to society and to the workers arising from the short work-day are found in Australasia. The movement for the eight-hour day began in Victoria over fifty years ago. In New Zealand the eight-hour day was established by law in 1901. In most of the other Australasian States, the wages boards or arbitration courts are empowered by law to fix maximum hours of labor. The general Australian standard is the forty-eight-hour week. In these colonies the short day has been in operation long enough to show its effects. The testimony of factory inspectors and other observers tends to prove that the workers have gained greatly in force and efficiency and that the social welfare of the entire community has been well served through the operation of the short working-day.

Political aspects. The welfare and safety of democracy rests upon the character and intelligence of its citizens. For the exercise of the elective franchise is determined by the mental and moral equipment of the voters. Under the conditions of modern industry, for the development of morals and intelligence, leisure is needed. Hence leisure is a prime requisite for good citizenship. If democracy is to flourish, the education of the citizen must not end at the 14th birthday, when wage-earning ordinarily begins. It must be a continuous process, to enable men to understand great issues when they arise, to discuss them, and to reach decisions upon them.

In the interest of the State, therefore, industrial labor must be limited: first, so that leisure may be provided outside of working hours; second, so that the worker shall not be too much exhausted to make use of his leisure.

There are a large number of foreign-born in the United States. The exact figure for 1920 was 13,920,692. A large proportion of these millions are employed in industry, especially in the great manufacturing establishments, such as the iron and steel mills, munition plants, textile factories, etc.

Throughout the country there is increasing recognition that the prime necessity for the immigrant is Americanization, that is, opportunity for acquiring the ability to speak and read the English language, and to become acquainted with American institutions. Americanization is the paramount need, not only for the immigrant, but for the very existence of the Republic. Unless the millions of immigrants present and future are made an integral part of the population, understanding our institutions, sharing the standards and ideals of the democracy, the Nation itself is imperiled.

No man can become a naturalized citizen unless he can speak English. Learning English is therefore the key to citizenship. It is indispensable for the adoption of American standards of living; for a participation in the life of the community. Ignorance of the English language is the greatest obstacle to industrial advancement. It prevents the distribution of congested immigrant populations. It increases the dangers of industrial accidents, injuries and occupational diseases, owing to the immigrants' inability to understand orders or hygienic regulations printed or orally given in industrial establishments.

The growing recognition of the need of Americanization has resulted in a country-wide movement to provide evening schools to teach English and give special instruction on American institutions. Federal, state, and city authorities are urging increased appropriations for these special facilities. Obviously this whole program of Americanization is impossible unless sufficient leisure is provided *after working hours* to enable the workers to take advantage of the opportunities offered. The task of teaching foreigners a new language is almost hopeless unless they can come to be taught with some freshness of mind. The project of Americanization is defeated when working-hours are so long that no evening leisure is left or the immigrant workers are too much exhausted to make use of it.

The State is dependent upon the quality of its citizens not only for its development in times of peace, but in the last resort, for military defense. Industrial conditions which result in physical degeneration of the population are thus a menace to the very existence of the State. In communities where excessive working-hours have long prevailed, progressive decline in stature, strength, and efficiency becomes markedly evident. This is conspicuously shown by the large percentage of recruits necessarily rejected from military service for physical unfitness. In 1915 there were 41,168 applicants for service in the United States Marine Corps. Of these, 3833 or 9.31 per cent were found physically fit for the service; in other words, one man out of every eleven examined. In New York City 11,012 men applied, and of these 316 were found fit for service, or 2.869 per cent. The experience of the draft under the Compulsory Service Act was to find 30 per cent of the men examined to be unfit for service. European experience has been similar.

Economic aspects of reducing hours. The experience of those manufacturing countries which have longest had the short working-day, shows that commercial prosperity is not hampered by the curtailment of hours. The increased efficiency of the workers due to shorter working-hours, together with the general improvement of industrial communities in physique and morals, reacts so favorably upon output that commercial prosperity is heightened rather than impaired.

The industrial competition of the nations is fast becoming a mere contest in the personal productive capacity of their laborers. The other conditions of the strife are getting equalized. Improved machinery is no sooner made in one country than it is imported or imitated in another; and as the material elements of the competition are growing equal, the supremacy must obviously go to the nation that can turn these elements to most account — the nation with the most vigorous, the most intelligent, the most productive working-class.

The New York Bureau of Labor Statistics admitted in 1900 that the cotton industry of Massachusetts had grown steadily throughout the period of short-hour legislation, and — what was far more impressive — had made larger gains than were shown by adjacent States with less radical short-hour laws.

The universal testimony of manufacturing countries tends to prove that the shortening of the work-day acts favorably upon output. The introduction of a shorter work-day does not result in lessened output. Wherever reliable statistics of output have been kept, before and after the introduction of a shorter work-day, they show that with rare exceptions the aggregate production under shorter hours has either equaled that of the long day, or risen above it.

These conclusions were long supposed to be true only of single individual manufacturing industries, such as the textile trade, in which the shorter work-day was first established, over seventy years ago. The most recent investigations have confirmed the facts, and have shown that what was true of a single industry applies to practically all industries, and is thus not a special but a general rule. The Commonwealth Steel Company reported that the change from twelve to eight hours in the open-hearth department, with a higher rate of wages per hour, resulted in more economical production, and an actually lower wages bill per day. The change to an eight-hour day in the mines of the four leading Eastern coal States — Illinois, Indiana, Ohio, and Pennsylvania — in 1897 did not cause any diminution in daily output. The president of the Solvay Process Company of Syracuse, New York, writes: "In general, I can say that the results of the change from a twelve-hour shift for an eight-hour shift were very satisfactory and have continued to be so. While the immediate result was to considerably increase the cost per unit of product, the efficiency of the men gradually increased, so that at the end of about one year the first increase had been overcome and the cost per unit of product fell to a point even lower than had been obtained under the twelve-hour shift, and further the time consumed per unit of product has been so reduced that we are to-day and for some time have been operating with a smaller number of hours per unit of product than we had under the twelve-hour shift."

Cause of increased productivity. The testimony from other countries is similar. The increased productivity of workers under shorter hours is due to their increased efficiency. Such efficiency springs from improved physical health and energy, together with a change of attitude toward work and employer. Greater promptness in starting in the morning and at noon, more interest and application on the part of the workers and the elimination of "soldiering" and lost time contribute to the increased output under shorter hours.

The introduction of the shorter working-day has acted as a stimulus to heightened efficiency on the part of employers as well as on the part of workers. The curtailment of hours has led to a new scrutiny of methods and organization in manufacture. It has proved possible for instance to lessen or eliminate "lost time" by securing a steadier flow of work and materials through the factory. An added incentive is provided for installing improved machinery and new processes of manufacture so that output may be maintained under shorter hours.

The introduction of the shorter work-day has not led in the long run to an increase in the cost of production. This is due to two causes: first, because the labor cost is only one item, and often a small item, in the total cost of manufacture; second, because the heightened efficiency of both employers and workers under shorter hours stimulates output and thus tends to equalize or even decrease the total costs.

With excessive hours of labor, the efficiency of the workers is so much reduced that output deteriorates both in quantity and quality. Over-fatigue results in "spoiled work" which must be done over again the next day. The early belief that profits were dependent on the last hours of the working-day has long been proved a fallacy. On the contrary, the output of the last hours shows a steady and marked decline.

Effect on wages. Statistical evidence tends to show that wages are not decreased by the reduction of hours. In some cases there may be temporary decrease for a short time, before industry adjusts itself to a change in hours, but after a short period the gain in the workers' efficiency from shorter hours and their consequent increase in output tends to balance completely the curtailment of their working time. Wages are almost universally higher in industries in which the short work-day has been established than they are in wholly unregulated trades. Moreover, even when the shorter day has resulted in a slight temporary decrease in wages, the majority of workers have willingly suffered the reduction, in order to gain the increased health and leisure consequent upon shorter hours of labor.

Wherever the hours of labor have been shortened employment tends to become more regular. In place of alternating periods of intense overwork and periods of idleness, employers have found it possible to distribute work more evenly throughout the year. No incident of industrial life is more disastrous to the worker than the irregularity which characterizes most industries. The "rush" season of long hours often strains health and vitality beyond the power of recovery during the slack season.

Few employers are able to grant their employees reduction of hours, even if they are convinced of its advantages, while their competitors are under no such obligation. The uniform requirement of limited working-hours, therefore, not only checks the unscrupulous employer, but makes it possible for the enlightened and humane employer to shorten the working-day without fear of underbidding competitors.

CHAPTER VI

THE PROBLEM OF CHILD AND WOMAN LABOR

1. WOMEN AND CHILDREN IN INDUSTRY

A modern problem. Like most of the problems of the modern industrial worker, the problem of the labor of women and children arose out of the Industrial Revolution. It is true that the lot of the women and children of the poorer classes in society has always been one of toil; nor can it be proved that in respect of either the conditions under which they work or of the rewards for their labor, the modern world deals less kindly with these more defenseless of its members than did society in the Middle Ages. This whole problem has been complicated by sterile attempts to compare the life conditions of women and children under the modern wage system with the circumstances of their lives under the economic conditions which preceded the Industrial Revolution — usually to the disadvantage of the modern world. Nothing can be proved by such comparisons. In some regards the sordidness of life in the Middle Ages surpassed the worst records of present-day industry; in other respects — especially with reference to the independence of the worker — a strong case can be made in favor of the condition of women and children under the domestic economy. But there is no accepted standard with which to measure the merits of these two modes of life in terms of the spiritual welfare of the worker. And, after all, an understanding of modern conditions is not to be reached by this method of approach. For the labor of women and children is a problem of modern industrial relations, not because it is more extensive, or more degrading, than formerly, but because its effects are different.

To grasp the significance of such a problem as this at any stage of societal development, it must be studied in its relation to the whole complex of customs, institutions and ideals which comprises the social structure at the time. It is because this relationship has been changed by the revolution of the social order which produced the modern industrial world that we are correct in speaking of the labor of women and children as a *modern* problem. This change, in part, has been due to an alteration in the ideals and principles which govern our political and social life. In a democracy, the tests of enduring social welfare are fundamentally different from those which obtain in an aristocratic order; conditions which deny to children opportunities for wholesome physical development and education, and interfere with the normal functions of motherhood or contribute to the spread of vice among unmarried women are recognized as constituting a problem of obvious social import. It is from this standpoint of its relation to general social welfare and to the ideals of the modern world that the extent of child and woman labor and the legal program for its solution will be presented in the articles which follow.

But there is another way in which this problem differs from that of an earlier social order: namely, in its effects upon the life conditions of male workers. Before the Industrial Revolution, the labor of women and children was supplementary to, not in competition with, that of men. With the perfection of the machine technique, however, processes were so far simplified that jobs formerly monopolized by men could be filled by children or by women who possessed no considerable skill or physical strength. At once craft lines began to dissolve; cheap labor began to compete for employment with the skilled worker; women and children with men. Thus began a lowering of the standard of life and an undermining of the security of employment for male workers. With the progress of the Industrial Revolution this condition spread from one industry or one process to another until to-day the menace of this form of competition confronts the workingman in many of the fields of industrial enterprise.

Attitude of labor. In general the attitude of the male worker toward the labor of women and children is based squarely upon his desire to defend himself from what he considers to be unfair competition. The policy of organized labor is formed much more in the spirit of antagonism toward, than of sympathy with, the woman and child who works in a factory. It must be granted in all fairness that such an attitude is understandable; indeed, it is the inevitable reaction of the propertyless man whose sole right to life consists in his control of a job; whose single source of support for himself and his family is his pay envelope. Nevertheless, it does not always contribute to clarity of economic reasoning nor to the efficacy of devices adopted for the solution of the problem.

To meet one phase of this problem, almost all male workers favor the absolute prohibition of child labor under a certain age. Organized labor is to be credited in large measure with the progress of child-labor legislation during the past half century. In this part of its program, it is moving in harmony with the social tendencies of the age and is gradually approaching its goal. The extent and character of the child-labor laws in the United States will be described in Article 2.

As regards the labor of women, the conflict is summed up in the trade-union slogan: "Equal pay for equal work." The meaning of this formula is not always clear when it is used in connection with a wage dispute. The most apparent meaning gives us a proposition whose justice is self-evident: namely, that the payment *for a given product* should not be less for women, solely because they are women, than it is for men. But as the formula is used by organized labor it seems, more frequently, to mean that the daily or weekly wage for the woman worker on a given job should be the same as that of a man on the same job, regardless of the relative productivity of the two. When applied in the first sense, the equal pay slogan would result, obviously, in lower day wages for women than for men to the extent that the productive efficiency of the former — because of physical weakness, or lack of skill, or susceptibility to sickness — was smaller than that of the latter. If the formula were to be applied in the second sense, the money wage, though the same in absolute amount, would be higher for women in relation to their productivity than for men, to the extent that the former were less productive. Now, employers are interested in the question of wages primarily from the standpoint of the relation of the payment to the performance of the worker — or, in other words, to the worker's productivity. If they are required to pay the same wage to two groups of different productivity, it is obvious that they will not willingly employ the less efficient workers at all.

The equal pay program. This seems to be the object in view in the case of many trade unions who press the demand for "equal pay" for women workers. Their desire is not to raise the wages of women employed in industry but to defend their members from the competition of women workers by loading the wage contract in their favor. The effectiveness of this device to expel women labor from industrial employment rests clearly upon the assumption that women workers produce less, in a given time and under the same conditions, than do men. But this is undoubtedly true with regard to most lines of employment. Women are physically weaker than men and are, in many cases, unable to perform all the operations embraced in a job; they have less incentive in perfecting their skill since the majority of them do not look forward to a full life of industrial employment; they are less regular in their attendance; they are incapable of the sustained effort required in the emergencies of overtime work. These factors, among others, make them, on the whole, less productive than male labor; consequently, a demand for absolute equality of wages must result in establishing a handicap in favor of the male worker in the competition for employment.

It is probable that few disinterested students will give approval to the doctrine of equal wages when it is applied with this meaning and with the purpose of excluding women from employment. At any rate, the program to restrict or prohibit woman labor which wins support from public-spirited citizens rests upon considerations of broad social welfare, not upon the desire to give artificial advantage to the male workers. So far as concerns the wages of the two groups, economic justice demands no more than that the rate of wages for both should be equal, in proportion to their productive efficiency. It is in the first of the two senses we have been considering that the "equal pay" slogan wins approval.

Wage discrimination against women. Even if we thus limit the meaning of the slogan, however, we are still confronted with a problem of economic justice in the actual working of the industrial world. The woman worker has consistently been underpaid, as compared with the male worker, relatively to her productivity. Exhaustive studies of the condition of women in industry carried out in England during the Great War, disclosed the fact that there was a tendency among employers everywhere to pay a lower wage for women than for men in exchange for the same service. In some cases, the piece rate for women varied from one third to one half of that paid to men. Certain factories paying wages on the piece-rate basis were found to have lowered their rates when women were employed to take the places of men who had left for military service, for no other apparent reason than that the new employees were women. Similar studies in this country, and elsewhere, have established beyond question the fact that it is not customary to pay "equal wages" to women, even in the first sense in which this term is used.

The discrimination explained. The fact that women workers are systematically victimized in this way is difficult to account for, except on the basis of their weaker bargaining power. As compared with men, women are notably weak in defending their interests when bargaining with an employer. To their naturally non-aggressive and timid disposition, are added other handicaps which arise from their social position and their economic environment. In the first place, their labor is concentrated for the most part in certain definite lines of employment where they must meet severe competition from a large and fluctuating number of women workers who seek part-time or temporary employment as a supplement to their labor in the home. Again, they are relatively "immobile" as compared with men; it is difficult for them to play off one employer against another when this involves a change of residence. Furthermore, they are often not self-supporting and make no pretense of demanding a "living wage"; as subsidized workers, they offer cutthroat competition to their self-supporting competitors, both male and female. Again they look upon their employment as a temporary expedient to fill in the time before their marriage, and, therefore, are less intent than men upon exacting the highest possible price for their labor. Finally, for reasons which will appear later in our study, they are unorganized and, to a great degree, unorganizable; their bargains are made as individuals, and they labor under all the handicaps which the isolated worker must bear in the modern labor market.

Bearing on wage theory. This customary discrimination against the woman worker in the wage contract has a bearing on our theory of the determinants of the wage rate under conditions of competition. In another place, we have examined the economist's law of wages, finding it to consist in the statement that money wages, under competition, will tend to equal the value of the marginal product of the labor group. Our discussion of this law led us to the conclusion that it, in reality, summed up the forces which determine the upper limit to the wage rate, under given conditions; and that the actual rate paid to any individual worker or class of workers would be fixed with reference to this maximum by the relative bargaining power of employer and worker. This conclusion is supported by the facts relative to the wages of women in industry. When we find that women are paid less for the same performance on the same job than men, for no other apparent reason than that they lack aggressiveness as bargainers, the importance of the element of bargaining in the establishment of actual wage rates becomes clear.

To the extent that women are paid a truly unequal wage, their competition with the male worker is "unfair" competition. Business men are familiar with analogous situations in the market for commodities. The practice of "dumping" in international trade — sporadic unloading on a foreign market of excess supplies of goods at prices below the cost of production — is generally considered unfair to the domestic producer, the temporary cutting of prices below cost by a would-be monopolist for the purpose of ruining small competitors, is condemned both by business morality and considerations of economic welfare; Government subsidies to certain favored producers in a competitive field are similarly condemned. These are conditions similar to that in which the male worker finds himself when forced to compete for employment with a supply of labor which may be bought for less than it is worth in terms of productivity. Such competition tends to lower the wage rate for all workers in the industry below the point which measures the laborer's economic worth; it nullifies the efforts of the organized workers to obtain economic justice through an increase of bargaining power; it gradually degrades the standard of life.

The remedy. The remedy for this situation is to apply, in its true sense, the doctrine of equal pay for equal work. This might be done through the medium of minimum-wage laws for women, though this device is unreliable in that it employs an arbitrary, and not an economic test of fair wages. The best and most permanent solution lies along the line of increasing the bargaining power of women workers by organization for collective action. Difficulties in the way of unionizing women workers are disappearing under the action of those forces in the modern industrial world — e.g., delayed marriage and the increasing economic independence of women — which tend to give the woman worker a recognized and a permanent place in the labor market.

2. Position of the Child and Woman Wage-Earner in the United States

Child labor. The economic importance of children has always been recognized, but it is since the advent of power machinery that their labor has become competitive with that of men and women. The modern factory has thus given rise to another serious social and economic problem. Before attempting to indicate the evils connected with, and resulting from, child labor, it is desirable to have at hand some of the facts concerning the nature and extent of it in our country.

Prior to 1870 there were no statistics compiled of the number of children gainfully employed; in that year there were reported 739,164 children between 10 and 15 years of age at work, of whom 114,628 were in manufacturing plants. In 1880 the census gave 1,118,356 children from 10 to 15 employed, or 16.8 per cent of that age group total. In 1900 the number was 1,750,178 or 18 per cent. In 1910 almost two million children between 10 and 15 were engaged in remunerative occupations; officially 1,990,225. They made up 12 per cent of all persons employed in agriculture, and over two per cent of persons engaged in other employments. About two thirds of them were boys. After 1910 there was a decrease in the number of child workers; this may have been a real advance, or merely due to the depression. Whichever it was, the War stopped it, and a rapid increase occurred. This increase, as indicated by school certificates, went as high as 400 per cent in at least one large city (Lowell, Mass.). After the War, when production was curtailed, the numbers employed again began to fall off. In 1920 there were only 1,060,858 child workers tabulated. This figure was abnormal, however, for several reasons. First, the Federal Child Labor Tax Law, later declared unconstitutional, was then in force; also, the census was taken in January when many children who work on the farms would escape enumeration. Nevertheless, the decade 1910–1920 was the first in forty years in which there was any indication of a decrease in the number of young folks at work.

Occupations of children. The question naturally comes to mind, What sort of work do these children do? A glance at the following brief tabulation answers this.

647,000 children work in agriculture
185,000 work in manufacturing
80,000 work in clerical occupations
63,000 work in trade
54,000 work in domestic and personal service
19,000 work in transportation
3,500 work in professional service
1,130 work in public service

The census takes no notice of children under 10, but investigations show that there are many of these at work in the beet fields, cotton plantations, cranberry bogs, and other farm work, as well as in street trades, tenement home work, domestic service, and canneries. Neither does the census take account of those who manage to attend school at least half time, no matter how much their earning may interfere with school work.

The States with the largest percentages of child workers are ten of the Southern States, Rhode Island, and Massachusetts. The Southern States stand in this unenviable position chiefly because of the predominance of agriculture there. The New England States have a larger proportion of children in non-agricultural work than any other section. Pennsylvania has the largest number employed in manufacturing, although her large population keeps the percentage low.

Child labor on farms does not mean doing a few chores; the census counts as child labor only that toil which constitutes a material addition to the labor income of the farm. Thousands of children are hired out as farm laborers to people quite outside of their own families. Furthermore, this is the easiest occupation in which to utilize the work of those under 10 years. In Texas local papers tell of cotton-picking contests between boys five years old. In New Jersey they crawl on their hands and knees in the cranberry bogs. In Michigan the beet growers give preference to contract laborers who have large families that can be used in the fields. It is in this phase of the problem that the law has so far failed to even attempt much improvement.

In the factories the law has been more active. The year 1920 showed a decrease of 29 per cent in the number of child factory hands, although 185,337 children between the ages of 10 and 15 were still at work. About 9500 of these were under 14, the usual legal minimum. The chief employing industries were the textiles, which used 54,000.

Industrial home work cannot be gauged by census figures, but there is no doubt that a great deal of it is carried on. Wherever it is found, child labor is also found, with results that can easily be imagined. A recent study in three New England cities showed 5000 children under 16, or 7.6 per cent of the entire child population engaged in industrial home work. Many of them admitted that they suffered from eye-strain. Half of these children earned less than five cents an hour; four fifths less than ten cents.

The canneries have long been known as exploiters of child labor. They require long hours and pay very poorly. The conditions of work are very bad. The mines are also users of children, although they can point to a decrease in the past decade. Not many children work underground, but the breakers claim many. There is a high rate of accident, which in itself should be sufficient to cause the exclusion of children.

No discussion of child labor would be complete without some mention of the children at work in the city streets. Newspaper selling is the leading trade, with bootblacking next. The census cannot give a complete enumeration of these trades, for the same reasons that make street trade laws hard to enforce. The big objection to street work is that it is so apt to lead to juvenile delinquency in one form or another.

Evils of child labor. The evils of child labor will be apparent to any one who will give the matter thought. The child is almost certain to be injured physically, whether it be from lifting too heavy loads, or from working in a posture of strain, or from contracting a disease from unhealthy surroundings. He is deprived of his natural period of play and development, which is coming to be held as absolutely vital to a proper maturity. He is deprived of an education. Even if he continues to attend school, he will be irregular and in danger of retardation. Agriculture is the worst offender in keeping children from school, although for those above fourteen the industrial States show an abrupt drop in school attendance. The States in which the most child labor is employed are almost without exception the ones showing the highest percentage of illiteracy.

From the point of view of society, there are equal objections. A physically unfit child is a social liability, with unpleasant prospects for the next generation; how much more so is mentally, or morally, an undeveloped one. Obviously such conditions are not compatible with the American system of democracy. And from the so-called purely practical viewpoint of the workingman, the child in industry is a competitor of the most insidious nature.

Legal regulation. What, then, have we as an organized Government done to improve matters? During the past decade two Federal Child Labor Laws have been in operation. Each was in turn declared unconstitutional by the United States Supreme Court. The only hope lay in an amendment to the Constitution to permit Congress to legislate upon this matter. This amendment has been passed, and is now (1924) before the States for ratification. This aims merely to permit legislation, which it is hoped will be early in forthcoming.

Practically every State has some laws in regard to the work of children. Forty-six of them fix the minimum age for factory work at 14 years or higher, while only one has no minimum. Thirty States limit the working-day for children under 16 to 8 hours, while 17 States permit 9, 10, or even 11 hours a day, and one has no limit. Thirty-eight States prohibit night work for children under 16; 5 more allow certain exemptions, while 4 have no prohibition at all. Twenty-six States prohibit children from working in mines and quarries, 7 more from mines only, while 15 States permit them to work in both mines and quarries. Only 10 States have state-wide laws applying to the street trades. Eighteen States have no definite educational requirement for children leaving school to go to work, and only 12 require the completion of the eighth grade. There is practically no legislation regarding work in agriculture or domestic service. School attendance laws are often a dead letter in the rural sections, and street trade laws are almost impossible to enforce. There is plenty of room for advancement along these lines.

Woman labor in the United States. Women have always been economically important to the industrial progress of the race. Since the beginning of the factory system, women have come to the front as an integral part of it. Even in the early days of this country, when women are popularly supposed to have stayed in the home, it is evident that over a hundred occupations were open to women. In the first half of the nineteenth century they entered the factories in increasing numbers. But no factory class had developed, and most of the women workers were simply there temporarily. During the Civil War many women were thrown upon their own resources, and entered the factories; thereafter, they entered into more active competition with the men.

In 1880 there were 2,647,157 females over 10 years of age engaged in gainful occupations; in 1900 the number was 5,319,397, or 19 per cent of all the women in the United States. In 1910 there were 8,075,000 women gainfully employed, or one fifth of all gainfully employed persons in the United States. In this decade the increase of women workers outside the home was 45 per cent; the increase of men workers was only 30 per cent. With the entrance of the United States into the War in 1917 another million women entered industry. It was estimated that in 1922 there were 12,000,000 women in gainful occupations in the United States.

Occupations of women. Women have invaded practically every kind of work. There is not an industry listed in the United States in which women are not employed. The list includes chemical works, clothing manufacture, corset, glove, and hat factories, candy factories, clock, watch, and jewelry factories, paint factories, munitions and fireworks factories, soap factories, the manufacture of food products, shoe factories, box factories, wagon and carriage manufacture, the production of leather and leather products, shoe factories, printing and publishing works, the manufacture of paper products, button factories, rubber factories, straw factories, laundries, cotton, knitting, woolen, lace, linen, silk, and carpet mills. More than half the workers in the textile and bookbinding trades, and one third of those in the canning industry, are women. Office staffs in every kind of business invariably contain many women. Over one sixth of the people in the wholesale and retail trades are females; and they make up one half of the workers in professional service, and two thirds of those in domestic service.

Wages of women. The wages of women in industry are quite inadequate, much below the remuneration of men even when the work done is of a similar nature. In 1900 the median rate of wages for women in all industries was 53 per cent of the rate for men. In California in 1915–16 a majority of the women workers received less than $10 a week, ranging from 48 per cent in the printing trades to 94 per cent in the 5 and 10 cent stores. In Minnesota in 1918–19 one third of 51,000 women wage-earners were getting less than $10 a week. In Kansas the median wage to women in 1919 and 1920 was $11.95, with 20 per cent of the women earning less than $9. In Ohio in 1919, 14 per cent of the women workers were receiving less than $10 per week, and 52 per cent less than $15 a week. The Bureau of Labor Statistics made a survey in 1920 which showed that several leading industries, such as the manufacture of candy, paper boxes, hosiery, knitted underwear, and overalls, the women employed received less than a living wage; and this in a period when the demand for workers was great, and wages high.

Legal regulation. The States also undertake to regulate the work of women to some extent. A number of them require an eight-hour day, or a forty-eight-hour week, although the majority permit nine, ten, or even more hours, and four have no limitation at all. Twelve require a day of rest; 14 specify as to the noon-hour; and 13 will not allow more than five or six hours of continuous work. Night work in at least one industry is prohibited in 13 States. Mothers' pensions are granted in 40 States.

Altogether it appears that not much progress has been made in labor legislation for women.

CHAPTER VII

THE PROBLEM OF INDUSTRIAL ACCIDENT

1. The Machine Process and Industrial Accident [1]

Extent of work accidents. Work accidents in the United States, according to the best attainable estimates, annually cause more than 35,000 deaths and about 2,000,000 injuries, whereof probably 500,000 produce disability lasting more than one week. To employ a telling comparison frequently made, the industrial casualties of a single year in this country alone equal the average annual casualties of the American Civil War, plus all those of the Philippine War, increased by all those of the Russo-Japanese War. As many men are killed each fortnight in the ordinary course of work as went down with the "Titanic." This single spectacular catastrophe appalled the civilized world and compelled governmental action in two hemispheres; while the ceaseless, day-by-day destruction of the industrial juggernaut excites so little attention that few States take the trouble to record the deaths and injuries.

The point especially to be emphasized in this connection is that the appalling waste of life revealed by the above cited estimates is, in great part, unavoidable. Doubtless the number of work accidents may be considerably reduced in the United States, as it has been reduced in Europe, by preventive measures. Yet when all possible precautions have been taken modern industry will continue to exact a fearful toll of life and limb. Even in the German Empire, which leads the world in accident prevention, there were reported in 1911, the last year for which statistics are available, 662,321 work accidents, whereof 9687 terminated fatally and 142,965 caused disability for more than thirteen weeks. Scientific accident prevention in Germany has produced a lower accident rate and a much lower rate of fatal accidents than obtains in the United States, but it has left the total casualty list of industry deplorably large. Indeed, the number of work in-

[1] Adapted from *History of Work Accident Indemnity in Iowa*, by E. H. Downey, pp. 1–5. The State Historical Society of Iowa, publisher.

juries in Germany, as elsewhere, is increasing, both absolutely and relatively to the numbers employed, as industrial development goes forward. The ugly fact is that work accidents, in the main, are due to causes inherent in mechanical industry on the one hand, and in the hereditary traits of human character on the other hand.

Causes of accident. In the first place, a high degree of hazard inheres in present-day methods of production. Modern technology makes use of the most subtle and resistless forces of nature — forces whose powers of destruction when they escape control are fully commensurate with their beneficent potency when kept in command. Moreover, these forces operate not the simple hand tools of other days, but a maze of complicated machinery which the individual workman can neither comprehend nor control, but to the movements of which his own motions must closely conform in rate, range, and direction. Nor is the worker's danger confined to the task in which he is himself engaged, nor to the appliances within his vision. A multitude of separate operations are combined into one comprehensive mechanical process, the successful consummation of which requires the coöperation of thousands of operatives and of countless pieces of apparatus in such close interdependence that a hidden defect of even a minor part, or a momentary lapse of memory or of attention by a single individual may imperil the lives of hundreds. A tower man misinterprets an order, or a brittle rail gives way, and a train loaded with human freight dashes to destruction. A miner tamps his "shot" with slack and dust explosion wipes out a score of lives. A steel beam yields to a pressure that it was calculated to bear and a rising skyscraper collapses in consequence, burying a small army of workmen in the ruins.

In the second place, human nature, inherited from generations that knew not the machine, is imperfectly fitted for the strain put upon it by mechanical industry. Safely to perform their work the operatives of a modern mill or railway should think consistently in terms of those mechanical laws to which alone present-day industrial processes are amenable. They should respond automatically to the most varied mechanical exigencies, and should be as insensible to fatigue and as unvarying in behavior as the machines they operate.

Manifestly these are qualities which normal human beings do not possess in anything like the requisite degree. The common man is neither an automaton nor an animated slide-rule. His movements fall into a natural rhythm, indeed, but the beat is both less rapid and more irregular than the rhythm of most machines — with the consequence that he fails to remove his hand before the die descends or allows himself to be struck by the recoiling lever. It requires an appreciable time for the red light or the warning gong to penetrate his consciousness, and his response is apt to be tardy or in the wrong direction. Fatigue, also, overcomes him, slowing his movements, lengthening his reaction time, and diminishing his muscular accuracy — thereby trebly enhancing his liability to accident.

The machine technology, in fact, covers so small a fraction of the life-history of mankind that its discipline has not yet produced a mechanically standardized race, even in those communities and classes that are industrially most advanced. And so there is a great number of work injuries due to the "negligence of the injured workman" — due, that is to say, to the shortcomings of human nature as measured by the standards of the mechanician. This maladjustment is aggravated by the never-ceasing extension of machine methods to new fields of industry, and the continued influx of children, women, and untrained peasants into mechanical employments. Accordingly, the proportion of accidents attributable to want of knowledge, skill, strength, or care on the part of operatives appears everywhere to be increasing.

There is, then, no prospect that the "carnage of peace" will be terminated, as the carnage of war may be, within the predictable future. An industrial community must face the patent fact that work injuries on a tremendous scale are a permanent feature of modern life. Every mechanical employment has a predictable hazard; of a thousand men who climb to dizzy heights in erecting steel structures a certain number will fall to death, and of a thousand girls who feed metal strips into stamping machines a certain number will have their fingers crushed. So regularly do such injuries occur that every machine-made commodity may be said to have a definite cost in human blood and tears — a life for so many tons of coal, a lacerated hand for so many laundered shirts.

2. The Incidence of Work Accidents [1]

Who bears the cost? Work accidents, in the nature of the case, are sustained principally by wage-earners, who are substantially propertyless as a matter of course, who have no savings to speak of, and whose incomes, for the most part, are too small to leave any adequate margin for accident insurance. The almost total absence of property or savings among wage-workers is abundantly demonstrated by tax returns and the records of savings banks and life insurance companies. But wages statistics are yet more conclusive to the same effect. More than half of the workmen injured in the Pittsburgh district in 1907 were earning less than $15 weekly (making no allowance for unemployment) at the time of injury. Of the men sustaining industrial injuries in Minnesota in 1909–10, 47 per cent were receiving less than $12.50 and 78 per cent were receiving less than $15 weekly.

It needs no argument to show that families in receipt of incomes such as these can have neither property, savings accounts nor insurance. And this conclusion, finally, is corroborated by investigations into the insurance actually carried by wage-workers. Of 132 married men killed in Pittsburgh, only 6 had insurance in substantial amount and only 25 out of 214 left savings, insurance, and trade-union and fraternal benefits to the amount of $500 each. In New York State 175 workingmen who suffered fatal or permanently disabling accidents had insurance in the aggregate sum of $18,635. Nor are these extreme instances selected to make out a case. The average value of 13,488,124 "industrial insurance" policies in force in 1902 was only $135. The unvarnished fact is that the wage-earner neither does, nor can, provide for the contingencies of sickness, accident, and unemployment.

To the wage-worker, then, even when no one but himself is dependent on his earnings, the loss of a few weeks' wages means serious privation, and permanent incapacity means beggary. But quite half the victims of work accidents are married men, and a majority of even the unmarried contribute to the support of others. For example, of 467 fatal accidents in Allegheny County, Pennsylvania, 258 were sustained by married men and 129 others by regular contributors to the support of relatives; whereas only

[1] Adapted from *History of Work Accident Indemnity in Iowa*, by E. H. Downey, pp. 6–8. The State Historical Society of Iowa, publisher.

80 of the 467 dead were wholly without dependents. Of 285 fatal accidents investigated in Cuyahoga County, Ohio, 176 were suffered by heads of families. Of 1476 men killed on the job in New York State, 679 were the sole supporters of 1775 dependents, 167 were the principal supporters of 520 dependents and 252 contributed to the support of 668 relatives — leaving but 378, or 35 per cent of the whole number of deceased, entirely without economic responsibilities. In Wisconsin 43 per cent of the injured workmen whose conjugal conditions could be learned by the State Bureau of Labor were married.

A serious work accident, therefore, commonly deprives a necessitous family of its sole, or chief, or at least a very important, source of income. The inevitable result, in the absence of systematic accident indemnity, is poverty, and the long train of social evils that spring from poverty. It is not only that victims of unindemnified work accidents suffer prolonged incapacity and often needless death from want of means to obtain proper care, not only that families are compelled to reduce a standard of living already low, and that women and children are forced into employments unsuited to their age and sex, with resultant physical and moral deterioration; but it is that the ever-present fear of undeserved want goes far to impair that spirit of hopefulness and enterprise upon which industrial efficiency so largely depends.

3. Needless Coal-Mine Accidents — A Program for Their Prevention [1]

Human costs in coal mining. My first trip underground in a coal mine was twenty-three years ago, but I became especially interested in coal-mine accidents at the time of the Illinois Cherry Mine Disaster in 1909. That catastrophe, where 259 were killed, resulted in some improvements in mine practice and, with other mine disasters of the period, led to the creation in 1910 of the United States Bureau of Mines. Its first director, Dr. Holmes, until his untimely death, was an officer of the Association for Labor Legislation. For fifteen years — in the midst of many other activities — we have attempted to follow the general progress of scientific research and to aid in the practical application of improved safety measures.

[1] Adapted from the pamphlet, "Needless Coal-Mine Accidents" by John B. Andrews. Published by the American Association for Labor Legislation.

Safety in this country has, up to this time, received most public attention in factories. Probably this is due in part to the presence of women and children in manufacturing establishments, but it is also because factories are, day after day in many thousands of communities, much more under the eye of our citizens. Coal mines are much more remote. They are thought of principally in relation to the price of coal. And the human cost of mining coal — the maimed bodies and shortened lives of those who dig down into the earth — has not received sufficient public attention.

There is a powerful labor organization in this industry, but it has concentrated its attention principally upon the obviously important matters of wages and hours. Some mine operators, we find, are making splendid efforts to reduce accidents; many others are "leaving safety to chance."

I have found among mining engineers as well as among coal operators a surprising readiness to assert that of course the cost of needed safety precautions must be added to the price of coal. Is this declaration warranted by the facts? The profits made by many coal companies do not suggest that all of the cost of preventing coal-mine accidents need be passed on to those who buy the coal. Moreover, accident prevention work, in thousands of instances, has paid for itself.

Indifference to safety in the United States. More intensive study of this problem during the past year, in Europe as well as in this country, I regret to say, has left me sorely troubled by the appalling and needless hazards in our coal industry.

In the United States we are killing coal miners three times as fast as they kill them in Great Britain. I have great interest in the safety movement in America. I point with pride to it at every opportunity. But we will probably all agree that the way to get the best results in any industry is to face the facts and then make use of them.

It happens that for 1919, 1920, and 1921, the latest years for which comparable statistics are available, our fatality rate per thousand coal miners employed has been a little more than three times as great as their fatality rate in the United Kingdom.

Voluminous government reports have been saying this in tabular statements. But the fact has not as yet "got over" to the public.

FATALITY RATE PER 1000 WORKERS

YEAR	UNITED KINGDOM	UNITED STATES	RATIO
1919..........	.94	3.03	3.22
1920..........	.88	2.92	3.32
1921[a]..........	.66	2.42	3.67

[a] In both countries during 1921 the mines were closed for a considerable period.

Moreover, one may point out, as did a leading statistician before the National Safety Council in 1923, that "More disturbing than the appalling greater fatality rate is the fact that the relative fatality rates, though fluctuating rather widely, show on the whole a decided increase."

As clearly brought out at the Chicago conference of the Association for Labor Legislation in 1922 by Geo. S. Rice, chief mining engineer, and Wm. W. Adams, statistician, of the United States Bureau of Mines, "Over a period of ten years (1911–1920) the average fatality rate has been 1.2 in Great Britain and 4.3 in the United States."

But in the United States the coal seams are in general much thicker and more accessible and we employ more and larger machinery. Naturally our output per man employed is several times greater. This has suggested to the apologists for our shameful fatality record that we should measure our fatality rate by output in tons rather than by the number of human beings killed per thousand of full-time workers. I am glad to note that the secretary of the Pennsylvania Department of Labor and Industry — a statistician of international reputation — has branded this suggestion "to measure deaths and disabilities of workers on a tonnage basis" as "utterly erroneous and bad statistics." Dr. Meeker properly adds: "The only just and accurate basis of reference is the man hours worked, during which time the workers were exposed to the hazards of industrial accidents. . . . The lower fatality rate per thousand tons is due to the fact that human lives are sacrificed to the God of Big Output."

But despite the unfairness of the tonnage basis, it may be interesting to note that while the American miner produces more than three times as much coal as does his British competitor, the comparative fatalities are as 1. to 1.16 per million tons mined.

Bituminous mine. Turning to the hazards in the bituminous coal industry of the United States we find the fatality rate still higher than for the coal industry as a whole. During the ten years to 1922, the United States Bureau of Mines reports that at the bituminous coal mines alone there were killed 18,243 miners, the average fatality rate being 4.30 per 1000 employed.

Of the average of 1824 bituminous coal miners killed each year about one half met their death from falls of roof and coal, about 18 per cent were killed by mine cars and locomotives, about 12 per cent by gas and coal-dust explosions, and the remaining one fifth lost their lives from other causes.

"No general statistics are available on non-fatal injuries in the bituminous coal industry, because there is no uniformity among the States in reporting such accidents." This "daily sniping" of miners underground is not yet counted for the whole country.

But from compensation insurance experience in Pennsylvania it is estimated that the bituminous coal industry in that State alone loses approximately 1,165,900 days' service yearly on account of about 28,800 serious non-fatal accidents, which result in a compensation cost of approximately $1,497,000 annually. There is also to be considered the property and production loss running into millions.

This is a record of striving for large output with less consideration for safety than for both high dividends and high wages. Officially it is a record of decentralized administration — of protective state regulations that differ almost as much in character as does the degree of their enforcement from State to State. It is a record at best of tardy adoption of safeguards — lagging years behind engineering knowledge of what can and ought to be done. It is a record of appalling and needless loss of property as well as human lives, which have been sacrificed to speed, greed, and indifference to the public interest.

As pointed out by occasional writers on this subject the loss of 150 lives at one mine disaster and 250 at another, as we read of them in the papers, "are mere figures to us, they have no human meaning. But if we could stand at the mouth of the mine upon its reopening after an explosion and behold the seemingly endless column of charred bodies borne hour after hour to the surface; if we could witness the long line of hearses on their way to the hillside burial ground; if we could hear the heartbreaking sobs of stricken widows mingled with the pitiful wails of little children bereft of their fathers; if we could go in the days that follow to the bare homes deprived of their bread-winners," we would then perhaps begin to appreciate the loss.

Mine accidents preventable. The United States Bureau of Mines, says a recent authoritative report, has demonstrated clearly how to avoid explosions, how to use explosives, what lamps are safe, how to install and use electrical equipment, when to declare a mine gaseous and how to reduce accidents from falls of roof and from transportation.

I believe it is a reasonable statement that two thirds of the fatal and serious accidents at the bituminous coal mines of this country could be prevented by the universal adoption of safety methods already in successful operation at some of the mines of this country or in Great Britain. As a result of practical experience with safety legislation during fifteen years, and through our own recent studies of this subject in Europe and America, our Association has gradually drawn up, from the public point of view, a suggestive program for prevention. This has been done after consultation with mine operators and engineers, representatives of the miners' organizations, state and federal mine inspectors, in addition to a careful study of published reports.

The very valuable reports of the United States Bureau of Mines, since its organization in 1910, have dwelt year after year upon needless hazards in the coal industry. Now we have received from a committee that is representative of coal-mine operators, coal miners, casualty insurance interests, mining engineers, mine inspectors and statisticians, a new and informing report prepared under the chairmanship of the well-known engineer, E. A. Holbrook, dean of the mining school, Pennsylvania State College. Let us consider briefly the findings of this representative committee of practical men submitted recently to the United States Coal Commission.

A practical program. It will economize space and unify the statement if our Program for Prevention and the findings of this latest official report are discussed together.

Our first proposal is:

I. The adoption of uniform legal minimum standards of safety.

Beginning with Ohio in 1874, most of the coal-mining States have adopted mining codes, the most comprehensive perhaps being that of Pennsylvania where the first official mine inspection was instituted in 1870. These codes — while differing widely in scope and effectiveness — include such provisions as were at the time of their adoption regarded as a step in advance, or the best that could then be passed through the state legislatures. Minimum requirements as to exits, ventilation, proper timbering, safety lamps, electric wiring and blasting regulations, are typical features of these state codes. Many of these laws now need thorough revision to bring them into line with modern engineering knowledge and the best mining and administrative practice. Our Association has noted a growing conviction that unless state regulations are generally and rapidly improved, the suggestion is to be expected that operations in this industry which are regarded as in the nature of a public service should be subjected to some form of federal control.

It is scarcely necessary to repeat here what is again tersely stated — that "non-conformity among States in their mining laws is a handicap to safety and a disturbing economic element in competing fields in adjoining States." The mine safety committee asks, "How can a safety law, costing, say five cents a ton, be enforced in one State, when the competing mines of a neighboring State have no similar law?" A fair question. Too much emphasis has sometimes been put on the interstate competition argument in protective legislation, but there is a real problem here that calls for uniformity of minimum legal standards.

Consumers are interested in this question. The coal miners argue that the extra hazardous nature of their occupation justifies a high wage. The coal-mine owners insist that higher wages must be reflected in a higher price for coal. Moreover, coal operators in one State object to safety requirements that result in added cost in their own mining operations when the same regulations are not uniformly placed upon their competitors in adjoining States. The public which ultimately pays the cost also of accident compensation, has a right to insist upon reducing the cost of needless accidents through the universal use of practical safeguards.

It is of course recognized by the safety committee that "accidents from falls of roof and from transportation are due to many different causes, each of which generally needs careful local study." And of course, "every company should foster first aid, provide a safety inspector, and provide instruction in safety." On the other hand "the expense of a complete approval system for gassy and dusty mines is large, too large for the individual States to carry out. Nation-wide uniformity," declares the committee, "is desirable." And the need of some additional authority is plainly apparent in view of the fact that "in 1922, only 18.2 per cent of the explosives used in coal mining were permissibles."

It is the belief of practical experts, who have just reported on this subject, that the various recommended safeguards will gradually be adopted by the industry, but they say "under present conditions it should be remembered that neither operators nor miners like to change customs and appliances with which they are familiar."

"While many of us oppose so-called government paternalism," concludes the safety committee, "yet we believe it is the duty of the Government to secure safety of life by wisely directed legislation. If the compulsion by the Government to use life-saving devices, as the air-brake and automatic coupler on our railroads, is proper, we believe the coal industry should prepare (especially in new operations) to universally adopt safety suggestions."

The second proposal is:

II. The use underground of no explosive that is not after scientific investigation numbered among the "permissibles"; the strict limitation of "shooting off the solid"; and the use of shale or approved rock dust to check the spread of coal-dust explosions.

In general it is a sound principle to encourage the greatest possible local and representative committee study and formulation of safety standards. Our Association has consistently recognized this. But it sometimes happens that necessary technical scientific research has reached positive conclusions supported by practical experience, at the same time that there is urgent call for efficient and direct application of measures to save human life. Such an example is found in the remedy for coal-mine explosions.

I was shocked during a visit this year to Middle Western States to learn how extensively black powder is still being used. Reference has already been made to the fact that despite the painstaking scientific work of the federal Government only about 18 per cent of the explosives used last year were permissibles. Does this condition not call for something more than the purely voluntary acceptance of safety precautions by isolated coal operators? Obviously, black powder should rarely if ever be used, and permissible substitutes should be adopted as is recommended by the coal safety committee. Moreover, the use of large quantities of powder, without undercutting the coal, should be discouraged.

Another important related problem is the extension throughout the mine of explosions, due to the throwing into suspension and the rapid ignition of coal dust. The remedy is to provide quantities of shale dust, the particles of which come between the floating particles of coal dust and arrest the process of ignition and explosion. Of the Federal Bureau of Mines' splendid research work of a dozen years at a cost to our taxpayers of millions of well-spent dollars, "the outstanding accomplishment is the practical demonstrations of the cause and nature of coal-dust explosions and the development of methods for their limitation and control by use of rock and shale dust. The cause and nature of coal-dust explosions has been 'sold' to the industry," continues the coal safety committee, but "an equal work remains of getting the industry to adopt the best methods for their prevention."

There are not, to my knowledge, more than three substantial coal companies in America that are using this simple, reasonably inexpensive, and effective safeguard against coal-dust explosions. While making inquiries in Europe I learned that at least France and England compel the use of shale or rock dust by national law. And in talking recently with the chief of the British Department of Mines I found that before the adoption of official regulations on the subject, British employers were not unlike the vast majority of our own coal-mine operators. At first they wouldn't believe coal dust is explosive. When it was conclusively demonstrated in experimental mines, they then said, "Well the coal dust in my mine is not explosive!" And when the explosibility of this too had been proven, they fell back upon the objection to the cost of adopting so simple a measure.

Says the committee on mine safety, "It has been clearly demonstrated" that "gas and coal-dust explosions can be limited and controlled by the intelligent use of rock and shale dust." Some coal mines in this country are doing it. And yet, sixteen times during the past twenty-three months the first pages of our newspapers have carried the grim story of the most recent fatal explosion. I submit that if it is necessary on this subject to have compulsory legislation in this country, it cannot come too soon.

As Director Bain of the United States Bureau of Mines has publicly stated: "The great explosions should not be considered to be normal occupational accidents. Investigations carried on by the Bureau of Mines for more than ten years have demonstrated beyond question of doubt that such spreading of explosions by coal dust can be prevented. Responsibility for this rests upon the mine managements.... Explosions can and must be prevented."

Our third proposal is:

III. Reward careful employers and penalize the less scrupulous, by the universal adoption of schedule rating for insurance under accident compensation laws, with a further graduated penalty for cases of willful failure to put into effect legal safety regulations.

Already schedule rating has demonstrated its value in inducing the employer to reduce hazards as a method of reducing his insurance premium. The Association for Labor Legislation has long been impressed with this development in workmen's accident insurance, and the safety committee likewise notes its bearing upon mine safety. By this means, says the committee, "the direct cost of a mine with low safety standards is brought home to the operator. The system has proven a real safety incentive."

In some mining States also there is a special penalty provided of from 15 to 50 per cent additional compensation to the injured worker where it is clear that the employer was guilty of serious or willful misconduct. The same penalty works inversely upon the injured workman in case he has offended, and he then loses a part of his accident compensation. In several States, with reference to certain other labor law violations, double or even triple compensation is assessed directly upon the offending employer.

Familiarity with danger has always bred contempt for it among workers in extra-hazardous occupations, and the coal miners need to feel their increasing responsibility to exercise every practicable safety precaution. But it is nonsense to say — as one editor does and as certain propagandists would have the public believe — that "the coal miner of this generation is in danger only through carelessness, his own or that of a fellow worker." We find refutation of such an assertion right at hand in one of the recent mine disasters — that at the Glen Rogers mine in West Virginia, November 6, where 27 miners were killed in an explosion. It has been determined that the tragedy was caused by a spark from the commutator brushes of a drill. "Disregard of the vital requirements of the mining law on the part of the company's representative in allowing the use of dangerous electric drill not approved by the mining department," was the finding of the coroner's jury.

The experts of the Coal Commission stress the importance of official inspection in influencing operating methods and working conditions. They report that those interviewed in many States believed that an increase in compensation benefits would result in a marked decrease in accidents, and they conclude that mining laws and compensation laws are the two great direct factors for mine safety.

The fourth proposal is for:

IV. An adequate mine inspection staff selected upon a merit basis of training and experience, fairly paid for reasonably long tenure of office, and protected from partisan interference whether political or industrial.

This proposal is in harmony with the best practical experience in factory safety as well as in accident prevention in mines. Its importance deserves elaboration, but its merits are well understood, and there is opportunity here only to refer to the fact that the coal safety committee also recommends it.

"For the country in general coal mining would to-day be a better and safer industry," the experts say in their report, "were inspectors in every State chosen through strict examination in principles and practices of mining, at a salary sufficient to hold high-grade men, and freed from any influence save those listed in the laws and that of their superior officer, and expectant of holding office until retired by natural causes."

Because much of the work is independent of state boundaries and constitutes a national problem, it can best be undertaken under national auspices.

"The (federal) Bureau of Mines, through its investigations, discoveries and recommendations," the Coal Commission investigators find, "has become the authority and leaven for mine safety work in this country."

A million dollars has been spent in developing and equipping, near Pittsburgh, an experimental mine where practical work on underground safety can be carried out by the federal bureau.

"It shall be the province and duty of said bureau," decreed Congress in establishing it, "to make diligent investigation of the methods of mining, especially in relation to the safety of mines and the appliances best adapted to prevent accidents."

But Congress stopped there without giving the bureau the necessary authority.

"The suggestion has been made," now reports the safety committee, "that the engineers and officials of the Bureau of Mines should have the right of entry to a mine, for the purpose of investigating mine accidents, and that their reports should be made public or delivered to the operator through the state department of mines. At present the bureau enters a mine on permission of the operator. The new thought is that an independent report on accident or disaster, by an agency not affected locally, would be beneficial to operators and to miners, and of service to the mining department of the State. . . . At least it would be valuable could the federal bureau coöperate with the state mining departments, by furnishing them confidential copies of reports on conditions investigated within their police jurisdiction."

Despite splendid work by this federal investigation bureau, and by a few of the state bureaus, there is still "little coördination in methods and technique of investigation and inspection of mines for safety." It is believed therefore that to a national agency should be given authority to improve and make more uniform the character and technique of mine inspection "and the improvement and adoption of more uniform safety standards underground." It is interesting to note that our federal experts already have up-to-date operating regulations in effect for the coal mines, now more than one hundred in number, owned by the United States Government and operated under lease on the public lands.

Any one familiar with the progress toward centralization in the administration of mine safety measures in recent years in other countries will, upon comparing their results with the American mine accident record, understand the growth of this sentiment.

Finally, we submit as the fifth proposal:

V. Greater public authority, federal and state, to procure and disseminate information, and to establish and maintain on a uniform basis reasonable minimum standards of safety.

In 1911, Dr. John Randolph Haynes, following his inquiry into coal-mine safety in America and abroad, addressed the annual meeting of the American Association for Labor Legislation on this subject. With eloquence and conviction he pictured the needless hazards in American mines. "Experience has shown at a frightful cost," he then said, "that these things can not be left to the volition of the operator or the miner or to the regulation of the individual States." He then urged that a federal enforcing agency, with powers like that of the Interstate Commerce Commission, be set up. "Shall we go on in this country," he asked, "clinging to our inefficient system of state regulation of an industry that is essentially interstate in character until we have uselessly sacrificed the lives of tens of thousands more poor miners, before we stop this slaughter under the only practical system of safety — the federal regulation of the mines?"

Twelve years later we can give part of the answer. We are again counting the dead.

If we really want to prevent this needless loss of human life the lawyers will find a way for us to act nationally, said Dr. Haynes in 1911.

Now comes, in 1923, a conservative federal commission — which after spending three quarters of a million dollars looking into the coal situation — notes that "coal is not primarily a commodity, it is a service"; the production and transportation of coal constitute a single service"; "coal is clothed with a public interest." And there follows logically a general proposal by this federal commission for the creation of a coal division in the Interstate Commerce Commission.

There is still difference of opinion among lawyers as to the possibility of securing effective results through federal action without a federal constitutional amendment. Three principal proposals are now being discussed.

(1) Shall we prepare a standard safety code for uniform state legislation? Upon this task a committee has been working and some further improvements can doubtless be made.

(2) Shall we provide for greater coöperation between the federal and state bureaus by means of federal-state financial aid as in the rehabilitation of industrial cripples? There are evident possibilities in such action. Likewise much local jealousy to be overcome.

(3) Shall we go directly for a federal constitutional amendment authorizing the establishment of national minimum standards of safety? Such amendment, which could be made only after a long campaign of education and favorable action by three fourths of the State, is nevertheless thought necessary by some who have studied the problem most carefully.

But by whatever additional public authority a national minimum of safety is finally assured, there will of course be not less but greater opportunity for the mine departments of our individual States to function effectively in the great work they have to do. Authoritative federal and state coöperation, with the continuous encouragement and assistance of employers, miners, and engineers, is urgently needed.

4. Workmen's Compensation under the Common Law[1]

The common law doctrine. Let us consider the principles which, only a quarter century ago, determined the right of a workman to recover compensation from his employer. Those principles still apply, with some modification, in all the States of the United States, and have but recently been discarded in part by the federal Government itself. The elementary theory of "the law of negligence," as it is usually called, in its relation to the liability of employers for financial loss to workmen and their families, was originally the same in all civilized countries. The development of the law of liability has not been identical in every country, but nowhere, probably, has the principle been pushed so far as in the United States. The doctrine has, however, been modified somewhat by decisions of the courts and by act of our legislatures.

The underlying principle of the law of negligence is that *the*

[1] Adapted from *Workingmen's Insurance in Europe*, Frankel and Dawson, pp. 5–7. The Russell Sage Foundation, publishers.

employer is liable only in case he is at fault; that is, *he must have been neglectful in some respect and this negligence must have been the proximate and sole cause of the accident.* In that case it declares that he alone must bear the financial burden of compensation.

Liability of the employer for his own negligence is qualified as follows:

First, it is not enough that he was the chief cause.

If the employee himself has been negligent and if this in any degree contributed to the accident, the employer is not held. This is known as the principle of "contributory negligence." The idea is that the courts, not being able to separate results flowing from these two causes and to determine how much was due to one and how much to the other, will refuse to grant compensation if the employee's negligence contributed to the accident even though only in a slight degree.

Second, the accident must not have been a consequence of the ordinary risks of the occupation.

If it can be shown or the conclusion fairly be deducted that the employee assumed this particular risk as a condition of his contract of employment, or as the ordinary risk of his occupation of which he knew or was bound to know, the employer is not held. If the employee was aware that certain danger existed and notwithstanding continued to work, this action on his part would bar recovery. As a corollary to this, the courts have held very generally that the employee must be presumed to know what are the ordinary dangers of his occupation, and even what are the unusual dangers connected with continuing to perform the duties of that occupation, when the place where it is carried on, or the machinery or tools with which it is carried on, are defective.

This is called the principle of "assumption of risk." Some courts have gone so far as to hold that, even though the employer is required by law to keep the machinery, tools, and the place in which the work is done in a certain condition of safety, and that although by failing to do so he has rendered himself liable to a penalty, the workman, notwithstanding, will not be able to recover if he has known of these defects and has nevertheless continued to work. The same courts have also held that the fact that he has called the defects to the attention of his employer and asked that they be remedied, will not render the employer liable if the workman, notwithstanding that the defects have not been remedied, continues to work. In fact, calling the defects to the attention of others prejudices his claim in that it is proof positive that he knows of them.

Third, the accident must have been the result of the employer's own negligence and not that of another employee or employees.

If the workman has been injured because one or more of the employees working with him were negligent, the employer will not be held. This proceeds from the idea that each workman whose negligence has caused the injury should himself be held financially responsible; and since in most cases he is in fact financially irresponsible and could not respond to a judgment, the result of the application of this rule is that the persons injured are not compensated at all. This is directly contrary to the rule which applies when the injury is to one not an employee; in that case the employer, under the general doctrine of principal and agent, is held liable.

The principle stated above is known in practice as the "fellow-servant" rule. It has been carried so far by some courts that it is difficult to see how a corporation employer could be held responsible at all, no matter what officer or other employee was negligent. Even an officer is an agent or employee, and therefore a fellow-servant with all other employees, although the courts have usually not so held. Except in the case of executive officers, however, the rule has been applied so sweepingly that, for instance, a scrubwoman washing out railway coaches might be held to be a fellow-servant with the superintendent of the road, and, therefore, without a good claim against the company for negligence attributable to him.

The "fellow-servant" rule grew up in the courts out of the simplicity of the common law, which in its origin did not know employers and employees in the modern industrial or commercial sense, but only "masters" and "servants." The law did not hold the master liable, even on the ground of negligence. It certainly would have refused to require him to compensate one servant for the negligence of another. This principle manifestly has little or no suitability for the uses of a commercial and highly organized industrial community, in which much the larger part of the services performed by employees is not for the direct enjoyment of the employer but is part of the aggregate cost of products or services sold by him to the public at a price to cover all the costs. In recent years the "fellow-servant" rule has been much relaxed, first by the courts and later by legislatures. In many States an employee who supervises the work and controls the workman is held to be a "vice-principal" and to represent the employer, so that his negligence is treated as if it were the negligence of the employer.

Under the rules of law just outlined, a very large proportion of the accidents which occur in the industries of the country go uncompensated. In some cases, on the other hand, the employer is held for substantial amounts, and occasionally very large verdicts are recovered, but in only a small percentage of the cases is the compensation adequate.

5. Workmen's Compensation Laws in the United States [1]

Changing viewpoints. We have seen how the common law doctrine of employer's liability provided the employer with such defenses against suit by the injured workman as to render the recovery of damages an extremely hazardous venture. One of these defenses was the "fellow-servant" rule, by which it was held that some other workman, not the employer, was responsible for the injury. Since most employees nowadays must work in large groups, this was very often the case, and the workman lost his suit. Another defense of the employers was "contributory negligence" which meant that the victim of the accident had brought it on himself by some want of care, however slight. Finally, the employer might claim immunity under the principle of "assumption of risk." According to this principle the workman, by accepting employment, took upon himself all the customary hazards of the occupation, and also any extraordinary risk of which he became aware, but in spite of which he continued working. Moreover, employers usually insured their liability with casualty insurance companies, which maintained strong batteries of expert legal talent for defeating workmen's claims.

[1] This article is in part an adaptation of chapter seven of *Labor Problems and Labor Legislation*, a pamphlet written in 1922 by John B. Andrews, Ph.D., and published by the American Association for Labor Legislation, of which Dr. Andrews is Secretary.

Investigations showed that of every $100 paid by employers in liability premiums, only about $28 ever reached the claimants, and so late that the worst of the need was past.

This entire mass of legal procedure was based upon a false point of view toward the problem of industrial accident. The attempt was primarily to fix the *blame* for the injury upon one or the other of parties to the suit and to apply the penalty of money damages to the employer as a punishment for proved culpability on his part. Where the employer could escape the blame, the workman was left to bear the suffering and financial loss involved in the injury on the grounds that he — or, at least, some other workman — was morally at fault. But no sound social policy can grow out of this method of judging industrial accidents on grounds of moral right or wrong. A certain minimum amount of accident is an inevitable product of modern high-speed industrial methods, and must be viewed as one of the necessary costs of producing goods under our present system. In a vast number of cases, no one is personally at fault. Correctly considered, the award of damages to the injured workman is not a punishment; but a payment for one of the costs of production, exacted, in the first instance, from the employer in the expectation that he will reimburse himself through the sale price of his goods.

Compensation acts in the United States. Rising dissatisfaction with earlier methods resulted in the American movement for workmen's compensation legislation similar to that which was already in force in some European countries for decades. Two pioneer statutes were declared unconstitutional, but in 1909 the first state compensation act to go into permanent effect was secured in New Jersey. In the period 1911–22 the legislation spread to forty-five States and territories, and the United States Government adopted a model act covering its own half million civilian employees. The validity of these laws has now been established beyond question by favorable decisions of the Supreme Court. They cover the entire area of the United States, with the exception of the States of Arkansas, Mississippi, Florida, North and South Carolina, together with the territories of Alaska, Hawaii, and Porto Rico.

The direct aim of these laws is twofold — to restore the injured man to industry as completely and quickly as possible, and to provide for the support of the family during the period of disability. Most American laws provide for medical care, but many hedge it in with limits ranging from one week to ninety days in time or from $25 to $250 in amount. To lighten the administrative burden and to discourage men from "laying off" unduly for minor injuries, most laws set a "waiting period" of from three days to two weeks during which no compensation is paid. As only about 25 per cent of accidents requiring medical care cause disability for more than two weeks, it is clear that the latter period is too long. For death and disability, the best laws, such as those of New York and Ohio, award 66⅔ per cent of wages within certain limits. Death benefits in good laws are paid until the widow remarries or dies, and disability benefits during the disability even if it be lifelong. For partial disability several sliding scales have been devised to apportion the compensation to the degree of incapacity. Important provisions in most of the acts require employers to insure their risk, sometimes in a state fund, in order to guarantee benefits to the injured, and provide for supervisory administration by a state bureau or commission. A beginning has also been made in providing re-education or "rehabilitation" for men who sustain permanent injuries which interfere with their continuing in their old occupations.

In about a dozen laws, including the Federal Employees' Act, occupational diseases are covered. It has been found that so doing staves off hardship in some meritorious cases, and increases the cost of the act only 1 or 2 per cent.

Effects of the laws. An incidental, though highly important, effect of these acts has been to decrease the number of industrial accidents. Opponents of this line of state policy were wont to predict that relieving the workman from the effects of carelessness would necessarily end in a multiplication of injuries. Accident has been proved to be a thoroughly "insurable risk." The so-called "moral hazard" is negligible. It has been found that workmen will not deliberately injure themselves for the purpose of gaining the indemnity, and that they cannot effectively feign injury where it does not exist. On the other hand, it has been found that the number of accidents can be reduced only through the medium of the employer. A workman's compensation law, applying in equal terms to all competitors in a given industry, arouses the profit motive of each employer to reduce to a minimum the tale of accidents in his particular enterprise, and thus to gain a saving of cost in comparison with his less alert competitors. Private and public funds have encouraged this effort by proportioning the premium charges to the accident experience of the employer who is insuring himself against liability for compensation.

The practical result of this policy of making it profitable to the employer to conserve the lives and limbs of the industrial wage-earners has been almost phenomenal. "If society and industry and the individual," said Louis D. Brandeis, in 1911, before he became a member of the Supreme Court, "were made to pay from day to day the actual cost of sickness, accident, invalidity, premature death, or premature old age consequent upon excessive hours of labor, of unhygienic conditions of work, or unnecessary risk, and of irregularity of employment, those evils would be rapidly reduced." The truth of this statement has been established beyond all question in the field of industrial accident. In one large factory after the passage of the compensation act the rate of accident fell progressively by twenty per cent during the first two years, fifty per cent at the end of the fifth year, until, after ten years' experience, the average number of accidents was only one quarter of the old experience. In another large plant in New York State, adjustment to the compensation law has resulted in an accident rate which is scarcely one fifth of that which obtained before the law was passed. These are extreme cases; but the same tendency is noticeable wherever the policy of compensation for accident is enforced. It is needless to say that these results represent an unalloyed gain for society which, of itself, justifies the policy.

The ideal law. Following is a description of an ideal workman's compensation act, as drawn up by the American Association of Labor Legislation: [1]

In the opinion of the American Association for Labor Legislation the following features are essential to satisfactory workmen's compensation laws:

I. SCALE OF COMPENSATION. Assuming machinery to insure the prompt payment of the compensation required by law, the scale

[1] See *Standards of Workmen's Compensation Laws*, published by the American Association for Labor Legislation, January 1, 1924.

of payments is the most important feature of the system. The strongest argument for compensation to all injured workmen or to their dependents is that shortened lives and maimed limbs due to industrial injuries are just as much expenses of production, which should be met by those conducting industry for their own profit, as are used-up raw materials or worn-out tools and machinery. The whole expense of losses to capital is necessarily borne by the employer. The whole expense of the personal losses due to injuries is the loss in wages sustained and the expenses for medical care during incapacity. The only logical reason for not imposing, through the employers, this entire expense on every industry that occasions it, is that injured workers must not be deprived of a motive for returning to work and to independent self-support as soon as they are able to do so. The compensation act, therefore, should provide for the expense of all necessary medical attendance and for the payment of such a proportion of wages to the victim of the injury during his incapacity, or to his dependents if he be killed, as will provide for the resulting needs and yet not encourage malingering. The following scale is believed to conform to these requirements and to be the lowest that should be inserted in any compensation law.

a. Medical attendance. Aside from humanitarian considerations the employer should, in the interest of economy and efficiency, be required to furnish all necessary medical, surgical and hospital services and supplies as determined by the Accident Board.

b. Waiting period. No compensation should be paid for a definite period — to be not less than three nor more than seven days — at the beginning of disability.

c. Compensation for total disability. The disabled workman should receive during disability 66⅔ per cent of wages; compensation not to be more than $25 or less than $8 a week, unless his wages are less than $8 a week in which case compensation should be the full amount of wages. If he is a minor, he should, after reaching twenty-one, receive 66⅔ per cent of the wages of able-bodied men in the occupation group to which he belonged.

d. Compensation for partial disability. The workman who

is only partially disabled should receive a percentage of his wages, proportioned to the degree of physical disability (taking into account age and occupation), and subject to re-adjustment only on account of changes in extent of disability; compensation not to exceed $25 a week, with provisions for minors, and for workmen earning less than $8, similar to those in the case of total disability. Awards for permanent partial disability should be in addition to total disability compensation paid during the healing period.

e. Compensation for death.

(1) Funeral expenses. The employer should be required to pay a sum not exceeding $150 for funeral expenses, in addition to any other compensation.

(2) Compensation for widow. If living with the decedent at the time of his death, or if dependent, the widow should be granted 35 per cent of his wages until her death or remarriage, with a lump sum on remarriage equal to two years' compensation.

(3) Compensation for widower. If living with the decedent at the time of her death and dependent upon her support, the widower should receive 35 per cent of her wages, or a proportionate amount if his dependency is only partial, to be paid until his death or remarriage.

(4) Compensation for widow or widower and children. In addition to the compensation provided for the widow and widower, 15 per cent should be allowed for each child under eighteen, not to exceed a total of 66⅔ per cent for the widow or widower and children. Compensation on account of a child should cease when it dies, marries or reaches the age of eighteen.

(5) Compensation to children if there be no widow or widower. In case children are left without any surviving parent 25 per cent should be paid for one child under eighteen, and 15 per cent for each additional such child, to be divided among such children share and share alike, not exceeding a total of 66⅔ per cent. Compensation on account of any such child should cease when it dies, marries or reaches the age of eighteen.

(6) Compensation to parents, brothers, sisters, grand-

children and grandparents if dependent. For such classes of dependents 25 per cent should be paid for one wholly dependent, and 15 per cent additional for each additional person wholly dependent, divided among such wholly dependent persons share and share alike, and a proportionate amount (to be determined by the Accident Board) if dependency is only partial, to be divided among the persons wholly or partially dependent according to the degree of dependency as determined by the Accident Board. These percentages should be paid in cases where there is no widow, widower, or child. In other cases members of this class should receive as much of these percentages as, when added to the total percentage payable to the widow or widower or child, will not exceed a total of 66⅔ per cent. Compensation to members of this class should be paid only during dependency.

(7) Compensation for Alien Non-Resident Dependents. Aliens should be placed on the same footing as other dependents.

(8) Maximum and Minimum Compensation for Death. The wages on which death compensation is based should be taken to be not more than $37.50 per week nor less than $12 per week; but the total amount of the weekly compensation should not be more than the actual wages.

f. Commutation of periodical compensation payments. If the beneficiary is or is about to become a non-resident of the United States, or if the monthly payments to the beneficiary are less than $5 a month, or if the Accident Board determines that it would be to the best interests of the beneficiary, the employer should be permitted to discharge his liability for future payments by the immediate payment of a lump sum equal to the value of all the future payments computed at 4 per cent true discount, compounded annually. For this purpose the expectancy of life should be determined according to a suitable mortality table, and the probability of the happening of any contingency such as marriage or the termination of disability, affecting the amount or duration of the compensation, should be disregarded.

II. EMPLOYMENTS TO BE INCLUDED. It is believed that sufficient progress has now been made in public education on the problem, and in the development of efficient and economical machinery for insuring the employer against his compensation liability, to justify the inclusion in the system of all employments. The only exception which should be made is of casual employees in the service of employers who have only such employees and who, therefore, cannot fairly be required to carry compensation insurance policies. Such policies, on payment of a small additional premium, are now drawn so as to embrace casual as well as regular employees. No serious burden is, therefore, entailed on employers, even of domestic servants, in making them liable to pay compensation to casual employees.

III. INJURIES TO BE INCLUDED. Compensation should be provided for all personal injuries in the course of employment, and death resulting therefrom within six years, but no compensation should be allowed where the injury is occasioned by the willful intention of the employee to bring about the injury or death of himself or of another. The act should embrace occupational diseases which, when contracted in the course of employment, should be considered personal injuries for which compensation is payable.

IV. OTHER REMEDIES THAN THOSE PROVIDED BY THE COMPENSATION ACT. One of the weightiest arguments against the outworn system of employers' liability is that it causes vast sums to be frittered away in lawsuits that should be used in caring for the victims of accidents. To avoid this waste the compensation provided by the Act should be THE EXCLUSIVE REMEDY. If the employer has been guilty of personal negligence, even going to the point of violating a safety statute, his punishment should be through a special action prosecuted by the state factory inspection bureau.

Likewise, if he has failed to insure, he should be penalized by being made subject to a penal action prosecuted by the accident board and by increasing his liability for compensation.

V. SECURITY FOR THE PAYMENT OF COMPENSATION AWARDS. The supreme tests of a compensation system are, first, the incentive provided for reducing accidents to the utmost, and, second, the promptness and certainty with which compensation claims are met. The strongest incentive toward prevention results from imposing the whole expense of compensation upon the employer. The irregularity and uncertainty of accidents, however, make this policy inexpedient for small employers with limited financial resources. Security can only be attained through some system of insurance. Employers should, therefore, be required to insure their compensation liability.

In accordance with the plans of insurance at present provided for, employers may either:

1. Maintain their own insurance fund subject to the approval of the Accident Board or other administrative authority;
2. Insure in a Mutual Association authorized to insure compensation liability;
3. Insure in a State Insurance Fund managed by the Accident Board upon the same principles and subject to the same general requirements as those governing Mutual Insurance Associations;
4. Insure in a commercial company, such companies to be subjected to the most rigid regulation to guard against insolvency, to insure just settlement of claims, to prevent wasteful practices and exorbitant rates, and to eliminate unfair competitive methods.

VI. Organization of Accident Board. It is essential to the successful operation of the compensation system that an Accident Board be created. This board should consist of three or five members appointed by the Governor with the consent of the Senate. The board should have power to employ necessary assistants. Its members should be required to devote their entire time to its work and should not be permitted to carry on any other business or profession for profit. The entire cost of administration of the Accident Board, including the administrative expenses of establishing the State Insurance Fund managed by the Accident Board, should be paid out of an appropriation made by the State.

VII. Procedure for Settlement of Compensation Claims. Provision should be made for the determination of all claims for compensation, either by the Accident Board, or, if the number of claims be large, by one member of the board or an authorized deputy. A decision by a member or deputy should be conclusive, unless appeal therefrom is taken to the entire Accident Board within a specified time. The Accident Board's disposition of the case should be final and conclusive unless appeal therefrom is taken within a specified time. Appeals from decrees of the Accident Board should not be allowed, except on questions of law, and should be carried direct to the highest court.

VIII. Reports of Accidents. The bill should direct the administrative board to use the Standard Accident Reporting Blank of the American Association of Labor Legislation, now in use for about half the industrial population of the country, requiring full and accurate reports of all industrial accidents as a basis for computation of future industrial accident rates and for future safety regulations to decrease or prevent accidents.

IX. Rehabilitation. Restored earning power is of more importance than distress relieved. The administrative board should therefore be authorized to encourage, coöperate with, or conduct enterprises for the re-education and rehabilitation of injured persons.

Thirty-six States already make provision for aiding industrial cripples to secure re-training, re-education or re-employment.

PART TWO
THE ORGANIZED LABOR MOVEMENT

CHAPTER VIII

DEVELOPMENT OF ORGANIZED LABOR

1. Background of the Labor Movement

Introduction. The preceding pages of this book have been devoted to analyzing certain of the life problems of the industrial worker. It has been shown that his normal experience is a series of struggles with conditions and forces which are, in large measure, natural features of the kind of economic order which has emerged from the Industrial Revolution. Unemployment, low wages, accident and disease — hazards which threaten without warning either to cut him off from the source of life, or to undermine his standard of living, or to destroy his productive capacity — are commonplace incidents in the life of the propertyless man. They are evils which he is, on the whole, powerless to remove or control so long as he relies upon his compeers as an individual in a competitive order. Our purpose in presenting these specific problems at the beginning of our study has been to make it clear that they form the background of the wage-earner's outlook on life and mould his life policy. Many aspects of the organized labor movement can be understood only in the light of this study of the problems of the industrial wage-earner.

But the labor movement is not solely a reaction to the evil influences of a life in industry. It is also an attempt to mobilize the competitive forces of our society to the betterment of the conditions of propertyless men and women. In a system of uncontrolled individual enterprise, material prosperity depends upon bargaining power, and this upon the possession of a position of advantage in relation to the other members of the social group. It has been demonstrated over and over again in the business world that not necessarily he who serves most, but he who is in position to take utmost advantage of the necessities of his fellow men, prospers most abundantly. Power and riches flow to those who control the supply of a good which, being in wide demand, is scarce. A strategic position in relation to the market makes for competitive power. We shall see in due course how the working classes of society have learned this truth about our competitive society and are attempting to turn it to their advantage. Many of the practices and policies of labor are to be explained not as adjustments to the hazards of life, but as devices by means of which to win for the workingman this position of competitive advantage whose importance all men of business appreciate.

The major purpose of this study is to throw light upon that conflict now going on in society to which we give the name, "The Labor Problem." As has been said, this conflict is the outward manifestation of a serious maladjustment within our order, a rebellion against certain of our established institutions, or against that group which has dominated in the functioning of these institutions. The conflict is waged chiefly in the field of industrial relations where the employer and employee meet in bargaining; but its effects spread throughout the entire range of society and are felt by all who are interested in the productive efficiency or public security of the social order — that is to say, by most of us. Since it is in the organized labor movement, with its theories and methods, its ideals, its economic and social programs, that we meet the problem in its most insistent form, the following pages will be given up to a description of this movement and its consequences. In order, however, to retain the right perspective in viewing the Labor Problem, we must avoid the error of believing that it is limited to the activities of the trade union. In the broadest sense, all industrial workers, whether unionized or not, are so affected by the labor problems we have been studying that they adopt very similar attitudes toward the business world and their relations with it. The organized labor movement is unique only in that it openly avows policies and gives emphatic expression to purposes which are congenial to the thought life of the great mass of wage-earners.

Natural causes of the labor movement. Two things must be made clear at the outset of our study of organized labor. In the first place, we must see that the whole movement is the product of natural causation. No useful knowledge can be gained about this great modern development, nor can any sound judgment be passed on its social utility, if we assume that it is the artificial creation of a few leaders, or an expression of the natural perversity or original sin of mankind. That these viewpoints are unsound is demonstrated by the extent to which the movement has spread over the modern world, following the path of the Industrial Revolution. The appearance of trade-unionism in any country is historically connected with the industrialization of that country. Springing up first in England, it arose independently in each of the countries of Europe, in the United States, and in every other country where the factory had established itself. In our own day it has attained formidable proportions in Japan, though that country in its feudal state sixty years ago was entirely free from it. We may also note its beginnings in India and Egypt and in every country where the industrial system of the West is gaining a foothold. The truth is that the wage-earners of all lands and cultures, when confronted with the hazards of a life in modern industry, spontaneously resort to some form of collective action to protect their interests.

No uniform type. Since the organized labor movement has this natural origin, we must not expect to find great uniformity between the different parts of the movement either as regards form of organization, final goals and ideals, or methods and tactics. It has not been built according to a preconceived plan, nor are its programs drawn to meet the specifications of doctrinaire theory. The simplest way to account for it is to say that the wage-earner in modern society is frightened by certain aspects of his life and embittered by others, and is experimenting, through the process of trial and error with various devices which he thinks may give him security or win him justice. Accordingly, the union movement takes different forms at different times; old policies are discarded as they prove ineffective and new ones are adopted. These variations appear also at any given time; in the United States at the present time, for example, we have many different structural forms of unions which differ in their policies from cautious conservatism to ultra-radicalism.

The common basis. Underlying these variations of structure and method, however, we find a broad principle which is common to all but the spurious forms of labor-unionism. The economic structure of society as it emerged from the Industrial Revolution, and before it had felt the modifying influence of the organized labor movement and other modern tendencies of similar import, was an order dominated by private initiative — by the principle of "free competition" or "free enterprise." The spur of private gain or advantage was almost the sole directing force in industry, determining the kinds and quantities of goods provided for the satisfaction of human wants, the forms of organization which industry would adopt, the technical methods used in production, the relations between the individuals coöperating in carrying through a productive process, and the rewards accruing to these coöperating factors. Along with this principle of free enterprise went certain tenets regarding the rights of private property. Within broad limits, the owner was free to "do what he willed with his own." A business or productive undertaking in its entirety was held to be the property of those who supplied it with capital; the owners' interest was not merely dominant in the councils of the enterprise — it monopolized authority to the exclusion of all other interests. It was expected that a similar condition of individual initiative and profit-seeking would characterize the activities of the propertyless members of society, those compelled to draw their living from wage labor; they were to compete with each other as individuals in seeking employment, in agreeing to accept a given rate of wages, and in the zeal with which they rendered service to their employer. We have employed the past tense in drawing this rough sketch of laissez-faire society only because it has passed its zenith and has entered, in our day, upon a process of compromise and modification which is gradually remodeling the social order. Despite these qualifications, however, free enterprise with all of its implications remains the dominant principle in modern industry; its place in shaping our philosophy of rights and duties and, especially, in moulding the law which governs human relationships in the business world is still supreme.

Clash with individualism. Now, the principle which underlies the organized labor movement in all of its branches is in conflict with this fundamental doctrine of a laissez-faire society. This is the second truth which we must grasp before attempting a study of organized labor. No trade union can be formed without rejecting the principle of free competition — at least in so far as it applies to the activities of those who do the work of the world. In its place, as a dominant motive, the union substitutes the principle of conscious, deliberate coöperation. It is essential to the purposes of organized labor that the workers in industry cease to contend with each other for individual advantage and unite their efforts in the pursuit of *group* interests and of goals deliberately chosen by the combined intelligence of the group. Membership in a union means, for the individual, discipline, a surrender of self-interest, conformity to the standards of his fellows.

As the organized labor movement grows in power and importance in the industrial system of any country, this clash of principle becomes apparent. The collective agreement takes the place of the individual wage contract; the rate of wages, the length of the working-day, the output of the worker in a given time, are matters to be decided with reference to the predetermined standards of the union of workers, not left to the free play of competitive forces. The union soon discovers that its purposes cannot make headway in an industrial order essentially competitive as long as the employer's monopoly on authority is left undisturbed. Then begins a gradual encroachment on the powers which, traditionally, have been bestowed on the owner of capital or the representative of the owner. The employer's right to "hire and fire," to introduce changes in the technique of production, to regulate with a free hand the volume of output and the conditions under which his employees will work, are challenged on the ground that they conflict with the chosen goal or the union, or interfere with its effort to maintain the coöperative spirit among its members.

It is this conflict of principle which gives us the Labor Problem in the broad social significance of the term. In the studies of organized labor which follow, we shall see the coöperative principle embodied in the structure of the labor union, in its program, its methods of bargaining, the means by which it carries on industrial warfare. We shall see how their efforts to give effect to this principle bring the organized workers into conflict with those interests favorable to the maintenance of free competition in industry and of the traditional rights of private property — a conflict involving a clash with the law of the land as interpreted by the courts. In many cases, it will be evident that neither the leaders nor the members of the union are aware of the social implications of their movement; in others, the union will be found to have accepted these implications and to be striving for the ultimate reorganization of the industrial structure along coöperative lines.

2. Origin of the Labor Movement [1]

Modern industrial society. In a very general and abstract sense there is such a thing as the labor problem, which may be defined as the problem of improving the conditions of employment of the wage-earning classes. Of course, this simplicity of definition is largely verbal. There is no one labor problem whose solution would carry with it the settlement of all others; and we shall always have labor problems so long as there are conditions of employment capable of improvement. The consequence is that when we begin to study the problem it divides up into a number of evils and abuses like sweating and child labor, for each of which in turn a number of practical remedies are in use or under active consideration. It is true, nevertheless, that most of the important labor problems have their roots in three or four great social institutions. These institutions it is desirable to keep firmly in mind, not only because of their exceptional importance, but in order that the somewhat overwhelming mass of details cited in the following chapters may be given a certain unity of

[1] From *Labor Problems*, chap. I, by Adams and Sumner. Copyright, by The Macmillan Company. Reprinted by permission.

meaning and import, without which they become unintelligible and wearisome.

First of all, naturally, is the wage system itself. If our industrial order rested either upon a basis of slavery or upon one of socialism the problem would be entirely different. Under those systems, if successfully operated, the laborer would be assured a place to work and a minimum, at least, of food, clothes and shelter. Under the wage system, on the other hand, the laborer takes upon himself the responsibility of securing work and of supporting himself and family. More important still, he must do this by selling his services to the great masters of industry. He has become not only a producer, but a merchant as well. He must acquire a certain strength or skill, and then sell it to the best advantage. Slowly and gradually institutions are perfected to strengthen his weakness and ignorance in this bargaining with the employer. Society creates customs which harden into standards of life or comfort, and assist the laborer to bargain more effectually. The laborers themselves combine in trade unions, by which these standards are more consciously fixed and more tenaciously maintained; and in time the laborer begins to bargain through agents — walking delegates. Underlying all the problems which will be discussed, however, is this system which casts upon the laborer the responsibility for his own maintenance, which makes him merchant as well as producer, and compels him to take his chances and stake his welfare upon successful bargaining in the labor market.

Second in order, and not less important than the wage system in accounting for the peculiar nature of the problem, is the highly capitalized form of modern industry. The introduction of the capitalistic system has been followed by great and unmistakable progress in many ways, such as a general increase in wages and a rapid elevation of the standards of life and comfort. These evidences of progress are discussed in some detail in the last chapter. At this point we desire to emphasize those more unpleasant characteristics of the present industrial system which aggravate and intensify the labor problem.

To work successfully to-day in most lines of industry, men must own or control a large capital, which is usually embodied in extensive, complex mechanical plants, and the plan under which production is carried on within these plants is usually called "the factory system." The factory system itself is directly responsible in a large degree for many labor problems — child labor, industrial accidents, factory regulation, the unemployment resulting from the invention of labor-saving machinery, and other evils. It is indirectly responsible, however, for more and sterner problems than these.

The great majority of men do not possess the abilities or the opportunities to secure the large capital necessary for the successful conduct of a modern business. For the masses, indeed, it is true and increasingly true, that once a wage-earner always a wage-earner. This permanency of status makes the labor problem in one respect a class struggle. The laborer feels that he is permanently held within a class whose interests are, in part, antagonistic to those of the employers with whom he bargains and higgles over wages. Fortunately or unfortunately, too, industry becomes more highly capitalized as time passes, making it increasingly difficult for men to acquire industrial independence, and steadily reducing the proportionate number of those who can set up establishments of their own. To some it seems that the complexity of industry has outrun human ability, leaving a smaller and smaller proportion of men who are fitted to direct and control. Others explain the phenomenon by asserting that, owing to a mechanical tendency towards centralization of business, a decreasing proportion of men have the exceptional means and opportunities to rise to industrial independence. Whatever the explanation, there can be no doubt of the fact that the ultimate control of industry is passing into relatively fewer and fewer hands, with the result that the power and wealth of the few who do reach the top are so enormously swelled that they would threaten — if misused — the purity and stability of the government itself. The labor problem is thus intensified by a grave social problem, arising from the strikingly unequal distribution of wealth.

These, then, are what may be called the fundamental factors of the modern labor problem — the wage system, the permanent status of the wage-earning class, the factory system — with all which that implies — and the extreme concentration and control of wealth in the hands of a very small proportion of the population. It is absolutely necessary to keep these fundamental conditions firmly in mind; but it is just as necessary to remember that, permanent as such institutions may seem, they are but steps or stages in a centuried process of evolution, whose past unfolding is as profoundly significant as its future course is fascinating and mysterious. Let us glance briefly at the genesis of the wage system and modern capitalism, the two pillars of the present industrial system.

Evolution of wage labor. Almost the first laboring class that historical records disclose was composed of slaves. In the development of human society from savagery to civilization there came a time when a comparatively sedentary agricultural life suggested a possible economy in the disposition of captives, by the substitution of slavery for slaughter and cannibalism. Thus it happens that in all the great militant nations of the world, the laboring population has passed through the stages of slavery and serfdom. At Athens, for instance, in 309 B.C. — though the statistics have been questioned by some authorities — we are told that there were 400,000 slaves in a total population of 431,000. In Ægina at the time of Alexander the Great, according to Aristotle, there were 470,000 slaves; and a little later, in Corinth, a citizen body of 40,000 owned and controlled 640,000 slaves. In Rome, after the second century before Christ, the same conditions prevailed — "everywhere the great part of the manual work in agriculture, mining, trade and commerce was performed by slaves"; — the institution of slavery was entrenched among the barbarian conquerors of Rome; and in England it lingered until about a century after the Norman invasion.

Slavery slowly softened into serfdom, and serfdom into the wage system. The last serf did not disappear from England until the eighteenth century, and in other countries of the world serfdom lasted well into the nineteenth century. We need not linger over these facts. The point which concerns us is why serfdom was replaced by the wage system.

Three causes stand out preëminent. In the first place, bondage is repugnant to the deepest instincts and highest ideals of the human race. The simple, animal instinct for freedom must have played an important part, aided as it was by the better teachings of the Church and the common law, whose leaning, in England at least, was always toward the side of liberty. Secondly, bondage as a system became socially wasteful and uneconomic. Freedom gave fuller play to the incentive of self-interest. Thirdly, it became profitable for the people who owned the land to which the serfs were bound, to commute the old personal services into money dues — to divest themselves of the responsibility for the welfare of their vassals, while retaining a money equivalent for the old feudal obligations. Serfdom, then, passed away because it was at once inequitable and uneconomic.

The modern system of capitalization is often explained as a direct and immediate result of the Industrial Revolution of the eighteenth century, the main features of which are now so generally understood that it is unnecessary to recite them here. This explanation is substantially correct, provided we do not misconstrue the nature of the Industrial Revolution itself. Many accounts of the Industrial Revolution greatly exaggerate the suddenness of the changes which characterized it, and give the impression that some mysterious stirring of the human mind caused a meteoric burst of new discoveries and inventions, from which flowed, as immediate results, the factory system, modern capitalism, and the separation of classes, with all their consequences and accompaniments. This interpretation disguises the real nature of the Industrial Revolution and of the modern labor problem, both of which are perfectly natural and logical results of economic progress and of the ceaseless effort to make more and better things at a lower cost. In order to emphasize this familiar, but very important truth, let us note in bare outlines the development of mechanical industry from the introduction of the wage system to the period of the industrial revolution.

As the feudal system disintegrated, industry passed from the manors to the free cities and chartered towns, where the escaped serf who eluded his master for a year and a day became free, and where trade and industry were regulated by the gilds. Industry under the gild system was at first simple and paternalistic. The master or manufacturer worked in his own home, assisted by a few apprentices, who moved in their employer's family on terms of equality, and might reasonably hope some day to marry into that family and so succeed to the business or in other ways to acquire independent establishments of their own. The authorities are singularly unanimous in agreeing that in the beginning the craft gilds were beneficial, not only to industry and the laborer, but to the consumer as well. They were monopolies and no man could practice a trade in a city who was not a member of the gild which regulated that trade; but they prevented conflicts of interest, guaranteed the quality of goods, stimulated the organization and division of labor, trained skilled workmen, regulated apprenticeship, and bestowed upon the artisans the military system demanded by the circumstances of the time. Moreover, their tone was distinctly moral and educational, while they served as the great benefit societies of the Middle Ages, lessening pauperism, promoting thrift and cultivating in their members the qualities of good workmanship and active citizenship.

As time passed, however, the gilds became close corporations, jealous of their rights and privileges. Membership and mastership both became hereditary; the dues were raised; production was limited to keep up prices; and onerous regulations were introduced, which hindered the march of progress in production and exchange. After the gilds became more aristocratic, too, the old transition from apprenticeship to journeymanship, and from journeymanship to mastership, which in the beginning had been easy and practically universal, became exceedingly difficult. A class of permanent journeymen was created, which became large and relatively numerous in western Europe during the sixteenth and seventeenth centuries. With its appearance the forces antagonistic to the gild began to obtain the mastery. In 1680 the author of *Britannia Languens* records that "most of our ancient corporations and gilds [have] become oppressive oligarchies," and a few years later in England their influence was at an end; though on the continent the gild retained its importance until the nineteenth century, while in Germany and Austria it has in recent years been revived.

Class separation. It is plain that the separation of the capitalistic and wage-earning classes was due in part to the desire, apparently ineradicable from the human mind, to maintain a social superiority, once gained by the erection of class barriers. When a few of the master craftsmen had accumulated fortunes, they began to ape the manners of the landed aristocracy, conceived the ambition of founding families, and began to marry chiefly within their own or a higher class. In the gilds the richer and more powerful masters separated themselves into a distinct class, while the gild government came under the control of a still smaller group, the "Court of Assistants," whose regulation of industry became monopolistic, avaricious, and harsh. Excessive fines or entrance fees were required upon the admission of apprentices into the mastership, the period of apprenticeship was excessively lengthened, and the custom sprang up of requiring apprentices to take oath that they would not set up competing establishments without the masters' permission, a practice that in England was prohibited by Parliament in 1536.

This innate tendency to class seclusion must undoubtedly be numbered among the causes which explain the appearance of capitalism and the segregation of a class of permanent wage-earners. A far more potent cause, however, is found in the great economies effected by the production on a larger scale. A man working with a tool is much more productive than a man without any mechanical assistance and a man aided by many and costly tools is immeasurably superior to the man with one. The superiority conferred by the possession of capital tends to grow and increase; its advantages are cumulative.

Whatever the explanation of the appearance of a capitalistic class, there can be no doubt of its existence long before the Industrial Revolution. On the Continent a class of wealthy entrepreneurs — the merchant clothiers — appeared in the woolen industry as early as the thirteenth century; and in certain parts of England that industry had passed beyond the domestic stage as early at least, as the beginning of the sixteenth century. Referring to the new system in England Mr. Cooke Taylor tells us in his *Modern Factory System* (page 48) that "the increase of machinery employed under it had already become so alarming by the time of Edward VI, that a statute (50 and 60 Edw. VI) was passed in that reign regulating its use, while long before, and even by the end of Henry VII's reign, a class of great capitalists had arisen, using its methods on a very large scale indeed."

The Industrial Revolution was not a cataclysm of mechanical inventions and social transformations. Natura non facit saltum. It came gradually. Thoughtful men were expecting it. The way was prepared for it. It was understood that industry was on the eve of great developments and that improvements in production were imperatively demanded. The possibilities of steam as a motive power in industry were well understood many years before James Watt patented a workable engine in 1769. Many of the inventions which transformed the textile industry in the latter half of the eighteenth century were long preceded by mechanical devices which differed from these inventions only in so far as they were impracticable or costly of operation. The spirit of the times is illustrated by the fact that the Royal Academy, realizing the handicap imposed upon the textile industry by the excessive time required for spinning yarn, "offered a prize for the invention of a machine that would spin several threads at the same time." The factory system was not accidental; it was the inevitable result of the unceasing effort to reduce the cost of production. Production by machinery, like production on a large scale in general, came because it was economical, uprooting old institutions, extinguishing tenacious customs, widening the gulf between the masters and the servants, dislodging the old landed aristocracy, doing an infinite amount of damage in an infinite number of ways, but rendering possible in the end a vastly greater production and consumption of material wealth.

The genesis of the labor problem is full of instruction for the student of that problem as it now confronts us. Time was when the wage system, private property in land, and the industrial combination did not exist, and the time may come when they shall no longer exist. No social institution is inherently immortal, or above and beyond the touch of the iconoclast or reformer.

The test of progress. Nevertheless, we may be certain that every deep-seated social institution will endure until a better substitute is provided, capable of performing the old function in a more economic way. The test of the possible reform is its power of decreasing cost or augmenting production. We may rebel against the materialism of this criterion, but deny it we cannot. If economic history teaches one lesson of indisputable meaning, it is the utter inevitableness of the method, machine or institution that makes for economy. We may — indeed, we must — ameliorate its temporary destructiveness, but thwart it we cannot. Such is the law of progress, and progress is inevitable. Not without interruption from men and institutions, and not without guidance at times by combinations of men in legislature, church, and trade union, but in its ultimate direction irresistible and irreversible, the car of industrial progress has traveled its appointed way, improving, enlarging, but always complicating the mechanism of industry, and so ceaselessly reducing the proportion of independent workers. Capitalism, the separation of the industrial classes, and the labor problem are the products of progress itself.

It is some comfort to reflect that our problems are the problems of progress, the growing pains of youth, and not the signs of approaching decay. Of course, it avails nothing to the man who is thrust aside or maimed by the car of progress, to be told that his suffering is a mere incident in the upward march of society. This truth, indeed, carries with it a supplementary lesson of the gravest consequence: society must learn to minimize the unfortunate incidents of progress, and systematically compensate those who are injured literally for humanity's sake, because it is just this incidental and temporary destructiveness of progress that accounts for the gravest economic and social evils of our epoch. Moreover, society must learn to restrain the capricious plunging, the unnecessary deviations of our figurative vehicle; and as invention crowds upon invention, and revolutionary methods replace those to which we are accustomed and to which we have accommodated ourselves, in a word, as progress becomes more rapid, social regulation must increase. No greater truth has ever been enunciated by an American economist than the proposition, so ably maintained by Professor Henry C. Adams in his *Relation of the State to Industrial Action*, that public regulation must proceed *pari passu* with the development of private trade and industry. The true ideal of society is not laissez-faire, but economic freedom, and freedom is the child, not the enemy, of law and regulation.

3. Development of the Labor Movement in the United States [1]

In reading the following account of the history of organized labor in the United States, it must be borne in mind that the or-

[1] The outline of this article follows that given by *Short History of the American Labor Movement*, by Beard. Harcourt, Brace & Co., publishers.

ganized labor movement is essentially empirical, both in structure and function; that it has evolved by the process of trial and error, adapting its form, its program, and its methods to changing industrial forces. Consequently, to reduce its history during any period of rapid industrial change to a simple chronological sequence involves some distortion of the facts. It is possible, however, with this caution in mind to divide the history of the labor movement in the United States into six rather well-marked periods.

The beginnings of trade-unionism, 1792–1827. There were no trade unions in the modern sense in the colonial period of American history. Industry at that time had not reached the factory stage of its development; no permanent class of industrial wage-earners existed; economic enterprise was, in large part, limited to agricultural pursuits. There were, it is true, some organizations among the workingmen of the town; but these took the form of friendly or benevolent societies whose purpose was, in part, to render financial aid to members in distress, in part to supply facilities for their social activities. These organizations made no attempt to interfere with wages, hours of labor, or other matters of importance in the trade.

At the time of the adoption of the Constitution, however, the United States felt the first effects of the Industrial Revolution. Manufactured goods, formerly imported from England began to be supplied from home industries. The new machine processes began to encroach upon the fields of enterprise formerly monopolized by the skilled craftsmen. The market widened and commerce sprang up between industrial cities which undermined the power of workmen and employers of any one locality to control prices and wages. A new figure appeared in the market, in the person of the "merchant capitalist," whose function it was to buy in the cheapest market and sell in the dearest, thus broadening the area within which competition worked out its effects upon prices and the wages of labor. Under the pressure of these conditions, the wage-earners gradually drew away from coöperation with their local employers and began to form unions among themselves for the protection of the wage rate.

These early unions were very narrow in their scope, being limited to a specific trade and a specific locality. In other words, they were what we would call in modern parlance "local craft unions." They were made up of skilled workers only: printers, shoemakers, tailors, carpenters. All records of many of these early local labor societies have disappeared; but we know that the shoemakers of Philadelphia were organized in 1792; that the printers of New York had their Typographical Society as early as 1794 and were organized in Philadelphia and Baltimore during the opening years of the nineteenth century. The Boston printers were associated on a permanent basis in 1809, and in New Orleans a year later.

"During the quarter century which followed the inauguration of Washington as first President of the United States in 1789, the skilled workmen of the American towns formed powerful local organizations to take part in the fixing of hours, wages and conditions of the industries generally. During the same period, trade unions drew slowly away from employers, finally excluding from membership those journeymen who became masters." The activities of these groups were still tinctured with the spirit of the friendly societies which had preceded them in the colonial period, but the importance of these features gradually declined as the struggle to protest the customary wage rate, to defend the craftsman in the prerogatives of his trade as against the encroachment of the machine and the apprentice, grew more intense. Selfish in their aims, limited in their outlook to the individual craft and locality, and devoid of broad social purpose, these early trade unions did little to arouse within the laboring population as a whole any consciousness of common class interests.

Political and social agitation, 1827–1830. "The first coördinated movement of several trades in the United States occurred in Philadelphia in 1827 when, as a result of a strike of building-trades workmen for a ten-hour day, there was formed the first effective city central organization of wage-earners in the world — the Mechanics' Union of Trade Associations. This in turn gave birth to the first labor party in the world — the Workingmen's Party, which led to the first industrial union, at least in this country — the New England Association of Farmers, Mechanics, and other Workingmen. For several years this movement was not only the expression of labor's unrest, but was also an important political force with which the old established parties were obliged to reckon and to which they were obliged to make concessions." [1]

The entrance of the organized labor movement into politics marks the close of the first period in the history of this movement in the United States, and the opening of its second phase. This was a period of social and political experiment when all classes of society were engaged in applying the new doctrines of democracy to a reform of the social order. It was the time of the Utopians and Humanitarians whose communistic and coöperative experiments spread over the country. Labor's attempt to accomplish its ends by political means was a response, in part, to this prevailing element in the thought life of the time; and, in part, a reaction to the competitive forces which were breaking down craft and community lines.

The Workingmen's Party, formed in Philadelphia in 1828, was at the outset a successful political venture. In the first year, it elected all of its candidates to the city council and captured a balance of power in that body. At the following election, however, its vote dwindled and it lost control. In 1831, its attempt to run independent candidates was a complete failure and it thereupon withdrew from the political field. At about the same time, as an outgrowth of a struggle over the ten-hour day in the building trades of New York City, a labor party was formed in that place. During the next two years, there was an active campaign on the part of wage-earners to elect independent representatives to the city council and the state legislature. Small towns in the State fell in with this movement which met with some local successes. Gradually the movement spread to other States throughout the country, every State in the Union, with the exception of New Hampshire showing some signs of the political activity of the laborers.

This first period of political activity on the part of the organized workers lasted until 1834. It ended everywhere in failure as far as its immediate objectives were concerned. Yet the movement had an influence on the trend of politics in the country as a whole, for many of the measures advocated by the labor parties were incorporated into the platforms of the older parties. Imprisonment for debt was abolished; the principle of universal education at

[1] *History of Labor in the United States*, by Commons, vol. 1, p. 169.

public expense was established; and other reforms, originally advanced by the workers, became a part of the law of the land. From the standpoint of the labor movement, its principal effect was to break down the narrow craft consciousness which had characterized the earlier unions and to prepare the way for attempts at broader forms of organization to follow.

After the failure of their political programs, the workers fell back upon industrial action and there set in a period of rapid increase in the numbers and effectiveness of the trade unions. This movement was aided by the prosperity which the country experienced during the early thirties as a consequence of the rising prices. By 1836 there were fifty-three trade unions in Philadelphia; sixteen in Boston; the same number in Newark; twenty-three in Baltimore; fifty-two in New York. It was then estimated that the union membership in the seaboard cities amounted to 300,000.

"As organization advanced by leaps and bounds in the individual trades, there developed a labor movement of wider significance — namely, the combination of the trade unions of a single city into central bodies for financial and moral support during strikes. These central bodies repudiated political action and bent to the task of controlling the trades in such a way as to improve their own economic conditions. In their strikes for higher wages and shorter hours, they sought to exercise some check on hasty and ill-considered action on the part of any union. Through common discussion of trade conditions in different industries, the workers learned more about the products of 'unfair' shops, other than their own, and thus were able to introduce the boycott of goods as well as the boycott of the 'scab.' The idea of the union label now crept in so that the workers might recognize in the open market the products of union shops and confine their purchases to such products wherever possible.

"The labor movement of the thirties tried to reach out toward still wider and more effective combinations through a national organization of local unions. An attempt in this direction was made in 1834 in New York City where a convention was called from all parts of the country 'to advance the moral and intellectual condition and pecuniary interests of the laboring classes, promote the establishment of trades unions in every section of the

United States; and also to publish and disseminate such information as may be useful to mechanics and workingmen generally; and to unite and harmonize the efforts of all the productive classes of the country. Trade unionists from the leading cities came together in a similar convention for similar purposes for two succeeding years before they realized that their attempt to consolidate the workers of the nation was premature. They were fully convinced that better groundwork would have to be laid in local and city organizations before the national movement became powerful and permanent."

This was the first attempt to *federalize* the workers in all the different crafts into one national organization. After it was given up, the organized labor movement fell back into the channels of craft unionism and began a process of national organization along craft lines. In 1835, the shoemakers met in national assembly representing the local unions of this trade in the different industrial cities and laid the foundations for a national organization. During the next two years, four other national unions were formed by the printers, the comb-makers, the carpenters and the handloom weavers. This development had scarcely got under way, however, when the disastrous Panic of 1837 dealt a body blow to the whole labor movement. With business at a standstill, the credit structure demolished, unemployment general, and prices and wages falling, the union leaders found it impossible to keep their local organizations together to say nothing of striking out on broader plans of development. All the national unions disappeared, most of the city centrals likewise vanished, and but a small fraction of the local units survived.

As a consequence of the Panic of 1837, the organized labor movement was turned again in the direction of political activity, and, during the remainder of this period — i.e., until about 1850 — its energies were absorbed in various social and political experiments. The wage-earners, powerless, in the face of the great industrial calamity, to improve their lot by economic methods, were a fruitful field for the labors of reformers and theorists of all schools. Many workmen became followers of Brisbane and Greeley, the American disciples of Fourier, and wasted their energies in futile attempts to found communistic colonies in different parts of the country. Others, under the leadership of intellectuals, joined political parties in opposition to monopolies, in favor of cheap money, for restriction of immigration, for land reform. The trade-union movement, as such, virtually disappeared.

Period of national organization, 1850–1866. With the industrial recovery of the country in the late forties, trade-unionism of the older type was revived. A decade of experiment with Utopian ventures and political agitation left the wage-earners in a mood to resort once more to coöperative action, strictly within their own class, upon the industrial field. Economic forces favored this tendency. The increasing industrialization of the country had begun to draw sharp class lines between the propertyless and the employer-capitalists; at the same time the broadening of the market under the influence of improved transportation gave strength to other tendencies which were working in the direction of national organization along class lines. In 1850 the Typographical Union formed a nation-wide organization of its craft. A similar national union was formed by the Stone-Cutters in 1853, the Hat Finishers in 1854, the Moulders in 1857, and the Machinists and Blacksmiths in the same year. As is always the case during periods of intense industrial activity, these years were marked by many strikes and other evidences of aggressiveness on the part of labor. The conflict centered around questions of wages and hours, questions of immediate economic advantage to the craftsman. The broad social philosophy of the preceding decade was given up, together with the attempt to effect a comprehensive organization of the entire laboring population into a single coöperative union; and the labor movement remained within the confines of the several specific trades or crafts.

This movement was gaining headway when a second disaster — the Panic of 1857 — again checked its growth. Union organization, as has always been the case, dissolved under the impact of hard times, and the recent gains in membership and more complete organization were swept away as unemployment, low wages, and distress undermined the economic power of the workers. The initial effect of the Civil War was also injurious to the labor movement. As a consequence of the inflationist policy of the Federal Government, prices rose faster than wages, and there set in a gradual degradation of the standard of life of the average man. The period from 1857 to 1863 records a low-water mark in the progress of organized labor when its slump both in membership and effectiveness reduced it to a point of insignificance comparable to its condition in the earliest stages of its growth.

The setback, however, was temporary in character; nor did it exert an immediate influence upon the direction taken by the labor movement, the type of organization which the workers strove to effect, or the tactics they employed when recovery set in. One truth is clearly established by the history of organized labor in all lands: namely, that strength of the movement varies directly with the economic prosperity of the workers and their social importance in the industrial system. Union labor is not the outgrowth of desperation but of strength; its periods of expansion coincide with times of business prosperity when there is a relative shortage of labor and an increase in the bargaining power of the wage-earner; conversely, decline in membership and power is recorded during periods of unemployment, falling wages, and general distress. After the first year of the war, the business world had begun to respond to the influence of wholesale government purchasing; factories were working overtime; new enterprises sprang up in the industrial cities of the North, and old ones expanded the scope of their operations. These developments, coupled with the drafting of workers into the army, resulted in a relative scarcity of labor which progressively strengthened the position of the wage-earner in the economic system. That the union movement quickly gained momentum under the influence of these favoring circumstances is shown in the accompanying table.

Until 1866, the end of the period we are describing, this expansion of trade-unionism took place within the craft lines which had marked out the path of union development after the disillusioning experience of labor with political and socialistic ventures in the forties. As locals increased in number, however, each craft undertook again the task of uniting its members on a national scale. During the period of intense business activity — which lasted from 1863 to 1866 — ten national unions sprang up in two years. At the close of the sixties there were in existence at least thirty-two national trade unions, some of them assuming the title "international" so as to include the locals organized in Canada.

States	Number of Unions 1863	1864
Connecticut	2	6
Delaware	..	1
Illinois	1	10
Indiana	3	17
Kentucky	2	8
Maine	1	7
Maryland	..	1
Massachusetts	17	42
Michigan	4	9
Missouri	4	9
New Hampshire	3	5
New Jersey	4	10
New York	16	74
Ohio	4	16
Pennsylvania	15	44
Rhode Island	1	7
Tennessee	..	2
Vermont	1	..
Virginia	1	1
Wisconsin	..	1
Total	79	270

Second attempt at amalgamation, 1866–1886. "All things conspired together to draw organized labor in war-time into closer union on a national scale. By the end of the Civil War every important city had its city trades assembly representing all the organized crafts. It had coöperative stores, free libraries and reading rooms, legislative lobbies, and a labor press. It held periodic meetings and helped those unions engaged in contests for better conditions. There were, as we have seen, thirty powerful national unions of specific trades and several of these trades had their own journals.

"The time seemed ripe for a grand consolidation of all labor's forces, such as had been tried thirty years before without permanent results. So in 1864 an attempt was made to federate the city trades assemblies. A national convention was called for this purpose, the idea being to form a national body on the General Confederation of Labor in France. . . . The main object of the promoters of this organization was to abolish strikes and establish trade agreements with employers in their place. In explanation of these objects, the promoters declared "that the capitalists or employers will cease to refuse our just demands and will, if we make any unreasonable demands, condescend to come down on a level with us and by argument and proof show us that our demands are unjust, but this will have to be explained to the satisfaction of the trades assembly of the city in which the demand was made." The outcome of this movement was the formation, in 1866, of the National Labor Union.

"The basis of the National Labor Union was the city assemblies of trade unions. It did not represent strict craft unionism, therefore. Moreover, it did not confine its efforts to the promotion of that type of union effort. Sylvis (the prime mover in this attempt at amalgamation), who was himself a workingman and a good unionist, was deeply interested in freeing labor from the control of capitalists by means of coöperative shops in which the workmen supplied their own capital and shared the profits. In 1867 he declared: "At last, after years of earnest effort and patient waiting and constant preaching, coöperation is taking hold upon the minds of our members and in many places very little else is talked about." A year later he was still urging the superior merits of coöperation as compared with unionism, insisting that unionism made war upon the effects of industrial distress and did not get at the cause, which was in the fact of the wage system itself. Sylvis's own union, the ironmoulders, made a number of experiments in coöperative production, opening ten or more coöperative foundries which failed. Similar attempts were made during this period by other trades, bakers, shipwrights, machinists, tailors, printers, needlewomen, etc. The unsuccessful strikes carried on in 1867–68 were followed in many instances by the establishment of independent coöperative shops in which the producer was to receive the "full product of his labor and the wages struggle was to be eliminated."

In addition to these ventures in the field of coöperative production, the National Labor Union soon became involved in politics. The difficulty in securing money capital with which to equip the experiments in production swung the movement into line with other organizations interested in "cheap money" and political alliances were made with the Grangers and the "Greenbackers." The inflationist program of these groups was partially successful, leading to the passage of the Silver Purchase Act at the end of the seventies; but this part of the policy of organized labor has left no lasting impress upon the legal system of the United States. This was not true, however, of other phases of labor's political platform. The agitation for Chinese exclusion led eventually to the exclusion act of 1882; after a protracted struggle, the eight-hour day was made the legal standard for federal employees; the demand for a Government Bureau of Labor was granted in 1884. As in the earlier period of labor's activities in politics, the principal effect of its agitation was to force upon the other parties an acceptance of its chief demands and eventually to enact them into law through this medium.

"Unluckily for the National Labor Union, most of the coöperative experiments on the part of workingmen failed, and the political gains made by agitation did not seem important or spectacular enough to hold the rank and file. The pure and simple unionists began to desert, and by 1872 the Union had ceased to function, having fallen almost entirely into the hands of political reformers. Another reason for its failure was its foundation upon city trades assemblies rather than upon the regular national craft unions. City assemblies were more interested in their local problems and in local politics than in national affairs."

One year after the dissolution of the National Labor Union came the Panic of 1873 whose effect upon the labor movement was the same as that experienced during earlier periods of industrial depression. To the best of their ability, the national craft unions resisted wage cuts and the loss of working standards won during the preceding decade; but were, on the whole, impotent in the face of underlying economic forces tending to depress the business prosperity of the country. The period from 1873 to 1878 was one of prolonged and bitter strikes, resulting in violence so widespread as to border on a condition of civil war. It was the time of the "Molly Maguires" who terrorized the Pittsburgh district; of the first great railroad strikes; of the first clash between organized labor and the federal troops called out to maintain order during an industrial disturbance. The national organizations of the craft unions were almost annihilated, but eight remaining of the thirty-two which were in existence in 1870. Craft-union membership the country over fell to something like one fifth of the former figure.

In this setting was born the Knights of Labor, successor to the National Labor Union in the attempt to amalgamate in one organization the working classes of the country, but destined to be more successful than its predecessor and to hold the center of the stage in the world of labor until the end of the period we are considering (i.e., until 1886). The Noble Order of the Knights of Labor was the outgrowth of a union formed among the garment cutters in Philadelphia in 1869. Taking the name by which it is now known in labor history in 1871, the Knights of Labor began to branch out to embrace within its membership other workers than those in the clothing trade and other localities than the city of its origin. By 1876 there were over a hundred local assemblies in different cities in Pennsylvania, and in 1878, after the organization had spread into other States, these scattered locals were drawn together into a single national union.

The structure of this national union was highly centralized. At the top stood the national assembly with its permanent officers, which was given absolute authority over the district assemblies — the next lower unit. In the terms of the constitution of the Order, the national assembly had full and final jurisdiction over all subordinate bodies and was made "the highest tribunal." In matters of local interest, the district assemblies were placed in a similarly dominant position as regards the local units. Thus was built up an autocratic system in which final authority to command or prohibit was lodged in the hands of permanent officers and standing committees at the top. The aim of the organization was to weld the labor movement into a single disciplined army subject to orders issued from a central office and mobile enough to act as a unit. The tests of eligibility for membership were so broad as almost to take in every worker by hand or brain. Any person over eighteen years of age "working for wages, or who at any time had worked for wages," could join, but "no person who either sells, or makes his living from the sale of intoxicating drink" could become a member nor could any lawyer, doctor, or banker. With respect to membership, it is apparent that the Knights of Labor stood in contrast with the narrow craft unions which had practically met their deathblow in the Panic of 1873. As a direct consequence of this all-inclusive membership, the program of the organization ran in terms of broad social reform, aimed at a general improvement of labor conditions all along the line.

"The Knights of Labor took no aggressive action as a national organization until 1880. After that year its principal activity consisted in the conduct of strikes. Many of these strikes were unsuccessful because the organization operated mainly among the unskilled and inexperienced in labor controversies, and because its centralized character was not well adapted to a strike of the members of a single trade. . . . Frequent railway strikes were a feature of the labor movement during the years 1884 to 1886. Some early successes of the Knights of Labor in the conduct of these struggles served as a powerful advertisement of the organization. The result was that strikes were declared and the strikers joined the Knights of Labor after they had struck. The almost unavoidable outcome of such a method was a second strike after a short interval to protect the existence of the new union. A strike on the Wabash Railway in August, 1885, was of this character. A lockout of the members of the Knights of Labor, under the guise of a reduction of forces, compelled the general executive board to issue an order which would have caused a general strike affecting Jay Gould's Southwestern System. Gould would not risk a strike at that time, and, accordingly, an agreement was made by him which satisfactorily settled the trouble. The effect of this victory was to give an exaggerated idea of the power of the Knights, both to the workingman and to the general public." [1] This overestimate of the influence of the organization among workingmen had been fostered during the early history of the Knights by its policy of secrecy. Until 1881, it made an effort to keep its name secret from the general public, using, in the place of its official title when referring to itself, five stars or asterisks. This gave it a mysterious character, and it came to be looked upon by the general public as an "invisible empire" with great and hidden power. After this policy had been given up in response to pressure of public opinion and the Catholic Church, its strike activities served to carry on the tradition of power, so that it figured in the discussion of political parties and in the press as one of the principal forces of the day.

The extent of the membership of the Knights at the height of

[1] *Social Politics in the United States*, by Fred E. Haynes, pp. 91–92. Houghton Mifflin Company, publishers.

its power has always been a matter of dispute. Fantastic claims were made for it, both by its friends and by its opponents. It is probable that its followers never numbered more than three quarters of a million at any time, though various estimates made at the time placed its membership as high as five million. The *New York Sun* in a leading article asserted that the five men who constituted the executive board of the organization had it in their power to throw 2,500,000 people out of work without warning, and referred to the Federal Government as a "petty authority" in comparison with this power.

"The outcome of the Gould strike of 1885, the exaggeration of the powers of the Knights by the press and public, and their successes at Washington provided the setting for the great labor upheaval of 1886. This upheaval marked the appearance of a new class in the labor movement — that of the unskilled. They felt that they had found a champion who could curb the most powerful capitalists of the country. Their accumulated bitterness and resentment now caused a rush to organize under the leadership of the Knights. The rapid pace at which the order grew, the wave of strikes, particularly sympathetic strikes, the use of the boycott, the violence of the movement — 1886 was the year of the Chicago anarchist outbreak — all were evidence of the rise of a new class — the unskilled worker. The outburst bore the aspect of a social war. A frenzied hatred of capital was shown in every important strike. Many of the leaders of the Knights realized the danger created by the attitude of the rank and file, but they were powerless to restrain them." [1]

After 1886, the Knights of Labor began rapidly to lose ground. By 1890, its membership had fallen from 700,000 to 100,000; during the succeeding years, more of its followers deserted the order, until there remained but a handful — and these principally middle-class political reformers — to carry on the tradition. The causes of its decline were, in part, circumstantial; in part, due to essential flaws in its structure and policy. In the first group of causes may be listed the disastrous outcome of its strike policy in 1886 — in fact, the strike policy itself, especially in the form of the sympathetic strike, was a constant drain upon the strength of the

[1] *Social Politics in the United States*, by Fred E. Haynes, pp. 93–94. Houghton Mifflin Company, publishers.

order, wasting its resources in futile struggles against the growing power of big business. At the same time, the violence of the order called forth the organized efforts of the employers in self-defense. Strong associations were formed to combat the Knights with lockout and blacklist, which received the support of an aroused public opinion in their efforts to break the power of this disturber of the public peace.

The more fundamental reason for the failure of the Knights of Labor, however, is to be found in its own inherent weakness of structure and the ineffectiveness of its program. Embracing within a single organization all workers regardless of craft or skill, it attempted to operate on the assumption of a community of interest among workingmen. But, in reality, the immediate interests of the skilled workers often ran counter to those of the unskilled; gains were to be made by the craft unions through the device of restricting numbers by stringent apprenticeship rules and thus pressing for a monopoly advantage in industry — a policy which operates to destroy the opportunity for self-advancement among the unskilled and to depress the lower rates of wages. During the eighties there was little class-consciousness among the industrial workers of the country as a whole, but much craft- or trade-consciousness. The time had not come when it was possible to organize the entire working population into a single mixed industrial union, without creating internal dissension. That time could come only when the progress of machine technique in industry had advanced so far that most wage-earners were reduced to a similar condition of unskilled factory operatives. An attempt to form such an organization, before the time was ripe, compelled the order to adopt policies which affronted a part of its membership, policies of broad social action — like the sympathetic strike — which, in the opinion of the skilled workers, were carried on at their expense and for the advantage of the unskilled. This conflict within the organization led to the gradual withdrawal of the craft-unionists; as for the unskilled, membership in the Knights was, with them, a prosperity policy; and they, too, deserted when the order began to lose its strikes.

The period of federated national craft unions, 1886–1924. During the period just discussed, we have seen how two attempts to organize the workers in a single comprehensive union failed.

Before the close of the period, a reaction against this effort had begun among the craftsmen of the country in the direction of a return to the older type of organization along trade lines. This revolt was led by the stronger national craft unions which had maintained their structure intact through the Panic of 1873. It resulted in the establishment of the American Federation of Labor which, from that time to the present, has been the centralizing force in the labor movement in this country.

The American Federation of Labor is a loose federation of national craft unions — a union of unions. Its members are self-contained, self-governed organizations, having each its own independent policy, system of dues and benefits, officers and governmental machinery. A dissolution of the Federation would leave intact these great national craft unions, each capable of functioning within the limits of its own specific trade. The loyalty of any individual union member of the country is to his own national organization; his wage demands conform to its standards; by it he is disciplined and controlled, aided while on strike, and represented in his bargaining with the employer. The Federation, accordingly, has partial jurisdiction only, and can wield no real authority over the organizations which constitute its membership; its policy is limited to coöperative action along lines favorable to all craft unions — the eight-hour day, collective bargaining, the union label, propaganda favoring union organization, and substantial aid through its own officers to any craft union seeking to increase its membership and power. Its independence as an organization rests upon its power to draw a permanent revenue from charter fees and taxes levied upon the members of the national craft unions. The income from these sources is expended on publicity, organizing expenses, and strike benefits supplementary to those paid by the national organization of the strikers.

As a consequence of the dissension within the ranks of the Knights of Labor there set in, as we have seen, a reaction toward craft-union organization. In 1885, there existed in the country about twenty national organizations within as many different trades. This number increased during the next five years as efforts were made by the skilled workmen to reconstruct the organizations which had been swept out of existence by the Panic of

1873. A return of good times strengthened this movement, and by 1885 the membership in the various craft organizations numbered over 300,000. The power and prestige of the national union were increased by several new lines of governmental policy which they adopted at this time. "Under their plan (1) complete authority over the locals was given to the officers of the international union; (2) membership dues were increased to build up a large benefit fund; and (3) a benefit system was created to tide the union over periods of industrial depression. By a system of fund equalization, the well-to-do locals were obliged to help weaker locals in times of crisis. Here was statesmanship in organization of a new order — practical, business-like, and substantial."

The attempt to federalize these craft unions was first made in 1881, when the "Federation of Organized Trades and Labor Unions" was formed by a convention of delegates at Pittsburgh. This organization proved to be a thing of little power, its policy drifting into lines of political and social activity which failed to interest the rank and file of union members. In 1886, five leaders in the craft-union movement — among them, Samuel Gompers — calling for a reorganization of the federal body, succeeded in erecting the present Federation of Labor, and in slowly winning to its support most of the great national unions together with other organizations of labor. For the first decade of its existence the growth in membership was slow, but with the beginning of the twentieth century there set in a period of steady increase. By 1900, its official roll of dues-paying members numbered 548,321; in 1910, this figure had risen to 1,562,112; and in 1920 to 4,978,740.

To-day, the American Federation of Labor, with certain exceptions presently to be noted, covers the entire field of craft-unionism in the United States. Since a description of its structure, policy, and powers is given in later articles in this book, we shall not enter into a discussion of these details at this point. The only craft unions of importance not embraced in the organization are those existing in the railroad industry, known as the "Big Four Brotherhoods": the locomotive engineers, railway conductors, locomotive firemen and enginemen, and the maintenance-of-way employees. The first three of these great craft unions were in existence prior to the formation of the American Federation of Labor and had developed a tradition, built up financial reserves, and succeeded in their bargaining and benefit policies to a point which made them hesitate to merge their identity in any larger union. Altogether the Brotherhoods have between four and five hundred thousand members. Despite their refusal to join the American Federation of Labor, their relations with that organization are cordial in the extreme.

Recent radical tendencies in the labor movement. This brief sketch of the history of organized labor in the United States would not be complete without some reference to certain modern tendencies which indicate a reaction against the narrower policy of craft-unionism. There are elements of weakness in the organization of workers by crafts in the setting of the modern industrial world. The maintenance of craft lines in the face of machine progress becomes increasingly difficult. The growth of the trust and giant corporation, embracing within its control the workers in many different trades and localities, reduces the power of any one craft union to effect lasting improvement in the economic well-being of a given group of wage-earners. The increasing injection of government forces into trade disputes, through the use of the injunction by the courts and of the militia, encourages political activity on the part of the workingmen as a class. These forces have led to a resurrection of the industrial-union movement — the movement, that is, toward organization of workers into groups larger than those determined by craft or trade lines. It has also stimulated radical social and political tendencies in some of these broader organizations which may be called revolutionary in contrast to the cautious, conservative, law-abiding policies of the national crafts.

For a time, the most spectacular of these industrial unions was the Industrial Workers of the World. Formed in 1905 in bitter opposition to the Federation of Labor, this organization sought to unite the unskilled workers into a single great union with avowedly revolutionary aims. A split occurred over a matter of government in 1908, and the present I.W.W. traces its history to the more radical of the two factions. From this date, the Industrial Workers of the World attracted widespread attention by their dramatic fights for free speech, the revolutionary violence of their language, and the bitter strikes they have waged. Their main strength is drawn from the migratory workers of the Western farms and lumber camps, with fluctuating support from the unskilled and largely foreign-born labor of the textile mills. This strength has been consistently overrated since the advent of the I.W.W. into the world of organized labor, both by the leaders of the movement and by the general public. At the present time it numbers not more than ten thousand.

Of much greater importance are the organizations in the clothing trades, a group of industrial unions comprising in all a membership of some three hundred and fifty thousand. In many respects, these recently formed organizations — only one has had a continuous history since before 1900 — are in the vanguard of American labor. Formed among a class of workers notoriously exploited, in an industry subject to cutthroat competition, seasonal unemployment, occupational disease, and among an impoverished and largely alien group, the unions of the garment workers have impressed all students of the modern labor movement with their statesmanlike policy, their able leadership, their solidarity, and the broadness of their social vision. In contrast to the conservatism of the craft unions in the American Federation of Labor, this group of organization in the clothing trades has been given the name — The New Unionism. Prominent among them are: The International Ladies' Garment Workers' Union (membership, 1920, 102,000); The Amalgamated Clothing Workers of America (membership, 1920, 200,000); The United Cloth Hat and Cap Makers of North America (membership, 15,000). The structure and policies of these important units of the American labor movement will be described in later readings.

Because certain powerful economic forces have been working in the direction of labor organization on industrial lines, the American Federation of Labor has been compelled to compromise with this principle, although it is foreign to the essential purpose of that organization. The "Departments" of the Federation are one evidence of this compromise. These are merely larger groupings of the crafts which commonly work side by side in a given industry. There is, for example, a Department of Railway Workers, embracing the skilled craftsmen of different trades — machinists, blacksmiths, etc. — who are employed in the railroad shops. Another Department takes in the carpenters, masons, bricklayers, and other craft unions engaged in the building trades. The purpose of these organizations within the Federation is to provide a structure to unite for common action those separate groups of workers whose interests are likely to be similarly affected by a given event or tendency in the industrial world; and to harmonize the differences and disagreements which arise among these organizations to prevent harmony. In this respect they represent an attempt on the part of craft unions to obtain the advantages peculiar to the industrial form of organization without a surrender of the narrower principle upon which they are based.

In addition to these signs that the labor movement is tending away from the structural form which has been dominant since 1886, there are evidences of revolt against the policies and tactics of craft-unionism. We have already mentioned the revolutionary program of the I.W.W. and the plans for broad social reform put forward by the Clothing Trades as evidences of this tendency. Another indication is to be seen in the recent inclination of organized labor to reënter the political arena as a separate party. The American Federation of Labor has studiously avoided politics, inferring from the past history of labor that attempts to engage in political activity as a body are bound to destroy any labor organization. No political discussion is allowed on the floor of the Convention of the Federation; the organization has limited its exercise of political influence to lobbying in support of measures favorable to all labor interests, and endorsing candidates, irrespective of party, who give pledges to support such measures. In 1920, however, the Convention endorsed the Plumb Plan for the reorganization of the railroads along lines favored by the Guild Socialists — a decidedly political program. Beginning at about the same time, a number of the national organizations have interested themselves in the organization of a separate labor party. The groundwork of an independent labor party had already been laid with the help of the farmers and certain Socialist groups in the country. Separate candidates were offered for election for state and local offices in 1920, with some measure of success; while plans are being laid at the present time (spring, 1924) for a nation-wide canvas during the presidential election of 1924.

4. Present Strength of Organized Labor in the United States

Most of the statements regarding the numerical strength of the union movement in the United States are false or misleading. Organized labor is still on the defensive in this country; there is much heated controversy about the aims and methods of the trade union, and not a little about the right of the unions to exist at all. In this setting the opponents of the movement are inclined to strengthen their case by making it appear that organized labor represents but a small fraction of the entire working population of the country. The proponents, on their side, are concerned to present the organized labor movement as representative of the great body of common people. We are not interested in the motives of either side of this controversy, it being our object to study the labor movement as a social phenomenon, not to condemn or to praise it. A careful analysis of the statistics of the movement will aid us to place it in its proper social perspective.

Trade-unionism — using the term to include all forms of organized labor — reached its high-water mark in 1920. Since that time, the country has passed through a panic and a business depression which have materially depleted the ranks of the union movement. Our previous study of the history of organized labor has shown us that this is the inevitable effect of the backward swing of the business cycle, and, furthermore, that this effect is temporary. No useful comparisons can be based upon the strength of the movement during an abnormal period; moreover, judging from past history, it may be predicted with safety that trade unions will recover the lost ground when once the industrial world is reëstablished on an even keel. The statistics which follow, therefore, refer to conditions obtaining in 1920.

In that year the total membership of the A.F. of L., as reported by that organization was 4,078,740. This membership includes only trade-unionists "in good standing"; i.e., those who paid their dues during the period covered by the report. Men temporarily dropped from union rolls, and those who, for one reason or another, failed to pay their dues, are not counted. If an allowance of 20 per cent — this is the proportion based on the past experience of the Federation — is made for this factor, the maximum strength of the American Federation of Labor would appear to have been very nearly four and three quarter millions. We must then add the membership of the unions not affiliated with the Federation. The five strongest of these unions — the Amalgamated Clothing Workers, Locomotive Engineers, Locomotive

Firemen, Railroad Trainmen, and Railroad Conductors — reported in 1920 a membership of 630,000. Certain smaller groups — the I.W.W., International Garment Workers, Cloth Hat and Cap Makers — bring the total union membership outside the Federation to approximately three quarters of a million. Thus we reach a grand total for the entire country of five and one half million organized workers.

Relative strength of unionism. The Census of 1920 reported 41,614,248 persons ten years of age or over "gainfully employed." But this figure includes all people who drew an income from personal service of any sort — active owners of business, farmers, doctors, ministers, lawyers, foremen, managers, and all others; many of these groups are certainly not material for unionization. Furthermore, it is almost impossible to organize many groups of wage-earners because of the nature of their work and surroundings; bank clerks, stenographers, domestic servants are examples. To discover the number of "organizable" workers in 1920, therefore, the Census figures must be analyzed with care. Such analysis will eliminate the following groups:

(1) Agriculture, forestry, animal husbandry All except 196,881 lumber workers.	10,756,277
(2) Extraction of minerals: foremen, overseers, inspectors, managers	71,256
(3) Manufacturing and mechanical industries: officials, owners, non-factory workers, etc.	1,073,131
(4) Transportation: proprietors, managers, officials, garage men, foremen, etc.	297,433
(5) Trade	2,600,774
(6) Public Service	612,774
(7) Professional Service All except actors, musicians, theatrical employees.	1,974,239
(8) Domestic and personal service All except barbers, bootblacks, elevator men, janitors, porters, waiters.	2,555,867
(9) Clerical occupations	3,126,541
Total deduction on account of occupation	23,068,292
Add child labor	1,060,858
Total deductions	24,129,150
Total gainfully employed	41,614,248
Total deductions	24,129,150
Organizable workers	17,485,098

We find, then, out of a total organizable working population in 1920 of 17,500,000, a union membership of 5,500,000. In other words, the union movement had enlisted the active support of 31 per cent of these industrial wage-earners. On this showing it is decidedly a minority movement in this country.

A final interpretation of these figures, however, must take account of certain other factors. The union movement, the world over, is predominately a movement among *male* workers. Even in such a country as England, it is still difficult to organize the female wage-earners. In a younger industrial country, the handicaps to organization among women workers are much more severe, for various reasons; the *permanent* female wage-earning population is relatively smaller; custom, habit, and social standards prevent the woman worker from joining a labor organization and thus announcing her commitment to a life in industry; the spirit of individualism and conservatism is stronger among women in such a country. In the United States, with few exceptions — notably in the clothing and textile trades — women workers do not belong to the trade unions at all. If, then, we reduce the number of organizable workers by subtracting the female element, the trade-union membership becomes 42 per cent of the residue.

Even in this most favorable light, trade-unionism remains a minority movement in the United States, though a large enough minority to merit serious consideration. To appreciate its full strength, however, still another factor must be taken into account. Organized labor flourishes chiefly in a few key industries, prominent among which are transportation, mining, clothing, building, and a few lines of metal working. In transportation, mining, and building, the unions are strong enough to cause an almost complete paralysis of these important industries in case of a general strike. The heart of American industry is the center of the trade, union movement. This must be borne in mind in appraising the social importance of organized labor.

5. Extent of Trade-Unionism in Great Britain [1]

The membership of the unions affiliated with the Trades Union Congress was over five million in 1922, which was a considerable decrease from the preceding two years, due to hard times. Thus it is seen that numerically British organized labor is more than twice as strong as the movement in the United States, in proportion to the population. It is stronger in other ways, also, notably in the fact that in Great Britain collective bargaining is accepted as the customary way of dealing between employers and workers.

[1] This article is based on *An Outline of the British Labor Movement*, by Paul Blanchard, chap. 4. George H. Doran Company, publishers.

Even the employees of the Government are for the most part organized. Just how strong the unions are is shown by the conduct of their great strikes. In the coal strike of 1921 about one million miners were on strike, while some three million other workers were unemployed, but no one seriously suggested the use of strike breakers in the mines.

The supreme body of the British unions is the Trades-Union Congress, which corresponds to the annual Convention of the American Federation of Labor, but which includes practically all the unions of strength and importance in Great Britain. It meets in an annual session, to which delegates come from all parts of the country to express their views on the broad general questions affecting the whole labor movement. It has no power to call a strike nor to impose on the local unions any definite policy. Nor has it any full-time officers.

To act in the interim when the Congress is not sitting, a General Council has been established. Within the labor movement it aims to settle the many disputes arising over jurisdiction, and the like. In meeting the common enemies of trade-unionism it aims to "formulate a common policy and secure the maximum of common action." It was created to conduct a general strike, but it is not clear that it will greatly facilitate such an affair. It is divided into six sections each including the trades which are naturally allied to one another. Thus one includes the miners, railroad workers, and transport workers, a reminder of the Triple Alliance. The whole Council is composed of thirty-two members elected each year by the Trades-Union Congress.

This General Council represents the industrial side of the labor army; there is also a National Joint Council of fifteen members which binds together the Labor Party, the Trades-Union Congress, and the Labor members in Parliament, having five members from each. The power of both these councils is quite limited, largely because the British policy has been to allow competing unions to affiliate, with the resulting tendency to weaken the central body. Moreover, the great British unions are jealous of their powers, and do not want any central body to direct their operations except in the most serious emergencies.

To meet the propaganda power of the Government and of the employing class, the Trades-Union Congress set up four special departments to manufacture mental dynamite for the labor movement. These are:

The Department of Research and Information
The Department of International Affairs
The Publicity Department
The Legal Department

This Big Four Intellectual Machine is able to provide statistics, and what is more present them to the public when desirable. It has also produced many valuable studies about the labor movement.

The real authority in the labor world rests with the national and local trade unions, which are controlled by the votes of their members. These unions do not yield to the Trades-Union Congress or to any other body the control of their policies. They may agree to a policy adopted by the Congress, but are not bound to obey it. They are organized in many ways; some are very democratic, of the town-meeting type; some are so highly centralized that the officers are able virtually to dictate all the policies. There are several union federations which are more important than the rest, such as:

The National Federation of Building Trades Operatives
The Iron and Steel Trades Confederation
The National Printing and Kindred Trades Federation
The Engineering and Shipbuilding Trades Federation
The National Association of Unions in the Textile Trades
The Northern Counties Textile Trades Federation
The United Textile Factory Workers Association

While some of these are mostly on paper, others are actual approaches to the "One Big Union" in their industry. On the whole they amount to amalgamations half completed. The most powerful unions in Great Britain are:

The Miners' Federation of Great Britain
The National Union of Railwaymen
The Transport and General Workers' Union
The Amalgamated Engineering Union
The National Union of General Workers
The Workers' Union

The Miners' Federation with 800,000 members is the largest. It is not a federation of national unions, but a combination of eighteen district unions which do not overlap. The Railwaymen are next in importance.

The national mutual benefit society of the British Labor movement is the General Federation of Trade Unions. Its chief function is to protect the workers against the risks of strikes and unemployment. It had in March, 1921, over 1,500,000 members, but the depression of 1922–23 caused it to decline rapidly.

The unions are also making gains in the ranks of the "white-collar workers." Over 100,000 teachers belonged to the National Union of Teachers in 1921, an organization which has even supported several teachers' strikes. The Post Office workers are organized, and have an aggressive policy. Clerks, insurance agents, foremen, and other brain-workers are becoming organized, some rapidly, some more slowly.

The British labor movement appears to be a kind of crazy-quilt at first glance, because the Trades-Union Congress admits competing unions and unions with overlapping jurisdictions to membership. There are over 150 unions represented in the cotton industry. Fortunately, in most matters of importance the different unions really act together, and the tendency is for the unions to amalgamate where the difficulties are not insuperable. This tendency is being encouraged.

British labor is represented at the sessions of the International Federation of Trade Unions at Amsterdam. It also exchanges delegates each year with the American Federation of Labor at their annual conventions. British workers are anxious to form a real alliance of the working classes of the two English-speaking peoples not only because such an alliance would have tremendous power in enforcing union standards but because the economic futures of Great Britain and the United States are bound up together. At present this is all the contact there is.

6. International Survey of Trade-Unionism [1]

A world movement. After the conclusion of the Armistice in 1918, the various direct and indirect hindrances to the develop-

[1] From the United States Bureau of Labor Statistics, *Monthly Labor Review*, vol. XIV (January, 1922), pp. 201–08.

ment of the economic organizations of workers due to the war were removed, and in the two years subsequent to the war trade-unionism experienced a phenomenal growth throughout the whole world. Trade-union membership reached its highest level at the end of the first half of 1920, but during the second half of that year the upward movement came to a standstill and in some countries there set in a retrograde movement which in 1921 seems to have become still more marked. Statistical data for this latest phenomenon are of course not yet available; data collected by the International Labor Office at Geneva make it, however, possible to follow the trade-union movement up to the end of 1920.

The total membership of the trade unions of 30 countries for which returns are available has trebled since 1913, having increased from 15,446,000 to 48,037,000 members. This very great increase in trade-union membership may be partly attributed to the fact that trade-union statistics are becoming more complete each year and thus reflect the real position more and more clearly. Allowance must also be made for a general increase in population, which plays a part in the increase of trade-union membership (probably about six per cent during the period). It should, moreover, be taken into consideration that Russia and Japan, in which countries in 1913 the trade unions were not yet legally recognized, are not included in the total for 1913, neither are Argentina, Greece, India, Poland, Portugal, and Spain, for which countries figures for that year were not available. Nevertheless, the above total membership figures indicate a very great increase in trade-union membership in the various countries of the world, more particularly in those which, since the Armistice have undergone great political changes. The future will show how far the trade unions will be able to adjust their organizations to the new conditions and to assimilate the hordes of new members. At present there seems to be a tendency among large parts of the trade-union membership to secede into new separate organizations.

Total trade-union membership of thirty countries. It is not possible to make anything more than a rough comparison between the totals of trade-union membership in various countries, as the degree of completeness and accuracy of the figures varies greatly. In most cases the statistics given here are based on returns voluntarily made by the trade unions to their Governments, or published in trade-union or other periodicals. In some countries the trade unions are centralized in great national federations, and in these cases the figures may be regarded as nearly complete, as the unions which are not affiliated to these central organizations are generally small ones. In the case of other countries, where there are a number of isolated local organizations, the available information is far less reliable.

The definition of the term "trade union" is somewhat difficult and varies from one country to another; an association which in one country would be called a trade union bears a different name in another. Account has here been taken rather of the idea than of the name.

For some years there are no available figures. In these cases approximate estimates have been made either from the figures of the preceding and following years, or from the calculations of the competent authorities of the country. All estimates contained in the following table are, however, designated as such.

Generally speaking, but especially as regards belligerent countries, the figures referring to the years 1914 to 1918 are not of great value. Trade-union statistics were almost everywhere disarranged by mobilization. In some countries mobilized members of the trade unions are omitted from the statistics, which thus show a great decrease in the membership; in other countries an attempt has been made to include them, but it has not been possible to arrive at such accurate results as formerly. Finally, some countries ceased entirely to publish statistics of this kind during the war.

The following table gives the total trade-union membership, so far as figures are available, in thirty countries for the years 1913, 1919, and 1920. Figures for the years 1914 to 1918 have been omitted for the reasons stated above.

The total membership figures given in the preceding table are not absolutely comparable. Only the total for 1919 is based on nearly complete information. For 1913 statistics are only available for twenty-one countries.

The third column of the table shows the total membership in 1920. For those countries (nine in number) for which no statistics are available the figures for 1919 were inserted in the column, as there has probably been no considerable decrease in membership in any of them. This gives us, according to most recent information, a total of 48,037,000 members in 1920 for all countries, a total which is probably not an overestimate. When com-

TOTAL TRADE-UNION MEMBERSHIP IN THIRTY COUNTRIES
1913, 1919, AND 1920

COUNTRY	1913	1919	1920
Argentine	[a]	40,000	68,000
Australia	498,000	628,000	684,000
Austria	260,000	803,000	901,000
Belgium	200,000	[b] 715,000	920,000
Bulgaria	[b] 30,000	36,000	[c] 36,000
Canada	176,000	378,000	374,000
Czecho-Slovakia	[a]	1,301,000	[b] 2,000,000
Denmark	152,000	360,000	[b] 400,000
Finland	28,000	41,000	59,000
France	1,027,000	[b] 2,500,000	[c] 2,500,000
Germany	4,513,000	11,900,000	[b] 13,000,000
Great Britain	4,173,000	8,024,000	[c] 8,024,000
Greece	[a]	170,000	[c] 170,000
Hungary	[b] 115,000	212,000	[b] 343,000
India	[a]	[b] 500,000	500,000
Italy	972,000	1,800,000	3,627,000
Japan	[a]	247,000	[c] 247,000
Netherlands	189,000	457,000	[b] 683,000
New Zealand	72,000	83,000	[c] 83,000
Norway	64,000	144,000	142,000
Poland	[a]	[b] 350,000	[b] 1,037,000
Portugal	[a]	100,000	[c] 100,000
Rumania (old)	10,000	[b] 75,000	90,000
Russia	[a]	3,639,000	5,220,000
Serbia (old)	9,000	20,000	[c] 20,000
South Africa	5,000	60,000	60,000
Spain	[a]	876,000	[c] 876,000
Sweden	136,000	339,000	[b] 400,000
Switzerland	[b] 95,000	[b] 200,000	292,000
United States	2,722,000	5,607,000	5,179,000
Total	[d] 15,446,000	41,605,000	48,037,000

[a] Figures not available.
[b] Estimates based on partial information.
[c] Figures for 1919.
[d] Not including figures for nine countries, not available.

pared with 1919, the figure for the total shows an increase of over 6,000,000 members in the course of a single year. It is estimated that in 1913 there were approximately 15,500,000 members, so that by 1920 pre-war membership had trebled.

Among the countries in which the increase has been greatest from 1913 to 1919, there must be mentioned Austria and Belgium, in which membership has more than trebled. Japan, Russia, and

Poland are in a somewhat peculiar position, for trade unions were not recognized by law in these countries in 1913 and therefore hardly existed at that time. In 1919, however, they had a large membership.

The countries in which the trade-union movement was most hampered by the war, namely, Germany, Austria, France, Hungary, Italy, and Czecho-Slovakia, have rapidly made up the deficiency since the Armistice. Their 1919 membership was at least double that of 1913, and their 1920 membership shows a further very considerable increase.

It is interesting to note further that of the total of 41,605,000 members in 1919, 34,061,000, or 82 per cent, belong to European countries. Of the remaining 7,544,000 non-European members, 5,985,000 belong to the North American Continent. A closer examination shows that the concentration of trade-union membership in certain countries is still more marked. Six countries, namely, Germany, Great Britain, the United States, Russia, France, and Italy, account in 1919 for 33,471,000 trade-union members, while the other 24 countries account for only 8,134,000. If, moreover, Russia, where the trade-union movement is of a peculiar nature, and Italy, where 60 per cent of the members are agricultural workers, metayers, and small farmers, are excluded, it is found that the four great industrial countries, Germany, Great Britain, the United States, and France, include more than 28,000,000 members, or 67 per cent of the recorded total of world trade-union membership in 1919.

The international movement. About one half of the membership of the trade unions of the world is, through their national central organizations, affiliated with one great international federation. Before the war this affiliation was affected in closest connection with the international organization of the Social-Democratic Party. After the international conference at Copenhagen in 1901 international conferences of the secretaries of the central trade-union organizations of the various countries took place at first every year, and later on every two years, and an international secretariat presided over by Legien, the president of the German General Federation of Labor, kept the various federations in contact with each other. The International Secretariat, which in 1913 assumed the name International Federation of Trade Unions, is an association of the national central organizations of the trade unions and recognizes only one trade-union federation in each country as the representative of organized labor in that country. It is due to this rule that the I.W.W. of America and the Federation of German Trade Unions of Czecho-Slovakia were not allowed to affiliate with the International Federation. In 1912 the number of national central organizations affiliated to the International Federation was nineteen. Their total membership was 7,400,000. In 1913 the central trade-union organizations of New Zealand and South Africa affiliated with the International Federation. The World War brought about the entire disruption of the International Federation, and in July, 1919, it was reorganized with a secretariat at Amsterdam. Not all of the countries formerly affiliated with it could, however, be induced to rejoin the reorganized International Federation. The American Federation of Labor reserved for some time its decision as to whether it would affiliate, and in the fall of 1920 it broke off definitely its relations with the International Federation, as it considered the political aims of the latter too radical. At the same time Russia issued a call for the foundation of a new "red" International in opposition to the "yellow" Amsterdam International. In spite of these secessions the International Federation had a membership of 23,662,000 at the end of 1920.

The Third International. Compared with the powerful organization of the International Federation of Trade Unions the "red" trade-union international, officially called the "International Council of Trade and Industrial Federations," but generally known under the name "Third International," lags far behind as to affiliated membership. Its membership is chiefly recruited from Eastern Europe. The declaration of principles of the Third International of July 15, 1920, is signed by trade-union federations of Russia, Italy, Spain, Bulgaria, and Jugoslavia, and by revolutionary minorities of the French and Georgian trade unions. The membership figures quoted by the Third International at the time of its foundation are without doubt very unreliable. The figure given for Bulgaria, for instance, is much too high, and the data as to the revolutionary minorities of federations not affiliated with the Third International are very arbitrary. It is, moreover, altogether impossible to give correct data as to the affiliated membership of the Third International because according to the resolutions adopted at its first congress of August, 1921, it is not the object of this organization to found new separate trade unions but to have its adherents "bore within" the old established trade unions until these declare themselves solidly for affiliation with the Third International. The statement made at the first congress of the Third International giving the number of affiliated members and adherents as between 17,000,000 and 18,000,000 must be considered as pure propaganda.

The refusal of the Third International to sanction the formation of independent trade unions has aroused strong opposition on the part of the syndicalistic and unionistic trade unions which exist as independent organizations. This opposition is especially strong in Germany and America. The attempt of the Third International to combine within its organization all the revolutionary elements among trade unions has therefore failed. Efforts of the unionists and syndicalists to form an international organization among themselves have likewise so far not led to any tangible results.

CHAPTER IX

FORMS OF ORGANIZED LABOR

1. Types of Unions [1]

From the popular viewpoint, trade-unionism is a simple, definite phenomenon upon which it is easy and safe to pass positive and sweeping judgments. Almost every one, in fact, who is at all interested in economic or social affairs is inclined to assume that he knows just about what unionism is, and just what ought to be done about it. The man in the street, the lawyer, the economist, the social worker, the teacher, the preacher, each has his positive concept and his positive scheme for union control or regeneration.

Conflicting concepts. Thus the student honestly seeking the truth about unionism is faced at the outset with a mass of confident but contradictory interpretations. He is told that unionism is a narrow group organization designed to benefit certain favored workmen at the expense of all others; that it is an artificial monopoly of labor, an impossible attempt to raise wages by unnatural and therefore socially inimical means; that it is the creation of selfish and unscrupulous leaders primarily for their personal gain and aggrandizement, a thing foisted upon unwilling workers and designed to disrupt the natural harmony of interests between employers and employees; that it is a mere business device for regulating wages and conditions of employment, by means of collective bargaining; that it is a great revolutionary movement, aiming ultimately to overthrow capitalism and our whole legal and moral code; that it is a universal expression of working-class idealism whose purpose it is to bring to all the toilers hope, dignity, enlightenment, and a reasonable standard of living; that it is, in short, selfish and altruistic, monopolistic and inclusive, artificial and natural, autocratic and democratic, violent and law-abiding, revolutionary and conservative, narrowly economic and broadly social.

And with each of these positive interpretations, a student is

[1] From an article by R. F. Hoxie, "Trade-Unionism in the United States — General Character and Types," in the *Journal of Political Economy*, vol. 22, pp. 201–17. University of Chicago Press, publishers.

commanded to subscribe to an equally positive and final solution of the union problem. He is informed that unionism will cease to be dangerous when it is boldly proceeded against as a trust; that the problem will be solved when once we have guaranties of industrial peace in the shape of universal arbitration schemes, voluntary or compulsory; that unionism is in any form a menace to social welfare and must, therefore, be destroyed by legal enactment and counter-organization; that the trouble with unionism is moral, and the obvious remedy lies, therefore, in moral suasion and the preaching of social obligation; that unionism is the expression of crass ignorance, and hence is to be quietly disregarded while schemes are formulated and put into operation for the welfare of society as a whole; that the real problem is one of encouragement and support, since unionism stands for all that is best in human conditions and relationships.

The mutual contradictoriness of these popular interpretations and remedies is sufficient evidence to warrant the rejection of any and all of them, pending the most unbiased and thoroughly scientific investigation of the facts. It must stamp them either as pure fabrications of the imagination or at best as partial truths, the outcome of narrow observation distorted by conscious or unconscious preconceptions derived from tradition, interest, or special environment. To accept them as final truths, therefore, is to block the way to a real comprehension of unionism and the union problem. For such acceptance must mean the coloring of the facts and the warping of the judgment, however sincere and painstaking the student may be. The first step, therefore, toward a scientific understanding of trade-unionism and the problems which it presents to us is to rid ourselves of the popular attitude toward it, and to root out of our minds as far as possible these popular conceptions of it. We must start by wiping the slate clean.

No uniform type. The very existence of these numerous contradictory interpretations, nevertheless, carries with it a pregnant suggestion for the student, namely, that trade-unionism may be, after all, not a simple, consistent entity, but a complex of the utmost diversity, both structurally and functionally. And, indeed, the most obvious facts of union status and history seem to warrant this conclusion, at least as a working hypothesis.

There are in the United States to-day hundreds of union organizations, each practically independent or sovereign, and each with its own and often peculiar aims, policies, demands, methods, attitudes, and internal regulations. Nor is there any visible or tangible bond, however tenuous, that unites these organizations into a single whole. Groups there are, indeed, with overstructures and declared common aims and methods. But group combats group with the bitterness that can arise only out of the widest diversity of ideals and methods.

A slight acquaintance with the history of organized labor shows that this situation is not unique, and at the same time furnishes the apparent clues to its explanation. It reveals the fact that unionism has not a single genesis, but that it has made its appearance time after time, independently, wherever in the modern industrial era a group of workers, large or small, has developed a strong internal consciousness of common interests. It shows, moreover, that each union and each union group has undergone a constant process of change or development, functionally and structurally, responding apparently to the group psychology and therefore to the changing conditions, needs, and problems of its membership. In short, it reveals trade-unionism as above all else essentially an opportunistic phenomenon.

For, if the history of unionism seems to admit of any positive generalizations, they are that unionists have been prone to act first and to formulate theories afterward, and that they have acted habitually to meet the problems thrust upon them by immediate circumstances. Everywhere they have done the thing which under the particular circumstances has seemed most likely to produce results immediately desired. Modes of action which have failed, when measured by this standard, have been rejected and other means sought. Methods that have worked have been preserved and extended, the standards of judgment being always most largely the needs and experiences of the group concerned. So that, prevailingly, whatever theory unionists have possessed has been in the nature of group generalization, slowly developed on the basis of concrete experience.

In making these statements, it is not intended to imply that general economic, political, and social theories have not played a part in the genesis of unions, or in the moulding of their function and structure. Nor is it intended to deny that some unions have been formed and dominated by individuals and small groups of leaders. Idealism has frequently been a genetic and formative force in union history and the autocrat has played an important rôle in union affairs. But apparently history warrants the general statements that unions, and especially unions that have lived and worked, have arisen mainly in direct response to the immediate needs and problems of specific working groups, and that they have developed characteristically by the trial-and-error method.

Thus the scope and character of union ideals and methods have been as broad and diverse as the conscious common needs and conditions of the groups of workers entering into organization. Some unions have confined themselves to attempts to deal directly with their immediate employers and their immediate conditions of work and pay; others have emphasized mutual aid and education; still others have enlarged their fields of thought and action to include all employers and all conditions — economic, legal, and social. In other words, the union program, taking it with all its mutations and contradictions, comprehends nothing less than all the various economic, political, ethical, social viewpoints and modes of action of a vast and heterogeneous complex of working-class groups, moulded by diverse environments and actuated by diverse motives; it expresses nothing less than the ideals, aspirations, hopes, and fears, modes of thinking and action of all these working groups. In short, if we can think of unionism as such, it must be as one of the most complex, heterogeneous and protean of modern social phenomena.

But can we thus think of it? If all that has been said be true, are we not forced to this pregnant conclusion as the basic hypothesis of our study — namely: that there is no such thing as unionism, either in the sense of an abstract unity, or of a concrete, organic, and consistent whole, which can be crowded within the confines of a narrow definition or judged sweepingly as good or bad, right or wrong, socially helpful or harmful? If, then, we dispense with narrow preconceptions and face things as they actually are, and are becoming, it is impossible to say that unionism as such is artificial or natural, revolutionary or conservative, violent or law-abiding, monopolistic or inclusive, boss-ridden or democratic, opposed to industrial progress or favorable to efficiency, the spontaneous outgrowth of legitimate needs or the product and tool of selfish and designing individuals. In short, there is unionism and unionism. But looking at matters concretely and realistically, there is no single thing that can be taken as unionism per se.

It follows as a corollary that the union problem is neither simple nor unitary. It is not a mere question of wages and hours, of shop conditions, and of narrow economic rights of employer and employee, and it cannot be solved by a mere resort to economic theory. On the contrary, it is a complex of economic, legal, ethical and social problems, which can be understood and met only by knowing the facts and the genesis of the viewpoint of organized labor in all its reach, diversity, contradictoriness, and shifting character, and by considering this viewpoint in relation to developing social conditions and social standards.

The study of unionism, therefore, if it is to be fruitful, that is, if it is to assist in the solution of our economic and social problems, must be realistic and scientific. Unionism is what it is and not what any advocate or opponent would have it to be. It is a matter of fact in the same sense that institutions, animal and plant species, or any other organic manifestations are matters of fact. There is no normal or abnormal unionism; no unionism that is artificial as distinguished from that which is natural. In short, there is no fixed union norm by which any concrete case is to be tested; for all unionism is, and is becoming by virtue of sufficient causation. The problems which it raises, therefore, like all other problems of a scientific nature, are to be solved, if at all, not through passion and prejudice, and formulations of what ought to be, but through an intimate knowledge of the facts as they exist and study of causes. It is for the student, then, to put aside his preconceptions and feelings, to get close to the realities, to be willing to follow the truth to whatever conclusions it may lead. Calmly and dispassionately we must seek to know unionism as it actually appears in all its phases and to search for its underlying causes. Only after we have studied it and its problems thus in the spirit of the biologist or of the student of social psychology and social institutions, shall we be in a position to say positively what unionism really is and what, if anything, should and can be done about it. It is in this spirit that the following tentative analysis is presented.

Structural types. The master key to the real character of unionism and union problems is to be found apparently in the existence of distinct union types. Though unionism itself is so pragmatic and therefore so protean as to warrant the rejection of all attempts to characterize and judge it as a whole, it has seemingly developed along certain fairly distinct general lines, giving rise thus to types sufficiently definite to allow of legitimate generalization in regard to them. It appears possible to distinguish such types, both as to function and structure. Structural types have, indeed, been recognized quite generally by students. Examination of the history and present status of unionism in the United States appears to reveal four such types, each objectified in a variety of concrete units; while, somewhat akin to these distinct types, may be distinguished other forms which may perhaps be regarded as modes of transition from one to the other.

Craft. Naming the structural types in what hypothetically may perhaps be considered their natural sequence of development, we find, first, what is ordinarily called the craft union. This is an organization of wage workers engaged in a single occupation, as, for example, in glass bottle blowing, horseshoeing, locomotive engineering. The occupation may be limited strictly to one simple task, or may include a number of closely allied tasks or crafts. The strict test of a craft union seems to be that each member of the organization performs or may perform all the tasks included in the occupation. Usually a craft union covers but a fraction of the work of a given industry. The craft organization has developed two principal units, or appears in two main forms; the local craft union, which usually unites the members of the craft or occupation working in a particular locality — a town, a city, or a section of a city; the national or international craft union, which unites into one organization the local units of a single craft or occupation throughout the country or neighboring countries.

Trades unions. Secondly, there appears what may be termed the crafts or trades union. This organization is a federation of unions in different crafts or industries. It has developed three principal forms or units: the local trades union, or city federation;

the state federation; and the national or international federation, which unite through delegate organizations, respectively, the unions of a locality, a State, or a larger territorial area. Examples are the Chicago Federation of Labor, the Illinois Federation of Labor, and the American Federation of Labor. The essential characteristic of the trades union is that the constituent organizations retain their individual independence or sovereignty.

Industrial. Thirdly, we may distinguish the industrial union. This type, as the name implies, is organized on the basis of the industry rather than the craft. That is to say, it attempts to unite into one homogeneous organic group all the workers, skilled and unskilled, engaged in turning out and putting on the market a given finished product or series of closely related products. For example, this type of union would unite all the craftsmen in the direct employ of brewing concerns, including not only actual brewers, maltsters, bottlers, and packers, but the engineers, firemen, teamsters, watchmen, etc.; or, again, it would organize into one union all the workmen in and about a coal mine, including actual miners, miners' helpers, shot-firers, drivers, spraggers, trappers, trackmen, timbermen, hoisting engineers, check-weighmen, dumpers, etc. The actual connotation of this type of unionism varies in different productive lines and with the integration of productive enterprise, but the essential test of industrial unionism seems to be that the industrial scope or area of the workers' organization shall be coterminous with that of the capitalistic enterprise or series of closely related enterprises. The main forms or units of this type of unionism thus far are: the local industrial union, a combination of all the employees of a single local industrial plant or of all the industrial enterprises of a like character in a given locality; the national or international industrial union, a combination of all the workers in a given industry throughout the Nation or the international economic unit; the district industrial union, an organization covering an area within which productive and market conditions are essentially similar. Thus, for example, the coal-mine workers are organized into local unions at the mines, into an international union including workers in the mines of the United States and Canada, and into district organizations covering adjacent bituminous or anthracite mines or fields.

Labor unions. Fourthly, there exists what is technically known as the "labor union." This type of unionism proposes the organization of all workers regardless of craft or industrial division into homogeneous groups by localities, by districts, and throughout the Nation or largest possible international area. At present the local labor union is the only existing unit of importance in the United States which realizes this ideal of organization, though attempts have been made, notably in the case of the Knights of Labor, to establish and maintain labor-unionism in all its ideal forms, local, district, and national.

Compound forms. Besides these four structural types of unionism, there exist in this country at least two varieties which can hardly be designated as distinct types, but which, strictly speaking, are apparently neither craft, trades, industrial, nor labor unions. The first of these varieties may be called the "compound" craft or crafts union. It is a centralized, homogeneous organization of the workers in a number of related crafts. It differs from the craft union in that it includes workers who do not engage in the same tasks or occupations. But it is not an industrial union, since it may be one of several labor organizations whose workers are engaged in turning out a given finished product, or are in the employ of a single capitalistic enterprise. On the other hand, it may overlap industrial divisions. It may be the outcome of a formal consolidation of two or more crafts or compound craft unions, in which case it is usually known as an "amalgamated" craft or crafts union. Examples of this variety of unionism are to be found in the Amalgamated Association of Iron, Tin, and Steel Workers of North America, the Amalgamated Meat Cutters and Butcher Workmen of North America, the International Association of Machinists, and the Amalgamated Association of Street and Electrical Employees of America. In fact, a large proportion of the unions, local and national, in the United States are to-day compound or amalgamated craft unions, whether or not so designated by title. As this variety of union has special representatives in all the intermediate structural stages between strict craft-unionism and industrial unionism, it would perhaps be not unreasonable to regard it, provisionally at least, as a mode of transition between these two distinct types. Later considerations, however, must determine the truth of this assumption and, if true, the general direction of the developmental tendency.

The second structural variety of unionism which is difficult to classify may, in the absence of any generally accepted designation, be termed the "quasi-industrial federation." It is generally a federation of industrially related craft and compound craft unions, appearing in local, district, or state, and national units. Examples of it are to be seen in local printing trades, and local building trades councils, in state building trades councils and system federations of railway employees, and in the building trades, metal trades, and railroad employees' departments of the American Federation of Labor. This variety of unionism is one in which the constituent craft or amalgamated craft unions retain their individual sovereignty, yet appear and act as a single organization with respect to designated affairs of common interests. It resembles both the trades union and the industrial-union types, but differs from each essentially. It is a narrower and closer association than the trades union and is vitally unlike it in the scope and character of its activities. On the other hand, it lacks the organic homogeneity and centralization of the industrial union. As it is in every case, roughly speaking, an organization within a particular industry, and as its aims and activities approximate — as far as they go — those of the industrial-union type, it may perhaps be regarded also as an intermediate phase — a mode of transition between the craft and the industrial union. Whether it represents thus a continuous evolutionary process, and, if so, what the nature of the process is, will appear from later consideration.

Functional types. As we have said, the existence of distinct structural types and varieties of unionism has quite generally been recognized, and it has been noted further that union function tends to vary somewhat with the variation in structure. It seems possible, however, to go much further than this in the general functional analysis of unionism. A penetrating study of the union situation, past and present, seems, in fact, to warrant the recognition of functional types quite as distinct in their essential characteristics as the diverse structural manifestations. It is true that these functional types do not in practice represent exactly and exclusively the ideas and activities of any particular union organization or group. That is to say, no union organization functions strictly and consistently according to type. Yet as representing as fairly distinct alternative programs of union action, and as guides to the essential character and significance of the diverse organizations and groups included in the heterogeneous union complex, these functional types apparently do exist, and are of the most vital concern to the student of unionism. There are seemingly four of these distinct types, two of which present dual variations.

Business unions. The first and perhaps most clearly recognizable functional type may be termed "business-unionism." Business-unionism appears most characteristically in the programs of local and national craft and compound craft organizations. It is essentially trade-conscious, rather than class-conscious. That is to say, it expresses the viewpoint and interests of the workers in a craft or industry rather than those of the working class as a whole. It aims chiefly at more, here and now, for the organized workers of the craft or industry, in terms mainly of higher wages, shorter hours, and better working conditions, regardless for the most part of the welfare of the workers outside the particular organic group, and regardless in general of political and social considerations, except in so far as these bear directly upon its own economic ends. It is conservative in the sense that it professes belief in natural rights, and accepts as inevitable, if not as just, the existing capitalistic organization and the wage system, as well as existing property rights and the binding force of contract. It regards unionism mainly as a bargaining institution, and seeks its ends chiefly through collective bargaining, supported by such methods as experience from time to time indicates to be effective in sustaining and increasing its bargaining power. Thus it is likely to be exclusive — that is, to limit its membership, by means of the apprenticeship system and high initiation fees and dues, to the more skilled workers in the craft or industry, or even to a portion of these; though it may, where immediate circumstances dictate, favor a broadly inclusive policy — when, for example, the unregulated competition of the organized and unskilled seriously threatens to sweep aside the trade barriers and break down the standards of wages, hours, and shop conditions it has erected. Under these circumstances it tends to develop a broad altruism and to seek the organization of all the workers in the craft or industry. In harmony with its business character it tends to emphasize discipline within the organization, and is prone to develop strong leadership and to become somewhat autocratic in government, though government and leaders are ordinarily held pretty strictly accountable to the pragmatic test. When they fail to "deliver the goods," both are likely to be swept aside by a democratic uprising of the rank and file. In method, business-unionism is prevailingly temperate and economic. It favors voluntary arbitration, deprecates strikes, and avoids political action, but it will refuse arbitration, and will resort to strikes and politics when such action seems best calculated to support its bargaining efforts and increase its bargaining power. This type of unionism is perhaps best represented in the program of the railroad brotherhoods, though these organizations, as we shall see later, present some characteristics of a vitally different nature.

Uplift unions. The second union functional type seems best designated by the terms "friendly" or "uplift" unionism. Uplift unionism, as its name indicates, is characteristically idealistic in its viewpoint. It may be trade-conscious, or broadly class-conscious, and at times even claim to think and act in the interest of society as a whole. Essentially it is conservative and law-abiding. It aspires chiefly to elevate the moral, intellectual, and social life of the worker, to improve the conditions under which he works, to raise his material standards of living, give him a sense of personal worth and dignity, secure for him the leisure for culture, and insure him and his family against the loss of a decent livelihood by reason of unemployment, accident, disease, or old age. Uplift unionism varies greatly in degree of inclusiveness, and in form of government. But the tendency seems to be toward the greatest practicable degree of mutuality and democracy. In method, this type of unionism employs collective bargaining, but stresses mutual insurance, and drifts easily into political action and the advocacy of coöperative enterprises, profit-sharing, and other idealistic plans for social regeneration. The nearest approach in practice to uplift unionism is perhaps to be found in the program of the Knights of Labor, though that organization has varied in many respects from the strict type.

Revolutionary unions. As a third distinct functional type, we have what most appropriately may be called "revolutionary" unionism. Revolutionary unionism, as the term implies, is extremely radical both in viewpoint and in action. It is distinctly class-conscious rather than trade-conscious. That is to say, it asserts the complete harmony of interests of all wage-workers as against the representatives of the employing class, and seeks to unite the former, skilled and unskilled, together into one homogeneous fighting organization. It repudiates, or tends to repudiate, the existing institutional order and especially individual ownership of productive means, and wage system. It looks upon the prevailing modes of right and rights, moral and legal, as, in general, fabrications of the employing class, designed to secure the subjection and to further the exploitation of the workers. In government it aspires to be democratic, striving to make literal application of the phrase *vox populi, vox Dei.* In method, it looks askance at collective bargaining and mutual insurance as making for conservatism and hampering the free and united action of the workers.

Of this revolutionary type of unionism there are apparently two distinct varieties. The first finds its ultimate ideal in the socialistic state and its ultimate means in invoking class political action. For the present it does not entirely repudiate collective bargaining or the binding force of contract, but it regards these as temporary expedients. It would not now amalgamate unionist and socialist organizations, but would have them practically identical in membership and entirely harmonious in action. In short, it looks upon unionism and socialism as the two wings of the working-class movement. The second variety of revolutionary unionism repudiates altogether socialism, political action, collective bargaining, and contract. Socialism is to it but another form of oppression, political action a practical delusion, collective bargaining and contract schemes of the oppressor for preventing the united and immediate action of the workers. It looks forward to a society based upon free industrial association, and finds its legitimate means in agitation, rather than in methods which look to immediate betterment. Direct action and sabotage are its accredited weapons, and violence its habitual resort. These varieties of the revolutionary type may be termed respectively "socialistic" and "quasi-anarchistic" unionism. The former is perhaps most clearly represented in the United States by the Western Federation of Miners, the latter by the Industrial Workers of the World.

Predatory unions. Finally, in the union complex, it seems possible to distinguish a mode of action sufficiently definite in its character and genesis to warrant the designation "predatory" unionism. This type, if it be truly such, cannot be set apart on the basis of any ultimate social ideals or theory. It may be essentially conservative or radical, trade-conscious or class-conscious. It appears to aim solely at immediate ends and its methods are wholly pragmatic. In short, its distinguishing characteristic is the ruthless pursuit of the thing in hand by whatever means seem most appropriate at the time, regardless of ethical and legal codes or effect upon those outside its own membership. It may employ business, friendly, or revolutionary methods. Generally, its operations are secret, and apparently it sticks at nothing.

Of this assumed union type also there appear to be two varieties. The first may be termed "hold-up" unionism. This variety is usually to be found in large industrial centers, masquerading as business-unionism. In outward appearance it is conservative; it professes a belief in harmony of interests between employer and employee; it claims to respect the force of contract; it operates openly through collective bargaining, and professes regard for law and order. In reality it has no abiding principles, and no real concern for the rights or welfare of outsiders. Prevailingly it is exclusive and monopolistic. Generally it is boss-ridden and corrupt, the membership for the most part being content to follow blindly the instructions of the leaders so long as they "deliver the goods." Frequently it enters with the employers of the group into a double-sided monopoly intended to eliminate both capitalistic and labor competition, and to squeeze the consuming public. With favored employers, it bargains not only for the sale of its labor, but for the destruction of the business of rival employers and the exclusion of rival workmen from the craft or industry. On the whole its methods are a mixture of open bargaining coupled with secret bribery and violence. This variety of unionism has been exemplified most frequently among the building trades organizations under the leadership of men like the late notorious "Skinny" Madden.

The second variety of predatory labor organization may be called, for want of a better name, "guerrilla" unionism. This variety resembles the first in the absence of fixed principles and in the ruthless pursuit of immediate ends by means of secret and violent methods. It is to be distinguished from hold-up unionism, however, by the fact that it operates always directly against its employers, never in combination with them, and that it cannot be bought off. It is secret, violent, and ruthless, seemingly because it despairs of attaining what it considers to be legitimate ends by business uplift or revolutionary methods. This union variant has been illustrated recently in the campaign of destruction carried on by the Bridge and Structural Iron Workers.

The writer is aware that, apparently, strong objections may be urged against the assumption that these diverse expressions of union viewpoint and action represent true functional types. It has been admitted that probably the ideals and modes of action of no particular union organization correspond exactly to any one of these so-called types. It is a fact, moreover, that the programs of most unions are undergoing a pretty constant process of change and sometimes shift rapidly. It is true further that the membership of any union may include representatives of all kinds of unionism — business, uplift, revolutionary, and predatory. It might then be argued that what have here been called types are mere individual attitudes, or, at most, aspects or tendencies of one and the same union species. It will be the purpose of succeeding chapters, therefore, to test the reality of these assumed types and varieties, and to interpret them causally by means of a brief study of the genesis and development of organized labor in the United States. Incidentally this study should reveal also the general laws of union development.

2. Structure and Government of the Craft Union[1]

The local union. There is now a strong tendency to unite all of the trades or divisions of a trade in any one industry into a single national federation of local societies. Thus the present

[1] Adapted from *The Government of American Trade Unions*, by T. W. Glocker. The Johns Hopkins Press, publishers.

national union of wooden shipbuilders includes shipwrights, joiners, caulkers, boat-builders, and ship cabinet-makers. For many years the International Typographical Union embraced bookbinders, compositors, pressmen, stereotypers and electrotypers, and photo-engravers, and to-day it has jurisdiction over compositors, proof-readers, machine-tenders, mailers, and type-founders.

The organization of the members of several trades, or branches of a trade in the same local union, has, however, been found undesirable. In the first place, each group of workmen in an industry resents the right of the other groups to vote upon the numerous matters which it considers its particular concern. If in addition one group of workers is in the majority and is able to dominate the general meeting, friction is almost inevitable. At the same time, the very close coöperation required to maintain a uniform scale of wages for journeymen performing the same work is unnecessary between groups of employees doing different kinds of work and hence receiving different wages.

In some national unions there has been urged the adoption of a rule requiring that the members doing a certain kind of work be always organized into separate local unions, and that in places where they are not sufficiently numerous to form a union they join the nearest local union of this branch of the trade. Such a rule was advocated but not passed by the Cigar-Makers' International Union after the admission of the cigar-packers about 1885. Most national unions charter a separate local union for each of the most important branches of the trade in the large cities, and in the small places unite all members in one union. In small communities there are too few of each division of the craft to warrant separation, and the boundaries between trades are not always so clearly defined as in the large cities. Thus the bricklayers, who in the large cities only lay bricks, in rural sections often do the work of stonemasons and plasterers.

Division of local unions. Experience has shown that whenever it is possible women should be organized separately. In the first place, women hesitate to join a union composed largely of men. Moreover, the claim is made that in mixed local unions the men do not accord the women full opportunity to discuss their particular class concerns, and show prejudice when allowed to vote on questions of interest to their female members. Certainly women's unions enroll a much larger proportion of the female section of the trade and arouse greater and more sustained enthusiasm than do mixed unions.

The appearance of the negro as an industrial competitor caused another division of the local union in a number of trades. After the close of the Civil War the competition of the newly emancipated negro was greatly feared by many American workmen. "The negro," declared the president of the Workingmen's Assembly of the State of New York in 1870, "will no longer submit to occupy positions of a degrading nature, but will seek an equality with the whites in the various trades and professions. For a time, we may not have to contend against their labor; and all may be well. Yet I feel impressed with the necessity of preparing for the future by organizing such colored workmen as may now or hereafter exist *into unions by themselves*, and recognizing their organizations. If we discard this element of labor and refuse to recognize it, capital will recognize it and use it to our great disadvantage." Already, indeed, in 1867 the importation of colored ship caulkers from Portsmouth, Virginia, to Boston during the struggle in that city for an eight-hour day had been a practical illustration of the way in which the negro might be used as a strike breaker.

At this time the white mechanics refused consistently to admit colored men into their own local unions; and in very few localities were there enough negroes employed at the same trade to make possible the formation of separate colored unions.

When the national associations have removed the ban of prohibition, subordinate local unions have frequently refused to admit negroes, and have demanded that they be organized under separate charters. As a rule, distinctions as to color are less frequently made in the North.

Friction between nationalities has led to further subdivision of the local union in a good many American trades. The Anthracite Coal Strike Commission found some nineteen nationalities at work in the mines. The employees of the Colorado Fuel and Iron Company include representatives, it is said, of thirty-two nationalities speaking twenty-seven different languages; in the meat-packing houses of Chicago, Germans, Bohemians, Lithuanians, Poles, Slovaks, Italians, and Greeks have succeeded one another in bewildering succession. Obviously, to organize each of these many races into separate local unions is frequently impossible, and national trade unions whose members speak many tongues often refuse to attempt it. Resort is had to various expedients in order that business may be transacted. Constitutions, circulars, and other documents are printed in several languages. Interpreters are used at the meetings of the local unions; a recording secretary is sometimes created for each language spoken by the members, and the officers are usually divided among the several nationalities. In a few instances the various races meet in adjoining rooms, and propositions are brought successively before each body. Such makeshifts are inconvenient; and, when race antagonism arises, the only solution is the subdivision of the local. Besides general race antipathy, ill-feeling between nationalities arises in various ways. In the late seventies a union of foreign cigar-makers, composed of Cubans, Spaniards, Mexicans, and Italians, with a preponderance of the Spanish element, was formed in New York City. Shortly afterwards, during the public agitation in favor of Cuban liberty, the members began to discuss current political questions, with the result that the local union went to pieces.

A local union, though its members comprise a comparatively homogeneous group, may be divided because it has become too large for good government. If the number of members is too great, the meetings degenerate into mob assemblages, and intelligent discussion of any important question is difficult. Men who advocate a sane and conservative policy are often hissed down. Factions are inevitably created, and threaten by their acrimonious bickerings to disrupt the organization.

Unscrupulous leaders also take advantage of such conditions to establish themselves in power. In the days of Sam Parks, the walking delegate of the Structural Iron Workers who was sent to Sing Sing Prison for blackmailing employers, there was only one local union of structural iron workers in New York City. The membership was nearly four thousand, and meetings were held in a small hall which seated only a few hundred. Sam Parks built up a small army of followers by using the power which his position gave over employers to secure the jobs as foremen and other choice positions for his favorites. When he desired reëlection or needed a vote of confidence, he would order his adherents to come early. The room would be packed with men who voted as he desired, and the other members would fail to find admittance. A somewhat similar condition of things has at times existed in the New York and Chicago unions of bricklayers and in other large local unions in other trades. For example, Local Union of Bricklayers No. 7 of New York City had in 1870 a membership of two thousand, and met in a hall with a seating capacity of three hundred and fifty. There were several factions within the organization, and, in order to secure the adoption of a particular measure, one clique would sometimes pack the hall. In this way a minority in the local union brought about, for a time, the withdrawal of the New York local union from the international union.

The size of the local union is greatly diminished in many organizations by division according to branch of the trade, sex, color, or nationality. For example, in New York City the local union of structural iron workers of Sam Parks' day has been replaced by three unions, one of housesmiths and bridge men, another of inside architectural bridge and structural iron workers, and a third of finishers. But in unions such as the Bricklayers and the Carpenters, where subdivisions according to trade, sex, color, or nationality are unimportant, the local unions are very frequently too large. The international secretary of the Bricklayers has several times proposed to prevent the growth of such large unions by limiting the membership of each local union to five hundred. A rule limiting the membership of each subordinate association to four hundred was adopted by the United Brotherhood of Carpenters in 1886. The provision proved unsatisfactory, however, and it was repealed a few years later. As far, then, as present indications show, the general tendency seems to be not to adopt rigid rules as to size, but to create additional local unions in any community as occasion appears to demand.

The federation of local unions. During the latter half of the nineteenth century the local societies of organized trades have as a rule been federated into district, state, national, and international unions. The most common form of federal association is the international union with jurisdiction over subordinate societies in Canada and sometimes even in Mexico as well as in the United States. There have been three important causes of the federation of local trade unions: first, the movement of workmen from one city to another; second, the competition between manufacturers in different places; and third, the need of a joint fund for the support of certain trade-union activities.

Probably the chief cause of the federation of local trade organizations has been the constant movement of journeymen from one part of the country to another. This form of labor competition existed, of course, from the birth of American trade-unionism, and in 1815 was already a very serious problem to the local societies of printers which had been formed by that date in all the large cities of the Atlantic seaboard. One writer, discussing the movements of the working population in 1847, just a few years before the era of federal unionism, says of the artisan class that they, too, like their richer neighbors, "must sometimes change their place. When work is dull in one town, they go to another, and there are thus two streams of workmen perpetually setting between our two great cities, while in a smaller degree a similar circulation is kept up through the whole country. There is also a current of emigrants to the west; and, in this, there is always a considerable infusion of mechanical labor."

Effect of labor mobility. With increased rapidity and decreased cost of railway transportation, labor has become continually more mobile. In nearly all trades there is a class of traveling craftsmen or "tramp" journeymen, mostly young men, who, imbued with the modern spirit of restlessness, travel from place to place, and work for a few weeks or months, now here, now there, as fancy or the hope of larger wages may direct. The amount of this shifting labor is especially large in the building trades, probably because of the intermittent character of the work, and regularly organized gangs move constantly to those localities where building operations are especially active. A few years ago a part of this shifting body of laborers may have been at work on the buildings of the World's Fair in St. Louis. Later, they were employed perhaps on the New York subway. Then, possibly, the building operations in Baltimore's burnt district attracted them; and still later they may have been engaged on the buildings of the Jamestown Exposition or upon the reconstruction of San Francisco.

Besides the labor current between the cities, there are smaller eddies from the country and small towns into the large cities, and *vice versa.* The union carpenters in large cities for years have complained bitterly of periodic invasions by the "hatchet and saw" carpenters from the surrounding country and the small outlying towns. On the other hand, the photo-engravers in the small towns of New England and of New York State fear the competition of the photo-engravers coming from New York City, who are in great demand on account of their superior skill, and replace, even at considerably higher wages, the poorer resident workmen.

An industrial depression, the introduction of machinery, or any other condition which increases the unemployment or decreases the skill required serves to intensify in any trade this interurban competition. About the year 1880 wood-working machinery was introduced in planing mills; and as a consequence the doors, sashes, mouldings, window-frames, and other fittings which the carpenter had formerly made by hand in his workshop were now made by machinery in the factory. Consequently, in every large city there was created a small army of idle members of the trade, ready to "scab" in their own or other towns. At the same time the work of the carpenter on a building had been minutely subdivided. For this reason the annual influx of relatively unskilled country carpenters assumed large proportions.

This movement of workmen from one place to another handicaps the local union greatly in its efforts to improve the conditions of employment. Frequently when a local union has succeeded in raising wages above the general level, union and non-union members of the trade in other cities who hear of it rush to the place, and by their underbidding force down wages possibly below their original level.

Sometimes local unions engaged in industrial war have discovered unexpectedly that their strike is lost because the employers have been able by advertisements to secure from other cities journeymen who were willing to act as strike breakers.

The movement of journeymen from place to place neutralizes the efforts of the independent local societies to control the supply of workers by limiting the number of those learning the craft. For example, a union in Baltimore may enforce the most rigid rules for defining the period of apprenticeship and the number of apprentices to each shop; but if the unions of the craft in Philadelphia and Washington have a lax apprenticeship system, probably the only result will be that Baltimore will serve as a convenient outlet for the constantly accumulating body unemployed in both cities. The need of some national regulation of apprenticeship, therefore, has been another cause for the federation of local unions.

As long as the local societies of a trade are not united, the member suspended for non-payment of dues or for some other violation of the union rules is able to escape his penalty by traveling to another city. There, upon payment of an initiation fee, he will probably be admitted to the union of the locality, and so will be able to find employment. Under such circumstances the threat of suspension loses some of its terror for the delinquent, and much of the coercive power of the union over its members is destroyed. The effective punishment of outlawed members has been an incidental purpose in the organization of federal trade unions.

On the other hand, from the point of view of the traveling journeyman some agreement between the scattered local unions of a trade is desirable, in order that he may be admitted more readily to the union of the place in which he hopes to find work. The ardent unionist is often unable to pay the high initiation fee required for membership in the association of the place to which he has journeyed in search of work. Consequently, he turns "scab," and accepts a much lower wage than he had previously earned, or, if the local union is strong, does not find employment.

Need of uniformity in local conditions. A second important cause of the federation of local societies has been the need of keeping wages and other conditions of employment affecting cost of production uniform in competing establishments. A typical illustration is afforded by the boot and shoe industry. Except for certain popular high-grade shoes, competition between manufacturers of footwear in various parts of the country has reduced profits to a very small amount. At the same time, one trust, by means of its ownership of patents, has been able to control the price of shoe machinery, and another trust, aided until recently by a prohibitive tariff on hides, has been able to fix the price of leather. Moreover, methods of production are very much the same in all parts of the country. The most important variable element in the cost of production is, therefore, wages; and a difference of a few cents per piece in several departments of a factory, or possibly even in a single department, may make the difference between ruin and prosperous business. Therefore, the boot and shoe manufacturer resists desperately any attempt of a local union to raise wages. If the union is strong and he is forced to yield, he may be compelled through the falling-off of sales to shut down his plant or reduce his working force.

The independent local unions have great difficulty not only in raising wages, but also in preventing them from falling in sympathy with reductions in other places. An employer calls together his employees, and informs them that his rivals in other cities are driving him out of business. If he continues to pay the same wages as before, he will be compelled, he tells them, to shut down his plant, certainly during the dull season. If, however, they will submit to a ten-per-cent reduction, he will be able to sell his shoes, coal, iron, or whatever the commodity may be, some cents cheaper, and will secure certain large contracts for goods. The men, he declares, will lose nothing by the reduction. The factory will continue to run at full time, and some may even recover the lost wages by working overtime. His employees in all probability yield, and then his competitors, who find themselves losing trade, propose in turn a reduction to their men, and so the movement spreads.

Effect of benefit features. A third important reason for the federation of local societies has been the need of a joint fund from which to pay strike, sick, death, disability, and out-of-work benefits. Such a joint fund has been greatly needed to support the members of a local union involved in a strike. If a strike has behind it the financial resources of all the local unions of a trade, amounting perhaps to a hundred thousand dollars, it has obviously much more chance of success than when supported by only one local union with perhaps fifteen hundred dollars in its treasury. With a hundred thousand dollars instead of fifteen hundred dollars to draw upon, the members involved in a difficulty with employers can be supported for a much longer time. "Scabs" can also be bought off and kept from taking the places of the strikers.

The payment of sick, death, or out-of-work benefits from the federal rather than the local treasury is urged for two reasons. In the first place, when each subordinate union maintains its own system of benefits, a member forfeits the right to enjoy them whenever he travels to another city in search of work, for even if the union in the city to which he journeys does pay benefits of identical amounts and character, a new member must usually be a member for six months or a year before he becomes entitled to receive them. In the second place, only the large local unions are able to maintain systems of benevolent relief. A single death during the first year would probably bankrupt the small union of ten or twenty members.

Industrial depressions have been the chief cause of the dissolution of federal trade unions in the United States. The union men who are thrown out of employment feel themselves unable to pay their dues, and so are suspended from the trade organizations; or, what is worse from a union point of view, many of them, demoralized by unemployment, lose faith in the system of collective bargaining and stand ready to take the places of their fellow workmen at wages far below the union scale. To add to the demoralizing influence of the depression, many trade unions, utterly unmindful of the rapidly thinning ranks of organized labor and of the hundreds who are vainly seeking employment, rush into strikes against reductions in wages. The strike is lost, the funds of the association are exhausted, the men, replaced by others, join the mass of the unemployed, and the association goes to pieces. The national unions show the effects of the depression more quickly than the local unions, since the strike funds of the national organization are the first to be exhausted, and the local unions which survive the first blast of the industrial storm abandon allegiance to the now impotent central association, and strive to fight on alone. After the depression, the local unions, which had dissolved, begin to reorganize, and these, together with the survivors, unite again into federal associations.

The American Federation of Labor, which displaced the Knights of Labor, has been active in forming national and international trade unions. A loose confederation, created and controlled by the existing national unions, it has not, like the Knights, aroused conflict and antagonism. In 1905 one hundred and eighteen of the one hundred and thirty national and international unions belonged to the Federation. Moreover, the number of national associations is being constantly swelled through the efforts of paid agents maintained by the American Federation of Labor. These agents are continually organizing local unions among the non-union workers in various industries and welding them together into international trade unions.

Nationalizing effect of A. F. of L. The influence of the American Federation of Labor has also tended to hasten materially the transition from local to national unionism. Formerly, local unions of a trade existed usually for some years before they were federated, often reluctantly, into national and international associations. Under the influence of the American Federation of Labor the organization of a federal union has sometimes followed almost immediately the appearance of local unions in the craft. When only a few isolated local unions exist in any trade, usually each of them holds a charter direct from the American Federation of Labor; but as soon as enough of these societies have been organized, they are federated into a national or continental union. When, however, the immediate creation of a federal association seems urgently desirable, a national charter is sometimes granted to a single local union, perhaps the sole existing one in the trade, or to a group of promising leaders of the craft. With the assistance of paid organizers of the American Federation, fellow craftsmen in all parts of the country are induced to form local unions. Soon a convention of representatives from these newly created local societies is held, a framework of government is established, and a full-fledged national or continental association emerges. In only a few trades are the local societies still disunited.

The government of local unions. The machinery of government of the shop meeting has always been simple and informal. Usually some one has been elected to preside at meetings held within the industrial establishment, and when the need has arisen, special committees have been created to lay the demands of the journeymen before the employer. At a very early date the journeymen in the printing shops of England and America were organized into "chapels." The chapel held meetings whenever a disagreement arose with the employer or between the journeymen themselves, and it was presided over by the so-called "father of the chapel."

Meetings held within the factory itself are so very inconvenient that they are rapidly disappearing and all functions are being delegated to some official or to a small committee.

The government of the local union is essentially government by mass meeting. The whole body of members, assembling once each month, once each fortnight, or oftener, is the final authority for the transaction of all business — legislative, executive, and judicial. The general meeting may adopt amendments to the by-laws, may suspend or expel a member, may order the purchase of an account book, or may declare a strike.

Usually the meetings of the local union are held in some convenient hall. Sometimes several local unions join together to hire or purchase a building where each may have its office and meeting room. Often the cheapest and most convenient place is a room over a store or perhaps over a saloon. The character of these meeting halls varies widely. Some are forlornly barren, uncarpeted, containing only a decrepit table and formidable rows of long dilapidated benches. Others are cozy and attractive. In one such room visited, for example, the floor was covered with rugs, and the chairs were not arranged in formal rows, but were disposed irregularly along the sides of the room. During the meetings the several officers were stationed in various parts of the room with something of the ceremony of fraternal orders. They sat upon raised platforms, before small round column-like tables painted in black and cream-and-gold. Cases filled with gay regalia and shelves lined with books and periodicals added to the attractiveness of the room.

In the trade union the faults of government by mass meeting are the ones common to all such assemblies. One difficulty is to secure regular attendance of members. Often in small societies a quorum can be secured with difficulty. Some local unions levy fines for inexcusable absences, or even deprive a member of the card which enables him to work at his trade with other unionists. Usually such measures are effective, though a few instances have been found where the fines are so frequent that they have become a regular source of revenue, and in consequence the weekly dues have been reduced in amount. Occasionally, difficulties result from revolts of the minority, who, disgruntled perhaps because a pet scheme has been rejected, revenge themselves by bitter denunciation, by filibustering, or by constantly stirring up factional feeling which may ultimately disrupt the union. The thoughtful and conservative allow themselves to be overawed into declaring unwise strikes by the taunt of cowardice from the "red-hot fire-eaters." Windy orators waste the time of the meetings in rambling, pointless discussion.

The mass meeting is a clumsy mechanism to use for rendering judicial decisions and for the transaction of executive business, and matters are continually arising which demand immediate consideration during the period between the regular meetings. The general meeting has been very reluctant to delegate any of its powers; but of necessity various boards and committees have gradually been created. Many of these committees are appointed for a particular purpose, and are discharged when that purpose has been attained. Nevertheless, certain standing committees have also emerged, the most important of which is the executive committee. This board exercises a wide though varying number of specially delegated powers, but any of its decisions may be overruled by the general meeting. The executive board appears at a comparative late date in the history of the local union.

The officers of the local union are commonly a president who is chairman at meeting of the society, a vice-president, a recording secretary, a treasurer, a corresponding secretary, and frequently also a financial secretary who keeps account of receipts and expenditures. Sometimes the recording secretary acts as corresponding or as financial secretary; sometimes the officers of corresponding secretary and financial secretary are combined. Usually the local officers are unpaid, or are paid a nominal sum. They work at their trade, and perform their official duties during spare time. The duties of the local and financial secretary are exceptionally onerous in unions which, like the Cigar-Makers, maintain a variety of benefits, and many of the larger local unions in such trades pay him a salary. The paid financial secretary devotes his entire time to the union, and receives usually the rate of wages prevailing in the trade. Not only does he keep the financial accounts, but he also performs in many instances the work of corresponding secretary, recording secretary, and treasurer.

The business agent. The other paid official in the local union is the walking delegate, or, as the trade-unionists prefer to call him, the business agent. The business agent adjusts disputes between employers and their workmen, and thus replaces the committees of the shops and local union which would otherwise perform this service. The policy of bargaining with employers through unpaid officials or committees has certain disadvantages. In the first place, the employers frequently look upon the members of delegations from their workmen as agitators seeking to stir up trouble, and sometimes discharge them at the earliest opportunity. Moreover, efficient bargaining with an employer requires shrewdness, diplomacy, and considerable knowledge of cost and methods of production in competing factories. Gradually the salaried official attains knowledge concerning conditions in the industry and also some skill in bargaining. At the same time he is not restrained in upholding the rights of his fellow workmen by the fear of being discharged by the employer.

The business agent performs also duties which in other unions are left to the shop steward. Like that official, he collects dues, detects and calls attention to violations of trade agreements, and prevents the employment of non-society journeymen in union shops. Another of his functions is to serve as the head of an employment agency. Employers who need additional journeymen apply to him in the early morning hours before he starts on his round of visits from one establishment to another, and he dispatches such men as are out of work to fill the vacant places. As an organizer he seeks to persuade workmen to join the union. Frequently he acts as financial secretary. Sometimes when the union pays sick benefits he visits sick members to determine their eligibility to receive such benefits.

Hated by employers, envied and often criticized by his fellow unionists, the position of the business agent is not always a pleasant one. Such is the common complaint of the business agents with whom the writer has talked. "I found the position anything but pleasant," said James Lynch, the early walking delegate mentioned above. "I was at once plunged into continual war. My presence on a job was an irritation to the employers as well as to the non-union men and not infrequently some of the union men envied me, little knowing the sorrows of my lot." Usually the business agent receives the same salary as he would if he were working at his trade. His expenses are increased, however, because of his office. At the same time he is vested with great authority and is subjected to dangerous temptation. From accepting bribes to levying blackmail was the short step which put prominent business agents of New York building trades unions in Sing Sing Prison a few years ago. The union is frequently not blameless. The statement has been made repeatedly, though with what truth it is difficult to say, that certain unions have condoned the blackmailing of employers by shrewd and energetic agents who have been successful in securing good wages for the trade.

One serious mistake has been to vest the business agent with power to call a strike, for this power has been the club which he has used to extort money from the employers. The policy of permitting the business agent to declare a strike has prevailed particularly in the building trades. In those trades he may order the workmen to leave the building immediately whenever he finds a non-union man at work or discovers some other violation of the agreement by the employer. As a consequence, the most flagrant cases of dishonesty among business agents have occurred in the building trades. These trades vest control over strikes in such officials for the same reason that they permit the men on a building to strike without the consent of the local union, namely, because the frequent shifting of the men from one building to another necessitates prompt action.

Government of district unions. In the district unions the representative assembly performs the functions of the general mass meeting in the local society. Equal representation on the district council for each society has sometimes been secured by the small local unions, which are watchful to prevent any encroachment upon their independence. The more centralized district unions, which hold the welfare of the majority paramount to the preservation of local authority, ordinarily permit representation in proportion to membership. The district council transacts all important business, though in some trades the members, wishing to retain control over the adoption of amendments to the constitution and of regulations governing the conditions of employment, require that the decision of the council on such matters be submitted to a referendum vote. The officers of the district union are commonly a president, a vice-president, a recording secretary, a financial secretary, a treasurer, and trustees. Sometimes a single official known as the "secretary-treasurer" performs the duties of the recording secretary, financial secretary, and treasurer. Frequently there is also an executive board, which transacts emergency business between the meetings of the district council. Often the district union maintains a business agent, since many small local societies lack sufficient money to maintain one of their own. Except the business agent, and occasionally the secretary-treasurer, the officers serve without pay or receive only a nominal sum. Quite commonly the business agent is elected by popular vote of the members of all the local societies, though sometimes the district council selects the business agent from a list of candidates submitted by the local unions. Almost invariably the other officers and the members of the executive board are selected by the district council, and as a rule only the delegates comprising the council are eligible to these positions.

The form of government and the problems of government of the district unions are very similar to those of the national and international associations. In both, for example, there is variety of opinion and practice concerning the use of the initiative and referendum. In both there is the struggle between those who favor equal and those who favor proportional representation. The problems of government of the national union are made more complicated, however, by its wider territorial jurisdiction. Thus, while the district council, which can meet weekly if necessary, transacts nearly all business of the district union, the national trade-union convention, which can be convoked, because of distance, only for a few days each year, transacts but a small part of the national business, matters arising during the long period between its sessions being considered by the officers or the executive board or referred to a general vote of the members.

The national convention. The convention of delegates from the several local societies is perhaps the most important part of the governmental machinery of national and international trade unions. In its general features it does not differ widely from the assemblies or conventions held regularly by church, fraternal, and other organizations. The delegates assemble at the time and place fixed by the preceding convention. They meet in some convenient public hall, are welcomed by municipal executives and local trade-union leaders, continue in session five days, or a week, perhaps a little longer, and then adjourn for a year, two years, or more.

The trade-union convention exercises executive and judicial as well as legislative functions, thus violating the political principles of those who hold that each of these three functions of government should be vested in a separate organ of government. In exercising its legislative power it has equal authority to pass every kind of rule. In fact, the trade unions ordinarily make no distinction between constitutional and statutory laws. All kinds of rules are adopted in exactly the same manner. At one moment, therefore, the convention may be remodeling the entire machinery of government, or transferring important functions from the local unions to the international union; at another, it may be passing an unimportant rule to the effect that the union label shall be printed on red instead of blue paper.

Acting as a judicial tribunal, the convention considers grievances brought by national officers, local unions, or members, and these grievances may involve violations of the rules of local unions as well as of those of the national union. In consequence, while some of the suits laid before convention are important, others are trivial. At one time the convention may be suspending a local union for serious violation of the rules; at another time it may be sustaining a subordinate union in imposing a fine of one or two dollars on a member for some petty misdemeanor.

The levy of taxes, the appropriation of revenue, the declaration of industrial war, and the ratification of agreements are the functions exercised by the trade-union convention.

That assembly fixes the amount of dues and assessments; it controls disbursements; it orders strikes against employers. The convention has the final power in making agreements. Even when collective bargaining is conducted by the local societies, the national union frequently fixes rules of apprenticeship, hours of labor, and other conditions of employment which the subordinate lodges must demand from employers. When the terms of the labor contract are determined by a national or district joint conference between employers and employees, the national or district convention practically always meets immediately before the joint conference and outlines the terms which its representatives are to demand. The convention performs many other functions. It elects officers, and audits their accounts. Through its committees it performs at times a wide variety of detailed administrative duties which in a political government are usually delegated to the executive officers.

The trade-union conventions almost outrival the state and federal legislatures of the United States in the bewildering number and variety of their committees. The committee on constitution, or the committee on laws, as it is variously termed, is perhaps the most important. To it all amendments to the rules are submitted. In some unions this committee reports concerning all amendments submitted to it merely with favorable or unfavorable comment. In other unions it follows the usual legislative practice of pigeonholing the amendments which it deems undesirable, and presents, perhaps in a reconstructed form, those which it desires the convention to pass. Besides this general legislative committee, special ones are created to consider or draft rules regulating strikes, sick benefits, the union label, or apprenticeship. A judiciary committee, sometimes known as the committee on appeals or grievances, considers appeals from judicial decisions of national officers and local unions. One committee sanctions strikes. Another audits the financial accounts of officers, There are committees to consider conditions of employment, wages, hours of labor, relations with other unions, printing, and the trade journal.

In fixing the basis of representation in convention, the same opposition has existed between the large and the small local societies as existed at the time of the founding of the American Commonwealth between the large and the small States. The members of the large local unions have demanded that representation should be proportional to membership. They point out the unfairness of allowing a society of twenty-five and one of a thousand members to have the same voting power in convention. They hold that the majority, not a small minority, should dominate. On the other hand, the small local unions have demanded that each society have equal representation. They fear that if representation were proportional to membership, two or three large societies would dictate policies to all the rest. Such a condition is not, indeed, a baseless fear, conjured up by the small unions. Instances of it may be found whenever the system of representation according to membership has prevailed.

The officers of the national union. Certain governmental machinery is needed to do administrative work which a representative body like a convention cannot perform. From the beginning of national trade-unionism some one has been required to collect revenue, and a corresponding secretary has also been needed to serve as the agent of communication between the local societies and the national unions. Some one has had to do a policeman's work in enforcing the observance of the national rules. As the activities of the federal organization have developed, an executive has been created to manage the complicated administrative machinery.

Certain machinery of government is also required to make decisions on matters the consideration of which cannot be postponed until the next convention. One question which must nearly always be decided immediately is the desirability of a strike. Sometimes, indeed, the postponement of a strike may preclude the necessity of its declaration, since greater deliberation may show the lack of necessity for it, or further conference with employers may secure its peaceful adjustment. When the declaration of a strike seems inevitable, the delay which furnishes the employer an opportunity for preparation may steal away most of its effectiveness. Industrial conditions change rapidly. At the moment, all may be propitious; if action is postponed until the next convention, the opportunity will be lost.

Moreover, the strike, the success of which seemed reasonably certain at the time when it was declared by the convention, may become a hopeless venture after the adjournment of that body because of an unexpected change in industrial conditions. For this reason, trade-union leaders dislike exceedingly to be bound by rigid and specific instructions of the representative assembly.

In other words, the trade union is a belligerent association nearly always engaged in a guerrilla struggle with employers, sometimes in wide-spreading general combat; and for success in war, industrial as well as military, prompt decisions and a flexible policy are requisite. The very life of the organization may be the penalty of long delay and rigid rules. Therefore, between conventions some governmental body must have authority to declare strikes, to conduct them, to call them off, or to levy special assessments when the funds are exhausted by a long struggle.

During the period between conventions some judicial authority must be created to interpret the meaning of vague or conflicting rules, otherwise the carrying-out of the activities of the organization may be abruptly halted. Some judicial authority must also be created to discipline local unions and individual members and to hear appeals of members from local unions. If no such authority exists, the guilty may delay their punishment and the acquittal of the innocent may be postponed.

Usually the representative assembly has jealously endeavored to retain exclusive legislative power, but its efforts have nearly always failed. Unexpected problems are continually arising for which the rules make no provision. Moreover, the rules, hastily adopted by the convention, are frequently worded vaguely and carelessly, and to put them into operation is difficult or impossible. It may easily happen, for example, that while provision is made for the payment of a sick benefit, the administrative machinery to carry out such a plan is not created or is wholly inadequate.

In most organizations efficient and expeditious machinery for the adoption of amendments to the constitution during the period between conventions has been gradually created, and with this development there have been fewer violations and a more wholesome respect for the rules by officers and members. Indeed, some of the officials of the older and better organized unions, when asked whether they exercised unconstitutional legislative power, seem as much shocked at the idea as might have been a law-and-precedent-loving judge of a superior court.

The two officers now found in the great majority of international unions are the president and the secretary or secretary-treasurer. The president acts as chairman at meetings of the convention and of the general executive board. He has supervision over the administrative affairs of the organization. He is a policeman enforcing the rules, and is frequently also a judge. He travels often to various parts of the country to organize new local unions, to encourage the weak ones, and to adjust disputes between the workmen and their employers.

The secretary or secretary-treasurer acts as secretary at meetings of the convention and of the general executive board. He serves as a medium of communication between the local societies and the central union. He edits the trade journal, save in a few organizations which have created a special official for this purpose or which entrust the president with this duty. He keeps the financial accounts, and in a large majority of unions also has charge of the funds. In about forty out of one hundred and thirty international unions, however, the secretary must turn over all funds to a treasurer. This system has grave inconveniences. The duties of the treasurer require only a small part of his time; and usually he is paid no salary or only a nominal sum. He works at his trade and lives in his home city, which is probably at some distance from headquarters, where the secretary is stationed, and much time and energy are wasted in sending money back and forth. When a strike has been declared, funds are usually needed immediately by the local strike committee, and delay in obtaining them may cause serious results. For these reasons, most unions require the secretary to take care of the funds. In these unions he bears the title of secretary-treasurer.

Trade-union leadership is a profession, and to make a success of it native ability and experience are required. The leader must learn to write, not necessarily grammatically, but with force and clearness. He is doomed to an unending succession of speeches, and so must develop self-possession on the platform and the power to hold audiences. He must know how to handle his men. He must learn that much profanity, particularly in dealing with employers, does not constitute forcibleness or diplomacy. He must know intimately the conditions of the trade and also much about the cost and methods of production. He must be resourceful, constructive, and patient; he must be constantly ready to meet new and unexpected situations with few resources to aid him, and perhaps with a discouraged and carpingly critical following at his back.

The trade unions have made little attempt, however, to impose qualifications on the candidates for international offices. Usually, of course, the candidate must have been a member of the union for a certain length of time. Some of the early unions provided also that only delegates to the representative assembly should be eligible, but this limitation on the selection of candidates was soon found to be undesirable and was abolished. Nevertheless, the important officials are usually picked men. Most of them have held some office, such as that of president, secretary, or business agent in the local union. Often they have also served as delegates at one or perhaps several conventions. Sometimes they have held minor offices in the international union; perhaps they have been organizers or labor agitators, have later been made vice-president, and finally have been promoted to the presidency or the secretaryship. Yet even with this preparatory education in subordinate positions, the newly elected leader comes to his office as very raw and crude material, and attains efficiency only after some years of experience.

For this reason the older unions have tended to lengthen the term of office and to reëlect officials for several terms.

The national officers were wholly unchecked by any higher authority during the period between conventions. Luckily the functions of the federated unions were so few that the officers had very little opportunity to display arbitrary power. But the functions of the national unions were increasing rapidly, and at the same time duties which had been divided among several unpaid officials were being vested in a single salaried officer. On his growing absolutism the infrequent conventions exercised little restraint. In the absence of a general executive board, therefore, he exercised despotic power, never hesitating even to overturn the old rules or to adopt new ones whenever an emergency demanded such a course of action.

After 1875 a tendency to form general executive boards became manifest, and by 1880 such boards were being maintained by practically all existing national unions.

In the Iron Moulders' Union the president was emphatic in expressing his antagonism toward the newly created executive board, which he denounced as a foreign device utterly alien to American trade-unionism. The president, led on by almost unlimited opportunity, had yielded to temptation, and had appropriated some of the funds. One of the first results of the creation of the executive board was the discovery of this malfeasance. The president strove desperately to maintain himself in power. He began with the declaration that he would not be the clerk of any board or committee. Restricted in authority by the new governmental reorganization, he was nevertheless not wholly impotent. His chief weapons of defense were power to expel from the organization and control over the trade journal. In the official trade journal he denounced the accusations made against him as libels inspired by the desire of his enemies to remove him from office and secure the position for a rival. He refused to publish any statements by the other side. When one member of the national executive board persuaded his local union to publish and distribute a circular containing a statement of the board's position, the president suspended the local society, and so made this member ineligible to hold office. Several members of the board who belonged to subordinate branches which were somewhat remiss in the payment of assessments were likewise rendered ineligible by the suspension of their local unions. Other members of the board were removed from office on the charge of failure to attend to their duties. The efforts of the president were fruitless. A special convention was called, and this convention removed him from office and elected his successor.

The creation of the executive board has limited greatly the judicial power of the president. In more than fifty of the one hundred and thirty unions he possesses no judicial power. Only in nine organizations can he discipline the local unions, such authority being reserved to the general executive board. To prevent the board from wasting its time in the consideration of unimportant complaints, the president is frequently given authority to hear appeals of members from decisions of local unions, but appeals may nearly always be made from any of his judicial decisions to the executive board.

The executive board levies assessments, appoints temporary officers to fill vacancies, and performs other duties which were vested in the president in the early days of the older organizations. The duty of declaring strikes, which none of the older organizations ventured to entrust to the president, has been delegated to the executive board by practically all unions save the few which submit this question to popular vote. Perhaps the most important function of the board is to bring to trial and remove officers for misdemeanors and neglect of duty, since control over officers depends so largely upon the ability of the board to exercise this power.

The executive committee transacts much of its business by mail or telegraph. A few organizations impose fines on members of the board for failure to telegraph their decisions on strike applications within twenty-four hours. Nevertheless, this method of transacting business causes some delay. It likewise handicaps the board in giving intelligent judgments, since its members have no opportunity to discuss with one another the various phases of the problems under consideration. Moreover, the board must depend largely on the paid officers for information concerning questions submitted for its decision, and hence it is limited in its ability to check the absorption of power by such officials.

3. The American Federation of Labor — Government [1]

The American Federation of Labor was formed in 1881 in Pittsburgh. I was elected its first vice-president. With the exception of three terms I have been president of the A. F. of L. since that time.

Membership of the Federation. The Federation covers practically the whole field of industry. There are no limitations as to membership. The only requirement, so far as the A. F. of L. is concerned, is that the organization desiring affiliation shall be composed of wage-earners.

The A. F. of L., as its name implies, is a federation, and not, as it is often mistakenly called, an organization. It is a federation of organizations, each of which has its own government, determined by its own needs and requirements, the result of the experiences of the members of the organization. This right to self-government was recognized in the beginning and has been reaffirmed and adhered to as consistently as possible. The Federation has no powers except those which are authorized and conceded by the organizations which compose it. These powers are enumerated in its written constitution and the definite direction of conventions.

There are affiliated to the A. F. of L. 107 national and international unions, 49 state federations of labor, 855 city central

[1] From the pamphlet *The American Labor Movement, Its Make-up, Achievements, and Aspirations*, by Samuel Gompers, published by the American Federation of Labor.

bodies or local federations of trade unions in a city or town, 458 directly affiliated local trade and federal labor unions whose chartered existence will continue until there are sufficient numbers belonging to each trade or calling to form a national trade organization. There are industrially four departments for the more effective coöperation of allied trades.

Government. The A. F. of L. holds annual conventions which for many years have been held in the month of November. The officers of the Federation consist of a president, eight vice-presidents, a secretary, and a treasurer. These eleven officers constitute the Executive Council. The convention is the supreme law-making body of the Federation, exercising all authority within the limitations of power conceded to the Federation by the constituent or affiliated sovereign organizations. If I may be permitted to draw a comparison, we modeled our A. F. of L. after the government of the United States, both as to federal jurisdiction within federal limitations and state sovereignty with local prerogatives and rights. The Federal Government exercises such powers as are conceded to the United States by the various States. In the A. F. of L. the right of secession remains with the affiliated unions. No one can question the right of a local organization within the Federation to secede.

Control of member unions. The affiliated organizations are held together by moral obligation, a spirit of *camaraderie*, a spirit of group patriotism, a spirit of mutual assistance.

There are no coercive methods used by the A. F. of L. to prevent the withdrawal or secession of any affiliated organization. The Western Federation of Miners, for instance, withdrew from the A. F. of L. about 1896. There were many efforts and many suggestions made to induce individual unions belonging to the Western Federation of Miners to join the A. F. of L. as local unions. Not only were these efforts discouraged, but the proposal was repudiated.

Similarly, no coercion is used in regard to national organizations which are not affiliated to the A. F. of L. We feel that it is the duty of every wage-worker to belong to the union of his trade or calling; that it is the duty of the local union of a trade or calling to belong to the national or international union of that trade or calling; that it is equally the moral duty of every national or international organization of *bona fide* workingmen to belong to the A. F. of L. But coercive methods are never employed.

When an international union affiliated to the A. F. of L. refuses to carry out convention resolutions applying to the members of that trade, the A. F. of L. has no power to enforce its judgment. I recall but one instance in which an organization, which had in advance agreed to abide by the decision of the Executive Council in regard to a dispute between it and two other organizations, refused to abide by the decision rendered against it. The Executive Council then decided that the organization's charter, or its chartered relations with the A. F. of L., should cease upon a certain date. However, a year afterward the organization reaffiliated upon a declaration by the convention.

All the actual power outside of the moral power that the A. F. of L. possesses is the power of expulsion from membership in the Federation. Expulsion can occur only upon a roll-call vote at a convention of the A. F. of L. in which two thirds of the votes are cast for revocation of charter or expulsion of the organization. The moral force of the A. F. of L. is the most effective influence or power it has in dealing with allied organizations.

The experiences of the men in our movement have shown one fact standing out in bold relief: that every movement of workingmen which had a system of government by which power, force, or compulsion was exercised aroused resentment, repudiation, and dissolution, while on the contrary an effort which was controlled by exerting moral force upon the doings of men and women has always exercised a beneficent influence. In other words, workingmen are just human beings. When men and women are told they must do something at the peril of their organized existence or their personal existence, there is always aroused in them a spirit to say, "I shall try to do the very opposite to that which you have commanded me to do." If the better judgment and the better feeling of men are appealed to, they are more ready to do and willing to do the best that they can. No member of any organization has the right to force another to take any certain action, and no trade union has the right to force a member to go on strike. The sole force that any organization has is moral.

The Executive Council of the A. F. of L. is an administrative committee for the purpose of carrying into effect the conclusions reached by the conventions, and to take initiative in any matter, particularly legislative, upon which the convention has not had an opportunity to express itself; to be helpful in any and every way to any activity contributing to the protection, benefit and welfare of the people, particularly the wage-earners. The powers of the Executive Council are set forth in the constitution.

Growth of membership. A chart which was prepared for the last convention contains the membership of the organizations affiliated to the A. F. of L. from the date of the formation of the Federation in 1881 up to and including 1924. You will observe in the chart that the membership in 1881 was small; that the growth up to 1892 was very slow; that the membership was then practically stationary up to 1898; that in 1899 there was a slight growth; that in 1900 there was a still greater growth which continued until 1904, when there was a recession. The report for 1904 was based upon the years 1903 and 1904 and shows the result of an industrial stagnation which existed at that time. You will observe also that at times there has been a recession or a fall in the membership of the affiliated organizations, but that as a rule the membership never receded substantially.

Another chart submitted in the same report illustrates the relationship of the various affiliated organizations to the A. F. of L. This chart shows that the integral part, the key, the heart of the Federation is the national or international union. The sovereign national and international unions are the primary elements. The four departments were created for the mutual protection, the advancement of the individual trades or callings of the industries interested in the departments. The chart as made up illustrates the ligaments, the heartstrings, we might say, of the Federation. The membership of the organizations affiliated to the A. F. of L. is composed of adults, chiefly men, but there are some women. If you allow five to a family it is only fair to assume that associated and identified with the A. F. of L. we have about 15,000,000.

4. Constitution of the American Federation of Labor

Preamble

Whereas, A struggle is going on in all the nations of the civilized world between the oppressors and the oppressed of all countries,

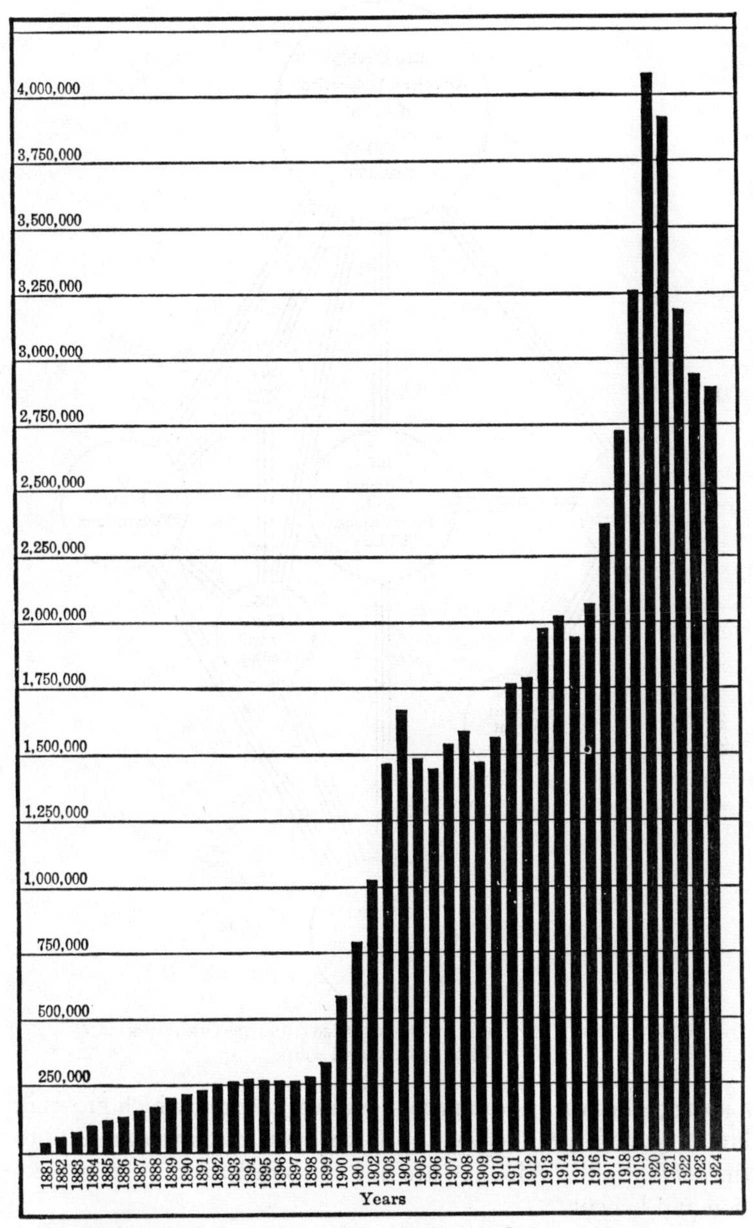

MEMBERSHIP OF AMERICAN FEDERATION OF LABOR, 1881–1922

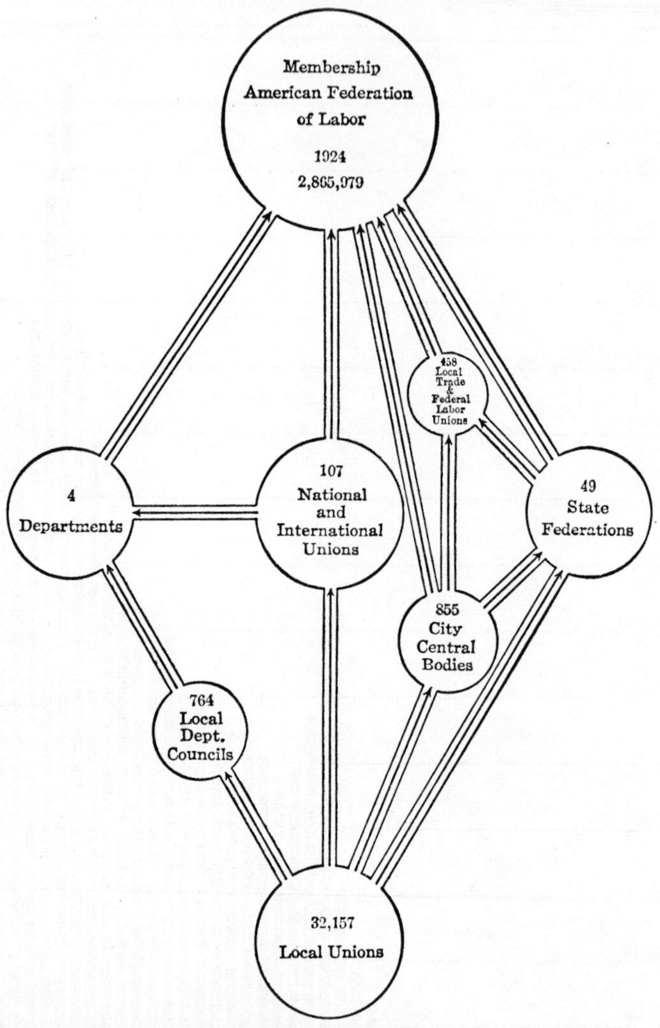

RELATIONSHIP OF AFFILIATED ORGANIZATIONS TO THE AMERICAN FEDERATION OF LABOR

a struggle between the capitalist and the laborer, which grows in intensity from year to year, and will work disastrous results to the toiling millions if they are not combined for mutual protection and benefit.

It, therefore, behooves the representatives of the Trade and Labor Unions of America, in convention assembled, to adopt such measures and disseminate such principles among the mechanics and laborers of our country as will permanently unite them to secure the recognition of rights to which they are justly entitled.

We, therefore, declare ourselves in favor of the formation of a thorough Federation, embracing every Trade and Labor Organization in America, organized under the Trade Union system.

CONSTITUTION

ARTICLE I. — NAME

This association shall be known as The American Federation of Labor, and shall consist of such Trade and Labor Unions as shall conform to its rules and regulations.

ARTICLE II. — OBJECTS

SECTION 1. The object of this Federation shall be the encouragement and formation of local Trade and Labor Unions, and the closer federation of such societies through the organization of Central Trade and Labor Unions in every city, and the further combination of such bodies into State, Territorial, or Provincial organizations to secure legislation in the interest of the working masses.

SECTION 2. The establishment of National and International Trade Unions, based upon a strict recognition of the autonomy of each trade, and the promotion and advancement of such bodies.

SECTION 3. The establishment of Departments composed of National or International Unions affiliated with the American Federation of Labor, of the same industry, and which Departments shall be governed in conformity with the laws of the American Federation of Labor.

SECTION 4. An American Federation of all National and International Trade Unions, to aid and assist each other; to aid and encourage the sale of union label goods, and to secure legislation in the interest of the working people, and influence public opinion, by peaceful and legal methods, in favor of organized labor.

SECTION 5. To aid and encourage the labor press of America.

ARTICLE III. — CONVENTION

SECTION 3. The following committees consisting of fifteen members each, shall be appointed by the President: First, Rules and Order of Business; second, Report of Executive Council; third, Resolutions; fourth, Laws; fifth, Organization; sixth, Labels; seventh, Adjustment; eighth, Local and Federated Bodies; ninth, Education; tenth, State Organizations; eleventh, Boycotts; twelfth, Building Trades (to which shall be referred all grievances and other matters pertaining exclusively to the building trades).

SECTION 8. Party politics, whether they be Democratic, Republican, Socialistic, Populistic, Prohibition, or any other, shall have no place in the Conventions of the American Federation of Labor.

ARTICLE IV. — REPRESENTATION

SECTION 1. The basis of representation in the Convention shall be: From National and International Unions, for less than four thousand members, one delegate; four thousand or more, two delegates; eight thousand or more, three delegates; sixteen thousand or more, four delegates; thirty-two thousand or more, five delegates, and so on. From Central Bodies, State Federations, National Departments, Federal Labor Unions, and Local Unions having no National or International Union, one delegate; provided however, that Local Unions and Federal Labor Unions herein referred to, located in one city, shall have the right to unite in sending a delegate to represent them unitedly. Only *bona fide* wage-workers who are not members of, or eligible to membership in, other Trade Unions, shall be eligible as delegates from Federal Labor Unions.

ARTICLE V. — OFFICERS

SECTION 1. The officers of the Federation shall consist of a President, eight Vice-Presidents, a Secretary, and a Treasurer, to be elected by the Convention on the last day of the session, and these officers shall be the Executive Council.

SECTION 2. The President and Secretary shall be members of the succeeding Convention in case they are not delegates, but without vote.

SECTION 3. All elective officers shall be members of a local organization connected with the American Federation of Labor.

SECTION 4. The terms of the officers of the American Federation of Labor shall expire on the first day of August succeeding the Convention.

SECTION 5. The President and Secretary shall engage suitable offices in the same building at Washington, D.C., for the transaction of the business of the organization.

SECTION 6. All books and financial accounts shall at all times be open to the inspection of the President and Executive Council.

ARTICLE IX. — EXECUTIVE COUNCIL

SECTION 1. It shall be the duty of the Executive Council to watch legislative measures directly affecting the interests of working people, and to initiate, whenever necessary, such legislative action as the Convention may direct.

SECTION 2. The Executive Council shall use every possible means to organize new National or International Trade or Labor Unions, and to organize Local Trade and Labor Unions, and connect them with the Federation until such time as there is a sufficient number to form a National or International Union, when it shall be the duty of the President of the Federation to see that such organization is formed.

SECTION 3. When a National or International Union has been formed, the President shall notify all Local Unions of that trade to affiliate with such National or International Union, and unless said notification be complied with, within three months, their charters shall be revoked.

SECTION 5. While we recognize the right of each trade to manage its own affairs, it shall be the duty of the Executive Council to secure the unification of all labor organizations, so far as to assist each other in any trade dispute.

SECTION 6. Whenever the revenue of the Federation shall warrant such action, the Executive Council shall authorize the sending out of Trade Union speakers from place to place in the interests of the Federation.

SECTION 10. All Local Trade Unions and Federal Labor Unions holding charters direct from the American Federation of Labor, desiring the assistance of the American Federation of Labor in trade disputes, shall submit to the President of the American Federation of Labor for approval by the Executive Council the full statement of the grievance, and shall receive within twenty

(20) days from the President an answer as to whether they will be sustained or not, and no benefits shall be paid where a strike takes place before the Local Union has received the approval of the Executive Council.

Article X. — Revenue

Section 1. The revenue of the Federation shall be derived from a per capita tax to be paid upon the full paid-up membership of all affiliated bodies, as follows: From International or National Trade Unions, a per capita tax of one cent per member per month; from Local Trade Unions and Federal Labor Unions, twenty cents per member per month, five cents of which must be set aside to be used only in case of strike or lockout; Local Unions, the majority of whose members are less than eighteen (18) years of age, two cents per member per month; from Central and State bodies, $10 per year, payable quarterly.

Article XI. — Local Central Bodies

Section 7. No Central Labor Union, or other central body of delegates, shall have authority or power to originate a boycott, nor shall such bodies indorse and order the placing of the name of any person, firm, or corporation on an unfair list until the Local Union desiring the same has, before declaring the boycott, submitted the matter in dispute to the Central Body for investigation, and the best endeavors on its part to effect an amicable settlement. Violation of this section shall forfeit charter.

Article XIII. — Defense Fund for Local Trade and Federal Labor Unions

Section 1. The money of the defense fund shall be drawn only to sustain strikes or lockouts of Local Trade and Federal Labor Unions when such strikes or lockouts are authorized, indorsed, and conducted in conformity with the following provisions of this Article:

Section 2. In the event of a disagreement between a Local Union and an employer which, in the opinion of the Local Union, may result in a strike, such Union shall notify the President of the American Federation of Labor, who shall investigate, or cause an investigation to be made of the disagreement, and endeavor to adjust the difficulty. If his efforts should prove futile, he shall take such steps as he may deem necessary in notifying the Executive Council, and if the majority of said Council shall decide that a strike is necessary, such Union shall be authorized to order a strike, but that under no circumstances shall a strike or lockout be deemed legal, or moneys expended from the defense fund on that account, unless the strike or lockout shall have been first authorized and approved by the President and Executive Council.

SECTION 3. When a strike has been authorized and approved by the President and Executive Council, the President of the Local Union interested shall, within twenty-four hours, call a meeting of said Union, of which every member shall be regularly notified, to take action thereon, and no member shall vote on such question unless he is in good standing. Should three fourths of the members present decide, by secret ballot, on a strike, the president of the Local Union shall immediately notify the President of the American Federation of Labor of the cause of the matter in dispute; what the wages, hours, and conditions of labor then are; what advances, if any, are sought; what reductions are offered, if any; state the number employed and unemployed; the state of trade generally in the locality, and the number of persons involved, union and non-union; also the number of members who would become entitled to the benefits therein provided should the application be authorized and approved.

SECTION 4. No Local shall be entitled to benefit from the defense fund unless it has been in continuous good standing for one year; and no member shall be entitled to benefit from said defense fund unless he has been a member in good standing in the American Federation of Labor for at least one year.

SECTION 5. When a strike has been inaugurated under the provisions of Sections 2 and 3, the American Federation of Labor shall pay to the bonded officer of the Union involved, or his order, for a period of six weeks, an amount equal to six ($6) dollars per week for each member. Each Local Union shall require its treasurer to give proper bond for the safe-keeping and disbursement of all funds of the Local. No benefit shall be paid for the first two weeks of the strike. The Executive Council shall have the power to authorize the payment of strike benefits for an additional period.

SECTION 6. No member of a Local Union on strike shall be entitled to weekly benefits unless he reports daily to the proper officer of the Local Union while the strike continues, and no member who shall receive a week's work, three days to be a week, shall receive benefits. Any member refusing other work while on strike (providing said work is not in conflict with labor's interests) shall not be entitled to any benefits.

SECTION 7. Any Union inaugurating a strike without the approval of the Executive Council shall not receive benefits on account of said strike.

SECTION 8. In case of lockout or the victimization of members, the Executive Council shall have power to pay benefits if, upon investigation, it is found that the Local Union whose members are involved did not by their actions or demands provoke the lockout by their employers.

SECTION 9. During the continuance of a strike the executive board of the Local Union shall make weekly reports to the Secretary of the American Federation of Labor, showing the amount of money distributed for benefits, and to whom paid, furnishing individual receipts to the Secretary of the American Federation of Labor from all members to whom such benefits have been paid, and all other facts that may be required.

SECTION 10. Before a strike shall be declared off a special meeting of the Union shall be called for that purpose and it shall require a majority vote of all members present to decide the question either way.

SECTION 11. In the event of the defense fund becoming dangerously low through protracted strike or lockout, the Executive Council of the American Federation of Labor shall have the power to levy an assessment of ten cents on each member of Local Trade and Federal Labor Unions, assessments to be restricted to not more than five per year; and further, that there shall always be a surplus of five thousand ($5000) dollars in the defense fund.

ARTICLE XV. — GENERAL RULES GOVERNING DEPARTMENTS OF THE AMERICAN FEDERATION OF LABOR

SECTION 1. For the greater development of the labor movement departments subordinate to the American Federation of Labor are to be established from time to time as in the judgment of the American Federation of Labor, or of its Executive Council, may be deemed advisable. Each department is to manage and finance its own affairs.

5. Policies of the American Federation of Labor [1]

Hours. The A. F. of L. is in favor of a shorter workday, and a progressive decrease of working hours in keeping with the development of machinery and the use of productive forces. The Federation has recognized the need for greater opportunities and more time for rest, leisure, and cultivation among the workers. It favors a rest of not less than a day and a half in each week. We insist upon one entire day of rest in each week. I may say that it was my great pleasure to have been president of the New York State Federation of Labor when the Legislature of the State of New York enacted the first law in the United States making Saturday afternoon a legal holiday.

The A. F. of L. favors fixing maximum hours of work for children, minors, and women. It does not favor a legal limitation of the workday for adult men workers. The unions have very largely established the shorter workday by their own initiative, power, and influence; they have done it for themselves. The A. F. of L. is opposed to limiting, by legal statutory authority, the hours of work for men in private industries. The A. F. of L. has apprehensions as to the wisdom of placing in the hands of the Government additional powers which may be used to the detriment of the working-people. It particularly opposes this policy when the things can be done by the workmen themselves.

It is in favor of a uniform shorter workday and would encourage and help affiliated organizations to secure it by collective bargaining and other methods employed by labor unions. For instance, the International Typographical Union undertook such a move. It gave employers more than a year's notice that after a certain day they would not work longer than eight hours a day. Almost immediately a large number of employers acceded to the request, others refused. The men struck. Covering a period of more than a year, employees and individual firms came to agreements providing for the eight-hour day and its enforcement, until

[1] Excerpts from a pamphlet by Samuel Gompers, "Policies of the A. F. of L.," published by the American Federation of Labor.

finally the eight-hour day has been accomplished, not only for the printers, but generally for all those employed in the printing trades.

It did not require any law for the printers to secure the eight-hour day, nor for the granite-cutters, nor for the Cigar-Makers' International, to which I have the honor to belong. There was no law establishing the eight-hour day in the building trades, nor in any other trades which now enjoy it. The A. F. of L. at various annual conventions, as early as 1884 adopted resolutions approving the movement for an eight-hour day and coöperated with the various affiliated organizations for its attainment.

It is necessary, however, for the organizations themselves to take the initiative. For instance, in 1888, when the A. F. of L. again took up the movement to encourage the inauguration of a shorter workday, the Executive Council was authorized by the Convention to concentrate its energies in helping any organization making application to be selected to conduct a special eight-hour movement. The carpenters' organization was among the organizations then making the application, and was selected by the Executive Council to make the fight.

The organized labor movement of Colorado and Utah, represented by the United Mine Workers and the Western Federation of Miners, has been very active in establishing by legislation a minimum workday of eight hours. The Federation has not taken any position in regard to this legislation, but I think, if called upon to approve a course, would say that those organizations acted within their rights. We would not deny their right to that line of action, although it arouses our apprehensions. The fact of the matter is that some men unconsciously and with the best of intentions grant others the opportunity to rivet chains on their wrists.

The A. F. of L. encourages the practice of its various affiliated organizations in endeavoring to secure a shorter workday by means of collective agreements with employers in the various industries, but it opposes reaching the same result by means of a law binding upon all employers in a given State, or throughout the Union. If there were a movement and a possibility of establishing an eight-hour workday and a minimum wage by legal enactment throughout the land, the Federation would oppose such policies, because it has in a large measure accomplished the same purposes and will accomplish them by the initiative of the associations or the organizations and by the grit and courage of the manhood and womanhood of the men and women of the A. F. of L. That these results have been accomplished through the initiative and voluntary association of the workers precludes the question of having legal enactment for the same purpose. In addition, the giving of jurisdiction to government and to governmental agencies is always dangerous when it comes to governing the working-people.

Opposed to minimum wages. The A. F. of L. is not in favor of fixing, by legal enactment, certain minimum wages. The attempts of the Government to establish wages at which workmen may work, according to the teachings of history will result in a long era of industrial slavery. There was a time in English history when the Government and the courts in quarter sessions established wages. During periods when there was a dearth of workmen and employers offered higher wages, both the workmen and employers were brought into court and punished by imprisonment and physical mutilation because the one asked, received, or demanded, and the other was willing to offer, or did pay, higher wages.

There is now a current movement to increase wages by a proposal to determine a minimum wage by political authorities. It is a maxim in law that once a court is given jurisdiction over an individual it has the power, the field, and authority to exercise that jurisdiction. "I fear the Greeks even when they bear gifts." An attempt to entrap the American workmen into a species of slavery, under guise of an offer of this character, is resented by the men and women of the American trade-union movement.

When the question of fixing, by legal enactment, minimum wages for women was before the Executive Council of the A. F. of L. for investigation and discussion, and subsequently before the Convention of the A. F. of L., there was a great diversity of views. I am betraying no confidence when I say that. The official decision of the Convention was that the subject was worthy of further discussion and consideration. In my judgment the proposal to establish by law a minimum wage for women, though well meant, is a curb upon the rights, the natural development, and the opportunity for development of the women employed in the industries of our country.

If the legislature should once fix a minimum wage it would have the opportunity to use the machinery of the State to enforce work at that rate whether the workers desired to render services or not. I am very suspicious of the activities of governmental agencies. I apprehend that once the State is allowed to fix a minimum rate, the State would also take the right to compel men or women to work at that rate. I have some apprehension that if the legislature were allowed to establish a maximum workday it might also compel workmen to work up to the maximum allowed. I ought to say, however, that I am in favor of the legal enactment fixing the maximum hours of labor for all workmen in direct Government employment and for those who work for contractors substituted for governmental authority.

The full value of production does not go to the actual workingmen to-day. A portion goes to investment, superintendence, agencies for the creation of wants among people, and many other things. Some of these are legitimate factors in industry entitled to reward, but many of them should be eliminated. The legitimate factors are superintendency, the creation of wants, administration, returns for investment in so far as it is honest investment and does not include watered stock or inflated holdings.

Whether or not dividends should be paid as an incident to stock ownership, regardless of the personal services performed, the activity or inactivity of the owner of the stock, depends altogether upon whether the investment is an honest one. An honest investment is an honest actual physical investment. I am out of harmony with and opposed to the manipulation of stocks and of the stock market and all manner of speculation. I will do whatever I can to eliminate speculation involved in stocks and the fundamentals of stock jobbery and stock sales. The vast sums of money paid annually in dividends on stocks and interest on bonds by corporations managing and operating important industries constitute a very large proportion of the incomes from these industries. This is an unfair distribution of the incomes from industries. The owners, stockholders, or bondholders of modern corporations receive from this distribution an unearned income which is taken from the product of the labor of those who produce it.

Struggle with employers. The efforts of the American labor movement to secure a larger share of the income are directed against all who illegitimately stand between the workers and the attainment of a better life. This class includes all who have not made honest investment in honest enterprises. Employers, capitalists, stockholders, bondholders — the capitalist class generally — oppose the efforts of the workers in the A. F. of L. and in other organizations to obtain a larger share of the product. Very much of the opposition to the efforts of the working-people to secure improved conditions has come from those who obtain what may be called an unearned share in the distribution. The beneficiaries of the present system of distribution desire to retain as much as possible of their present share or to increase that proportion. But an additional reason that leads to opposition is that there are employers who live in the twentieth century, yet who have the mental outlook of the sixteenth century in their attitude toward the working-people, and who still imagine that they are "masters of all they survey." These employers think that any attempts upon the part of the working-people to secure improvements in their condition is a spirit of rebellion that must be frowned down. But we organized workers have found that after we have had some contests with employers, whether we have won the battle or lost it, if we but maintain our organization there is less difficulty thereafter in reaching a joint agreement or a collective bargain involving improved conditions of the workers.

The stronger the organization of the workers the greater the likelihood of their securing concessions. These concessions are not altogether because of the strength shown by the employees, but result in part from the changed attitude of the employer.

An employer changes his policy when he is convinced that the workingmen have demonstrated that they have a right to a vote in determining questions affecting the relations between themselves and their employers. For instance, this was demonstrated in the case of the late Mr. Baer, who, as may be recalled, once declared that he would not speak with nor confer with the representative of the miners or any one who stood for them; that he and his associates were the "trustees of God" in the administration of their property and in taking care of the rights and interests of the working-people. He, as well as many other employers, lived to revise his judgment and to see the necessity of making agreements with workers.

Because employers as a class are interested in maintaining or increasing their share of the general product and because the workers are determined to demand a greater and ever greater share of this same general product, the economic interests between these two are not harmonious. Upon this point I have been repeatedly misrepresented by socialist writers and orators whose frequent repetitions of that misrepresentation have finally convinced them of the truth of their assertion. No amount of emphatic repudiation of that statement, no matter how often that repudiation and denial have been expressed, has secured a change in the assertion that my position was contrary to the one I have just stated.

From my earliest understanding of the conditions that prevail in the industrial world, I have been convinced and I have asserted that the economic interests of the employing class and those of the working class are not harmonious. That has been my position ever since — never changed in the slightest. There are times, when, for temporary purposes, interests are reconcilable; but they are temporary only.

When a fair and reasonable opportunity presents itself for continued improvement in the conditions of the workers, the movement of the workers must necessarily go on and will go on. It will not be dominated by the so-called intellectuals or butters-in. The working-class movement to be most effective must be conducted by the workers themselves. It is conducted by the working-people in the interests of the working-people. It is conducted against those who stand in the way, hostile to the advancement of conditions for the working-people. It is conducted against those employers whoever they may be — the employers who refuse to understand modern industrial conditions and the constant need for the advancement of the working-people and who refuse to accede to the demands of the workers.

All the demands upon employers are not made by organized labor. There are frequently demands made by workingmen and working-women who are unorganized and who then become organized after they have made their demands. The number of employers who refuse to accede to labor's demands is growing smaller and smaller. As a matter of fact, there are more employers to-day who live under collective bargains with their organized employees than at any other time in the history of the industrial world.

In the initial stages of the altered relations between workers and employees improvements are forced upon the employers by collective bargains, strikes, and boycotts. Later there is a realization upon the part of the employers that it is more costly to enter into long strikes and lockouts than to concede conditions without interrupting the industry. As the vision and the understanding of the employer change, his attitude toward his workmen and the relations between employer and workers also change, so that the sentiments and views of employers are often in entire accord with those of the organizations of working-people.

However, the gains made by the organized labor movement in this country have generally been wrung from the employing classes. What the workingmen of America have obtained in improved conditions, higher wages, shorter hours of labor, was not handed to them on a silver platter. They have had to organize, they have had to show their teeth, they have had to strike, they have had to go hungry and to make sacrifices in order to impress upon the employers their determination to be larger sharers in the products of labor.

There are some exceptions to the general rule that the achievements of the American labor movement have been accomplished by the organized struggle of the workers against their employers. One instance is that of the coal miners. In their first strike in 1897, not three per cent of them were organized. Yet upon the initiative of the union and the recommendation of the officers of the A. F. of L. a movement was inaugurated to present a scale to the mine operators in the bituminous fields and to state that unless the proposed increase in wages and other conditions were granted upon a certain day, there would come a call urging all the miners to lay down their tools.

The employers, realizing the unorganized conditions of the miners, never for a moment imagined that the small union would have any influence upon their so-called "independent workingmen" who were really workingmen over whom they had exercised domination for a long time. Though unorganized, the miners responded. There was among them the group patriotism to which I referred in the early part of my testimony — a group patriotism, a *camaraderie*, an understanding of their common interests. They received the assistance of their fellow workers in other industries and the full assistance of the A. F. of L. The movement proved to be the initial step in the regeneration of the miners. They finally won and established the eight-hour day, the right to purchase their necessities wherever they chose, the right to act like all ordinary citizens. The spirit and influence of that movement spread until they reached the anthracite coal fields, extended beyond West Virginia into the competitive fields of bituminous coal mine operation in many other States.

In their struggle to obtain lasting improvements the workers have occasionally been aided by employers whose interests for the time being were identified with theirs. For it sometimes occurs that the competitive interests of employers may impel some of them to aid the workingmen in the establishment of what have become known as standardized conditions of the trade — the minima of standardization. Such assistance is only an incident in the struggle, of which the workers take advantage.

On the whole, the A. F. of L. recognizes that the struggle for improvement in the conditions of the workers is the struggle of the workers themselves. The unions affiliated to the A. F. of L. and the A. F. of L. in dealing with directly affiliated locals do not permit employers to become members of the unions. I know of no means of harmonizing in full the interests of employers and workers.

Pensions. The A. F. of L. favors a system of non-contributing old-age pensions for workers who have reached a certain age, to be established by legal enactment and maintained by governmental machinery. The Federation favors a general system of state insurance against sickness, disability, and accidents. It has not endorsed state insurance of unemployment. In regard to the problem of unemployment the Federation proposes to shorten the workday of the employees, that they may share with the unemployed the work that is to be performed and thereby tend constantly toward the elimination of unemployment. The

American workman refuses to regard unemployment as a permanent evil attending the industrial and economic forces of our country. The American workmen propose to share work with those who are unemployed and thereby to help to find work for the unemployed.

Opposition to labor parties. The A. F. of L. has an independent political policy — a policy so independent politically that it is independent of the Socialist Party, too. It is concerned more about achievements than it is about the instrumentality for achievement. We have achieved through the American labor movement more real betterment for the working-people than has been accomplished by any other labor movement in the world.

The entire trade-union movement of America is absolutely without any parties and without political affiliation. The large national organizations not affiliated to the A. F. of L. are also absolutely independent politically. The labor interests most intimately associated with the A. F. of L. during the entire period of its national legislative activities have been the Railroad Brotherhoods.

Wherever the Federal Government has undertaken industrial legislation in this country, that legislation has affected the men engaged in interstate commerce, men engaged as workmen on the railroads, men in the engine and train service, and of course seamen.

The logical tendency is to extend to the States in some degree the legislative principles tried by the Federal Government. There has been for many years an insistent effort to establish for these men some tribunal that would fix by legislation the wages, conditions of service, and hours of labor. Insistence for the enactment of legislation placing in a Government board such power is always traceable to the larger interests that employ men. There is an underground process constantly at work to devise ways and means ostensibly and superficially well-sounding, but which contain a process and a method by which the status of the workmen can be fixed. The purpose is to tie them to their tasks, that the right of freedom of action shall be first impaired and then denied. Our friends, the members and leaders of the Socialist Party, would gladly establish that in the wholesale. They do not understand the real struggle for freedom.

Political program. The Federation is in favor of absolute freedom of press, speech, and assemblage. It stands for freedom of speech, freedom of press, freedom of assemblage, and has undertaken great risks to assert and maintain these rights. In addition to this, the A. F. of L. looks askance upon any effort to curb the inherent as well as the constitutional rights of free press, free speech, and free assemblage. It holds that though these rights may be perverted, may be improperly exercised, exercised for unlawful purposes, yet these rights must not be interfered with in advance. The right of assemblage, the right of free expression by speech or through the press, must be untrammeled if we are to maintain a republican form of government. If anybody utters that which is libelous, seditious, or treasonable, he may be and must be made to answer for those transgressions, but the right to free expression of opinion must be unimpaired. The A. F. of L. has stood and will stand unalterably and unequivocally in favor of free assemblage, free speech, and free press.

The A. F. of L. favors unrestricted and equal suffrage for men and women, and has done much to advance that cause.

It favors the initiative, referendum, and recall. It not only advocates these measures, but a member of an affiliated organization, Mr. James W. Sullivan, was the author of the first book published in the United States upon direct legislation, the initiative and referendum.

The A. F. of L. has not taken any official position in regard to the system of proportional representation. The proportionate representation employed in voting in the conventions of the A. F. of L. is not proportional representation as that term is usually used. Proportional representation denotes a system by which votes are cast and rights are exercised by representatives in proportion to the total numerical strength of the constituents.

It favors the election of the President and the Vice-President of the United States by direct vote of the people without the intervention of an electoral college.

It favors restriction of the powers of judges to nullify laws and to set them aside as unconstitutional.

The Federation favors making the Constitution of the United States amendable by an easier method than is provided at present. The present method of amendment is very cumbersome and slow. A written constitution is a chart which ought not to be subject to changes at every ebb and flow of the tide, but ought to be more easily changed than is now possible. The Federation favors curbing the powers of courts to punish for alleged contempts committed in connection with labor disputes.

Education. It favors the enactment of further measures for general education and particularly for vocational education in useful pursuits.

It is not generally known that to the organized labor movement of Massachusetts belongs the credit of establishing public schools in Massachusetts and the general public school system as it has since developed. Prior to that time there were schools which children of poor parents could attend, but attendance at such schools carried with it the stigma of the poverty of the parents. Such poverty was a stigma then. The labor movement of Massachusetts secured the enactment of a law removing as a requirement for attendance at these schools that the parents of the children must declare that they could not afford to pay for the tuition of their children. Thus came into existence the first public school in the United States.

The A. F. of L. has had for the past ten years a committee composed of many of its own representative men and women and a number of public educators acting for the A. F. of L., yet independent of it, that has worked out a system of vocational training for industries, agriculture, and household economy. The report shows the relation between these vocations and civic duty. That report has been made a public document by the Senate of the United States.

CHAPTER X

ECONOMIC PROGRAM OF ORGANIZED LABOR

1. Collective Bargaining [1]

Need for collective bargaining. In its fundamental principle trade-unionism is plain and clear and simple. Trade-unionism starts from the recognition of the fact that under normal conditions the individual, unorganized workman cannot bargain advantageously with the employer for the sale of his labor. Since the workingman has no money in reserve and must sell his labor immediately, since, moreover, he has no knowledge of the market and no skill in bargaining, since, finally, he has only his own labor to sell, while the employer engages hundreds or thousands of men and can easily do without the services of any particular individual, the workingman, if bargaining on his own account and for himself alone, is at an enormous disadvantage. Trade-unionism recognizes the fact that under such conditions labor becomes more and more degenerate, because the labor which the workman sells is, unlike other commodities, a thing which is of his very life and soul and being. In the individual contract between a rich employer and a poor workman, the laborer will secure the worst of it; he is progressively debased, because of wages insufficient to buy nourishing food, because of hours of labor too long to permit sufficient rest, because of conditions of work destructive of moral, mental, and physical health, and degrading and annihilating to the laboring classes of the present and the future, and, finally, because of danger from accident and disease, which kill off the workingman or prematurely age him. The "individual bargain," or individual contract, between employers and men means that the condition of the worst and lowest man in the industry will be that which the best man must accept. From first to last, from beginning to end, always and everywhere, trade-unionism stands unalterably opposed to the individual contract. There can be no concession or yielding upon this point. No momentary ad-

[1] From *Organized Labor*, by John Mitchell, pp. 2–11. The American Book and Bible House, publishers.

vantage, however great or however ardently desired, no advance in wages, no reduction in hours, no betterment in conditions, will permanently compensate workingmen for even a temporary surrender in any part of this fundamental principle. It is this principle, the absolute and complete prohibition of contracts between employers and individual men, upon which trade-unionism is founded. There can be no permanent prosperity to the working classes, no real and lasting progress, no consecutive improvement in conditions, until the principle is firmly and fully established, that in industrial life, especially in enterprises on a large scale, the settlement of wages, hours of labor, and all conditions of work, must be made between employers and workingmen collectively and not between employers and workingmen individually.

To find a substitute for the individual bargain, which destroys the welfare and the happiness of the whole working class, trade unions were founded. A trade union, in its usual form, is an association of workmen who have agreed among themselves not to bargain individually with their employer or employers, but to agree to the terms of a collective or joint contract between the employer and the union. The fundamental reason for the existence of the trade union is that by it and through it, workmen are enabled to deal collectively with their employers. The difference between the individual and the collective or joint bargain is simply this, that in the individual contract or bargain one man of a hundred refuses to accept work, and the employer retains the services of ninety and nine; whereas in the collective bargain the hundred employees act in a body, and the employer retains or discharges all simultaneously and upon the same terms. The ideal of trade-unionism is to combine in one organization all the men employed, or capable of being employed, at a given trade, and to demand and secure for each and all of them a definite minimum standard of wages, hours, and conditions of work.

Trade-unionism thus recognizes that the destruction of the workingman is the individual bargain, and the salvation of the workingman is the joint, united, or collective bargain. To carry out a joint bargain, however, it is necessary to establish a minimum of wages and conditions which will apply to all. By this is not meant that the wages of all shall be the same, but merely that equal pay shall be given for equal work. There cannot be more than one minimum in a given trade, in a given place, at a given time. If the bricklayers of the city of New York were all organized and the union permitted half of its members to work for forty cents an hour, while the other half, in no wise better workmen, were compelled or led to ask for fifty cents, the result would be that the men receiving fifty cents would be obliged either to lower their wages or get out of the trade. To secure to any union man fifty cents an hour, all union men of equal skill must demand at least an equal sum. The man who wants fifty cents an hour is not injured by other unionists asking or getting ten or twenty cents in excess of this minimum, but he is injured by fellow craftsmen accepting any wage less than the minimum. The same rule of collective bargaining applies to the hours of labor. If all union bricklayers in New York City were to receive four dollars a day and some were, for this pay, to work eight hours, others ten, and still others twelve and fifteen hours, the result would be that the employers would by preference employ the men who were willing to work fifteen hours. As a consequence, the men willing to work only eight or ten hours would lose their positions or be obliged either to reduce their wages or to work as long as their competitors, who were employed for twelve or fifteen hours. What is true of wages and of hours of labor is equally true of all the conditions of work. If some members of the union were allowed to work with machinery unguarded, whereas others insisted upon its protection; if some were to work in any sort of factory, under any sort of conditions, with any sort of a foreman or master, while others insisted upon proper surroundings; if some were willing to be so overrushed as to do more than a fair day's work for a fair day's wage, or would allow themselves to be forced into patronizing truck stores, to submit to arbitrary fines and unreasonable deductions, whereas others would rebel at these impositions, it would result that in the competition among the men to retain their positions, those who were most pliant and lowest-spirited would secure the work and the wages, hours of labor, and conditions of employment would be those set or accepted by the poorest, most cringing, and least independent of workers. If the trade union did not insist upon enforcing common rules providing for equal pay for equal work and definite conditions of safety and health for all workers in the trade, the result would be that all pretense of a joint bargain would disappear, and the employers would be free constantly to make individual contracts with the various members of the union. The trade union does not stand for equal earnings of all workmen. It does not object to one man's earning twice as much as the man working by his side, provided both men have equal rates of pay, equal hours of work, equal opportunities of securing work, and equal conditions of employment. The union does not object to an employer's rewarding especially efficient workers, or even favored workers, by paying them more than the union scale, or granting them shorter hours than provided for by the joint agreement. What the union does stand for is merely equal rates of pay — equal pay for equal work; and while it will allow a man to receive twice as much as his fellow craftsmen, it will not permit him to do so by underbidding them in wages or by working under less favorable conditions or for longer hours. Neither does the union oppose competition among unionists for positions, although it demands that this competition be solely upon the basis of efficiency and not upon that of reduced wages, lengthened hours, or any abatement from the conditions fixed by the collective bargain.

Reason for standard rate. This principle of trade-unionism will explain many of the seeming peculiarities and many of the numerous rules of labor organizations. It will supply an answer to the question, so naïvely put by many people, as to why the union will not allow a man to accept two dollars a day, while all other workers in that trade are receiving three dollars, or to accept forty cents for mining a ton of coal, when the minimum scale is fifty-six cents. "Why," it is inquired, "should not a man be allowed to accept a reduction of wages if he wish? Why should a man be compelled to take more wages than he wants?" The answer of the unions is that, as a result of such individual bargains, the employer would give all the work to the men who were satisfied with two dollars a day, and, consequently, the men who demanded three dollars would be thrown out of employment, and therefore forced to accept a lower rate of remuneration. It is this necessity of equal pay for equal work that compels trade unions to say to the employer: "Either you shall pay three dollars to the man who only asks for two, or we will not work for you. We recognize your right to employ or not to employ whomsoever you wish, but either you must pay *at least* three dollars, or else all the members of our union will refuse to work for you."

This necessity of defending the collective bargain, or contract, explains many features of trade-union policy. If the union is to maintain its standard of wages by collective bargaining, it must prevent the employer, by individual bargains with individual workmen, from making deductions from wages and thus breaking down the minimum wage agreed upon between the union and the employer. If trade unions are to tolerate truck stores, not only will unfair and extortionate prices be charged, but individual men desiring the favor of the employer will compete for their jobs by purchasing more and more goods in the company store. Instead of offering to work for two dollars a day when the standard rate is three, a man may simply take for his work an order on the store, which, though nominally worth three, will actually be worth two dollars. It is well known that companies, operating truck stores for profit in connection with their factories, invariably give the preference in the matter of jobs to men who best patronize the stores, with the result that competition for jobs among workmen becomes as severe as ever, and the consequent undercutting or underbidding takes the vicious form of spending as much as possible at the company store. The toleration of the company store may thus come to mean a series of individual agreements, real but not expressed, by which individual workingmen permit themselves to suffer deductions from their real wages in the form of profits on the goods which they are obliged to buy.

The prohibition by unions of arbitrary fines and docking is due to this same desire to maintain a common minimum standard of wages and conditions. Apart from the direct evil and oppression that result from the unlimited powers of employers arbitrarily to levy fines or make deductions from wages, there is the added danger that, by this means, the employers will break down the collective bargain and substitute for it a series of individual bargains. If the trade unions secure from the employer a minimum daily three-dollar wage, the effect of this common action will be nullified and destroyed if some individual workmen submit in any form to an average deduction of ten cents a day, whether for fines or docking, others to a deduction of twenty cents, and others to one of fifty cents or a dollar a day. The union is not opposed to a deduction from wages in case of proved negligence or poor workmanship; but as these fines and this docking affects the union wage, they should be jointly determined upon by the employer and the union, and not by the employer alone, nor between the employer and the individual workman. If the individual employee is permitted to make any rebate or allow any deduction whatsoever, under whatever guise, from the wages fixed as a minimum by the union, then the whole principle of a union scale of wages will fall to the ground.

The necessity of maintaining the collective, rather than the individual, bargain explains why the trade union is sometimes opposed to the piece system and sometimes not. When the piece price can be regulated collectively, as in bituminous coal mining, the unions are not antagonistic to, but actually in favor of, this system. Where, however, each separate job differs and a price must be put upon it separately, payment by the piece degenerates into a system of underbidding and undercutting and to the resurrection of individual bargaining in one of its worst forms. Where the price cannot be fixed collectively and where time wages cannot be paid, the union has solved the problem, at least partially, by having the shop foreman, a representative of all the men in the establishment, fix the price of the work in concert with the employer or foreman.

Like the wage scale, the length of the working-day, as determined by the union and employers, must be protected from changes made by individual workmen. The individual workman cannot be allowed to work longer hours than the union prescribes as a maximum, or to work more overtime, or at different times, or for less compensation than is fixed by the collective bargain. If the individual workman is to decide for himself how much overtime he will work, and at what rate of compensation, he can just as surely underbid other workmen as by accepting a lower wage at the start.

There is hardly an action taken by the trade unions, hardly a demand made, which does not either immediately or ultimately, directly or indirectly, involve this principle. Whether the union demand a higher standard of healthfulness, comfort, or decency in the factories, or a greater degree of protection from machinery, or any other concession ministering to the health or safety of the employee, the demand is always in the form of a certain minimum for all workers. The union does not prohibit a man from being paid more wages for less hours than his fellows, but it does claim that no man shall work in union shops for less than a certain rate, for more than a certain number of hours, for more than so and so much overtime, or at a lower rate for overtime, or with less than a given amount of protection to his health, comfort, safety, and well-being. The employer may, if he wish, make special provision for the health of a favorite workman, just as he may pay above the union rate or allow an employee, in return for the minimum wage, to work less than the maximum number of working hours prescribed by the union. What the union insists upon, however, is that certain minimum requirements be fulfilled for the health, comfort, and safety of all, in order that the workingmen shall not be obliged to compete for jobs by surrendering their claims to a reasonable amount of protection for their health, and for their life and limb.

The trade union thus stands for the freedom of contract on the part of workingmen — the freedom or right to contract collectively. The trade union also stands for definiteness of the labor contract. The relation between employer and employee is complex in its nature, even though it appear simple. The workingman agrees to work at the wage offered to him by the employer, at, say, fifteen dollars a week, but frequently nothing is said as to hours of labor, pauses for meals and rest, intensity of work, conditions of the workshop, protection of the workman against filthy surroundings or unguarded machinery, character of his fellow workmen, liability of the employer for accident, nor any of the thousand conditions which affect the welfare of the workman and the gain of both employer and employee. There has always been a general tacit understanding between employers and employees that these conditions shall roughly conform to the usual and ordinary custom of the trade, but in the absence of an agreement with the union it is in the power of the employer to make such rules absolutely, or to change or amend them at such time as he thinks proper. Like the railroad time-tables, the individual contract reads, "Subject to change without notice."

Meaning of "recognition." The recognition of the union is nothing more nor less than the recognition of the principle for which trade-unionism stands, the right to bargain collectively and to insist upon a common standard as a minimum. Workingmen have a nominal, but not a real freedom of contract, if they are prevented from contracting collectively instead of individually. The welfare of the working classes, as of society, depends upon the recognition of this principle of the right of employees to contract collectively. An employer, be he ever so well-meaning, stands in the way of future progress if he insist upon dealing with his workmen "as individuals." While in his establishment wages may not by this means be reduced, owing to the fact that other establishments are organized, still the principle for which he stands, if universally adopted, would mean the degradation and impoverishment of the working classes. There are many employers who surrender the principle of the individual bargain without accepting the principle of the collective bargain. These employers state that they do not insist upon dealing with their employees as individuals, but that they must retain the right of dealing with "their own employees solely," and that they must not be forced to permit a man who is not their own employee to interfere in their business. The right to bargain collectively, however, or to take any other concerted action, necessarily involves the right to representation. Experience and reason both show that a man, even if otherwise qualified, who is dependent upon the good will of an employer, is in no position to negotiate with him since an insistence upon what he considers to be the rights of the men represented by him may mean his dismissal or, at all events, the loss of the favor of his employer. Not only should workingmen have the right of contracting collectively, but they should also have the right of being represented by whomsoever they wish. The denial of the right of representation is tyranny. Without the right to choose their representative, the men cannot enjoy the full benefit of collective bargaining; and without the right of collective bargaining, the door is opened to the individual contract and to the progressive debasement of the working classes, and to the deterioration of conditions of work to the level of conditions in the sweated and unregulated trades. To avoid this calamity and to raise the working classes to a high state of efficiency and a high standard of citizenship, the organized workmen demand and insist upon "the recognition of the union."

2. THE STANDARD RATE [1]

Among trade-union regulations there is one which stands out as practically universal, namely, the insistence on payment according to some definite standard, uniform in its application. Even so rudimentary a form of combination as the "shop club" requires that all its members shall receive, as a minimum, the rate agreed upon with the foreman for the particular job. The organized local or national union carries the principle further, and insists on a standard rate of payment for all its members in the town or district. The standard rate, it should be observed, is only a minimum, never a maximum. The Friendly Society of Operative Stonemasons, for instance, agrees (1897) with the London Central Master Builders' Association that all its able-bodied members shall receive not less than tenpence halfpenny per hour. But the Society has no objection to an employer offering a particular stonemason, whose skill or character is valued, any higher rate that he may choose. The Amalgamated Society of Tailors, in conjunction with the Master Tailors' Association of the particular town, settled a "log" fixing the payment for each kind of garment. But this does not prevent West End master tailors, with the full sanction of the union, paying some members far above the London log rates. In fact, though there are certain seeming exceptions with which we shall deal separately, we know of no case in which a trade union forbids or discourages its members from receiving a higher rate of remuneration, for the work actually performed, than the common standard rate fixed for the whole body.

The standard not a maximum wage. But although the standard rate is a minimum, not a maximum, the establishment of this minimum necessarily results in a nearer approximation to equality of rates than would otherwise prevail. Trade-union officials who have had to construct a piecework list, or to extend such a list from one shop to the whole town, or from one town to the whole trade, know that, in order to secure a standard list of prices, they

[1] From *Industrial Democracy*, by Sidney and Beatrice Webb, pp. 279–296. Longmans, Green & Co., publishers.

have had to pare down the rates hitherto enjoyed by particular shops or even particular towns. It is exactly this willingness on the part of the more fortunately situated sections of the trade to forego, for the sake of a standard rate, the higher rates which happen, by some accident, to have become current for a particular line of work, that makes uniformity possible. We have already cited, in describing how trade-unionism breaks down local monopoly, the case of the Cotton-Weavers, who discovered that, in order to secure a uniform list of piecework prices — meaning, to the majority of members, an advance of wages — one or two districts had to consent to a positive reduction of the rates they had hitherto enjoyed. The powerful society of Flint-Glass Makers has recently afforded us an even more striking example. When in 1895 the Flint-Glass Makers concerted with their employers a uniform "catalogue of prices" for all the glass works in Yorkshire, the York branch, which enjoyed higher rates than any other in the county, at first vehemently protested. A uniform list, they urged, "was impracticable, unless by some section of us making enormous sacrifices"; and its enforcement would involve the "edifying spectacle of a trade union compelling its members to work at a reduced wage, when neither they nor the employer desired it." Notwithstanding this protest, the members of the union approved the preparation of the uniform list, which was submitted to general meetings of all the Yorkshire branches. The issue was thus put before the York members, and, though it was made clear that the new list would involve a reduction of their own earnings, the feeling in favor of uniformity was so strong that, as the general secretary records, out of a total of eighty-four members in the branch at the time, "the vote against the catalogue was only the miserable total of nine."

Relation to collective bargaining. This conception of a standard rate is, as we need hardly explain, an indispensable requisite of collective bargaining. Without some common measure, applicable to all the workmen concerned, no general treaty with regard to wages would be possible. But the use of a definite standard of measurement is not merely an adjunct of the method of collective bargaining. It is required for any wholesale determination of wages upon broad principles. The most autocratic and unfettered employer spontaneously adopts standard rates for classes of workmen, just as the large shopkeeper fixes his prices, not according to the higgling capacity of particular customers, but by a definite percentage on cost. This conception of a consistent standard of measurement the trade union seeks to extend from establishments to districts, and from districts to the whole area of the trade within the kingdom.

This trade-unionist insistence on a standard rate has been the subject of bitter denunciation. The payment of "bad and lazy workmen as highly as those who are skilled and industrious," "setting a premium on idleness and incapacity," "destructive to the legitimate ambition of industry and merit," that "worst kind of communism, the equal remuneration of all men," are only samples of the abusive rhetoric of capitalists and philosophers on the subject. Even as lately as 1871 a distinguished economist poured out the following tirade against the assumed wickedness of the trade unions in this respect: "Not yet, but in course of time, as economic principles become popularly understood, we shall see trade unions purged of their most erroneous and mischievous purpose of seeking an uniform rate of wages without regard to differences of skill, knowledge, industry, and character. There is no tenet of socialism more fatal in its consequences than this insidious and plausible doctrine — a doctrine which, if acted upon rigidly for any length of time by large classes of men, would stop all progress. Put in plain language it means that there shall not be in the world any such thing as superior talent or attainment; that every art and handicraft shall be reduced to the level of the commonest, most ignorant, and most stupid of the persons who belong to it."

Such criticisms are beside the mark. A very slight acquaintance with trade-unionism would have shown these writers that a uniform standard rate in no way implies equality of weekly wages and has no such object. For good or for evil, the typical British workman is not by any means a communist, and the trade-union regulations are, as we shall see, quite free from any theoretic "yearnings for equal division of unequal earnings."

Piece rates as a standard. The misapprehension arises from a confusion between the rate of payment and the amount actually earned by the workman. What the trade union insists on, as a necessary condition of the very existence of collective bargaining, is a standard rate of payment for the work actually performed. But this is consistent with the widest possible divergence between the actual weekly incomes of different workmen. Thus we have the significant fact that the standard rate insisted on by the great majority of trade-unionists is, not any definite sum per hour, but a list of piecework prices. The extent to which these piecework lists prevail throughout the country is seldom realized. Even those who have heard of the elaborate tonnage rates of the ironworkers, steel-smelters, and coal miners, and the complicated cotton lists, which together govern the remuneration of a fourth of the trade-union world, often forget the innumerable other trades, in which (as with the tailors, bootmakers, compositors, coopers, basketmakers, brushmakers) lists of prices, signed by employers and employed, and revised from time to time, date from the very beginning of the century. When, as in all these cases, the standard rate takes the form of a schedule of piecework prices, it is clear that there can be no question of equalizing the actual earnings of different workmen. One basketmaker or one coal miner may be earning two pounds a week, whilst another, receiving the same standard rate and working the same number of hours, may get less than thirty shillings; and another, putting in only half-time, may have only ten or fifteen shillings for his week's income.

Nor can it be assumed that in the industries in which the trade-union rate is not based on piecework, but takes the form of a definite standard wage per hour, this necessarily implies equality of remuneration. Even where workmen in such trades put in the same number of hours, their weekly incomes will often be found to differ very materially. Thus, whilst ordinary plumbing, bricklaying, and masonry are paid for at uniform rates per hour, directly the job involves any special skill the employer finds it advantageous to pay a higher rate, and the trade union cordially encourages this practice. The superior bricklayer, for instance, is seldom employed at the standard rate, but is always getting jobs at brick-cutting (or "gauge work"), furnace-building, or sewer construction, paid for at rates from ten to fifty per cent over the standard wage. In all industries we find firms with special reputations for a high class of production habitually paying, with full trade-union approval, more than the trade-union rate, in order to attract to their establishment the most skillful and best conducted workmen. In other cases, where the employer rigidly adheres to the common rate, the superior workman finds his advantage, if not actually in higher money earnings, in more agreeable conditions of employment. In a large building the employer will select his best stonemasons to do the carving, an occupation not involving great exertion and consistent with an occasional pipe, whilst the common run of workmen will be setting stones under the foreman's eye. The best carpenters, when not earning extra rates for "staircasing" or "handrailing," will get the fine work which combines variety and lightness, and is done in the workshop, leaving to the rougher hands the laying-down of flooring and other heavy mechanical tasks. These distinctions may seem trivial to the professional or business man, who to a large extent controls the conditions under which he works. But no workman fails to appreciate the radical difference in net advantageousness between two different jobs, one involving exposure to the weather, wear and tear of clothing, monotonous muscular exertion, and incessant supervision, and the other admitting a considerable share of personal liberty, agreeably diversified in character, and affording scope for initiative and address. Though there may be in such cases equality in the number of shillings received at the end of the week, the remuneration for the efforts and sacrifices actually made will have been at very different rates in the two cases.

We do not wish to obscure the fact that a standard rate on a timework basis does, in practice, result in a nearer approach to uniformity of money earnings than a standard rate on a piecework basis. Nor is there any doubt that a considerable section of the wage-earning class have a deeply rooted conviction that the conscientious, industrious, and slow mechanic ought in equity to receive no less pay than his quicker but equally meritorious neighbor; more especially as the normal earnings of even the quickest mechanic do not amount to more than is demanded for the proper maintenance of his household. It is often assumed that this conviction has produced, in the trade-union world, a fundamental objection to piecework. Had this been the case, it would have been strange that we should have had to quote, as typical instances of unions strongly enforcing a standard rate, so many trades in which piecework universally prevails.

Among the trades in which piecework is either insisted on by the men, or readily accepted by them, we find the largest and the most powerful trade unions. The miners and cotton operatives, who would instantly strike against any attempt to introduce time wages, are only paralleled in the strength and extent of their trade unions by the boilermakers and iron shipbuilders, who adopt piecework as the basis of the greater part of their wage contracts. And so far is piecework from being objected to by trade-union officials, that we find, in these trades, that the preponderating part of the trade-union machinery, including the ablest and most influential officials, has been called into existence for the express purpose of dealing with piecework lists. The district delegates of the boilermakers, the secretaries of the cotton operatives, the investigators of the boot and shoe operatives, and the check-weighmen of the coalminers spend their whole lives in arranging remuneration on a piecework basis.

On the other hand, though the time workers are in the minority, we have among them some very strong unions, such as the stonemasons, the bricklayers, and the plumbers, who have always vehemently denounced piecework as the bane of their trades. How can we explain this divergence?

When piece rates are favored. On asking a leading official of the cotton-spinners' union why he objected to time wages, he replied that, in his opinion, it was only the system of piecework remuneration that had saved his trade from the evils of sweating. The work of a cotton-spinner, he explained, varies in intensity (and his product in quantity) according to the number of spindles which he has to attend to, and the speed at which the machinery runs, conditions over which the operative has no control. Owing to the introduction of mules bearing an increased number of spindles, and the constant "speeding-up" of the machinery, the amount of work placed upon the operative is steadily, though often imperceptibly, increased. If he were paid by the hour or the day, he would need, in order to maintain the same rate of remuneration for the work done, to discover each day precisely to what degree the machinery was being "speeded-up," and to be perpetually making demands for an increase in his time wages. Such an arrangement could not fail to result in the employer increasing the work faster than the pay.

Under a system of payment by the amount of yarn spun, the operative automatically gets the benefit of any increase in the number of spindles or rate of speed. An exact uniformity of the rate of remuneration is maintained between man and man, and between mill and mill. If any improvement takes place in the process, by which the operative's labor is reduced, the onus of procuring a change in the rate of pay falls on the employer. The result is, that so effectually is the cotton-spinner secured by his piecework lists against being compelled to give more work without more pay, that it has been found desirable deliberately to concede to the employers, by lowering the rates as the number of spindles increases, some share of the resulting advantages, in order that the trade union may encourage enterprising mill-owners in the career of improvement. The cotton-weavers have a similar experience. The weaver's labor depends upon the character of the cloth to be woven, involving a complicated calculation of the number of "picks," etc. Time wages would leave them practically at the employers' mercy for all but the very easiest work. But by a highly technical and complex list of piecework rates, every element by which the labor is increased effects an exactly corresponding variation in the remuneration. Only under such a system could any uniformity of rate be secured.

In another great class of cases piecework is preferred by the workmen, with the same object of securing a standard rate, but under entirely different conditions. The coal miners have, in some counties, had a long experience of both time wages and piecework, with the result that, wherever there is a strong trade union, piecework is insisted on for all hewers. The explanation is to be found in the circumstances under which the work is done. Employers have found it impossible to supervise by foremen or managers the numerous hewers scattered in the recesses of the mine. The only possible alternative to paying the hewers at piecework rates, was to let out the different parts of the mine to working contractors, who engaged hewers by the hour to work alongside them. This was the notorious "butty system," against which the organized hewers have persistently struggled. It was found that, whatever was the customary standard of daily time wages, the "butty master," who set the pace, was always increasing the quantity of work to be done for those wages by himself putting in an unusual intensity of effort. It is obvious that, under this system, the ordinary hewer lost all security of a standard rate. It paid the "butty master" to be always "speeding-up," because he received the product, not of his own extra exertion alone, but of that of all his gang. The only method by which the ordinary hewers could secure identity of rate was to dispense with the "butty masters," and themselves work by the piece.

We shall find exactly the same preference for piecework wages in other trades among men who work under a sub-contractor, or in subordination to another class of workmen paid by the piece. The strikers, for instance, who work with smiths paid by the piece, were themselves formerly paid time wages. In most parts of the country they have now been successful in obtaining the boon of a piecework rate proportionate to that of the smiths, so that they are secured extra remuneration for any extra spurt put on by the smith. Another large class of workmen in a somewhat similar position have not been so fortunate. The shipyard "helpers," who work under the platers (iron-shipbuilders), are paid by the day, whilst the platers receive piecework rates. The first object of any combination of helpers has always been to secure piecework rates, in order that their remuneration might bear some proportion to the rapidity and intensity of work, the pace being set by the platers. But owing to the strength of the boilermakers' union, to which the platers belong, the helpers have never been able to attain their object. The iron and steel industries afford numerous other instances in which workers paid by the day are in subordination to workers paid by the piece. In all these cases, the subordinate workers desire to be paid by the piece, in order that they may secure a greater uniformity in the rate of payment for the work actually done.

Why piece rates are opposed. Coming now to the trades in which piecework is most strongly objected to by the operatives, we shall find the argument again turning upon the question of uniformity of the rate of remuneration. The engineers have always protested that the introduction of piecework into their trade almost necessarily implied a reversion to individual bargaining. The work of a skilled mechanic in an engineering shop differs from job to job in such a way as to make, under a piecework system, a new contract necessary for each job. Each man, too, will be employed at an operation differing, if only in slight degree, from those of his fellows. If they are all working by the hour, a collective bargain can easily be made and adhered to. But where each successive job differs from the last, if only in small details, it is impossible to work out in advance any list of prices to which all the men can agree to adhere. The settlement for each job must necessarily be left to be made between the foreman and the workman concerned. Collective bargaining becomes, therefore, impossible. But this is not all. The uncertainty as to the time and labor which a particular job will involve makes it impossible for the foreman, with the best intentions in the world, to fix the prices of successive jobs so that the workman will obtain the same earnings for the same effort. And when we remember the disadvantage at which, unprotected by collective action, the individual operative necessarily stands in bargaining with the capitalist employer, we shall easily understand how the Amalgamated Society of Engineers should have been led to declare that, under this system of settling a special price for each job, "it is well known that piecework is not a bargain, but a price dictated by the employer and lowered at will." And the report adds that "the system has often been made the instrument of large reductions of wages, which have ended in the deterioration of the conditions of the workmen. . . . If an expert workman, by his skill and industry, earns more than his neighbor, and much more than his daily wages come to, a reduction is at once made, and made again until eventually the most expert is only able, by intense application and industry, to earn a bare living, whilst the less skillful is reduced below living prices."

We could cite from the reports of the great national unions of the engineers, ironfounders, and carpenters innumerable similar protests against piecework in their trades, all based upon the proved impossibility of maintaining a standard rate, if each job has to be separately priced. It is, however, more interesting to watch the same conviction being gradually borne in upon the mind of an exceptionally able employer. In 1876, William Denny, the well-known Clyde shipbuilder, who had put his whole establishment on piecework rates, delivered a remarkable lecture on the advantages of this method of remuneration, alike to the employer and to the workmen, specially commending the intensity of competition which it secured. He was utterly unable to understand why the workmen objected to a system which, in giving an "increase of from twenty-five to fifty per cent in his wages — and this increase my experience confirms as a rule — puts at once within his power a more comfortable and easy style of living, combined with an opportunity of saving, which, if he is a sober and careful man, will enable him to enjoy a pleasant old age, and even to lay by sufficient money to enable him to refuse on his own account any rate of payment which he deems insufficient."

Notwithstanding all these allurements, the trade unions persisted in their objection. After ten years' further experience of the working of piecework, William Denny at last perceived the real root of the men's protest. In an interesting letter written in 1886 he described his own conversion:

> At the time I published my pamphlet *The Worth of Wages*, I was under the impression piecework rates would regulate themselves as I then assumed time wages did. A larger experience of piecework has convinced me that, excepting in cases where rates can be fixed and made a matter of agreement between the whole body of the men in any works and their employers, piecework prices have not a self-regulating power, and are liable, under the pressure of heavy competition, to be depressed below what I would consider a proper level. You must understand there is a broad and very real distinction in piecework between the kind of work which can be priced in regular rates and that in which contracts are taken by the men for lump jobs of greater or less extent. In the former kind of piecework it is easily possible for the rates to be effectively controlled by the joint efforts of the employers and the work-people, as it is in the case of time wages. In the latter, owing to there being no definite standard, it is quite possible that the prices may be raised too high for competitive efficiency, or depressed to too low a point to recoup the workmen for the extra exertion and initiative induced by the very nature of piecework. In such work as that of riveters, iron fitters, and platers and in much of

carpenters' work standards of price or rates can be arranged or controlled, and the workers are not likely to endure any arrangement they may consider inequitable. They are, indeed, much more likely by insisting on uniform rates for a whole district to do injustice to the more intelligent and energetic employers, who, by introducing new machinery and new processes, are directly influential in drawing work to their district. It is evident that if piecework rates are not reduced so as to make the improvements in machinery and methods introduced by such employers fully effective in diminishing cost of production, there will be a tendency on their part to abandon these attempts, with diminished chances of work for their districts. In the case of such improvements it is possible to reduce rates without in any way reducing the effective earnings of the work-people. I may say that in our own experience we have almost invariably found our workers quite willing to consider these points fairly and intelligently. Frequently they themselves make such suggestions as materially help us to reduce cost of production. Such cases of invention and helpfulness on their part are rewarded directly through our awards scheme of which you have particulars.

In the second kind of piecework, involving contracts which cannot be arranged by rates and controlled by the whole body of the workers, the prices are necessarily a matter of settlement between individual workmen and small groups of workmen and their foreman. Here it depends upon the control exercised by the heads of the business whether this kind of piecework drifts into extravagances, or into such reductions of contract prices as either to reduce them to less than the value of time wages or to so little above time wages that they do not compensate the men for their extra exertions. We have found in testing such piecework that the best method is to compare the earnings made by these pieceworkers in a given period with the time wages which they would have received for the same period; and it is the duty of one of our partners to control this section of the work, and he does it almost invariably to the advantage of the men. Our idea is that the men should be able to average from twenty-five to fifty per cent more wages on such piecework within a given time than their time wages would amount to. There are occasional and exceptional cases where the results are less or more favorable. Where they are less favorable, we consider them to be not only a loss to the men, but disadvantageous to ourselves; and our reason for this is very clear, as unless the men feel that their exertions produce really better wages, and that increased exertions and better arrangements of work will produce still further increases of wages, there is an end to all stimulus to activity or improvement.

I know an instance in which a well-meaning foreman, desirous of diminishing the cost of the work in his department, reduced his piecework prices to such a point that he not only removed all healthy stimulus to activity from his workmen, but produced among them serious discontent. Our method of piecework analysis and control enabled us to discover and remedy this before serious disaffection had been produced. I know another instance in which a foreman, while avoiding the mistake I have just mentioned, gave out his contracts in such small and scattered portions, and under such conditions as to the way in which the work was to be done and as to the composition of the co-partneries formed by the men, that he not only reduced their earnings to very nearly time rates, but created very serious disaffection among them. He was in the habit of forcing the men to take into their co-partneries personal favorites of his own, who very naturally became burdens upon those co-partneries. As soon as our returns and inquiries revealed to us these facts, we insisted that the contracts entered into with the men should be of a sufficient money amount to enable them to organize themselves and their work efficiently. We removed the defective arrangements above referred to, and laid down the principle that their co-partneries were to be purely voluntary. We were enabled by these means, and without altering a single price, to at once raise their earnings from a level a little above what they could have made on time wages to a very satisfactory percentage of increase and to remove all discontent. These two instances will show you how necessary it is in this kind of piecework that there should be a direct control over those who are carrying it out. When the heads of a business are absentees or indifferent the most effective way in which the workmen can control such piecework would be by taking care that the standard of time wages was always kept perfectly clear and effective, and that regular comparisons per hour on piecework were made. Such comparisons would immediately enable them to arrive at a correct conclusion as to whether the prices paid them were sufficiently profitable.

There is besides a mixed kind of piecework in which skilled workmen employ laborers at time wages to do the unskilled portion of their work for them. Here, too, some kind of control is required, as instances occasionally occur in which the skilled workmen treat their laborers, either intentionally or unintentionally, with harshness. I have even known an instance in which such piecework contractors reduced their laborers' time wages on the pay day without having given them any previous notice. On the other hand, there are instances in which these laborers behaved in an unreasonable and unfair spirit to the skilled workmen who employ them.

In conclusion, I would say that the method of piecework is one which cannot be approved or condemned absolutely, but is dependent upon the spirit and the way in which it is carried out for the verdict which should be passed upon it. It is imperative in such kinds of piecework as by their nature cannot be reduced to regular rates that either the employer should take the responsibility of safeguarding his workmen's interests, or that the workmen themselves should, by such a method as I have suggested, obtain an effective control over them.

3. Restriction of Output [1]

In a recent market letter issued by a prominent business house the following statement occurs in connection with a survey of current economic conditions: "The most important of the favor-

[1] From "The Philosophy of the Restriction of Output," an article by L. Ardzooni, in the *Annals of the American Academy of Social and Political Science*, vol. 91, September, 1920.

able factors are the world shortage of goods, the present low prices of investment securities and the expenditure of the greatest wage fund ever received by a nation's workers." Another high authority on present-day business conditions remarks with significant nonchalance: "The war consumed more men, more food, more clothing and more raw and wrought material than all the wars since 1760, though it left the United States richer than ever before." To substantiate this opinion he adduces a statistical array of a few score thousand war millionaires and the present estimated per-capita wealth of the United States.

The object of restricting output. Under the régime of money and price economy such factors as "the world shortage of goods" or "the expenditure of the greatest wage fund" are familiar concepts as evidences of business prosperity and national welfare. The primary purpose in modern business and industrial activity is merchandising — buying and selling with a view to securing as wide a margin of net money returns above cost as possible. As a result it often happens that a superabundance of merchantable goods is inconsistent with business success which is invariably measured in terms of net price returns. Overproduction is the nightmare of business and though the children of common folks may starve for want of a sufficient supply of milk, as a matter of sound business policy it is better not to have too much milk to sell than to have enough milk to drink.

A normal business policy. Restriction of output and limitation of supply of goods are normal and legitimate phenomena in business. In fact, the life of modern business enterprise depends on such performances. The established governments sanction these practices and the courts protect the practitioners. In its stricter and more technical application, however, "restriction of output" refers not to the business man's method of monopoly control with a view to profitable merchandising; it has reference rather to the trade-union policy of interference with the processes and guidance of production with a view to standardizing the volume of employment and the rate of remuneration of the wage workers. Regarded in this light, "restriction of output" is a phenomenon in the modern industrial system which presupposes a high degree of organization of material and mechanical equipment and an equally highly organized group of workers subject to collective discipline and governed by common standards of work and working conditions.

As a phenomenon operating within the framework of modern industrial system the working-class method of "restriction of output" is a habit of thought acquired through contact with the discipline of modern business enterprise which imposes on all that come under its influence the necessity of getting without serving. In modern Christendom men do not go into business "for their health," nor do they seek out employment to fashion and produce goods. The purpose of work is to get wages as the purpose of business is to "make money." By the test of money and prices, scarcity of product and shortage of labor are blessings without disguise, since the one condition is good for business, and the other, good for the workers. Through the magic of the price system the loss of one is the gain of another and the hunger and destitution of the multitude is transformed into private profits and higher prices, so that business profits and prosperity are not necessarily synonymous with national exuberance or welfare of the masses. On the contrary, private gain and national grandeur feed on the misery and privation of the public.

Conversely, to secure a tolerable measure of comfort and contentment for the large masses often involves heavy private losses and often the sacrifice of business solvency; for example, it is becoming more and more evident in these times of reversion ("reconstruction") that the degree of success or failure of the war-time food, fuel, and railway administrations was in direct proportion to the degree of sacrifice of or subservience to the interests of private business. The efficient transportation of troops and war materials, for instance, was made possible only at the cost of handsome railway receipts which resulted from the elimination of cross freights and the embargo on luxurious private trains and cars, not to mention the enforced retirement from their cynosures of the bewildering multitude of railroad presidents and office-holders. On the other hand, the case of a young deputy fuel administrator in one of the larger Middle Western States serves as an object lesson, illustrating the extreme risk and hazard of an absolute and conscientious subordination of business profits to community welfare which came to be professed as a rule of conduct during the war. In this instance it happened that a large coal operator, who was at the time serving his country for a dollar a year, was more interested in an exclusive market for winter vegetables which required the use of several carloads of coal than in transportation of troops and war equipment. The young fuel administrator, by the scrupulous but indiscreet application of war-time rules governing the distribution of coal, prevented the diversion of several carloads of coal for such a purpose, though to the operator the coal for this purpose had a higher market value than the comfort of the East-Siders in New York or the life of a doughboy in the trenches. The young fuel administrator was presently relieved of his responsibilities presumably "for indiscretion in the conduct of his duties" and was drafted into the army.

This somewhat disjointed and more or less anecdotal recital of incidents in the conduct of modern business and industry has seemed necessary in order to emphasize the distinction between money gains and price returns — the real ends of business and industry, on the one hand, and the production of goods and personal services, the supposed ends of business and industrial activity, on the other. It would serve no good purpose here to enter upon a recital of the circumstances which have attended this subversion of the end and aim of economic activity. Let it suffice to point out that the modern conception of welfare in terms of price equivalents is so well grounded in the habits and practices of modern civilization that not only does the notion find expression in the daily conduct and manner of life of all classes of people, but that it has also been crystallized into one of the fundamental economic doctrines of modern times and is to be found in articulate form in the theoretical formulations of the common run of economists.

Limitation of supply and increased price. The fundamental problem in current orthodox economic theory is the problem of value and the point of departure as well as the final resting-place of this problem is the theory of marginal utility. According to the marginal-utility theory of value, given the human desire for a commodity, the utility of the commodity to the individual is to be measured by the utility of the marginal increment of the commodity in question. In the nature of the case, the greater the number of these increments the lower the marginal utility and the lower, therefore, the marginal utility of the commodity to the individual. In other words, the greater the scarcity of the object involved the higher the esteem or worth in which it is held by the individual. As a further corollary of the main proposition it is held that the individual's own estimation of the goods constitutes the real income of the individual; that is to say, the question of the utility of an object is a matter for individual estimate and, therefore, individual, "subjective" psychology. In other words, income in the final analysis is "psychic" in nature and character. The unavoidable conclusion of the argument then is that the less one has of goods and services, the greater the marginal utility of those goods and therefore the greater the individual's "psychic" income. So that whereas the common-sense view of welfare would have it that half a loaf is better than none, according to the logic of current economic theory fortified by business practice, half a loaf is better than one, or that the Spanish caballero who stinted himself and finally died of starvation in order to maintain a well-fed and well-groomed doorkeeper is "psychically" better off.

> "To man propose this test
> Thy body at its best
> How far can that project thy soul on its lone way?"

As has been intimated more than once in the course of this discussion, the limitation of supply to enhance the price is a normal and legitimate business practice by business men. The modern captains of industry — those whom "God in his infinite wisdom has placed to watch over the welfare of the community" — through careful training and long experience have been emancipated from the notion of viewing welfare in any other light than that of price equivalents. Recently, however, the business method of turning an honest penny has affected the methods and policy of the working classes as well.

Although the method of the restriction of output has been on the trade-union statute books as a means of standardizing wages and working conditions, not until within quite recent years has it meant more than trade-union rules regarding apprenticeship and membership. At the present time, restriction of output refers to the widespread and menacing practice of what may be characterized as the "conscientious withdrawal of efficiency" by the working classes regardless of trade-union affiliations. It is the art of substituting salesmanship for workmanship which the working classes have learned from the employers and are applying as wage-workers. It is the strategic maneuvering of the working classes to sell their time and energy for the highest price possible. It is the policy of enhancing the price of labor by limiting the supply.

Among the many preoccupations that beset the mind of the modern workingman is the belief that, through organized effort, the economic and social conditions may be altered to the advantage or disadvantage of one class or another. There exists the conviction among the working people that the problem of distribution is a problem of price manipulation and that it is all a matter of human arrangement rather than the result of immutable and preëxistent economic laws which bind mankind and out of which no one can stir. One method of converting a wage bargain to one's advantage in the view of the worker, is, therefore, the deliberate and conscious restriction of output. The worker's idea of stock watering is to dilute one's labor power by giving less service for a stipulated wage.

The trade-union theory. Another of the business principles which the trade-unionist is coming to appreciate more and more is the principle of patrimony or vested rights. The institution of private ownership is hedged about and protected by a legal system of which the foundation is presumed to be a balanced arrangement of rights and obligations. For the most part, rights are of positive character, are impersonal, and have to do with property; obligations are of negative character, are personal, and have to do with persons. The net outcome of this general system of law and ownership is that the possessing classes are vested with positive rights and with little or no obligations, while the dispossessed classes are blessed with obligations and with little or no rights; for instance, the law recognizes and enforces the right to the use and enjoyment of an item of property by the owner. It also recognizes and enforces the obligation of persons not to interfere with such right, but the law does not recognize and therefore cannot enforce the right of an individual to a livelihood. Livelihood unless attached to an item of property is not a legal right, but a personal obligation at best.

The modern trade union appears to have overcome this discrepancy, however, by the same logic and pettifoggery which has invested property rights with stability and respectability. By way of an offset to the property rights of the owning classes, the trade-unionist invokes the patrimonial rights of the worker in his particular trade and particular job. Consequently, any move whatever, such as innovations in the processes of production and introduction of machinery, which disturbs the "established expectation" of the worker with respect to wages and conditions of employment is conceived to be a violation of the vested rights of the workers. Similarly, any one who has not attained his place and position in the trade through the regular channels of apprenticeship and trade-union membership is regarded as an "impostor," a "quack," and deserves the contumely of mankind much the same way as one who has come into possession of an item of property through deceit and thievery. At any rate, it is in this light that the trade-unionist views the situation.

The trade-union theory of vested rights and the less articulate but more formidable theory of "conscientious withdrawal of efficiency" operate to "restrict output" and "retard progress." But modern trade-unionism partakes of the nature of business enterprise which implies that its members are more interested in wages — price per hour, per day, per week — than in output of goods — tons and yards per day, per week, per month.

Modern industry is controlled and managed by a small group of the propertied class who are at no time and at no point in contact in any way with the mechanical and technical processes of production, but who, nevertheless, are secured in their use and abuse of the usufruct of the industrial system; that is to say, the managers of modern industry and the guardians of the community's welfare are in the position of absentee owners without responsibility to God and without obligation to man.

So long as the working population remains in blissful ignorance of the magic potency of business principles to make something out of nothing, the community may be tolerably assured a safe margin of subsistence, despite the continuous interference and pestering of business men with processes of production. But with the taste of the fruit from the tree of knowledge the working classes are gradually assuming the rôle of absentee workers and are falling in the position of irresponsible agents in emulation of the absentee owners and their irresponsible principles. Under these conditions, notwithstanding the unlimited natural resources and the unprecedented advance in the arts of industry, the existence and welfare of modern civilized communities is likely to become precarious.

All the while the disinclination on the part of the wage-earners to produce anything but wages grows with a growing distrust of their well-wishers — the employing classes, the social uplifters, and the reformers, and so long as the price system endures there seems to be no help for it. Moreover, the practice of "conscientious withdrawal of efficiency," engendered and stimulated by modern business principles, is likely to become habitual and enduring even to the disappearance of the narrowest margin of production over cost. On the other hand, the trade-union theory of the workman's patrimony in his trade and position is not likely to prove of serious consequence, since new inventions and mechanical refinements are destined to render nugatory and obsolete the "skill, judgment, and dexterity" of any one worker in relation to another upon which rests the trade-union theory of vested rights. So that with the gradual disappearance of the distinction between skilled and unskilled trade, the conventional rules regarding apprenticeship and trade-union membership are most likely to be discarded.

Allowance is to be made, of course, for the extension of such devices as scientific engineering, bonus systems, welfare work, educational and philanthropic adventures and the like, to keep the industrial system in repair, and it may well be that some device may yet be found to preserve the price system and at the same time meet the bewildering demands of an increasing standard of living throughout the civilized world. At best, the devices hitherto tried cannot be said to have met with anything like a crowning success. Of these devices, scientific management and efficiency engineering gave perhaps the greatest promise, but these devices have so far worked to the greater advantage of the employing classes — at least, so the workers think — and to that extent they have failed to enlist the coöperative support of the workers.

4. Effect of Collective Bargaining on Volume of Production [1]

As a general proposition, the desirability and need of securing increased production cannot be questioned. Even in normal times that may be accepted as a foremost aim of industry; for increased production means potentially, at least, a larger measure of well-being for all within the industry as well as for the community. To-day, with all the wastage and losses of the war to be made good, the need is peculiarly urgent.

Worker's attitude toward greater production. In the face of this undoubted need, what do we find to be the actual situation? The productivity of labor, generally, has fallen off; that a large measure of deliberate restriction of output is practiced by workers, non-union as well as union; that the wage-earners frequently are not merely indifferent, but are actually antagonistic to the introduction of machinery or methods aimed to increase production; and that production is being hampered and often completely interrupted by numerous strikes and stoppages, and by the constant shifting of workers which reflects itself in a large turnover of labor.

Moreover, we know with reasonable certainty that most wage-earners are capable of greater productive effort without injury to themselves. We know, too, from the progress made in the past, that there are vast possibilities of increasing output through the introduction of improved machinery and methods. Our problem then lies in the discovery of means whereby this greater productive effort may be secured and the way may be made easier for the introduction of these improvements.

Is that means to be found in forcing him to work? Will talking to him, lecturing and exhortation get him to produce more? Hardly, when we now find textile mills and shoe factories shutting down because people would not buy at the prevailing high prices. Here the wage-earner has had the fact hammered into his ears for two years that prices cannot come down until he produces more goods, and just as soon as prices do begin to go down, manu-

[1] From "Collective Bargaining and its Effect on Production," an article by W. M. Leiserson, in the *Annals of the American Academy of Social and Political Science*, vol. 91, September, 1920.

facturers who have been clamoring for production shut down their plants so as not to "overproduce" as they call it. Are the manufacturers to be blamed now as the workers were before, and shall we, by injunction, compel them to keep their factories open?

Perhaps, however, the forces that make for increased or lowered production are more deep-seated than the mere will of men, be they wage-earners or employers. Herbert Hoover, upon his return from Europe, did not place the blame upon the workers in discussing the lack of production in Russia. He charged it to the system of management that the Soviets had provided for Russian industry. In the same way, may we not find that our lowered production is due to the kind of management we provide for our industries and to the lack of proper incentives to increased effort?

Why should the wage-earner respond to the plea for more production? He is told by the people who presume to teach him what they call "sound economics" that he should do so because the world needs more goods, and because prices can be reduced only by increasing the supply of goods. But does the investor furnish more capital simply because more production is needed and so that prices may be reduced? Does he invest in railroads because we need more and better transportation, and does he lend money to home-builders so that rents may come down? On the contrary, the railroads to-day cannot get the money they need for new equipment and extensions. Building is almost at a standstill because capital can secure a better return in the automobile business or in the manufacture of perfumes and other luxuries. Will the manufacturers of shoes, clothing, and other necessaries continue to produce these articles in slack seasons and in periods of falling prices? On the contrary, it is not considered good business to invest in unprofitable enterprises and to continue keeping factories running full time when buying is slack and prices are falling. Why, then, should we expect the wage-earner to respond to an appeal for more production based on social need, when manufacturers and investors cannot be appealed to in that way? May it not be that the workers, too, have had experiences which taught them that producing more under certain conditions was unprofitable and not good business?

The workers in many a seasonal industry have learned from

bitter experience that to increase their efforts during busy seasons was merely to be laid off a few weeks earlier than usual and to lengthen the period of their unemployment. Those who work piecework have often had the experience that when they turned out more pieces and their earnings were increased, the employer assumed that the rate of pay was too high and cut the piece rate, or so changed the operation as to get the same result. Then, too, people in the so-called "sweated trades" have found that when production was increased it meant that more "cheap" labor was brought into the industry, the market was undercut, and prices were reduced to a point where living wages could not be paid to the regular workers. Wage-earners also remember that even the patriotic stimulus of the war was not sufficient to induce the farmers to grow more wheat or manufacturers to produce more supplies. The farmer had to be guaranteed a higher price than usual, the manufacturer had to be assured bigger profits. It cannot be expected, therefore, that the wage-earner will increase his efforts simply because more production is needed and he is told to produce more. Very naturally he says: "I want to be sure that it is profitable for me to produce more." And when he assumes that attitude he is merely following the example that business men have set him. He is refusing to invest his labor in unprofitable work.

Participation in management essential to production. In the past it was possible for the employer to exact additional output, to speed up his workers, under threats of dismissal. However, the shortage of labor, the lack of immigration, and the growing independence of wage-earners make this impossible. The employer now finds that his authority to get production is breaking down. Industry has to-day reached the point where the employer finds himself incapable of getting work done by means of a mere mandate. He is in a situation much the same that the King of England faced one hundred and fifty years ago when the American colonists refused to pay taxes unless they were represented in the making of the tax laws. With the coming of political liberty and of free popular education, the workers now are no longer content that all the power over the terms and conditions of their employment should be in the hands of the employer. They look upon him as an industrial monarch, and as soon as the opportunity comes that shortage of labor and strong union organization gives, they say to the employer, "Unless we have a voice in determining the working conditions that control our industrial lives, we will refuse to obey the commands of industry."

While those who have hitherto controlled industry naturally do not want to give up their power, any more than the monarch wanted to yield his political power to the people, they confront the absolute necessity of sharing their control with the workers if production is to be maintained, not to say increased. Until such participation is granted by the employer, the workers may be expected to withhold production. With the employer's power to compel obedience to his orders fast going, participation by the workers in the control of industry becomes a condition not only for increased production, but also for maintaining the production of the past.

That the wage-earner's demand for a voice in the control of production is a fact and not a theory is proved by the zeal with which employers in every line of industry are establishing shop committees, work councils, and so-called "industrial democracy" plans. No employer who is frank with himself will deny that in inaugurating such a scheme he is hoping to head off the necessity of having to deal with a trade union. But with all the publicity that the so-called "industrial democracy" plans have received and with all the progress that the shop committee movement has made, it must be remembered that by far the more common form of participation of wage-earners in control of working conditions is that provided by organized labor in collective bargaining with employers. The number of plants having work committees is insignificant compared with the number of shops that deal with regular trade unions. During the last four years, when the shop committee movement has made such great headway, very many more wage-earners have joined the regular labor unions than are included in all the company plans put together. Even if all of these plans gave a real and effective voice to wage-earners in the control of industry, and most of them do not, they would still be far from meeting the demand of the workers for participation in industrial government, because organized labor is growing very much faster in numbers, in prestige and in power, than is the competing movement launched by employers.

Is collective bargaining an incentive to production? Modern industry, therefore, if it is to get production, is face to face with the problem of adjusting its management methods to provide for collective bargaining. Collective bargaining implies a questioning of the absolute authority of the management in governing the productive efforts of the employees. It says there must be no rules or orders affecting the interests and welfare of the wage-earners without the consent of those who must obey them. It is further based on the principle that an individual employee cannot effectively question the authority of the management; therefore, the aim is to join all the employees in a union which together with representatives of the employer will form a legislative body for the purpose of giving to those who have to obey the laws of industry a voice in determining those laws.

No matter how insistent the demand of wage-earners for a voice in industry may be, and no matter how powerful labor unions may become, they cannot establish collective bargaining as a permanent method of industrial control unless such democratic control of industrial processes is more efficient, economical, and productive than individual bargaining with an employer having absolute authority over his business. Trade unions, with their method of collective bargaining, cannot survive if this method does not bring greater production and greater economic welfare.

Recalling now that it is lack of profit from their labor and lack of incentive, not mere laziness, that causes workmen, like farmers and business men, to slow down production, the question arises as to whether collective bargaining and democratic control of industry offer to wage-earners greater incentives to labor than individual bargaining, and will it make greater effort and increased production more profitable to the wage-earners?

While there are many incentives to industry, all human experience has shown that there is no incentive quite so powerful for the great masses of men as private ownership of the results of one's labor. Private property in industry finds its justification primarily in the universal experience that men have more interest in working for themselves than in working for society in general, and that by letting each work for himself better results are secured for all. But what of the laborer in the steel industry, packing-houses or on the railroads where individual ownership of the business by the worker is out of the question? Working, as he does, for a wage that is fixed not by what he produces but by the competition of other laborers who want his job, what sense of ownership can he have in the results of his labor? He sees the results of his efforts distributed by a few directors in the form of dividend payments or stock dividends, surpluses of various kinds laid aside or reinvested in the business to which he has no title of any kind. What incentive can there be for such a wage-earner in the large modern industrial establishment to "take an interest in the business"? Certainly there is little of the incentive of private ownership for him.

Other devices. This has been recognized by many employers, and some of them have tried to supply this incentive by establishing profit-sharing plans in their plants. Others have sold stock to their employees on easy payments, built homes for them, provided pensions and insurance, and many have resorted to various other forms of "welfare work." Their experiences have shown, however, that while these measures may sometimes serve a valuable purpose to meet particular needs, they do not provide the wage-earner with a sufficiently direct incentive to take an interest in his work, stick to his job and give increased production.

Many have thought that where it was impossible for the great masses to enjoy individual ownership this sense of ownership might be supplied through public ownership by the municipality, State, or Nation. But, obviously, there is no more direct sense of ownership in being a citizen than in being a wage-earner or even a holder of a share or two of stock in a $100,000,000 corporation. Moreover, the experience of the past few years has shown that the public, as an employer, takes no more interest in its employees than does the capitalist. Even in publicly owned industries, therefore, some more direct sense of ownership is needed if the workers are to feel a sufficiently direct incentive to increased production.

The stimulus of collective bargaining. Wherever collective bargaining is established, however, the wage-earners have an equal vote with the employers in the fixing of wages, which is, in effect, deciding on the division of the wealth produced by the industry. Without depriving the owners or directors of the legal title to the business, collective bargaining limits their absolute property rights. When an organization of the workers has a fifty per cent "say," the owners must consult with labor before dividing the product. In substance, this "say" of labor becomes the same sort of right that the owner possesses. In addition, collective bargaining involves the surrender by the employer of his absolute right to discharge without proper cause. To some people this may appear dangerous, as if the workers were taking over the industry in bolshevik fashion. But these features of collective bargaining combine to give the worker a sense of ownership in the industry closely akin to the feeling of the man who works his own farm or conducts his own business. And if what the world needs is the powerful incentive to industry that comes only from a sense of ownership in the industry, then why should we not have collective bargaining when nothing else seems to provide that needed incentive? To employers who have to share their power over industry with those who formerly had to obey orders without question, collective bargaining may indeed appear dangerous. But if the public finds that this method of dealing with labor organizations does promote peace and production in industry without suddenly overturning all our social arrangements, it may be expected to support this movement for the democratization of industry.

But is it true that collective bargaining in practice results in increased interest and increased production? The objection will immediately be raised that to give a share of control to the unions is to give power over industry to those who traditionally oppose greater production. But is it true that unionism stands in opposition to higher productive efficiency? The fact that curtailment of production exists to-day in every industry in the country belies that charge, for the vast majority of working people are unorganized. Thus, in the textile industries, where unionization has met defeat after defeat, production is conspicuously low. The tendency of the union to restrict production is simply the articulation by organization of the individual workman's attitude. Moreover, the individual workman withholds production because he has no guarantee that increased production will be profitable to himself. On the other hand, given the assurance of a strong union that will protect him in the fruits of his additional effort, the worker gradually gets away from that tendency to restrict output which he develops as the only method of protecting himself against the arbitrary fixing of his income by the employer under individual bargaining.

An example. This was amply proved by the increased production secured during the war, where government agencies dealt with organized labor or required employers engaged in war work to do so. It is further illustrated by a case involving a group of pressers in the Rochester Clothing Industry. These pressers wanted to earn more money. They were getting $29.00 a week then and wanted $35.00. All the other workers were getting a $3.00 raise at that time. The employers told these pressers that they could not give them more than the others were getting, but that if they would undertake to increase their production ten per cent they would be given an additional ten per cent increase in salary. The pressers accepted the proposal and increased their production accordingly. There were some individuals who wished to withhold production after the raise in wages was granted; but the union saw to it that they lived up to their obligation on penalty of having their wages reduced. The union was able to do this by insisting that every individual must live up to the rule of the majority. Moreover, employers in Chicago and Rochester, who have within the last year or two entered into collective bargaining arrangements with the union of clothing workers, have stated that the production per man an hour in their shops has actually increased under this arrangement, although this was a time when most other industries have been suffering from curtailment of production.

Under such an arrangement the workers can no longer preach the idea that anything they can get from the employer is justifiable, for they now have as much to say as the employer in determining the division of the product of the industry. The union, as an organization, can no longer defend restrictive practices, for it has assumed a responsibility for the maintenance of output. The union, in fact, must exercise a discipline upon its own members in the interest of keeping up production. It is a common occurrence in industries where collective bargaining prevails for a union representative to convince a workman or group of workmen that they must maintain production. In a Cleveland plant which recently entered into a collective bargaining agreement with an international union of the American Federation of Labor, the superintendent found at first that the union shop committee in the plant was continually bringing complaints against the management in behalf of individual employees. The superintendent thereupon took advantage of the agreement with the union to file complaints with the committee against employees whose efficiency or whose production was not properly maintained. He then found that the committee was as quick to discipline its own people when the case was clear as it was to take up complaints for them. And where the discipline was democratically imposed by fellow employees, it was much more effective in getting results than orders of the employer.

Collective bargaining and machine processes. Collective bargaining has brought about a similar change in the attitude of the workers toward the introduction of machinery and improved methods of production. Here, again, the individual workman's feeling acquired under individual bargaining is falsely ascribed to organized labor, for the man who joins a union cannot rid himself, in a day, of the feelings acquired through years of experience. A certain degree of antagonism to improvements must always be expected, for it is the instinctive opposition of all human beings to changes in their habits or methods — common to employers as well as to workers. The introduction of pressing machines has been quite a problem in the clothing industry, but the unions have taken a stand with the employers in approving the use of these machines, and with the aid of the unions the introduction of the pressing machines has been made much more easy, even though some men have to operate two or three machines. Recently in Boston, however, one factory wanted to return to the use of hand irons. The workmen objected most strenuously to this, showing conclusively that it is not machinery, but change to which wage-earners object. It was the representatives of the union who succeeded in getting the pressers to use hand irons; the employer could not do it.

Opposition to machinery and improved methods has been much accentuated by many years of bitter experience under individual bargaining when employers used these to the workers' detriment. It will be recalled, in this connection, that the destruction of textile machinery in England during the thirties was done not by organized labor, but by unorganized enraged workmen.

The reason for this is plain when we bear in mind the statement of such a careful historian as Professor E. P. Cheney, of the University of Pennsylvania, who, at a recent meeting of the American Academy of Political and Social Science in Philadelphia, stated that the immediate result of the Industrial Revolution in England that ushered in the factory system was to bring more misery and poverty to the great masses of working people than they had suffered before, although it also enriched a greater number than had previously enjoyed riches.

With the protection to the workers' interests afforded by collective bargaining, the fear of the loss of job or wages, resulting from improved machinery or methods, is gradually eliminated. What may be accomplished when such a guaranty is provided is illustrated by what happened at the time of the introduction of the linotype into the printing industry. Union labor withdrew its opposition and assisted in the introduction of these machines when it received assurances that the former typesetters would be employed as operators of the linotype machines.

It has already been intimated that a collective bargaining arrangement may actively assist the employer in introducing new methods and machines. Under an arrangement whereby the workers are guaranteed an equal "say" with the employers in distributing the product of the industry, the wage-earners acquire an interest in anything that will add to the size of the amount to be distributed. In the introduction of scientific management in a shop, a union may be especially helpful. I know of a shop where scientific managers introduced practically a complete system without any serious objection, because the matter was previously taken up with officials who called meetings of the employees and explained fully the nature of the changes to be made and that the employer had a right to make such changes under the agreement with the union. On the other hand, the same employer a short time previously had a great deal of trouble in another shop when an order was issued, without previous consultation with the employees, requiring daily records of work to be kept which had never been done before.

It is, of course, a common occurrence for employees to become unreasonably aroused over some change proposed or instituted in the shop by the management. Any one familiar with collective agreements between unions and employers, however, can cite instances of such employees going to union officials for advice, and on receiving assurances from these that the change would not hurt them and their interests would be protected, returning to work under the new conditions.

Piecework. Collective bargaining also has an important bearing on the wage-earner's attitude toward piecework or other forms of payment for measured production. Most workmen do not believe in equal pay for all. They, who do the same work, want to get the same pay, but they also insist that those who do more than others should be paid more. When workmen have opposed piecework, generally, it has not been because they were opposed to it in principle, but rather because they were opposed to the practice of employers of regulating the piece rate by what they consider the workman ought to earn. When, under collective bargaining, the workers feel sure of the strength of their organization to protect their earnings, they do not object to piecework or other forms of measured production. In fact, when the workers have something to say about the distribution of the wage bill they begin to feel strongly that the distribution ought to be according to each worker's contribution. Thus, we find the tonnage basis and piecework accepted without question as the method of wage payment under the agreements of the United Mine Workers of America and of the United Shoe Workers. Where unions are opposed to piecework, it will usually be found either that they are not strong enough to contest the power of the employer, or else the quality of the product is an important factor in the industry and that quality is measured by an examiner's opinion rather than a mechanical test. In both the women's and the men's clothing industry, however, where such quality is most important, and the unions have insisted on week-work, they have also agreed that standards of production shall be established for every weekly scale of wages, which, if not exactly piecework, is payment for measured production.

Industrial interruptions. A highly important gain to production from collective bargaining, which is commonly overlooked, is the lessening of interruptions to industries caused by strikes, lockouts, stoppages and also by high rates of labor turnover. Trade-union agreements with employers usually run for a year or other stated period and during these periods strikes, stoppages, or lockouts are prohibited and arbitration of disputes provided. Between these periods the general tendency is for strikes and lockouts to decrease as soon as collective bargaining relations have been established in an industry. In the matter of labor turnover, no data has been collected to enable us to compare accurately the percentages of labor turnover in plants dealing with unions and those which do not deal with unions. It is strikingly noticeable, however, that the high labor turnover, which has been a matter of great concern to industrial managers during the last few years, is most common in the so-called "open-shop" industries, whereas the industries and occupations which are unionized have a comparatively low labor turnover.

There is a common superstitious belief that democracy is always less efficient than autocracy, and therefore industrial efficiency is bound to suffer to the extent that democracy is introduced into the industry. To the boss, the foreman, the superintendent or the employer, whose word has been law to his employees, it may appear most absurdly inefficient that he should have to discuss his orders with his employees and consult them about his policies. But when we remember that it has been his rule that brought us opposition to machinery and improved methods from the workers, restriction of output, strikes and lockouts, labor turnover of 400 or 500 per cent and more and the great decrease in production that most industries now suffer, it must be quite plain that there is nothing efficient about autocratic control of industry.

On the other hand, it is not sufficient merely to curb the employer's absolute power and establish the wage-earner's rights in industry through collective bargaining. This is the negative democracy that confuses liberty with freedom from interference. To be efficient, democracy must be positive and constructive, and deliberately organized to do the things which autocracy has failed to accomplish. Collective bargaining and trade-unionism in industry must have administrative agencies for seeing to it that the problems of labor management, such as increasing production, progressive improvement in methods and technique, wage-payment for service rendered and discipline of employees, are properly and efficiently handled.

Administration of collective bargaining agreements. Have the collective bargaining agreements between employers and trade unions developed such administrative agencies? No one who has studied the history of trade agreements in the coal-mining industry, stove-moulding, printing trades, on the railroads and in the clothing and building trades, can have any doubt that such agencies are developed where the collective-bargaining relations are maintained for a sufficient length of time to permit it. In the first place, the unions in their own local units, district council, conventions and executive boards establish that control and discipline of individual members which is essential in industry, and which because it is democratic, is more effective than the employer's efforts at control. Secondly, when the agreements are made there are always joint meetings of representatives of the employers and the workers who have a mutual veto on each other's acts and who together legislate for the industry. Thus, the point of view of both labor and capital are considered in all legislation and each gets a thorough understanding of the problems and purposes of the other.

Then, during the intermission between meetings, officials of the organizations of both parties and committees of both employers and employees are in constant contact for the purpose of adjusting disputes and settling complaints and grievances of both sides. Thus, there are trained in a school of experience expert labor administrators who are able to give to employers that technique and knowledge of handling human beings which has been conspicuously lacking in the management of industry. At the same time, it gives to the wage-earners labor officials who are not only expert union organizers, but who understand also the problems of the management and the financial side of the industry.

Finally, practically all trade agreements between unions and employers contain arbitration clauses. This is the rudimentary form of the judicial function in the constitutional government of industry. It has been the weakest point in the collective bargaining machinery because both employers and wage-earners were most interested in establishing and defining their rights. They rightfully objected to any outsider, coming in as an arbitrator, doing that for them. In recent years, however, it has become more and more plain that the agreements made and amended from time to time by representatives of the employers and the workers are the real constitutions and laws of the industries. Not an arbitrator, in the sense of umpire or referee, is needed, but a man or board that will be partly a court and partly an administrative agency to carry the laws into effect. The Workmen's Compensation Commissions offer a good analogy. It was found that compensation laws do not work out unless there is good administrative machinery to make them work, and trial boards, without all the legalistic methods of the courts, to adjudicate disputes under the laws. In such a manner trade agreements entered into by collective bargaining do not work out satisfactorily of themselves. They need administration, interpretation and application to particular cases from day to day, and for this a labor adjustment board or industrial court of some kind is necessary.

With this developed, to complete the administrative machinery of collective bargaining, we have a complete system of constitutional government in industry, modeled on the basis of experience, and capable of handling efficiently and constructively all the problems of modern production. It is bound to grow and survive as the prevailing type of labor management, because industrial monarchy with its insistence on individual bargaining has already broken down in its inability to get production from the wage-earners.

5. Union Attitude Toward Machinery [1]

Labor's attitude toward machinery. A generation ago it was assumed, as a matter of course, by almost every educated person, that it was a cardinal tenet of trade-unionism to oppose machinery and the introduction of improved processes of manufacture. "Trade unions," said a well-known critic of the workmen in 1860, "have ever naturally opposed the introduction of machinery, such introduction tending apparently to reduce the amount of manual labor needed, and thus pressing on the majority. No trade union ever encouraged invention." In support of this opinion might

[1] From *Industrial Democracy*, by Sidney and Beatrice Webb, pp. 392–400. Longmans, Green & Co., publishers.

have been quoted, for instance, the editor of the *Potters' Examiner*, an influential leader of the Potters' Trade Unions, who in 1844 could still confidently appeal to experience in ascribing all the evils of the factory operatives to this one cause. "Machinery," he wrote, "has done the work. Machinery has left them in rags and without any wages at all. Machinery has crowded them in cellars, has immured them in prisons worse than Parisian bastilles, has forced them from their country to seek in other lands the bread denied to them here. I look upon all improvements which tend to lessen the demand for human labor as the deadliest curse that could possibly fall on the heads of our working classes, and I hold it to be the duty of every working potter — the highest duty — to obstruct by all legal means the introduction of the scourge into any branch of his trade."

Nowadays we hear no such complaints. When, in 1892, Professor Marshall published a careful criticism of trade-union policy and its results, he deliberately refrained from taking into account, or even mentioning, the traditional hostility of trade unions to inventions or machinery. And when, in 1894, the Royal Commission on Labor reported the result of its three years' elaborate and costly inquiry into the claims and proceedings of the workmen's organizations, it found no reason to repair this significant omission. The Commissioners heard the complaints of employers in every trade, and certainly exhibited no desire to gloss over the faults of the workmen. But if we may trust the summary of evidence embodied in the lengthy majority report, resistance to machinery no longer forms part of the procedure of British trade-unionism. Although the Commissioners analyzed the "rules and regulations" of hundreds of separate trade unions, in none of them did it discover any trace of antagonism to invention or improvement.

The fact is that trade-unionism on this subject has changed its attitude. It is quite true that during the first half of the century the trade-unionist view was that so forcibly expressed in the *Potters' Examiner*. But in 1859 it was noticed by a contemporary scientific observer that neither the trade unions in general, nor even those in the same industry, showed any real sympathy with the Northamptonshire bootmakers' strike against the sewing-machine, "deeming it neither desirable nor practical to resist the extension of mechanical improvements, although very sensible of the inconvenience and suffering that are sometimes caused by a rapid change in the nature and extent of the employment afforded in any particular trade." In 1862 the Liverpool Coopers, who had formally boycotted machinery in 1853, resolved "that we permit any member of this society to go to work at the steam cooperage." During this decade the Monthly Circular of the Friendly Society of Ironmolders contains numerous earnest exhortations by the executive committee to the members not to resist "the iron man," the new machine for iron-molding. "It may go against the grain," they say in December, 1864, "for us to fraternize with what we consider innovations, but depend upon it, it will be our best policy to lay hold of these improvements and make them subservient to our best interests." The United Society of Brushmakers, which had in 1863 and 1867 supported its members in refusing to bore work by steam machinery, and had formally declared that they must "on no account set work bored by steam by strangers," revised its rules in 1868, and decided "that should any of our employers wish to introduce steam power for boring, no opposition shall be offered by any of our divisions, but each division shall have the discretionary power of deciding the advantage derived from its use." These conversions gain in emphasis and definiteness from decade to decade, until, at the present day, no declaration against innovations or improvements would receive support from the Trade Union Congress or any similar gathering. Among all the thousand-and-one rules of existing trade unions we have discovered only a single survival of the old irreconcilable prohibition, and that in a tiny local industry, which is rapidly fading away. The Operative Pearl Button and Stud Workers' Protection Society, established at Birmingham in 1843, and numbering about five hundred members, enjoys the distinction of being, so far as we are aware, the only British trade union which still prohibits working by machinery. Its latest "Rules and Regulations" declare "that the system of centering by the engine be annihilated *in toto*, and any member countenancing the system direct or indirect shall be subject to a fine of two pounds. Any member of the society working at the trade by means of mill-power, either direct or indirect, shall be subject to a fine of five pounds."

Causes of present opposition. But every newspaper reader knows that the introduction of machinery still causes disputes and strikes; and no doubt many excellent citizens still pass by the reports of such disputes as records of the old vain struggle of the handworker against the advance of industrial civilization. An examination of the reports would, however, show that the dispute now arises, not on the question whether machinery should be introduced, but about the conditions of its introduction. The change has even gone so far that there are now, as we shall show, instances of trouble being caused by trade unions putting pressure on old-fashioned employers to compel them to adopt the newest inventions. The typical dispute to-day is a dispute as to terms. The adoption of a new machine, or the introduction of a new process, in superseding an old method of production, usually upsets the rates of wages based on the older method, and renders necessary a fresh scale of payment. If wages are reckoned by the piece, the employers will seek to reduce the rate per piece; if by time, the workers will claim a rise for the increased intensity and strain of the newer and swifter process. In either case the readjustment will involve more or less higgling, in which the points at issue are seldom confined merely to the amount of remuneration. The degree of difficulty in any such readjustment will depend on the good sense of the parties to the negotiations; and in this as in other matters good sense has to be acquired by experience. Some industries, cotton-spinning, for example, have had a century of experience of readjustments of this kind, which have accordingly become a matter of routine. But in trades in which the use of machinery, and even the factory system itself, are still comparatively new developments, the readjustments are seldom arrived at without a struggle.

An example. As a typical instance of a trade in this stage, take the modern factory industry of boot and shoe manufacture, which is notorious for incessant disputes about the introduction of machinery. In this trade the compact little union of handicraftsmen, working for rich customers, has long since been outstripped by its offshoot, the National Union of Boot and Shoe Operatives, formed exclusively of factory workers, and numbering, at the end of 1896, 37,000 members. We have here an industry which is being incessantly revolutionized by an almost perpetual stream of new inventions and new applications of the old machines. The workmen are noted for their turbulence, want of discipline, and lack of education. The employers, themselves new capitalists without traditions, exposed to keen rivalry from foreign competitors, are eager to take the utmost advantage of every chance. The disputes are endless, and the prolonged conference proceedings, the elaborate arguments before the arbitrators, and the complicated agreements with the employers are all printed in full, affording a complete picture of the attitudes taken up by the masters and the men.

The employers' indictment of the operatives has been graphically summed up by their principal literary spokesman. "It is true," says the editor of the employers' journal, "that objection does not take the form of rattening or direct refusal to work with the machines; experience has taught the union a more efficacious way of marshaling the forces of opposition. To say openly that labor-saving appliances were objected to would be to estrange that public sympathy without which trade-unionism finds itself unable to live. So other methods are adopted. The work done by the machines is belittled; it is urged that no saving of labor is effected by their use; the men working the machines exercise all their ingenuity in making machine work as expensive as hand labor. There exists among workmen what amounts to a tacit understanding that only so much work shall be done within a certain time, and, no matter what machines are introduced, the men conspire to prevent any saving being effected by their aid. It is of no use to mince words. The unions are engaged in a gigantic conspiracy to hinder and retard the development of labor-saving appliances in this country. The action of their members in failing to exercise due diligence in working new machines is equivalent to absolute dishonesty. It is, indeed, positively painful to any one who has been accustomed to see, for example, finishing machinery running in American factories, to watch English operatives using the same machines. In America the men work, they run the machines to their utmost capacity, and vie with each other in their endeavor to get through as much work as possible. But in an English factory they seem to loaf away their time in a manner which is perfectly exasperating. If they run a machine for five minutes at full speed, they seem to think it necessary to stop it and see that no breakage has occurred. Then they walk about the shop, and borrow an oil-can or a spanner, wherewith to do some totally unnecessary thing. This occupies anywhere from five minutes to an hour, and then the machine is run on again for a few minutes; and if the operator is questioned, he says, 'machines are no good; I could do the work quicker and better by hand.' And so he could, for he takes care not to allow a machine to beat a shopmate working by hand on the same job, and, in short, does all he can to induce manufacturers to abandon mechanical devices and go back to hand labor. The spirit of comradeship is carried to a ridiculous extent, and no man dare do the best he can, lest his fellow workmen should be, as he foolishly thinks, injured. . . . It seems to be a settled policy with the men, not to try to earn as much money as possible per week, but as much as possible per job, in other words, to keep the cost of production as high as possible."

The clue to the difficulty. Assuming all this to be true in fact — and, so far, at any rate, as times of strained relations are concerned, there is no reason to question its accuracy — let us supplement it by two other facts which would hardly have been inferred from it. First, that in the American boot factories which work at such high pressure, the high pressure is invariably paid for by piecework rates. Second, that in England it is the workmen who demand that, in conjunction with the new machines, they should be allowed to work by the piece, as they have hitherto been accustomed, and that it is the employers who have resolutely insisted on taking the opportunity of changing to fixed day wages. Here lies the clue to the whole difficulty. We have already explained, in connection with the cotton-spinners, how piecework is the only possible protection of the standard rate for men who are working machines of which the rate of speed is always being increased. On such machines payment by the hour, day, or week involves the exacting from the operative an ever-increasing task of work in return for the old wages. In the case of the boot operatives the question is complicated by the fact that the new machines have introduced a new organization of the factory, the workman steadily becoming less and less of an individual producer working at his own speed, and more and more a member of a "team," or set of operatives each performing a small part of the process, and thus obliged to keep up with each other. This enforced "speeding-up" would be all very well if the old plan of paying by the piece were continued. But when the "more efficient organization of labor" is coupled with the introduction of a fixed day wage, the workmen see in it an attempt to lower the standard rate of remuneration for effort, by getting more labor in return for the old payment.

This position the employers fail even to comprehend. "I know," said the President of the Employers' Association in 1894, "that it will be said it is slavery, pace-making, and driving, and that sort of thing. . . . But the manufacturers contend that that is not so. For instance, when men are put to work in a team, they are waited on hand and foot, and they are never kept waiting for anything, whereas when they have to 'shop' their [own] work a waste of time is involved. That time is saved under the team system." It is part of the brain-worker's usual ignorance of the conditions of manual labor that the leaders of the employers could naïvely imagine that to be "never kept waiting for anything" is an advantage to the man paid a fixed daily wage. To the workman it means being kept incessantly toiling at the very top of his speed for the whole nine hours of the factory day. When this high pressure is demanded for the old earnings, it amounts to a clear attempt to lower the standard rate. How this attitude strikes an employer in the same trade, conversant with American conditions, may be judged from the following instructive letter written in reply to the editorial first quoted: "Let us take a look into an English machinery-equipped factory. What do we see there? Precisely what you state, only much worse. The workmen, or very often boys, who work on weekly wages, try how little work they can do and how badly they can do that little. They don't seem to care a scrap so long as they get the time over, and are glad when the time comes to clear out of the factory and the day's monotony is over. They are continually meddling with their machines and throwing them out of order. Then the engineer has to be called in. The result is a loss of time, a loss of work, and expense also. All this to my mind arises from a mistaken policy which English manufacturers adopt in employing so much boy labor and the weekly wages system. If the piecework system were adopted, and only expert men employed on the machines, better work would be the result, at less cost, and the workman would earn higher wages. Is not that the secret why an American manufacturer can produce his goods at a lower labor cost than similar goods can be produced in this country, while at the same time the American operative is earning much higher wages than his English brother?"

6. The Closed Shop [1]

Argument for the open shop. To many persons the closed shop seems an arbitrary institution which could well be abandoned without injury to the cause of organized labor. In their view the exclusion of non-unionists from employment is for no ostensible reason except to exercise accidental power or wantonly to deprive certain workmen of a livelihood. The friends of union labor who take this view wish to see the open shop universally established. Under the open shop it is claimed that both union and non-union men would receive fair treatment, as discrimination in employment would not exist. Employers, it is said, would not try to abolish collective bargaining, since they are not only ready but anxious to make contracts with the "proper kind" of unions. Finally, the friends of the open shop declare that a properly conducted union can attract non-unionists to itself by means of beneficial, social, and educational features. To illustrate how well labor organizations can succeed without discriminating against non-members, attention has usually been called to the four great railway brotherhoods, the Locomotive Engineers, the Railway Conductors, the Locomotive Firemen and Enginemen, and the Railroad Trainmen. These organizations are admittedly strong and vigorous beyond the majority of American trade unions, although they do not refuse to work with non-unionists.

The case of the unions: Discipline. In answer to such criticism the closed-shop unions have explained at some length their motives in requiring the exclusive employment of union members. In the first place, they claim that the closed shop is necessary to enforce discipline over union members. If the union scale and the rules are to be enforced, there must be some sufficient penalty attached to their violation. The fear of exclusion from employ-

[1] From *The Closed Shop in American Trade Unions*, by Frank T. Stockton, pp. 153–64. The Johns Hopkins Press, publishers.

ment is considered the "best possible means" of holding members "to fidelity to the union." There is no penalty which a workman fears so much as that of being deprived of his employment and possibly of his livelihood. This is the punishment administered to him in case he violates union rules or wage scales in an establishment where the closed shop is enforced. Neither social ostracism nor loss of the right to share in accumulated union funds can compare in rigor with exclusion from a trade.

Protection of standard rate. Moreover, it is argued that unless a union has complete control over the workmen in a shop it cannot prevent non-unionists from rendering its rules ineffective. Particularly is this the case if the open shop involves the use of individual agreements. Non-union men are then not restrained from working under whatever conditions they see fit. Although union men may agree among themselves to work only for certain wages, non-unionists often prove "subservient" enough to work for less. The employer naturally favors the cheaper men and will endeavor to fill his shop with them. Accordingly one by one union men will be discharged when non-unionists can be secured. The open shop, therefore, "means only an open door through which to turn the union man out and bring the non-union man in to take his place." "Weak-kneed" union men who do not wish to lose their jobs will follow the example of the non-unionists and accept reductions in their wages. In a short while the wage scale has been hopelessly undermined. "The result of a number of non-unionists cutting wages or the price of work is like the existence, in a community of healthy people, of a man afflicted by a contagious disease." The open shop thus compels organized workmen to give way to the unorganized.

Enforcement of collective bargain. The closed-shop unions also claim that the open shop makes collective bargaining to a large extent ineffective. Employers in trade agreements are "constantly seeking to extend the responsibility of trade unions." "To meet this responsibility it is incumbent upon the labor organizations to exercise jurisdiction over all the men employed in the same shop, over all those working at a given trade or calling, otherwise the unions will be powerless to enforce any contract." A bulletin of the American Federation of Labor sets forth that "the agreement . . . of organized labor with employers depends for its success not only upon the good will of the union and the employer toward each other, but that neither shall be subject to the irresponsibility or lack of intelligence of the non-unionist or his failure to act in concert with, and bear the equal responsibility of, the unionists." Only when the closed shop is enforced are all workmen in an establishment equally responsible for the observance of a collective contract with the employer, since all are then parties to it and can be severely disciplined if they violate its provisions. Only under such conditions do the unions consider that collective bargaining becomes "complete, effective, successful."

Defense against victimization. The unions also claim that the continued presence of non-union men in a shop is likely to make for a completely non-union shop. A prominent spokesman for the unions recently said: "The promotions, the easy place, the favors, all fall to the non-union workman, whose presence and whose attitude is ever helpful to the employer and a menace to his fellow workman. If some one is to be relieved for a day, if a laborer is given extra work, if a workman is specially commissioned for an important duty, and if some one is to be promoted, it is always the non-union man. This is his reward for minding his own business. . . . Union men are much like other men. They cannot long be persuaded to pay dues, to make sacrifices for their organization, when they find that others are favored or promoted over them, or receive special privileges because they are non-union men."

That many open-shop employers have discriminated against union men cannot be denied. Although they have usually avoided "victimizing" them openly, yet they have easily found pretexts on which to discharge union men, especially officers and "agitators." The laws passed in several States and by Congress against the discharge of workmen because of union membership have been for the most part held to be unconstitutional. The only effective defense that a union can make against an employer who discriminates against its members is to discriminate against non-unionists. In closed shops the danger that the employer will gradually eliminate the unionists is not present. In these shops all workmen of a certain class receive uniform pay, and work the same number of hours under identical conditions. The advocates of the closed shop contend, however, that even if all employees are paid at the same rate and no preference is shown to non-unionists, there would still be, in most trades, a disastrous falling off in union membership in such shops. Non-union men would receive all the advantages of the improvement of working conditions obtained by the union, and yet contribute nothing to the support of the organization. When union members see that they are bearing burdens from which the non-unionists escape, they will be likely to drop their membership.

A "sentimental" argument has also been advanced in favor of the closed shop as a trade-union device. Non-union men, it is said, are "industrial parasites" who do nothing to help organized labor fight its battles. "To say that the fruits of victory should come without effort, nay, as a reward for cowardice and disloyalty, is neither right in the realm of ethics or in the practical work-a-day world." Consequently the non-unionist "should not consider it a grievance if at the conclusion of a successful strike he should be invited to join the union or work only with other non-unionists. . . . All that is demanded is that the cost and burdens of union management and action be fairly shared by these men in the future." This argument fails to take account of the real motives for excluding non-unionists. Although resentment has often been aroused against non-unionists because they escape paying dues, as, for example, among the paper makers, there would be no discrimination against them if their presence did not endanger the enforcement of union wages and shop rules. Among the railroad trainmen, for instance, there have been no protests against the employment of non-members for "sentimental" reasons. This is because the open shop is not a menace in railroad work.

Increase of union membership. An argument for the closed shop of which much has been made is that it increases trade-union membership. Experience has shown that there are always a large number of workmen "in and out of the union." They are "in the union" when they obtain a job in a closed shop; they are "out of the union" when they work in a shop where a union card is not necessary. It has been said that "the mere closing of one door to the non-unionist is the best argument to him for application." Instances of marvelous growth in membership following the introduction of the card system have also been frequently reported.

A recent writer, in dealing with a typical American trade union, indicates the two ways in which the closed shop increases union membership. "In the first place, when the union has once unionized an office, it is able by requiring the exclusive employment of unionists to affiliate with itself every workman who thereafter obtains work in the office. The rule thereby tends to continue a control once obtained. The closed-shop rule can be viewed in another aspect as a device for securing the unionizing of offices, and of thereby bringing in new members. If a local union controls a large part of the labor supply, the influence of the closed-shop rule as a means of increasing the membership may be very considerable. If, for example, in a community where 500 printers are employed, 400 are members of the union, both the non-unionist workmen and their employers will be at distinct disadvantage. A non-unionist workman, if he can earn the minimum rate, will be eager to secure access to the wider opportunities for employment which the unionist possesses. The non-union employer under such circumstances cannot discharge his workmen and thus reduce expenses so readily in times when business is slack as he otherwise would, for he cannot easily replace his employees from his restricted labor market. At times, for the same reason, he must go outside his home labor market, at expense and inconvenience, to supply himself with printers. But just as the closed-shop rule is a powerful instrument for unionizing offices when the union is strong and controls a great part of the labor supply, so it is a hindrance when the union is weak. The unionist and the employer of unionists suffer in this case under the same disadvantage of a restricted labor market as non-unionists and the non-union employer do when the union is strong.

"Fellow-servant doctrine." Finally, it has been asserted in defense of the closed shop that the exclusive employment of union men is necessary in many trades because of the legal principle known as the "fellow-servant doctrine." In dangerous employments, it is said, skilled union men run constant risk from having to work with unknown non-unionists. If the latter, by careless acts, injure unionists, no redress is ordinarily to be had. If the shop is an open one, their discharge cannot be forced. As the common law requires "each to be responsible for the rest," it is maintained by unionists as in accord with the "most elementary principles of self-preservation" that they should seek through the union to have some voice in choosing their fellow employees. The fellow-servant argument, like the "sentimental" argument, is an afterthought on the part of zealous unionists and their sympathizers. No union was ever led by such an argument to introduce the closed shop. There are probably few employers who would continue to hire an habitually reckless workman. In a few cases, however, the argument has been seriously considered by the courts.

It will thus be seen that the closed shop is used by trade unions as a device to gain certain ends. It is not an end in itself. It cannot be explained on the grounds of unreasoning prejudice against non-union men. It is an utterly mistaken view to regard it as a mere "passing phase" of unionism. It is also probably safe to say with Mr. John Mitchell that "with the growth of trade-unionism in the United States the exclusion of non-unionists will become more complete."

Economic argument against the closed shop. In recent popular discussion of the closed shop, much emphasis has been put upon its uneconomical character. The charge is made that the demand for the exclusive employment of union men, by interfering with the right of an employer to "run his own business," makes high efficiency impossible. This argument is based on the fact that the employer, under the competitive system, is alone responsible for the successful conduct of business undertakings. If he fails to produce as well and as cheaply as others do, the loss is his. It is necessary, therefore, for the most economic conduct of business that the employer "should have power to order his own affairs." He "should not be influenced by any other consideration in the hiring of men than the ability, fitness, or loyalty of the applicant." At the same time he should be free to reward exceptional workmen and to discharge those who are inefficient or insubordinate. He should be the sole judge as to the kind of machinery, tools, and material to be used. Only in this way, it is argued, can the employer secure that "effective discipline" which is essential in bringing about the "highest measure of success . . . in industry."

The "essence" of the open shop is that the employer is entirely free "to hire and discharge." It gives him, therefore, the opportunity for initiative, and subjects him to the control of no influence save that of the market. The closed shop, on the other hand, is attacked because it does not leave the employer free. It denies him the "right to hire and discharge." If the employer wishes to hire competent non-union men, he is prevented from procuring their services if they cannot or will not obtain union membership. Often he is compelled, because of a "waiting list," to hire the union men who have been longest out of employment regardless of their ability or fitness. The "walking delegate" in some cases, it is said, usurps the employer's prerogative.

The employer complains that under the closed shop, instead of being able to secure workmen regardless of whether they are union or non-union, white or black, Catholic or Protestant, Jew or Gentile, he is compelled to draw from a definitely fixed labor market. Very often, too, this market is severely limited by the refusal of the unions on one ground or another to admit competent workmen to membership. He cannot hire members of other unions who are competent to do the work because this will at once involve him in a jurisdictional dispute. One trial is enough to demonstrate the fact that members of rival unions tolerate each other's presence less than they do that of non-unionists. There is then no practicable way in which he can secure additional help when his work increases except by bidding for workmen against other union employers. It is also said that the closed shop serves to prevent the discharge of inefficient employees. If such persons are dismissed from employment, they try to make it appear that they have been "victimized" on account of union membership. Often they secure a sympathetic hearing from their union, and the latter forces their reinstatement.

Another evil attributed to the closed shop is that it establishes a minimum wage which becomes virtually also a maximum wage. This is said to produce a disastrous "dead level" of efficiency throughout an establishment and to discourage effort. Accordingly union control is declared to be "absolute death to individual effort and ambition," and to cause the degeneration of "mental and moral fiber." Restriction of output is the direct result of such conditions. Especially harmful does the closed shop become, in the opinion of its opponents, when a union requires foremen to obey its rules and to serve the union rather than the employers. All closed-shop unions, it is represented, "define the workman's rights, but say nothing of his duties. . . . They destroy shop discipline and put nothing in its place."

Defense of the unions. To these indictments the advocates of the closed shop have made vigorous rejoinder. They assert that while the unions do not allow employers to "victimize" their members, they do not interfere otherwise with the "right to hire and discharge" as long as all persons who are hired become union members. It is also flatly denied that the minimum wage is usually the maximum, and that production is restricted in closed shops.

The reconciliation of these conflicting statements of facts is possible. The opponents of the closed shop in discussing its economic effects always assume that the closed shop is everywhere the same, and take as typical those unions in which the restrictions on employment are most severe. The advocates of the closed shop assume as typical those unions in which the restrictions are mildest. If reference is made to a preceding chapter, it will be noted that the unions vary widely in this respect. In some unions, employers are allowed to hire only such persons as have already become union members. In fewer cases employers are restricted to hiring persons who have been union members for a fixed period. That such rules are injurious cannot be denied. Compulsory "waiting lists," too, are found in a few unions. Where such lists are in force, the employer's right to hire and discharge is almost entirely destroyed. In the majority of closed-shop unions, however, we have seen that the employer is allowed to hire non-unionists when competent unionists are not available, or even in many unions when they are available. It is also customary to allow such non-unionists to work a certain period in a shop before being required to join the union. There is little basis for the claim, therefore, that employers are restricted to hiring union men only. It is true that "scabs" and members of rival unions are rarely allowed to work. "Scabs," however, form but a small part of the men in any trade, and agreements between rival unions have now to some extent solved the problem of jurisdictional disputes.

If the union itself is closed — that is, will admit new members only with great difficulty — union employers have no means of obtaining additional help when their business increases. The closed union, however, although it is usually found with the closed shop, is not identical with it. To say that no more members shall be admitted to a union is an entirely different thing from saying that union men shall not work with non-unionists. It cannot be denied that the effect of "closing" a union is made economically important by the requirement that only members of the union shall be employed. If the union is closed but the shop is open, the excluded workmen alone are affected. But if a closed union enforces the closed shop, workmen, employers, and the consumer suffer loss. A highly objectionable feature to be found in certain closed-shop agreements is the provision that employers shall hire only members of a certain local union. The only economic method is to allow the employer to "take on" any one he will as long as such persons join the local union having jurisdiction.

There is much truth in the charge that some closed-shop unions have prevented the discharge of inefficient workmen on the score of "victimization." The older unions have come to understand that nothing is gained by such a policy. They realize that employers cannot destroy the union by "victimizing" members if the persons they hire are required to become members. The closed-shop rule does not necessarily require any infringement on the employer's right to discharge. In instances where this right has been limited, use has been made of the power derived from the closed shop to enforce a union rule. It is quite possible for open-shop unions to seek to prevent their members from being dismissed from employment, even though they are incompetent or insubordinate.

The unions have also denied in a general way that their shop rules have been unduly restrictive. As a matter of fact, the great open-shop movement which began in 1901 was caused primarily by the rapid increase in rules regulating the number of apprentices, the kind of machinery that should be used, the methods of shop management, and the like. The connection between the closed shop and arbitrary shop rules is close, but the two are not identical. Arbitrary rules can rarely be enforced except in closed shops. If the union is strong enough to secure the one, it can, if it sees fit, enforce the other. Obviously, however, a closed-shop union need not, and many of them do not, have hurtful shop rules.

How the closed shop may benefit employers. The defenders of the closed shop, however, have not contented themselves with endeavoring to answer their opponents. They have tried to show that the closed shop is an advantage to an employer. In the first place, they claim that the closed shop protects fair-minded employers from "cut-throat competition." If an industry is thoroughly unionized, every manufacturer or contractor can tell precisely what his competitors are paying in wages. As wages form the largest item in the average employer's expense account, it therefore becomes possible for him to "figure intelligently on his work," something which he "could never feel certain of were the open shop to prevail." The same shop rules also apply in all union establishments. Under the open shop not nearly the same uniformity in competitive conditions can be secured. The closed shop is a device absolutely essential to the rigid and wide enforcement of union rules. Without it, the "check which the union rules have placed on the unscrupulous employer will be swept aside," and the "fair competitive basis" established under the closed shop will be destroyed.

This argument can be valid only when applied to a sharply competitive industry which is thoroughly unionized. It would be absurd to claim that the closed shop tends to protect employers in the steel industry from "cut-throat competition." Likewise it would be extravagant to represent that one employer was put on a "fair competitive basis" with others if his shop alone were unionized. The argument is therefore chiefly applicable to trades, like the building trades, which are highly competitive and fairly well organized. Even in the building trades only the larger contractors have ever been placed on a "fair competitive basis" with each other. The small contractor who runs a "one-man shop" is still free to cut prices.

Secondly, those who uphold the closed shop affirm that it tends to create a greater *esprit de corps* among the men than the open shop does. Union and non-union men represent two diametrically opposed ideas. The first stand for collective, the second for individual action. Consequently, there is constant conflict between the two in the endeavor to obtain control over a shop. Because his men do not coöperate, the employer is likely to lose money. Therefore as a business necessity open shops must become either union or non-union. That there should be ill-feeling between union and non-union men is easily understood when we consider why unions desire the closed shop. Non-union men are the economic enemies of unionists as long as employers resort to individual bargaining or express a dislike for full union control. In most open shops, therefore, there is an element of unrest and dissatisfaction. Even in the organizations which do not enforce the exclusive employment of members there is usually not the same coöperation between union and non-union men that there is between the unionists themselves. In particular, efforts are put forth to make the employment of "scabs" unprofitable. For this reason, after a strike of the trainmen or firemen has been settled, railroads have almost always discharged their strike breakers quietly, but as quickly as possible.

Finally, unionists say that the closed shop is advantageous to employers because in many unions it carries with it the privilege of using a label that has a distinct market value. In the building trades it is represented that a contractor profits by employing unionists exclusively, since business agents always endeavor to secure jobs for "fair" employers. No union solicits work for an open shop. A label, however, is an advantage to an employer only under certain conditions. It can be used to best advantage on articles largely purchased by the laboring classes. That a label increases sales on such goods is evidenced by the fact that manufacturers, solely for the purpose of obtaining the use of the label, have often asked that their establishments be unionized. The labor journals not infrequently contain statements from employers that the closed shop is a "good business proposition." But the label rarely effects an increase in the demand for expensive goods or for articles sold to women. It is evident, therefore, that the number of employers who can find an advantage in the use of the labels is small relative to the total number of employers. Business agents are often able to secure jobs for "fair" building contractors, but if the building industry were thoroughly unionized, one employer would be able to secure no advantage over others in this way, since all would be equally "fair."

Effect of the closed shop on non-union labor. The opponents of the closed shop also declare that the closed shop is an injustice to unorganized labor. They assert that the demand for the closed shop "is in fact the demand for the installation of a labor monopoly." For a union to exclude non-members from employment is denounced as an act of "criminal selfishness" because it deprives the latter of a property right in which they have as great an interest as unionists. Ten or fifteen per cent of the working class, it is said, are trying to prevent the remaining eighty-five or ninety per cent from obtaining employment, although the latter consists more largely of persons, like women and immigrants, who have special need of protection and assistance. Trade unions are therefore as "tyrannical" as capitalistic trusts, for they violate the principle of equal opportunity by aiming to "gain an advantage for the insiders over the outsiders." The closed shop itself, therefore, is said to be "far from . . . a democratic invention," as it is "a means of promoting the interests of a certain group or class against the interests of the mass."

In reply the unions have answered that it is not their purpose to establish a labor monopoly through the closed shop; that on the contrary it is the purpose of every union "to get every man following or engaged at a business to affiliate himself." To this end vigorous campaigns for members are conducted among non-unionists, and "hundreds of missionaries are at work, in and out of season, urging and pleading with them to enter the wide-open doors of the union." Furthermore, it is said that even if it is true that ninety per cent of the wage-earners in America are non-union, the great majority of non-unionists are "in occupations in which there are no unions at all, or in which the unions are too weak to think of challenging a contest over the employment of workers outside their organizations."

Confusion of closed shop with closed union. Here again it seems to the writer that many of the critics of the closed shop have identified it with the closed union. If non-union men have no difficulty in obtaining union membership, it is hard to see how the closed shop can be condemned as a "criminally selfish" device. Only when a union declares that it will not work with non-members and then refuses to admit the latter to membership can monopolistic motives properly be charged. Closed unions, however, are rarely found at present except in decaying trades. The closed shop is ordinarily intended not to restrict membership, but to increase it, as has already been shown. Even a union which is "closed" and refuses to work with non-members lacks many of the attributes of a capitalistic trust, as it does not aim to undersell non-members or to "exterminate men to raise wages as trusts have destroyed an excessive stock of goods."

When all shops are unionized, however, not only will employers be completely at the mercy of organized labor, but non-unionists will also be compelled to obtain union membership whether they wish to do so or not. Thus "liberty," "freedom of contract," and the "inalienable right" of a workman to secure employment "where and when he pleases" will be denied. The closed shop, therefore, is said to be "un-American," "un-democratic," and contrary to the principles embodied in the Declaration of Independence and in the Constitution of the United States. It injures individuals by impairing their privileges as citizens, and therefore it is pronounced to be against public policy. In reply the unions which enforce the closed shop maintain that they do not deprive non-unionists of their "right to work" in any real sense, since no man is privileged to take up any employment that appeals to him regardless of the desire of employers. The only "right" which an individual mechanic has, if he does not see fit to accept such terms as are offered him, is the right to look for another job. The unions argue, moreover, that even if they do exercise some compulsion upon non-unionists in order to bring them into membership, it is with a view to conferring benefit upon them. The workman who refuses to join a union, therefore, is said to be injuring himself, since he gains his livelihood "at the expense of the permanent interest of all workingmen."

Attitude of non-union labor. Only on rare occasions have non-union men protested in a body against the establishment of the closed shop. In most of these instances, such as the appeal of non-union miners to the Anthracite Coal Strike Commission, there is strong suspicion that the non-unionists took action at the instance of their employers and not upon their own initiative. There is no doubt, however, that many non-unionists in various trades have felt that to be required to become union members has been an imposition. Those who have been most firmly opposed to joining the union have probably been the exceptional mechanic and the workman of less than usual efficiency. The former feels able to shift for himself, and fears that the rules of the union may keep him from selling his skill as dearly as he might in a free market. The latter is hostile to the closed shop because he is excluded from employment in case he has not sufficient competency at his trade to obtain admission to membership, or, if admitted, to receive the minimum rate.

In the long run the question will probably resolve itself into a consideration of the value of labor organization. Individuals may properly be made to suffer some loss by being compelled to act with others, or by being excluded from acting with others of their class, if it appears that the class as a whole is advanced by such action. What the non-unionist loses in "individual liberty," therefore, may be made up to him if his membership is necessary to enable the union to protect the conditions of work in its trade.

The closed shop and trade-unionism. The final argument directed against the closed shop is that it will ultimately prove the destruction of trade unions themselves. It is claimed that, if workmen are induced to join a union through coercion, "the same process which deprives them of their freedom deprives the labor organization of that spirit of brotherhood which is at once the justification of its existence and the inspiration of its power." Collective bargaining, it is urged, is highly desirable, but it will be "more speedily and permanently secured by the maintenance of free labor unions than by swelling the ranks of labor unions through processes of compulsion." A combination of workmen to be "permanently efficient" must be composed "of members who believe in unionism and are loyal to it; it must be an army of volunteers and not of drafted men."

In answer to the charges that their members are largely obtained through compulsion, some union leaders have retorted that "the scruples that the non-unionist is supposed to have against joining the union evidently exist only in the mind of the employer." In the opinion of these writers, only "scabs," professional strike breakers, and semi-criminals dislike to join a labor organization. Other unionists admit that "it is a fact much to be regretted that a large per cent of all trade unions in this country consists of so-called forced membership." They recognize that by means of the closed shop, social ostracism, and even physical force, union membership has been substantially increased.

We have already noted that one of the trade-union motives for enforcing the closed shop is that new members may be recruited. It would undoubtedly be disastrous if members were gained in no other way. But it is probably safe to say that most non-union men are not hostile to organization, but are merely indifferent toward it. Consequently it is wrong to assume that every man who is compelled by the closed shop to become a union member remains anti-union at heart. Forced members have become in many instances ardent trade-unionists. In fact, some of the men who are now national union officers originally joined their respective unions because they were compelled to do so or leave their jobs. On the other hand, many workmen resent having been forced to join an organization. Their resentment may even be carried so far as to induce them to act as informers for employers. Certainly no union can afford to neglect the development of social, beneficiary, and other features that will induce men to join of their own accord. Voluntary membership is by all means the best, and a trade union cannot exist long if built on compulsory membership.

If it be true, as has been said, that "the excesses of unionism which have done and are still doing the greatest injury to the prospects of the movement are all traceable to the uses of the arbitrary and coercive power of the closed shop," it is equally true that the closed shop is responsible for the greatest advances made by unionism. On the one hand, the closed shop, if universally enforced, would afford unions the opportunity to commit gross excesses by virtue of the power lodged with them. On the other hand, the closed shop opens the way to the highest and most efficient form of collective bargaining.

Since regulation of employment is a matter of public concern, and since there is danger that trade unions may become arbitrary in exercising control over a trade, it has been suggested that the State should control their "constitution, policy, and management." In this way requirements for admission to union membership and working rules could be regulated. State regulation, however, is likely to be introduced only after the closed shop has been widely enforced. At present, in the majority of trades, it is but partially enforced, and only with great difficulty.

CHAPTER XI

SOCIAL AND POLITICAL PROGRAM OF ORGANIZED LABOR

1. Introduction

Early trade unions had no definite social or political aims. They were concerned with the immediate practical problems of the workers; and their programs were "dollars and cents" or "bread and butter" affairs, looking no further than the momentary improvement of the standard of comfort among their members. A desire for broad social reform, such as the abolition of the wage system or a change in the control of industry, came later in the history of the movement.

The appearance of these newer aims in the program of trade-unionism might be the result of either of two causes. Unions formed late in the progress of the Industrial Revolution, or in industries in which the Revolution had reached an extreme point of development, originate among workers who are class-conscious. As the industrial system matures, it tends to increase the number of propertyless; to destroy, for the great mass of wage-earners, the hope of becoming independent of the wage system; and to resolve the working population into a more or less uniform and homogeneous group of semi-skilled. Advancement for such a group means advancement *en masse*, not by sections or crafts; and their plans for social progress as a class bring them at once to a consciousness of the powers, privileges, and legal rights possessed, in the modern industrial systems, by the class of employers and the capitalists whom they represent. They soon learn that their hope of social progress is limited by the *system* under which they live, and, unwilling to accept these limitations, their thought turns toward a reorganization of the system itself. Thus the younger unions — those formed in our own time among workers previously unorganized — are likely to start their life with broad social and political aims and with avowed radical or revolutionary purposes.

On the other hand, the older craft unions may, as they grow mature, adopt social aims which were absent in their earlier programs. Pressing day by day for economic gains in hours, wages, and other conditions of employment by collective action, they reach the point where further progress is stopped by fundamental economic forces at work in a competitive order. To advance further requires a change in the organization of industry. The Railroad Brotherhoods, for example, have been among our most conservative craft unions, relying upon collective bargaining alone, keeping their contracts faithfully, disclaiming all revolutionary purposes. Yet in the past five years they have committed themselves to a program for a thorough change in the ownership and operation of the railroads — a change which would institute a system closely approaching the social ideal of the Gild Socialists. This broadening of viewpoint on the part of the craft union may be stimulated by accidental social or political events. Unions, for example, which had studiously eschewed politics, might suddenly find the forces of the State arrayed against them in their struggle with the employer, or their efforts outlawed by the reverence of the courts for the traditional rights of the property owner. The employment of the militia or the State constabulary to crush a strike, or the use of the injunction to prevent union organization, or the nullifying of a statute favorable to labor interests by the Supreme Court would be typical events impressing the craft union with the futility of relying solely on economic action.

Since 1886, the labor movement in the United States has been, on the whole, averse to political action and devoid of conscious social aims of broad import. It has been dominated by the craft-union spirit, conservative, narrow in its outlook, relying upon economic action. There are signs, however, that this situation is changing. This will be made clear by the readings which follow.

2. The New Unionism [1]

Functional types. Robert F. Hoxie, in his *Trade-Unionism in the United States*, contends that unions are not of one or two kinds simply, but assume many forms, according to the function for which they exist. Among these forms he has identified four basic types, to which in some degrees all unions in the United States have approximated. "Business unionism," in this classification, is the kind formed to serve the material interests of its members within the existing industrial structure; its main object is to practice collective bargaining. "Uplift unionism" is characterized by broad humanitarian purposes; its main methods are friendly benefits and mutual insurance; it was prominent during the early stages of union history and was roughly typified during the latter half of the nineteenth century by the Knights of Labor.

[1] From *The New Unionism*, by G. M. Budish and G. Soule, pp. 8-13. Harcourt, Brace, and Company, Inc., publishers.

"Revolutionary unionism" aims to prepare for a new social and industrial order; it is divided into two subsidiary types — socialistic, which lays more emphasis on political action, and quasi-anarchistic, which eschews political action, and looks forward to abolishing entirely the State as we know it. The I.W.W. may be taken as an example of the latter. "Predatory unionism" has no large aspirations, but preys on the employer through secret and illegal methods such as blackmail and bribery, sometimes for the benefit of the members, sometimes for the benefit of the dishonest union official. This type flourished twenty years ago in the United States, but has now almost disappeared.

To the present writers it seems that this classification is not wholly illuminating, because it is not based on a sufficiently dynamic conception of the labor movement. The types are not, after all, quite coördinate. In the light of the intensification of the industrial conflict which takes place with the growth of the capitalist order, neither uplift unionism nor predatory unionism seem fundamental enough types to set beside business unionism and revolutionary unionism. At bottom the labor movement is one, because it represents a protest, unconscious or conscious, against the status of the wage-worker. Whatever the avowed purpose and policies of the union under consideration, its activities are bound to affect the structure of society to a greater or less degree. Its particular creed and method are dependent on a variety of circumstances. Unions holding to creeds and methods which become unsuited to the advancement of labor tend to disappear as the environment alters. As we have seen, the most revolutionary unions employ collective bargaining; the characteristics of uplift unionism are displayed sometimes by business unions and sometimes by socialist unions; predatory unionism is practiced, if at all, by business unions corrupted by boss politics, or by little cliques in revolutionary unions driven underground through suppression.

The modern contrast of types. The most significant distinction, in our opinion, is that between unions which are unconcious that their efforts tend toward a new social order and so adapt their strategy solely to the immediate situation, and unions which are conscious of their desire for a new order, and so base their strategy on more fundamental considerations. These two types in turn have many variants, but the nature of every variation bears the impress of the primary type. It is the former type, roughly corresponding with Professor Hoxie's "business unionism," which we have chosen to call "the old unionism," and the latter which we have called "the new unionism." G. D. H. Cole has given this distinction a phrasing which brings out its meaning in an objective way. In *The World of Labor* he writes, 'Regarded merely as instruments of collective wage-bargaining, the unions are the most powerful weapon in the hands of labor; if they are in addition the germs of the future organization of industry as a whole, their importance becomes at once immeasurably greater."

In spite of the decline of the I.W.W., the new unionism in other forms is by no means waning in the United States. Various kinds of old unions in the course of their natural development are being forced to approach it by one route or another. The conservative Railway Brotherhoods have little by little been obliged to coöperate with unions of the unskilled; the railway "system federation" is a unit through which craft action has been superseded by industrial action; and the enunciation of the Plumb plan is a long step toward the acknowledgment of the need for a new economic order which can be attained, not through collective bargaining, but only through combined political and economic action. The United Mine Workers have long been a union industrial in form and practicing industrial rather than craft strikes; socialist influence has been strong within the union, though not dominant in its government. The time is rapidly approaching, as even its conservative officials admit, when no further gains of importance can be made for the members without pressing actively for the nationalization of the mines, a measure already endorsed several times by the convention. Similar tendencies can be observed everywhere in the conservative American Federation of Labor. Thus does the old unionism merge into the new, by force of sheer economic and social pressure.

No strong and important groups of unions in the United States, however, have whole-heartedly accepted the new unionism and consciously modeled structure and strategy accordingly, except the unions in the clothing industry. For this reason they may be considered the nearest approach to the pure type now existing in America. They sprang into power about the time of the port strike of 1911 in London, and the course of their development has been much closer to that of the new unions in England than to that of the I.W.W. They arose from mass movements of the unskilled and semi-skilled, carrying the skilled along with them. They have built up a strong and highly centralized industrial structure, but one sensitive at the same time to the will of the rank and file. They skillfully use collective bargaining, not primarily as a means of gaining material concessions, but as a means of solidifying the workers and retaining victories that will make possible further progress along the main highway. While prepared for the most extended economic action, they at the same time take an active part in independent political action. They do not preach sabotage or ca' canny, but on the contrary assist in every sound project that may improve the industrial machine and increase productivity. Upon the cultural aspects of the labor movement — the press, education, and art — they lay great stress. In short, their whole tendency is in the direction of training the workers for assuming control of production, and of accepting the social and economic responsibility which such control involves.

However different in theory and method, all forms of "new unionism" have had one trait in common. They have always come into being during a period in which the labor movement as a whole seemed to have exhausted its resources and was felt to be in danger of decline if not of destruction. They have all represented a divergence from the established practice, and, more significant than that, all have brought to the movement a new breadth of sympathy and vision, a new ideal, and a new hope. An exposition of a new unionism as exemplified by the clothing workers of America may give further light to those who have been stirred by the expressed aspirations of British labor, the present unrest in the American labor movement, and especially by the ideal of national gilds.

3. Social Aims of the New Unionism

The following excerpts from the Manifesto of the I.W.W., and the Constitutions of that union and the Amalgamated Clothing Workers, state the ultimate social aims of radical industrial unionism. To understand correctly the purposes of these organizations and their tactics, these statements of their social aims should be read with the thought in mind that they formulate a theoretical program in the broadest possible terms. This program does not mean, necessarily, that the unions adopting it favor immediate and violent revolution. The Amalgamated, for example, decries violence, practices collective bargaining, lives up to its contracts, and relies upon opportunistic measures for the immediate economic improvement of its members much as do the craft unions. The I.W.W. is much given to violent language, but its members are at heart pacifists and practice non-coöperation and non-resistance more frequently than they do violence. Both unions, however, look forward to an ultimate reorganization of society, and in their plans for this distant future are governed by the theories summarized in the preambles to their Constitutions.

Social philosophy of the I.W.W. The working class and the employing class have nothing in common. There can be no peace so long as hunger and want are found among millions of working people and the few, who make up the employing class, have all the good things of life.

Between these two classes a struggle must go on until the workers of the world organize as a class, take possession of the earth, and the machinery of production, and abolish the wage system.

We find that the centering of the management of industries into fewer and fewer hands makes the trade unions unable to cope with the ever-growing power of the employing class. The trade unions foster a state of affairs which allows one set of workers to be pitted against another set of workers in the same industry, thereby helping to defeat one another in wage wars. Moreover, the trade unions aid the employing class to mislead the workers into belief that the working class have interests in common with their employers.

These conditions can be changed and the interest of the working class upheld only by an organization formed in such a way that all its members in any one industry, or in all industries, if necessary, cease work whenever a strike or lockout is on in any department thereof, thus making an injury to one an injury to all.

Instead of the conservative motto, "A fair day's wages for a fair day's work," we must inscribe on our banner the revolutionary watchword, "Abolition of the wage system."

It is the historic mission of the working class to do away with capitalism. The army of production must be organized, not only for the everyday struggle with the capitalists, but also to carry on production when capitalism shall have been overthrown. By organizing industrially we are forming the structure of the new society within the shell of the old.

Social forces promote industrial unionism. Social relations and groupings only reflect mechanical and industrial conditions. The great facts of present industry are the displacement of human skill by machines and the increase of capitalist power through concentration in the possession of the tools with which wealth is produced and distributed.

Because of these facts trade divisions among laborers and competition among capitalists are alike disappearing. Class divisions grow ever more fixed and class antagonisms more sharp. Trade lines have been swallowed up in a common servitude of all workers to the machines which they tend. New machines, ever replacing less productive ones, wipe out whole trades and plunge new bodies of workers into the ever-growing army of tradeless, hopeless unemployed. As human beings and human skill are displaced by mechanical progress, the capitalists need use the workers only during the brief period when muscles and nerve respond most intensely. The moment the laborer no longer yields the maximum of profits, he is thrown upon the scrap pile, to starve alongside the discarded machine. A dead-line has been drawn, and an age limit established, to cross which, in this world of monopolized opportunities, means condemnation to industrial death.

The worker, wholly separated from the land and the tools, with his skill of craftsmanship rendered useless, is sunk in the uniform mass of wage slaves. He sees his power of resistance broken by class divisions, perpetuated from outgrown industrial stages. His wages constantly grow less as his hours grow longer and monopolized prices grow higher. Shifted hither and thither by the demands of profit-takers, the laborer's home no longer exists. In this helpless condition he is forced to accept whatever humiliating conditions his master may impose. He is submitted to a physical and intellectual examination more searching than was the chattel slave when sold from the auction block. Laborers are no longer classified by difference in trade skill, but the employer assigns them according to the machines to which they are attached. These divisions, far from representing differences in skill or interests among the laborers, are imposed by the employer that workers may be pitted against one another and spurred to greater exertion in the shop, and that all resistance to capitalist tyranny may be weakened by artificial distinctions.

Crafts-unionism weakens labor. While encouraging these outgrown divisions among the workers the capitalists carefully adjust themselves to the new conditions. They wipe out all differences among themselves and present a united front in their war upon labor. Through employers' associations, they seek to crush, with brutal force, by the injunctions of the judiciary and the use of the military power, all efforts at resistance. Or when the other policy seems more profitable, they conceal their daggers beneath the Civic Federation and hoodwink and betray those whom they would rule and exploit. Both methods depend for success upon the blindness and internal dissensions of the working class. The employers' line of battle and methods of warfare correspond to the solidarity of the mechanical and industrial concentration, while laborers still form their fighting organizations on lines of long-gone trade divisions. The battles of the past emphasize this lesson. The textile workers of Lowell, Philadelphia, and Fall River; the butchers of Chicago, weakened by the disintegrating effects of trade divisions; the machinists on the Santa Fé, unsupported by their fellow workers subject to the same masters; the long-struggling miners of Colorado, hampered by lack of unity and solidarity upon the industrial battlefield, all bear witness to the helplessness and impotency of labor as at present organized.

This worn-out and corrupt system offers no promise of improvement and adaption. There is no silver lining to the clouds of darkness and despair settling down upon the world of labor.

This system offers only a perpetual struggle for slight relief from wage slavery. It is blind to the possibilities of establishing an industrial democracy, wherein there shall be no wage slavery, but where the workers will own the tools which they operate and the products of which they alone should enjoy.

It shatters the ranks of the workers into fragments, rendering them helpless and impotent on the industrial battlefield.

Separation of craft from craft renders industrial and financial solidarity impossible.

Union men scab upon union men; hatred of worker for worker is engendered, and the workers are delivered helpless and disintegrated into the hands of capitalists.

Craft jealousy leads to the attempt to create trade monopolies.

Prohibitive initiation fees are established that force men to become scabs against their will. Men whom manliness or circumstances have driven from one trade are thereby fined when they seek to transfer membership to the union of a new craft.

Craft divisions foster political ignorance among the workers, thus dividing their class at the ballot box, as well as in the shop, mine, and factory.

Craft unions may be and have been used to assist employers in the establishment of monopolies and the raising of prices. One set of workers are thus used to make harder the conditions of life of another body of laborers.

Craft divisions hinder the growth of class-consciousness of the workers, foster the idea of harmony of interests between employing exploiter and employed slave. They permit the association of the misleaders of the workers with the capitalists in the Civic Federation, where plans are made for the perpetuation of capitalism, and the permanent enslavement of the workers through the wage system.

Previous efforts for the betterment of the working class have proved abortive because limited in scope and disconnected in action.

Universal economic evils afflicting the working class can be eradicated only by a universal working-class movement. Such a movement of the working class is impossible while separate craft and wage agreements are made favoring the employer against other crafts in the same industry, and while energies are wasted in fruitless jurisdiction struggles which serve only to further the personal aggrandizement of union officials.

A movement to fulfill these conditions must consist of one great industrial union embracing all industries — providing for craft autonomy locally, industrial autonomy internationally, and working-class unity generally.

Social philosophy of the Amalgamated Clothing Workers. The economic organization of labor has been called into existence by the capitalist system of production, under which the division between the ruling class and the ruled class is based upon the ownership of the means of production. The class owning those means is the one that is ruling; the class that possesses nothing but its labor power, which is always on the market as a commodity, is the one that is being ruled.

A constant and unceasing struggle is being waged between these two classes.

In this struggle the economic organization of labor, the union, is a natural weapon of offense and defense in the hands of the working class.

But in order to be efficient, and effectively serve its purpose, the union must in its structure correspond to the prevailing system of the organization of industry.

Modern industrial methods are very rapidly wiping out the old craft demarcations, and the resultant conditions dictate the organization of labor along industrial lines.

The history of the class struggle in this country for the past two decades amply testifies to the ineffectiveness of the form, methods, and spirit of craft-unionism. It also shows how dearly the working class has paid for its failure to keep apace with industrial development.

The working class must accept the principles of industrial unionism or it is doomed to impotence.

The same forces that have been making for industrial unionism are likewise making for a closer inter-industrial alliance of the working class.

The industrial and inter-industrial organization, built upon the solid rock of clear knowledge and class-consciousness, will put the organized working class in actual control of the system of production, and the working class will then be ready to take possession of it.

4. Political Policy of A. F. of L.[1]

In the political efforts, arising from the workers' necessity to secure legislation covering these conditions, and provisions of life

[1] From A. F. of L. pamphlet, *A Reconstruction Program*, pp. 6–7. Published by the American Federation of Labor.

not subject to collective bargaining with employers, organized labor has followed two methods: one by organizing political parties, with the determination to place in public office representatives from their ranks; the other to elect those who favor and champion the legislation desired and to defeat those whose policy is opposed to labor's legislative demands, regardless of partisan politics.

The disastrous experience of organized labor in America with political parties of its own, amply justified the American Federation of Labor's non-partisan political policy. The results secured by labor parties in other countries never have been such as to warrant any deviation from this position. The rules and regulations of trade-unionism should not be extended so that the action of a majority could force a minority to vote for or give financial support to any political candidate or party to whom they are opposed. Trade-union activities cannot receive the undivided attention of members and officers if the exigencies, burdens, and responsibilities of a political party are bound up with their economic and industrial organizations.

The experiences and results attained through the non-partisan political policy of the American Federation of Labor cover a generation. They indicate that through its application the workers of America have secured a much larger measure of fundamental legislation, establishing their rights, safeguarding their interests, protecting their welfare, and opening the doors of opportunity than have been secured by the workers of any other country.

The vital legislation now required can be more readily secured through education of the public mind and the appeal to its conscience, supplemented by energetic independent political activity on the part of trade-unionists, than by any other method. This is and will continue to be the political policy of the American Federation of Labor if the lessons which labor has learned in the bitter but practical school of experience are to be respected and applied.

It is, therefore, most essential that the officers of the American Federation of Labor, the officers of the affiliated organizations, state federations, and central labor bodies and the entire membership of the trade-union movement should give the most vigorous application possible to the political policy of the A. F. of L. so that labor's friends and opponents may be more widely known, and the legislation most required readily secured. This phase of our movement is still in its infancy. It should be continued and developed to its logical conclusion.

5. Program of the British Labor Party [1]

Future of labor parties. Democracy is awake and aware of its own power. It sees things in a better perspective, and realizes that at home and abroad the triumph of democratic principles in politics and industry and social life is a matter simply of wise and capable leadership and resolute and united effort on the part of all sections of the organized movement. There never was a bigger opportunity for democracy to achieve its main aims than the one which now offers. It is time that we should begin to think not only of the great social and economic changes that are to take effect in the coming period of reconstruction, but of the methods and means of securing them. The war has proved to democracy that a dictatorship, whether with one head or five, is incompatible with its spirit and its ideals even in war-time. It has also revealed many serious defects in the structure of society. And it has shown the need for drastic change in the composition and organization of political parties. It is generally acknowledged that the old party system has irretrievably broken down. Evidence of this is afforded by the clamant call for new parties. The appearance upon the horizon of a National Party and a Women's Party, the probability of separate groups forming in Parliament around the personality of political leaders who have lost or are losing their grip upon the more or less coherent and strongly organized parties of pre-war days, are symptoms of this disintegration. Political power is about to be redistributed, not only amongst the electors under the Franchise Bill, but amongst the political parties in Parliament which will claim to represent the new democratic consciousness. Minor readjustments designed to adapt orthodox Liberalism or Unionism to the changing psychology of the electorate will not avail. A thoroughgoing transformation of the machinery of the parliamentary parties and a

[1] From *Aims of Labor*, by A. Henderson, pp. 22–30. B. W. Huebsch, Inc., publishers.

fundamental revision of their programs are in my judgment not merely timely, but necessary.

Organization of the British Labor Party. The Labor Party, at any rate, has proceeded upon the assumption that reconstruction is inevitable. It has formulated a scheme which is deliberately designed to give the enfranchised millions full opportunity to express their political preferences in the choice of members to represent them in the Reconstruction Parliament which will have to deal with the vast problems arising out of the war. The outline of the new party constitution is now familiar to every attentive reader of the newspapers. It contemplates the creation of a national democratic party, founded upon the organized working-class movement, and open to every worker who labors by hand or brain. Under this scheme the Labor Party will be transformed, quickly and quietly, from a federation of societies, national and local, into a nation-wide political organization with branches in every parliamentary constituency, in which members will be enrolled both as workers and as citizens, whether they be men or women, and whether they belong to any trade union or socialist society or are unattached democrats with no acknowledged allegiance to any industrial or political movement. We are casting the net wide because we realize that real political democracy cannot be organized on the basis of class interest. Retaining the support of the affiliated societies, both national and local, from which it derives its weight and its fighting funds, the Labor Party leaves them with their voting power and right of representation in its councils unimpaired; but in order that the party may more faithfully reflect constituency opinion it is also proposed to create in every constituency something more than the existing trades council or local labor party. It is proposed to multiply the local organizations and to open them to individual men and women, both handworkers and brainworkers, who accept the party constitution and agree with its aims. The individually enrolled members will have, like the national societies, their own representatives in the party's councils and we confidently believe that year by year their influence will deepen and extend. The weakness of the old constitution was that it placed the center of gravity in the national society and not in the constituency organization; it did not enable the individual voter to get into touch with the party (except in one or two isolated cases, like that of Woolwich or Barnard Castle) except through the trade union, the socialist society, or the coöperative society. The new constitution emphasizes the importance of the individual voter. It says to the man or woman who has lost or never had sympathy with the orthodox parties, "You have the opportunity now not merely of voting for Labor representatives in Parliament, but of joining the party and helping to mould its policy and shape its future."

Appeal to brainworkers. Under the old conditions the appeal of the party was limited. It has seemed to be, though it never actually was, a class party like any other. It was regarded as the party of the manual wage-earners. Its program was assumed, by those who have not taken the trouble to examine its whole propaganda, to reflect the views of trade-unionists not as citizens with a common interest in good government, but as workers seeking remedies for a series of material grievances touching hours of labor, rates of wages, conditions of employment. This misapprehension rests upon a too narrow definition of the term "labor." On the lips of the earlier propagandists the word was used to differentiate between those whose toil enriched the community, and those who made no productive effort of any kind, but lived idly and luxuriously upon the fruits of the labors of others. The Labor Party is the party of the producers whose labor of hand and brain provide the necessities of life for all and dignify and elevate human existence. That the producers have been robbed of the major part of the fruits of their industry under the individual system of capitalist production is a justification for the party's claims. One of the main aims of the party is to secure for every producer his (or her) full share of those fruits — and to insure the most equitable distribution of the nation's wealth that may be possible, on the basis of the common ownership of land and capital, and the democratic control of all the activities of society.

Program of the British Labor Party. The report on the general policy of the party (which was adopted in a series of embodying resolutions at the Conference of June, 1918) dealing with reconstruction covers a very wide range of problems. It lays down the doctrine that what has to be reconstructed after the war is not this or that Government Department or piece of social machinery, but society itself. This party declares that whether in opposition or in office it will not tolerate the revival of the social and economic system which the war has destroyed, but will seek to build up a new social order based on a deliberately planned coöperation in production and distribution for the benefit of all who labor by hand or by brain. Four propositions are laid down in the Memorandum upon which the party proposes to establish the democratic control of all the activities of society:

(a) The universal enforcement of the national minimum;
(b) The democratic control of industry;
(c) The revolution in national finance; and
(d) The surplus wealth for the common good.

The national minimum. Applying the first principle, the Labor Party proclaims its resolve to secure for every member of the community, both in good times and bad, all the requisites of a healthy life and worthy citizenship. It proposes to do this by enforcing the universal application of the policy of a prescribed minimum of health, leisure, education, and subsistence by the extension of such legislation as the Factory Acts, Truck Acts, Public Health Acts, Housing Acts, Education Acts, Minimum Wage Acts, and Trade Board Acts.

The policy of the party in regard to the problems of demobilization is briefly to insure that the demobilization and discharge of the eight million wage-earners now in the fighting forces or engaged in war work shall be so regulated as to avert the peril of widespread unemployment involving the whole wage-earning class in economic ruin. The party insists that the obligation to find suitable employment in productive work for all these men and women is national, and that until work is found it is the duty of the Government in the interest of the community as a whole to provide them with adequate maintenance, either through the out-of-work benefit afforded by the trade unions or in some other way.

In order to prevent the occurrence of unemployment, either in the course of demobilization or in the first years of peace, the party urges that all necessary preparations should be made by the Government for putting in hand at once, directly or through the local authorities, urgently needed public works, including the building of a million new cottages, new schools, and training colleges; the making of new roads, railways, canals; afforestation, the reclamation of land, the development of ports and harbors; and the establishment of coöperative small holdings; whilst steps ought also to be taken, for the purpose of relieving pressure upon an overstocked labor market, to raise the school-leaving age to sixteen and substantially to shorten the hours of labor for all young people; to reduce wherever practicable the hours of adult labor; and to limit the amount of overtime.

Democratic control. The policy of the party as applied to industry contemplates a great extension of the principle of democratic control. It demands the progressive elimination of the private capitalist from the control of industry and the scientific reorganization of the nation's industry on the basis of the common general ownership of the means of production, the equitable sharing of the proceeds among all who participate in any capacity, and the adoption of such methods of administration and control as experience has shown to be practicable and necessary.

Social and political reforms. The party's policy of nationalization is applied not only to great undertakings like railways, mines, shipping, canals, and the like, and to the super-power stations for the production of electricity which are in contemplation, but to the whole business of retail distribution of commodities like household coal and milk; and the party also demands that the activities of the profit-making industrial insurance companies shall be undertaken by the departments charged with the administration of health insurance in its various aspects.

In the sphere of political reforms the Labor Party demands complete adult suffrage with absolutely equal rights for both sexes, shorter Parliaments, and the same civic rights for soldiers and sailors as for officers. For the complete emancipation of women it affirms the principle of equal pay for equal work on the industrial side and full equality of civic rights with men.

In education, the Labor Party is not satisfied with the meager advance made by the Act of 1918. It demands a systematic reorganization of the whole system on a basis of social equality. For this, education must be provided for child, youth, and adult, schools and colleges, irrespective of social class and wealth, must be regarded solely from the point of educational efficiency, and the teaching profession, without distinction of grade, must be recognized as one of the most valuable to the community.

In the matter of temperance reform the party proclaims the policy of public right, which it proposes to assert over the liquor traffic by giving localities power to prohibit the sale of liquor within their boundaries, to regulate the conditions under which liquor may be sold, and to determine how the popular refreshment houses shall be conducted.

In housing, the Labor Party considers it essential that all funds should be supplied and all plans should be made ready for the provision of a million new houses immediately on the outbreak of peace.

Standing, as it does, for the democratic control of industry, the Labor Party announces its intention of resisting any attempt to abandon the present profitable centralization of the importation and distribution of raw material used in indispensable industries, and will insist upon maintaining the elaborate system of costing and public audit which has been set up.

Taxation. The party's proposals for dealing with the problems of national finance involved the institution of a system of taxation designed to obtain the revenue necessary for meeting war charges and the cost of reconstruction from the largest incomes and the biggest private fortunes. It proposes that the income tax and supertax should be levied in such a way as to make the real sacrifice of all the taxpayers as nearly as possible equal, raising the present unduly low minimum income assessable to the tax, and steeply graduating the scale of taxation from 1*d*, in the £ [pound] on the smallest assessable income up to 16*s*. or even 19*s*. in the £ [pound] on the highest income of the millionaires. To free the nation from the greater part of its new load of interest-bearing debt for loans the Labor Party proposes a special capital levy to pay off a substantial part of the entire national debt, chargeable like the death duties on all property, with exemption of the smallest savings and with very steeply graduated rates which will take only a small contribution from the people with small incomes and a very much larger percentage from the wealthy.

In the interests not only of the wage-earners, but of every grade and section of producers, the absorption of the wealth of the community by individual proprietors must in future be stopped, and the party proposes that this constantly arising surplus wealth, to be secured on the one hand by steeply graduated taxation of private income and riches, shall be used for social purposes; including provision for the aged, the sick and infirm, for the establishment of a genuine national system of education, and for the organization of public improvements of all kinds, including a great development of the means of recreation for the people, the encouragement of scientific investigation and original research in every branch of knowledge, and for the promotion of music, literature, and the fine arts.

Problems of the Empire. Upon the broader problems of political reconstruction the Labor Party stands for a repudiation of the Imperialism which seeks to dominate other races and countries, and looks forward to an ever-increasing intercourse, a constantly developing exchange of commodities, a steadily growing mutual understanding, and a continually expanding friendly coöperation among all the peoples of the world. Not only does it demand Home Rule for Ireland immediately. It presses also for separate legislative assemblies for Scotland, Wales, and even England. Indeed, the development of a system of Home Rule all round, within the Empire, and the fullest possible extension of the principle of democratic self-government is an essential feature of the Labor Party policy, which safeguards the absolute autonomy of each self-governing part of the Empire, while it also permits a continuous participation by Ministers of the Dominions, of India, and eventually of other dependencies, in the control of foreign policy and Imperial affairs.

Beyond the maintenance of the British Empire in harmony with these principles, the Labor Party looks for the immediate establishment of a universal league or society of nations with suitable machinery for judicial arbitration and conciliation, which will enable the nations to settle their disputes with one another without resort to war. In relation to foreign countries, the Labor Party disclaims all idea of economic war; it objects to all protective customs tariffs; it believes that nations are in no way damaged by one another's economic prosperity or commercial progress; and it looks ultimately to the establishment of universal free trade as one of the ultimate safeguards of world peace.

The party stands for the abolition of secret diplomacy, the control of foreign policy by Parliament, and the substitution of a policy of international coöperation for the policy of the balance of power involving the creation of hostile alliances and combinations.

6. Why there is no Labor Party in the United States [1]

It is a common practice for members of the American intelligentsia frequently to bewail the "backwardness" of the American labor movement in political matters in comparison with the advanced development of the British movement. Here, we not only do not have a political labor party, but all attempts to form one seem doomed to speedy failure. The Labor Party across the seas, on the other hand, with over 190 members in Parliament, has assumed power and now constitutes His Majesty's Government. The conclusion that is generally drawn from this comparison is that the American movement must be much more lacking in intelligence and in the capacity to organize and to coöperate for common objectives — or, in a word, that the American worker is inferior to the British.

Such critics have perhaps never tried to reconcile this conclusion with the undeniable fact that in the industrial field the American unions, organized into the 112 component international unions of the A. F. of L., and the half dozen national unions outside that body, far surpass in compactness of structure and efficiency of organization the many hundreds of sovereign English unions which overlap each other in wild confusion, both sectionally and industrially.

If we are to explain the relative slowness of American labor to create a political party of its own, we must then search for less superficial causes than that frequently ascribed, and it is that which this article attempts to do.

Economic influences. In the first place, it should never be forgotten that England experienced the Industrial Revolution several decades before we did. The modern factory system which began to come into being in England around 1780 had become firmly and widely established by 1830, and by that time had created its large attendant class of propertyless industrial wage-earners. On the other hand, although we had cotton and woolen

[1] From an article by Paul H. Douglas in *American Labor Monthly*, February, 1924.

mills before the Civil War, the factory as a pervasive industrial type did not become predominant until approximately 1880. It is probably not an exaggeration to say that we were half a century slower in the development of the industrial system than was Great Britain. Moreover, in England, manufacturing has come so far to outshadow agriculture that the industrial population is not balanced by farmers and farm workers to anywhere near the degree that it is in this country.

In consequence of this, individual opportunity for the workers to rise in the industrial scale, not merely to become millionaires, but to become small masters or farm-owners, is and always has been much greater in the United States than in England. The condition of the English workers has always been far more degraded and the alternative of free land has not been present. Although the opportunities in America for rising in the industrial scale are rapidly narrowing, we have not yet reached the stage of a rigid caste society, to which England has virtually come.

Since the American workman has far more hope of rising by his own merits, he tends to rely more upon individual effort than the England worker who, on the contrary, sees his salvation only in group struggle and coöperation. It is this which makes the percentage of industrial wage-earners, who are organized at all, far smaller in this country than in Great Britain. And the smaller the union membership, the less energy and strength there is to form a political labor movement.

Nor is this all. The type of workers now organized in this country is much the same as in England forty years ago — namely, the skilled. The organization of unskilled and common labor which has proceeded at so rapid a pace in England during the last twenty years has not as yet occurred in the United States to any appreciable degree. In consequence, those who are union members are in the main able to obtain their demands through industrial action alone and do not need legislation to give them better wages, shorter hours, or better conditions. Hence they conclude that if the State will only let them alone, they will look out for themselves. Such in the main is the position of Mr. Samuel Gompers to-day.

Mr. Gompers's political and social philosophy is essentially that of Herbert Spencer. Such a philosophy is indeed quite admirably adapted to the purposes of economically powerful groups — for if the State will only stop any regulation of industry, whether of employer or employee, then the strong, by refusing to provide their services, save on terms satisfactory to themselves, will be able to wrest from society at least as much and generally more than they could secure were the State to interfere. We all realize that this is eminently true in case of the large employer; but it is also applicable, although of course to a lesser degree, to the aristocracy of labor. There is small reason, then, for the skilled trades to advocate the policy of using the State as an agency of social reform, since they neither need nor want social reform for themselves. That is why President Gompers and his associates have so steadily opposed the State regulation of hours and of wages, and why they have opposed health insurance, and turned a deaf ear toward old-age pensions and unemployment insurance. If they are given the unlimited right to strike, to boycott, and to picket, they can, so they believe, secure all these things for themselves. That there are millions of unskilled workers who cannot secure these conditions, because of their lack of economic power, does not seem greatly to influence the dominant forces within the A. F. of L. As long, indeed, as such skilled trades as the building crafts, the molders, and the more skilled printing crafts control American labor policy, we cannot expect a labor party in any real form to eventuate. For if a labor party were formed, it would be led inevitably by the very laws of its being not to stop merely with freeing the economic power of the unions. In order to provide itself with campaign material to secure the vote of unskilled labor, it would inevitably be led to advocate collectivism and State control of industry. Political labor parties, like trade unions, must have something with which to occupy themselves. Once such an organization is set up, it will be forced to create issues which run strictly counter to the political philosophy of the present leaders. Forays into the primaries of the old parties in order to redress individual grievances can, on the other hand, be controlled more effectively and no machinery is created to hunger for further political power once the immediate end has been obtained.

British parallelisms. British labor during the seventies and eighties was dominated by similar crafts and had an identical policy. The carpenters, the masons, the ironmolders, and the engineers (machinists), together with the cotton-weavers and spinners, under the leadership of Henry Broadhurst, George Howell, and John Burnett, controlled the Trade-Union Congress. Having secured what they believed to be immunity from the law by the Employers' and Workmen's Act of 1876, just as Mr. Gompers believed he had attained immunity for American labor by the passage of the Clayton Act, the English leaders settled back and proceeded to oppose the State regulation of hours of work, to vote down proposals for universal manhood suffrage, and of course to regard collective ownership as anathema.

It was the organization of the unskilled, first in 1886 and increasingly since 1900, that swept these leaders and their followers from power and replaced them with Ben Tillett, J. R. Clynes, Will Thorne, Robert Smillie, and others representing the humbler workers, who had come to demand that the State should cease its sham neutrality and should be used to redress the weakness in the economic bargaining power of the unskilled laborers.

The extraordinary similarity of Mr. Gompers to Henry Broadhurst is indeed most striking, and those who think that Mr. Gompers's policy is an anachronism should reflect upon the fact that Broadhurst was the idol of the British labor movement less than forty years ago.

A further reason for the difficulty of uniting American labor upon either a common political or economic program is the great racial heterogeneity of the working population, as contrasted with the relatively uniform racial stock of any given English locality. The skilled trades in this country are predominantly manned either by Anglo-Saxon stock or by the children of former immigrants from northwestern Europe. The lower varieties of industrial labor, on the other hand, are performed in the main by those "newer" immigrants from southeastern Europe and increasingly of late by the negroes. American industry largely rests, indeed, upon these two helot classes, for whom a large proportion of the skilled workers have only racial contempt and animosity. Political coöperation between the various groups is therefore at present extremely difficult.

The influence of political structure. But there are other causes for the non-development of a political labor party in this country. The political structure and institutions of Great Britain are such as logically to necessitate the formulation of a separate labor party, while the American political structure chiefly operates to delay and to prevent it.

National parties. Thus, in America, our parties are national, but most legislation that vitally affects the worker must be passed by the forty-eight States. In England, on the other hand, one Parliament is the lawgiver for the land. In the United States, therefore, a large national vote and the election of a number of representatives to the National Congress is no assurance that legislation beneficial to the workers will result. It is from the States that the workers must primarily expect relief and to State politics that they must predominantly address themselves. This preoccupation with State affairs, however, operates against the formation of a national party and causes the adoption of varying political methods in the different States. Thus, in 1920 the organized forces of labor in North Dakota supported the Republicans, in Montana the Democrats, while in Washington they were allied with the Farmer-Labor Party. Such a variety of tactics may have been the wise method so far as the political situation in each State was concerned, but, from a national standpoint, its effect was to have the votes of men with almost identical political ideals neutralize and cancel each other. In England a more or less uniform national policy must necessarily be followed, and this uniformity fosters the development of a separate labor party.

Presidential Government. Another barrier is created because of the fact that the executive in this country is elected directly by the people, and is therefore outside the control of the legislature, while in England, with her cabinet system of government, the executive is virtually chosen by Parliament and is dependent upon Parliament for its continuance. Consequently, the executive in this country can represent only one party, while in England the cabinet may be formed by varying shades of opinion. There, as in all Continental countries, a handful of representatives, on the contrary, may be of tremendous importance. They may determine who shall form the cabinet as well as dictate some of its members. Thus, in the 1909 English Parliament, the Labor Party and the Irish Nationalists held the balance of power, and it was their support alone that enabled the Liberals to continue in power. The Liberals, in return for the support of the Irish, were forced to push Home Rule, while to retain the support of Labor, they were driven to the advocacy of social reform. The creation of the system of employment exchanges, the passage of the Old-Age Pensions Act, and of the Trade Boards (Minimum-Wage) Act, as well as the installation of health and unemployment insurance, were all predominantly due to the pressure of the Labor Party, which forced the Liberal politicians to pass such measures if they were to remain in office. The social reform program of Lloyd George would indeed have been relatively helpless against the opposition of the two older Liberal Imperialists, Asquith and Grey, had it not been for the ever-present menace of a separate group of Labor members, upon whose good favor Messrs. Asquith and Grey depended in large part for their continuance in power. In a similar fashion, the Socialist members of the French Chamber of Deputies have been able to exercise a great deal of influence upon the formation of cabinets, and upon cabinet policies, which was perhaps most notably evidenced in the case of the Waldeck-Rousseau Cabinet.

The cabinet system of government, therefore, lends itself to the creation of many parties, while our system of an independent executive tends to prevent the permanent existence of more than two parties. The anonymous author of *Behind the Mirrors* states this point succinctly:[1] "Groups will not be able in this country as in Europe to elect members of the national legislature independently and then form a combination and pick their own executive. They are under compulsion to elect the executive at large by the votes of the whole people. They must hold together enough for that purpose. The centrifugal tendency of minorities in the American system is thus effectively restrained. Groups must work within the parties, as the agricultural bloc has done and as the proposed workers' bloc promises to do."

The Supreme Court. In the third place, the presence and powers of our Supreme Court, operating as it does under a written constitution, has tended powerfully to discourage political action. Of what use is it to wage a political struggle and finally to pass a law, many ask, if all one's efforts are rendered nugatory by a decision of the Supreme Court declaring the law to be unconstitu-

[1] *Behind the Mirrors*, pp. 215–16. G. P. Putnam's Sons, publishers.

tional? The large number of social reform measures that have thus been overthrown by the Supreme Court has convinced large groups of workers of the futility of political action, particularly in view of the virtual impossibility of popularly determining the appointees to the Court. The absence of any Supreme Court or written constitution in England has made Parliamentary legislation the supreme law of the land. By removing the power of judicial review it has been made possible for the labor movement to concentrate upon political action with the assurance that once a measure is enacted, it will remain until repealed by a future act of Parliament.

The direct primary. A still further obstacle to the creation of a labor party is the fact that the direct primary makes it possible for the American labor movement actively to enter politics without creating a separate party, while its absence in England virtually compelled the creation of such a party. In England the Liberal and Conservative nominations for Parliament are largely made by the national committees of the two parties, subject to ratification by the more or less closed organizations of the stalwart party members in the various localities. Nominations are thus largely dictated from the center and there is little or no possibility of Labor capturing the political machinery of the old parties on any large scale. Without a labor party, the workmen were largely compelled to take such candidates as the two old parties offered. It is, of course, true that after much pressure, the Liberal whips did consent to grant a number of candidacies to representatives of the working class and that a small Liberal-Labor (Lib-Lab) bloc developed in consequence in Parliament. But the Liberal central organizations naturally would not provide for many such representatives. When the conservative English trade unions, therefore, felt themselves endangered by the Taff-Vale decision, which declared the unions and their members to be financially responsible for the acts of their officers, and which, in addition, more rigidly restricted the rights of picketing and boycotting, they had little power of recourse within the old parties. To elect a large number of Laborites, it became necessary to form a new party which would run independent candidates. The old-line unionists thus felt themselves to be forced to combine with the Independent Labor Party and the British Labor Party thus came into being.

Far different is the situation in this country. Here labor, in virtually all the States, can invade the primaries of the old parties, and, if it is powerful enough, nominate its men under Democratic or Republican labels. It is probable, indeed, that this has been the chief reason why the workers have not felt the necessity of late of forming a separate party. It is doubtful whether Mr. Gompers would have been able to satisfy the movement in this country by the policy of "reward your friends and punish your enemies" had it not been for the rapid spread of the system of direct primaries. Formerly, nominations were almost exclusively in the hands of the party machines and the workers were faced with candidates in whose selection they had had little or no choice. Friends were few to reward and enemies were many. No real alternative presented itself to the voters. With direct primaries, it is possible, however, for labor, as well as for other progressive groups, to enter the primaries of the two old parties and try to nominate their favorites. The A. F. of L. has in recent years broadened the scope of its political activities to do this very thing, along the lines which have been followed by the Non-Partisan League. A considerable number of labor representatives have thus been elected to our legislative bodies, without the creation of a separate labor party — a development which would have been virtually impossible in England.

The single-member district. Finally, the fear in this country of throwing away one's vote or of actually helping the least desirable of the candidates of the two major parties, by running a third ticket, has restrained many such candidates from being advanced and large groups of electors from voting for those that have run. Under our system of electing representatives from single-member districts by plurality or majority vote, men are afraid to divide the more or less progressive groups by running a third party, since such a party would generally permit the more conservative candidates to be elected. The national leaders of labor have therefore preferred to conclude a more or less implicit alliance with the Democratic Party, rather than, by creating a new party, enable the Republicans to sweep the country more completely and decrease the number of representatives with labor sympathies.

Such an obstacle to the development of a vigorous third party is, of course, inevitable wherever proportional representation is not used, for the necessity of a candidate commanding a plurality predominantly condemns the voters with labor sympathies to the thralldom of the second-best, or, more often, to a choice between the lesser of two evils.

This situation was mitigated in England by the little known gentlemen's understanding between the Liberal and Labor campaign committees in 1909 and 1910, to the effect that they would not "cut each other's throats" by running many candidates against each other. A certain number of uncontested seats were thus assigned to the Labor Party, which in turn refrained from running candidates in the vast majority of the other constituencies. The area of electoral conflict between the two parties was thus closely circumscribed. This policy on the part of the Liberal whips saved the elections of 1909 and 1910 for them, although it raised the Frankenstein of a strong Labor Party that may yet devour official Liberalism. Such an agreement would be impossible in this country, both because of the election of an independent executive and because the political machinery of our parties is so much more decentralized that any such division of territory would be impossible.

It should not be thought from the foregoing that a political labor party is an impossibility. On the contrary, the writer believes that such a party is distinctly desirable and that it will come in the not too distant future. But it has many real obstacles to face which will probably delay its advent and long militate against its acquiring great political power.

7. Prospects for a Labor Party in the United States [1]

Why a labor party? Again and again groups of belligerent American wage-earners have attempted to break into politics, but hitherto American workers have refused to be weaned from trustful allegiance to the Republican and Democratic parties. The anti-political and purely syndicalist policy of the American Federation of Labor derives from a recollection of the past futility and danger to American labor of political agitation, from fear that such agitation will divide the workers against one another and from a conviction of the salutary effect on the unity of the

[1] From *The New Republic*, vol. 18, pp. 397–400. April 26, 1919.

labor movement of an exclusive policy of direct class trade-union action. Are there sound reasons for believing that these considerations are losing their force?

Increasing importance of politics. In our opinion there are such reasons. In the past the relation of the American laborer to his employer and his employer's business was vastly more important to him than his relations to the Government. Although the State frequently interfered in industrial controversies and almost always to the disadvantage of the wage-earner, the State was not his worst enemy: nor was its friendship indispensable. The wage-earner was struggling tenaciously to maintain himself against the powerful employers' organizations and against the competition of a constantly increasing volume of European immigration. He was not strong enough to put up a political as well as an industrial fight, and unless he selected his ground prudently and paid careful attention to the economic stamina of his union associates he was in danger of suffering a complete defeat. Under such conditions the American Federation of Labor may have been justified in eschewing politics and in concentrating its attention on organizing the skilled trades and fighting exclusively for the increased economic power of its own limited membership. During the last few years these conditions have changed. The American Federation of Labor is no longer the harried and almost outlawed organization that it was for so many years. The Federal Government recognized it during the war and asked its coöperation in organizing the production of the necessary volume of war supplies. Immigration has ceased and will not return to its former volume. The wage-earning class won a substantial increase in economic power and independence. No doubt the relation of the wage-earners to their employers is still of more importance to them than their relation to the State, but under the new conditions the attempt to keep the two relationships separate will suffer from manifest artificialities. The Government interferes in all considerable industrial controversies, and this interference has only begun. When the wage-earners demand union recognition, a universal eight-hour day, a national minimum of health and security, and the nationalization of the railroads and the coal mines, they are putting forth a program with political aspects whose fulfillment will depend in the end upon their ability to exercise political power.

If the American Federation of Labor does not recognize the meaning of these changes and assist instead of opposing the formation of an American Labor party, it will in the long run forfeit its leadership of the American wage-earner. The conditions are favorable and the time has come for the American worker to take the aggressive, and to insist on those changes in our political institutions which will vindicate his claim to industrial citizenship. American labor leaders have preached for years the doctrine that wage-earners should not be treated as a commodity. They have organized and agitated and fought in order to force on industrial managers the recognition of wage-earners as human beings whose welfare should not be subordinated to the making of profits. They must continue to organize, to agitate, to negotiate, and to strike for the purpose of insisting on the prior claim of their needs as human beings upon the product and process of industry. Indirect political action, as they know, affords no substitute for direct action. But the converse is also true. If they try by direct action alone to prevent labor from being treated as a commodity, they will either fail or they will land in revolution. The reorganization of American social and industrial life for the purpose of subordinating the mechanical and capitalistic element in industry to the human element is in large part a political problem. The wage-earners cannot trust the Democratic and Republican parties to carry on the work. Its accomplishment demands the coöperation of the hand and brainworkers of the Nation, consciously organized and educated for participation in this essentially political task.

Post-war influences. The existing industrial situation illustrates the need of supplementing direct with political action. During the war the wage-earners benefited by an inexhaustible demand for commodities which enabled them to obtain uninterrupted employment at increased wages. Since the end of the war the demand for commodities, particularly in the metal industries, has diminished. The volume of production has diminished with the demand. The price of metal products is coming down and will come down still further. Hitherto no general reduction of wages has taken place, but many wage-earners are being discharged and employers are insisting upon lower wages as a necessary corollary of lower prices. But if wages are lowered and unemployment increased, even though rent, food, clothing remain at their present high prices, the industrial management of the country will have treated labor as a commodity. They will sacrifice the public interest in maintaining high standards of living to the avoiding of losses or the making of profits. What else can the managers of particular industries do? They can, of course, devote much more intelligence and consideration to handling the problem of hiring and firing and dealing with their employees than they have done in the past, but they cannot risk bankruptcy by operating at a loss. The better employers are frequently obliged to follow the example of less scrupulous competitors and to ask their employees to choose between work under hard conditions at low wages or no work at all. The opponents of political action expect by striking to prevent such a clear assertion of the principle that labor is a commodity, and under prevailing conditions the strike is a more powerful weapon than formerly. But the strike is not a powerful weapon for the unskilled workers outside of the A. F. of L., and by basing their whole campaign on it the wage-earners will accomplish their end, if at all, with a maximum of loss, bitterness of feeling, and social friction. Another supplementary way of breaking down the time-honored practice of treating labor as a commodity is to follow the example of the English workers and seek the sanction of the law for certain national minimum standards of work, wages, and union recognition. The legalizing of such standards, and the industrial reorganization which must accompany it, is a task of industrial statesmanship in which the workers, organized and educated for participation in politics, must coöperate, and which the politicians will evade unless labor prepares for effective political action.

Old parties unreliable. They cannot trust the job to the Republican and Democratic parties. Both of the older parties are committed by the instinct of self-preservation to prevent the adoption by the State of a principle which would be so subversive of existing privileges as that of testing the management of industry by its success in promoting the welfare of the wage-earners as human beings. The Democrats in their anti-trust legislation affirmed the principle that labor was not a commodity, but the affirmation in question was a perfect example of the gold bricks with which politicians are always willing to placate get-rich-quick social or labor reformers. Since 1868, when reforming agitation started in this country, the political machines of the two parties, by keeping in their own hands the framing and carrying-out of "progressive" legislation, have frustrated every attempt to liberate American politics and business from subservience to special interests. The agitation of the last fifty years has, indeed, clipped the wings of the State and National political "bosses." It has hampered the accumulation of fortunes such as those of the Rockefeller and Vanderbilt families. But it has not removed any of the fundamental abuses of American politics or business. Future agitation will not succeed any better until it undermines the governing power of the political and business machines. As long as they continue to exercise control over politics and business, the whole system of privilege is safe. The machine bosses can always yield, as they have so frequently yielded in the past, to temporary pressure; but if they participate in drafting the legislation and control its administration, they know they cannot come to serious harm. The social ideals of the working class will never have a chance of success as long as the country is governed by two national parties, the underlying object of whose machines necessarily is to keep political and economic power in the safe custody of its present possessors.

Independent labor party needed. If the American wage-earner wishes, consequently, to humanize American industry, he must organize for this partly political task by qualifying and equipping himself to become a power in politics. He is learning the futility of political democracy unless sustained by industrial democracy; but he has still to learn the other half of the lesson. Industrial democracy needs to be sustained by the practice of political democracy. Effective political democracy for the wage-earner demands the organization of a national party of brain and hand-workers to conduct constitutional agitation on behalf of those larger modifications of American institutions which are required by industrial democracy. By entering into politics in the interest of their own program they will act in obedience to the American democratic tradition which is that of using political agitation as an indispensable educational agency of social adjustment. It is the alternative method of banking on a combination of direct action plus the solicitation of concessions and favors from the lords of party politics which carries with it dangerous and subversive consequences. For the politicians will frustrate labor progressivism just as they have frustrated all the other progressive movements of the last fifty years. When they realize they are being fooled, the labor unions will become exasperated and insurgent. They may succumb to the temptation of enforcing their demands by such extreme forms of direct action as a general strike, and in a nation whose political constitution is as rigid as that of the United States a general strike or a strike in a group of key industries might lead to revolution.

Considering the predestined increase in power of the wage-earners and the substantial justice of their demands for the humanization of industry, it is of the utmost importance for themselves and for the Nation that they organize and educate themselves for effective political action. The one agency of effective political action is a national party organization. By forming a labor party they will at once clarify their own program, deposit it on the table for nation-wide and serious political discussion, and assume the responsibility of adjusting the program to that of the other economic classes. The political effort of organizing a labor party will tend to nationalize the American labor movement. It will force the trade-unionists to seek the assistance of the unskilled workers, of the increasing body of coöperatives, and of the minority of brainworkers who wish to share the aspirations and would like to contribute to the success of their brothers-in-labor. But above all it will force them to adjust their program to that of the discontented farmers who form such a large part of the American electorate and whose own economic grievances the political parties have so often smothered. For the first time in the history of American politics, the clear political possibility exists of an alliance between the representatives of agrarian and industrial discontent. A national labor party which emphatically repudiates revolutionary socialism and which commits itself to an experimental program of industrial and agrarian coöperative democracy, reinforced by democratic community organization and so far as necessary by direct trade-union action, has become a necessary and a salutary agency of American social progress.

CHAPTER XII

THE INDUSTRIAL CONFLICT

1. The Strike Problem [1]

The trend of strikes. Many conflicting estimates are made of the extent of industrial disturbance due to strikes and lockouts, as well as of the causes of these disturbances, and their effects upon society. The following brief statistical summary is offered as a guide to a proper appraisal of this great industrial problem. As will be seen, the various tables present information on three phases of the strike problem: (*a*) the development of strikes during recent years; (*b*) the extent of strikes as measured by the number of strikers; (*c*) the loss caused by strikes as measured by the number of days of work lost.

The Development of Strikes in the United States, 1881–1921.

Table One

Years	Average per Year		Relative Movement of Strikes (Average 1881–85 = 100)	
	Strikes	Strikers	Strikes	Strikers
1881–1885	498	124,005	100	100
1886–1890	1336	255,863	268	206
1891–1895	1337	278,868	276	225
1896–1900	1351	406,639	271	227
1901–1905	2793	1,547,087	561	324
1915–1921	3043	1,744,502	611	1407

The first half of this table records the average number of strikes per year, and the average number of men on strike per year during each of the five-year periods indicated in the first column. It will be noted that the table is not chronologically complete; the ten-year interval between 1905 and 1915 is omitted. This is due to the unreliability of the statistics covering the omitted period. The loss of information is not vital, since the

[1] Statistics based on an article by Paul H. Douglas, "The Trend of Strikes," *Journal of the American Statistical Association*, September, 1923.

purpose of the table, after all, is to provide a basis of comparison between present and past years and to show the major sweep of the strike problem in recent history. The table shows that, whether measured in terms of strikes or in terms of strikers, the problem is growing in magnitude.

This is best shown by the second half of the table which presents the matter in the form of an index number. Taking the average number of strikes during the five-year period, 1881 to 1885, as unity, and comparing with this the average number during the later periods we obtain the percentages recorded in the two columns of the table. In the period from 1886 to 1890, for example, there were 268 per cent (2.68 times) as many strikes as from 1881 to 1885; and 206 per cent (2.06 times) as many strikers in each year. From 1915 to 1921, each year showed on the average 611 per cent (6.11 times) as many strikes, and 1407 per cent (14.07 times) as many strikers as the yearly average from 1881 to 1885. This is a startling increase in the magnitude of the strike problem.

Increase of strikes in relation to expansion of industry. But, of course, industry was expanding during this period and the number of industrial workers was continuously on the increase. Before we have reached a stable basis of comparison, therefore, we must allow for this factor of industrial expansion. If strikes increased sixfold during the forty years under review, while industry and the number of wage-earners expanded more than sixfold, the relative importance of the strike problem is actually less to-day than formerly. The following table undertakes to place the comparison on a more exact basis than that which underlies the preceding table.

TABLE TWO

YEARS	AVERAGE YEARLY NUMBER PER 1,000,000 WORKERS		RELATIVE INCREASE IN NUMBER PER 1,000,000 WORKERS	
	Strikes	Strikers	Strikes	Strikers
1881–1885	84	20,990	100	100
1886–1890	193	37,050	230	177
1891–1895	167	33,880	199	161
1896–1900	140	29,030	167	138
1901–1905	240	34,900	286	166
1915–1921	179	102,440	213	488

The essence of this table is the comparison between the average number of strikes and strikers and the number of workers engaged in industry during the periods recorded in the first column. The table is derived by taking the data given in Table One and comparing them with the statistics of industrial workers. Taking a group of one million workers as a unit, this comparison shows that the strike problem increased during the period even when weighted to allow for the expansion of industry. The increase, however, was not so great as might have been inferred from the preceding table. Nor was it continuous. Looking at the last half of the table, it will be seen that during the period 1901 to 1905, for example, the average number of strikes per year *in proportion to the number of industrial workers* was 286 per cent (2.86 times) the number in the period 1881 to 1885; and that the average number of strikers during the later period was 166 per cent (1.66 times) the number during the earlier period. This increase in both cases is much smaller than that shown by the cruder measurement of the preceding table. Instead of a continuous growth in magnitude, the history of the strike problem, when pictured against the background of industrial expansion, shows periods of decline; and though the general trend is upward, the rate of increase is not as great as would be supposed if one examined only the absolute figures.

The social loss caused by strikes. Many attempts have been made to estimate how much society loses because of strikes. The standard method of computing this loss is to estimate the workers' loss of wages, the employers' loss of profits, and the loss to the general public in higher prices, add these elements together, and present the sum as an index to the gravity of the strike problem. This, of course, is fallacious. There is but one way of estimating the loss to society due to cessation of work during strikes and that is in terms of the *amount of product lost.* When the coal mines shut down, the social loss is so many tons of coal; not so many millions of dollars in wages, profits, etc. When factories are closed, the general public loses a portion of its supplies of shoes, clothing, furniture, or what not. As the best manner in which to present this real social loss, the following table records the waste in terms of working days. This may be an unreliable index; but, at any rate, the working day is one measure of the productive power of labor, and the loss of a day's work roughly indicates the injury to society through a diminished product.

TABLE THREE

Years	Average Duration of Strikes 1881–1921	
	Average in days	Relative duration
1881–1885	22.7	100
1886–1890	23.4	103
1891–1895	26.8	118
1896–1900	21.5	95
1901–1905	28.2	124
1915–1921	28.8	127

This table requires very little explanation. The periods covered are the same as in the preceding tables. The first half shows the duration of strikes, on the average, measured in absolute number of days. The second half shows the relative increase in the duration of strikes measured in percentages, the average for the period 1881 to 1885 taken as a base. The outcome of this comparison discloses a rather steady, though moderate increase in the seriousness of the strike problem when measured by the number of days lost in the average case.

Loss in production. Clearly, however, this gives only a partial index to the social loss caused by industrial disputes. All strikes of the same average duration do not inflict a like damage upon society in terms of lost productivity. The seriousness of the strike depends quite as much upon the number of strikers involved as upon the duration of the strike. Hence to measure the social loss caused by strikes with any degree of accuracy these two factors must be combined as in the following table:

TABLE FOUR. TOTAL NUMBER OF DAYS' LABOR LOST IN STRIKES

Years	(Combining Tables One and Three)
1881–1885	2,814,913
1886–1890	5,987,194
1891–1895	7,473,662
1896–1900	8,742,738
1901–1905	13,627,853
1915–1921	50,241,657

The striking feature of this table is the enormous increase in the total loss of working days during the period following the opening of the twentieth century. In searching out the cause for this increase, we find that it does not consist in marked degree in the tendency of strikes to be prolonged. The major factor is the rapid expansion of the number affected by the average strike — the tendency of an industrial dispute to attain nation-wide dimensions. The growth of large-scale industry with the consequent broadening of the segment of the working population affected by the controversies arising within a given enterprise, the development of strong national unions formed for united action in trade disputes, the unsettled conditions of certain of our key industries — for example, the railroads and the mines — have brought about this great increase in the total number of days lost during the year.

In summary of the information contained in the foregoing tables we may say that, in the average year during the period 1915 to 1921, the number of strikes was sixfold as great as in the average year from 1881 to 1886; the number of strikers fourteen-fold as large; and that these figures become twofold and fivefold, respectively, when an allowance is made for the general industrial expansion of the country between these dates. The loss caused by strikes, measured in the waste of labor power, increased in absolute terms seventeen-fold.

2. Labor and the Courts

Reasons for conflict. One prominent feature of the Labor Problem is the conflict which has arisen between organized labor and the concepts of justice which dominate in modern society. Such a conflict has been inevitable in the nature of the case. Law and the courts of justice which give effect to law are a conservative force. They arise after the fact to sanction institutions and norms of conduct which have developed in harmony with the prevailing economic and social forces of the time. The labor movement, as we have seen, is to a large degree a reaction against these institutions and norms. The motive and aims, the policies and methods, the standards of conduct which prevail in the ranks of organized labor are not in harmony with those which dominate in capitalistic society. From this point of view, the labor movement has been a non-conformist movement in every country in which it has developed. It has found the existing system of law and legal rights antagonistic or antipathetic to its purposes. As it has grown in strength, its pressure has been exerted in the direction of modifying the law to the end that its own purposes might find a place in the prevailing system of legal rights. Failing this, or in the interval during which the modification was being worked out, the labor movement has adopted an attitude of aggressive or passive opposition to constituted authority in its existing form.

Legal status of organized labor in England. The history of the relation of the labor movement to the law in England is an epitome of its history in other countries. England was the birthplace of organized labor. Here the factory system had its origin and here it first produced on a large scale those conditions of life for the propertyless man of which the labor movement is the natural product. With a history longer by at least a generation than its history in other countries, the labor movement in England has more profoundly affected the legal system of the country.

Unionism at first illegal. When the modern labor movement began in England during the closing decades of the eighteenth century, it met a blank wall of opposition from the law. Its essential purpose — collective agreement — was condemned as a conspiracy by the common law; the courts held that all combinations to raise wages were criminal. Statutes passed at the opening of the nineteenth century prohibited the formation of unions, as the earlier common-law doctrine of conspiracy had condemned their activities. From the beginning of the nineteenth century, therefore, the history of labor law in England has been marked by the gradual removal of these prohibitions.

Legalized in 1824. The Combination Acts which prohibited the formation of unions in 1800 were repealed in 1824 and 1825. From this point onward the legal right to combine was conceded to the industrial wage-earners. The older doctrine of conspiracy, however, still remained in force and was brought into play to condemn as criminal many of the activities of the unions upon which they relied to win material gains through their right of collective action. The coercive weapons of the union were taken by the courts as proof of criminal intent to restrain trade or destroy property. Though legal in form, the trade unions remained largely impotent.

This situation was changed in the seventies. By a statute passed in 1871, labor organizations were specifically declared not to be illegal combinations in restraint of trade. This Act was supposed to exempt the unions in their corporate capacity from the operation of the conspiracy doctrine. When it was found that the courts interpreted the Act in terms which did not concede this complete exemption to labor organizations, a supplementary

Act was passed in 1875 by which labor was held to be entirely immune from the operation of the law of criminal conspiracy. The question was not again raised until 1901, when a decision of the House of Lords acting as the final court of appeal in Great Britain levied damages of over $200,000 upon a union of railroad workers for injury to company property during a strike. This famous decision, known as the Taff-Vale case, had far-reaching results in shaping the labor law of England. It appeared to undermine an immunity which had been conceded by statute law twenty-five years before, and which had become one of the foundation stones of legal right as viewed by organized labor. After an active political campaign which shook the whole country and brought forth the British Labor Party as a significant force in British politics, the decision was nullified by the Trade Disputes Act of 1906.

Trade Disputes Act. This law is now the determining factor in the relation of trade-unionism to the courts in Great Britain. Its far-reaching import is shown in the following statement of its provisions as summarized by the leading American authority on the subject:[1]

It provides that acts done by a combination, either of employers or employees, in contemplation of a trade dispute, shall be lawful unless they would be unlawful if done by one person. It provides further that such acts shall not be deemed unlawful because they interfere with another's free access to the labor and commodity markets, or because they amount to meddling by third parties with contractual rights. Thus the law of conspiracy in all its forms of statement, is declared not to be applicable to labor disputes. Moreover, in lieu of vague prohibitions of "violence," "intimidation," and "coercion," England has a definite statutory declaration as to the conduct which is lawful. The dividing line between lawful persuasion and unlawful coercion is fairly definite, so that all who read may know. Picketing for the purpose of peacefully obtaining or communicating information, or of peacefully persuading another to work or abstain from working, is lawful. On the other hand, it is unlawful to commit acts of violence or sabotage, or persistently to follow another. Nor may one quit work in violation of a contract when he has reason to know that the consequence of his leaving will be to endanger human life, or

[1] From *Principles of Labor Legislation*, by Commons and Andrews, p. 123. Copyright by *Harper and Brothers*. Reprinted by permission.

to expose valuable property to injury, or to deprive a city of gas or water.

Both the lockout and the strike are legal, as are the boycott and the blacklist. Parallel to the right of employers to get new workmen is the right of the strikers to picket peacefully and to induce them to abstain from working. England's policy is to allow both sides a free hand for a fair fight. . . .

The most radical departure in the British Trade Disputes Act must still be noted. It is the exemption of trade unions and employers' associations from all liability in tort for wrongful acts alleged to have been committed in their behalf. This was Parliament's answer to the Taff-Vale case. It made it impossible to maintain any damage suit against a trade union or an employers' association. This is a greater privilege than the limited liability of business corporations. The liability is not merely limited; it is removed *in toto*. Even though a trade union may be responsible for acts of violence, it cannot be sued for the damages it causes. . . . Exemption of trade unions and employers' associations from actions in tort does not mean that wrongs they commit are allowed to go unpunished. The union members who are guilty of acts of violence can be held therefor, both criminally and in tort; but the members who have not been direct participants in the wrongdoing cannot be held civilly liable as principals.

Legal status of organized labor in the United States. In our country the industrial workers have found the law less antagonistic to their purposes than was that of England at the opening of the nineteenth century. The union, as such, has always been legal in the United States. There have been, it is true, two court decisions which have declared the formation of a union to be a criminal act in itself; but these decisions, issuing in both cases from inferior courts, have never influenced the general attitude of the courts. The only true exception to the statement that unions have always been lawful in the United States appears in the recent enactment of anti-syndicalism laws by about twenty of our States. These laws make it a criminal act to organize or belong to an association which advocates the policies of syndicalism — that is, practices, as an accepted and normal policy, the destruction of property or the violent interference with individuals. But these laws affect but one, and that an insignificant, type of labor organization in the United States — the Industrial

Workers of the World. The vast majority of our unions, and all those which have acquired a position of power in the labor world, are lawful organizations and always have been so.

The real conflict between the unions and the courts, however, has not been over the right of the former to exist, but over their right to adopt policies which are necessary to make their existence of any account to the workers. Among these policies which are in dispute are the strike, the boycott, and the picket, the principal weapons upon which labor relies to support its demand for collective bargaining. The legality of these policies, even when they are free from the taint of violence and intimidation, is still a matter of dispute. Furthermore, the liability of unions in their corporate capacity for damages caused by the activities of their members remains as a menace to all members of the organized labor movement.

Conflict of laws. There is no law of national scope covering the activities of trade unions in the United States. This matter lies within the province of the States. It is therefore impossible to formulate with any degree of accuracy a general statement of the legality of union activity which will hold true in all parts of the country. Even within a given State, there is confusion due to the existing conflict of decisions issued by different courts, or by the same court of different times, with regard to the strike, the boycott, and other phases of trade disputes. And between States, the confusion is worse confounded both by conflicting interpretations of the law and by the practice of employing the terms "strike," "boycott," and "picket" in different meanings. Recognizing this condition of the law, we can attempt no more than a summary statement of the essential points on which all courts appear to agree.

The strike: definition. With regard to the *strike*, the usual statement of the law is that it is lawful to strike "for any reason or for no reason." But laymen should not infer from this that no strike will be condemned as illegal; on the contrary, there exists a long record of court decisions which have held specific strikes unlawful. The confusion arises over the meaning of the term "strike." When the courts hold that all strikes are lawful, they define the term as "simple collective quitting of work," and their statement resolves itself into the truism that no man can be forced to labor against his will in this country. By the Thirteenth Amendment, involuntary servitude has been made unconstitutional. Accordingly, workmen cannot be forced to remain at their tasks against their will, even when they have entered into definite contracts to perform service for a stated length of time.

If they leave their work while under contract to remain, the workmen will be held liable to civil action for the recovery of damages by the employer; but the fact that most workmen have no definite time contracts, together with the fact that those who have entered into such contracts rarely possess material wealth sufficient to justify suit for damages, virtually exempts all workmen from interference by the court when they decide to quit their jobs. This is all that is meant by the statement that the strike is always legal. As one writer states the matter, "What is really meant is that quitting work cannot be directly prevented."

But the definition of a strike as collective quitting of work is not broad enough to embrace all the implications of that weapon of trade-unionism. With rare exceptions, a strike is something more than a spontaneous and simultaneous surrender of their jobs by a group of workmen. It is preceded by a collective agreement among these workers to strike unless certain of their demands are granted. Before the strike occurs, the workers engage in concerted action through the union to bring pressure to bear upon the employer under threat of strike. The strike itself is a response to orders issued by the officials of a combination of workmen. While it is in operation, the strikers retain their coherence and continue to act as a unit with the intent to recover their jobs after the period of disturbance has passed. In all its phases, the essence of the strike consists in the *combination* of the workers for concerted and predetermined action.

Now the courts distinguish this element of combination from the overt act of striking and treat it as a separate legal question. Though the act of striking may be an exercise of constitutional right by the workers, the *agreement* to strike and the *combination* formed to give effect to this agreement may be held civilly and criminally unlawful as evincing malice. Here the test of legality is not the act itself, nor yet the fact that a combination exists, but the purpose or motive which actuates the combination. Few such combinations can function without interfering with contractual or property rights, with freedom of action on the part of the employer or some other party, with the free flow of goods and services in the channels of trade. Such interferences are, on their face, contrary to common law and, in many cases to statute law.

Basis of courts' attitude toward strikes. A combination formed to engage in these activities, then, must be as privileged to act as is the employer, the non-union workman, or any other party whose rights are violated to be protected from the strike. Where two legal rights clash, the law does not attempt to enforce one at the cost of the other. If the union can show that the purpose of the strike is primarily to benefit the strikers and not primarily to injure the employer or some one else, the court will hold the combination innocent of malicious intent and the strike will be declared legal. If, on the other hand, this direct personal interest of the strikers cannot be shown to the satisfaction of the court, it is probable that the union will be held guilty of interfering with the rights of others without legal justification. Applying this general principle to the various types of strikes, we may say that strikes for immediate improvement of hours or wages for the strikers are legal; strikes for the closed shop, strikes to secure the discharge of a non-union man, strikes against the use of open-shop material, and sympathetic strikes are often held illegal. There are exceptions to all of these propositions in the court decisions of various States; but the principle as laid down is generally valid. The most important exceptions are to be found in Kansas where all strikes are forbidden in essential industries under the Industrial Court Act; and in California where all types of strikes have been legalized by statute.

The boycott: primary boycotts legal. The *boycott* has been divided, for legal purposes, into two categories. The first of these called the "primary boycott," embraces those cases in which workmen withdraw their patronage from an employer with whom they have a grievance. Here only two parties are engaged in the dispute: the union on the one hand and the employer, in his capacity of vendor of merchandise, on the other. With regard to this type of boycott the law is clear. No merchant has a legal right in the patronage of any class of buyers; accordingly, this patronage can be withdrawn at any time, for any reason or for no reason, without committing tort. This reasoning legalizes the primary boycott. It does not legalize, however, all the incidents connected with such a boycott; for example, the advertisement of the union's intent to cease patronizing the offending employer; the soliciting of recruits to the boycott; applying moral pressure upon disloyal union members may be held unlawful as constituting coercion of third parties or evincing malicious intent. Nevertheless, if used with caution, the primary boycott is a legal weapon of trade-unionism.

Ineffectiveness of primary boycott. This, however, is a matter of little significance in the industrial conflict. The increasing division of function which characterizes capitalist society has brought it to pass that very few employers of labor are engaged in selling completed goods directly to consumers; and it is this type of employer alone who can be reached by the primary boycott. The vast majority of wage-earners are engaged in the intermediate stages of production. Their employers find the market for their goods among other employers of labor. In the metal trades, for example, it is rarely that one finds an industrial establishment patronized directly by the ultimate consumer. Construction material is sold to building contractors who are employers of labor; steel rails find their market in the railroad industry; completed machines are bought by the owners of factories to be used in the production of other types of goods. So it is in other branches of our great industrial society. The workmen with a grievance against their employer can rarely apply pressure to that employer by withholding their patronage, for the sufficient reason that they do not buy his goods at all. They must first induce a third party — another employer — to aid them in the dispute by refusing to buy the goods of the producer who has given them offence.

Secondary boycott. It is the attempt to apply pressure in this indirect manner which gives rise to the *secondary* boycott. The union threatens to strike against an employer with whom they have no dispute unless he withdraws his patronage from another employer against whom the union is carrying on a strike. To illustrate, a strike occurs in a factory which makes printing presses. Union men in another city employed by newspapers and publishing houses threaten to strike unless their employers cease using the printing presses made by the employer who is party to the original dispute. Or, while a trade dispute is in progress in the steel mills, the building-trade laborers in other places strike against the use of construction material made in the offending shop. Thus the secondary boycott always involves coercion of a third party. It may be defined as "pressure brought to bear upon a second employer to compel him to boycott another employer who is party to a trade dispute."

This type of boycott is illegal in all jurisdictions in the United States with the exception of California, where it has been legalized by statute law, and, possibly, in Oklahoma, where an inferior court has sustained it. The courts hold that interfering with, and inflicting damage upon, an employer against whom no direct grievance is lodged, merely to force him to cease exercising his legal right to bestow his patronage as he sees fit, is clear evidence of malice. This is also the position of the Supreme Court of the United States which, in a recent decision, held that the boycott (meaning the secondary boycott) had always and universally been condemned in this country.

Damage suits. Though this has long been the law, it is only within fairly recent years that the unions have had anything to fear from flouting the opinion of the Court. In 1908, however, a Federal court in the Danbury Hatters case awarded damages amounting to approximately $300,000 against the members of a union which had been held guilty of practicing the secondary boycott. It would appear that every union convicted of practicing the secondary boycott is liable for damages. Since this act is viewed as malicious, every agreement to practice it becomes an illegal conspiracy to destroy property; and under the Sherman Anti-Trust Law the victim of these conspiracies may recover triple damages. In contrast with the position of the English unions under the Trade Disputes Act of 1906, labor organizations in the United States are liable in their corporate capacity for illegal acts done by their officers or members. Furthermore, their individual members are liable without limit for illegal acts of union officials which the members appear to have authorized. This was the position taken by the Supreme Court in the Danbury Hatters, case (1917) and later (1922) in the Coronada case. In the former case, damages of $300,000 were assessed against 175 members of the Hatters' Union. In the latter case, though the Court could find no cause for the assessment of damages, it emphatically asserted the liability of the union. In view of this danger, the secondary boycott is no longer used on a wide scale, though it is practiced locally.

Legality of the picket. The *picket* is incidental both to the strike and to the boycott. It is an attempt to make the strike effective by preventing the employment of workers to fill the vacant jobs; and to strengthen the boycott by persuading others to join the union in withholding patronage. The method is to station union members on the scene of the dispute who, in case of a strike, attempt to induce non-union workers to join forces with the strikers, and, in case of a boycott, accost passers-by and possible patrons of the establishment with the intent of inducing them to go elsewhere.

On the face of it, the law relating to picketing seems clear. It is generally agreed that peaceful persuasion is lawful, except when it results in the breaking of preëxisting contracts. On the other hand, it is also generally true that intimidation and violence in furtherance of the purposes of the picket are unlawful. Confusion, however, arises over the distinction between peaceful persuasion and intimidation. There is no exact definition of either of these terms in our law; the line between them is exceedingly shadowy; and the distinction is open to varied interpretation according to the personal judgment of the court. One judge has said: "The peaceful, law-abiding man can be and is intimidated by gesticulations, by menaces, by being called harsh names, and by being followed, or compelled to pass by men known to be unfriendly." Such a definition of intimidation amounts to saying that, although peaceful picketing may be lawful, there can be no peaceful use of this weapon, and hence its use may always be illegal. In fact, this was the conclusion of the judge quoted above: "There is and can be no such thing as peaceful picketing, any more than there can be chaste vulgarity or peaceful mobbing or lawful lynching." On the basis of this reasoning, at least ten of the States have forbidden the picket, among them being the State of California which legalizes the strike and boycott.

On the other hand, Arizona, Indiana, Minnesota, Missouri, Montana, New Hampshire, New York, Oklahoma, and Virginia have held that peaceful picketing is lawful, and have attempted to define the type of picketing which can be called peaceful. This is also the position taken by the Supreme Court which, in two recent cases, has attempted in detail to prescribe rules to insure the peacefulness of the picket line. In these States, and in the Federal jurisdiction, however, the courts give an extremely wide definition to the term "intimidation"; and their attempts to prevent the picket from precipitating violence directly or indirectly have the effect of rendering that weapon virtually impotent. The Supreme Court, for example, has reduced the number of permissible picketers to two, prescribed for them a fixed station in the vicinity of the shop where the dispute is under way, and forbidden them from conduct more aggressive than that of accosting passers-by in an ordinary tone of voice. With its use thus restricted, the picket becomes virtually ineffective to accomplish the purpose for which it is intended.

Summary. We may summarize the attitude of the law in the United States toward these weapons of organized labor in the language of the authors previously quoted: [1]

Strikes, boycotts, and picketing have often been held illegal. These are the weapons through which labor secures and maintains collective bargains with employers. Collective agreements are worthless without a strong union to back them up. They are not enforceable in courts of law. The unwilling employer is kept from violating them only through fear of a strike. *Real* collective bargaining implies equal strength upon both sides. It results only when each side is aware of the strength, ability, and willingness of the other. Then a joint conference is held and a

[1] Commons and Andrews, *op. cit.*, p. 112.

compromise is effected. Neither will violate the agreement while the other party maintains its strength. Thus, it will be seen that restrictions upon the weapons which Labor may employ in trade disputes are in fact limitations of its right to bargain collectively.

The law in this country has not yet adjusted itself to the fact that collective interests and collective action are a natural product of the industrial system as it has developed in modern society. Legal rights and processes are still dominated by the prevailing philosophy of individualism, and of the supremacy of property and contractual interests, which characterized the early stages of the capitalistic order. That the interest of the public in the prevention of violence and the preservation of peace in the industrial world is supreme over all other interests, may be conceded without question. This is conceded in England where organized labor is much less fettered by legal restriction than in our country. But in England a recognition of this supreme interest has not prevented a thoroughgoing acceptance of collective bargaining with its indispensable concomitants — the right to strike, boycott, and picket. There reliance is placed in a balance of power between labor unions and employers' associations to preserve the peace; and in a careful definition of those actions which are condemned as subversive of public order and safety. In the United States, on the other hand, apart from the confusion which results from the lack of uniformity among the laws of our different Commonwealths, there is also a general maladjustment between the whole system of law and the underlying economic forces of the social order.

The use of injunction in trade disputes. The standard device of the court to prevent a strike, boycott, or picket which has been declared illegal is the issue of an injunction. The injunction is an order by a court of equity commanding certain persons to perform, or to abstain from performing, certain specified actions. It is issued on plea of an individual that his property will be damaged irreparably unless the defendants be constrained in the manner requested. All such property losses will not be prevented by the issue of an injunction, however. It must be shown that the defendants are not privileged to pursue the course of action complained of. Where equal rights clash, the law is silent. Only when irreparable loss to property can be shown to result from a line of action which is in itself unlawful, will the court move to prevent the loss by enjoining the defendant.

Accordingly, the applicability of this device to trade disputes is determined by two factors: the definition of property by the court and the court's opinion as to the innocence of the motive which underlies the activity of the union. The injunction has had a long history in Anglo-Saxon jurisprudence. Its utility to society, when employed within its proper sphere, has never been questioned. But the injection of this device into labor disputes has been of recent origin. Until the closing decade of the nineteenth century, the definition of property was such as to make the injunction inapplicable to the strike or boycott. At that time, however, the courts began to broaden the concept of property to include intangible elements, such as the right of the employer to undisturbed access to the market for labor and goods, his right to free contract, and so forth. Under the narrower concept of property, a labor union by adhering rigidly to peaceful methods could avoid the inflicting of obvious property losses upon the employer. With the definition of property widened to include these intangible elements, however, it has become literally impossible for any strike or boycott, however peaceful, to avoid the destruction of property. Every action of this sort on the part of the union obstructs the employer's access to market and frequently interferes with contractual rights. These types of "property" are always damaged by a trade dispute.

The rôle of motive. This being so, the question whether an injunction will be issued to restrain a strike or boycott will turn on the court's view of the motive of the union. It would seem that in every case where the action of the union is held tainted with criminal conspiracy, that action may be enjoined if it clearly damages property rights. Now the writ of the injunction is a weapon of peculiar and far-reaching potency in the hands of the court. It confers powers upon the judge which for their absolutism are without parallel in any other department of modern government. In the first place, the judge alone has power to decide whether the cause merits the issue of an injunction. In this capacity he acts as legislator, specifying acts which are prohibited. Violation of the injunction is punished as contempt of court by fine or imprisonment. The judge decides whether a violation has occurred and the accused is denied jury trial. After hearing the case, the same judge applies the penalty. As has been said, when wielding the writ of injunction the court acts as "legislator, judge, jury, and lord high executioner." These powers are too great to entrust to any man unless it is assured that he will act without prejudice. Yet, as has been shown above, the original decision to issue the injunction must be based, not on overt acts, but upon an interpretation as to the motive of the union. Here there is much room for bias, conscious or unconscious, which may react disastrously to labor.

Reaction against the injunction. The use of the injunction in trade disputes has caused more bitterness in the ranks of labor and more far-reaching antagonism to the courts of justice than any other phase of our law. In the Buck Stove and Range case, union officials were enjoined from acts which appeared on their face to be the exercise of constitutional rights — such as, the communication of information to each other and to their members, the publishing of statements regarding the strike against the Stove Company, and so forth. For violation of the injunction the president and two vice-presidents of the American Federation of Labor were sentenced to imprisonment without jury trial. During the coal strike of 1919, a sweeping injunction was issued against the Miners' Federation which again forbade the officials to engage in routine activities of the union. Again, in 1922, an injunction nation-wide in its scope was issued in an effort to stop the shopmen's strike on the railroads. Multitudes of instances of the use of this weapon on a smaller scale could be cited. Labor, organized and unorganized, is prone to interpret its use as evidence on the part of the court of bias in favor of property interests and against elemental human rights.

The Clayton Act. The last concerted effort on the part of organized labor to bring the law into harmony with their aims led to the passage of the Clayton Act in 1914. This Act limited the use of injunctions in trade disputes by prescribing that no one should be enjoined "from doing an act which might lawfully be done in the absence of such dispute by a party thereto." Jury trial was prescribed in cases of contempt of court when the act occurred outside the immediate presence of the court. Federal courts were not to prohibit by injunction quitting of work, peaceful persuasion, peaceful picketing, or refusal to patronize. "The labor of a human being was not to be considered an article of commerce"; trade unions were specifically exempt from the charge of conspiracy in restraint of trade under the Anti-Trust laws. This law was hailed by labor as "labor's Magna Carta." Yet, as was pointed out at the time, it did not alter the doctrine of conspiracy which has proved the greatest menace to active trade-unionism. And a line of court decisions issued during the past three years have clearly shown that the position of labor before the courts has been altered in no material respect by the Clayton Act, with the possible exception of the right to jury trial in contempt cases.

PART THREE
AGENCIES OF INDUSTRIAL PEACE

CHAPTER XIII

CONCILIATION, MEDIATION, ARBITRATION

1. Basic Concepts [1]

Social cost of industrial war. Any stoppage of work due to a strike or lockout must injuriously affect the national dividend. In the industry concerned the capital has to lie idle and the workmen must lose wages. But the effects of disputes do not end with the industry directly involved. Other industries, and the general public, suffer in more or less direct ways. In important basic industries, such as coal mining and the transport services, the loss of output caused by a strike or lockout quickly affects the other industries in the country affected. Most industries depend on coal for power, and on the transport facilities to bring the coal to them. The loss of their raw material quickly forces them to close down, so that more capital is made unremunerative and more workmen lose wages. The extent to which strikes cause such losses in other industries of course varies with the industry involved. A coal strike causes much more loss than, say, a strike among compositors in a printing press. But every strike involves primary or secondary losses in some way, and the necessity of their prevention hardly admits of dispute.

In all stoppages of work, great and small, the purchasing power of the people as a whole is diminished. The loss of wages and of returns on capital must lessen the demand for the products of industry. Apart from more or less measurable losses, however, industrial disputes create a psychological condition which directly affects the power of production. The constant irritation, antagonism, anxiety, and ill-feeling, engendered by lockouts or strikes, result in irksome work and sullen service. Unwilling or grudged service is usually bad service, and is reflected either in the amount or quality of output. Apart from trade-union rules imposing restrictions on output, the psychological effect of strife on output must always be reckoned as one of the most anti-eco-

[1] Bulletin of Indian Industries and Labor, no. 23, *Conciliation and Arbitration*, pp. 2–12, by R. N. Gilchrist.

nomic aspects of industrial warfare. Industrial society is like an organism. The whole organism functions well only when each part functions harmoniously with the whole. It is to this aspect of the problem that the Whitley Reports specially addressed themselves. The underlying principle of their recommendations is harmony or good feeling within each industry or works, with the corollary of willing, and, therefore, productive service.

The theory of force. Lockouts and strikes are really an application of the theory of force to industry. Just as war has often been held to be beneficial to society on the plea either of the survival of the fittest or of its beneficial action in cultivating the finer qualities in man, so strikes have sometimes been commended from the economic point of view for good by-products. A strike in one area, it is said, results in intensified activity in another area, or in an allied industry. The actual deduction in the national dividend is, therefore, not a net fall in output or wages. It is only a local and temporary deduction. This may be true of small and localized strikes; it certainly is not true of strikes in basic industries. Further, it has been argued that industrial unrest is a direct incentive to invention. This is no doubt true. But it is very questionable whether such invention would not have come independently of strikes. Normally competition is incentive enough to invention, and the less the ordinary forces of supply and demand are interfered with by strikes the more do the ordinary forces of competition impel managers and capitalists to seek new processes. To argue that strikes are justifiable for this end is on a par with arguing that war is justifiable because it may produce some good effects on society. Certainly strikes lead to *substitution:* but this is quite another matter. The recent coal strikes in Britain, for example, have already led to a big diminution in the demand for coal. Oil fuel has been substituted for coal, not only because of the enormous rise in the price of coal, but because the coal supply has become uncertain owing to stoppages of work. This, of course, on the whole may be a net gain to industry in the long run. It represents a direct and perhaps a permanent loss to the coal industry. The dislocation of industry due to the diversion of capital and labor, moreover, must be taken into account. To make new channels requires the expenditure of power, and it is always a matter of argument whether such new channels will ultimately be productive or not. Sudden and forced changes are at least temporarily unproductive. The gradual erosion made by supply and demand is usually productive. Dislocations and fractures rarely increase the strength of the body; gradual adaptations of physical strength to the necessities of environment do.

Kinds of disputes. Industrial disputes, like the methods of settling them, admit of some general lines of classification. By far the greater number of disputes is concerned with wages. Another class of disputes concerns the demarcation of functions, which, in countries where labor is strongly organized, includes the question of employment of unionists or non-unionists, or, as this is usually called, preference to unionists. Professor Pigou subdivides the two main divisions of disputes thus:

(1) Those connected with the reward of labor, generally raising an issue as to the money rate of wage, but sometimes touching such matters as workshop fines or the amount of special allowances, whether in money or in kind;
(2) Those connected with the doing and bearing of the employees, generally involving the question of hours.

Differences as to demarcation of functions include, besides the well-known but relatively unimportant "demarcation disputes" between kindred trades, all quarrels arising out of claims by the work-people to a larger share in the work of management. This latter class of disputes generally relates to —

(1) the way in which work is apportioned between different classes of workmen and machine tools; or
(2) the sources from which the employer draws his work-people; or
(3) the voice allowed to work-people in the settlement of working conditions.

In many disputes both these types are involved at the same time. In regard to wages, the most important basic issue nowadays is the minimum wage. The relation of wage to price of product made is also an important factor. This, however, is an indeterminate area of dispute, and the question of price variations in relation to wages may be settled by means which more properly may be studied under methods of industrial remuneration. Doubtless, marked variations between scales of wages and profits lead to unrest. The modern working man has assimilated sufficient Marxian philosophy to make him impatient of stationary or slowly advancing wages, coexisting with high profits. More and more he is demanding a larger share of the product of industry for himself, irrespective of minimum-wage standards. The more he gets, too, the more indeterminate becomes the definition of a minimum wage. The minimum wage varies directly with the standard of life. As that standard rises, so also must rise the minimum wage.

The problem of minimum wages. The many questions connected with the minimum wage do not directly concern us here, save in so far as it has now become recognized that wages must be such as enable the earner to live in comfort and respectability without injury caused by long hours or bad conditions. In Australia, as we shall see, minimum-wage regulation is now generally a statutory duty of the Government. The principles of the fixation of the wage vary from place to place, but the existence of the minimum wage is important for our present purpose inasmuch as it represents a common ground of agreement among parties to a dispute — employers, workers, and public. Every one recognizes the justice of the worker's claim to such a wage as will enable him or her to live decently. What a standard actually is or should be in any district or country is quite another matter. Whether it be a statutory duty of wages boards, trade boards, or courts, the "right to live" in the economic sense is conceded by all, and the safeguarding of this right has often been taken up by governments independently of industrial disputes. In fact, the action of governments in this respect has often not been forced by industry itself, but by public opinion, or a sense of natural justice. The legal enforcement of a living wage, or, to put it in the opposite light, the prevention of sweating, has been adopted in those industries where the likelihood of strikes is at a minimum owing to the weak bargaining power of the workers and their lack of organization.

The fixation of wages under such conditions is not the normal sphere of modern industrial disputes. It is true that frequently the stronger industrial groups lend a helping hand to their weaker brethren, but the modern dispute, with its lockout and strike, has become possible by means of collective bargaining. With the organization of workers into trade unions and federations of trade unions, and with the similar organization of employers, disputes have become disputes of combinations, not of individuals. The individual workman is a weak bargainer: he can be easily forced to accept the terms of the employer. But when the worker is a member of a strong organization he can afford to fight. Similarly, organized employers can fight, and fight stubbornly, when individual employers might not be able to hold out. The stronger the combinations are, the more strongly they maintain their claims and the more ready are they to adopt extreme measures. The dispute thus becomes more uneconomic; and it may be added that this brings out more clearly than ever the claim of the third party, viz., the public. Nor is a dispute of highly organized workers confined to the "natural justice" claim of a living wage. It becomes a fight for a fair wage, and the word "fair" is very elastic. It admits of many interpretations. It may mean a "living wage," or it may mean the pre-dispute wage plus a share of the growing profits of the employer. An absolutely fair rate of wages, as Marshall says, belongs to Utopia. This uncertainty opens the field to disputes, and the better organized the dispute the more uneconomic it is. Were all disputes merely to obtain a fair *living* wage, in all probability they would serve a high economic end, except for the bitterness and ill-feeling that they engender. Better wages mean better health and strength, better education, and, perhaps, better character. All of these are useful economic assets, which may be looked on as offsets to lost hours and diminished production. But such beneficent ethical results of industrial disputes are as doubtful as their baneful economic effects are certain. Hence it is that the community as a whole demands methods of settling disputes which both secure ordinary human fairness to the parties involved and prevent the economic losses which lockouts and strikes entail.

Organization for peace. Conciliation and arbitration normally presuppose organization among both employers and workers. Where such organization is absent, negotiations for the settlement of disputes must be irregular. It is difficult to organize methods of industrial peace where industry itself is inchoate. It may be possible by factory laws and wage laws to prevent abuse of power by employers where industry is unorganized or conducted on a small scale, but no government could undertake to settle every dispute between employers and workers where the issues were merely personal or parochial. The services of government, the chief organization of all, can only be usefully invoked where the issues are clearly defined and where they affect a considerable section of the community. The development of machinery for the settlement of disputes has followed the growth of large-scale production and the organization of large-scale or national services. Historically, it is true, there has been machinery of various types for dealing with small disputes. These experiments, however, have only an historical value. Modern conciliation and arbitration imply modern industrial conditions which are based on large-scale production and organization of employers and employees.

Three stages of development. Historically, in older countries the methods for securing industrial peace have been of three types. In the first stage, there are irregular negotiations. These negotiations are the result of interruptions of work caused by strikes or lockouts. In this stage both parties are unorganized. Each party tries to use such force as it possesses to obtain its own terms, and the result usually favors the employer, as he has longer staying power. At this stage, each party tries to get a drastic cure for an evil. In the second, there is conciliation and arbitration. In this stage an attempt is made by discussion and argument to reach amicable settlements either before or after the intervention of the forcible measures of strikes and lockouts. Prevention as well as cure comes in at this stage. The third, and final, is compulsion, or compulsory prevention of lockouts and strikes, with recognized principles for cure.

These three stages represent similar stages in social psychology. The first stage is the primitive notion that might is right, that the stronger must survive and the weaker go to the wall. The second and more advanced stage represents the recognition of common interests. Conciliation is possible only when the feeling that the interest of masters and men are antagonistic is replaced by the idea that their interests are complementary or common. The third stage represents the still more advanced notion of a homogeneous community, where the interests of all sections are bound up together in an organic unity. At this stage the communal consciousness extends beyond the immediate boundaries of the dispute to the community as a whole.

In actual practice, few countries have actually passed through the three stages. In Australasia the third stage has been reached without any long experience of the first and second. But Australasia had the big advantage of starting where others had left off. Its accumulated experience was the experience of other countries. Great Britain nominally is at the second stage, but the first draft of her most recent Act (the Industrial Courts Act) made provision for compulsory arbitration. This was dropped, and Britain switched off into other experiments, the aim of which is to prevent disputes by more suave means. The United States is either at the second or third stage, according to the laws of the individual States on the subject. Canada may be said to have reached the third stage, though Canada is not wholly a "compulsory" country.

Methods of organizing. The Royal Commission on Labor, which presented its report in 1894, found in practice some eight methods of settling trade disputes by means of institutions internal to trades. Beginning from the bottom of the scale and working upwards to the most highly organized institutions, the Commission classified these methods thus:

(1) Negotiations between individual employers and deputations or representatives of their own workmen.
(2) Negotiations between individual employers and trade-union officials from outside on behalf of their workmen.
(3) Negotiations between officials of trade unions and officials of employers' associations.
(4) Occasional meetings with reference to wage rates and other general questions between committees of trade unions and committees of employers' associations, with, possibly, at the same time a standing joint committee to settle minor questions of the judicial orders.
(5) More or less regular and periodical meetings between such committees for the despatch of current business.
(6) Formation of joint committees or wages boards composed

equally of employers and workmen, and meeting at more or less regular intervals for the settlement of general questions, with a regular constitution and rules of procedure, and usually with a standing sub-committee to deal with minor and local disputes in a judicial manner. The wages board or joint committee might either be for a whole trade, or for a district section of a trade, or for a single establishment.

(7) Reference of special cases to an arbitrator, approved by both parties.

(8) Embodiment in the constitution of joint committees, wages boards, or other courts of conciliation of the principle of referring to arbitration questions on which such bodies fail to agree. Such rule of reference might be either with regard to all questions or with regard to a certain class of questions only; and the arbitrator or arbitrators might either be standing referees or be selected upon each occasion *ad hoc*.

The general principles underlying these methods are very similar to those of the three classes noted above. The earlier stages are those of irregular negotiations in industries in which there is a low level of organization, both of trade unions or employers' unions. The later stages are those of advancing, or advanced organization.

With the stage of irregular negotiations, except incidentally, I do not propose to deal. The main issues concerning us are Conciliation and Arbitration. The word "mediation" is often used in the same sense as "conciliation," especially in the United States, but it is convenient to use "mediation" in a definite sense.

Basic concepts. As a basis for the definition of our terms we may adopt the definition of the Royal Commission on Labor:

Arbitration is the settlement by one or more presumably impartial persons of an issue on which the parties have failed to agree.

Conciliation is the coming together of the parties for the discussion of questions with a view to amicable settlement. This word is often used where we should properly speak of mediation.

Mediation means the exercise of good offices by some outside agency, with a view to avert an impending rupture between the parties, or, if the rupture has taken place, to bring them together again as soon as possible, without itself acting as arbitrator, or making an award, though it might sometimes make and even publish recommendations as to the course which should be followed. In the latter case its action facilitates what may be called arbitration by public opinion.

An American definition of conciliation and mediation (that of Drs. Commons and Andrews),[1] although interchanging the terms, brings out the particular function of mediation.

> By mediation or conciliation is usually meant the bringing together of employers and employees for a peaceable settlement of their differences by discussion and negotiations. The mediator may be either a private or an official individual or board, and may make inquiries without compulsory powers, trying to induce the two parties by mutual concessions to effect a settlement. The successful mediator never takes sides and never commits himself as to the merits of a dispute. He acts purely as a go-between, seeking to ascertain, in confidence, the most that one party will give and the least that the other will take without entering on either a lockout or a strike. If he succeeds in this, he is really discovering the bargaining power of both sides and bringing them to the point where they would be if they made an agreement without him.

Arbitration. In the various definitions of arbitration which have been given in reports of commissions and other sources, the definition of the British Royal Commission has been considerably changed. In the first place, arbitration may not be by impartial persons. The Australian courts, for example, are usually so constituted as to represent the parties concerned. Even where there is only one judge, Australian employers and employees hold very different views as to his impartiality. In the second place, arbitration is often defined as implying compulsory awards. The essence of arbitration is the existence of an authority specifically

[1] From *Principles of Labor Legislation*, by Commons and Andrews. Copyright by Harper and Brothers. Reprinted by permission.

set apart to adjudicate on disputes under recognized conditions. Arbitration may be of two kinds — voluntary and compulsory. Voluntary arbitration implies that two parties, unable to settle their differences between themselves, or by the help of a mediator, or conciliation authority, agree to submit their cause to an arbitrator, whose decision they agree to accept. The essential item in voluntary arbitration is the voluntary submission of cases to an arbitrating authority. The subsequent attendance of witnesses and investigation may or may not be attended by compulsion. The subsequent compulsion does not make the arbitration compulsory.

Compulsory arbitration means that parties must submit their cases to an arbitration authority. This implies compulsory attendance of witnesses, compulsory powers of investigation, and compulsory award, with penalties for breaches of awards.

Compulsory conciliation. The three chief terms which concern us thus are "conciliation," "arbitration," and "mediation"; but another term frequently used in the literature on the subject requires notice, viz., "compulsory conciliation." This term seems self-contradictory; and it has been used to denote several phases in the organization of industrial peace. It may mean the compulsory reference of disputes to conciliation boards, or it may mean the semi-compulsory Canadian system. Still another meaning has been given to compulsory conciliation — the settlement of disputes between the parties by arbitrators without a definite arbitration award being made. This is often done by disinterested chairmen of boards in Australia, who, gauging the feelings of the parties, persuade them to come to an agreement by "splitting the difference."

The term "compulsory conciliation" is an awkward one, and it would be better were it abolished from the technical language of industrial peace. Conciliation, voluntary arbitration, and compulsory arbitration cover such cases as may be denoted by compulsory conciliation. The Canadian system is best termed "compulsory investigation." Such compulsory investigation implies (*a*) the power of the investigating authority to compel the attendance of witnesses, the production of papers, etc., and to enter premises, and (*b*) the making of a recommendation as distinct from an award. In practice compulsory investigation further implies (*c*) the publication of the proceedings of the investigating authority, and (*d*) the postponement of strikes pending this publication.

Value of mediation. Before we proceed to the examination of existing systems of conciliation and arbitration, a reference may be made to the value of mediation, as distinct from conciliation. Mediation is rather a haphazard method of settling disputes. It may be brought into the quarrel at any stage. The friendly offices of a well-meaning outsider or agency may help parties to come to an understanding in the early stages of a dispute; or they may be useful in the later stages when conciliation has failed or where arbitration is not desired. Mediation in an industrial dispute is much the same as mediation in a private quarrel. It may stave off the estrangement which quarrels engender, or it may bring the parties back to friendship after the estrangement has taken place.

Generally speaking, there are three types of mediators — government agencies, private boards or individuals, and, to use Professor Pigou's handy term, the "eminent outsider." The methods of mediation are many. Mediators may try to settle disputes, "off their own bats"; or they may make acceptable suggestions to the parties about further inquiries, pending which the *status quo* will continue; or they may be able to persuade the parties to submit to arbitration. Naturally much depends on the personality and experience of such mediators. Hence arises the value of the "eminent outsider." English industrial history contains many examples of this type of mediator. The more eminent the mediator, the greater is the likelihood of his success. But the method is adventitious and unreliable. The "eminent outsider" method should be a method of last resort, a method of reserve, not a real and regular part of the machinery of industrial peace.

2. Conciliation and Arbitration in Great Britain [1]

In spite of her large industrial population and manifold industries, Great Britain has very few statutes affecting industrial peace. The modern legislation dates from 1896, the year in which the Conciliation Act — still in force — was passed. This Act satisfied British needs till 1909, when the less organized trades

[1] Adapted from *Conciliation and Arbitration*, by R. N. Gilchrist. Government of India, Calcutta, 1922.

were brought under the Trade Boards. From 1910 to 1914 there was marked industrial unrest, but the only new institution that was created was the Industrial Council of 1911. New lines of development were in contemplation when the war broke out. The industrial legislation of the war period was abnormal, and when conditions were restored, a short new Act — the Industrial Courts Act of 1919 — was passed. The Trade Boards Act was extended in 1918. A survey of the development of this legislation, therefore, shows that it falls into three periods: (1) the period up to 1914, recording the methods adopted in peace times; (2) the exceptional measures taken during the war; and (3) the constructive proposals of the Whitley Commission after the war, together with the legislation built on these proposals. Since the second period was one of abnormal circumstances, very little attention will be paid to the war-time laws in the discussion which follows.

The First Period, 1896–1914. During this period, three attempts were made to set up by law machinery for the settlement of industrial disputes: (*a*) the Conciliation Act, 1896; (*b*) the Trade Boards Act, 1909; (*c*) the Industrial Courts Act, 1911. The last named was short-lived and of small practical effect; hence, it may be disregarded in any attempt to understand the present legal machinery of Great Britain applicable to industrial unrest. The Conciliation Act and the Trade Boards Act, on the other hand, have become a permanent part of the law.

The Conciliation Act, 1896. Prior to 1896 there had been a series of laws regulating industrial disputes, most of which were practically dead letters and were repealed by the Conciliation Act. This law, passed in 1896, was more a codification of informal practice existing in the country than the result of new recommendations or principles. The voluntary system of conciliation boards which is embodied in the Act was in vogue in England for many years prior to its passage; and in many industries these voluntary boards had achieved noteworthy success in maintaining peaceful relations between employer and employee. The expedient of sliding scales had also achieved wide popularity as a method of securing industrial peace. The sliding scales of this period were based on the general principle that wages should vary with the market price of the commodity. According to this theory, a standard wage is paid for a standard price of a given commodity, and a rise or fall of the selling price automatically leads to a rise or fall of wages. For the regulation of these sliding scales, joint committees were required which lessened the need for boards of conciliation and arbitration.

The sliding scales were adopted in several important industries in England, but from 1880 onwards their popularity declined, and many of them were abolished. Since the conclusion of the Great War, another type of sliding scale has become very common — that based on the cost-of-living index numbers published by the Ministry of Labor. In August, 1921, the Ministry of Labor estimated that the number of workers covered by such agreements was about 2,750,000. The agreements between employers and workers providing for the automatic adjustment of wage rates according to the index number cover about fifty-five trades and occupations, as well as a large number of local authority non-trading services. This type of scale by its nature is a temporary measure, and in all probability wages and the cost of living will soon be stabilized.

The immediate cause of the Conciliation Act of 1896 was the findings of a Royal Commission of Labor, whose researches lasted from 1891 to 1894. Just before the Commission was appointed there was a period of marked unrest in England, which was succeeded by a period of trade depression. Among several big strikes one in particular — the dockers' strike of 1889 — had far-reaching results. This strike showed the workers the value of organization and collective action as a remedy for their ills. It gave a big impetus to both the trade-union and the labor movements. The membership of the unions, which had hitherto been languishing, increased considerably, and the political side of the labor movement — The Labor Party — found many new supporters. This combination of circumstances prepared the ground for a measure of industrial peace. From the evidence given at this Commission, it was clear that a large body of influential opinion in England favored the creation of some definite means for the settlement of trade disputes. Influenced by these various circumstances, the Government ventured to pass the Conciliation Act.

The Act provides for the registration and functions of conciliation boards. Any board established either before or after the

Act, constituted for the purpose of settling disputes between employers and workmen by conciliation or arbitration, or any association or body authorized by agreement in writing, may apply to the Board of Trade (now Ministry of Labor) for registration under the Act. The Labor Ministry keeps a register of such conciliation boards and it generally conducts the ministerial work connected with registration. The registration feature of the Act may be dismissed with little notice; it has been almost wholly inoperative. Thus, at the end of 1919 nearly five hundred conciliation boards were known to exist, but of these only thirteen were registered.

The Act lays down that where a difference exists or is apprehended between an employer or any class of employers and workmen, or between different classes of workmen, the Board of Trade (Ministry of Labor) may:

(*a*) inquire into the causes and circumstances of the difference;

(*b*) take such steps as the Board deems expedient to enable the parties to assemble, either by themselves or through their representatives, under a chairman mutually agreed upon or nominated by the Board of Trade or by some other person or body, with a view toward an amicable settlement of the difference;

(*c*) on application of employers or workmen interested, and after taking into consideration the existence and adequacy of means available for conciliation in the district or trade and the circumstances of the case, appoint a person or persons to act as conciliator or as a board of conciliation;

(*d*) on application of both parties to the difference, appoint an arbitrator.

The Act thus confers power on the Board of Trade (Ministry of Labor) to help in establishing conciliation boards. If it appears to the Board that in any district reasonable facilities for settling industrial disputes do not exist, they may appoint a person or persons to inquire into the conditions of the district and trade with a view to determining the expediency of establishing a conciliation board.

As will be seen from its provisions, this Act is very elastic. The operative sections of the Act are those which authorize the Minister to inquire into the causes and circumstances of a dispute and to appoint a conciliator at the request of *either* party or an arbitrator at the request of *both*. The arbitration provisions were extended in 1908, when the Board of Trade set up a Court of Arbitration. Panels of chairmen, of employers and labor representatives were established, and the courts were selected from these panels on the application of both parties to a dispute. The court consisted of three to five members. Technical assessors, to give the court expert advice on technical matters, could also be appointed if deemed expedient.

The chief feature of the Act is its purely voluntary nature. It is often quoted as a good example of purely voluntary methods in the settlement of trade disputes. It may also be noted that the Act allows wide discretion to the Labor Department to deal with cases as circumstances demand. Such permissive provisions require an experienced and well-trained labor staff. The possession of such staff by the Board of Trade, and later by the Ministry of Labor, is largely responsible for the success of this non-compulsory English measure.

The number of cases dealt with under the Conciliation Act from 1896 to 1913 is shown by the table on page 456.

The chief work of conciliation boards is the prevention of lock-outs and strikes, although in some cases the actual settlement of stoppages is one of the objects of the board. Most of the boards provide in their rules that no stoppage of work shall take place until the difference has been referred to the board of conciliation. In some cases, as in the manufactured iron and steel trade, it is provided that, if a stoppage has taken place, the board will refuse to discuss the question until work has been resumed. Some boards inflict fines for stoppage of work by either party under given conditions. It must be recalled that these boards are not government organizations, but voluntary arrangements set up in the trade by agreement between workers and employers. The Conciliation Act merely facilitates this trade practice and provides aid in perfecting it.

As conciliation boards usually are constituted on the basis of equal representation between employers and workers, it some-

Year	Number of Cases		
	Total	Involving stoppage of work	Not involving stoppage of work
1896[a]	11	9	2
1897	37	23	14
1898	12	8	4
1899	11	5	6
1900	21	13	8
1901	33	20	13
1902	21	10	11
1903	17	8	9
1904	12	4	8
1905	14	3	11
1906	20	8	12
1907	39	15	24
1908	60	24	36
1909	57	24	33
1910	67	27	40
1911	92	57	35
1912	73	34	39
1913	99	53	46
Total	696	345	351

[a] Five months only.

times happens that the opinion of the board is equally divided on the question at issue. In many cases such deadlocks are overcome within the board itself, but it is obvious that in many cases some definite machinery is necessary to solve the difficulty. With regard to this question, the conciliation boards of England fall into the following classification:

(1) Boards with complete automatic machinery for the settlement of disputes;
(2) Boards with complete machinery to be used only by mutual consent of the parties;
(3) Boards with no provision for avoiding a deadlock in the settlement of disputes.

A study made in 1910 showed that at that time, out of 252 boards and committees, 153 belonged in the first class. With them, failure to adjust a dispute within the board led to the reference of the matter either (*a*) to the Board of Trade for appoint ment of a final authority; (*b*) to a permanent neutral chairman, president, arbitrator, umpire or referee; (*c*) reference to an arbitrator appointed *ad hoc;* or (*d*) reference to three arbitrators with decision by majority. Of the second class, there were 81 in 1910; the majority of these referred for final decision to the Board of Trade upon mutual consent of the parties.

Trade Boards Act, 1909. This Act established the minimum wage in certain selected trades in England, setting up boards for the purpose of determining the wage and administering the provisions of the Act. The system of trade boards is an example of industrial organization which is the outcome, not of industrial disputes, but of a general public feeling that wage-earners who are not in a position to defend themselves should be protected by the community. This minimum-wage procedure is not properly to be considered a part of the system of conciliation and arbitration, yet its incidental purpose is to maintain peaceful and healthful relations in industry, and this purpose has been recognized especially in the recent extensions of the Act.

When the Act was passed in 1909, the industries to which it was meant to apply were specifically mentioned. The immediate effect of the Act was so beneficent — "sweating" immediately disappeared from the designated trades — that its scope was broadened. Up to 1918, about 500,000 workers had been brought under the boards. In that year, the policy of minimum wages, fixed and enforced by the Government, was extended to many other industries, so that by 1920 thirty-seven new boards applicable to a million and a half workers had been established. Since 1920 trade-board organization has been vigorously conducted and the numbers now affected by them must be considerably above two and a half millions.

In 1921 a backward step was taken when the wage boards established in behalf of the agricultural laborers were abolished. These boards had been created by an extension of the Act at a time when the prices of farm produce were guaranteed by the Government. The withdrawal of this guarantee after the war led to a demand that the costs in agriculture, stabilized so far as wages were concerned by the wage boards, should be freed from government control also. The Act by which this repeal was effected provides that, in the place of the agricultural wages boards and district wages committees, new quasi-statutory conciliation committees should be set up on which the farmers and farm servants should be represented equally, and on which there should be no independent members as there are on trade boards. The functions of these committees are limited to wages, hours, and conditions of work. The committees may, if necessary, appoint an independent chairman to act as conciliator, or, if they think fit, they may confer voting powers on him such as will make him a compulsory arbitrator. The decisions of the committees are enforceable at law after confirmation by the Minister of Agriculture and advertisement in the districts to which they apply.

The Industrial Council Act, 1911. The great labor unrest of 1911 led to the establishment of another unit in the conciliation machinery of Great Britain — the Industrial Council. Although the Conciliation Act had been effective in settling many disputes, opinion was gaining headway that a body representative of employers and employees was necessary to consider industrial unrest in its larger as well as its smaller aspects. Accordingly, there was created a central court or council composed of two panels of members — thirteen representatives of employers and an equal number of representatives of employees. These members were nominated by the Government, at first, for periods of one year.

The Industrial Council never became a live organization for the settlement of industrial questions. Its eminent Chief Commissioner, Lord Askwith, has accounted for its failure partly on the grounds of its bureaucratic nature and its failure to represent the parties immediately concerned in a dispute; partly because of its lack of power to enforce its findings; and partly because of its inept and cumbrous procedure which caused it to blunder in its attempts at strike settlement. The Council was soon abolished by a repeal of the Act of 1911.

The War Period, 1914–1918. During the three years previous to the war there had been a marked increase in industrial unrest in Great Britain. The Conciliation Act had been frequently brought into action, and the Board of Trade was seriously considering strengthening the machinery of the Act. When the war broke out, there were upwards of a hundred strikes in progress. The outbreak of the war completely upset industries for a time, but a wave of patriotic feeling which spread throughout the country brought about a conciliatory feeling amongst both employers and employees. Soon after the outbreak of hostilities, the great majority of strikes were settled. Recruiting seriously depleted the supply of labor, and the industries more intimately connected with the supply of war material required an additional number of men. Strikes and lockouts had to be avoided at all costs. The procedure — conciliation, arbitration, or anything else — was not of first importance; what mattered was the result.

Certain developments growing out of the war soon upset this condition of industrial tranquillity. The increased demand for labor placed the workers in a strong bargaining position which they were the more ready to exploit because of their conviction that employers were practicing wholesale profiteering; the influx of women into industry broke down the restrictive agreements made by the trade unions; the rising cost of living gave the wage-earners a real grievance founded on immediate economic interest. Hence, in 1915 labor unrest again appeared.

The legislation of the war period consisted in the prohibition of strikes and lockouts in certain essential industries; the provision of machinery for compulsory arbitration; and the authoritative determination of wages, privileges, and conditions of work in certain fields of industrial enterprise. The Munitions of War Act was passed in 1915 and amended in 1916. From the point of view of industrial unrest, the Act compelled the Board of Trade to promote settlement of disputes by arbitration or agreement between the parties. Any award or agreement thus reached was made binding and enforceable at law. No strike or lockout could take place in any dispute to which the law applied unless the dispute had been reported to the Board of Trade and twenty-one days had elapsed from the date of the report. The amendment in 1916 empowered the Minister of Munitions to set up special arbitration tribunals in important war industries. This Act, therefore, introduced compulsory arbitration at the option of the Board of Trade and, under given circumstance, prohibited strikes and lockouts. It is to be noted that compulsory arbitration is made a matter of last resort, however.

This legal prohibition of strikes and lockouts and enforcement of arbitration stiffened as the war went on. The Munitions of War Act, 1917, set up an arbitration commission in war industries to which was given the power of initiating arbitration in case of dispute. The Defense of the Realm Regulations prohibited incitement to strike. The Treasury agreement between the Government and the unions provided that no strikes should occur in munitions works and that the unions should surrender, for the period of the war, certain of their privileges which restricted production. All of this machinery for compulsory arbitration was intended to be temporary and it disappeared after the close of hostilities.

The Whitley Councils and the Industrial Court Act, 1919. In anticipation of the difficulties of the period of reconstruction which would follow the war, the British Government appointed in 1917 a special commission to study the relations of employers and employees. The report of this commission has been incorporated in an elaborate system for promoting industrial good will, known, from the name of the chairman of the committee, as the Whitley Councils.

The principle underlying the system of Whitley Councils is that peace in industry requires a recognition that employers and employed have an equal interest in the smooth functioning of the productive system, and a provision of machinery whereby these two parties may be brought into permanent and continuous consultation over matters which concern their mutual welfare. Trade-unionism, on the one hand, and the associations of employers, on the other, are recognized as indispensable conditions of the success of the plan. In the words of the Commission: "An essential condition of securing a permanent improvement in the relations between employers and employed is that there should be adequate organization on the part of both employers and workpeople. The proposals outlined for joint coöperation throughout the several industries depend for their ultimate success upon there being such organization on both sides; and such organization is necessary also to provide means whereby the arrangements and agreements made for the industry may be effectively carried out."

Machinery of the Whitley Councils. The Whitley Councils, in their perfection, can be established only in industries where this bilateral organization already exists. In such industries, it is recommended that a nation-wide organization be set up consisting of three divisions — a National Joint Standing Council representative of the industry as a whole; a District Joint Standing Council in each of the natural territorial divisions of the industry; and a

Works or Factory Joint Standing Council in the individual enterprises. Each of these councils is to be equally representative of organized labor and organized employers; they are to be in permanent existence, bringing the two interests together for conference over matters which arise within the respective fields of their operation. Thus the larger units of the scheme will consider such matters as legislation affecting the industry; devices for stabilizing employment, establishing standards of production, and promoting the security of the wage-earner, on the one hand, and the productive efficiency of the industry, on the other; and general improvement of technical processes. The committee established in the individual plant will provide machinery for joint negotiation of wages, hours, and conditions of employment, and thus give the worker a larger share in the control of his industrial life. The system as a whole will function as a medium for the clearance of difficulties and the settlement of grievances on a local, district, or national scale.

In industries partially organized, it is urged that the scheme be applied, with the aid of the Government, to those sections where organization has proceeded far enough to supply the framework for the councils; and that complete organization among employers and employed be encouraged to the end that the council system might be made national in scope. For industries in which no organization existed, it was recommended that the trade boards, instituted under the Act of 1909, be made the medium for introducing the scheme; but this perversion of the original purpose of the trade boards did not receive the approval of the Government.

The Whitley Councils are in no sense compulsory. The system is adopted by any industry only upon the motion of both parties concerned and is not enforced upon an unwilling interest by action of Government. In fact, the Government has no connection with the system, unless requested to appoint members in an advisory capacity to any one of its units, or to aid in the establishment of councils in a backward trade. Though provision is made for negotiation between labor and employer throughout the entire range of a given enterprise, from the smallest unit to the entire industry, decisions reached are binding only through voluntary acceptance. The plan does not embody the principle of compulsory arbitration, nor, in fact, of any type of arbitration. It merely gives frank recognition to the existing state of affairs in large-scale industry: namely, that both parties to the wage contract are tending to organize for mutual protection and that both demand a share in the determination of working conditions. On the basis of this recognition, the Whitley Councils provide for smoothly functioning negotiation in the hope that differences may be settled without resort to open warfare. The machinery adopted by any industry is voluntary and elastic, adapted to the prevailing conditions of the industry, and able to determine its own functions and methods of operation.

Progress of the system. There has been considerable progress in England along the lines mapped out by the Whitley Commission. Joint industrial councils have been set up in certain government departments which resembled in nature an industrial establishment: e.g., the Admiralty, War Office, and Office of Works. At first the better organized industries were not enthusiastic about the Whitley scheme, but by the end of 1919 several of the largest had accepted its principles. By the publication of a Joint Industrial Councils Bulletin the Ministry of Labor has tried its utmost to popularize the new movement, and it is noteworthy that a large number of foreign countries have made inquiries regarding the system. The time has not come to judge of the real utility of the joint standing councils; but it may be said with certainty that they have aided materially in tiding over difficult times.

Immediately after the cessation of the war there was a violent outburst of labor trouble. Once the tension of the war period was removed, there was a tendency on the part of the wage-earners to slack off work. This tendency was reflected in the new demands made on employers. The unrest was not only connected with higher wages; it was associated with demands for a shorter working day and for the elimination of systematic overtime. Gradually, in both public-utility services and privately owned industries the demand for a shorter working day or week was conceded, but in the period of reconstruction the diminution of output that this meant made it all the more difficult for industry to bear the higher wages that were demanded. The prevalent unrest brought about many strikes culminating in the strike of the coal miners in 1919

— one of the most protracted and bitter labor controversies that Great Britain has known.

To study this situation a national conference was summoned by the Minister of Labor, representatives of employers, trade unions, and joint councils. The main recommendations of this conference urged, among other things, that the questions of wages and hours be settled on a nation-wide scale by legal enforcement of the eight-hour day in all industries with few exceptions, and universal enactment of a standard minimum wage. It was also recommended that there be established a permanent national industrial council, to supplement the existing sectional machinery, and to advise the Government on general questions affecting the welfare of industries. The recommendations regarding wages and hours were not adopted by the Government, but the suggestion of a national industrial council was incorporated in the Industrial Courts Act passed in November, 1919.

Industrial Courts Act, 1919. This Act sets up a permanent court of arbitration, officially known as the Industrial Court, to which both parties to a dispute may have recourse if they both consent. The constitution of the court is elastic. According to the Act it may consist of persons to be appointed by the Minister of Labor, of whom some shall be independent persons, some representing the employers, some the workmen. One or more women may be added. The Minister is empowered to fix the term of office for a member of the Court, and to determine the make-up of the Court for the purpose of considering any particular problem referred to it. The headquarters of the Court are in London, but it may move into the provinces for the purpose of hearing cases, or delegate this local task to individual members.

The Act also empowers the Minister of Labor, in cases of disputes either in existence or apprehended, to appoint a court of inquiry, one of the objects of which is to place before the public an impartial account of the merits of the case. Such a court of inquiry consists of a single person or of a group headed by a chairman, as the Minister may decide. An important provision of this part of the Act is that the Court may, by order, require any person who, in its judgment, appears to have knowledge of the subject under inquiry to furnish this information in writing, or to appear before the Court for testimony given under oath. This section is notable, as it is practically the only compulsory item in the whole of the modern English peace-time legislation on industrial disputes.

Conclusion. The foregoing general survey of English legislation and practice will show that the dominant principle has been voluntary conciliation. On the principle that desperate diseases require desperate remedies, compulsion was tried for a short period during the war, but, even under such circumstances, it was not successful and was given up with the return of peace. In Britain nothing is more certain than that compulsion is not desired and that it would not be suitable.

During the last ten years the machinery of industrial peace in England has assumed the chaotic character of English law. The various expedients which have been tried have left permanent traces in the form of different types of machinery all aiming to promote voluntary negotiation between employers and employed, with voluntary recourse, as a last resort, to conciliation or arbitration by persons appointed by the Government. Of this nature are the conciliation devices of the Act of 1896; the Joint National Councils of the Whitley scheme, and the Industrial Court of 1919. The latter measure, as we have seen, contains provision for compulsory investigation in the interests of the public, though not for compulsory arbitration. The Trade Boards of 1906 are not essentially a part of the machinery of conciliation and arbitration, though they indirectly promote industrial peace by caring for the interests of the weaker classes of wage-earners. Owing to the official policy of leaving the settlement of disputes, as far as possible, to industries themselves, there must continue to be individuality and, therefore, lack of uniformity in the actual as distinct from the official machinery of industrial peace.

3. Compulsory Arbitration in New Zealand [1]

Background. New Zealand has had an unbroken history of compulsion since 1894. In the history of industrial legislation her laws occupy a unique place, but it must be remembered that her industrial conditions when compulsion was first introduced were also unique. The first Industrial Conciliation and Arbitra-

[1] *Conciliation and Arbitration*, chap. IV, pp. 122–37, by R. N. Gilchrist. Bulletin of Indian Industries and Labor, no. 23.

tion Act of New Zealand was passed in 1894. It is one of the most notable Acts in the whole history of industrial legislation, but it can be properly understood only by a study of its industrial setting. For some years prior to 1894, industrial conditions in New Zealand were depressed. From 1885 to 1890 there was actually a net loss of population of nearly 20,000 people. Scarcity of employment had led to low wages and emigration. Many work-people, however, in preference to emigration accepted lower wages, and by the end of the eighties there were numerous complaints of sweating, especially with regard to women workers. A commission was appointed to examine these complaints, and, although the majority declared that sweating as understood in England did not exist in New Zealand, three out of the nine commissioners considered that sweating did exist. This commission, among other recommendations, suggested that steps should be taken to set up boards of conciliation based on the equal representation of capital and labor. Considerable impetus was given to this idea by the maritime strike of 1890, which had spread from Australia. The maritime strike, which ended in the victory of the employers, was a severe blow to labor, but it also brought home to the community as a whole the necessity of some sort of legislation for the regulation of disputes. Abandoning faith in the efficacy of the strike weapon, the Labor Party of New Zealand turned its attention toward legislation as a means of securing its ends.

Minimum wage. The first "labor" Act was the Factory Act of 1891. This Act prescribed a legal minimum wage. The minimum wage applied to both sexes, and it stamped out sweating. This bi-sexual minimum wage also explains why in later years there has been very little reference to women's work and wages either in the Arbitration Acts or in the awards of the Arbitration Court. Women's work, moreover, was on a special footing in New Zealand. The chief difficulty of New Zealand employers was to secure women workers at all. There was no local supply of female labor, and women were imported from England in considerable numbers on special terms. Subletting of outwork was also prohibited by law. These were by no means the only exceptional features of New Zealand. Her geographical isolation, the size of her population, her abundant natural resources, the type of her exports (mainly agricultural produce), and her tariff must also be kept in mind when comparing New Zealand legislation with that of other countries.

Early form of conciliation. The first New Zealand Industrial Conciliation and Arbitration Act was introduced by the Ballance Government in 1891, and passed in 1894 by the Seddon Government. Its sponsor was Mr. Pember Reeves, then Minister of Labor. The compulsory provisions of the Act were at first strongly opposed by employers; they were twice deleted in the Assembly, and a general election, in which the principle of the Act was the chief subject before the voters, was necessary before compulsion could finally be accepted. The Act, as Mr. Reeves said, had three objects: (*a*) to prevent strikes, (*b*) to strengthen trade unions, and (*c*) to improve the conditions of labor generally. Naturally, therefore, the trade-unionists supported the measure all along, and although the Act was repeatedly amended, the general principles of the first Act have continued throughout.

By the 1894 Act, New Zealand was divided into eight industrial districts, in each of which a conciliation board was set up. Each conciliation board consisted of five members; two were nominated by unions, two by employers, and they together elected an impartial person as chairman. If the four could not agree on a person as chairman, power was conferred on the Governor to nominate. The members of a board held office for three years. The Act also made provision for the creation of *ad hoc* boards for particular disputes. Boards of experts could also be appointed. In 1901 provision was made for special boards, to be constituted if either party asked for one. This clause did not come into operation at all for six years.

Early form of arbitration. The main statutory duty of conciliation boards was to try to make the parties come to an agreement. The boards had power to summon witnesses and to compel evidence. If a settlement was arrived at and accepted by both parties, it was registered as an industrial agreement binding for a fixed period not exceeding three years. It might remain in force after the three years unless one of the parties applied for a revision. If the parties failed to come to an agreement, the boards of conciliation were empowered to issue a particular settlement which either party — employers or workmen — could dispute and refer to the Court of Arbitration. The Court of Arbitration was a single court for the whole country. Prior to 1901 disputes had first to proceed to boards of conciliation before they could come before the Court. After 1901 the disputes were allowed to go straight to arbitration. The Arbitration Court consisted of three members appointed by the Governor. The President used to be a Judge of the Supreme Court, but now he is specially nominated as President of the Court. The other two appointments were made on the recommendation of the employers and workers.

The Act made provision for the registration of unions or societies of seven or more workers. These unions *on registration* could come under the provisions of the Act; i.e., the Act was operative only if the unions themselves wished to come under it.

As in the case of most similar Acts, the original New Zealand Act was often amended. The direction of the amendments was largely determined by the political pressure of different periods. During the first ten years of its existence, labor opinion favored the extension of the Act. The original definition of "worker" was widened to include persons engaged in any kind of employment, and all kinds of disputes concerning conditions of employment were brought under the Act. In the period following 1906 the powers of the Act for the enforcement of the Court's awards were strengthened. More stringent penalties were introduced in 1907. Failure to obey awards was made punishable by imprisonment as well as fine, and subsequently imprisonment was actually inflicted in several cases.

In regard to the actual working of the 1894 Act, Mr. Pember Reeves proved a very false prophet. He reckoned that ninety-nine out of every hundred cases would be settled by conciliation. In practice the conciliation boards were largely neglected; in fact, they were criticized as having raised more trouble than they settled. Their procedure was cumbrous, tedious, and expensive, and their constitution led to partisan feeling. Nearly all the cases brought before them were taken on appeal to the Court of Arbitration. The inevitable result was congestion of work in the Court. Between 1894 and 1907 the binding agreements and awards imposed by the Court reached the number of 535, affecting 78 industries. The delay due to this congestion was used as a plea for strikes, and in 1908 the Government was forced to amend the machinery.

The present system. In 1908 the previous legislation was consolidated in the Industrial Conciliation and Arbitration Act. This Act was amended in 1908, 1910, 1911, 1913, and 1920. As the law stands at present, it provides for the registration of any society consisting of not less than two employers or seven workers "lawfully associated for the purpose of protecting or furthering the interests of employers or workers" under the usual registration conditions. Every society so registered becomes *ipso facto* a body corporate, and members may be sued for fines or dues by the secretary or treasurer of the society in any competent court. The usual provisions for the prevention of multiplicity of unions in an industry or a locality, for cancellation of registration, for periodic returns, etc., are included.

Provision is made for the making, varying, renewing, and cancellation of industrial agreements. These agreements may be made for a term specified in the agreement, but not exceeding three years. They are binding on the parties, and are enforceable in the same way as are awards of the Court. For the purposes of conciliation and arbitration the principal Act empowers the Governor to divide New Zealand into industrial districts. In every district a clerk of awards must be appointed, whose duties are to receive and register all applications for reference to the board or Court, to convene the board, to issue summonses to witnesses, and generally to do the office work connected with the board and Court.

Councils of Conciliation. By the original Act, a conciliation board was established in every district constituted as in the earlier act. Special boards may be created on the application of either party to a dispute. By the Amending Act of 1908 the conciliation boards were abolished. Councils of conciliation were set up in their place. The Governor may appoint conciliation commissioners as necessity arises. Each commissioner is appointed for three years, and exercises jurisdiction over such district or districts as the Governor may determine. Any dispute may be referred by any of the parties concerned, under prescribed conditions, to the commissioner, to be heard by a council of conciliation. One of the conditions of application is that the parties give the number and names of persons (one, two, or three) whom they desire to be appointed as assessors to sit with the commissioner for the hearing of the dispute. Normally these persons must be *bona fide* engaged as employers or workers in the industry concerned, but the commissioner may appoint one outsider as an assessor. The outsider must be recommended by the party concerned. The commissioner and the assessors constitute a council of conciliation.

The powers and duties of these councils are elaborately defined by the 1908 Amendment Act. The chief points are:

(1) It shall be the duty of the council to endeavor to bring about a settlement of the dispute, and to this end the council shall, in such manner as it thinks fit, expeditiously and carefully inquire into the dispute and all matters affecting the merits and the right settlement thereof.
(2) In the course of inquiry the council shall make all such suggestions and do all such things as it deems right and proper for inducing the parties to come to a fair and amicable settlement of the dispute.
(3) The procedure of the council shall in all respects be absolutely in the discretion of the council, and the council shall not be bound to proceed with the inquiry in any formal manner, or formally to sit as a tribunal, or to hear any addresses or evidence save such as the council deems necessary or desirable.
(4) The council may hear any evidence that it thinks fit, whether such evidence would be legally admissible in a court of law or not.
(5) The inquiry shall be either public or private, as the council thinks fit.
(6) Meetings of the council shall be held from time to time at such times, and at such places, within the industrial district in which the dispute has arisen as the commissioner appoints.
(7) No such meeting shall be duly constituted unless the commissioner is present thereat, but the absence of any of the assessors shall not prevent the exercise by the council of any of its powers or functions.

(8) In all matters other than the making of a recommendation for the settlement of a dispute the decision of a majority of the assessors present at the meeting of the council shall be deemed to be the decision of the council, but, if the assessors present are equally divided in opinion, the commissioner shall have a casting vote, and the decision of the council shall be determined accordingly.

(9) A record of the proceedings of every council of conciliation shall be made and preserved in manner prescribed by regulations, or, in default of such regulations, in such manner as the commissioner thinks fit.

(10) The Commissioner shall have the same power of summoning witnesses and of taking evidence on oath, and of requiring the production of books and papers, as if the inquiry were the hearing of a complaint heard before a justice of the peace, and all evidence given on oath before the council shall for all purposes be deemed to have been given in a judicial proceeding before a court of competent jurisdiction.

(11) No person shall be bound at any inquiry before the council to give evidence with regard to trade secrets, profits, losses, receipts or outgoings in his business, or with respect to his financial position, or to produce the books kept by him in connection with his business.

(12) If any person desires to give any such evidence as is mentioned in the last section, or to produce any such books as aforesaid, he may, if the commissioner thinks fit, do so in the presence of the commissioner alone sitting without the assessors; and in such case the commissioner shall not disclose to the assessors, or to any other person, the particulars of the evidence so given, or of the books so produced, but may inform the assessors whether or not, in his opinion, any claim or allegation made by the applicants of respondents in the inquiry is substantiated by the said evidence or the said books.

The parties may appear before the council. An employer may depute an agent to appear for him, but "no barrister or solicitor, whether acting under a power of attorney or otherwise, shall be allowed to appear or be heard before the council." Barristers and solicitors may appear before the Court of Arbitration. The council is empowered to proceed with its inquiry notwithstanding the absence of applicants or respondents. If the parties come to an agreement during the inquiry, the terms must be drawn up as an industrial agreement. If no agreement is reached, the council must try to make a temporary arrangement pending the reference of the case to the Court of Arbitration. The commissioner *at any time* may take steps to secure a voluntary settlement. If no settlement is effected, the council must so notify the clerk of awards, but, prior to each notification, the council may make a recommendation for settlement, and state in the recommendation whether in their opinion, the failure was due to the unreasonableness or unfairness of any of the parties to the dispute. The Act of 1913, to which reference is made later, amplifies this provision. The council may also send a memorandum of partial settlement to the clerk of awards. This official must forthwith refer the case to the Court of Arbitration.

Court of Arbitration. The Act, with its amendments, continues the earlier arbitration machinery. It constitutes a single Court of Arbitration for the whole of New Zealand. The Court consists of three members appointed by the Governor. Of these members one is a Judge of the Court, and the other two are members nominated to represent employers and workers. No one is eligible for appointment as a Judge of the Court unless he is eligible for appointment as a Judge of the Supreme Court of New Zealand, and, if one person is at the same time a Judge of the Supreme Court and a Judge of the Court of Arbitration, he must give priority to his duties as Judge of the Court of Arbitration. Detailed provision is made in the Act for the appointment of the nominated members by the recognized industrial unions. If one of the nominated members is a party to the dispute, an acting nominated member may be nominated in his place. The Act also lays down in detail the jurisdiction of the Court, its procedure, and the regulations regarding evidence. The Court is empowered to compel the attendance of witnesses and the production of books, documents, and other papers relevant to the case under consideration. The Judge and one other member constitute a Court. The decision of a majority of the members present at the

Court is the finding of the Court, but the Judge has the final word if the parties are equally divided. The Court may refer matters before it to a board for investigation and report. Frivolous cases may be dismissed and the parties compelled to pay the costs. The award of the Court on any reference must be made within one month after the Court begins to sit for the hearing of the reference, but provision is made for the extension of the time under special circumstances. Elaborate statutory provision is made regarding the terms of the award and the powers of the Court to extend the award or to add parties to it. The Court is also empowered to prescribe the minimum rate of wages.

Every inspector appointed under the Factories Act of 1908 is an inspector of awards under the Act. It is his duty to see that the provisions of any industrial agreement, award, or order of the Court are properly observed. Inspectors of mines are similarly empowered. Special powers are conferred on these officials to compel employers or workers to produce wages books and overtime books, but they are forbidden to disclose any information which they acquire in the performance of their duties, under a penalty not exceeding £50.

Penalty features. The Act also contains elaborate provision for the enforcement of awards, orders of the Court and industrial agreements. In the principal Act of 1908 any industrial union or industrial association or employer or any worker, whether a member of any such union or association or not, who strikes or creates a lockout or takes part in a movement intended to produce a strike or lockout, is declared guilty of an offense and made liable to a fine. The fine shall not exceed £100 in the case of a union, association, or employer, or £10 in the case of a worker. The strike and lockout provisions were considerably amplified by the Amendment Act of 1908.

The definition of strike in the Amendment Act is notable as one of the most complete definitions in the whole course of Australasian legislation:

> In this Act the term "strike" means the act of any number of workers who are or have been in the employment, whether of the same employer or of different employers, in discontinuing that employment, whether wholly or partially, or in breaking their contracts of service, or in refusing or failing

after such discontinuance to resume or return to their employment, the said discontinuance, breach, refusal, or failure being due to any combination, agreement, or common understanding, whether express or implied, made or entered into by the said workers —

(*a*) with intent to compel or induce any such employer to agree to terms of employment or comply with any demands made by the said or any other workers; or

(*b*) with intent to cause loss or inconvenience to any such employer in the conduct of his business; or

(*c*) with intent to incite, aid, abet, instigate, or procure any other strike; or

(*d*) with intent to assist workers in the employment of any other employer to compel or induce that employer to agree to terms of employment or comply with any demand made upon him by any workers.

The term "lockout" is also fully defined. It means:

The act of an employer in closing his place of business or suspending or discontinuing business or any branch thereof —

(*a*) with intent to compel or induce any workers to agree to terms of employment or comply with any demands made upon them by the said or any other employer; or

(*b*) with intent to cause loss or inconvenience to the workers employed by him or of any one of them; or

(*c*) with intent to incite, aid, abet, instigate, or procure any other lockout; or

(*d*) with intent to assist any other employer to compel or induce any workers to agree to terms of employment or comply with any demands made by him.

The 1908 Amendment Act continues the penalties prescribed in the principal Act for strikes and lockouts, but the fine in the case of lockouts is raised to £500. No worker or employer is liable to more than one penalty in regard to the same strike or lockout. An additional penalty, not exceeding £10 for workers and not exceeding £200 for employers, is prescribed for persons who incite, instigate, aid, or abet unlawful strikes or lockouts. Every person who makes a gift of money for the benefit of a person who is a party to a strike or lockout is declared to be guilty of aiding or abetting the strike.

When a strike or lockout takes place and a majority of the members of any industrial union or industrial association are parties to it, the union or association is to be deemed as having instigated the strike or lockout. An unlawful strike or an unlawful lockout means a strike or lockout of any workers or employer who are bound at the commencement of the strike or lockout by an award or industrial agreement affecting the industry concerned.

The same Amendment Act lays down special penalties for strikes and lockouts in certain specified industries. These industries are:

(*a*) the manufacture or supply of coal gas;
(*b*) production or supply of electricity for light or power;
(*c*) the supply of water to the inhabitants of any borough or other place;
(*d*) the supply of milk for domestic consumption;
(*e*) the slaughtering or supplying of meat for domestic consumption;
(*f*) the sale or supply of coal whether for domestic or industrial purposes; and
(*g*) the working of any ferry, tramway, or railway used as a public carriage for goods or passengers.

If any person employed in any of these industries strikes without having given to his employer, within one month before so striking, not less than fourteen days' notice in writing of his intention to strike, the striker may on summary conviction be fined up to £25. A penalty not exceeding £500 is prescribed for lockouts under similar circumstances. Incitement, instigation, etc., are also made liable to heavy penalties. Provision is also made for the suspension of registration of industrial unions or associations convicted of offenses under the strike and lockout provisions of the Act.

Every industrial union and association and every employer who commits a breach of an award or industrial agreement is made liable to a penalty not exceeding £100 in respect of every such breach. Every worker is liable to a penalty not exceeding £5 for the same offense. These penalties are recoverable by action in a magistrate's court, with the right to appeal, in certain cases, to the Court of Arbitration, the decision of which is final.

The 1908 principal Act makes provision for the appointment of experts as assessors to boards or to the Court.

The 1908 principal Act makes special provision for the Government railways. The Amalgamated Society of Railway Servants of New Zealand is specifically named in the Act as registered under the Act. This society is enabled to enter into an industrial agreement with the Minister. In cases of disputes between the parties the matter may be referred to the Court of Arbitration, before which the Minister may be represented by any officer of the department whom he appoints to act on his behalf. The Court is exempted from interfering with the Amalgamated Society except for purposes as defined in the Act. The Act does not apply to the Crown or any other department of the Government of New Zealand except the railways.

The Amendment Acts of 1910, 1911, 1913, and 1920 do not introduce any fundamental new features. They deal mainly with the procedure and the extension of awards to parties other than those directly connected with the dispute or to the Dominion as a whole.

Results in New Zealand. The working of the New Zealand Acts is illustrated by the following statistical tables, taken from the reports of the New Zealand Department of Labor. The tables cover two periods — 1905–09 and 1910–14:

Year	Recommendations in Conciliation	Awards in Arbitration
1905	10	26
1906	7	52
1907	12	59
1908	15	98
1909	9	88
Total	53 (14 per cent)	323 (86 per cent)
1910	102	89
1911	87	74
1912	119	80
1913	118	94
1914	166	93
Total	592 (56 per cent)	430 (42 per cent)

Strikes and lockouts during the same periods were as follows:

Year	Number
1905	*Nil*
1906	1
1907	12
1908	12
1909	4
Total	29
1910	11
1911	15
1912	20
1913	23
1914	46
Total	115

The most recent figures show that out of a total of 184 disputes dealt with by the commissioners and conciliation councils during 1920, 171, or ninety-three per cent, were settled or substantially settled by them without recourse to the Arbitration Court. During the same year fifty-one industrial agreements, including thirty-five made between parties without having had recourse to a conciliation commissioner or council were made, compared with thirty-one in 1918–19. In 1918–19 and 1919–20, 137 and 168 recommendations of councils of conciliation, respectively, were made, and 130 and 131 awards of the Arbitration Court. During 1919–20, 777 prosecutions were instituted by the Department, of which two were against workers for breaches of awards and 119 were against employers for breaches of awards, agreements, and various other provisions of the Act. Proceedings were taken in nineteen strikes, nine against unions and ten against workers, numbering about 650. Fines varying from £1 to £10 each were imposed in the case of workers and from £10 to £20 on unions.

The foregoing Acts on the whole have secured the support of both employers and labor in New Zealand, although on general principles employers have consistently complained of the interference of a court with their private affairs, and in each individual case they have objected either privately or publicly to compulsory appearance before the boards or the Court, and to the subsequent rearrangements in their businesses which have been forced upon them. On the other hand, the New Zealand system has not thwarted the growth of industry. New enterprises have been started and old enterprises expanded. Profits have not fallen below a reasonable level, and, in spite of their complaints, employers now generally recognize that even the inconveniences of compulsion are preferable to the dislocations of industrial strife. It is to be remembered, of course, that New Zealand is a new country, and that, since the introduction of the first compulsory measure, times on the whole have been good for both capital and labor.

Early attitude of labor favorable. That industrial conditions have been favorable is also borne out by the fact that during the last thirty years wages in New Zealand have steadily been rising. It is true also that prices have risen during the same period, and that labor has not enjoyed a net increase. The majority of the decisions of the boards and courts have been favorable to the workers, although in several cases "no change" has been decreed; in a small number of cases there has been an actual reduction in wages. In other respects the laws have fulfilled the three original objects of Mr. Reeves, although, with regard to the first (the prevention of strikes), it is by no means certain that the compulsory legislation has been the only or even the main cause. In the first ten years of the existence of the 1894 Act, wages were steadily rising owing to flourishing economic conditions. There were no strikes because the causes of strikes were absent. The Legislation has certainly achieved Mr. Reeves's second object (to strengthen trade unions). Preference to unionists is now consistently granted by the Court. Mr. Reeves's third object (to improve the conditions of labor generally) has also been achieved. Labor conditions have certainly improved, and at least one of the causes of such improvement has been the way in which the Arbitration Court has determined the fair wage. Sweating has also been abolished. In the earlier years of the Act, too, labor as well as capital benefited by the absence of strikes.

Recent change in labor's attitude. As the records of strikes from 1910 to 1914 shows, the Act has not been so popular with labor in its later years. Even before the passing of the 1908 Act, there had been several strikes, but this tendency was mitigated when the new Act was passed. From 1912 onward strikes became more frequent. In spite of the apparent fullness of the previous legislation, there was still a loophole which permitted unions to remain outside the scope of compulsion. The Acts of 1894 and 1908 had enabled practically all workers to invoke their help in the settlement of disputes; but trade unions which were dissatisfied with the existing conditions could escape from the provisions of the Act if they cared by omitting to register, or by canceling their registration under the Act. The New Zealand system in this respect was only nominally compulsory. In actual practice workers were never compelled under the Industrial Conciliation and Arbitration Acts. But it was only after the strikes occurring in the period 1910 to 1913 that the Government deemed it necessary to provide for the investigation of disputes in which unions which had withdrawn from or which had chosen not to come under the existing Act were concerned. The Labor Disputes Investigation Act of 1913 was the result.

Disputes Investigation Act, 1913. The Act of 1913 is an application of the Canadian theory to New Zealand conditions. Originally the New Zealand Government meant to include the 1913 Act as part six of a consolidated Industrial Conciliation and Arbitration Act. Owing to pressure of business, however, the main measure was held over, and the section was passed as a separate Act. The Act provided that a society or union of workers must give notice of a dispute to the Minister of Labor. On receipt of this notice the Minister must (*a*) refer the matter to a conciliation commissioner appointed under the 1908 (Amendment) Act, or (*b*) refer it for investigation to a labor dispute committee. This labor dispute committee must consist of not less than three and not more than seven members, as determined by the Minister. The members of the committee, other than the chairman, are appointed by the parties to the dispute in equal numbers. These members must elect their chairman, but, in case of failure to elect, the Minister may nominate.

Upon the appointment of the committee the chairman must fix a time and place for the investigation, advertising notice of it in the newspapers circulating in the district, or in any other suitable way. The committee must investigate the dispute, try to settle it, and, as soon as practicable, send a report to the Minister. If a settlement is not effected, the committee must include in its report such recommendations for settlement as it thinks fit. If the members of the committee are equally divided in opinion, the committee may submit to the Minister not more than two proposals for the settlement of the dispute. On the receipt of the report, the Minister must publish the recommendations or proposals in the newspapers circulating in the district affected, or in any other way he thinks fit.

If a settlement is not arrived at within fourteen days after the delivery of the notice to the Minister, the Registrar is enjoined to conduct a secret ballot of the workers implicated in the dispute to ascertain (*a*) whether a strike shall take place where recommendations for the settlement of the dispute have not been made by a labor dispute committee, and (*b*) whether the recommendations (where such recommendations have been made) should be accepted. Detailed statutory regulations for the conduct of the ballot are laid down. The Act also makes provisions for the making of voluntary agreements.

If the members or any of the members of a union or "society" of workers, to which the provisions of the Act apply, take or takes part in a strike, whether arising out of a dispute with their employers relating to the conditions of their employment or not, (*a*) without notice having been given and before the expiration of seven days after the publication of the result of the secret ballot, or (*b*) at any time before the expiration of the currency of a voluntary agreement, every member is deemed to be party to an unlawful strike and is liable to a penalty not exceeding £10.

At any time during the continuance of a strike which is not an unlawful strike, on the requisition of not less than five per cent of the workers concerned who are members of a union or unions of workers, the Registrar may conduct a secret ballot to ascertain the opinion of all the workers on the continuance of the strike.

The same provisions, *mutatis mutandis*, apply to employers and to lockouts. Penalties are also laid down for aiding or abetting unlawful strikes or lockouts.

The chief differences between the New Zealand and the Canadian Acts are as follows:

(1) The New Zealand Act applies to all trades, the Canadian only to public utilities.
(2) The New Zealand Act provides for more elasticity in the constitution of tribunals for the investigation of disputes.

Canada provides for only one class of board, comprising one representative of each side with an independent chairman.

(3) The New Zealand Act fixes a limit of fourteen days for the investigation of disputes. The Canadian Act fixes no time limit.

(4) The New Zealand Act provides for a secret ballot after the investigation of the dispute has taken place and before a strike may take place. There is no such provision in the Canadian Act.

The 1913 Act came into force on the 1st April, 1914, but no dispute arising under its provisions has yet been reported.

Verdict on the system. In his recent book, *Modern Democracies*, Lord Bryce sums up the present opinion of New Zealand as a whole regarding the compulsory system in these words:

> This opinion seemed to me to be in favor of maintaining the Acts. It is not so proud of them as in the first few years of their working. It admits that they have not solved the industrial problem as a whole, that they are used by the labor leaders to gain something by way of compromise, and soon after to reopen the dispute, and that a still longer experience than twenty-five years have supplied is needed to test them, but it conceives that, by invoking a trusted authority, they have enabled the public to hold the balance fairly between the parties, and have brought its judgment to bear on each dispute. Thus the Acts have made for peace, one of the highest interests both employers and employed can have. Things would be worse without them, because no means at all of settlement would be left, and the disposition to uphold them is all the stronger because they are denounced by the revolutionary Communist Party. I saw no likelihood of their being repealed in the near future.

His own summary of the results of the New Zealand system may also be quoted:

> It has had little success in the line of mere conciliation, and has perhaps done something to discredit that method of set-

tling disputes, which, to be sure, was effecting but little in New Zealand when compulsion was introduced.

It began by strengthening the labor unions, but has latterly tended to create a division between them, some, under the influence of extremists, repudiating any pacific methods of settling industrial disputes.

It has raised wages, yet perhaps no more than they would have risen, ultimately, if not so quickly, by the action of economic causes.

It has not, to any appreciable extent, injured business or retarded the progress of the country.

If it has not extinguished strikes, it has reduced their frequency and their severity.

It has been a mitigation, not a panacea. But, I must again repeat, the results have been attained during a period which has been, as a whole, a period of prosperity and expansion. The real test will come with hard times. Two dangers must not be ignored. One is the growth of a party among the workers which avows its wish to have done with peaceful methods. The other is the possibility that a government might some day, yielding to the pressure of the labor vote, appoint judges virtually pledged to decide according to its wishes. In the present healthy conditions of public opinion such a danger seems remote.

4. The Canadian Industrial Disputes Investigation Act [1]

Background. The Canadian Industrial Disputes Investigation Act of 1907 does not embody the whole of Canadian law for dealing with labor disputes, but was enacted as a supplement to two other laws both of which are still in force. The Conciliation Act of 1900 followed in a general way certain usages long in operation, first as custom, and later as law, in the coal-mining districts of England. That Act created a Department of Labor and provided machinery for mediation or arbitration, but its use was left to voluntary action of the parties to a dispute. The Railway Disputes Act of 1903 gave to the Minister of Labor a limited power of compulsion with respect to the establishment of concili-

[1] From *The Canadian Industrial Disputes Investigation Act*, National Industrial Conference Board Research Report no. 5.

ation boards in labor disputes between railroad companies and their employees. Where such a dispute arose, a board of conciliation could be appointed by the Minister of Labor on the request of either of the parties, without consent of the other. In 1906 these two Acts were consolidated, forming the Conciliation and Labor Act of 1906, in which form they are still operative.

In 1906 a bitter and prolonged strike closed the coal mines of Lethbridge, Alberta. The Deputy Minister of Labor, the Honorable W. L. Mackenzie King, succeeded in bringing about a settlement, but not until much public hardship had developed. The failure of the existing Conciliation Act to prevent this strike revealed the need of further legislation, and the Industrial Disputes Investigation Act of 1907 was a direct result of the sentiment thus aroused.

This Act was amended in 1910, and again in 1918, but since the latter date no alteration or addition has been made, although some changes are contemplated at the approaching session of Parliament.

Procedure under the Act. While the Canadian Industrial Disputes Investigation Act of 1907 applies specifically only to transportation companies, other public utilities and mines, it may also be invoked for settlement of disputes in other industries on application of both parties to a dispute; that is, by mutual agreement. During the war, industries supplying war materials were brought under the action of the provisions previously applying only to transportation companies, other public utilities and mines. The principal provisions of the Act are as follows:

On application in due form by either party to a dispute in an industry covered by the provisions of the Act, the Minister of Labor is required to appoint a board of reference consisting of one nominee of each party and a chairman selected by the two. The Minister of Labor has exercised a certain freedom of judgment as to whether or not the application falls under and meets the requirements of the law, and his right to do so is expressly affirmed in the Amendment of 1918. No person having a direct pecuniary interest in the dispute may be appointed. To prevent a deadlock, in case all other provisions of the Act governing applications for a board have been complied with, but where either or both of the parties fail to agree on nominations, the Minister of Labor may both select and appoint a board.

An application for a board must be made in writing by a party to the dispute, and must be accompanied by a statement setting forth the parties to the dispute, its nature and cause, an estimate of the number of persons affected, an account of the efforts that have been made by the parties to adjust it, and by a statutory declaration that

> failing an adjustment of the dispute or reference thereof by the Minister to a board, to the best of the knowledge and belief of the declarant, a lockout or strike will be declared, and (except where the application is made by an employer in consequence of an intended change in wages or hours proposed by said employer) that the necessary authority to declare such lockout or strike has been obtained; or where a dispute directly affects employees in more than one province and such employees are members of a trade union having a general committee authorized to carry on negotiations in disputes between employers and employees and so recognized by the employer, a statutory declaration by the chairman or president and by the secretary of such committee setting forth that, failing an adjustment of the dispute or the reference thereof by the Minister to a board, to the best of the knowledge and belief of the declarants, a strike will be declared, that the dispute has been the subject of negotiations between the committee and the employer, that all efforts to obtain a satisfactory settlement have failed, and that there is no reasonable hope of securing a settlement by further negotiations.

The Act expressly provides that applications for boards of reference may be made by trade unions, and specifies the manner in which such applications shall be legally presented.

The Act requires that

> Employers and employees shall give at least thirty days' notice of an intended change affecting conditions of employment with respect to wages or hours, and in every case where a dispute has been referred to a board, until the dispute has been finally dealt with by the board, neither of the parties

nor the employees affected shall alter the conditions of employment with respect to wages and hours.

In this connection it is also provided that

If in the opinion of the board either party used this or any other provision of this Act for the purpose of unjustly maintaining given conditions of affairs through delay . . . such party shall be . . . liable to the same penalties as are imposed for a violation of the preceding section.

By the Amendment of 1918 it was provided that

Where in any industry a strike or lockout has occurred, and in the public interest or for any other reason it seems to the Minister expedient, the Minister, on the application of any municipality interested, or of the mayor, reeve, or other head officer, or acting head officer thereof, or of his own motion, may, without application of either of the parties to the dispute, strike, or lockout, whether it involves one or more employers or employees in the employ of one or more employers, constitute a board of conciliation and investigation under this Act in respect of any dispute or strike or lockout, or may, in any such case, if it seems to him expedient, either with or without an application from any interested party, recommend to the Governor in Council the appointment of some person or persons as commissioner or commissioners under the provisions of the Inquiries Act to inquire into the dispute, strike, or lockout, or into any matters or circumstances connected therewith.

The Minister, where he deems it expedient, may, either upon or without any application in that behalf, make or cause to be made any inquiries he thinks fit regarding industrial matters, and may cause such steps to be taken by his department and the officers thereof as seem calculated to secure industrial peace and to promote conditions favorable to settlement of disputes.

The board of reference fully investigates the dispute, and no strike or lockout may legally occur before or during such investigation. Boards are given power to summon witnesses, administer oaths, and to compel witnesses to testify and produce books and other evidence in the same manner as courts of record in civil cases.

If settlement of a dispute is reached by the parties during the course of its reference to a board, a brief memorandum drawn up by the board and signed by the parties is filed with the Minister of Labor. If settlement is not arrived at during the reference, the board is required to make a full written report to the Minister of Labor, setting forth the details of its investigation and its recommendation for settlement of the dispute. The report is filed in the office of the Registrar and copies are sent free of charge to the parties and to any newspapers in Canada which apply for them. The minister may also distribute copies in such manner as he considers desirable, as a means of securing compliance with the board's recommendation. In addition to this, for the information of Parliament and the public, a copy of the report must be published without delay in the *Labor Gazette*,[1] and be included in the annual report of the Department of Labor to the Governor General.

If a question shall arise concerning the interpretation of a recommendation or agreement drawn up by the board, the Minister of Labor may cause the chairman of the board to reconvene the board and make a report on the question.

Not compulsory arbitration. It cannot be too strongly emphasized that the Act of 1907 is not a compulsory arbitration law. While the Act undertook to carry the element of compulsion a step farther than the Conciliation and Labor Act of 1906, it did not alter the principle of voluntary adjustment on which that law was founded.

A Canadian official, who was engaged in the settlement of the Alberta strikes out of which the demand for the law arose, and who was one of its authors, said:

> In the dispute in Alberta referred to in the report [i.e., the one leading to the adoption of the Act], we spent nearly a week trying to get the parties together. We spent nearly another week finding out from each what they were prepared to do. Meanwhile, settlers and others were freezing in their

[1] An amendment to the Act declares that this requirement is met if the *Labor Gazette* publishes a summary of the report.

> homes. We had no powers other than that of a voluntary conciliator to fall back upon. Had we had legislation providing powers of *compulsory investigation*, we could have effected in two days what took nearly two weeks. It was this experience, and similar experiences in other strikes which made us seek to get from Parliament powers of *compulsory investigation*, which meant, to labor, power at the expense of the State, and with the machinery of the State back of it, to choose its own investigator, to summon witnesses, to compel the production of documents, to take evidence under oath, and to give to the public the fullest possible kind of a view of its case, including any injustices under which it might be suffering. This is *the really important compulsory investigation feature* of the Act, not the penalties which we laid to strikes and lockouts.

In pursuit of this aim, and to avoid difficulties involved in compulsory arbitration, the machinery was changed to consist of boards of conciliation and investigation, and although it was the duty of these boards to do all in their power to effect conciliations, and to offer recommendations of settlement, compulsion was restricted to their investigatory function. Compliance with the recommendations of the reference boards is optional; the weight of public opinion alone is relied on to make settlements effective.

The only provision giving mandatory power to the finding of a board is that if, at any time before or after a board has made its report and recommendation, both parties to the dispute agree in writing to be bound by the recommendation of the board in the same manner as parties are bound in the case of a reference to arbitration on the order of a court of record, the recommendation shall be made a rule of the court on application of either party, and shall be enforceable in like manner. Canadian courts, however, have hesitated to regard a recommendation in case of such an agreement as constituting a rule of court.

Reliance on public opinion. The commonly accepted statement that the Canadian Industrial Disputes Investigation Act of 1907 was based on Australian labor legislation is historically incorrect, and tends to give a mistaken conception of its nature. Indeed, this erroneous view has not been without influence in the development of a hostile attitude toward the Canadian Act, which, unlike the Australian legislation, avoids compulsion, as far as possible, and instead is frankly based on an appeal to the power of public opinion.

The Honorable F. A. Acland, Deputy Minister of Labor for the Dominion of Canada, says:

> The theory of the Act is that the board's findings, being based on what is presumed to have been a fair and impartial investigation, will bring an informed public opinion to bear on the matters which have been in dispute, and that either of the disputants who is unreasonable in his attitude will thus be induced to yield a point and accept the recommendations of the board, rather than fly in the face of a public opinion which might be expected to sustain the view of the board; acceptance of the findings, however, no matter how urgent the apparent advantage or necessity, is not legally compulsory.

The text of the Act is brief, and makes no effort to exhaust either the scope of its provisions or the details of their application. In the first important litigation to which it gave rise, and which occurred while the general sentiment in accord with which it was formulated was still active, the decision of the Court contains these words:

> The legislation is tentative, broad and beneficial, and it cannot be expected to cover at once all the little difficulties which may be imagined to arise.

Much, therefore, was left to be determined by departmental decisions.

Administrative interpretations. The Minister of Labor, who is responsible for the administration of the Act, thus far has taken the stand that the penalty provided for strikes or lockouts prior to investigations will be imposed only where prosecution is initiated by one or the other of the disputants. As a matter of fact, although there have been many "illegal" strikes since the Act became effective, the penalty seldom has been imposed. This fact has led to the rather hasty assumption in the United States that the compulsory feature of the Act is a failure. Thus the author of one of the most widely circulated studies of the subject declares:

> The Canadian Act is a compulsory one mainly because penalties are provided for the calling of such illegal strikes, and the essential test of any compulsory law is the extent to which it is enforced. Yet it is in this very important aspect that the Act has failed as a compulsory measure.

While this is to some extent true, it fails correctly to reflect the spirit and intention of the Canadian Act, which should be interpreted in the light of its original purpose.

The Honorable W. L. Mackenzie King has said:

> The Government has never laid particular stress on the penalty end of it. The penalty part . . . has always been treated much in the same light as penalty for trespass.

Examination of the reasons for such opposition to the Act as exists in Canada reveals that only in theoretical discussions do they rest on the failure to impose penalties. On the other hand, one at least of the instances in which a penalty was imposed is prominent among the sources of discontent. This was a case in which an agent of the United Mine Workers was fined for paying strike relief to union members who had violated the law.

One employer has been fined for an illegal lockout, and a few union officials have been fined for inciting strikes, but no effort has been made to penalize a large body of men for striking. The conclusion seems justified, therefore, that criticisms of the Act in the United States, on the basis of its failure to impose penalties, arise from a misunderstanding of its spirit and intention.

A procedure which appears to be responsible for much of the opposition to the Act on the part of organized labor in Canada is the use made of the discretion which it allows to the Minister of Labor to grant or refuse boards of investigation. Boards have been refused in a number of cases where the workers felt that they had a real grievance. The Amendment of 1918, however, expressly conferring this authority on the Minister of Labor is in the nature of a confirmation of his actual practice. In strikes involving several employers or several unions where these employers or unions could not agree on a single representative, the

Minister of Labor has declined to appoint a board. A strike involving many companies is regarded by the Minister of Labor as a separate dispute for each company, and, where the various interests agree on a single nomination, although one board is appointed to investigate the whole trouble, it is legally considered that there are as many separate boards as there are independent employers.[1]

An instructive instance is that of the Thetford mines dispute in 1915. The facts in this case were discussed at the Trades and Labor Congress of Canada, which met at Toronto in September, 1916, and was a factor in the subsequent action of that Congress in calling for abrogation of the Act. The chairman of the Congress described the situation as follows:

> There are five companies controlling the asbestos mines of Thetford. After the miners made an application for a board under the Industrial Disputes Investigation Act, they were informed through a letter from the Department that the industry in which they were employed came under the Industrial Disputes Investigation Act, and that it would be a criminal act on their part to go out on strike. The letter stated that there was not the slightest doubt as to the Act applying to the Thetford mines, and the inference was that the provisions of the Act dealing with penalties for violations would be rigidly enforced if a strike was declared. While that attitude was assumed by the Minister of Labor, the men were prevented from taking any further action in their own interests, other than complying with the law. Suddenly, however, the Department switches and points out that there are five companies controlling the mines at Thetford in which the applicants for a board were employed, and that, because the owners of the mines could not agree upon a representative for the board under the Industrial Disputes Investigation Act, a Board could not be appointed.

The Minister of Labor, who was present at the Congress, in reply said:

> There were five companies to deal with when the request to

[1] An amendment to meet this difficulty is being prepared for presentation to Parliament.

> appoint a board was made. I hold that the Act does not lend itself to the conditions where there are several employers not agreeing. We had a case in Cobalt where there were forty-two companies and I refused to grant a board when application was made by the miners' union. I would refuse to-day.

A delegate then inquired if the men had the "legal right to strike after a board had been refused because the five companies at Thetford mines could not agree upon a representative." The Minister answered that the men could not legally strike, but were compelled to resort to the provisions of the Act and apply for the appointment of a board to deal with each company. Another delegate asked the Minister if a board would have been granted each group of employees in each mine if they had applied separately. The Minister replied that he would not answer the question, because such a situation had not arisen. This, then, appears to be a fixed ruling of the Department of Labor, and one which the workers believe operates to their disadvantage.

During this same discussion of the Thetford mines dispute, the Minister of Labor said:

> At Thetford mines there were two unions, the local union being there before the local of the Western Federation of Miners. . . . I have refused to appoint boards before when there were two unions quarreling among themselves as to what should be done.

Although contrary to previous practice, in at least two notable instances it appears to be the latest ruling of the Department of Labor that boards will not be appointed where two unions exist unless they are in agreement with each other. Both of these rulings are purely administrative and do not arise directly from the provisions of the Act.

Difficulties and objections. The operation of the Act has shown that the opinion of the chairman usually controls the finding of the board. This arises naturally from the fact that employers and employees each select a representative favorable to their respective cause, and it has gradually come to pass that, in almost all cases, these two members of the board disagree and the decision rests with the chairman. On this account it has even been suggested that, in the case of important disputes involving large public issues, the position of the chairman be strengthened by appointment by the Minister of Labor of three outside representatives. It is believed that decisions of a board so constituted would inspire greater public confidence.

In some instances where the report is distinctly favorable to one side, the representative of the other makes use of his legal right to put in a minority report. Mr. Carl H. Mote, in a recent volume, says that even

> public opinion is futile to avert a strike, particularly in those cases where there is a divided report of an investigating committee.

The operation of the Act has further developed the fact that boards are most successful when least formal, and particularly when least legalistic in their attitude and procedure. Boards of which prominent jurists have been chairmen have notably failed. The difficulty of securing acceptable chairmen is very great. Dr. Victor S. Clark, in his investigation for the United States Bureau of Labor of the working of the Canadian Act, says:

> The tendency is to select the same board members repeatedly so that several boards have been identical in different disputes, and one chairman — a professor of economics — has served acceptably on eleven of the twenty-eight boards that have been established.... A judge who organizes a board after the fashion of a court, sets it up on a dais, takes testimony according to legal rules of evidence, enforces legal technicalities, and checks up his witnesses by stenographic proceedings, so far as Canadian experience goes, leaves the parties at the end of their negotiations farther apart than at the beginning, and crystallizes tentative issues into insolvable difficulties.

Dr. Clark, in the same report, quotes an experienced board chairman as follows:

> The most important work is often done outside of regular sessions of the board. We talk to the different parties individually and get to a mutual understanding that way. We

never allow the disputants to leave important matters to the board. We insist that they themselves shall agree on main points.

The informality of procedure is furthered by the Amendment of 1918, which provides that the Minister of Labor, at any stage of the proceedings, may introduce matters other than those appearing in the application and statement, if, in his opinion, it is necessary in order that the board may deal satisfactorily with the dispute.

Yet another source of difficulty that has arisen in the operation of the Act, and not directly from its provisions, but apparently contrary to them, is the delay which may occur in the appointment of a board. The Act says that the Minister of Labor

> shall, within fifteen days from the date on which the application is received, establish such board under his hand and seal of office, if satisfied that the provisions of this Act apply.

For the nine-year period ended March 31, 1916, 191 applications for boards were made, and 169 were established. Of this number only 60 were established within the 15 days. In 14 cases, between 46 and 61 days elapsed between the application and the establishment of the board; in 21 cases, between 31 and 46 days; in 66 cases, between 16 and 31 days.

Commenting on this phase of the administration of the Act, an officer of an international railway union, referring to a specific strike, is reported to have said:

> Our case was begun by notice of a revision of contracts October 1st. The board met December 3d and the decision was given December 20th, allowing the company over two and one half months to prepare for a strike.

Dr. Clark, from whose report this quotation is taken, adds:

> From the men's point of view this particular delay was peculiarly unfortunate, as a financial crisis bringing on a period of unemployment occurred in the interim.

The Act also states that employers or employees shall give at least thirty days' notice of an intended change affecting conditions of employment with respect to wages or hours, and provides a penalty for disregard of this provision. Emphasizing yet further the intention of the Act to avoid delay, the clause allowing this period of thirty days adds:

> But if in the opinion of the board either party uses this or any other provision of this Act for the purpose of unjustly maintaining a given condition of affairs through delay, and the board so reports to the Minister, such party shall be guilty of an offense and liable to the same penalties, etc.

In spite of this provision no complaint among workmen is more common than that wages and hours are changed without notice, and are followed by delays in appointment of boards.

Recent experience under the law undoubtedly is reflected in the amendments that are now being proposed.[1]

One of these amendments seeks to prevent the possibility of a minority of members in a trade union, or a minority of workmen affected where they are not organized, from making an application for a board.

Another proposed amendment would make it impossible for an unlawful organization to claim protection under the Act by contending that it is a trade union within the meaning of the Act.

Yet another amendment is proposed that would extend the time during which a strike is illegal until a copy of a board's report has been delivered to both parties through the Registrar. This would prevent workmen from claiming that their obligations under the Act had been fulfilled before the employers had an opportunity to know the contents of a board's report or to decide whether or not they could accept its recommendations.

An amendment that has not yet taken definite form would make it possible for the Minister of Labor, at his option, to establish one board to deal with a dispute that affects employers and employees in several plants of a given industry. If the employers affected agree to the establishment of a board, it can be done under the present Act, but if the employers disagree and will not nominate a representative on the board, then the Department has no alternative but to establish one board for each com-

[1] April 30, 1920.

pany affected, a procedure which has been found expensive and undesirable.

It is clear that these proposed amendments seek to correct minor defects in the law and to strengthen its central principle of preventing disputes until an investigation shall have been made and the public informed of the merits of the case. None of them seek to overthrow the law or alter its substance.

Results achieved. The number of applications for boards each year since the adoption of the Act shows a gradual decline until the latter years of the war, during which conditions were not normal and the data concerning which calls for special analysis and separate treatment.[1]

	1907 9 mos.	1908	1909	1910	1911	1912	1913	1914	1915	1916 3 mos.	Total
Applications	25	27	22	28	21	16	18	18	15	1	191
Boards refused	3	2	1	5	5	0	3	0	3	0	22
Boards granted	22	25	21	23	16	16	15	18	12	1	169
Strike not averted	1	1	4	4	4	3	1	1	1	0	20

It is apparent from the above figures that in 88 per cent of the disputes referred to boards, strikes or lockouts were averted or ended. If the number of applications refused is added to the number of cases in which strikes or lockouts were not prevented, as also indicating failure on the part of the Act to meet the situation, the proportion of successful conciliations is reduced to seventy-eight per cent. These figures, taken from reports of the Labor Department of the Dominion of Canada, make no reference to the strikes and lockouts occurring during this period in which no application was made under the Act for a board of investigation. The United States Bureau of Labor Statistics, in a report published September, 1917, covering almost the entire period of ten years of the operation of the Act, from March 22, 1907, to December 31, 1916, states that 222 disputes resulting in strikes and lockouts occurred within the jurisdiction of the Act. The number of employees affected in these disputes was 100,608 and the time lost 4,838,647 working days. In 44 of these, involving

[1] In 1919 there were 95 boards in operation, of which 17 were operating at one time. Whether this reflects an abnormal condition due to the war, or is the beginning of a more general use of the provisions of the Act, can be determined only in the light of further experience.

44,086 employees and a time loss of 3,665,969 working days, application was made for investigating boards under the Act. In 18 of the disputes the strike or lockout did not occur until after a board made its investigation and report, while 204 strikes occurred either before or pending board action, and were thus illegal under the Act; of this latter number, 178 strikes or lockouts involving 56,522 employees and a time loss of 1,172,678 days were instituted without either party to the dispute making application for a board.

The number of applications for boards under the section of the Act which allows voluntary application for boards in other than public-service industries and mines, may be regarded as a measure of public confidence in the Act. According to the same report, 691 strikes and lockouts, affecting 149,812 employees with a time loss of 3,254,332 working days, occurred in the period March 22, 1907, to December 31, 1916, in industries falling under this section of the Act. Of this number, in only 26, or about 4 per cent were applications made for a board, and in only 12 of these, affecting 5534 employees, were boards constituted. That is to say, where the Act was left to be voluntarily invoked, only about 1.75 per cent of the disputes occurring were referred to boards.

Reviewing the operation of the Act as thus outlined, it would appear that where boards have been actually constituted they have been reasonably successful in ending or averting strikes or lockouts. Sir George Askwith, who was sent by the British Government in 1912 to investigate the workings of the Act, reached the following conclusions:

> Where it was frankly adopted as a means of preventing disputes, it has worked extremely well, but where for reasons, some apparent and others which can only be guessed at, its introduction has been resented, it has not succeeded to the same extent. In such cases where, by the imposition of penalties efforts have been made to enforce the Act, the results have not been satisfactory.

Attitude of labor toward the Act. For the first two years of the operation of the Act but little opposition appeared; but from that time to the present, hostility among organized labor unions has steadily increased. This opposition is most outspoken on the part of the international labor organizations. The United Mine Workers of America, at their Indianapolis Convention, January, 1909, endorsed the following resolution:

> That we, the delegates from Canada, having had almost two years' experience with said bill, herewith advise our brothers on this side of the line to oppose any such measure of like nature to the utmost of their powers.

The legislative board of the Brotherhood of Locomotive Engineers in November, 1916, passed a resolution:

> That this board do all in its power to have the Industrial Disputes Investigation Act wiped off the statute books.

The president of the Order of Railway Conductors of America, writing on the subject of this Act in the *Proceedings of the American Society of Political Science* in January, 1917, said:

> It only succeeded in breeding an almost universal disgust of, and contempt for, legal machinery designed to settle troubles that should be settled by the parties thereto. . . . The Railway Brotherhoods are almost the only large class of employees who in the Dominion have scrupulously conformed to the provisions of this Act, and they have done this at an immense disadvantage to themselves. . . . It has been demonstrated time and again (and out of this demonstration has grown the attitude of the laborers toward this Act) that the period provided for investigation during which men must remain at work is almost invariably utilized by the employer, regardless of the spirit or letter of the Act, to reinforce himself against efforts of his men to better their condition, and at the end of the period he coolly repudiates the finding of the commission.

On the other hand, the Provincial Workers' Association, an organization of miners in Nova Scotia not associated with the international organization, has "coöperated cordially with the Government and with employers to make it [the Act] a success; and the general officers of the Union commend its influence." But no recent utterance from them on this subject is available.

At the convention of the Trades and Labor Congress of Canada, held at Ottawa September 17, 1917, feeling ran so high as to give rise to a spirited protest against the appearance of the Minister of Labor on the platform of the convention on the opening day. The report of the Fraternal Delegates appointed by this convention to the American Federation of Labor Convention at Buffalo, in speaking of the Act, said:

> A demand was made for the repeal of the Lemieux Industrial Disputes Law, because it was a source of advantage to the employers and hampered the employees. This Act seeks to prevent strikes and lockouts in certain occupations by prohibiting a man's right to stop work, and making it a crime for a union to provide its members with food while out on strike. This, coupled with the absence of an eight-hour law for Government contract work, made the work of the executive officers unusually difficult and created bitter feeling among the involved workers.

The rank and file of Canadian labor express little opposition to the principles of the Act, although some modifications are desired; the official attitude of the international labor organizations in Canada, however, is increasingly hostile.

The State of Colorado has a law which is not dissimilar in principle to the Canadian Act.

The American Federation of Labor, in its report of the proceedings of the Buffalo Convention, in November, 1917, states that:

> Every possible assistance was rendered to the organized workers of Colorado in their effort to secure the repeal of the Industrial Commission Act, which provides for compulsory investigation before the inauguration of a strike or lockout in that State.

This statement may be taken as fairly indicative of the attitude of the American Federation of Labor toward the Canadian Act as it has been administered.

It should not be forgotten that incidents arising in the course of investigations, while actually of minor importance, cause great bitterness in the ranks of workers, however trivial and however casually related to the actual operation of the Act.

Thus, in the opinion of the fraternal delegate to the Buffalo

Convention of the American Federation of Labor, reference is made to a court decision in Nova Scotia in 1912 in which a single union official was convicted of awarding strike benefits to men striking illegally and when four miners, employed by a small coal company, were fined forty dollars each. This was done by action of a Provincial court, but the incident appears never to have been forgotten or forgiven by organized labor. The same may be said of the refusal of the Department to grant boards in the Thetford mines dispute.

Another incident, constantly quoted by laboring men, is that of a decision by a board in a coal-mining strike in Nova Scotia which the workers claimed was interpreted in a manner not in accordance with their understanding of it when they accepted the decision. So influential are these minor incidents that it would not be far from the truth to say that upon scarcely more than five or six such insignificant events the bitterness of feeling, if not the substantial reason for the opposition to the Act on the part of labor in Canada, rests.

It is difficult to escape the conclusion that, whether or not the penalties of the Act are enforceable against workers, the very existence of the Act and the manner of its administration is felt by them to hamper the operations of the unions, and particularly to limit use of the strike to enforce demands.

This conclusion is strengthened by the fact that, of the recommendations of boards since the enactment of the Act, 90 per cent favored the employees and granted a major part of their demands. Also, more than 90 per cent of the boards have been instituted on application of employees. It is not, therefore, dissatisfaction in general with the recommendations of the boards that can account for organized labor's opposition. This must arise from the general operation of the Act and the effect of its continued existence on the statute books, which deprives striking employees, who have not applied for a board of investigation, of the moral support of the community. But perhaps the fundamental reason for this opposition, not to speak of possible antipathy to certain officials, is the fact that the settlement of disputes apart from the manipulation of the union leaders tends to weaken their hold on the rank and file, and their relative importance in gaining concessions for their followers.

It is a noteworthy fact that the representatives of employees on the committee of the Canadian National Industrial Conference which considered the recommendations of the Royal Commission on Industrial Relations, passed a resolution recommending "that employees of all Government bodies should be entitled to the right of appeal under the Industrial Disputes Act so long as that Act remains upon the statute books of Canada."

Attitude of employers toward the Act. It is more difficult to secure frank and definite expressions of opinion from employers in Canada. This reticence may be partly caused by a belief that if they express strong approval of it such an attitude may increase the feeling of organized labor that the Act operates in the interest of the employing class.

A report by G. M. Murray, secretary of the Canadian Manufacturers' Association, made in 1909, after two years' operation of the Act, is not at all enthusiastic as to the benefits derived from it. At that time 49 disputes had been referred to boards under provisions of the Act. In regard to these cases, Mr. Murray says:

> The Labor Department is careful to point out that accompanying each application was a sworn statement to the effect that a strike or lockout (they might have omitted all mention of lockouts, for there were none threatened) would take place in the event of a settlement not being reached. But the Act requires such a statement before a board can be granted and it may well be argued that employees, who have nothing to lose and possibly something to gain from an investigation, will foment trouble and secure from their union a snap verdict to strike, simply in order that their application for a board may be made in proper form, whereas, without the machinery afforded by the Act, the thought of striking would never enter their minds.

This report also complains that the Act

> is readily enforceable as against the employer, for if he locks out illegally, he can be promptly prosecuted and fined, but it is unenforceable as against the employees; for not only is it impracticable to institute proceedings against each of several hundred, or perhaps several thousand employees, but it

> would be the height of folly for an employer to put the law into operation against even a single offender. What he wants is to get his men back at work, not to put them in jail, and the surest way to defeat his own purpose would be to prosecute or persecute the fomenters of the trouble.

Not a few employers believe that compulsory incorporation of all labor organizations would greatly strengthen the Act at this point. Some employers would even have the compulsion which now applies only to the investigation made applicable also to the award. Such a change would, however, amount to a new law operating on a different principle. In general, employers are apt to feel that the Act binds them, but does not bind the worker.

Although Mr. Murray's statement was made only two years after the Act went into effect, it undoubtedly reflects the general opinion of the same group of employing interests to-day.

Summary and conclusions. In conclusion, the following points appear to be substantiated by the evidence that is available:

(1) The commonly expressed opinion, that the failure to impose penalties for illegal strikes is the principal weakness of the Act and the cause of its comparatively infrequent application, is not borne out. The position taken by the Department of Labor in regard to initiating prosecutions for infractions of the Act, in which they leave this to be done by prosecution of the aggrieved party, appears to be the only practicable attitude, and has probably saved the Act from early repeal. The penalty always exists as a possibility, and the entire attitude of organized labor indicates that it feels the restraint which the Act exercises. This restraint, however, arises quite as much from the mere fact of declaring the strike illegal under the Act as from the penalty provision. The Act might be quite as strong if the penalty provision were repealed. The few cases in which penalties have been imposed are responsible for much opposition to the Act.

(2) The operation of the Act has signally failed to inspire complete confidence of workers. It has led them to believe that the Act was not immune from legalistic manipulation, and that under it their rights or claims may be thwarted, not on reasonable grounds, but by legal technicalities. As evidence of this they cite the administrative delay which, although contrary to the

spirit of the Act, has occurred perhaps in the majority of the disputes that have been referred under it; also the refusal of the Department to appoint boards in a number of instances where the men felt that they had real grievances, particularly where two or more employers, or two or more unions involved in an individual dispute, cannot agree on a single representative. As the operation of the Act has largely covered a period during which the international labor organizations have been struggling for a foothold in Canada, sometimes in sharp opposition to the established local trades unions, this ruling has caused much discontent, the workers feeling that it interferes with what they believe to be their right to organize.

(3) The requirement of the Act, that a board may not be applied for unless one or the other of the disputants makes a statutory declaration that a strike or lockout will otherwise occur, has not operated advantageously, and is no doubt chargeable with some of the illegal strikes that have occurred. A group of organized employees cannot declare that a strike will occur as the result of any dispute without an official vote of their organization. Such a vote is not obtained without considerable effort, and having been obtained the men are but little inclined to forget the authority which it gives them to declare a strike. It is difficult to see what particular strength this provision adds to the Act, but it is quite easy to see the difficulty which it occasions. The employer in order to make application for a board must make a statutory declaration that, to the best of his knowledge and belief, his firm will otherwise declare a lockout, and few employers are ordinarily willing to make such a declaration, for by so doing they immediately forego the good-will and backing of the public.

(4) Owing to the fact that incidental administrative rulings tend to become fixed as precedents, and further that, especially among workers, incidental causes of irritation are held in memory for many years, opposition to the Act is cumulative and tends to become stronger, despite the fact that its operation may have been generally beneficial to the workers themselves.

(5) The existence of the Act on the statute books has acted as a wholesome restraint both on employers and employees through a period of great industrial unrest; it has served in some degree to

crystallize public opinion and in particular cases to make it effective for maintenance of industrial peace.

(6) Investigations have been most successful when most informally conducted; introduction of legal machinery is almost certain to destroy their usefulness.

(7) Where investigations have been fairly conducted, with no unfortunate administrative irritations, and with tactful, informal procedure, resultant recommendations have been almost universally backed by public opinion and accepted by the disputants.

(8) The Act after thirteen years of operation has sufficient support in Canadian public opinion to retain a place on the statute books, and to invite legislative consideration for its improvement without vital alteration.

5. Conciliation through Trade Agreement [1]

The foundations of the joint conference. Knowledge of the rise of the miners' organization, its evolution into a thoroughly organized and well-administered body, and the development of operators' organizations along similar lines, affords a basis for understanding the full significance of the interstate joint conference. The joint conference of the central field is the central market for mine labor. Collective bargaining has here reached as high as point of development as in any other industry in our country. An insight into its complexity makes one realize how far removed the average miner is from the old days of individual dealing with his employer. Under individual bargaining the employee was forced to take the wages the employer offered, and his inability to control the sanitary arrangements and dangers under which he worked put him at the mercy of his employer. In short, it is the contrast between the policy of expecting the self-interest of the employer to work out to the best interests of society and the growing modern concept that human life and public warfare should be held in higher esteem than mere acquisition and preservation of property. Nor does collective bargaining mean that a dead level of uniformity must exist among the laborers. According to Mr. John Mitchell, trade-unionism stands for competition among workmen on "the basis of effi-

[1] From *Conciliation and Arbitration in the Coal Industry in the United States*, by A. E. Suffern, pp. 142–52; 170–73. Houghton Mifflin Co., publishers.

ciency and not upon that of reduced wages, lengthened hours, or any abatement of the conditions fixed by the collective bargain."

The "right" of organization and representation. A chief foundation stone in the structure of the interstate conference is the "right" of the employee to organize which carries with it the right to be represented in bargaining with the employer. Labor thus becomes a product for sale, and, except for the fact that it is a perishable commodity, the seller of the same is on a par with the coal operator. Organized labor is coming to the point where it deplores strikes as much as any other group in the community. The fact that these elemental rights are disputed or not recognized is the cause of most of the strikes. This is because employers are unwilling to allow labor the benefits of coöperation and representation. Strikes are to be used only as a last resort in obtaining justice, for "the victories won in conference halls, where the elements of strength are the enlightened logic of the combatants, are the victories which leave no wounds to heal and are the greatest victories of them all."

The encouragement of good feeling. As we have seen, there was a period when the miners had to be educated in regard to the benefits of conciliation and coöperation. In the early days of the interstate conference the leaders on both sides felt called upon to impress upon the minds of their constituents the importance of the conciliation movement. Hard experience had taught them that they had hit upon something worth considering by the rank and file on either side. The occasion of electing a permanent chairman was generally used to lay a groundwork. "This is not an arena where foe meets foe, but it is a friendly meeting-place of those who are interested for the benefit of all. And happy will be the day when capital and labor can meet on the same platform and shake hands with true friendship." President Ratchford at the miners' convention laid emphasis on the importance of maintaining the joint conference by pointing out that "the man or men who throw a single obstacle in its way [are] undeserving of a place in the councils of miners or operators, and will be adjudged guilty of a crime against hundreds of thousands of men, women, and children whose comfort depends so largely upon its consummation." The evolution in attitude of both sides is plainly shown, in the conferences of recent years, by the brevity with which each side exchanges felicitations and proceeds to the necessary business.

Formulation of principles. Although the joint conferences had begun in 1898, it was not until 1902 that a clear formulation of their basic principles was adopted. The following resolutions were presented by Mr. Herman Justi, commissioner for the Illinois Coal Operators' Association:

> First. That this movement is founded, and that it is to rest, upon correct business ideas, competitive equality, and upon well-recognized principles of justice.
>
> Second. That, recognizing the contract relations existing between employer and employee, we believe strikes and lockouts, disputes and friction, can be generally avoided by meeting in joint convention and by entering into trade agreements for specified periods of time.
>
> Third. That we recognize the sacredness and binding nature of contracts and agreements thus entered into, and are pledged in honor to keep inviolate such contracts and agreements made by and between a voluntary organization, having no standing in court, on the one hand, and a merely collective body of business men doing business individually or in corporate capacity on the other, each of the latter class having visible and tangible assets subject to execution.
>
> Fourth. That we deprecate, discourage, and condemn any departure whatever from the letter or spirit of such agreements or contracts, unless such departure be deemed by all parties in interest for the welfare of the coal-mining industry and for the public good as well, and that such departure is first definitely, specifically, and mutually agreed upon by all parties in interest.
>
> Fifth. Such contracts or agreements having been entered into, we consider ourselves severally and collectively bound in honor to carry them out in good faith in letter and in spirit, and are so pledged to use our influence and authority to enforce these contracts and agreements, the more so since they rest in the main upon mutual confidence as their basis.

A sixth resolution providing for arbitration by a board of referees was thrown out.

The conference at work. The conference has generally been held during the latter part of January and the beginning of February. The miners' convention is held previous to this and their demands are formulated. This gives the joint conference plenty of time to reach an agreement before the previous agreement expires, usually April 1st.

Until 1908, the interstate joint conference was made up of miners and operators from the States of Illinois, Ohio, Indiana, and Pennsylvania. In that year the miners and operators of Illinois failed to attend the conference, for reasons which will be taken up later.

The operators not only expect the miners to keep their own members within the agreement, but rely on them to coerce a delinquent operator. This they can do by calling a strike, which may be more effective than any fine by an operators' association. But the cost of the procedure falls upon the miners, and it is a losing fight if the operator can get plenty of non-union labor. In fact, the chief burden of the cost of making competitive conditions uniform in the various district comes on the miners. "No attempt is made to make wages uniform or the earning capacity of the men equal between the different districts, or within the districts themselves, the principal object being so to regulate the scale of mining as to make cost of production practically the same in one district that it is in another, regardless of whether or not the earnings of the miners are equal."

Organization and rules. The organization and work of the conference is unique and interesting. The president of the miners is generally elected temporary chairman, which gives him a chance to extend felicitations on the continuation of the movement and to introduce local and national men of prominence who have been asked to address the conference. A committee on credentials and a committee on rules and order of business and permanent organization are then selected. These committees are made up of two operators and two miners from each State. A recess of a couple of hours is taken in order to give the committees time to make up their report. In connection with the report of the committee on rules and order of business and permanent organization the name of an operator is suggested as permanent chairman, a miner as secretary, and a representative of the operators as assistant secretary. The rules of the convention contain provisions for definite hours of meeting and adjournment, but special meetings or an evening session are allowable, which provision is often made use of at critical times when an agreement seems about to be reached. The miners' representatives occupy the right of the hall and the operators the left. Each State has the same number of voters, four votes for the operators and four votes for the miners. No vote is declared carried except upon the affirmative vote of both operators and miners from all the States. The unanimous vote shows that each side fears to trust the issue to the other side plus perhaps one vote from its own. In questions of mere procedure the rules in any standard manual of parliamentary procedure are in force. But the rule requiring unanimous vote on all main and principal questions is never suspended. "Main and principal questions" are "all questions affecting the proposed scale and agreement." Each State has four operators and four miners on the scale committee, who are appointed with the understanding that each representative shall have an alternate who has all the privileges of the scale committee, but cannot "vote except in the absence of his principal." In the formation of this method of representation on the scale committee in the conference of 1898, the minority of the committee on rules and regulations stood out strongly for representation on the basis of tonnage of the respective States, "one vote, miner and operator, respectively, for each five million tons or major fraction thereof, mine-run coal, produced in the year 1896." The majority insisted that their method was fairer to all concerned, and that it was not desirable that "conclusions" should "be forced on any State." The sessions are open to the public except when otherwise ordered, and as a result of this both sides suffer misrepresentation at the hands of newspaper reporters. But undoubtedly it is a considerable asset to the conciliation movement in convincing the public that their proceedings are open and above board and in winning support for the side which has the right of it.

The order of business. The order of business consists of the report of the credentials committee, report of the rules and regulations committee, appointment of the scale committee, report of the scale committee, and adjournment. This appears rather a simple order of business, but what seems at the most to be a few days' work has lengthened into weeks at critical times in the industry. After the report of the credentials committee has been accepted, each side learns what the other is expecting by the presentation of formal demands. These demands generally pertain to an increase or decrease in the mining rate, uniform mining system (the miners generally asking for mine-run rather than screen system), uniform wage scale for outside and inside day labor, differential per ton between pick and machine mining, advance in payment for yardage and deadwork, a check-off system by which the dues and assessments are deducted from the miners' wages and paid to the United Mine Workers, settlement of internal difficulties and inequalities in the various districts, etc. Discussion of these demands brings out the dissatisfaction that both sides have felt during the life of the previous agreement, and one would imagine that such diametrically opposite views as are there expressed could never be reconciled. On a vote to accept either the miners' or the operators' demands, the miners vote unanimously one way and the operators unanimously the other. If the demands had to be reconciled there in open convention, they probably never would be settled, but the machinery of the scale committee is now set in motion, and the discussion is carried on by thirty-two men and their alternates instead of by several hundred. The convention adjourns subject to call by the scale committee (or chairman) when the committee is ready to report. The scale committee is governed by the rules of the convention, and here the minutest details of the industry are taken up. It does not take long for each party to discover that there are two sides to every question which is brought forward. The only hope for an agreement lies in a willingness to recede from the arbitrary positions which each side has taken. Usually each side has certain demands which it will not withdraw, but others which it is willing to trade on. These demands are generally discovered by discussion and consideration, in the form of a motion of the formal demands that each has presented. Both sides are desirous of carrying full and unanimous conviction of the reasonableness of their demands before they are allowed to come to vote, for they always have hanging over them the knowledge that one dissenting vote will kill their proposition. Here one has a chance to see all the foibles of human nature at play, but withal mixed up with banter and good fellowship. Out of it comes a respect for the man for his real worth. Both sides realize that they cannot be governed by the personal concessions they are willing to make, for ultimately they are held responsible by their constituents. They must present an agreement to the convention that both sides feel will be accepted and lived up to by the rank and file. If the scale committee reaches an agreement, the convention is called to order and the report of the committee presented. If there is any dissatisfaction it is sure to be heard, but the leaders of both sides on the scale committee defend their course of action and advise acceptance of the agreement that has been reached. If the scale committee has been unable to agree, this is reported to the convention and there is another period of general discussion in the conference.

The leaders of the miners prove themselves just as capable and well informed as the best of the operators. It was in 1902 that the miners established a department of statistics to keep themselves in touch with prices and conditions of trade. They have used the information obtained in this manner in a very effective way. In 1906, when the operators offered to open their books for inspection, that a scale might be made on the basis of profits and selling prices, Mr. Mitchell very properly wished to know the connection between the coal companies and the railroads, who owned the stock, and how much of the profits of the coal companies were absorbed to pay freight rates, etc. At the most critical times and when the heat of the discussion runs highest the speaker on the floor is given a fair hearing. We give here a report of a convention incident:

Mr. —— (evidently from the miners' side, interrupting Mr. R., an operator). What are you doing, Mr. R.?

Mr. R. I am working, and you would be a great deal better off if you were doing the same thing.

Mr. W. (miner). I protest against any unfair treatment from this convention to any man who has the floor.

Mr. D. (miner). I move that the first man who does anything of this kind be put out. If the operators, when Mr. Mitchell or Mr. Lewis were on the floor, would act as our delegates are doing, would you like it?

Mr. L. (miner). I believe it is time to appoint a half-dozen sergeants-at-arms in this convention. Any man who interrupts any speaker on the floor ought to be ejected from the hall, I don't care who he is.

Mr. R. (operator). They needn't do that to protect me; I can take care of myself.

Mr. K. (chairman). I believe it is the feeling of the members on both sides, with a few exceptions, that every speaker should be given a fair hearing.

After further discussion in general convention the scale committee is recommitted to the task of reaching an agreement. Such modifications as each side are willing to make are brought forward, but here as elsewhere the unanimous vote required results in a process of elimination until something is brought forward upon which all can agree. If it becomes evident that such a large number as are in the scale committee cannot agree, a sub-scale committee, of two operators and two miners from each State, is selected by the scale committee. Stenographic reports of the convention and scale committee deliberations are made, but no record of the sub-scale proceedings is kept. The last thing that either party wants is a failure to agree, because it means loss of money. They realize that they must get together and undergo the difficult process of changing their minds — in part, at least. Various sources of information seem to indicate that this is a rather heating and exciting process. In the past it has been part of a sort of gentlemen's agreement that the participants should not reveal the difficult contortions some individuals have had to go through with in order to accomplish this result, but in the conference of 1910 the rather disagreeable practice was begun of making reference in general conference to what went on in the committee meeting. This called for an explanation on the part of the individual accused, with the result that it all went down on the record. It does not look well, and is likely to cause distrust. The sub-scale committee is appointed with the feeling that it is a last resort. When it brings forth an agreement after much labor and discussion, its report is accepted by both the scale committee and the convention. Neither side has received all it wanted, but each feels that it has obtained all it can get and that work may as well begin on this basis. In cases where even the sub-scale committee has failed to agree, the convention has adjourned and a suspension of work takes place until the leaders could succeed in getting together another conference.

Results of collective bargaining. During the time the joint agreement has been in force it has not been without its fruits for both sides. The operators have been able to maintain more stable industrial conditions and less fluctuation in prices. The miners have been able to build up an organization which has bettered their conditions and helped the operators to equalize competition. In the Southwest and Northwest the miners have reached out and forced state and interstate agreements whose scales are governed largely by the scale of the central field. The miners, by extending their organization so widely, have made it possible for the operators to grant conditions of labor which they would never have conceded had they not gone into effect generally. This is shown by the hardship which the various States inflict on industries when they pass laws compelling their industries to compete with conditions in other States where such laws do not exist. The joint movement has brought, by unity of action, the abolition of company stores and company tenements, the inauguration of the eight-hour day, regulation of screens, equalization of wages of different classes, and the improvement of working conditions and safety appliances. Dockage has been lessened and checkweighmen are employed, so that the miner is paid for the coal he produces. The principle of conciliation is ramifying every part of the industry, strikes have been lessened, and the movement is working out a better understanding of the difficulties with which both sides have to contend.

Although capitalization, production, number of mines, and the total of employees in the industry continued to increase, wages did not rise to a new level until collective bargaining became effective. When wages are once on this level we see no steady absorption of the value of the product, but wages fluctuate with the varying prosperity of the industry. In fact labor is engaged in a constant struggle to maintain this new level and make wages more responsive to changes in prices and cost of living.

There are several factors which make this struggle difficult. We have seen that the effect of machinery has been to decrease wages by helping to glut the market and lessen the number of days the miners could work. Added to this element is the constant increase in the number of employees, which causes a further reduction in the number of working days for those already in the industry. These conditions are made possible because the demand does not keep pace with the ability to supply the market. Aside from the advantages which might have accrued to the operator from the miner's patronage of company stores, there is another urgent reason for desiring to retain a surplus of men on the premises — the seasonal demand for coal. Further, it does not pay to mine coal and store it, thus giving fewer men steady employment, for the handling is a great expense and the coal deteriorates in appearance and quality. For this latter factor in the situation the public is largely responsible because consumers are very slow about buying coal ahead of the season, even though they are offered rates that are equal to good interest on the money invested.

The full import of the new level of wages for the worker is seen when we consider that in spite of the reduction of possible working days by the above factors, we find that in 1911 he gets a larger yearly wage for working 167 days than he did for 229 days in 1893. This result is obtained by gradually forcing up the average daily wage. The same general principle is shown in the other States, though not quite so strikingly. The force of collective bargaining is further shown by the fact that the prices paid for mining were more responsive in the bituminous field than in the anthracite region and also by the fact that the general level of average daily wages in Illinois and Ohio is kept on a higher plane than those of West Virginia. Another interesting consideration is that in spite of the eight-hour day the production continues to increase, although the men are working a less number of days. Besides the increased efficiency that may result from shorter hours, the increased use of machinery and a greater number of men in the industry accounts for this.

In connection with the increase of capitalization, production, and number of mines it may be observed that we have an exception here to one of Professor Moore's laws of wages, "that the more rapid the increase of capital in industry, the more rapidly do wages increase." The situation may be partly explained by another of his laws, "that the fluctuations of wages about their general trend are inversely correlated with the machine power with which the laborers work." But the trouble is that there is not a general trend, and the only power which the laborer has to make wages respond to prosperity is his united stand for higher wages. Nor in this case does the "rate of wages, amount of employment, and length of the working day" necessarily improve "with the increasing concentration of industry," but rather with the increase of the bargaining power of the laborer.

6. Conciliation and Arbitration in the United States [1]

State laws. In the United States most of the individual States have legislation dealing with industrial disputes. In one of them, Wyoming, there is a constitutional provision to that effect. It is impossible here to give any detailed analysis of the voluminous State legislation on this subject. Most of the States have permanent boards of conciliation and arbitration. These boards, as a rule, consist of two to six members. The usual number is three. Usually the State law provides that one member shall be representative of employees. All but two States provide for the representation of employers. In some States the particular local circumstances have dictated a peculiar constitution, e.g., in Oklahoma the farmers are represented on the board. In several States not more than two members of the board may be chosen from the same political party. In some States the Labor Commissioner acts as a board of conciliation or as a mediator. In States with industrial commissions a mediator is usually appointed with temporary powers for arbitration.

It may be noted that a favorite instrument of labor administration in America has been the industrial commission of inquiry. For many years the various Governments in America have conducted systematic inquiries into labor conditions and problems. During the period 1910 to 1915 there were, in all, close on thirty State commissions and one Federal commission in the United States, the purpose of which was to study industrial accidents and workmen's compensation law. Notable amongst these commissions has been the Factory Investigation Committee of New

[1] From *Conciliation and Arbitration*, by R. N. Gilchrist, chap. VI, pp. 164–72. Bulletin of Indian Industries and Labor, no. 23.

York, the reports of which led to the enactment of a large number of labor laws. These commissions originated usually in the demands of private parties for legislation or for inquiry, and the reports have served a very useful purpose in providing information to the public on labor matters and in aiding the legislatures.

In regard to compulsion the practice of the various States is by no means uniform. Compulsory investigation is provided for in several States. In these cases the State Board of Arbitration must conduct an investigation on the occurrence of certain circumstances as prescribed in the State law. These circumstances may be failure to settle a dispute by mediation or arbitration, or a demand by the Governor, or when the dispute is brought to the knowledge of the board. In other States such investigation is not obligatory, but may be carried out. In New York the Industrial Commission may direct that such an investigation should take place. In some States compulsory investigation may be employed when, after both parties refuse to go to arbitration, the dispute is likely to cause inconvenience to the public, in other States simply when both parties cannot agree to go to arbitration. In one or two cases compulsory investigation must take place whenever a dispute occurs.

The practice also varies in regard to the enforcement of awards. In some States, if arbitration has been agreed upon by both parties, the award is obligatory. In some cases a breach of the award may be treated as contempt of court. In other cases an option is given of a fine or imprisonment.

It may be noted that in only one State, Colorado, has the principle of the Canadian Act been adopted. But in several States a voluntary agreement to go to arbitration must include a promise to abstain from a strike or lockout pending the arbitration proceedings. In some States notice must be given of an intention to stop work. In others, strikes during arbitration and for some time after an award, without a specific number of days' notice, are altogether unlawful, and render the organizers and participants liable to damages.

Federal Acts. In the United States there have been passed five principal Federal Acts dealing with industrial disputes. The first Act was passed in 1888. It provided for voluntary arbitration on the initiative of the President, with compulsory investigation and the publication of the decision of the investigating authority. This Act empowered the President to appoint two commissioners, who, acting with the United States Commissioner of Labor, could investigate disputes and make a report. This investigation could be made on the application of either of the parties concerned, or on that of the Governor of the State in which the dispute took place, or on the President's own initiative. This Act was practically never brought into operation.

Erdman Act. The second Act, the Erdman Act, was passed in 1898. This Act repealed the 1888 Act. The Erdman Act applied specifically to transport workers. When a dispute was threatened, the Chairman of the Interstate Commerce Commission and the United States Commissioner of Labor, on the application of either party, were enjoined to make an attempt to settle the dispute by mediation. If mediation was unsuccessful, it was the duty of the mediators to try to bring the case to arbitration. If the parties agreed, a board of arbitration of three members was formed; one represented each party, and the third was nominated by these two, or, failing their nomination, he was nominated by the Commissioner. The award of this court was made binding, and neither side was permitted to cease work for three months after the award without at least thirty days' notice. It was directed that each award should continue in operation for at least one year and that no new arbitration should take place on the subject during that time. The arbitrators were given powers of compulsory investigation. Violation of the compulsory clauses made the guilty parties liable to damages.

In actual practice, although the arbitration clauses were regarded as the most important features of this Act, the mediation provisions proved of most value. Conferences were arranged with the parties separately. Neither party knew what the other was doing, and a joint meeting was held only after a settlement had been reached or the parties had decided to go to arbitration. These conferences proved to be much more useful than the judgments given in the few cases in which the arbitration machinery was invoked. In all, during the currency of the Act, only twelve cases were submitted to arbitration, of which only eight passed the mediation stage. Four of the cases were submitted directly. It is reported that in these twelve cases, in only three instances were the two arbitrators nominated by the parties concerned able to agree on the third member. But it is noted that, where an arbitration award was actually given, there is no case reported of an actual breach of the award. From 1898 to 1912, in all, forty-eight applications for mediation or arbitration were received. Of the 44 cases in which mediation was invoked, only eight ultimately went to arbitration.

Newlands Act. The third Act, the Newlands Act, was passed in 1913. In this Act provision is made for a Commissioner of Mediation and Conciliation, to be appointed for seven years by the President, with the advice and consent of the Senate. This Act enjoins the President to nominate two other Government officials who, acting with the Commissioner, constitute the United States Board of Mediation and Conciliation. Provision is also made for the appointment of an Assistant Commissioner. The duties of this Board of Mediation and Conciliation, as prescribed in the Act, are similar to those prescribed in the previous Acts, but the Newlands Act gives more detailed statutory prescriptions in regard to the procedure and form of arbitration. The Board was empowered to offer its services in any dispute which was likely to lead to the interruption of traffic, and, on the failure of mediation, a board of arbitration was to be formed with either three of six arbitrators. With the consent of both parties the board of arbitration was given powers of compulsory investigation.

Later developments. The Newlands Act did not have a long life. It broke down in 1916, when a railway dispute required the special intervention of Congress. The Board of Mediation and Conciliation offered to mediate in the dispute after the parties had failed to agree to go to arbitration and a date had been fixed for a strike. The mediation failed, and, to save the situation, the President tried to compromise by offering the concession of an eight-hour day and a commission to examine the other points in dispute. The men agreed, but the managers demurred. As a result, Congress passed an Act, the Adamson Act, which incorporated the proposals of the President. Later in the same year, the Newlands Act again broke down, and compulsory Federal legislation was contemplated. The entry of America into the war, however, turned the attention of Congress to more urgent matters. Under war conditions the failure of the Newlands Act was covered up by emergency war measures. The railways to all intents and purposes were taken over by the Government. A wage board was set up to advise on railwaymen's wages, and boards of adjustment, on which there was equal representation of workers and the administration, were created to settle disputes. A division of labor, at the head of which was a railway union official, was created to act as a connecting link between the boards and the men. These boards proved acceptable to the men, who, it may be noted, steadfastly refused to submit their cases to arbitrators.

A fourth agency for settling disputes was set up in 1913, when the Department of Labor was created. The Act creating the Department empowers the Secretary of Labor to act as a mediator and to appoint conciliation commissioners when he considers that such appointment is necessary in the interests of industrial peace. Power is given in the Act to refer cases to arbitration when mediation fails, but the mediators do not act as arbitrators. From 1915 to 1919, nearly 3650 cases were dealt with by the Secretary of Labor, and of these agreements were effected in nearly 2550 cases. In the first year after the armistice 1780 cases, of which 1223 were settled, were dealt with by the departmental machinery.

Railroad Labor Board. The purely war machinery, the chief part of which was the National War Labor Board, need not concern us here. In the Transportation Act of February, 1920, however, we have an interesting peace-time measure, the fifth of its kind, which incorporates some of the war-time lessons. The main features of this measure, which declares that it is the duty of railwaymen to do all they can to avoid interruption of traffic, are: (*a*) if a dispute arises, if possible it must be decided in a conference representative of both sides; (*b*) if grievances regarding rules and working conditions cannot be settled in this way, they must go before boards of adjustment, to be established by agreement between any railway or group of railways and its employees. The composition of the boards is left mainly to the parties themselves. The Railway Labor Board, the management, the organized workers, or a hundred workers by a written petition may set the machinery in motion. The Act also establishes a Railway

Labor Board. This is the final court for the settlement of railway disputes. The members of the Board, nine in number, equally representative of workmen, employers, and the public, are appointed for five years. The representatives of employers and workmen are chosen from a list of nominees (not less than six) submitted by their respective groups. During their tenure of office the members cannot be active members of unions or have financial interest in railway stock. Cases may be referred directly to the Board, or after failure of reference to the boards of adjustment. Decisions are by majority vote, but in cases directly referred to the Board, at least one of the representatives of the public must agree to the decision. It may also be noted that the Board is empowered to revise a decision of an earlier conference, if that decision is likely to increase costs and to raise railway rates.

The powers and duties of the Board of Mediation and Conciliation (established in 1913) do not extend to any dispute which is received for hearing by an adjustment board or by the Railway Labor Board.

One of the notable features of this Act is the place it gives to the public, the third party in disputes. In public-utility services like railways this aspect of the American Federal law is coming more and more into prominence, and many American observers look with much favor on the compulsory investigation provisions of the well-known Lemieux Act of Canada.

From a survey of American legislation it appears that the best results have been achieved by conciliation or mediation. Even in the war, compulsory arbitration was avoided, save in a few extreme cases. Up to the present, the powers of compulsory investigation and public report which are granted by many of the American laws have been little used, though much favored in certain quarters. It is stated that the American worker is still very suspicious of the impartiality and ability of the American official, whether Federal or State.

The Kansas Court. Special note may be made of the Kansas law, which has attracted wide attention in America, and the Colorado law, the only law in the United States drawn up on the basis of the Canadian Industrial Disputes Investigation Act.

The Kansas law, which was passed in January, 1920, was the

result of a strike of coal miners. It met with strong opposition from both capital and labor, but Louisiana, Texas, Michigan, New Jersey, Oklahoma, and Illinois have drafted bills on the Kansas model. The Kansas law sets up a Court of Industrial Relations. This Court is composed of three judges appointed for three years by the State Governor. The Kansas Court is not a joint but a neutral body. The interests of the consumers and the public are chiefly represented. The scope of the law explains the neutral nature of the Court. The Act declares that a large number of public utility services and industries concern the public interest, and, therefore, ought to be subject to supervision by the community as organized in the Government. Food production, the manufacture of clothes, transport services, mining and production of fuel, all come within the ambit of the law. When a dispute arises in any of these industries, the Industrial Court, on its own initiative or on the request of any ten citizens in the locality who pay taxes, may summon the parties to appear before it and inquire into the conditions of the industry affected. The Court is enjoined by law to lay down the conditions on which the industry is to be conducted. The Court may also enforce its decision by bringing a suit in the Supreme Court to compel compliance. Provision is made for appeal against unreasonable orders. Strikes, picketing, and the boycott are prohibited, but the right of workmen to leave their work individually is not prohibited. If an actual strike or lockout takes place in any of the industries within the scope of the Act, the Court is empowered to take the industry over and operate it by itself. This is a novel experiment which deserves more than passing notice. The pertinent section of the Act runs thus:

> In case of the suspension, limitation, or cessation of the operation of any of the industries, employments, public utilities or common carriers affected by this Act, contrary to the provisions hereof, or to the orders of said court made hereunder, if it shall appear to said court that such suspension, limitation, or cessation shall seriously affect the public welfare by endangering the public peace or threatening the public health, then said court is hereby authorized, empowered and directed to take proper proceedings in any court of compe-

tent jurisdiction of this State to take over control, direct and operate said industry, employment, public utility or common carrier during such emergency: *Provided*, that a fair return and compensation shall be paid to the owners of such industry, employment, public utility or common carrier, and also a fair wage to the workers engaged therein, during the time of such operation under the provisions of this section.

This section of the Kansas law is, of course, meant to provide against stoppages of work in public utility industries and services; but it may contain the key to the solution of the more general question of cessation of work, either by lockout or strike. The Kansas Industrial Court, as has been noted, is a *neutral* authority. In the early stages of a lockout or strike the feelings of the parties are usually too embittered to allow them to settle matters coolly and amicably. The parties are like belligerent nations. Confident of success, each refuses to give way till the burden of war becomes irksome or unbearable. The process of "climbing down" is unpalatable. The psychological is almost as necessary as the industrial solution. The stubbornness, confidence, and self-righteousness of the parties coincide with a real desire for settlement. The employer does not wish to close his works and lose his profits; the employee has no wish to lose his wages. Both parties would be glad to see the works going could a means be devised which would not injure their vanity or prospects of a successful issue to the fight.

A possible method of keeping the works going is for a neutral authority to step in, and, without prejudice to either party, take over the industry till the whole matter is threshed out and a settlement reached. The arrangements of terms of wages and returns on capital should not be beyond the wit of man. This solution, at least, would take the edge off the belligerent feelings of the parties, and would prepare the psychological ground for the final industrial settlement.

It may be added that employers and employees in industries not covered by the Act may voluntarily refer disputes to the Industrial Court. The Act also authorizes judges of the Court to make a special study of industrial conditions in Kansas or other States or countries.

Colorado law. The Colorado law of 1915 empowers the Industrial Commission to inquire into a dispute and make an award, which is not obligatory. No change of terms of employment and no strike or lockout may take place unless thirty days' notice is given and until an inquiry takes place (if the inquiry takes place within the time of notice). The Colorado Act, unlike the Lemieux Act, is not confined to public utilities. It covers all workers save those in agriculture and domestic service, and in establishments where less than four hands are employed. The reports on the working of the Act show that it has been as successful as any piece of similar legislation in the world. In very few cases have strikes taken place against the law, and in many cases the law has completely prevented strikes. In only 9 cases out of 145 did strikes take place without the statutory notice. The Industrial Commission has also been very successful in settling disputes, either by its own awards or by conferences convened at the instance of the Commission.

Movement toward outlawing strikes. In the State of Nebraska, the constitution was recently amended to permit of the passing of laws to regulate industrial disputes and to prevent unfair gains in any industry or calling affecting the public interest. Anti-strike legislation is also reported to be under consideration in Oregon and Montana. The "Open-Port Act" of Texas, passed in October, 1920, makes arbitration compulsory for transport services, and some other industries connected with transport. The prohibition of picketing is an outstanding feature in several of these proposed laws. The States of New York, Tennessee, and Missouri have drafted bills on the model of a bill drafted by the League of Industrial Rights, a body representative of employers. This bill seeks to make illegal strikes and lockouts (*a*) in public utility services, (*b*) in violation of agreements or arbitration awards, (*c*) without reasonable notice, and (*d*) sympathetic lockouts or strikes. The bill also proposes to make picketing, advertising, and other methods of furthering such disputes illegal.

An anti-strike bill was also recently reintroduced into Congress. This bill, which failed to pass last year, provides a maximum penalty of ten thousand dollars, or ten years' imprisonment, or both, for acts deliberately obstructing the movement of commodities in interstate or foreign commerce, or in any way attempting to induce employees of transportation services and industries to leave their employment. It also lays down penalties for persons injuring or destroying equipment used in interstate commerce. The compulsory tendencies of recent American legislation are strongly opposed by the trade unions.

Mr. Davis, the new Secretary of Labor of the United States, declared last April that his policy is to be "stopping labor disputes before they begin." He intends to propose to Congress a plan to maintain a special conciliation expert for each of fifteen industrial groups. These groups are mining, steel and iron, petroleum, packing-house, timber, leather, textiles, building, metal manufacturing, public utilities, needle trades, water transportation, wholesale and retail trades, publishing, and miscellaneous trades. These conciliators, who are to possess expert knowledge of the industry with which they deal, are to spend their time making adjustments in labor disputes before the disputes reach an acute stage.

7. Summary of Experience with Conciliation, Mediation, and Arbitration [1]

The foregoing survey of modern methods of industrial peace has established one central truth, namely, that there is no absolutely successful method of preventing industrial strife. It is true that the various systems which have been analyzed have not exhausted the possibilities of such methods. It has been noted that for a time the system of sliding scales was extensively adopted in England. Other methods of payment have been devised from time to time to harmonize the relations of employers and employees. But these methods, like the methods of industrial peace we have been studying, have been unable to bring unqualified peace to industry. A more detailed examination of the methods of industrial remuneration, including profit-sharing and copartnership, is left for a subsequent chapter.

Contrast between conciliation and arbitration. The main issue in conciliation and arbitration is between force and voluntary methods. Compulsion has many advocates, whose attitudes vary from an uncompromising enmity to all strikes and

[1] From *Conciliation and Arbitration*, by R. N. Gilchrist, chap. x, pp. 221–28 Bulletin of Indian Industries and Labor, no. 23.

lockouts to a modified antagonism only to strikes in public utility services or to strikes the causes of which have not been investigated. At the moment, the temper of the world as a whole is hesitating between voluntary methods and the modified compulsion of the Canadian Lemieux Act. The more thorough compulsion of Australia does not seem to be gaining in popularity. Even in Australia there are signs that compulsion may be modified by the more democratic methods of Whitley Councils. On the other hand, the Kansas compulsory measure indicates a contrary tendency in the United States.

The public's interest. One thing is very evident. In the aftermath of war, the number of strikes has been legion. They have occurred in all quarters of the globe. Many of these strikes have been national in extent. Several attempts have been made at international strikes. Individual industries and national services have alike been implicated. From the welter emerges a very clear universal demand that in industrial disputes the third party, the public, must be considered. More and more is it coming to be recognized that employers and workers have obligations to the public as well as to themselves. The more they strike the more they strengthen the power of the organization which represents the community, viz., Government. Many strikes in the last two or three years have been political. They have been in the nature of "direct action" to force Government to adopt some policy dictated by the workers. At the present stage of industrial development the workers of the world are not sufficiently organized, nor is the word "worker" sufficiently defined, to secure either such national or such international harmony among themselves as could force Governments to definite action. The stronger such attempts become the more will the community demand recognition of its own rights as against the demands of sections, and the more powerful will become the agent of the community, or Government. To attempt a forecast of how far the community will enforce compulsion from this point of view is beyond our present limits; but the formation in recent years of various civic federations, patriotic leagues, etc., to safeguard essential industries is not without significance. Hitherto the public has been passive; now it is asserting its own claims.

The growing popularity of legislation of the Canadian type is undoubtedly due to the claims of the public. It has been noted several times in the above survey that even where there are no laws on the Lemieux model, a distinction is drawn between ordinary industries and public-service utilities or basic industries. This distinction is made in compulsory Australia and in the voluntary United States. It is extending and is likely to extend.

Need of expert governmental machinery. Another point which emerges from the above study is the necessity in all modern Governments of having highly organized labor machinery for the administration of labor questions. Whatever be the powers of a Government or the utility of a Ministry in actually settling disputes, one point is universally conceded, viz., the necessity of an expert Government department for investigation and publicity. Government also must act as the central and coördinating authority in all administrative questions arising out of labor laws.

Compulsion not often successful. It is now generally recognized that compulsion is possible only where it is desired by the common consciousness. Even in countries where labor politically predominates, compulsion has been unsuccessful. It was unsuccessful in England during the war, when many abnormal factors might have been expected to come to its aid. For a legislature to force compulsory measures on an unwilling people, particularly unwilling workers, would be to court disaster. The law might, indeed, be passed; it could not be enforced. In theory no doubt the State is all-powerful, but in practice Government cannot consistently go against the popular consciousness without risk to itself. No Government has yet had the courage to carry the penal clauses of compulsory acts to their legal conclusion. Compulsory legislation thus becomes inoperative — a pernicious evil in all legislation.

Outcome always doubtful. The history of legislation for industrial peace brings out another fact, viz., the impossibility of predicting how any measure will work. This is particularly borne out by the experience of New South Wales, where many Acts and their amendments indicate how temporary may be the conditions which a law is passed to meet. Nothing illustrates this better than the earlier predictions regarding compulsion in New Zealand. Mr. Pember Reeves, the author of the 1894 measure, predicted that the Arbitration Court would be only a reserve power. "I do not think," he said, "the Arbitration Court will be very often called into requisition; on the contrary, I think that in ninety-nine cases out of one hundred in which labor disputes arise, they will be settled by conciliation boards, but, unless you have in the background an Arbitration Court, the conciliation boards will not be respected and they will be virtually useless." In actual practice the bulk of work became concentrated in the Court. In connection with the same Act, Mr. Reeves said: "I cannot help thinking, after devoting many hours to the study of this subject, that the ideal board is one consisting of three persons appointed by the State, paid an annual salary, and able to go to any part of New Zealand." This was the method of the Compulsory Arbitration Act. Mr. Reeves's successor, speaking on the 1908 Act, said: "Having studied the different methods throughout the different parts of the world, it appeared to me that the best solution as far as conciliation is concerned was to provide machinery whereby we will get both parties affected to come together" — the method of voluntary conciliation.

Composition of boards and courts. Where organizations for settling industrial disputes are set up, it is now a recognized principle that employers and workers should be equally represented on them. We have seen how in some cases the public may also be represented. The public, however, are not the immediate parties to the dispute, and from the point of view of either workers or employers they may be looked on as neutral. In existing organizations, too, the maximum possible amount of weight is placed on non-official action. Where industry is well organized, the functions of Government are reduced to the minimum consistent with good administration. Government is a registering authority; it keeps the machinery in good order, and sets it going, but it does not interfere with the product. Government interference, of course, is more or less welcome according to the predominence of the political parties. But, as no party expects always to be in power, Government as such is not welcome in disputes. This has raised an important question regarding the constitution of industrial courts. As a rule, they are established under a Ministry of Labor; but in the opinion of many they should be set up as divisions of existing High Courts such as the Railway and Canal Commission Court in England. Whatever be the authority that sets them up, or however they may be constituted, one point should be made certain — the independence of the courts. Every shadow of subservience of a court either to a ministry or to a political party should be removed, otherwise the one reason of its existence — impartiality — would be defeated.

Danger of Partisanship. Arbitration courts, and other industrial courts, must always differ from ordinary law courts in one important respect. Industrial courts of all kinds must deal with each case on its merits, within the general limits of the law. Only a limited use can be made of case law. Another point must particularly be noted. The legislature should not place the courts in such a position that a judge is made liable to attack on the ground of partiality. It is the duty of the legislature to word the laws in such a way that it is the duty of the court only to interpret. This is admittedly difficult for the parliamentary draftsman, but Australian experience gives a pointed warning. The Commonwealth Court is enjoined by law to prescribe "fair and reasonable" wages, etc. Obviously the words "fair and reasonable" admit of wide interpretation, and two Presidents of the Court (O'Connor and Higgins) have both protested against the duty imposed on them. Justice Higgins said:

> It is to be regretted that the legislature has not given a definition of the words ["fair and reasonable"]. It is the function of the legislature, not of the judiciary, to deal with social and economic problems; it is for the judiciary to apply, and, when necessary, to interpret the enactments of the legislature. But here, this whole controversial problem, with its grave social and economic bearings, has been committed to a judge who is not, at least directly, responsible, and who ought not to be responsible, to public opinion. Even if the delegation of duty should be successful in this case, it by no means follows that it will be so hereafter. I do not protest against the difficulty of the problem, but against the confusion of functions — against the failure to define, the shunting of legislative responsibility. It would be almost as reasonable to tell a court to do what is "right" with regard to real estate, and yet lay down no laws or principles for its guidance. In the course of the long discussion of this case, I have become

> convinced that the President of this Court is put in a false position. The strength of the judiciary in the public confidence is largely owing to the fact that the judge has not to devise great principles of action, as between great classes, or to lay down what is fair and reasonable as between contending classes in the community; but has to carry out mandates of the legislature, evolved out of the conflict of public opinion after debate in Parliament. I venture to think that it will not be found wise thus to bring the judicial department within the range of political fire.

The result was that, in Australia, Justice Higgins, whose economic theories favor the employee, used to be looked on by employers as a partisan. It would be almost impossible for any one in a similar position not to be a partisan of some kind. In such a case, the difficulty might partly be met by committing cases, not to one judge, but to a bench of judges. The real solution is for the legislature to enact proper laws, setting up administrative machinery to deal with minimum wages, to make inquiries, and generally to guide the courts.

No single system the best. It will also be obvious from the foregoing survey that there has been no definite line of development in legislation for industrial peace either in individual States or in the world as a whole. In what may be called conciliation States, or voluntary States, the eyes of both governments and people have sometimes been turned longingly toward coercion; in coercion States attempts are usually made to utilize the methods of voluntary States. All States at the present moment are busily engaged in finding the *best* method; but as yet not one has found it. In comparing the legislation of various States it is of the utmost importance to remember that the comparative success of any method must be read closely with the previous history of the people, the present social composition, the political complexion of the Government, and the other labor laws of the country. Even if a system is successful in one State, its success in another alone is by no means a guarantee that a similar method will succeed in another State.

It may happen that certain types of law are more suitable to the nature of a people than other types; e.g., laws which may be suitable for the robust and independent workers of New Zealand might not be equally suitable for the more mercurial and more ease-loving Italians. Laws which suit people in temperate climates may not suit people in extreme climates. Again, a system of industrial peace legislation must be studied in relation to other laws; e.g., laws of conspiracy and the general penal system, trade-union laws, workmen's compensation laws, and factory laws. In Great Britain, for example, compulsion may almost be said to be illogical so long as the Trade Disputes Act is in force. In Australasia, with a legally enforced eight-hour day and minimum wage, the universe of discourse for the arbitration courts or other agencies is considerably reduced. Comparison of countries thus must take into account the existing conditions of the worker. It makes a considerable difference if disputes are narrowed down within certain limits. The area of just claims is much widened, say, in a country in which there is no recognized limit of working hours and where the social consciousness is not sufficiently strong to prevent the worst forms of sweating.

Another thing which must be taken into account in comparison is the level of education among workers. In general terms it may be said that the degree of virility of workers' organizations varies in direct ratio to the level of education among the working classes. It is quite a different thing for organizations to deal with workmen whose ordinary literature consists of university textbooks in economics and social science and workmen who have not reached the stage of reading at all, not to speak of reading a daily or weekly newspaper.

Political factors. In comparing countries, still another point has to be noted, viz., whether States are unitary or federal. In federal States the type of federal union and the powers of the federal government as compared with state governments must be kept in mind, as well as the constitutional limitations under which both federal and state governments work.

The most important point of all to remember is the political complexion of a country. In this respect it may be noted that the most compulsory States at the present moment are those in which labor has the biggest voice in Government. Where labor rules naturally there is on the part of the workers much less suspicion of the Government and much greater readiness to commit labor disputes into the hand of Government than there is in countries where labor is as yet in a political minority. In a country where what are usually called the upper classes or the non-manual working classes control the legislation and administration, not unnaturally there is a suspicion on the part of labor that compulsion enforced by such a Government would be such as would not be favorable to them. Thus, in Australia and New Zealand the working classes have not hesitated to accept the legal prohibition of strikes, but in Great Britain and in America it will be a long time before the trade unions and workers as a whole, under any system of compulsion, will surrender their most powerful weapon. It is possible that their attitude may change when their own political party comes into power.

Economic and geographic factors. Another point of comparison may be noted, viz., whether a country is a new country or an old country. In a new country there are opportunities for more rapid development than in old countries, and often the big and sudden returns which labor receives make the workers relatively less jealous of the bigger and even more sudden returns which capital gets. In new countries, moreover, there is a tendency on the part of individual workmen to reckon that they themselves may one day become small or large capitalists. In new or undeveloped countries, too, much depends on the amount of labor available, and the amenities open to the laboring classes. Where labor is scarce, capital must bid against capital for its labor supply, and the keener is the competition for labor the higher will be the wage. So long as this competition is keen there is not likely to be much industrial unrest, for wages are always rising.

Labor unrest also may be affected by counter-attractions; e.g., an agricultural population may be persuaded to go into factories only by very high wages, and if the wages and conditions are unsuitable the workers may again revert to agriculture. Such alternative occupations, provided they are not overcrowded, very materially affect both capital and labor. In new countries, again, capital may have to import labor. Imported labor, or immigration, often leads to special difficulties, especially after importation has led to a settled laboring class. Settled labor, even though in origin it was itself imported, is very suspicious of further importation, especially where immigration leads to a "mixed" population.

In old countries, with a settled labor population, a population which is independent of the land, or has no alternative occupations, labor competes with labor for occupation. Such competition tends to bring down wages and otherwise affects labor conditions unfavorably. The weakness of individual competition, then, is gradually replaced by the strength of collective bargaining. The workers organize themselves into unions to save them from themselves.

PART FOUR

MODERN INDUSTRIAL RELATIONS POLICIES

CHAPTER XIV

PROFIT AND OWNERSHIP SHARING

1. Introduction

In recent years, the labor problem has been forced upon the attention of employers of labor and managers of enterprises in all industrial countries. Recognition of the existence of this problem, knowledge of its basic causes, and the ability to formulate business policies which effectively solve it, have become pre-conditions of successful management in the modern industrial world. The human factor in industry has grown in importance until it now ranks with the material and financial factors in its claim upon the skill and ingenuity of the enterpriser. Special branches of study and a special literature dealing with this factor of human relations have sought to spread among the managers of industry knowledge of the essentials of the problem and of its solution.

Present system inefficient. The aspect of the labor problem of most concern to employers is its injurious effect upon the efficiency of industry. There is general complaint to-day that the wage-earner — whether a union member or not — has developed an attitude of indifference, if not of positive hostility, toward the welfare of the enterprise with which he is associated; that he nullifies the efforts of the manager to promote efficiency by policies and habits of work which tend to restrict output, wastes time and materials, and increases friction within the enterprise. These things are condemned as contrary to the social interest; what is of more immediate importance to the employer, however, is the fact that they multiply costs and reduce profits. With the aid of science and inventive genius, managers of business enterprise in the modern world have progressed far toward a mastery of the material factors in industry; appropriation of forces from nature, utilization of raw materials, perfection of capital equipment, efficient organization of these factors and of the marketing mechanism are among the achievements of the society in which we live. But it is becoming increasingly evident that the benefits of these achievements in the field of business management are offset, in large part, by the failure of the system to stimulate the energy and arouse the interest and loyalty of the workingmen, without whose coöperation the industrial structure cannot function at all.

Breakdown of the drive policy. With regard to this problem of industrial relations, modern business management is distinguished from that of a generation ago by the fact that the employer is gradually perceiving the true reasons for the inefficiency of wage labor, and adjusting his policies of management to the essentials of the situation rather than to its superficial aspects. The preceding generation of employers too frequently viewed the slackness of labor as evidence of defect in the character of the workingman, to be eradicated by the application of measures of strict discipline. As long as this view persisted, sole reliance was placed in the "drive" system of management. The industrial relations program was summed up in the formula: "Catch 'em young, treat 'em rough, tell 'em nothing." But this simple program broke down before the stolid, intransigent opposition of the unorganized workers and the open rebellion of the trade unions. It was the utter collapse of the drive system as a means of promoting efficiency that, more than anything else, brought about a more enlightened viewpoint on the part of employers. There are even to-day some employers of Bourbon traits who, "learning nothing and forgetting nothing," rely solely upon two-fisted, strong-arm foremen and a militaristic discipline in the plant to promote the smooth functioning of their industry. But the system of ideas which they represent is becoming an anachronism in the modern world; their method is condemned as heartily by the more progressive employers as by the leaders of organized labor.

The modern viewpoint. Modern industrial relations policies are based upon a recognition of the fact that the behavior of labor is the natural outgrowth of the conditions of his life in industry; that the roots of the labor problem are embedded in the system itself. The wage-earner refuses to respond to efficiency movements because, in a system of refined division of labor, the quantity and quality of his product seem to bear no relationship to his own personal welfare; because his job is meaningless or distasteful to him, he performs his service grudgingly and seeks to escape from it entirely when he can; because he shares neither the ownership nor the control of the enterprise, its welfare is the concern of an interest alien to himself; because his life in industry is beset by menaces and insecurities whose burden society as a whole does little to lighten, he adopts policies which, though they are calculated to surround him with safeguards against unemployment, degradation of the standard of life, and destruction of his skill, sometimes work toward the general impoverishment of society. In preceding sections of this book we have studied these causes of the labor problem and traced their effects upon the welfare of the wage-earner and upon his program of action. We shall now consider them anew from the standpoint of the employer who is seeking a practical solution of the problem within the limits of his individual enterprise. The modern devices of profit and ownership sharing, employee representation, miscellaneous welfare and benefit plans are to be considered as adjustments to the social forces which have produced the labor problem, whose success depends upon the degree to which they counteract the effects of these forces.

Classification of employer's policies. Before studying the different devices in detail, it may help us to make clear the social bearings of the whole modern program of industrial relations if we attempt to classify them on the basis of their relation to the causes of the labor problem. A complete industrial relations program — such, for example, as that of the Standard Oil Company of New Jersey — consists of three groups of policies, each adjusted to one of the features of the modern industrial order which conduces to unrest or inefficiency among wage-earners. In the first place, there is that phase of the program which attempts to replace the bond of direct personal relationship between employer and employed which was destroyed by the growth of large-scale industry. Recognizing the impossibility of reëstablishing this simple relationship in modern industry, this phase of the program proposes to substitute for it a bond of mutual financial interest in the profitableness of the corporate enterprise. Schemes for the sharing of profits or ownership are examples of this. Secondly, there is that phase of the program which acknowledges the correctness of the principle of collective bargaining in an industrial system where workers are massed together in large groups under a single employer and are, as isolated individuals, powerless to protect their interests. Of this character are the different types of employee representation. They aim to restore a measure of that control over the conditions of his life of which the worker was deprived when the Industrial Revolution wiped out the household industry. Thirdly, there is a group of welfare provisions — sickness benefits, old-age pensions, safety schemes, employment guarantees — which are offered as aids to the propertyless man in his combat with the menaces of a wage-earner's life. They remove the incentive to the "make-work" practices of the industrial wage-earner and tend to promote efficiency.

Contrast with trade-unionism. The social philosophy which underlies the industrial relations program of modern employers is in sharp contrast with that upon which is based the program of organized labor. Trade-unionism sees industrial society divided into two opposing classes — the workers and the employers — whose interests are mutually antagonistic. It aims to organize one of these classes into a nation-wide union for coöperative action, accepting, if it does not encourage, a similar organization on the part of the employers. This horizontal division of society will cut across the boundaries of separate business establishments. The employee of a given employer will owe allegiance, not to the industry to which he is attached nor to his employer, but to other wage-earners throughout the field of industrial enterprise. Between the two classes thus organized, conflict will be joined over the division of the income of business, determination of conditions of work, and other details of management — a conflict whose peaceful manifestation is the collective bargain and whose active phase takes the form of the strike and lockout. In contrast with this, the industrial relations policy of the employer views society as divided vertically into competing industrial units, within each of which the interests of employer and worker are mutual. It organizes each enterprise separately for coöperative action, devising arrangements for smoothing out differences between the employer and his work force, for arousing loyalty to the industry among the workers, and increasing his interest in its welfare. The aim is to promote the efficiency of the enterprise to the point where it will surpass its competitors in the struggle for profits.

2. Fundamental Principles of Profit Sharing [1]

What profit sharing is. The term "profit sharing" is used to indicate many different methods of payment. There is little uniformity in plans going under this name, but in all cases they provide for certain payments to employees in addition to their regular wages or salaries. It is these additional payments which are ordinarily regarded as the participation in profits. But there are many plans for extra remuneration which cannot properly be called profit sharing. Perhaps the best definition of profit sharing is that used by the British Board of Trade, in its special report on *Profit Sharing and Labor Copartnership in the United Kingdom* (1912). This report states, "Profit sharing is understood to involve an agreement between an employer and his work-people under which the latter receive, in addition to their wages, a share, fixed beforehand, in the profits of the undertaking." In other words, the essence of profit sharing is that the amount of the

[1] From *Profit Sharing; Its Principles and Practice*, by A. W. Burritt *et al.*, pp. 4–16. Harper & Brothers, publishers.

special payments received by employees is directly contingent upon the earnings for a specified period, and varies directly with those earnings, upon a prearranged basis.

Types of profit sharing. The most usual form of the plan involves a distribution of a portion of the profits of the business as a whole. This may be termed *general* profit sharing, because it is the general or total profits, arising from all sources, which are divided. But profit sharing does not necessarily take this form. The profits to be shared may be those arising from a part or separate unit of the business, as, for example, when the manager of a department in a retail establishment shares in the profits of his department, or when the manager of a branch store shares in the profits yielded by that store. Such an arrangement may be called *unit profit sharing*. Again, the profits to be divided may be those attributed exclusively to the individual's own efforts, as, for example, when traveling salesmen share in the profits shown upon the orders they secure. This may be termed *individual* profit sharing. Although the last two forms are not so common as the first, they are none the less true profit sharing. Profit sharing, let us repeat, is an arrangement whereby *any portion* of the employees' remuneration varies directly with the net profits of the business, or any part or unit of the business. The essential feature of profit sharing is that the employees' earnings are not definitely fixed, and that the basis upon which they vary is net profits — as distinguished from output, total sales, or any other factor.

Pseudo-profit-sharing plans. This conception of profit sharing is much narrower than the popular one. In common terminology the term "profit sharing" is frequently applied loosely to all forms of compensation which represent an addition to guaranteed wages or salaries. An increasingly large number of employers are paying a periodic bonus consisting of a certain percentage upon wages. Such payments are frequently called profit sharing, although they represent merely a form of wage, or deferred wage payment, the amount of which has no direct relation to the profits earned during the period. Other firms announce that they will pay a bonus upon all wages at the end of the year, the employees being given to understand that the amount of the bonus will depend somewhat upon the prosperity of the business for the year. Under this plan the percentage of bonus to wages is not announced in advance, but remains entirely at the company's discretion. The Youngstown Sheet and Tube Company used this method for several years. It was abandoned after the violent labor outbreaks experienced by this corporation in 1916. Other firms occasionally pay a bonus on wages without having announced in advance their intention of so doing, and without having obligated themselves to do so. It is clear that such plans do not come within the meaning of the term "profit sharing" as here defined, or within any strict interpretation of that term. Unless the method of computing the amount of profits available for the individual participant is definitely established at the outset, he does not systematically "share" in profits. The employer may arbitrarily grant an extra payment. Such bonus grants in addition to regular wages presumably come out of what might otherwise go to profits. But they do not represent profit sharing in any real sense, since the amount of additional compensation obtained by each employee does not vary directly, and upon a prearranged basis, with the profits earned during the period.

Other firms have introduced stock-purchasing or stock-distribution plans for their employees, which are mistakenly regarded as profit sharing. In some of them the profit-sharing feature consists simply in the fact that the stock is sold to employees at less than its market value, or that it is sold to them upon installments. It is noticeable that some corporations are more anxious to make the employees feel that a profit-sharing plan is in effect than they are to introduce a genuine profit-sharing arrangement.

In spite of the fact that these various plans of compensation additional to fixed wages do not represent true profit sharing, it has seemed best, for the purposes of this study, not to exclude them from consideration. Important results may be produced by some of these pseudo-profit-sharing plans. But whatever the results obtained, they are not the results of profit sharing. When such plans are discussed, it should be understood that they do not constitute profit sharing in the technical sense of that term. But the advantages and disadvantages of these methods of making additional payments will be considered and compared with those of true profit sharing.

Essentials for success. It would be difficult if not impossible to formulate any generalization regarding the probable success or effectiveness of profit sharing which would be uniformly applicable to all businesses and to all groups of employees. But it is believed that there are certain general principles regarding profit sharing which are fundamental, and which apply with equal force, whether it is introduced to stimulate efficiency or to promote social justice.

Market wages must be paid. The first principle is that effective profit sharing must ordinarily presuppose the payment of the full going rate of wages to participants. If profit sharing is primarily introduced to improve the conditions of the workers, it must clearly begin by the payment of full wages, for the economic condition of employees cannot be advanced by lessening the amount of wages upon which they can definitely rely. Likewise, if the business point of view prevails, the full market wages must be guaranteed. For the object in this case is to induce a special degree of effort, efficiency, coöperation, or some other desirable result, not usually obtainable by the payment of a flat wage. Obviously these special results cannot be expected unless the rewards which call them forth can be counted on to exceed the regular and usual wage.

If the profit-sharing employer fails to pay a fixed wage at least as great as that paid by his non-profit-sharing competitors, the resentment among his employees caused by this act may more than counteract any desirable results which might have been secured. It may be confidently asserted that no employer can secure important results through profit sharing unless the profits which he distributes represent a payment over and above the market wages of the district and industry. As has been pointed out by Babson's Statistical Organization in a special report upon this subject, as on the farm it is the top bushels that count, so in industrial enterprises it is the amounts over and above the usual that secure the unusual devotion of employees.

Some employers and corporations have sought to use profit sharing for the purpose of keeping wages down or of paying wages less than would otherwise have been necessary. For example, the head of one profit-sharing concern writes: "On January first of each year our profits are distributed, and wages adjusted. On that day we consider the question of the wages of employees.

Any who insist on securing an advance in salary are dropped from the profit-sharing list." The owner of a retail store conducted on a profit-sharing basis, when asked to enumerate the results achieved by his profit-sharing plan, stated that "It has succeeded in keeping the salaries the same as they were when the plan was introduced several years ago, in spite of the fact that the general scale of salaries, the prices of commodities, and everything else has gone up." The president of a corporation employing over five thousand men indicated a similar attitude of mind. This corporation had for several years practiced what it regarded as profit sharing, but what was in reality an annual bonus distribution. The bonus was the same percentage upon wages for all employees, but the percentage was determined at the company's discretion, although understood to be in relation to earnings. The president of this concern, in an interview during our investigations, said: "My idea is to pay men as regular wages an amount slightly less than the actual value of their services, and then to make additional payments to them, dependent in amount upon the success of the business and the earnings of the company."

If the employer endeavors to use profit sharing to "nibble off" the existing wage scale, or to depress wages, he will find, sooner or later, that it fails to produce the hoped-for results. It is significant to note that only a few months before the above remark was made by the president who favored paying men "less than they are worth," his corporation experienced one of the most violent strikes and labor disturbances in the history of the industry. A New England manufacturer lamented the fact that his profit-sharing plan did not prove sufficient to secure stability of his labor force, and that his female profit sharers were regularly leaving his employ. Inquiry revealed that the wage he was paying to these young women was much less than the usual wage for such labor. In this instance, as in others, it is apparent that profit sharing used to depress wages, instead of being an evidence of good management, is a sign of poor business judgment. A profit-sharing plan cannot be operated with this purpose for any length of time before the design will be perceived, and the result will be other than beneficial.

Exception in the case of managerial employees. In the above discussion the existence of a "going wage" or "market wage" has been assumed. But for some higher-paid employees there is no easily ascertainable "market wage," because the work, and therefore the pay, cannot be standardized. This is particularly true of those whose functions partake of the managerial nature and among whom there are wide variations in salary. For these it may not prove equally necessary or possible to establish a fixed "market" salary. For example, profit sharing is sometimes applied to important employees in the managerial group who are placed upon comparatively small salaries, which merely serve the purpose of a drawing and expense account, with an arrangement under which they derive a large portion of their income from profits. This plan is not open to the objections which apply to cutting wages among the lower-paid groups. For under such circumstances the participants become, in a limited sense, partners in the business. They contribute their managerial ability, the owners contribute the capital, and both share in the profits. Furthermore, since such participants actually exercise functions of management, it is not improper that they should be permitted to assume some of the risks of the enterprise, if they care to do so, and frequently they are glad to do it. Therefore, when profit sharing is applied to the discretionary or managerial group, where little standardization of results or salaries is possible, it is not absolutely necessary that it shall begin with the payment of the "market wage." Clearly such an arrangement would be inapplicable when, as is sometimes the case, it is understood that a substantial or large proportion of the total income of the participant is to come from profits.

Payments must be substantial. A second principle essential to the success of any profit-sharing plan relates to the size of the prospective profit distribution. The payments provided must be adequate. It is impossible to prescribe any particular percentage which will prove most stimulating. But in profit sharing for business purposes there must be the prospect that the profits to be obtained under normally successful conditions will represent an appreciable addition to wages. The employer must not lose sight of the fact that he expects to obtain certain valuable results in larger degree than under a straight wage system. If these results are worth having, they are worth paying for. Indeed, he cannot secure them without paying for them. He must offer an incentive which appeals to the participants as worth while. The payments over and above wages or salaries must be commensurate with the additional interest or effort expected from and displayed by the participants. This does not mean that a profit-sharing plan will fail if, under unusual circumstances, the profits available for distribution prove to be small or non-existent. For example, the N. O. Nelson Manufacturing Company was compelled to suspend wage dividends entirely for several years after the Panic of 1893, but continued its plan in operation. Such circumstances, however, must be recognized as distinctly unusual and extraordinary. A profit-sharing plan which is to prove permanently successful as a business arrangement must be designed so that in normal times there may be an expectancy of a fair and adequate distribution of profits. Although, as has been stated, no exact percentage can be prescribed that is applicable to all concerns, yet experience indicates that an additional share amounting as a minimum to five or six per cent of wages is required to excite and sustain the interest and effort of any group of employees. Similarly, if social purposes are paramount in the employer's mind, the profit share must be considerable, in order to advance the standard of living, to promote thrift and savings, and to improve the conditions of life.

Plan should be definite. Further, profit sharing will not achieve its greatest effectiveness unless there be a definite plan or agreement under which the proportion or share of profits to be distributed is determined and established in advance. There are many concerns using so-called "profit-sharing" plans under which, at the end of the year, the employer simply determines in the exercise of his own discretion the amount or proportion of profits which shall be paid out. A contracting firm in Ohio, in the announcement of its profit-sharing plan, states: "Out of the net profits of the business for said fiscal year, beginning February first, 1915, remaining after deducting all costs and expense incident to said business, including payment of wages as shown by said payroll, there shall be first set aside such sum as the board of directors may determine to be a fair return upon capital invested, and that out of the balance remaining, one half thereof shall be distributed among such employees as may be deemed worthy by the board of directors."

Such plans are of questionable value viewed as instruments either for the promotion of efficiency or of social welfare. The arbitrary decision of the management, made after and not before the extra exertion, robs the plans of a large part of their stimulating power. It is not to be expected that men will concern themselves to increase profits and keep down costs, when they have no knowledge as to what portion of the profits, if any, they will receive. From the standpoint of social betterment such arbitrary distributions are also to be condemned. When the money is paid out simply as a voluntary and discretionary payment, the amount of which depends upon the judgment, whim, caprice, or generosity of the employer, it is difficult to regard it as anything other than charity. A widespread use of profit sharing of this character would inevitably work undesirable social results among members of the employed class, by making them more dependent upon the bounty and charity of employers than upon their own initiative and bargaining power.

Nature of the plan must vary with its purpose. Another of the fundamental principles regarding profit sharing, a principle never to be lost sight of, is that the nature of the plan must be arranged in accordance with the special purpose or purposes which it is expected will be promoted. A system which may be well devised to promote one purpose may be ill adapted to promote another purpose. Profit sharing aiming at length and stability of service might fail to promote increased efficiency. A plan organized to assist savings for old age might not be so successful in elevating the standard of living. The specific purpose or purposes must first be decided upon, and then the details of the plan must be arranged accordingly. A manufacturing establishment in New York recently announced that henceforth it would distribute twenty per cent of its net profit to employees. At the time this announcement was made, no arrangements had been made as to any of the details of the plan. This is placing the cart before the horse. If the inauguration of profit sharing is contemplated, it is necessary that the employer should first decide what he wishes to accomplish by the additional payment, and then he should adopt the method which appears most likely to achieve this purpose.

Summary. In short, profit sharing to be effective, whether it be general, unit, or individual, must begin with the payment of full going market wages or salaries, unless it be applied to those managerial employees whose compensation is not standardized. The payments must be substantial, and must be made in accordance with a definite plan, which is so worked out as to promote the particular purposes in mind. There are several important purposes which it is believed may be promoted by profit sharing. These purposes, together with suggestions as to the best methods of realizing them, are discussed in the following chapters.

3. Why I Share My Profits [1]

Profit sharing has spread slowly. Most of the starts are wrong. Because they are wrong, they do not work, and they are usually given up at the end of a year or so.

The simplicity of genuine profit sharing is one of the obstacles. Because the idea is a distinct innovation, the business men fancy that it must be intricate; they more often than not hamper it with needless restrictions.

The expression itself describes clearly and completely the idea, but men do not take it in.

It means to share profits; it does not mean to sell stock or to give bonuses, or anything else, but to share the profits.

Clearly, therefore, whatever profits are made in any given period, usually a year, are to be shared with employees. The particular terms of the sharing may vary. The essential fact must not vary.

This is the simple formula: the plan must be stated in advance; it must state the proportion of the profits that is to be allowed to wages compared with capital; it must be a dividend on the salaries and wages of all who have worked a reasonable part of the calendar year; it must state whether payment is to be in cash or stock; and it must leave nothing optional with the management.

Captains of industry do not profess to be either economists or philanthropists. Many of them are either or both without knowing it, or without a label. They are much more so now than twenty, thirty, or forty years ago.

A large number of them have set up beneficial arrangements in

[1] From *System, The Magazine of Business*, July–December 1915, pp. 339–44. Article by N. O. Nelson under this title.

behalf of employees, with philanthropic motives. The muck-rakers deny the motive, but admit the facts. They are economists to the extent of recognizing that it pays to hire good workmen and satisfied workmen.

Step by step they are learning that the actual partnership idea brings out better relations and better work. When the dividend on the wages paid out of the profits is handed out in stock, it does actually make a partner of every man who receives the dividend certificate.

In every partnership there is a senior head and the juniors. In the profit-sharing partnership the rank and file are the juniors. They do not run the business, but they are interested in making it pay. The head of the house recognizes, and the lowest employee in the concern recognizes, a mutual interest, an interest not alone of dollars, but of fellowship.

No captain can long be the head of a profit-sharing concern without getting a real human interest in all the employees for whom he is the manager. Not the lowliest employee will long fail to recognize that he is a part of the concern in the profits of which he shares.

Mr. Carnegie has said in his books, Mr. Roosevelt has said in his presidential messages, and other high authorities have said in effect, that a nation based upon business without some form of partnership cannot survive. They are undoubtedly right. Were captains of industry to continue to take all the profits and make all the accumulations of their ability, the date would not be far distant when our dear United States would repeat the history of Rome and every other wicked nation.

Profit sharing is so easy and simple and neighborly.

When a captain gets liberal pay for his time, when he gets interest on his own and his capitalists' investments, and when he gets a share of the still additional profits, can he fail to feel good over giving a share of the profits to all the employees who have helped to make them and whose attention necessarily increases them?

Genuine profit-sharing concerns are numerous in England and France. A majority of the English gas companies use the plan, the Consolidated Company having about twenty-five thousand employees, the Metropolitan about five thousand.

In this country some railroads and business corporations sell stock to employees on easy payments and with special inducements. This attracts the provident few, it leaves out the mass. It is not automatic, it is not profit sharing. Many banks give a bonus of one or two weeks' pay at the end of the year. It is generous, but it is not profit sharing.

There is, however, a growing list of genuine profit-sharing concerns, employing substantially the principles of my company's plan, though not all its details.

The N. O. Nelson Manufacturing Company — we are located at St. Louis — adopted plans for sharing profits with its employees in 1886, and has continued them without interruption since.

At the beginning of that year a notice was put in the pay envelopes saying that the net profits of the business, after allowing a commercial rate of interest on the capital, would be divided by equal percentages of the capital and the wages and the salaries of employees who had worked with us as long as six months within the year.

Two weeks later the employees were called together and the matter fully explained. They were asked to elect an auditor to verify the dividend figuring, and they chose a department head.

Owing to the big strike on the Gould Southwestern Railroad System the year was a poor one and the profits barely allowed a five-per-cent dividend. This was paid in cash, with the option of leaving it on deposit — which about one half did.

The next year allowed a ten-per-cent dividend on wages and provided a surplus besides. It was then announced that thereafter the dividends would be paid in stock.

The dividends continued at eight per cent or ten per cent for several years, then fell to four per cent, and, following the Panic of 1893, were suspended for several years. When times became better, dividends were resumed, and four per cent allowed on the suspended years.

In 1905 the customers were taken into the arrangement, their share being based on the gross profits obtained from their purchases. Capital received six per cent, but no further share of the profits. That is the present plan.

This arrangement has yielded dividends to employees of from ten per cent to thirty per cent, the average being about eighteen per cent. A surplus has been laid by equal to about fifty per cent of the capital stock issued, and liberal depreciation taken on all fixed property.

The capital at the beginning was about one hundred thousand dollars, and the employees numbered about two hundred. The capital and surplus is now about two million dollars and there are one thousand employees.

The business was then nine years old and occupied one rented building in St. Louis. It now has its own buildings in St. Louis; five factory buildings in its own town of Leclaire, Illinois; factories in Bessemer, Alabama; Noblesville, Indiana; and branch houses in Memphis, Houston, Los Angeles, Salt Lake, Pueblo, New Orleans, and Joplin.

The employees own about one third of the capital.

The plan has worked satisfactorily, has caused no trouble, and has undoubtedly increased the effectiveness and profits of the business.

No restrictions of any sort were coupled with the plan aside from its own terms. To prevent improvident men from bartering away their dividends, we in recent years have issued certificates only after a period of three years has elapsed, and we prohibit any employee, while in our employ, to buy or sell "employee" stock. In meritorious cases we buy the stock.

When for any reason an employee becomes disabled, we cash his stock by installments for as long a period as is needed. No employee or his family are allowed to suffer.

Taking in the customers is not a part of the customary profit-sharing systems — it is better known as coöperation. This variation has in it the economic merit of enlisting a steadier trade at less expense. This arrangement gives the employees and the customers a factory and organization of their own, and they simply pay interest for that part of the capital which they do not own. There is perfect freedom, for any employee may quit or be discharged, and a customer may trade elsewhere or be refused credit, and nevertheless retain their stock for the sake of its income, or sell it.

The officers and managers and department heads are all employees and their incomes depend upon their work in proportion to its importance, coming through salaries and profit-sharing dividends.

It cannot be claimed that every profit-sharing employee and customer will do his utmost, but it goes without saying that he will do better than when in instinctive opposition.

Interested coöperation is more efficient than warlike competition.

4. Examples of Profit Sharing [1]

The Filene plan. "Drones got just as much as workers. There was no way to reward individual merit when I shared my profits. So I simply stopped sharing them." This is the explanation made by an Eastern manufacturer who undertook a profit-sharing plan a few years ago, in order to secure more permanent and efficient employees, but abandoned it later. Yet, to-day, the Wm. Filene's Sons Company, which conducts a specialized department store at Boston, has under consideration a plan which solves this problem and provides a means for rewarding the workers more than the drones. It is based on nine years' experience in sharing profits.

First of all, the Filene organization divides its net profits half and half, after paying dividends on the capital invested in the business and providing such sums as are required for the retirement of stock. The members of the management — the president, the general manager, the merchandise manager, the comptroller, the store manager, the publicity manager, and the like — get half, and the employees get the other half after dividend charges and so forth have been taken care of.

The employees all belong to the Filene Coöperative Association — the "F.C.A." There is no obligation for them to join the "F.C.A.," but the fact that they are on the Filene payroll automatically makes them members if they so desire — and they do desire. The profit-sharing regulations provide that awards may be made to the "F.C.A." before the profits are split between the management and the employees. There are also special provisions for awarding bonuses — based on percentages of the sales — which come ahead of the division of the profits in order to provide a way to stimulate directly those who come in closest contact with the merchandising activities of the store. Individual contracts with buyers that provide for increased remunera-

[1] From *System, The Magazine of Business*, July–December, 1915, pp. 344–50.

tion, if profits in their departments come to certain levels, also take precedence over the profit-sharing division of the profits.

But in the end the Filene profits are split two ways. Half goes to the management. The employees' half goes to a board of apportionment, which has power to award the extra bonuses mentioned above prior to the distribution of the profits. It is this board that is depended upon to sift the drones from the pluggers.

There are seven members of the board of apportionment. Three of them are appointed by the "F.C.A." Three of the remaining four are appointed by the directors. These directors are really "The Management," although the "F.C.A." has representation on the board of directors. The seventh member is selected by these six.

The board of apportionment divides up the employees' half of the profits among the individual employees. The division is roughly based on salaries. But — here is the Filene innovation — the board is at liberty to disregard this basis absolutely, and to give those whom it desires — the workers — sums in excess of the proportions of the employees' half of the profits to which their pay envelopes would normally entitle them. When merit is rewarded in this way, it is at the expense of the drones. The office man stands as much chance as the star buyer.

The Farr Alpaca Company. The Farr Alpaca Company has a profit-sharing plan which differs considerably from the Filene arrangement. It depends upon the management's observation to prevent drones from staying on the payroll long enough to benefit from the profit-sharing plan. The Farr Alpaca Company says that it decided to share profits "with a view of interesting its three thousand employees in the financial results of the company's business, and of leading them to exercise the greatest possible care to guard against bad work and waste of time and material."

The Farr plan provides for dividends to labor as well as to capital. The dividend on labor will be a percentage of the payroll corresponding with the percentage of the stock paid to the shareholders as cash dividends. It is estimated that this percentage will be eight per cent.

The profit sharers on the Farr payroll are those whose names appear on the payroll on January first of each year, and who remain continuously in the employ of the company during the following twelve months. Furthermore, the services of the employee must be satisfactory. A notice of the assignment of his wages is held to justify his exclusion from the profit sharing.

The amount forfeited by the discharge of an employee, or by his leaving voluntarily, or by his exclusion on account of unsatisfactory service, is credited to a benefit fund out of which the directors of the company may grant assistance to aged and disabled employees. The company also reserves the right to decide whether or not absence from work resulting from sickness or disability constitutes a break in the continuity of an employee's service. But a dividend is never paid on wages not actually earned. In the event of the death of an employee eligible to share in the profits, the company may pay a dividend to the husband, wife, or other members of the family.

Lever Brothers. A third type of profit sharing — more familiarly known as "copartnership" — is used in the soap manufacturing plant of Lever Brothers, at Cambridge, Massachusetts. The plan was first undertaken in 1909, by Sir William Lever, at Port Sunlight, England, the headquarters of the company. There it applied only to the plant at Port Sunlight, but it has since been extended, until now it embraces all the Lever plants throughout the world. There are one hundred employees at the Cambridge works, and thirty-three of them are copartners.

Partnership certificates having a face value of two million five hundred thousand dollars, but not representing cash, were created by Sir William in 1909. An approximate proportion of these certificates, estimated on a basis of ten per cent of the salaries or the wages involved, was credited to each of the following four classes of employees: (1) directors, (2) managers and foremen, (3) salesmen, and (4) the general staff.

Annually each eligible employee receives partnership certificates equal to ten per cent of his salary or wage. The certificates draw dividends amounting to five per cent less than those paid on the company's ordinary shares. In other words, after the regular shares receive dividends of five per cent, the partnership certificates rank equally with them.

Sir William's plan extends to both male and female employees, provided they are twenty-five years of age, have been in the service of the company five years, and have signed an agreement to work faithfully.

Boston Consolidated Gas Company. During recent years there has been a marked tendency among profit-sharing firms to distribute in the form of stock what they estimate to be labor's share of the profits. The Boston Consolidated Gas Company, which has been paying a wage dividend since 1906, has followed this plan.

The dividend to the eligible employees is called a "premium" by this New England concern. The "premium" is fixed at the same rate as the dividend on the stock of the company for the corresponding year. Each employee's "premium" is figured on the amount of his salary or wages for the twelve months, and is applied toward the purchase of one or more preferred shares of capital stock at market prices. Any odd balances remaining after the stock is taken up are credited to the employee on the books of the company, and bear interest at the rate of four per cent per annum.

The shares bought for the employees are their absolute property. However, these shares cannot be sold without the approval of the directors, as "the success of the plan is dependent upon an accumulated interest in the stock of the company."

The management, acting through the department heads, selects very carefully those who participate in the profits. Only employees who have shown the greatest regularity, intelligence, and energy are rewarded. The Boston Consolidated Gas Company has the following to say about this provision: "We believe that this restriction is a very important part of the success of any plan of profit sharing with employees, as it prevents the employees from accepting the apportionment merely as an increase of their salary instead of a reward for actual merit applicable only to the best employees."

The results of this plan are already very promising. The percentage paid on the wages — the "premium" — has increased from seven to nine per cent. With the exception of two years, the average amount received by each profit sharer has steadily grown. In 1914, more than half of the employees held stock in the company — in all, 3147 shares, valued at $366,786. They also had $20,677 to their credit. Each of these profit sharers now has an interest in the business amounting to about one half of his annual salary. In 1911, the company extended the scope of the plan considerably. As a result, the profit sharers now have a representative of their own selection on the board of directors.

In this plan a very direct relation between the efficiency of the employees and the amount of the wage and capital dividends is noticeable. The Massachusetts Sliding Scale Act, under which the Consolidated Gas Company sells its product, provides that the dividend on the company's stock may be increased one per cent for each reduction of five cents below ninety cents per thousand cubic feet of gas. Hence, an increase in the dividends is dependent upon a reduction in price. Since price reductions can normally only come with business expansion and improved economies in operation, a strong incentive exists for the employees to endeavor to lower expenses.

Provisions of this type for regulating the rates charged by public service corporations are becoming more and more prevalent. For this reason the plan of the Boston Consolidated Gas Company is of peculiar interest. Undoubtedly it will be carefully studied all over the country. Many gas companies throughout England have found profit sharing a very successful venture. Water and light companies abroad have also recently tried out the system. Every indication points to further growth for it.

The Dennison Company. All grades of regular employees normally participate in the profits under the three plans just discussed. A venture along entirely different lines, however, is sponsored by the Dennison Manufacturing Company, of South Farmingham, Massachusetts. Only those who earn at least one hundred dollars a month, and have been on the Dennison payroll a specified number of years, are included under this plan. The main objective here is to secure managers and workers of long training and a peculiar natural aptitude by giving them a share of the profits, and placing upon them the detailed responsibility for wise management and the continued protection of the quality of the product.

The total authorized capital of the Dennison Manufacturing Company is $5,600,000 — first preferred stock, $4,500,000; second preferred stock, $50,000; and industrial partnership stock, $1,050,000. A cumulative dividend at the rate of eight per cent is allotted to the first preferred stock. The second preferred stock enjoys a fixed rate of dividend at or above four per cent. It may be issued in exchange for industrial partnership stock under conditions mentioned below. After the payment of dividends on the first and second preferred stock, a small fund is set aside annually for the purpose of buying in shares of the first preferred stock under favorable circumstances.

The industrial partnership stock is issued to employees who in the previous year have: (1) been paid twelve hundred dollars or over and served the company seven years; (2) been paid fifteen hundred dollars and served the company six years; (3) been paid eighteen hundred dollars and served the company five years. The shares, each representing ten dollars, are issued in proportion to the value of the services of the employee as expressed in terms of wages or salaries.

Out of one half of the remaining net profits, after the deductions have been made as outlined above, dividends are paid to the holders of the industrial partnership stock. So that there may be frequent issues of this stock, the dividend rate on it cannot exceed twenty per cent during any year. On the other hand, no new issue is made unless a five-per-cent cash dividend has been paid on the outstanding industrial partnership stock during the preceding twelve months. The remaining net profits are finally allotted to the principal employees by issuing, out of the authorized industrial partnership stock, shares in proportion to the wage or salary value of their services.

There are at present two hundred and twelve "industrial partners" in the Dennison organization. They hold more than a third ($450,000) of the authorized industrial partnership stock. When industrial partnership stock to the amount of $1,000,000 has been issued, the controlling voting power will fall into the hands of the holders of it. So long as the dividend on the preferred stock is earned, their control will be absolute.

There are, then, two standard types of stock profit-sharing plans. The labor dividend may be paid by the issue of special employees' stock — this is the Dennison Manufacturing Company's plan — or it may be applied toward the purchase of the regular shares of the company — the Boston Consolidated Gas Company's management. The plan favored by the Lever

Brothers' Company is quite different, for its certificates do not represent cash.

Other plans. Still other methods of interesting employees in their employer's welfare through the issue of stock are used by the National Carbon Company, the United States Steel Corporation, and the Illinois Central Railroad Company. The Procter and Gamble Company, of Cincinnati, Ohio, also uses a plan of this type. While this method does not provide for the distribution of a fixed share of the profits to all the employees, it does enable the workers to purchase stock on favorable terms. Generally a bonus is given if the stock is held a specified length of time, say five years.

In some instances, furthermore, it may be found expedient to include the managerial or office force in the distribution of profits; in other cases experience may dictate an opposite course. At first the Simplex Wire and Cable Company, which instituted a profit-sharing plan several years ago, did not allow its superintendents to participate in the profits because it desired an unbiased opinion from them as to the real merits of sharing profits. Later, they were included. Again, at first it was not considered that the plan was applicable to the office force. But a few years later the office forces at both Boston and Chicago were included.

If it is desired to recognize special merit, the Filene method of reserving part of the employees' share of the profits for such a purpose may be followed. If you wish to eliminate the assignment of wages or to create a fund for the care of disabled and aged employees, the Farr Alpaca Company's plan contains many suggestions. If you want to provide a pension system, Sir William Lever's management should be closely analyzed. If you desire to build up quickly a staff of employees of more than average morale, the Ford Motor Company's plan is promising, for the basis of its distribution of profits to employees is efficiency in the home and the community, as well as in the factory.

The division of the profits between the employer and employee may be annually, semi-annually, or more frequently. The annual distribution method is quite general among profit-sharing firms. Occasionally a six-months' basis is used. In support of these arrangements, it is urged that profits paid in a lump sum are more likely to be saved or to be used for permanent home improvements.

The Ford profit-sharing plan. It is also pointed out that business is generally done on an annual or semi-annual basis, and that a more frequent accounting is not feasible. The Ford Motor Company, however, distributes a share of its profits to employees semi-monthly. It is able to do this because of its unusual financial condition. One half of the estimated profits for 1914 was set aside at the beginning of the year, and semi-monthly employees were given a share of it in addition to their wages. The main advantage of this plan is that the confidence of employees who might otherwise take a short-sighted viewpoint is at once secured. It is true that recent tendencies in profit sharing indicate that the Ford plan of remuneration has an exceedingly wide range of adaptability to particular conditions in the individual store or shop, and that other industrial measures can often be instituted advantageously in connection with it.

Case of the small business. Most of the instances already discussed happen to refer to rather large concerns. How about the small organization — the shop or store office with only a few employees? The basic principles of the plans tested out by the larger concerns can be studied, and then adapted to the smallest business. Many small concerns have found profit-sharing of one type or another extremely worth while.

If a small concern decides to incorporate and sell stock to employees, it is, of course, necessary to provide that this stock will be returned at a specified price — or one to be fixed by appraisement — when employment ceases. It is also necessary to take into consideration that in many States a minority stockholder can cause a great deal of petty annoyance to the management if, for any reason, he becomes provoked, and sets out to do so.

It is not hard to guard against these possible difficulties when planning a profit-sharing arrangement for a small concern, particularly if a capable lawyer is consulted. The Filene plan of dividing up one half the net profits among employees can be adapted to the needs of the smallest concern, even without incorporating. If it is felt absolutely necessary to hide the amount of the profits, the proportion which the employees' share bears to the total need not be specified, and can be treated as a secret.

Many small retail concerns are introducing commission plans while considering the advisability of adopting profit-sharing arrangements. They give their salesmen and saleswomen commissions on all sales above certain amounts, and guarantee them a definite minimum wage. In two or three instances this plan is known to have increased sales over thirty per cent. Large concerns use it, too, and often with similar success.

So much for the detailed methods by which profit sharing can be carried out. Why is it often so profitable from a dollars-and-cents angle? Probably this employee's reply to "What is your opinion of Henry Ford's profit-sharing plan?" is as good an answer as any: "It makes an employee feel different from a hired man. It makes a man feel as if he was working in his own business."

CHAPTER XV

EMPLOYEE REPRESENTATION

1. Development of Shop Committees [1]

Extent of system. There are to-day in the United States between three and four hundred business establishments, employing between half a million and a million workmen, that have organized shop committees. Practically all of these committees have been installed within the last four years. Although most American employers consider this system to be of most recent origin, it was set up on the Continent during the last quarter of the nineteenth century in an attempt to check the growing power of the trades unions, and, failing, decayed (save in the mining industry), only to be reincarnated after the armistice in a far more radical guise as a method of securing control by the workers' over-production.

Contrast with Whitley system. Many, however, who are ignorant of the Continental experience with shop committees are acquainted with the Whitley Councils of England, and believe the American shop-committee system to be similar. The two plans differ, however, in the following basic respects: (1) The American shop-committee system is confined to individual plants, or at most to the plants of one employer, whereas the Whitley system provides for district and national councils for each industry, and indeed in practice has placed greater emphasis upon them than upon the formation of local works councils. (2) Whereas the overwhelming majority of American shop committees are not in any way affiliated or connected with the trade unions as such; in England the trade unions are recognized as the spokesmen of labor and select the representatives to meet the representatives of the employers. Stated more simply, the shop-committee system in America has grown up outside the unions, while the Whitley system is based upon them.

Contrast with trade-unionism. What, then, is the difference

[1] "Shop Committees," by Paul H. Douglas. *Journal of Political Economy,* February, 1921. University of Chicago Press, publishers.

between the shop committee and the trades union? They are similar in that they are both organizations whereby the wishes of the workers may be expressed and both constitute a means of substituting a collective bargain between employer and workmen concerning the wage contract in place of the individual bargain. They differ, however, in three respects: (1) The shop committee represents the workmen of only one plant or company, while the union represents the workmen of many plants in a given trade or industry. (2) The management is not excluded from the meetings of the shop committee, whereas it is from the meetings of the unions. (3) The shop committees, in the United States, at least, are initiated by the employers, while the unions are initiated by the workers. Of these three points of difference the first is, of course, the most important.

One of the most important issues in the labor world to-day is as to the proper relationship between the two. Should the shop committee be a substitute for the union, and thus make the plant or concern the final unit of organization on the part of the men, or should it be a supplement to the union and perform certain functions while retaining the wider organizations?

There can be but little doubt that the recent enthusiasm for shop committees on the part of the employers has been due to their belief that here was a ready substitute for the unions. They were thus enabled to admit the principle of collective bargaining, which was becoming accepted by the public as equitable and necessary, and yet avoid the necessity of dealing with the unions. This attitude was clearly manifested in the President's First Industrial Conference of 1919, when the representatives of the employers insisted that the unit of collective bargaining should be the shop, stating that "the establishment rather than the industry as a whole or any branch of it should, as far as practicable, be considered as the unit of production and mutual interest on the part of employer and employee." In the Canadian Industrial Conference the employers took a similar attitude and argued that they "should not be required to negotiate except directly, with their own employees." Both of these statements seem somewhat oblique, but no one who followed the two conferences could be in doubt as to their meaning. In both cases it was a refusal to recognize collective bargaining with the unions and an expression of willingness instead to set up, if necessary, shop units for collective bargaining.

Shop committees as an anti-union weapon. It is always difficult and often unprofitable to speculate concerning the motives of men, but if one studies the circumstances surrounding the installation of shop committees by individual firms, he is forced to the conclusion that the dominant motive in the vast majority of cases has been the desire to supplant or "head off" the unions. This is not to imply that this purpose need always have been consciously pursued; oftentimes it was undoubtedly subconscious. But it is most significant and indeed practically conclusive that the vast majority of shop committees are in plants that have been operating on the non-union shop basis.

Thus the pioneer plan of any size in America, that of the Colorado Fuel and Iron Company, was adopted in 1915 after a bitter struggle with the miners' union during 1914, while the Standard Oil Company's system came not long after the strike which tied up their Bayonne, New Jersey, plant. The establishment of such committees by governmental bodies, as the Shipbuilding Labor Adjustment Board and the National War Labor Board, was almost uniformly in plants which refused to recognize or deal with the unions. The adjustment boards used the shop committees as a means of obtaining non-union collective bargaining where union collective bargaining could not be secured. The adoption of the shop-committee plan by many steel companies, such as the Bethlehem Steel Corporation, the Midvale Steel Company, and others in 1916 and 1919, followed closely upon the campaign to organize the iron and steel workers launched by the American Federation of Labor. It will be remembered that one of these companies took its shop committee on a trip to Atlantic City, and there succeeded in inducing the committee to denounce the claims for decreased hours and increased wages which were being made by the union representatives. In a similar fashion the shop-committee plans of the International Harvester Company, the Willys-Overland Company, and the Goodyear Rubber Company cannot be understood without a knowledge of labor experiences of these firms and their very real fear that their plants might become unionized. The shop-committee plan of the Western Union Telegraph Company was installed after the trouble caused by their refusal to recognize the telegraphers' union and assisted the company in fighting the strike of 1919. Turning to street railways, we find that the organization of shop committees by the Philadelphia Rapid Transit Company and the Interborough Rapid Transit of New York came in each case soon after the attempts by the unions to secure recognition, while the shop-committee plans instituted by the Kirschbaum Clothing Company of Philadelphia and the Michael-Stern Company of Rochester were clearly designed to prevent organization by the Amalgamated Clothing Workers. Similarly, the shipyards of San Francisco Bay announced a shop-committee system during strikes conducted against them, while the plans instituted near Seattle have come shortly after the conclusion of strikes conducted by unions and in plants the owners of which are steadfast in their opposition to dealing with the unions. The shop-committee system recently instituted in the California oil fields comes after a long struggle between the employers and employees. One could multiply these cases, but the foregoing are sufficient.

A frank statement of the purposes of the movement has been made by Mr. D. R. Kennedy, an adviser on industrial relations to some of the largest concerns in the country. "After all, what difference does it make whether one plant has a 'shop committee,' a 'works council,' a 'Leitch plan,' a 'company union,' or whatever else it may be called? These different forms are but mechanisms for putting into practice . . . 'family factory relations' and local shop expression. They can all be called 'company unions,' and they all mean the one big fundamental point — *the open shop*." All of this, of course, does not affect the question whether the shop committee is a satisfactory substitute for the unions, but it does indicate that committees are being used for this purpose, and that a consideration of the relative merits of these two forms of organization is far from being an academic matter.

Practical defects. In evaluating the worth of the shop-committee system, one must be on one's guard to distinguish between the merits of plans already in operation and the inherent worth of the system. The fact that there are certain grave defects in many existing plans which might make it impossible to approve of them specifically does not in itself prove that a shop-committee system purified of these defects might not be desirable, since it is, of course, possible to have many incorrect applications of a correct principle. Certainly, however, the vast majority of the present plans have such serious flaws in the protection which they afford the workers that it seems improbable that the workmen will permanently accept them in their present form. Some of these defects are:

1. In many cases the employers control or influence the election of committeemen. While practically all plans pledge the employers to keep hands off the elections, more or less covert pressure is frequently exercised to defeat men suspected of radicalism and to elect those favorable to the employers' point of view. This was clearly evidenced in several steel mills during the early winter of 1919, when the companies concerned were anxious to keep unionism out of their plants and feared that active union men might be elected to the shop committees and use these as a lever to force union recognition. Even where the management, as such, does not take an active part, its general sentiments can be easily perceived by foremen and other minor officials and by the men themselves, causing an indirect but no less real influencing of the result.

2. The function of many shop committees is limited to non-vital matters. Many so-called shop committees are nothing more than welfare committees, while still others are only grievance bodies which may take up with the management individual complaints concerning wages, hours, and conditions of employment, but which have no power to negotiate a general wage scale for the plant as a whole. Many others, such as the Youngstown Sheet and Tube Company, specify that "the right to hire and discharge and lay-off for lack of work or other legitimate reason is vested exclusively in the management." The omission of these topics leaves the workers with absolutely no collective protection on those matters which concern them most.

3. Frequently the control in the joint committee is held by the employers. Thus the plan of the San Francisco shipyards gave one more vote to the representatives of the employers than it did to the workmen. The industrial democracy plan of Mr. John Leitch operates in much the same way. Here a house of representatives elected by the workmen, and a senate composed of foremen and minor executives, deliberate on matters of interest, and

refer their decision to the cabinet of executives for approval. It is apparent that the senate, which is certainly more representative of the employer than of the employees, virtually can negative any action by the house, and prevent it from even being referred to the cabinet for approval.

4. In many, although probably not in the majority of, cases the decision of the joint committee is not final, but must be approved by the executive before taking effect. This is not only the case in the Leitch plan, but in many others as well. The shop committee is, therefore, under these conditions, made merely advisory to the management, and should the management disagree with the committee there is little further recourse, save in those cases where arbitration is provided. The argument that even here the employer will seldom reject the findings of the joint committee does not meet the question. The fact remains that he has the power to do so, and that the asserted democratic government exists only on sufferance.

5. The qualifications for voting and holding office are such as to debar a large number of employees. It is typically provided that a workman must have been employed in the concern six months or a year before he is eligible for election as a shop committeeman and must be employed sixty days or more before he can vote. Many plants, moreover, limit office-holding to citizens, or to those having first papers, while others require this for voting as well. These requirements, of course, have the effect of barring out a large class of floating and foreign labor from representation, and while no more unjust than our political requirements for voting, may prevent the shop committee from becoming truly representative.

6. Shop committeemen are frequently prevented from pleading the case of the workmen very strongly because of their fear of being discharged or discriminated against. The rules of practically every shop committee state that perfect freedom is to be given the committeemen to express their opinions and that no discrimination shall be practiced against them. Many employers, nevertheless, do coerce the committeemen who take a radical or combative stand in the meetings, while many others, although they believe themselves to be fair, become prejudiced against the active proponents of the workmen's side and this prejudice leads

naturally into discrimination. Moreover, even where these dangers to free expression do not exist, the workmen often believe that they do, and consequently moderate their claims and their method of presentation, because of their fear that they may be covertly punished if they are too active or question the employers too closely. This is particularly the case where the employer reserves to himself, as he generally does, complete decision as to promotion, demotion, and discharge.

Wherein unions are better protection for labor. As I have said, although many plans do have these grave blemishes, it is perfectly possible to conceive of a shop committee which would not have them. The scrupulously conscientious employer, who seeks diligently and intelligently to deal fairly with his employees, would undoubtedly remove nearly all of the defects. Even here, it is questionable, however, whether he could completely eradicate the subconscious fear of the workmen to put their case strongly when they feel no forces outside their shop supporting them. Moreover, the less scrupulous employer may choose to perpetuate some of these very defects for the purpose of weakening the bargaining power of the workers. While in theory, therefore, these faults could be remedied, in practice some of them may be expected, in a greater or a less degree, to continue. Furthermore, careful analysis of the situation will show that even a model shop committee, void of the above-mentioned blemishes, is inherently not as effective a bargaining agency as the union, and hence from the standpoint of the workmen cannot be an adequate substitute.

1. Since it is limited to one shop or to the employees of one concern, it does not protect the "fair" employer from the "nibbling of competition" and the underbidding of the meanest man. It is thus likely to drag the conditions of labor in all plants down to the level of the conditions granted by the meanest man. This may be illustrated as follows: Employer A has a shop committee in his plant and pays high wages under good working conditions, while employer X, who does not have a shop committee, bargains with each of his employees individually and by reason of his greater bargaining strength pays much lower wages and affords poorer working conditions. Employer X, therefore, will be able to produce more cheaply than A, unless A's higher wages call out correspondingly greater production, which is not at all likely.

The only way A can protect himself is to reduce wages correspondingly. Other employers with shop committees will be obliged to do the same. Clearly the only way to protect the workmen in A's factory is to organize the employees of X and to push their wages up to the level of A's wage. Under the shop-committee system, however, this would be impossible, since the employees of one concern could not organize the employees of another or because independently affiliated with them. Through a union, however, the employees of A, B, C, etc., would furnish the moral and material resources to organize the workmen in X's plant and thereby protect themselves from the menace of low wages. In other words, despite the opinion of any well-meaning employers, no one plant under our present competitive industrial system can maintain proper standards of wages and hours by itself alone. There must be a general minimum for the industry as a whole below which no plant can fall, and the unified pressure of the unions is the chief means whereby the workmen may protect themselves against the attempts of employers to secure trade by depressing wages. The employer, indeed, should not be blamed for this, since he is merely striving to get business and in order to do so must make low prices which will attract the consumer.

It has been just this necessity of preventing competitive encroachments upon wages which has caused the unions to evolve from local shop organizations to the national and international unions of to-day. With our ever-widening market, the unit of labor organization must expand equally in order to maintain basic standards everywhere and to protect those already in its folds. To propose a return to the shop as the final unit of labor organization is, therefore, as much of an anachronism as to propose that our industrial system should return to the period of village self-sufficiency.

2. Since under the shop-committee system employers treat only with their own men, the workmen are deprived of expert outside advice in putting their case and conducting their negotiations. The modern wage contract needs a great deal of skill in negotiating. The owners of a concern hire skilled experts to represent them. The general manager, the personnel expert, the industrial engineer, and the lawyer are all the hired outside representatives of the shareholders. It is only fair, therefore, that the

workers should be allowed outside representatives as well. Men who work with their hands all day are seldom capable of driving as good a bargain as a skilled and shrewd negotiator. The union business agent or "walking delegate" is this expert negotiator for the workmen, and, despite his many faults, performs on the whole exceedingly valuable functions for those whom he represents. Indeed, it might be said that the union is in part a device whereby individual workmen are able to pool small amounts and hire a professional expert to represent them. This opportunity the shop committee virtually denies them.

3. It does not furnish the instrumentality which the unions do provide for the enactment of labor laws to better the conditions of labor. The labor question cannot be settled on the economic field alone. Protective legislation has been found necessary to protect men as well as women from the effects of unrestricted competition. Such legislation is generally opposed by the organized employers, and its passage and subsequent enforcement depend largely upon the efforts of labor itself, together with that of independent humanitarian groups. The unions, representing as they do a wide constituency, are enabled to apply a considerable measure of pressure for these purposes which unconnected shop committees would be totally unable to muster.

4. Save in a very large plant, the shop-committee system cannot afford the protection against sickness and unemployment that the union with its insurance funds, drawn from a wide area, can offer.

5. In the event that it became necessary for the workmen of a given plant or company operating under the shop-committee system to put pressure upon the employer to compel the acceptance of a demand, they would be in a very weak position to enforce their claim. Should they collectively leave work, they would not have the moral or financial backing of their fellow workers in other plants. They could not secure strike benefits to assist them, nor would other workers aid them by putting pressure upon the employer to accede to their requests. The union, however, buttresses the workers in an individual plant through strike benefits, assistance in picketing, moral support, and frequently through sympathetic strikes and boycotts. Should a break come with the employers the workmen's chances of success, therefore,

would be much greater if they were organized in a union than if they were merely organized in a shop committee.

6. Finally, it may be asked, why should the workmen be expected to organize only within plants when their employers are organized between plants? Practically every large city has its chamber of commerce through which the employers of the locality try to work out a common labor policy for their various concerns. In addition there are the many employers' associations which deal exclusively with labor matters, such as the Associated Industries which have been formed in so many cities in the last eighteen months. Moreover, practically every State has its manufacturers' association, while there are national and sectional bodies in nearly every trade and industry. In addition to these are such national organizations as the United States Chamber of Commerce, the National Manufacturers' Association, the National Industrial Conference Board, the Anti-Boycott Association, etc. Employers join these bodies in the main so that they may take common action in labor matters.

If workmen, therefore, should be organized only within the plant and should not be joined with the employees of other plants, should not all employers withdraw from these employers' organizations and not combine on labor matters? This, of course, few, if any, employers would do, and it is not proposed here that they should withdraw. Quite the contrary. It is very desirable that they should organize and take common counsel and adopt common measures. But if they do so, how can we or they legitimately deny to their employees the right to do the same?

Weakness of labor's position. The plain truth of the matter is that in our modern industrial society the interests of the worker cannot be protected adequately by the public opinion of the consumers, who are seeking low prices and who are generally ignorant of, and often careless about, conditions of employment; they cannot be protected by the benevolence of employers, not only because the modern impersonal wage relationship is not conducive to benevolence, but also because the employers themselves are in the grip of competitive pressure forcing them to cut costs wherever possible in order to secure trade. The interests of the workers can ultimately only be protected effectively by an organization of the workmen themselves to resist the pressure for lower wages and sweated conditions brought to bear upon them through the market structure. The success with which they can offset and overcome the personal and impersonal pressure already exercised against them will depend in direct ratio upon the strength of the organization they can set up. To substitute disconnected shop committees for the well-knit union forms would be to deal a severe and perhaps deadly blow at effective working-class organization, and to render them almost helpless before the opposing forces.

Therefore, while the creation of a shop committee is a real step forward in plants now bargaining with their employees individually, and even here only as a transitional stage to a more desirable relationship, it is almost invariably retrogressive when used to displace collective bargaining with the unions or to delay or prevent such dealings.

Those who have irrevocably resolved that the growing movement of labor should be checked cannot be expected to favor unions in preference to shop committees. Rather will this class prefer shop committees precisely because they *will* weaken the power of labor. Those, however, who know the conditions of life and work of the typical modern workman and his family and are sincerely desirous that he may have an opportunity to lead the better life, will realize that shop committees are not and cannot be a just substitute for unionism.

Federation of shop committees. It may well be asked whether a federation of shop committees and the creation of a council for the industry as a whole, outside the existing unions, is not an adequate substitute for the unions. Such is the plan of organization of the Loyal Legion of Loggers and Lumbermen, which has been functioning in the lumber industry of the Pacific Northwest for the last three years, and it is evidently some such plan that Mr. W. L. Mackenzie King regards as a possible solution. This method would enable a minimum scale of wages and working conditions to be set for the industry as a whole, and would consequently protect individual employers against the competition of their fellows. It would therefore be a vast improvement upon the uncoördinated shop-committee system. Is it then a substitute for the unions?

In the first place, it may be remarked that such a plan of organization would be a union of a sort. It is not necessary for an organization to have the *cachet* of the American Federation of Labor to be a union. Secondly, the question whether it would be preferable to the existing type of union would depend upon the opportunities granted the workmen under it. If both the rank and file of the workers and their representatives on the shop committees and on the industrial council were allowed to meet separately from the employers; if the organizations of the various industries were allowed to federate; if each body were allowed to accumulate funds for insurance and unemployment and to assist the workers in other shops or industries if they believed them to be in the right; if the workers through their organizations were permitted to present their program of legislation to legislative bodies; if they were allowed to hire experts from without a plant or industry who would not be dependent upon the employers for their jobs; if all these conditions existed, then such a system would be a sufficient protection to the workmen. It is extremely doubtful, however, whether the great mass of employers, in their present frame of mind, would allow such freedom to the workers. What, indeed, would be the advantage in replacing the present union organization by bodies every whit as formidable in bargaining power?

On the whole, then, it seems most dangerous to replace the existing union structures by the shop committee, or even by the industrial council system. It is better to build, in an evolutionary fashion, upon the existing union forms, trying to rid them of their evils, than to risk the protection of the workmen exclusively upon these newer methods of organization, which for a long time at least must depend for their effectiveness almost entirely upon the generosity of the employers.

True functions of the shop committee. The foregoing remarks should not be construed as meaning that the shop committee has no legitimate place in industry. Quite the contrary. It is because the shop committee has such very significant and important functions to perform that the attempt to use it as a union substitute is especially dangerous. While the shop committee may replace many unions for a time, the union type of organization cannot permanently be displaced by such an incomplete structure, since the logic of the situation will ultimately lead the workers to organize in ever larger and more effective units. A greater danger than the temporary weakening of the workers' bargaining strength is the probability that, if the shop committee is used as a union substitute, the minds of the workers will become so inflamed that they will refuse to see its good points and will reject it utterly. In other words, if it becomes a question of shop committee or trade-unionism, it will be the shop committees and not unionism that ultimately will disappear. If the valuable possibilities of the shop committee are to be preserved, it must be clearly envisaged that it is to be a supplement to the union and not a substitute for them.

What, then, are the functions which the shop committee can perform, once the union has been recognized as the body with which the collective bargain is to be made?

1. It would furnish an excellent instrumentality for applying and interpreting the terms of the labor agreement made with the unions and would enable grievances to be settled with a minimum of friction. Any labor agreement necessarily creates vexatious problems of administration, such as the correct classification of workmen into trades, the interpretation of overtime, the determination as to whether discharges are made for cause or for union membership or activity, the enforcement of rules as to piece-rates, hourly wages, etc. Ordinarily these adjustments are made in behalf of the men by the business agent, who is generally both ignorant of the details of plant administration and, however excellent as a combative negotiator of the original contract, is seldom tactful in bringing grievances to the attention of the management. In a large percentage of the cases he interferes with and impedes production unnecessarily in his attempt to settle grievances. Indeed, much of the opposition to unions on the part of the employers is due, not so much to fundamental opposition to the principle of collective bargaining, as to their fear of a "walking delegate" interfering unnecessarily with the operation of their plants.

Under the shop committee, this irritation would be reduced to a minimum, since the shop committeemen would know the particular situation and could make the adjustments with the management. In those few cases where disagreement would occur between the employer and the committee, appeal could be taken to a higher board, set up for the local industrial district, before which the business agent could appear (with the shop committee) to represent the workmen. The shop committee, moreover, could settle many grievances, such as abuse by foreman or fellow workers, which in the nature of the case are now impossible to settle even in a union shop. The equitable adjustment of these grievances by a body in which the workman has confidence will result in a much-improved plant morale, in greater individual effort, and consequently in heightened production.

2. It would permit workers and employers to meet on a common ground and understand each other. The representatives of both groups can meet face to face in discussion over common problems. From this meeting a better mutual attitude is almost invariably created than would be secured by dealing only through intermediaries.

3. It would enlist the workers' interest in production to a much greater extent than at present and would make the plant more efficient. Once protected by the collective bargain, workmen can be brought to realize that the greater the production, the higher will be their real wages. The shop committee is the effective local agency whereby this may be impressed upon the men and their appeal will have far greater effect than if it came directly from the management. Not only can the general appeal for production be made by the shop committee, but it can also set up coöperative relationships with the management along a number of different lines, whereby an increase in quantity and an improvement of the quality of the goods can be effected. Some of the concrete subjects which a truly representative shop committee, or its subcommittees, can deal with are: (*a*) the better utilization of the practical knowledge and experience of the employees, which under ordinary conditions are now untapped; (*b*) elimination of the waste of materials; (*c*) better coördination of work between departments; (*d*) introduction and utilization of new processes and machinery; (*e*) coöperation in the fixation of standards of normal quantity and quality expected at various tasks; (*f*) methods for the reduction of labor turnover and absenteeism; (*g*) active coöperation in accident and occupational disease prevention; (*h*) active development of trade training in the shop and supplementary training outside the plant.

4. It would train the worker in the real problems of industry

and would acquaint him with the actual conditions of affairs. Much of our present industrial unrest comes from a lack of knowledge of what the basic facts of business are. Much of it, whether consciously or unconsciously, comes from the desire of workmen to have a share in the conduct of the work at which they are employed. The shop-committee system, by admitting the workmen to a partial control in the actual government of production, would not only be extremely educative to its members, but to all the electors as well. Just as the ballot leads citizens to become more interested in political matters, so would the very act of industrial suffrage cause the workers to take a more intelligent interest in the affairs of the workshop. Industry would thus become educative in a real sense, turning out better men as well as more goods. With the increased knowledge of actual conditions, impossible demands upon the part of the workmen would become less frequent.

5. It would lay the basis for a more effective organization of the workers, with the plant as the unit of organization rather than the present heterogeneous local composed of workers from different plants. As the report of the New Jersey State Chamber of Commerce well says:

> All the meetings and all the business of the union are conducted in its various headquarters, central or local, which are located more or less remotely from the workshop in which the constituency of the union is located. In other words, the organization is to a considerable degree detached from its foundations. Instead of coming to their constituency in the places where it is located, i.e., in the workshops, the leaders must depend upon the constituency coming to them, i.e., to the headquarters, whenever its participation in organization affairs is desired. A large proportion of the members fail to come and the attendance of the meetings is usually very poor. The union leaders of to-day must not be blamed for this fundamental defect of their organization. It had been in existence long before they started their activities. It grew up under conditions when employers would not allow the unions to transact their business in the workshops and would discharge the men who were active in the union movement.

If the workshop is used as the basic local, this difficulty will be overcome and there will be a better attendance at meetings and more interest in union affairs.

The strength of the coal miners' unions, both here and abroad, is due in no small measure to the fact that they are largely organized with the pit as the typical local and that they thus have a cohesive and interested group of members. The clothing unions in this country are coming more and more to use the shop as the basic local unit of organization, while the printing unions have their "chapel" or shop organization as well. Such a type of organization would, of course, lead to industrial rather than to craft-unionism, since the entire plant would be the unit and not a specific trade. This development squares on the whole with the progress of machine industry and would effect the practical elimination of jurisdictional disputes. It is worthy of note that it is precisely this desirability of the workshop as the basic unit of unionism that Guild Socialists, such as Mr. G. D. H. Cole, strongly advocate.

Conclusions. Modern industry needs both the shop committee and the trade union, since both are necessary for the effective carrying-out of the relationship between workmen and employer. This relationship is neither one of complete antagonism nor one of absolute harmony. Neither the I.W.W. preamble, with its statement that "the working class and the employing class have nothing in common," nor the belief of the liberal employer that "the interests of labor and capital are identical," is completely correct, although each expresses a glittering half-truth. Paradoxical as it may sound, the interests of employer and employee are at once both harmonious and antagonistic. They are harmonious in that it is to their mutual interest to have the profits of an individual concern and the total production of society as large as possible. The larger the industrial pie, the more there is to divide; the higher the profits, the greater the possibility of higher wages. Their interests, however, are antagonistic in the division of the product. Each wants to get as large a share of the pie as possible, and the more one secures, the less will the other receive.

The unions hitherto have been chiefly combative organizations designed to protect and enhance the workmen's share in distribution. This is still a necessary function, and one that must be performed by the strong organization of the unions; to substitute the shop committee or even the industrial council for them would be a tragedy. The coöperative features of the relationship between employer and employee, however, need to be developed equally, in order that the size of the pie may be increased as much as possible, and in performing this function the shop committee is invaluable. The relationship of the two bodies, in other words, is properly complementary, and not mutually exclusive. We can only hope that in practice this harmonization will be secured.

2. An Example of Employee Representation [1]

I can best set forth the new method of coöperation between employers and workers in America — generally called the "shop-committee" system — by telling the extraordinarily interesting story of what has happened in one small industry where it has been applied.

Before the war this new method was practically unknown either in America or elsewhere, although there were several pioneer experiments in progress; but to-day there are several hundred industries — or, if individual plants are counted, many thousands — varying all the way from huge steel plants, like the Colorado Fuel and Iron Company and the Midvale Steel Company, to little factories of a few hundred hands, where the new plan is being practically tried out. In a following chapter I shall present a general survey of the present state and promise of the entire movement — for the experiments vary widely in detail and still more widely in spirit — but the actual living operation of the new method can best be understood by looking at its application to a small industry in a small town where all the factors are plainly visible.

Wappingers Falls is a very old town, as towns go in America. It lies back from the Hudson River a few miles below Poughkeepsie, where a fine stream comes down out of the hills to supply power for its mill. In earlier days before the railroads came, its only communication with New York was by way of Hudson River sloops which in summer worked in through the narrow inlet, or in winter by the stage-coach along the river road.

[1] From *The New Industrial Unrest*, pp. 149–65, by Ray Stannard Baker. Published by Doubleday, Page & Company.

Here long ago a bleachery and cotton printworks was established (now called the Dutchess Bleachery). I asked a bent old man I saw working over one of the vats how long he had been there.

"What's that?"

"How long have you worked here?"

"Fifty-nine years," he said, "in this one place."

So it was long ago. It was like many if not most such plants in America. It had its Royal Family that owned everything — mill, houses, land — and lived little there, but had leisure for education and European travel—opportunity written large. And the people worked long hours — as long, they say, as fourteen — then twelve, then ten, and wages were low. There was never any incentive upon their part to work hard, or improve methods, or increase production, because no surplus of their common toil ever by any chance reached their pockets, for their income was inexorably set by the iron law of supply and demand in the wage market. On the other hand, they did help bear whatever losses the state of the trade or the inefficiency of the management might entail upon the industry — for whenever business was "dull" the mill could be slackened down or closed, and they thrown out of employment. Their labor was as much a commodity as the chlorate of lime they used in bleaching the new gray cloth or the starch in stiffening it.

A few years ago the mill was purchased by a new company, the chief owners of which were men with social imagination. They were among the many employers in America who are beginning to be troubled about their relationships to their business and to their workers.

When the war came to Wappingers Falls, there was that sudden lift of common effort, common enthusiasm, which for a moment fired the soul of America. For a moment we forgot ourselves; we were greater than ourselves. There are those who mourn over the reaction and the present wave of unrest, but nothing can ever rob us of that great moment, nor wipe out the effect of it. We shall never go back to the ante-bellum ways or times. Whether we like it or not we are entering a new world.

The war jogged Wappingers Falls, as it jogged so many other towns, into a sudden self-consciousness. It had, for once, a good look at itself. Here it was, a rather outwardly attractive town of some thirty-five hundred people — with comfortable shady streets and picturesque hills all about. Most of the people lived in pleasant but more or less dilapidated houses, a few of which were miserably built of sheet iron, roofs and all, as cold in winter as they were hot in summer. There was one big Roman Catholic Church — for a majority of the people are of Irish and Italian origin — and four struggling, competing Protestant churches, most of them without vision or leadership. Its schools were no better, nor worse, perhaps, than those in other mill towns like this — more a habit, a routine, than a source of power. Its politics was without issues or ideas: had degenerated into local factional strife for trivial authority and small rewards. Its saloons were the saloons of any small manufacturing town, and the less said of them the better. As for the mill in which all the people worked, for which the town existed, it was owned almost exclusively (its capital is $1,350,000) by people who did not live in Wappingers Falls and never had.

Not an especially pleasant portrait, you say; and yet this town was probably better than the average of mill towns in America. It might be called 'A Portrait of an American Town at the Beginning of the Twentieth Century.' There was not enough emotion below the surface to make its aspect tragic — there was only blankness, dullness, uncreativeness — boredom!

In the summer of 1917 a young minister named James Myers went to Wappingers Falls. He was sent by the owners of the company to see what he could do to change the conditions. When the new company had taken the property, it had been much run down physically; they had built it up, got it on a profitable basis, and they wanted now to attack the problem of a new relationship with the personnel.

Mr. Hatch, the treasurer of the company, had been for some time interested in experiments in "industrial democracy," and had begun the introduction of the new system in a mill in which he was interested in Abbeville, South Carolina. He wanted to try out something of the same sort in Wappingers Falls. He had only two general ideas regarding the method of going about it — both fundamental; one was to go slow, not make changes too abruptly; the other was to be honest with the workers at every step, that is, not to give them something that looked like a "new deal," merely as a screen for a closer riveting upon them of the old system — or to prevent unionism.

A meeting of the five hundred operatives was called and the new representative plan was explained to them, and they elected by secret ballot six representatives (afterwards eleven) from the various departments. These were organized into a board of operatives, and James Myers was chosen executive secretary, his salary being paid by the company. It is to his enthusiasm, vision, and organizing ability that the plan owes much of its success.

There was one small labor union of skilled men in the mill, and they joined in the enterprise and elected their president, Mr. Bennett, to the board, where his experience as a union leader was of great value. The board, at the beginning, was given three groups of powers:

1. To solve the problem of housing. The company houses were out of repair and there was constant complaint. The company agreed to give the board of operatives entire charge of these houses and to supply the money for all repairs they should recommend.

2. To take up the matter of education and recreation in the community, and especially the matter of a clubhouse to take the place of the saloons when they should be closed.

3. The board was also empowered to suggest methods of improvement to the management in other matters — living conditions, wages, and the like, but it was without power to enforce its recommendations.

A survey of housing conditions was immediately begun, and the practical knowledge of the operatives on the board was at once apparent — and also their desire to maintain a businesslike attitude toward the problem. That is, they held that the houses ought to return a fair interest on the capital invested. At once a great transformation began to take place in the village: reconstruction of old houses, new paint, new conveniences; and even the removal of several antiquated tenements. All this was entirely managed by the board of operatives, but paid for by the company. The board also established a fine baseball and athletic field in a natural amphitheater, and a playground for the children, and by winter they had taken possession of one of the old saloon buildings and changed it into a well-equipped village clubhouse which is, to-day, one of the most popular places in town — a center of its life. They also began the publication of a monthly paper called *Bleachery Life* — dealing not only with the new plans, but with all sides of mill life, including certain news printed in Italian for Italian workers. This has been a real agency in awakening mutual interest. Plans have now been made for selling all company houses to workers at low prices with deferred payments: and a savings system has been instituted.

The officials of the company kept in close contact with these developments. In November, 1918, they were ready to lay the foundations for the next step. Mr. Hatch addressed a mass meeting of the workers and outlined the broader aspects of his new plan which he called a partnership between workers, management, and capital.

In a partnership each partner, he explained, shares the responsibility of management by taking charge of the business he is best qualified to handle; partners are also entitled to know the general results of their joint efforts; and he said that in the future the board of operatives would receive the report of the net earnings of the company just as did the board of directors; and, finally, partners share in the final net profits of the company, and he outlined a new plan of profit sharing between the owners and the workers which I shall describe later.

Finally he summed up his attitude toward the whole problem in words which merit careful reading as a fine expression of the new point of view:

> Why am I not satisfied with the system of paying wages as determined by supply and demand; i.e., with paying the market price for labor and making as large profits for the company as market conditions will permit? Because I am convinced that this system has been weighed in the scales of human experience and found wanting. It treats every employee as a means to an end, the end being the enrichment of the employer, whereas every man, every woman, and every child is an end in himself or herself, the most valuable creations in the universe. To phrase it differently: Because this system has on the one hand resulted in poverty for many in this glorious land of plenty, and on the other causing, as it

> does, the concentration of great wealth in the hands of a few, has enshrined the pursuit of material wealth as the dominant life motive of men.

This was a general outline of principles: as yet there was no real machinery for working them out. But such machinery cannot be created out of hand: it has to develop out of the needs of the situation. As the board of operatives broadened its scope of activity, it came again and again into contact with the deeper problems of the mill itself: wages, hours, and real coöperative control. As yet it could only make suggestions to the management: but by May, 1919, it was ready to ask for more power. The board explained to the company that "the apathy and lack of interest with which the employees view the board of operatives" were due to the fact that its powers did not affect directly those "things in which many employees are most vitally interested — matters within the mill, question of hours, wages, and the various conditions by which they are surrounded in their daily work." In response to suggestions from the management, which was already considering the reduction of the hours of labor in the plant, they also asked for a forty-eight-hour week instead of the prevailing fifty-five-hour week and for an increase of wages by fifteen per cent. At the same time the board of operatives now felt enough of the new spirit of coöperation and partnership not to stop merely with a demand for better wages and shorter hours for the workers, but they offered to do their part in keeping up production. They expressed their determination to produce as much in eight hours as formerly in ten, and actually suggested the installation of time clocks to keep a record of all employees. Their resolutions are well worth considering:

> While feeling its responsibility in making these suggestions (about decreasing hours and increasing wages), the board of operatives believes that in addition to the saving which will be affected in power and light, the plant can be so managed, and its efficiency so improved in other ways, as to result in turning out practically the same production in forty-eight hours as it turns out at present in fifty-five hours. To this end the board of operatives wishes specifically to recommend the following methods of increasing efficiency:

That time clocks be installed, covering all operatives.

That regular monthly foremen's conferences be held for mutual discussion, with the agent, of the problems of mill management, in order to harmonize the working of the various departments of the plant with each other; to improve working conditions which may effect plant efficiency; to promote the spirit of coöperation among all departments, and with the management, and to increase the efficiency and production of the entire plant.

That a mass meeting of all employees be called and full explanations made in regard to the importance of coöperation on the part of every one in order that production may be kept up and no loss sustained by us all as partners, on account of reduction of hours.

The next step was a long one. The company decided to establish a board of management, consisting of three members representing the employer's side (the manager of the mill, the New York agent, and the treasurer of the company — Mr. Hatch) and three members chosen by the board of operatives, Mr. Aurswald, Mr. Beasley, and Mr. Clark. This board was given absolute power "to settle and adjust such matters of mill management as may arise" — practically complete control of the mill. In case of a deadlock between the two groups over any question, they are empowered to elect a seventh arbitrating member whose deciding vote shall be final. This board went into control in August, 1919.

A profit-sharing system was adopted on these terms: After all expenses are paid, including six per cent interest on capital, the net profits, whatever they may be, are divided, half and half, between the stockholders and the workers. Mr. Hess, the agent (manager) of the mill, has introduced a very complete cost-accounting system, so that net profits can be known monthly and dividends are therefore now declared monthly. The first dividend to the wage-workers was paid last August and represented four per cent upon wages earned in the previous six months.

No sooner, however, is any profit-sharing plan discussed than the problem arises as to what will happen when losses come. The company has met this problem by establishing two sinking funds to be built up out of profits until each reaches $250,000: one to pay half wages to workers if the mill is forced to close down, the other to maintain regular interest on capital.

These new responsibilities, coupled with the new opportunities for a real share in any increased effort, have awakened a wholly new spirit in the mill. There is a reason now for "getting busy," for pushing up production. Instead of opposing the introduction of efficiency schemes in the plant — as workmen so often do — they welcome them. For more production, more efficient work, means more profits — and half of all profits go to them.

I want to give one example of this. Last winter the New York office "came back" at the board of operatives at the mill because of damage to one large shipment of cloth through "pin-cuts." It had cost the company $6000. In former times this loss would have been "swallowed" and not much said; perhaps some employee "fired" if the guilty one could be found. Here is the way the New York office expresses its feelings to the operatives at the mill:

> Let's just for the fun of the thing figure this out for each of us. Increased expenses mean decreased profits, and in this instance our decrease in profits amounts to about $6000, less what we can get for the salvage. Under our partnership agreement the stockholders stand half, or $3000, and the other $3000 is at the expense of the operatives. You all can easily figure out for yourselves just about what your individual share of this is, and can ask yourselves if you got your money's worth. We are sure the stockholders did not. We haven't written you a letter for some time, but this subject sure did drag us out of our shell.

It was no trouble for the five hundred operatives at the mill to calculate what that piece of carelessness cost, on an average, each of them. It was $6. It went through the mill like a shock and it was known just how and where the damage occurred. It can be seen what the public opinion of the mill would be toward those workers who had been so careless as to reduce by $6 the profits of every employee in the mill.

Another thing the board of operatives has done is to offer

prizes for suggestions from workers — in order to get the minds of every one to working upon the common problems of the shop. This has already resulted in a number of improvements. At the payment of each month's dividend, also, Mr. Hess proposes to hold a mass meeting and go over all the affairs of the mill and show the workers where they can improve processes, cut corners, save money. With both managers and men working at improvement of methods, something is bound to happen at Wappingers Falls!

But this is not all. The company has now gone still a step further upon the road to "industrial democracy." It has recognized its own board of directors. It has now five members, three representing capital and management, one elected by the board of operatives, and one representing the community of Wappingers Falls — who is the president of the town. This is aimed to draw together all the interests concerned: the management, the workers, the town. Especially is the last a novel idea — community representation; for in all old mill towns there is a heavy weight of dull local suspicion of the mill and the company. If the town can *know* what is going on, it is the theory of Mr. Hatch that the town also will help. He wants good-will all the way round. The company has now also made arrangements to sell shares of its stock to its operatives at a price somewhat below market value.

The greatest source of difficulty, suspicion and jealousy, leading to war in international affairs, is secret diplomacy. And so it is in industrial affairs: secret deals, back-stairs agreements, sly bookkeeping, dishonest profit sharing. The men behind the Wappingers Falls experiment recognize this, and have provided for a wide degree of publicity. With representatives of the board of operatives sitting on the board of management of the mill, nothing relating to the manufacturing end of the business can be covered up — and now with a delegate of the operatives and of the town in the board of directors the entire inside of the company's business will be known. This is a very advanced step — taken, so far as I know, by only two other employers: one the Filene Store in Boston, the other the Procter & Gamble Soap Company of Cincinnati. It is perhaps practicable yet only in relatively small industries, but it is a tremendous demonstration of the absolute sincerity of the employer in approaching his problem. It is also the best insurance to the employer that his industry will weather hard times and the possible necessity of reducing wages with the full coöperation of the workers — for they, also, will be on the inside and know of the difficulties and problems that confront the industry as well as he does.

This, in brief, is the new plan as applied at Wappingers Falls. It is, of course, very new — as are all of these experiments. As Mr. Hatch himself says: "We cannot really know how it will work until it has been under way for three or four years and we have passed through a period of hard times and losses. That will be the test of it!"

The great point, however, is that here the spirit of *approach* is honest on both sides: there are the beginnings of real coöperation, of real democratic control. With such a spirit new adjustments can be made to meet new difficulties. Like any other human scheme it can be attacked and criticized at many points, but the great thing here is that the problem is being approached with a genuine scientific desire to know the conditions and a spirit of good-will in meeting them. If this does not work, nothing else will — and we might as well toss over civilization, retire to the cynic's corner, and rail at the wickedness of men!

I should also like to add just this observation: and it applies as well to most of these new experiments, *where they are genuine*, and that is that both sides seem to be "having the time of their lives" — downright enjoyment of the new adventure. For it is real creative work in a new field — the most fascinating kind of creative work: with human beings. As one employer in another industry said to me, "It's the most interesting thing I ever did in my life. It beats mere money-making all hollow!"

Like any other truly creative work its results exceed expectations, and yield unanticipated rewards.

3. A Comprehensive Industrial Relations Policy

The Standard Oil program. The Standard Oil Company of New Jersey offers a good illustration of what can be done along the line of a workable industrial relations policy. This corporation has a well-formed policy touching as nearly as possible every point of contact with its employees. It is not the policy of an extremist — the Standard Oil Company is large enough to take care of itself, and does not have to make concessions to labor that it feels are unwarranted. For instance, the company insists upon the maintenance of the open shop. But the company finds it good business to form closer contacts with its employees than the old-fashioned autocracy of industry was accustomed to have. No plan which is held out to the workers to "do them good" can truly succeed; the employee is human, and does not want any one to officiously "do him good." His relation to his employer is one of business, and he prefers to keep it so. If the employer has a scheme that will be profitable to both sides, the worker feels that he can trust it a little farther. It is upon this basis that the Standard Oil Company of New Jersey has built its plan. They phrase it in this manner:

> The labor policy of the Standard Oil Company (New Jersey) is based upon certain well-established principles which have been developed on the fundamental proposition of a square deal for all concerned: the employees, the management, the stockholders, and the public. Several features of this policy have been part of the company's policy for many years; other features have been the outgrowth of joint conferences held during the past few years, but the entire program has been subject to review and amendment by the joint conferences in order that it may continue to express the united judgment of both employer and employee. The outstanding features of this program as at present established at the refineries are as follows:
>
> 1. No discrimination by the company or its employees on account of membership or non-membership in any church, society, fraternity, or union.
> 2. Collective dealing as to all matters of mutual interest, made effective through the industrial representation plan.
> 3. Paying at least the prevailing scale of wages for similar work in the community.
> 4. The eight-hour day, or its equivalent.
> 5. One day's rest in seven, preferably on Sunday, or the equivalent of such period.
> 6. Sanitary and healthful working conditions.

7. Just treatment assured each employee, with opportunity for submission of all grievances for adjustment through the industrial representation plan.
8. Continuous effort to eliminate accidents through effective safeguards and active coöperation of employees and committees, under expert supervision.
9. Payment of disability benefits in case of accidents incurred while at work.
10. Health supervision by a competent medical staff.
11. Payment of sickness benefits after one year's service.
12. Opportunity for special training to qualify employee for better work, with standard system of keeping record of service performed.
13. Promotion according to ability demonstrated and length of service.
14. Partnership through stock ownership made easily possible for the thrifty employee after one year's service, through a stock acquisition plan open until December 30, 1925, the company adding fifty per cent to the amount invested by the employee.
15. Assurance of a generous annuity at the age of sixty-five, guaranteed for life after twenty years of service, with special consideration for those who become disabled before that period.
16. Death benefits, or insurance, providing $500 to $2000 for dependents of employees of one year or more of service.

These are the Standard's sixteen points, set forth in briefest fashion. An analysis will show them to be more comprehensive than they appear on the surface.

The program analyzed. The first plank in the platform is the industrial representation plan, the underlying purpose of which is said to be justice for both sides. It attempts to provide a point of contact between the management and each employee, and regular opportunities for collective action by representatives of the employees and of the management on all matters of mutual interest. Such a plan, honestly carried out, would obviously be of great advantage to the workers; the company also expected to gain, believing that "a system which would create an opportunity for the honest expression and fair consideration of the views of all, which would send the men about their work with the consciousness that so long as the industry flourished their interests were safeguarded, must, in the long run, bring results in contentment, efficiency, coöperation, harmony, and mutual profit."

Joint conference. The plan provides for the election by the employees, by secret ballot, of men to represent them in a joint conference with representatives of the management. There is one representative for every one hundred and fifty employees, with at least two from each division of the works. These workers meet with representatives of the company, and this joint conference is authorized to handle all matters of mutual interest, such as wages, hours, working and living conditions. The conference appoints committees and divisional joint conferences, which can settle particular problems, often without bringing them into the works conference; the last-named is, however, the open court of appeal, with the further right of appeal to the highest officials of the company.

Under a joint agreement adopted by the joint conference, certain matters were settled and set down in black and white. First, an employment department was provided for, with the duties of: (1) Engaging all employees. In this, no discrimination is permitted between union and non-union men; the absolute open shop prevails. By a personal interview, the fitness of the applicant, intellectually and by experience, is learned. A physical examination is required, before the applicant is finally hired. (2) To act as a clearing-house in transfers of employees, from departments where work is slack, to other departments needing men. (3) To advise employees on personal matters, upon request, and to listen to reasons for desiring to be transferred to another department.

The agreement is definite on the subject of discipline, as this is so often the starting-point of friction. There is a list of offenses which automatically result in discharge. These include violations of the civil law, with particular attention to fighting, immoral conduct, stealing, and the like; violations of certain necessary safety rules, mostly in connection with the handling of railroad equipment and plant machinery; failure to report accidents;

insubordination; absence from duty without permission; willful lack of care in handling company property; and similar offenses. The advantage of such a list lies not in its completeness or laxness; its value is that it is perfectly definite, and every worker knows just what to expect when he conducts himself in a certain way. No other offenses than those on the list, which is posted conspicuously throughout the plant, can cause immediate discharge. Other offenses may bring a warning, and, if persisted in, discharge by the employment department, not the foreman.

Any employee who feels that he has not had a fair deal may place his case before the joint conference, either in person or through his representative. If he is still dissatisfied after their settlement, he may appeal to the higher officials of the company.

Wage adjustments are made in the joint conferences between the employees' representatives of the division affected and the representatives of the company, although the approval of the board of directors is required before any adjustment becomes effective.

The actual workings of the plan appear in following a case through the possible channels of adjustment. A grievance is first referred to the employee's own particular representative, who takes it up with the foreman. Failing in this, either the representative or the foreman will take it to a division conference, which is a duly elected and appointed conference for that one division. If it fails to make a decision, the matter goes to the works joint conference, which meets quarterly, or in the interim to its standing understudy, the executive council; if the latter cannot settle it, then it has to go to the joint conference. As a place of last resort, the case may be taken to the higher officials of the company in order, but this is almost never necessary. At any step, appeal may be taken if the decision of the conference is not unanimous. The actual use of all these steps is unheard of, and there is the added advantage that employees feel free to take up matters with their own foreman, knowing that there is always the possibility of appeal if necessary.

It is the policy of the company to encourage its workers to get ahead, and it provides evening classes whenever there is enough interest in a subject to warrant it. Americanization classes are also available, and insisted upon for those needing them.

The company maintains a medical service, to give treatment for injury and for sudden sickness. It attempts to enlist the workers in a continuous campaign of sanitation and prevention. It gives every new employee a physical examination, which may be repeated when desired.

Benefit features. The second big feature of the Standard Oil Company (New Jersey) program relates to annuities and benefits. If employees of at least one year's service are unable to work because of sickness for more than a period of seven days, the company will pay half-pay benefits from the date of first absence for a period of from six to seventy-eight weeks, according to length of service. This must be approved by the company doctor. Larger benefits are allowed in the case of tubercular patients, because of the nature of the disease.

Great stress is laid on the prevention of accidents, with safety inspectors and safety committees constantly at work. But when an accident does happen to a man while at work, the company furnishes all necessary medical care and treatment. Furthermore, it pays greater benefits than required by law — full pay for sixteen weeks of total disability, and two-thirds pay for the next thirty-six weeks, and thereafter compensation as required by the State law. Those failing to observe the rules made for the prevention of accidents forfeit all claim to benefits.

After a year of service, every employee's life is insured, and at his death his dependents receive from $500 to $2000, depending on the length of his service. This lapses, of course, if the employee leaves the company's service.

A pension scheme is also in operation. At the age of sixty-five and after twenty years of service, an employee is retired on a pension, the size of which is based on the wages earned during the previous five years and the length of service. In no case is it less than $300 a year, and may go as high as seventy-five per cent of the annual earnings.

Copartnership. The final point in the program is a scheme enabling the workers to invest in the company. After being with the company for a year, any worker may have as much as he wishes deducted from his pay, up to one fifth of his earnings, and credited toward the purchase of common stock of the Standard Oil Company (New Jersey). For each dollar so saved, the company adds fifty cents, feeling that a thrifty employee is worth more to them. The present plan terminates in December, 1925, and its extension will depend largely upon the favorable reaction of the workers to it.

Such is the employee relations policy of the Standard Oil Company of New Jersey. It is not perfect; in fact, it contains some features that might well be eliminated, and there is room for much improvement. But it is a working plan, and has been well received by the employees. Some of their representatives expressed it in these words:

> In the industrial representation plan the wage-earner has a channel through which his aims, aspirations, ideals, and his hopes are brought to the forefront, and discussed in a sane, sober, sensible manner. You don't have to be dubious about going down and asking for your rights. You have a channel through which you can do it.
>
> After all, the first demand of labor is not bigger wages, although you may think it is. The men want their bosses to recognize that they are men with all the pride, the self-respect, and the right to happiness of every other human being. The company encourages a representative to perform his duties properly so that the management and the men will get a square deal. This makes the plan interesting and worth while, and gives men a new feeling and spirit about their work. Hence it has achieved results which people call incredible.

4. Attitude of Organized Labor toward Works Councils [1]

Opposition to "company unions." Organized labor is officially against all plans of industrial government that do not provide for union recognition, though it does not object to a system of employees' committees elected within a shop if those committees are supplemental to a trade-union agreement. At the Atlantic City Convention of the American Federation of Labor in 1919,

[1] From *Experience with Works Councils in the United States*, National Industrial Conference Board, Research Report no. 50, pp. 138–47. New York, 1922.

"company unions," as works councils were termed, were condemned as "a delusion and a snare,"[1] set up by employers "for the express purpose of deluding the workers into the belief that they have some protection and thus have no need for trade-union organization." The trade union was stated to be the "only kind of organization" fitted for the purpose of collective bargaining, and all trade-unionists were advised "to have nothing to do" with "company unions."

This attitude toward employee representation plans still characterizes the speeches and writings of the leaders of the American Federation of Labor, and a general propaganda against works councils has been constantly conducted by the Federation.

In the discussion of the cases that follow, it will be noted that, in spite of this fact, individual trade-unionists in many instances have taken part in works council activities, and have not followed their leaders in the latter's opposition toward "company unions."

Union men as representatives. Most representation plans make no discrimination against employees because of membership in a labor organization. Trade-union employees are eligible for election as representatives — not as representatives of an outside labor organization, but as representatives of the employees in the plant. In some instances trade unions have been successful in creating committees composed entirely of union employees, and this has often been followed by an endeavor to secure benefits for the unions irrespective of the effect upon the industry. In some cases plans have had to be abandoned because of the determination of trade unions to utilize the committees for their own ends.

This has not been true, however, in the majority of plants. Employers have reported that members of trade unions as employee representatives have been quite as satisfactory as non-union employees. They have appreciated the benefits that accrue from a works council animated by a spirit of fairness on both sides, and have not attempted to convert the councils into organs for the propagation of trade-union principles.

The experience of a largo company with works councils in twenty-four plants is of particular interest in this connection. No

[1] American Federation of Labor. *Report of the Proceedings of the Thirty-Ninth Annual Convention*, June, 1919, pp. 249, 250. The other quotations in this and the following paragraphs are from the same source.

direct attempts have been made by organized labor to undermine or overthrow the works councils at any of the plants. The only direct influence exerted by organized labor has been "the general propaganda of the American Federation of Labor on the subject." One of the company officials stated that probably "fully fifty per cent of our employee representatives are union men."

> There has never been any indication from their attitude or acts in council that they were not as fully in accord with the principle underlying the plan as have been those employee representatives who are not members of trade unions.

A western coal and iron mining company reported a varied experience with regard to the attitude of the employee representatives who were members of trade unions. The councils in the five plants of this company were first formed in 1915, following a serious strike. Both the United Mine Workers and trade unions connected with the steel industry have endeavored to induce the employees to ignore the representation plan, and in some instances these attempts have met with a temporary success. At the time of the steel strike in 1919, the employee representatives at one of the company's plants were largely union men and "apparently interested in promoting union policies." This condition has not prevailed since the steel strike, although, wrote a company official, "probably some of the representatives are members of unions."

Despite the action of the National Machinists' Union, who decided to oppose the works council of the "committee" type in a Mid-Western arsenal, the individual machinists have taken an active part in the council's activities. The chairman and vice-chairman and one other member of the joint conference committee are machinists. It is noteworthy that the other trade unions represented in the arsenal have "lent their support, interest, and coöperation to all moves in connection with the council."

In an Eastern plant in which a number of local unions are represented, the union employees have taken the lead in securing representatives on the works committees. The works council was introduced into this plant under exceptionally trying circumstances following a strike. The National War Labor Board, under whose jurisdiction the case came, ordered the formation of "shop committees." A carefully prepared plan of representation, drawn up between representatives of the employees and the management, was agreed to by both parties and has been working successfully since its inception in 1919. Some of the employees who led the strike which precipitated the intervention of the War Labor Board are now ardent supporters of the works council. These men are trade-unionists and occupy prominent positions in the local trade-union movement. The company reported itself as well satisfied with the type of employees elected as representatives, ninety per cent of whom are trade-unionists. Management characterized them as "the recognized leaders in each department." One of the employee representatives, who is also an official in the local Trades and Labor Council, gave his opinion of the relation between the council and the union as follows:

> In a plant where the employer won't recognize the unions and won't deal with them, I think the unions should make all the use they can of a works council. It's the only way we have of getting in touch with the management, and why shouldn't we use it? There is nothing to be gained by standing off and refusing to take part in the council.
>
> We see to it that union men are elected to the committees. We can bring up before the management in that way the things we want them to do. If we didn't make use of the council plan, our point of view wouldn't receive any consideration at all.

A different attitude was found to characterize the business agent of one of the local trade unions. The plan was assailed by this union official as being simply a means of getting union employees to drop their memberships in the unions. Those representatives who were trade-unionists were accused of having "sold out" to the company; they were getting in well with "the boss," so as to get a "white-collared" job. An international officer of the same union attacked the plan on the ground that it broke down the workers' solidarity, leaving them powerless and at the mercy of the employer. In the eyes of this official the workers would sooner or later see through the employers' "little game" and then there would be an immense rush to join the trade unions again. In August, 1919, the plant was said to be ninety per cent unionized. Since that time, however, a large number of the employees have dropped their union memberships, till at the present time it is believed that not more than sixty per cent of the employees belong to trade unions.

In another plant with a plan of the "industrial democracy" type, the president of the company, writing with regard to the relations between the trade unions and the works council, stated there was a constant tendency, ". . . for questions which might come under union action to be referred directly to the union by the house of representatives previous to discussion by the House on the matter."

Investigation at this plant revealed that a certain group of the employees was well organized into a local union. This union did not pay for the services of a business agent, the members selecting their officers from among their own number. At the time of elections for the house of representatives in this plant, these employees nominated certain of their numbers in different departments and from those who were elected were chosen the officials of the union. In this way the union always had some of its members in the house of representatives. At the regular union meetings, those who were members in the house of representatives reported to the rest of the union employees the proceedings of the house.

The union employee representatives interviewed at this plant spoke highly of the plan. They did not believe that it had been introduced in order to do away with the union. On more than one occasion the president of the plant had urged employees to take a real interest in the union if they were members, to attend the union meetings, and to give it their support.

In one company, where it was stated that there had been no noticeable opposition on the part of the union employees to the representation plan, trade-unionists are allowed to choose representatives equal in number to those chosen by the non-union employees.

A Western company, on the other hand, reported that there was a desire among the union men in the plant, to "convert the shop through its union representatives on the shop committee into a closed union shop." One of the company officials wrote:

> There has been no well-organized attempt to do this, but the desire exists. Organized labor is not opposed to our shop committee and, in fact, the strong union men in our shop are the ones who first proposed it and served as charter members. I believe that union members understand thoroughly that there will be no recognition of the union in our shop and therefore we expect their activities along this line to gradually lessen, as they have already done.

A serious crisis in the history of this council occurred shortly after it was formed, when nearly all of the local industries were tied up with a general strike. Although a large percentage of the employees belonged to trade unions and pressure was brought on them from outside the plant to join the strike, the employee representatives unanimously refused to take part in it. In addition the works council members appeared before the local trades and labor council, and their statement of the issue involved was so convincing that the strike was soon called off. Recently, when a wage reduction was made in this company, the efforts of local unions to call their members out on strike was unsuccessful.

Refusal to serve as representative. In some plants trade-unionists have been unwilling to act as employee representatives. Whole departments of employees, the majority of whom belonged to unions, have sometimes refused to take any part in the activities of the council. This has been changed in some instances, after the plan has been in operation for some time, and the employees came to realize they were depriving themselves of benefits which were theirs for the asking. This was the case in an Eastern silk mill where, when the plan was introduced, a certain group of highly organized workers refused to take any part in the council. The representation plan in this concern is of the "industrial democracy" type, and the "collective economy dividend" is included in it. After three months' operation of the plan, during which time the other employees had received dividends amounting to five per cent of their weekly wages, the trade-unionists who had refused to take part in the council requested the management to allow them to share in the dividends, expressing a desire to take their place along with the rest of the employees under the representation plan.

In a Western motor concern, one department which consisted almost entirely of union employees refused to elect any representatives, and maintained this attitude for over two years. Recently, when a wage reduction was necessary in that plant, those employees refused to accept it and were accordingly discharged. The employees hired to take their places have manifested an interest in the council and have joined the rest of the employees in supporting it.

An Eastern tanning company, which introduced its representation plan at the time the local union was endeavoring to enforce a closed shop, reported that union men who were elected representatives refused to serve as such. Shortly after the plan was put into operation, a union agitator caused trouble in the plant and, on his refusal to have the matter referred to the works council, was discharged. The union demanded his reinstatement, but the company refused to do so unless the case was submitted to the works council. This the discharged employee refused to have done, and a strike was called against the plant. After one week's time the strike was called off by the union. Since that time, ". . . several officials of the union have worked for us in various departments and expressed satisfaction with the relationship existing between employer and employees here."

In an Eastern plant the introduction of a works council of the "committee" type was followed by an energetic campaign to organize the machinists in the plant, and ninety per cent of these employees joined the union. Although they had elected a representative on the council, they also set up a separate committee and asked for an increase in wages, along with recognition of the trade union. The company placed the matter before the works council, who appointed a special committee to investigate and report. The employee representatives took the stand that the machinists, who comprised one electoral division, were unfair to the representative they had elected. The special committee recommended that all the machinists should be paid up in full, and that they should not be rehired "until they were willing to pledge themselves that they would give the committee system a fair trial before calling on the union for help." The committee stated that in their minds

. . . the firm had no ulterior motive in introducing the committee system and that so long as the management was "on the level" there was no need of a business agent to speak for the men and create dissatisfaction.

Regarding this, an official of the company stated:

> It will be noted that the action of our committee was not because our men were opposed to labor unions, but rather because the action of the unionized men in the machine shop did not line up with the committee's idea of a square deal all around. As one of our old employees told the writer at the time: "Quarreling and striking is old stuff. It may be necessary in some plants, but none of it for me, so long as the boss shows himself willing to meet me half way. Reasonable men should be able to compose their differences without a strike that nearly always ends in a compromise. Why not compromise at the start?"

Other instances have been furnished the conference board in which the efforts of trade unions to induce employees to abandon works councils have failed, because of the spirit of loyalty among the workers toward their representation plan.

An Eastern steel company reported:

> Efforts were made from time to time by labor organizations to get a foothold here, but the men gave very little heed to them, our plant committee saying that "if we can't get along together amongst ourselves there would be little use for any outsiders to come in to try to accomplish anything." At the time of the steel strike in 1919 the plant committee stood loyal to the company and refused to affiliate with the outside labor organization.

The vice-president of a Middle Western textile company wrote:

> Organized labor has talked against our plan, but our people are so well sold on the system that "unionism," as at present constituted, is not at all in favor, especially since the committee system has been attacked. Awhile ago I took up a vote of our men and found that only 5 out of 175 favored a

closed shop with no committee. Our women are almost all opposed to unionism. We employ 550 women.

A Middle Western machinery company wrote that the efforts of the local union to organize its foundry failed because the men preferred the works council organization to the trade union. The president of the company stated:

> We have really done some remarkable things in this small town community in the way of staving off unionization of the foundry. This was done in the face of determined efforts by the union to organize the entire town. We have at least one union man on our committee of six or eight, but the union gave up in despair when they found they had not only the management of the organization to fight, but also the men.

One company with representation plans of the "industrial democracy" type in four plants, whose committee system has been the object of continual opposition on the part of organized labor, said that it considered the failure of either employees or management to live up to the requirements of the plan was much more dangerous than opposition direct against the plan from outside.

> There has been constant knocking of our plan by representatives of organized labor, but we cannot see that it has had any material effect up to the present time. We feel that such opposition is not a bad thing, as it keeps us studying all the while to make our plan more potent. We feel that the dangers from within, the hazards which arise from arbitrary measures, lack of consideration, etc., are more to be feared than the hazards from without.

The system as an anti-strike weapon. A Middle Western rubber company, with a plan of the "industrial democracy" type, related the following experience in connection with an attempt of the local machinists' union to call a city-wide strike. The machinists employed in this company presented their demands to the management, who in turn referred them to the "industrial assembly." The latter agreed to deal with the machinists after they had stated they came as "company employees, and that they were not being guided by outside influences." The grievance committee of the assembly recommended that rates be increased, and that overtime be paid on the basic eight-hour day instead of on the forty-eight-hour week. This recommendation was accepted by the management, who immediately put a large force of men at work reviewing the rates with a view to giving a higher rate to all men deserving it.

The industrial assembly then called a mass meeting of machinists and explained what had been done. In addition, each machinist was visited personally by a member of the assembly and informed what his new rating was, or was given a reason why he did not receive a new rating. When the city-wide machinists' strike was called, sixty per cent of the company machinists upheld the action of the representatives whom they had elected to the industrial assembly, and remained at work.

One firm reported that at the time of a city-wide strike, which affected the union employees working in two departments of the plant, not only did its union men remain at work, but they denounced the wage demands of the union as being "excessive."

In another plant the action of the works council in condemning a general strike was said to be responsible for the failure of the strike.

> About a year ago, when a general strike was ordered by the Millworkers' Union of this city, our house of representatives, composed largely of union men, went on record against it, giving their reasons, and sent a copy of the resolutions to both of our daily papers, and their action killed the general strike in the city. At the time of this action of our house of representatives, I think at least ninety-five per cent of our men belonged to this union, although we run an open shop.

Distinct from these cases, in which trade unions directed strikes against plants where works councils were operating, are the experiences of another group of employers who reported organized labor as confining itself to an attempt to ridicule the plans. This was often done only when the plan was introduced. After it was seen that the plans were satisfactory to the employees, no further action was taken by the trade unions. A Western construction company stated that, while there had been no direct and open attempt made by organized labor to discredit the works council, there had been, for over six months after the plan was initiated, "a whispering campaign" which was "rather annoying and difficult to overcome." This had been successfully met, however, with the result that the great majority of the workers had accepted the works council "as an entirely satisfactory substitute for the labor-union organization."

Shop committees in relation to trade agreements. Organized labor, while opposed to the formation of "company unions," does not object to a system of employees' committees elected within the shop if those committees are supplemental to a trade-union agreement. This was the subject of the resolutions of the Executive Council of the American Federation of Labor at the annual convention of the Federation in 1918. The Executive Council placed itself on record as being in favor of a "regular arrangement" in all "large, permanent shops" whereby:

> First, a committee of the workers would regularly meet with the shop management to confer over matters of production; and whereby:
>
> Second, such committee could carry, beyond the foreman and the superintendent, to the general manager or to the president, any important grievance which the workers may have with references to wages, hours, and conditions.

These demands were predicated upon "the basic principle of the right and opportunity of workers to organize and make collective agreements."

Three instances have come to the attention of the conference board, of works councils in firms which have agreements with labor unions covering wages and working hours.

At the time the "industrial democracy" type of council was introduced into an Eastern shoe company factory, the company had an agreement covering wages and working hours with the United Shoe Workers of America. The original constitution of the council provided for the discussion of wages and working hours. This provision was not looked upon favorably by the employees, nearly all of whom belonged to the trade union. Consequently the subjects of wages and working hours were removed from the jurisdiction of the works council. With this change made, the company reported that the employeės took much more interest in the committee system.

In the case of another company, an Eastern fishery, the "committee" type of plan works in conjunction with a union agreement covering wages and working hours. The company reported the elected representatives were "a very fair type of men." With regard to the attitude of the employees toward the committees which discuss neither rates of pay nor hours of work, a company official stated:

> The employees who are union members do not look to the committees to secure changes or to protect them against cuts, but rather continue to look to the unions. The non-union men are content to let their fellow union workers make arrangements with the unions and accept any changes made. The non-union workers do not . . . take any more interest in the representation plan than do the union men.

No attempt has been made by organized labor to induce the employees to abandon the plan, "principally because our method does not come in contact with the union." The company feels, however, that if a firm is obliged to deal with the union, ". . . the employees' conference will not have as much importance in the eyes of the workers as it would if the company dealt directly with the employees."

In another plant, an Eastern printing company, agreements as to hours of work and conditions are made with a trades council made up of representatives of the several trade unions working in the plant, and wage agreements are made with each one of the local unions. The employees' committees ". . . do not discuss union matters such as base rates or hours of labor, but frequently do take up matters such as a particular job, where a special element enters not common to other jobs."

The committees are not permanent, "but are appointed when a matter comes up for discussion." Each committee is composed as follows: A representative of each department affected (this representative being chosen by the members in that department), the representative of the particular union involved, the works manager representing the firm, and the employment manager, who is a neutral member. The "representative of the union involved" is usually the president of the local trade union. These committees have been functioning since 1915. One of the company officials wrote that they had functioned satisfactorily and had been helpful "in establishing a coöperative feeling between management and workers."

Difficulty of obtaining reliable information. In view of the reluctance of employers to furnish information regarding the attitude adopted by trade unions toward works councils, it has been difficult to form an accurate judgment as to the relative number of cases in which organized labor has opposed councils and those in which it has made no attempt to discredit the plans. The conference board has found that a large number of employers either disregarded the question, or simply stated that if any steps to oppose the plans had been taken by labor organizations, such steps had not been obvious or had been unsuccessful.

Field investigation, moreover, showed that in some cases the accounts given by employers of the attitude of local unions toward works councils were at variance with the statements of union officials themselves. Although the local unions may not have endeavored to disrupt the councils by any organized assault upon them, it was found that they regarded the councils very unfavorably and were doing much to induce employees to put no faith in them. The common belief among union officials was that, under a works council system, the work of organizing the employees was made more difficult; employees tended to drop their union membership because they could gain advantages through the works council that cost them nothing, whereas there was a fee demanded of them from the unions.

In view of this reluctance on the part of employers to furnish information and of the discrepancies found between the information furnished the board and that gained by investigation in the field, no reliable statement can be made as to the extent to which trade unions have combated works councils.

5. Summary of Experience with Employee Representation [1]

General results. It appears from an account of experience with works councils that, of a total of about one hundred and fifty reported upon, sixteen have lapsed entirely and several others have had only a perfunctory existence. Aside from one "Shipbuilding Labor Adjustment Board Committee" and three councils voluntarily introduced by employers, all of those which lapsed were "National War Labor Board Committees."

In six cases the lapse of the committees may be attributed to a disinterested or unsympathetic attitude on the part of the management. In a nearly equal number of instances, on the other hand, obstructive tactics on the part of organized labor evidently account for the failure of the committees. In one case a lack of interest on the part of employees is reported as the cause. The lay-off of workers following the cancellation of war contracts explains the lapse of committees in several other establishments. As previously noted, two plans instituted by employers passed out of existence with changes in the control of the companies.

Of those works councils herein classed as active, about fifty have functioned to a limited extent only. A number of "National War Labor Board Committees" ceased their activity with the completion of adjustments under the board's awards. In other instances only a few meetings were held or a few matters handled.

In many plants, works councils have been established so recently that they have had little opportunity to become active. This is true notably of those plants in which the "Bridgeport Plan" has been introduced and of a considerable number of establishments in which employers have instituted plans upon their own initiative.

Attitude of employers. Approximately three fourths of the employers having works councils, from whom statements were secured, either declared specifically that they favored these organizations or reported having had favorable experience with them.

Favorable statements were furnished by practically all of the

[1] From *Works Councils in the United States*, National Industrial Conference Board, Research Report no. 21, October, 1919, pp. 106-15.

establishments in which plans of employee representation have been voluntarily instituted by employers. In addition, about half of the employers who have had experience with "National War Labor Board Committees" and two thirds of those having experience with "Shipbuilding Labor Adjustment Board Committees" reported favorably.

The statement was frequently made that the works council "has demonstrated its usefulness." A large concern, in which a works council was voluntarily instituted by the employer, wrote that the "experience of almost four years has convinced the management that the 'industrial representation plan' is a success." The president of a small plant also expressed the belief that the plan has been "beneficial both to the company and to the workers." One company reported that "so far the results have been extremely satisfactory," and another was confident that "the plan is going to be very helpful in the solution of the problem of industrial relations." An establishment in which a "company union" plan has been effective for four years reports that the "experience in general is quite satisfactory; the operatives' council is an increasing success."

A large shipbuilding company declared: "The result so far has been an unqualified success in our yard." A Southern concern operating under the plan of Shipbuilding Labor Adjustment Board Committees wrote that "experience with joint shop committees has always been satisfactory"; and an Eastern company having similar committees reported "very satisfactory results for both sides." It was frequently stated by companies which have adopted the National War Labor Board plan that "results altogether have been very satisfactory." Another establishment in this group wrote that "no case has arisen where the management and the shop committee could not agree." "The plan," according to another concern, "has in every way proved extremely satisfactory," and still another wrote, "We believe . . . that it will be the best thing that has happened in our plant."

With few exceptions, the establishments which reported unfavorably upon their experience with works councils are plants in which committees were set up by the National War Labor Board. On the basis of its experience one concern concluded that "the committees are of no particular benefit." Another company wrote: "Our experience has not been satisfactory." According to the management of another company, "The committee represent the teachings of the walking delegate." One company was reported as unfavorable to the shop committee because its "committee was picked from the strictest union agitators." The management of one establishment stated that "it would not have started the employees' committees had it not been forced to do so" — an attitude quite common among establishments in the National War Labor Board group.

However, expressions of an unfavorable character from employers were relatively infrequent. The general attitude of employers who have had experience with works councils was favorable.

Character of representatives chosen. Obviously the success of works councils depends in no small degree upon the character of the representatives selected by employees to serve on such councils. In this respect the experience reported by employers for this investigation was predominantly favorable. With comparatively few exceptions it was stated that the men selected had been of an intelligent, fair-minded, and, on the whole, somewhat conservative type. Instances where extremists had been chosen were relatively few.

Thus, in several instances it was reported that "very good men" had been elected; in another, that "the type of employees chosen was satisfactory in a surprising degree." In still another establishment, "the selection of the majority of workers" was reported as "generally good." Another employer stated that "the employees elected have been conservative and have carried the employees along with them in their judgment." The management of another plant declared that the "type of employees elected on the committee is the best in the factory."

In the statements of a number of other establishments, approval of the employees chosen to serve on the works councils was qualified. Thus, one company "generally found the committees disposed to be fair, but lacking in broad vision in promoting coöperation and good-will." Another report stated that there have been "cases where it appeared to the management that the shop committee was overzealous for its interests, but on the whole a very fair spirit was displayed." According to another company, committee members show "usually one of two very pronounced and widely differing characteristics: the sober-minded, industrious, thinking man who has inspired his fellow craftsmen with confidence through his common sense, or the loudest, most vociferous talkers against the management."

The generally satisfactory character of employees elected as members of works councils is further exemplified in the following experience of a number of Bridgeport establishments which held elections under the "Bridgeport Plan":

> Conservatism has appeared to mark the shop committee elections; that is, the committeemen elected are usually of long company service, and thus apparently are of more set and conservative character. This is shown to be actually the case in practically every instance of the 422 departmental committees elected under supervision of the writers. For example, the average length of service of members of the executive committees of the Locomobile, Remington Typewriter, Singer, and U.M.C. factories in Bridgeport is a little more than seven years and eight months, while the chairmen of these four committees have an average service record of thirteen years each. In the Singer committee the chairman has been in the company's employ more than nineteen years, one member almost nineteen years, one fourteen years, one more than eleven years, and one a year and a half — an average of thirteen years for the company. The U.M.C. committee's chairman has been in that company's service sixteen years, and the Remington Typewriter Company's chairman has worked there fifteen years, while the Locomobile Company's chairman has been directly in that company's service two years.

A further instance of the type of representatives chosen is furnished by the following table, showing the personnel of the employees' representatives in three plants of the Bethlehem Steel Corporation.

In some cases unfavorable experience in this respect was reported. Thus, committee members were characterized as "union agitators" or "radical spirits" by four companies, three of which

Personal Record of Employees' Representatives in Plants of the Bethlehem Steel Corporation

	LEBANON	MARYLAND	STEELTON
Number	33	26	45
Age			
25 to 30	6	5	5
31 to 35	2	9	15
36 to 40	8	5	9
41 to 45	9	5	9
46 to 50	2		6
Over 50	6	2	1
Married	32	24	37
Single	1	2	8
Property owner		7	23
Naturalized	2	3	2
Alien	None	None	None
Nativity			
United States	31	23	43
Ireland	1	2	1
England	1		
Austria			1
Germany		1	
Length of service			
1 to 2 years	11	11	4
3 to 5 years	2	1	10
6 to 10 years	5	3	2
11 to 15 years	1	2	4
16 to 20 years	7	5	5
21 to 25 years	3	2	10
26 to 30 years	2	2	7
Over 30 years	2		3

operate under the National War Labor Board plan. In one instance the management wrote that the committee-men were "probably dictated by the union . . . to make trouble," and, in another instance, that the committee was "fixed up by the union."

While, therefore, the experience in this particular has not been universally favorable, the evidence indicates that in a great majority of cases members of works councils have been fair-minded and of high character.

Works councils and attitude of workers. Testimony as to the effect of works councils on the attitude of workers was almost universally favorable. A "better feeling between management and workers" was the gist of reports received from twenty-five companies. Some employers merely reported that the spirit of the workers was "much better" or "generally improved," or that the existence and activities of the councils "tended to create a good spirit." More emphatic statements were secured from some establishments to the effect that works councils had produced a "decided change for the better" and "had developed a strong feeling of mutual confidence." Several other companies characterize the attitude of their employees in such terms as "excellent spirit," "fine sense of coöperation," and "keen interest on the part of employees." "The men have always felt," wrote one company, "that committees form the medium for expressing all grievances and suggestions." Another company declared: "Our willingness to coöperate with the men through their committees has developed a fine spirit of harmony."

Somewhat less favorable judgment was expressed by the management of an establishment having a "company union," who reported that the spirit of the workers since the introduction of the plan had been "sometimes critical, sometimes disbelieving or scornful, sometimes appreciative and approving." One establishment, moreover, stated explicitly that "the spirit of the men is not as good as formerly." In three other instances field investigators found that the employees had a suspicious attitude toward the employee representation plan.

Works councils and labor difficulties. A particularly significant measure of the value of works councils lies in the effect which their operation has upon the occurrence of labor difficulties.

Twenty-three establishments reported specifically that labor difficulties have decreased, partly or wholly, because of the formation of works councils. Thus, a number of employers who had voluntarily introduced plans of employee representation stated that the committees have been "helpful" in meeting labor difficulties. The management of one company declared that all labor difficulties have been "promptly settled by a frank consideration of the trouble with the committee." Another company reported that "labor misunderstandings which might lead to difficulties are handled more efficiently and quickly through craft committees than otherwise." Two concerns have had no serious difficulties since the shop committees came into existence although one of these cautions: "This may not have been the means of their prevention." One employer reported that the committees "smoothed out many difficulties." In at least four instances establishments reported that their employees failed to join in strikes occurring in the industry or locality and attributed this action to the existence of works councils.

A small number of establishments, most of them plants in which "shop committees" were introduced by the National War Labor Board, reported specifically that labor difficulties had increased following the institution of works councils. In four of these plants strikes occurred and in one other a strike was threatened when the plan was in effect. Strikes of part or all of the employees have taken place in four other establishments, in which plans of employee representation have been introduced upon the initiative of employers. In two of these cases the strikes occurred immediately following the introduction of the plans. In each of the four instances, however, the managements reported that strike conditions were mitigated by the works councils, and that the occurrence of strikes had not altered their judgment of the value of the councils.

While, therefore, experience in this respect has not been uniformly favorable, the evidence indicates that works councils have been potent in reducing labor difficulties, and, at least in several instances, have been effective in bringing about an amicable settlement of differences which had arisen.

Works councils and labor turnover. The extent of labor turnover, like the occurrence of labor difficulties, forms a measure of the effectiveness of works councils. On this point, however, the evidence available is scant. In four of the six establishments which reported, a decrease in labor turnover was noted. In one case only was an increase in labor turnover reported. In the remaining establishment reporting on this point, it was stated that no effect was observed.

Works councils and output. The effect of works councils on production was commented upon by only nine establishments, eight of these being plants in which plans of employee representation had been voluntarily introduced by employers. All of the eight establishments reported that output had been increased, and attributed this result in part or entirely to the existence of the works councils. It is to be noted that four of these establishments had a "governmental" type of plan, which included a bonus feature to which the effect on output must be largely attributed. The only establishment which reported an unfavorable effect upon output was a shipbuilding yard in which the plan of the Shipbuilding Labor Adjustment Board was in effect.

In view of the limited evidence and the abnormal war-time conditions under which most works councils have operated, a general conclusion as to the effect upon output is not possible at this time.

Works councils in relation to trade-unionism. The institution of works councils has been followed in some cases by an increase, and in other cases by a decrease, in unionization among the employees of the establishments. Also the relations of works councils with trade unions have varied in character. In some instances, the unions have actively interested themselves in the operation of works councils; in other cases they have actively opposed them.

A definite effect upon the extent of unionization among employees in establishments having works councils was reported in thirteen cases. Increases in union membership occurred in seven of these instances and decreases in the remainder. Some other establishments reported merely that no discernible effect upon unionization had been observed.

All but two of the establishments which noted increases in unionization among their employees were plants in which the National War Labor Board had instituted "shop committees." One establishment in this group, on the other hand, stated that the "men have since dropped membership in the union."

Of establishments in which works councils were voluntarily introduced by employers, two having "company unions" and one a plan of the "governmental" type, reported decreases in unionization. In two other establishments of this group the institution of works councils was followed by decreases in union membership. In one plant, on the other hand, it was observed that "unionization has been stimulated."

While works councils provide for no recognition of trade unions, a close relationship has frequently developed between the unions and the employees' committees. In at least eight establishments, elections are so controlled by the union element that "all of the committeemen are union members." In two other plants "practically all of the committee members belong to unions." In a number of instances this relationship has served as the means of establishing more amicable relations with organized labor. In other cases, as previously noted, the attempt on the part of union members to "dominate" or "dictate the policy" of the committees has created bad feeling between management and workers. It is noteworthy that the ten establishments in which union members actively concerned themselves in elections are all plants in which "National War Labor Board Committees" or "Shipbuilding Labor Adjustment Board Committees" were established.

In this connection mention may again be made of the agreements between the American Shipbuilding and Bethlehem Shipbuilding Companies with the Metal Trades Department of the American Federation of Labor.

The evidence thus far available is so varied that no fixed relationship between works councils and trade-unionism can be said to have developed. The official attitude of organized labor has become increasingly hostile toward plans of employee representation.

INDEX